Y0-BKI-933

Anesthesiology and the Law

health administration press

The Press was established in 1972 with the support of the W. K. Kellogg Foundation as a joint endeavor of the Association of University Programs in Health Administration (Washington, D.C.) and The University of Michigan Program and Bureau of Hospital Administration

Editorial Board

John R. Griffith
Chairman
The University of Michigan

Gary L. Filerman
Association of University Programs in Health Administration

Donald C. Riedel
University of Washington

R. Hopkins Holmberg
Boston University

Lee F. Seidel
University of New Hampshire

David G. Warren
Duke University

Ronald Andersen
University of Chicago

Arnold D. Kaluzny
University of North Carolina

Anesthesiology and the Law

J. Douglas Peters, J.D.
Keith S. Fineberg, J.D.
Donald A. Kroll, M.D., Ph.D.
Vincent Collins, M.D., M.S.

Health Administration Press
1983

Copyright © 1983 by the Regents of The University of Michigan. All rights reserved. Printed in the United States of America. This book or parts thereof may not be reproduced in any form without written permission of the publisher.

Library of Congress Cataloging in Publication Data

Anethesiology and the law.

   Includes index.
   1. Anesthetists—Legal status, laws, etc.—United States. I. Peters, J. Douglas, 1948-   [DNLM:
1. Anesthesiology—Legislation—United States.
2. Anesthesiology—Standards—Legislation—United States.
WO 232 AA1 A5]
KF2910.A5A94 1983   344.73'0412   82-11994
ISBN 0-914904-79-5   347.304412

Health Administration Press
The University of Michigan
School of Public Health
Ann Arbor, Michigan 48109
(313) 764-1380

The authors dedicate this work to their wives: Chris Consales, Lynn Barr, Marlene Kroll, and Florence Collins.

Contents

Abbreviations xii

Foreword xiii

Preface xv

PART I: LIABILITY

Chapter I: The Law of Malpractice 3

§ 1.10 Introduction 3
§ 1.20 Elements of Negligence 6
§ 1.30 Duty 7
    § 1.31 Physician-Patient Relationship 9
    § 1.32 Standard of Care 13
    § 1.33 Consent and Informed Consent 19
§ 1.40 Breach of Duty 27
§ 1.50 Causation 30
    § 1.51 Legal Principles of Causation 30
    § 1.52 Res Ipsa Loquitur 34
§ 1.60 Damages 44

Chapter II: Other Theories of Liability 61

§ 2.10 Introduction 61
§ 2.20 Contract Theory 61
§ 2.30 Vicarious Liability 65
    § 2.31 Anesthesiologists 71
    § 2.32 Nurse-Anesthetists 73
    § 2.33 Hospitals 77
    § 2.34 Joint Enterprise 79

§ 2.40	Liability Arising from Medical Records 80
§ 2.50	Products Liability. 82
	§ 2.51 Defective Devices 88
	§ 2.52 Defective Drugs. 91

Chapter III: Defenses 100

§ 3.10	Introduction 100
§ 3.20	Contributory Negligence 100
§ 3.30	Comparative Negligence 103
§ 3.40	Assumption of Risk 105
§ 3.50	Statute of Limitations. 106
§ 3.60	Res Judicata and Collateral Estoppel 112
§ 3.70	Release from Liability Forms. 114

Chapter IV: The Lawsuit in Court 118

§ 4.10	Introduction 118
§ 4.20	Pleadings 118
	§ 4.21 The Patient's Complaint. 119
	§ 4.22 The Physician's Answer. 119
§ 4.30	Discovery. 120
	§ 4.31 Depositions 120
	§ 4.32 Subpoena. 122
	§ 4.33 Written Interrogatories. 122
	§ 4.34 Production of Documents and Things 123
	§ 4.35 Physical Examinations. 123
	§ 4.36 Protective Orders 124
§ 4.40	Evidence and Witnesses. 124
	§ 4.41 Expert Testimony. 124
	§ 4.42 Court-Appointed Experts. 129
	§ 4.43 Hypothetical Question and Opinion Testimony 129
	§ 4.44 Textbooks. 130
	§ 4.45 Adverse Witness Provisions. 131
	§ 4.46 Physician-Patient Privilege 132
	§ 4.47 Medical Records 133
§ 4.50	Countersuits. 134

PART II: REGULATION

Chapter V: Governmental Regulation 141

§ 5.10 Introduction 141
§ 5.20 State Licensure 142
         § 5.21 Requirements 144
         § 5.22 Relicensure and Continuing Medical Education 148
         § 5.23 Disciplinary Proceedings 149
§ 5.30 Professional Standards Review Organizations 157
§ 5.40 State and Federal Controlled Substances Acts 163

Chapter VI: Professional Regulation 176

§ 6.10 Specialty Certification in Anesthesiology 176
§ 6.20 Regulation of Nurse-Anesthetists 182
§ 6.30 Regulating Competing Professions 191

Chapter VII: Hospital Regulation 196

§ 7.10 Introduction 196
§ 7.20 Origin and Development 196
§ 7.30 Types of Hospitals 197
§ 7.40 Legal Bases for Hospital Operation 200
         § 7.41 Corporations 200
         § 7.42 Bylaws 201
§ 7.50 Organization and Administration 203
         § 7.51 Governing Board 203
         § 7.52 Hospital Administrator 205
         § 7.53 Medical and Other Staff 205
§ 7.60 Services and Procedures 206
         § 7.61 Admissions 207
         § 7.62 Emergencies 207
         § 7.63 Discharge 209
         § 7.64 Utilization Review Committee 209
         § 7.65 Abortion and Sterilization 210
§ 7.70 Regulation of the Hospital 211
         § 7.71 Joint Commission on the Accreditation of Hospitals 212
         § 7.72 Licensure 213
         § 7.73 Certificate of Need 213
         § 7.74 Professional Standards Review Organization 214

§ 7.80 Anesthesiology Services 214
    § 7.81 JCAH Standards 214
    § 7.82 State Regulation 217
§ 7.90 Medical Staff Privileges 217
    § 7.91 Substantive Due Process 218
    § 7.92 Procedural Due Process 220
§ 7.100 Exclusive Contracts 221

PART III: ANESTHETIC PRACTICES

Introduction 231

Chapter VIII: Preoperative Anesthetic Care 232

§ 8.10 Preanesthesia Visit and Evaluation 232
§ 8.20 Preoperative Medications 237

Chapter IX: Monitoring and Records 241

§ 9.10 Monitoring 241
§ 9.20 Records 245

Chapter X: General Anesthesia 255

§ 10.10 Principles of General Anesthesia 255
§ 10.20 Airways and Ventilation 258
    § 10.21 Airway Management without Intubation 258
    § 10.22 Airway Management with Endotracheal Intubation 259
§ 10.30 Volatile Anesthetic Agents 268
    § 10.31 Halothane 268
    § 10.32 Penthrane 275
§ 10.40 Intravenous Anesthetic Agents 276
§ 10.50 Muscle Relaxants 282

Chapter XI: Regional Anesthesia 292

§ 11.10 Spinal Anesthesia 292
§ 11.20 Epidural (and Caudal) Anesthesia 301
§ 11.30 Regional Nerve Blocks 305
§ 11.40 Infiltration (Local) Anesthesia 308

Contents

Chapter XII: Anesthesia Mishaps 313

§ 12.10 Human Error and Preventability 313
§ 12.20 Electrical, Gas and Fire Hazards 316
        § 12.21 Ether 317
        § 12.22 Burns 318
§ 12.30 Improper Management of Fluid and Electrolyte Imbalances 322
§ 12.40 Blood Transfusions 327
§ 12.50 Faulty Patient Positioning 328
§ 12.60 Malignant Hyperthermia 334
§ 12.70 Cardiac Arrest 336
§ 12.80 Postoperative Anesthetic Care 342

Appendix A: Controlled Substances Schedule 351

Appendix B: California Anesthesia Service Regulations 357

Appendix C: Massachusetts Anesthesia Service Regulations 361

Appendix D: Illinois Anesthesia Service Regulations 362

Appendix E: Joint Commission on the Accreditation of Hospitals
Anesthesia Services 364

Appendix F: Sample Release from Liability 371

Appendix G: Sample Complaint 373

Appendix H: Sample Answer 377

Glossary 380

Selected Bibliography 389

Index 391

Abbreviations

AANA	American Association of Nurse Anesthetists
AOA	American Osteopathic Association
ASA	American Society of Anesthesiologists
CAT	Computerized Axial Tomography
CPK	Creatine phosphophinase
CPR	Cardiopulmonary resuscitation
CRNA	Certified Registered Nurse Anesthetists
CSF	Cerebrospinal fluid
ECG	Electrocardiogram or Electrocardiograph
FCSA	Federal Controlled Substances Act
FDA	Food and Drug Administration
FMG	Foreign Medical Graduate
JCAH	Joint Commission on the Accreditation of Hospitals
NAIC	National Association of Insurance Commissioners
NAS	National Academy of Sciences
NRC	National Research Council
PSRO	Professional Standards Review Organization
SGOT	Serum Glutamic-oxaloacetic Transaminase
UCSA	Uniform Controlled Substances Act

Foreword

As an attorney who instructs health administration and other students and also interacts in the practice of law with hospital executives and medical personnel, my experience has been that comprehension of the law's relation to clinical activities is often poor. In *Anesthesiology and the Law*, the authors, J. Douglas Peters, Keith S. Fineberg, Donald A. Kroll, and Vincent Collins have achieved a synthesis of law and medicine oriented to anesthesia practice. However, the basic material in this book deals with a wide variety of matters, such as the function of the expert witness, the physician-patient privilege and the principles of liability, and thus constitutes a fund of information useful to all physicians, regardless of clinical specialty. Specifically, surgeons need to know just about everything in this volume, given the interdependence of surgical and anesthesia services.

The authors have judiciously used case illustrations—summaries of actual decisions in litigation—to emphasize, dramatize and clarify important elements of their text. Perhaps of greatest value in this book are the discussion of the scope of practice issues and the emphasis upon the cruciality of the factual questions in litigation. With respect to the former, there is considerable uncertainty surrounding who may provide and who is responsible for anesthesia service when an anesthesiologist is not the provider. Matters of licensing, legislation definitions, customary medical delegation practices, etc. abound in the area of scope of practice issues, and these issues are not handled uniformly in the various states.

As for the importance of the facts in litigation, a frequent concern expressed by physicians, regardless of specialty, is that the jury or the court will be "wrong" on the basic medical issues in a particular case. Attorneys have difficulty in conveying to physicians that the jury and judge are bound by the evidence submitted at trial. When the events in a case—elasped time, presence of signs of patient distress, etc.—are disputed, or when the standard of care applied to the anesthesia service provider is the subject of conflict, the result of litigation may offend physicians who read media accounts of such litigation or the court reports themselves.

In Part III, the device of organizing both medical and legal authority respecting the standard of care for various aspects of anesthesia services has many advantages. It works well for reference purposes, and for readers with specific concerns about the currently recognized standard of care. The authors frankly acknowledge that the device requires the reader to exercise caution, particularly with regard to legal authority. Because the trier of fact is bound by evidence of the standard of care specific to a given point in time, changes in practice standards reflecting new developments or questionable expert testimony occasionally make legal authority unreliable guidance respecting professionally appropriate medical services. On several occasions members of an audience have come up to me after a talk to inform me that though the legal principles in the case I discussed were correct, the standard of medical practice reflected in the court's opinion no longer is, and perhaps never was, in conformity with recognized standards of practice.

The authors have also made it possible for anesthesia providers to understand how changes in their performance can build a better fact situation and minimize the potential for liability in the event an untoward occurrence precipitates a claim, or even litigation. This may well reflect the experience of one of the authors, attorney J. Douglas Peters, a shareholder with Charfoos, Christensen, Gilbert & Archer, P.C., a Detroit law firm actively engaged in professional liability litigation. To the extent the number and severity of incidents involving apparent or actual harm are reduced by greater awareness, the interests of providers and the public they serve are fostered.

The contribution made by the authors is an extremely valuable one, and the availability of this book as a source of information in this period of renewed attention to enhancing patient care and concern about liability should be welcomed by all involved in the health and medical services field. I will add in conclusion that this volume will most certainly be a welcome addition to the libraries of both plaintiff and defense attorneys who specialize in malpractice litigation.

Nathan Hershey
Professor of Health Law
Graduate School of
Public Health
University of Pittsburgh

Preface

The authors have designed this text to serve as a reference and resource text for anesthesiologists and surgeons, attorneys with medical-legal practices, hospital administrators, and medical-legal educators and students. The underlying assumption of this text is that informed physicians, like well-informed patients, are able to choose courses of action consistent with their own best interests and those of society in general. The physician is able to evaluate both the medical and the legal implications of a medical situation can avoid possible unexpected legal consequences that may follow a well-intended medical action. Seeing how and where liability has been imposed on anesthesiologists may also help the physician user to avoid medical malpractice suits.

The material presented in this text is referenced to reported anesthesia cases, statutes, regulations, court rules and rules of evidence from the fifty state jurisdictions, as well as United States Supreme Court decisions and federal statutes and regulations which apply to the practice of anesthesiology.

In approaching the legal system, two thoughts should be kept in mind. First, the legal system is not a unity; rather, it consists of many federal and state jurisdictions, each with their own rules and case law. Second, not all questions of law, whether relevant to the practice of medicine or private lives in general, have been decided in any one particular jurisdiction. Therefore, gaps and uncertainties permeate the field. For instance, in response to the same question, Wisconsin may have answered in the affirmative, New York in the negative and, to complicate matters even more, California may not have taken a position on the question at all. Where divergent doctrines exist, each is presented because the law is subject to change: one jurisdiction may approve of and eventually adopt the law of another. Which doctrines apply to an individual anesthesiologist depend largely on the jurisdiction where the anesthesiologist practices.

The reader should be aware this text is not intended as a substitute for competent legal counsel. Because the entire field of law and medicine is one of the most highly legislated, regulated and litigated areas of law, it changes daily. And because the changes are often significant, competent legal counsel should always be consulted for definitive answers to questions of law.

Preface

The main purpose of this volume is to define and demonstrate the standard of care concept. With this concept as a framework, specific anesthesia standards of care governing anesthetic agents and induction techniques have been articulated in legal decisions, and by medical authority. The authors recognize that medical standards are never static and that leading authorities may differ on the validity of a particular treatment procedure. Accordingly, the authors invite debate and comment on the validity and relevance of the standards stated by offering this text to those who make daily life and death decisions. The authors hope these written standards will stimulate discussion resulting in further clarification and accuracy for the benefit of both practitioner and patient.

An extensive staff was involved in the preparation of this text. Staff members included: Elaine Brock, M.H.S.A., J.D., and John F. Gillespie, J.D., staff attorneys, Jody Aaron, J.D., Phillip L. Dutt, M.D., J.D., James Kalyvas, J.D., Michael Keeley, Brad Kuster, Jacqueline Kuster, Peter Manbeck, Marcia Murray, Pat Steele, Fred van Hartesveldt, Avery Williams, and Gary Woodard, research assistants, and Sherri Gorelick, Sharon LeGoullon, Alison Novick, Jill Taber, Julie Valentine and Gail Zumstein, secretaries and materials coordinators. The authors wish to recognize and thank each of these individuals for the time and effort they contributed toward the production of this text.

J. Douglas Peters
Keith S. Fineberg
Donald A. Kroll
Vincent Collins

Ann Arbor, Michigan
June 1982

Part I
Liability

Chapter I

The Law of Malpractice

§ 1.10 INTRODUCTION

In the American legal system, patients have always been entitled to sue their physicians, but until the 1950s malpractice lawsuits were relatively rare. From 1950 until the mid-1960s malpractice lawsuits steadily increased at a rate of two to five percent per annum. Within the mid-1960s the rate of increase jumped suddenly to 15 percent per annum, and has remained there.[1]

The term "malpractice" refers to any professional misconduct, including the unreasonable lack of skill or fidelity in carrying out professional or fiduciary duties.[2] The purpose of the medical malpractice lawsuit is to afford recovery for injuries suffered when physicians fail to exercise ordinary and reasonable care in the diagnosis and treatment of patients.[3]

Currently, malpractice theory is the predominant vehicle for imposing liability, although physicians may find themselves involved in suits brought on other legal grounds. Patients may sue a physician for disclosing confidential medical information (see § 2.40, Liability Arising from Medical Records), for injury resulting from the use of a defective drug or medical product (see § 2.50, Products Liability) or for the negligent acts of health care personnel providing treatment under the direction of the physician (see § 2.30, Vicarious Liability). However, most suits brought against physicians on such other theories usually involve malpractice principles as well. The purpose of this chapter is to acquaint the physician with the legal concepts at play in the typical medical lawsuit and provide the legal vocabulary necessary to apply these principles to the practice of anesthesiology.

From its beginnings, the law has imposed liability on the physician if his or her conduct failed to reflect professional skill and care. As the law of contracts developed, the courts increasingly chose to analyze the physician's liability in terms of emerging contract concepts.[4] (See § 2.20, Contract Theory.) The negligence action developed later; negligence as a separate tort has been recognized only for about one-and-a-half centuries. As this branch of law took shape, the courts began to adopt its principles and apply them to medical malpractice cases.[5] In most jurisdictions, both contract and negligence theories may currently be used in a malpractice suit; often, the outcome of the suit can depend upon which theory the patient-plaintiff adopts.

In many jurisdictions, contract as a basis for the malpractice suit has fallen into disfavor. The courts are disinclined to interpret a physician's words of reassurance as a contractual obligation to attain certain results.[6] Some states, such as Michigan, have gone so far as to legislate that the contract must be expressed rather than implied, and in writing, for a patient to recover against a physician on a breach of contract claim.[7]

Limiting the legal theories under which malpractice lawsuits may be brought has not, however, had much of an impact on the number of suits brought. The incidence of malpractice litigation increased to such an extent in the mid-70s that many commentators labeled the phenomenon a "malpractice crisis." Although this label suggests a deterioration of quality in medical care, it actually reflects a number of factors, including the increasing unavailability and high cost of malpractice insurance coverage, double digit inflation, increasing health care costs, and the higher claims consciousness of the public. One outgrowth of the malpractice crisis has been the efforts of various groups to develop statistical analyses of the phenomenon. With statistical data categorized according to specific medical procedures, medical specialties, and other such isolated contributing factors, some groups have proposed so-called "risk management" programs to alleviate the problem, relying on subsequent data to validate their efforts. These data also provide another perspective: even if the incidence of malpractice is on the decline, as some observers currently maintain,[8] the data identify the relative "malpractice risk" associated with various medical procedures.

The St. Paul Fire and Marine Insurance Company, a well known malpractice insurance provider, has compiled a list of allegations and causes of loss for malpractice claims. The list begins with those claims unsettled as of September 1973. As of December 1978, of a total of 12,590 cases tabulated, 1,067 or 5.4 percent arose out of anesthesia mishaps. Of these cases, 345 or 32 percent arose from cardiac arrest, 311 or 29 percent arose from adverse reactions to the anesthetic agent used, and 265 or 24.8 percent arose from damage to teeth.[9]

In June 1975, the National Association of Insurance Commissioners (NAIC), a voluntary, unincorporated association of insurance commissioners of 54 states and territories, adopted a statistical program for medical malpractice and initiated the collection of comprehensive data on claims closed since July 1, 1975. The data considers a total of 399 anesthesia-related claims. Of these claims, 183, or 45.8 percent, arose from inhalation anesthesia; 68, or 17 percent, arose from intravenous anesthesia; 45, or 11.3 percent, arose from spinal anesthesia; and 43, or 10.7 percent, arose from regional nerve block anesthesia. Additionally, the NAIC study included a "severity of injury" scale for classifying the degree of injury that resulted in suit. Of the ten anesthesia procedures considered, the

§ 1.10   Introduction   5

average severity of the injury was of a permanent, though minor,* nature with the exception of topical anesthesia, which resulted in only one claim for an injury of a temporary, minor nature.[10]

Another study, conducted by Harold Hirsch and Edward White, considered 1,566 cases reported from April 1971, through November 1977. Of these cases, 78 or 4.9 percent stemmed from anesthesia mishaps. Of these, the most common allegations were negligence in specific treatment or procedure in 35 cases or 44.8 percent of the total and negligence in postoperative care in 32 cases or 41 percent of the total. Hirsch and White shed additional light on these categories by stating that the primary sources of anesthesia-based malpractice claims were negligence in the induction of anesthesia and in the observation of the patient during anesthesia and postoperative care. Alleged negligence during anesthesia was found to be due, in part, to inexperienced personnel and inadequate monitoring, often because a supervising anesthesiologist had too heavy a case load.[11]

Anesthesiologists may be viewed as particularly susceptible to malpractice lawsuits because their professional tasks are fraught with major risks. These tasks include relieving patient pain during operations, thus providing surgeons with optimal operating conditions.[12] Anesthesia is accomplished through a deliberate, artificial, physiologic disturbance such as loss of consciousness, loss of response to painful stimuli, and loss of muscular tone. The risks involved, depending upon the anesthesia used, include respiratory disturbances, serious circulatory disturbance including sudden cardiopulmonary arrest, gastrointestinal upsets, depression of liver function by anoxia, necrosis of the hepatic lobules by chloroform, depression of kidney function, and a variety of other serious effects to the nervous system.[13]

More than one commentator has stressed that establishing good rapport with the patient does much to avoid litigation.[14] If this assertion is true, the anesthesiologist labors under an inherent disadvantage. He or she has less exposure to patients outside the operating room than other physicians, and consequently less opportunity to develop good rapport. Furthermore, the fact that the patient is unconscious during the period when the anesthesiologist contributes most to treatment may tend to create a feeling of resentment toward this unfamiliar physician.[15] An anesthesiologist's best protection is complete documentation. During the preoperative visit, he or she should take a thorough history and carefully explain the anesthesia procedure** to the patient.[16] Treatment alternatives, e.g. local, regional

---

*The study defines permanent, minor injury by providing examples of loss of fingers, loss or damage to organs, including non-disabling injuries.

**Preprinted standard form consents are in common use today. Care should be taken to modify these forms according to the facts of a given clinical situation or as technology or new information supplants

or general, and the risks and benefits of each should be described and offered prior to securing the patient's consent. (See § 1.33, Consent and Informed Consent.)

At regular intervals during the course of the operation and anesthesia, a complete and accurate record containing written observations should be recorded. If information must be added, this should be clearly indicated and if corrections must be made, a line should be drawn through the error and the correction added.[17] The line drawn should not obscure the erroneous information.

The malpractice crisis has generated various responses in both the medical and legal fields. Medicine has responded by imposing continuing medical education requirements in an attempt to ensure that high quality medical care is provided by the profession and that the profession is kept abreast of new developments. Some physicians have begun to practice "defensive" medicine leading to unnecessary tests and treatment conducted in a fruitless effort to avoid legal liability. Some authorities, however, challenge this conclusion.[18]

As an alternative to conventional litigation, legal responses have included arbitration, mediation, or both procedures to attempt the resolution of a conflict by an impartial third party selected by the contestants. Some state legislatures have limited malpractice attorneys' fees and the amount of damages that may be claimed in the malpractice complaint. Others have shortened the statute of limitations. At best these "band-aid" measures relieve the symptoms. As one study stated:

> Our conclusion, based on patient complaints, is that most of the cases could have been prevented if the health care providers had exercised greater vigilance, diligence, and attention to the details of patient care particularly in communicating with the patient. Proper drug therapy and timely testing are also very important in preventing malpractice, and these can be accomplished relatively easily . . . In conclusion, prophylaxis can beat malpractice.[19]

§ 1.20 ELEMENTS OF NEGLIGENCE

Generally, when a patient sues a physician for an injury stemming from the physician's treatment, the patient is suing for malpractice. Negligence is the legal theory most commonly used by malpractice plaintiffs. To succeed under a negligence theory or, in legal jargon, to present a cause of action for negligence, a patient-plaintiff must prove four things:

Continued.

the information contained in the preprinted form(s). Patients should sign these forms and, as a general rule, signature must be secured before the administration of any anesthetic drugs which might impair the patient's decision-making process.

1. DUTY—the patient-plaintiff must show that the anesthesiologist in question owed him or her a particular duty or obligation. This duty, recognized by law as created by the physician-patient relationship, requires the anesthesiologist to act in accordance with specific norms or standards established by the profession, commonly referred to as standards of care, for the protection of patients against unreasonable risks.
2. BREACH OF DUTY—the patient-plaintiff must show that the anesthesiologist failed to act in accordance with those norms by any commissive or omissive act violating the standard of care owed to the patient-plaintiff.
3. CAUSATION—the patient-plaintiff must show that a reasonable, close causal connection exists between the acts of the anesthesiologist and the resulting injury. This is commonly known as "legal cause" or "proximate cause" which differs from medical causation in that it refers to *a* cause and not necessarily *the* cause or even the most immediate cause as is the case with medical causation.
4. DAMAGES—the plaintiff* must establish that because of the anesthesiologist's acts, actual loss or damage has been incurred. Damages may include physical, financial or emotional injury to the patient or related others (i.e., spouse, heirs, etc.).[20]

In order to recover, the plaintiff must prove by a preponderance of the evidence that *all four* of these elements exist. Preponderance of the evidence means proof that leads the trier of fact (the judge or jury) to find that the existence of the fact at issue is more probable than not.

§ 1.30 DUTY

The definition of duty, stated above, refers to the duty component of negligence as it is applied to anesthesiologists. The general concept of duty, as an element of negligence, presupposes some uniform standard of behavior. Because of the infinite variety of situations that may give rise to negligent conduct, it is virtually impossible to prescribe specific standards for all aspects of human behavior. The law has responded to this difficulty with something in the nature of a formula that it leaves to the jury or the court to apply. Certain necessary qualities of such a formula have been recognized by the law: the standard must be objective and not

---

*On occasion, the plaintiff is someone other than the patient, e.g. a patient's spouse, or the estate of a dead patient.

left to the individual judgment of the actor; it must be uniform to avoid any semblance in the law of favoritism; and it must allow for the risk apparent to the actor, the actor's capacity to respond to it, and the circumstances under which he or she must act. In response to these considerations, the law has created the reasonable man of ordinary prudence who acts with reasonable and due care in any given situation. The actor has the duty to conform his or her behavior to that of this ideal individual, the reasonable man, placed in the actor's shoes.[21]

Within the confines of malpractice, the courts have provided greater focus with respect to duty. The reasonable man becomes the reasonable physician. This legal fiction requires that every physician possess or exercise the requisite skill, care, and diligence the particular case demands.[22] The patient may show that the physician failed to exercise the required care by doing something that should not have been done or by failing to do or order something which should have been done.[23] It may not be sufficient that the physician has performed at full potential and in the utmost good faith. Rather, the physician must have conformed to the standard of a "reasonable physician" under like circumstances.[24]

The circumstances may have a direct bearing on the duty owed. In a case where an anesthesiologist was unsuccessfully sued, a child undergoing a tonsillectomy suffered a cardiac arrest resulting in brain damage. The court recognized that the cardiac arrest presented the anesthesiologist with an emergency situation. The court stated that although a physician confronted with an emergency is bound to use due care, there is not the usual time for the same thought and consideration of his actions as in a nonemergency situation.[25]

While such statements provide a general standard of care or duty, they are insufficient in and of themselves to determine what the duty of a particular physician is in a particular case. Because most medical malpractice cases involve a highly technical evaluation of the propriety and skill of a physician in the treatment of a patient, it is considered necessary that witnesses with special medical or scientific qualifications provide guidance to a lay jury by furnishing them with the necessary knowledge to render a just verdict.[26]

Consequently, the standard of medical care must be ascertained from expert testimony in nearly all instances.[27] And that standard of care is the care and skill commonly possessed and exercised by similar specialists in like circumstances.[28] This specialty standard may often be higher* than that required of general practitioners[29] and has been applied by various courts to anesthesiologists.[30] (See § 1.32, Standard of Care.)

---

*While some courts characterize a national specialty standard as "higher" than that applied to a general practitioner, it is more accurate to state that the specialist does not owe a *greater amount* of care than the general practitioner; rather, the specialist, like the general practitioner, owes the patient due care in the application of the skill actually possessed. Consequently, by virtue of the specialty, the specialist is thought to possess greater skill in his or her specialty than the general practitioner.

§ 1.31 Physician-Patient Relationship

Whether a physician owes any legal duty to a patient depends upon the existence of a physician-patient relationship. Unless such a relationship exists, the physician cannot be held liable for medical malpractice.[31]

According to the American Medical Association's "Principles of Medical Ethics," a physician is free to choose whom he will serve.[32] Consequently, the physician is under no obligation to engage in practice or to accept professional employment,[33] but when the professional services of a physician are accepted by another person for the purpose of medical or surgical treatment, the physician-patient relationship is created.[34]

The physician-patient relationship is fiduciary in nature based on the notion that the physician is learned, skilled and experienced in an area of vital importance to the patient, about which the patient knows little.[35] Such a relationship may be created by the express or implied agreement of the parties.[36]

An implied agreement to enter into the physician-patient relationship may be found where a patient seeks medical assistance and the physician offers treatment without any specific reference to an agreement or the relationship.[37]

While express agreements are rarely made between physicians and patients, they are generally enforceable and the anesthesiologist has the right to impose certain conditions or create obligations additional to those inherent in the legal relationship.[38] (See § 2.20, Contract Theory.) However, an express agreement the patient signs to absolve the physician from any liability for injury resulting from negligent treatment has been held to be contrary to public policy and does not protect a physician from liability.[39] (See Appendix F.) Such an agreement differs from the duty to obtain the patient's informed consent to treatment. Where informed consent has been obtained, it is recognized by the courts. (See § 1.33, Consent and Informed Consent.)

Frequently, patients do not select particular anesthesiologists. The surgeon performing the operation may select the anesthesiologist. Alternatively, the hospital at which the operation is performed may provide anesthesiologists for all operations. In either of these cases, the critical element of the physician-patient relationship is the assent of the parties. By selecting a particular surgeon, or the particular hospital, the patient implicitly accepts the designated anesthesiologist.[40] Similarly, by agreeing to perform the operation with the surgeon, the anesthesiologist accepts the patient.

Mutual assent is not absolutely required to trigger a physician-patient relationship. An unconscious patient may have no opportunity to select a particular hospital or surgeon. Nonetheless, whenever a physician undertakes to render care to another, a professional relationship and its corresponding duty of care are created.[41] In cases of overt conduct by the physician, courts have had little trouble in finding a sufficient undertaking to create a physician-patient relationship.[42]

In certain situations, a physician may treat or serve a patient without creating a physician-patient relationship. One such situation, which possibly applies little to the anesthesiologist, occurs when medical services are provided for the benefit of a third party rather than the patient, for example, when a physician examines a patient for an insurer,[43] for a potential employer[44] or for purposes of a worker's compensation claim.[45] Furthermore, when a physician who is treating a patient discusses the patient's case with a second physician for advice or consultation and the patient receives no direct treatment or service from the second physician, there is no physician-patient relationship between the patient and the second physician.[46]

State statutes have limited the creation of the physician-patient relationship in certain situations. In many states, the rendering of treatment outside of the hospital emergency room in an emergency situation by a physician who does not already have an ongoing physician-patient relationship with the emergency victim does not establish a physician-patient relationship.* Except for acts or omissions amounting to gross negligence or willful and wanton misconduct, the physician is usually not liable for any civil damages resulting from acts or omissions in the rendering of such emergency care. This is a general statement of the statutory law in all but four states** which have enacted so-called Good Samaritan statutes.[47] The justification for such statutes stems from the fact that without them a bystander who renders aid to a stranger in distress assumes a legally enforceable obligation to exercise reasonable care and skill in the task voluntarily assumed; this obligation has been viewed as a deterrent to voluntary assistance. By providing treatment, the volunteering physician would create a physician-patient relationship with all its attendant obligations, without regard to whether or not the services rendered were gratuitous or compensated.[48]

While the Good Samaritan statutes are designed to alleviate this problem, they vary in their approach to the solution. Variations appear in what constitutes the scene of the emergency; some limit the statute's application to motor vehicle accidents,[49] while most states provide protection for the Good Samaritan at the

---

*The emergency admission situation is distinguishable from the in-hospital emergency situation. If physicians, nurses, or other hospital personnel respond in good faith to life-threatening emergencies within the hospital where their actual duties as defined by hospital rules do not require a response, by state statute they may be immune from liability for damages resulting from an act or omission, unless the act or omission amounts to gross negligence or willful and wanton misconduct. For example, see, Mich. Comp. Laws Ann.§ 691. 1502 (Supp. 1980-81).

WARNING: This immunity from liability usually does not apply to a physician where a physician-patient relationship existed between the patient and the physician prior to the advent of the emergency. For example, see, Mich. Comp. Laws Ann. *supra*.

**The four states which currently do not have Good Samaritan legislation on the books are Colorado, Kentucky, Minnesota and Missouri.

§ 1.31   *Physician-Patient Relationship*   *11*

scene of an accident or emergency generally.[50] Some states only provide immunity from liability if the physician-volunteer receives no compensation from the emergency victim.[51] A number of states extend immunity only to those licensed under the enacting state's own laws,[52] while others immunize licensees of any state.[53] Most of the statutes restrict immunity to cases where the actions of the physician-volunteer do not amount to gross negligence or willful and wanton misconduct.[54]

The following Good Samaritan statute, which has been adopted in Indiana, represents typical Good Samaritan legislation:

> From and after the effective date of this act, no civil action may be brought against a person licensed to practice the healing arts in the State of Indiana, who has gratuitously rendered first aid or emergency care at the scene of an accident, casualty, or disaster to a person injured therein, for the recovery of civil damages as a result of any act or omission by the said person rendering such first aid or emergency care in the rendering of such first aid or emergency care. This immunity does not apply to acts or omissions constituting gross negligence or willful or wanton misconduct.[55]

If nothing prevents the creation of the anesthesiologist-patient relationship, once it has begun, the anesthesiologist is obligated to attend the case as long as is medically necessary.[56] Though the anesthesiologist's primary role occurs during an operation, pre- and postanesthetic care are important parts of the anesthesiologist's overall duty. In fact, leaving the patient prematurely may give rise to an action for abandonment. Abandonment has been defined as the unilateral severance without adequate notice of the professional relationship with the patient despite the need for continuing medical attention.[57] The physician may not terminate the physician-patient relationship at will. The relationship continues until it is ended by either the patient's lack of need for further care or the withdrawing physician's replacement by an equally qualified physician. Withdrawal from the case under any other circumstance constitutes a wrongful abandonment of the patient and if the patient suffers any injury as a proximate result of such wrongful abandonment, the physician is liable for it.[58]

CASE ILLUSTRATION

The patient was admitted to the hospital for a dilatation and curettage. The defendant-anesthesiologist injected the patient with sodium pentothal, two or three minutes after which the patient developed a laryngospasm. Attempts to break and relax the spasm, manually and through injections, were unsuccessful. Fifteen minutes later a second anesthesiologist inserted an endotracheal tube down the patient's throat so that oxygen could be forced beyond the obstruction caused by the spasm, enabling the patient to be ventilated. Improvement was noted immediately, although the patient continued to be cyanotic and hypotensive.

Intubation was finally accomplished some 50 minutes after the initial injection of sodium pentothal had been given. However, only 35 minutes after the initial injection, the defendant-anesthesiologist left the operating room. He left upon the request of another anesthesiologist to attend another operation. The patient sustained severe brain damage and sued the first anesthesiologist. At the trial, the defendant-anesthesiologist claimed that when he left the operating room he did so only upon being replaced by an equally qualified physician, a second anesthesiologist. Evidence was introduced in the form of a hospital record that this second anesthesiologist was not present in the patient's operating room at all but was attending a birth taking place in another operating room. The Court of Appeals upheld the jury finding that the first anesthesiologist was negligent in abandoning the patient and was, therefore, liable for the injuries she sustained. (*Ascher v. Gutierrez*, 1976)[59]

The physician who has abandoned a patient may not assert that there is no way to prove that his or her efforts would have made any difference since it is the conduct of the physician, not the patient, that makes such proof speculative.[*] The patient is entitled to rely on the best efforts of the physician to reduce or eliminate the injury.[60] If abandonment can be proved, the patient may be entitled to an award of punitive damages in some jurisdictions.[61] (See § 1.60, Damages.)

Occasionally, a patient may sustain an injury resulting from a complication that occurs postoperatively, as the anesthesia wears off and the patient achieves semiconsciousness.[62] Generally, where the anesthesiologist has taken the necessary precautions in such situations, extubation and transfer of responsibility to recovery room supervision after surgery does not constitute abandonment.

A physician does have a right to withdraw from a case, provided the physician gives the patient reasonable notice to secure other medical assistance,[63] and all conditions for the physician's rightful withdrawal have been met. These include a release of the patient that is sufficiently complete and formal to allow another physician to take the case.[64] A physician may furnish a substitute,[65] provided that the substitute is acceptable to the patient.[66] In this situation, the physician owes the patient the duty to provide his or her successor with all the relevant medical data available.[67]

---

[*]An anesthesiologist responsible for the supervision of multiple CRNAs may be liable for abandonment if he or she is unavailable to the CRNA in a crisis. The greater the number of CRNAs to be supervised, the greater the risk the anesthesiologist will be sued for abandonment.

§ 1.32   Standard of Care

§ 1.32   Standard of Care

As physicians, anesthesiologists are not insurers against harm nor guarantors of favorable results.[68] According to a leading treatise on anesthesiology, "[t]he major objective of those in the discipline of anesthesiology is to possess knowledge and expertise so that those needing assistance in the control of their vital functions on an acute basis, which includes the state of anesthesia itself, can be properly and safely managed through the critical periods of their disability."[69] When an anesthesiologist owes a duty to a patient, he is legally obligated to possess and exercise the knowledge and skill necessary to perform these tasks. The "standard of care" is the legal term used to describe this required expertise.

The standard of care is a general formula employed by the court or jury to determine whether an anesthesiologist has properly performed his or her duties. One court has said that in an action for negligence a qualified medical practitioner should be subject to liability for failure to exercise that degree of care and skill which is expected of the average practitioner in the same class, acting under the same or similar circumstances.[70]

CASE ILLUSTRATION

The patient underwent a spinal anesthesia just prior to a hysterectomy. The anesthesiologist initially attempted to insert the needle into the L-2, L-3 interspace, but the patient immediately manifested pain. The anesthesiologist thereafter used the L-3, L-4 interspace. The patient sustained permanent injury to her left leg. The court held that the anesthesiologist must prove that he had that degree of skill and care which is usually possessed by practitioners of his profession. Several physicians testified that it is contrary to existing professional standards to inject spinal anesthesia directly into the spinal cord. Since the patient's symptoms did suggest a direct injection, and no other reasonable explanation for the condition was offered, the court rendered a verdict for the patient. (*Buras v. Aetna Casualty and Surety Company*, 1972)[71]

Every standard of care formula requires comparison of one physician's acts to the practices of some pool of physicians. Historically, the pool has consisted of physicians in the same community. Courts reasoned that medical sophistication is a function of community size and resources and no physician should be held liable for failure to meet more sophisticated standards. As one court noted, the community standard rule does not require a small office of rural medical practitioners to possess either the skills or equipment of a sophisticated clinic; but the standard demands, at least, that one exercise ordinary care commensurate with the equipment, skills, and time available.[72]

The pool was later expanded in many jurisdictions to include physicians in *similar* communities, rather than just those in the same community. As one court reasoned, it is frequently difficult to find local physicians willing to testify against their colleagues.[73] Moreover, should several careless practitioners settle in the same locality, the resultant community standard could significantly deviate from accepted practice.

Today medical specialists are held to a uniform standard regardless of the practices in a particular community.[74] As stated by a Connecticut court, the standard of care applicable to anesthesiologists depends on "the standard of their art at the time that they were allegedly negligent."[75*] In justifying the recognition of a national specialty standard for specialists, the courts have noted: (1) the refusal of physicians in the medical community to testify against one another, a condition identified by the courts as a so-called "conspiracy of silence";[76] (2) the fact that the various specialties of medicine have set up uniform requirements for certification of specialists, i.e., the length of residency training, subjects to be covered, and even examinations are established by the national specialty boards;[77] (3) the existence of continuing medical education requirements, as a result of which physicians continue to study and attend refresher courses and have access to journals which afford them the opportunity to keep current in the latest treatments and procedures.[78]

Because the standard of care cannot be determined without some understanding of accepted medical practice, there are few exceptions to the general rule that expert testimony regarding those practices is essential in a malpractice lawsuit.[79] One case held that "proof of [the] standard of care must be made by the testimony of a physician qualified to speak as an expert, having the basic education and training as a foundation and the practical knowledge which is of controlling

---

*With regard to this legal doctrine, the judge, in an appropriate case, may read the following instructions to the jury: "There is evidence tending to show that the patient involved in this action sustained injury from the improper administration of an anesthetic by the defendant. If you find that the injury complained of did result from such cause, in determining whether or not the administration was negligent, you must pay regard to the expert testimony as to whether or not defendant's conduct constituted a deviation from the standard of skill and care which is required of one in his situation. In so determining, you should consider whether, in view of his training and background, the standards required are higher than those of an ordinary practitioner who administers an anesthetic. . . . If you find that the results, or the injuries which plaintiff sustained, were due to peculiar conditions or temperament of the patient of which defendant, having regard to his training and experience, could not have been reasonably expected to have known, your verdict should be for the defendant. If, on the other hand, you find from the opinion evidence that such results ought reasonably to have been anticipated by one with the professional background of the defendant, your verdict should be for the plaintiff." (G. Douthwaite, Alexander's Jury Instructions on Medical Issues, § 6-1 ((2d ed. 1980).)

§ 1.32   Standard of Care   15

importance in determining competency of the expert to testify as to the standard of care.[80] Normally, the applicable standard of care is established by the testimony of someone with a background or training similar to that of the defendant. However, expert witnesses need not be medical doctors nor medical school graduates if they have received other appropriate training. For example, some courts have accepted the testimony of nurse-anesthetists[81] and pharmacologists.[82]

The plaintiff in a malpractice action has the burden of establishing a case of negligence by the preponderance or greater weight of the evidence.[83] Experts commonly disagree on the proper course of action in a particular case. The plaintiff can succeed only by showing that the greater weight of medical opinion goes against what the anesthesiologist did under the circumstances.

CASE ILLUSTRATION

A three-year-old girl underwent an operation to remove decayed teeth. Demerol, vistaril, and atropine were administered before the operation, and succinylcholine was used to aid nasal intubation. After the operation, the anesthesiologist used one-quarter cc. of tensilon to restore spontaneous breathing. The girl later died due to adrenal insufficiency. At trial, one expert witness in anesthesiology testified that giving succinylcholine followed by tensilon was a gross error. A pharmacology professor supported this view. On the other hand, a world-renowned expert in the field of pharmacology and anesthesiology testified that what was done was proper. Another anesthesiologist concurred. The court held that in light of this conflicting testimony, the plaintiff had failed to show by a preponderance of the evidence that medical specialists in the field of anesthesiology would generally regard the treatment given as improper. (*Chapman v. Argonaut-Southwest Insurance Company*, 1974)[84]

Additionally, the physician's duty is dependent upon the state of knowledge existing at the time of the alleged negligence. Thus, since physicians cannot be held to a standard which exceeds the limits of scientific advances existing at the time of their allegedly negligent conduct, expert testimony tending to show the scope of duties owed should be limited to scientific knowledge existing at that time.[85]

There are recognized exceptions to the expert testimony requirement. First, when the physician's lack of care is obvious and easily comprehensible to the layperson, experts are not needed to reveal the deficiency.[86] The most common example of this exception is physician caused injury to a part of the body not involved in the treatment.[87] Second, where issues raised in a malpractice case are not of a scientific or technical nature, the jury can assess the existence of negligence as it would in a non-malpractice case, without the assistance of expert testimony.[88]

CASE ILLUSTRATION

The patient entered the hospital for a cholecystectomy. The physician-defendant visited the patient on the day prior to surgery and advised her that she would be given general anesthesia. He further told her that tests taken at the hospital showed her physical condition as generally normal but because of her history of hepatitis there were "anesthetics that we probably would not be using." The physician testified that he decided to avoid using halogenated anesthetics, specifically Penthrane, and he informed the nurse-anesthetist of this decision. The nurse-anesthetist's testimony acknowledged that she was obligated to follow a physician's direct orders relating to an anesthetic; however, she claimed that the decision not to use Penthrane had *not* been communicated to her. Penthrane was administered and the patient developed a liver dysfunction and subsequently died.

The trial court instructed the jury that it could consider only the testimony of experts on certain factual issues regarding whether the physician had arrived at a medical judgment not to use Penthrane, whether he communicated his decision to the nurse-anesthetist, and whether the nurse-anesthetist disobeyed or disregarded the physician's directions. The appellate court overturned the trial court's verdict in favor of the physician and nurse-anesthetist and awarded a new trial to the plaintiff stating that while expert testimony on these questions might help in explaining the obligations of physician and nurse, the lay jury is perfectly capable of deciding these fact questions and should not be precluded from doing so. (*Carlsen v. Javurek*, 1975)[89]

Additionally, expert testimony may not be required in cases involving the issue of informed consent. (See § 1.33, Consent and Informed Consent.)

The testimony of expert medical witnesses is not the only way to establish the applicable standard of care. Standards announced in manuals for hospital employees, for example, are evidence of accepted medical practice and are therefore material and relevant.[90] In some cases the recommendations of a drug manufacturer may be used to establish the standard of care applicable to the use of that drug.[91] In many jurisdictions, however, manufacturer recommendations may be used to prove that a physician should have been aware of the risks involved in the use of a drug or other medical product, but may not be used by themselves to prove a specific standard of care.[92] The Minnesota Supreme Court has stated that where a drug manufacturer recommends to the medical profession (1) the conditions under which its drug should be prescribed, (2) the disorders it is designed to relieve, (3) the precautionary measures which should be observed, and (4) warns of the dangers which are inherent in its use, a physician's deviation from such recommendations is prima facie evidence of negligence if there is competent medical testimony that his or her patient's injury or death resulted from the physician's failure to adhere to the recommendations.[93]

CASE ILLUSTRATION

The patient was anesthetized with halothane in preparation for an operation to repair a diaphragmatic hernia. Approximately 13 minutes after anesthesia was begun by the nurse-anesthetist, it was discovered that the patient was cyanotic and had suffered a cardiac arrest. Resuscitation was attempted but no reversal of the cardiac arrest occurred and the patient was pronounced dead.

The patient's family sued the operating and assisting physician and the nurse-anesthetist, alleging that the patient's injury was caused by the failure of the nurse-anesthetist to administer a four-liter per minute flow of carrier gases (two liters of oxygen and two liters of nitrous oxide) with halothane continuously. The nurse-anesthetist testified that she never administered or increased the rate to as much as a two liter flow. The manufacturer of the machine by which anesthesia was administered recommended a four liter flow per minute. The court refused to permit use of the manufacturer's recommendations to impeach other expert testimony that what was actually done was proper. The court reasoned that the manufacturer, a corporation which was not shown to the court to have been a medical expert, could not by its literature have established any medical standard for purposes of trial in a court of law. The court found the physicians and nurse-anesthetist to be not liable. (*Webb v. Jorns*, 1975)[94]

Another source of the standard of care is the medical textbook. The admissibility of such evidence as proof of the standard, however, varies among jurisdictions. The traditional rule is that medical texts may be used in a malpractice lawsuit only to cross-examine a medical expert.[95] This is accomplished by framing a proposition in the exact language used by the author of the medical text and then asking the witness whether he or she agrees. The expert being cross-examined need not initially agree that the text is standard or authoritative. The courts have recognized that if the rule were otherwise, the witness would have complete control of the cross-examination and could conceivably preclude the use of any text.[96] Even in those jurisdictions which adhere to the old rule, there is an emerging trend which allows for such evidence to play a greater role at trial. The Supreme

Court of Michigan, a state which maintains the old rule, has stated that the testimony of an expert witness is, in all probability, far less reliable than testimony derived from textbooks since ordinary expert witnesses derive their knowledge not from personal experience but from studying scientific literature. The Court also pointed to the circumstances attending the publication of learned treatises and concluded that there is a fair probability that the work is trustworthy. The Court rejected the dangers of using passages which are explained away or contradicted in other parts of the book and noted that opposing attorneys, with the aid of the expert witness, may ask questions to point out the inaccuracy of the questionable text or to explain the meaning of technical passages. However, despite the Court's recognition of the validity of these arguments, the Michigan Supreme Court has refused to extend the permissible role of medical texts beyond the area of cross-examination.[97]

The Supreme Court of Wisconsin, in abolishing the old rule for that jurisdiction, observed:

> The rule that medical and scientific textbooks are inadmissible as independent, substantive evidence has worked hardship in many cases, particularly because of the difficulty of obtaining medical testimony. Where the foundation is laid that the work is authoritative, recognized by the medical profession, and one which has influence upon medical opinions, such works have now been admitted as independent evidence . . . (The Uniform Rules of Evidence,) . . . provide that '[a] published treatise, periodical or pamphlet on a subject of history, science or art' should be admitted in evidence as an exception to the hearsay rule 'to prove the truth of a matter stated therein if the judge takes judicial notice or if a witness expert in the subject testifies, that the treatise, periodical, or pamphlet is a reliable authority on the subject.' . . . we consider this to be the better rule and adopt it for future cases. This is but another example of accepting the scientific process in the search for truth instead of reliance upon the efficacy of an oath as a guarantee of trustworthiness.[98]

If a malpractice case is tried in a federal court, the Federal Rules of Evidence which adopt a more liberal view will apply, allowing statements from texts to be read directly into evidence.[99]

Standard of Care Variations: It is often the case in medical practice that the physician is faced with multiple options for treating the patient, any of which would be appropriate. The standard of care concept does not penalize the physician for choosing one treatment option over another if the propriety of the chosen treatment can be proved. Propriety of a chosen course of treatment may be shown in a number of ways.

Where different schools of medical thought exist, the law does not attempt to settle the debate; rather, the physician is held to the tenets of the school he or she professes to follow.[100] Thus the osteopathic anesthesiologist may conduct his or her practice differently from the allopathic anesthesiologist so long as the osteopathic practice conforms to principles governing the practice of osteopathic anesthesiology (see § 5.21, Requirements). Generally, the patient who seeks treatment from an osteopathic physician is assumed to know that the osteopath will follow the methods and practices observed by that school of medicine and the courts will not entertain the complaint that the osteopath failed to adhere to the standard of practice of another school.[101] However, where procedures in different schools of medicine are similar, members of the different schools of medicine may be held to the same standard of care.[102] The Texas Civil Appeals Court has articulated that physicians of different schools may testify as to the applicable standard in malpractice cases where: (1) the particular subject of inquiry is common to and equally recognized and developed in both schools of practice; and (2) the subject of inquiry relates to the manner of use of mechanical or electrical apparatus commonly used in both schools.[103]

Within a single school of medicine, a physician will not be found negligent for using a treatment method recognized as good practice even though a different physician of the same school might have employed another method.[104] The physician has a duty to use his or her best judgment in determining what treatment to provide[105] and will not be held liable simply because the exercise of such judgment fails to bring about the desired result.

§ 1.33 Consent and Informed Consent

Before a physician may treat or operate on a patient, the physician must obtain the patient's consent if the patient is competent to give it; if the patient is not competent, the physician must obtain consent from someone legally authorized to give it on the patient's behalf.[106] The requirement for consent has been said to arise from the contractual nature of the physician-patient relationship: consent specifies what the parties understand will be done.[107] The law imposes this requirement because it acknowledges that every human being of adult age and sound mind has a right to determine what shall be done with his or her own body.[108]

Liability for failure to obtain the consent of the patient may be imposed under one of two different legal doctrines, depending upon the nature of the consent actually obtained. If the patient gives no consent to medical treatment, the physician who nevertheless renders such treatment may be legally liable for assault and battery. If the patient consents to medical treatment, but does so without a fully informed understanding of the risks and hazards of the proposed treatment, the physician who fails to provide such information may be liable for breach of the duty to obtain the patient's informed consent.

Assault and Battery: Assault is defined as the act of placing a person in apprehension of a harmful contact;[109] battery is the actual contact. In other words, battery is the offensive touching of another without the consent or authorization of that person.[110] In most jurisdictions, the distinction is blurred and the legal action is one for assault and battery under either definition.

In order to be held liable for assault and battery, a defendant must have committed some affirmative act which is intended to cause an unpermitted contact.[111] Assault and battery is an *intentional* tort (as opposed to negligence which is an *unintentional* tort) in that it involves the planned and conscious touching of the patient-plaintiff's person. It is enough that the physician-defendant sets in motion a force which ultimately produces the result. The gist of the action for assault and battery is not the hostile intent of the defendant, but rather the absence of consent to the contact on the part of the plaintiff.[112] Thus, a plaintiff's cause of action for assault and battery must allege: (1) the defendant's intentional act, which resulted in (2) the offensive contact with the plaintiff's person and (3) the plaintiff's lack of consent thereto.[113]

The primary issue considered is what constitutes adequate consent. For the anesthesiologist, specific written consent to anesthesia is the most desirable form. However, consent to surgery has been held to include consent to anesthesia.[114] Oral consent to anesthesia has been deemed valid even though the patient later had no memory of the anesthesiologist or the injection.[115*]

Under certain circumstances courts have found an implied consent in the patient's act of seeking treatment or voluntarily submitting to a particular course of treatment.[116] Such a finding is generally limited to a situation where the patient knows what is to transpire.[117]

The courts have recognized that in an emergency the anesthesiologist will find it necessary to treat a patient despite the patient's inability to consent. In these situations, the emergency abrogates the consent requirement or, alternatively, constitutes implied consent.[118]

CASE ILLUSTRATION

The female patient was admitted to the hospital with abdominal pain, and was initially treated with various medications including sedatives, pain-relievers, antibiotics, anti-nauseants, euphorics, vitamins, and tranquilizers. Two days later, the nurse-anesthetist administered spinal anesthesia prior to an emergency laparotomy. An intestinal obstruction was found during the operation and corrected. After the operation, the patient suffered a number of physical disabilities including bladder trouble, phlebitis of the left leg and partial paralysis. The patient sued the hospital, her physicians,

---

*Where oral consents are secured incident to oral explanations, the medical record should *show* the fact and extent of the oral consent. The record should also *show* the time and date as well as the fact that the patient was clearly coherent, i.e., the patient was not in the preoperative preparatory area.

§ 1.33   Consent and Informed Consent   21

and the nurse-anesthetist, basing her suit in part on assault and battery due to lack of consent to the anesthesia. The court relied on evidence that from the time the patient was admitted to the hospital to the time of the operation she was under heavy sedation and under the influence of pain-killing drugs, and was quite groggy. She testified at trial that she did not know what was happening about 80 percent of the time prior to the operation and did not recall anything that happened on the morning of the operation. The court stated that due to the patient's condition it would have been impossible to obtain a valid consent. Furthermore, there was testimony that the surgery was performed due to the emergency nature of the patient's condition and was agreed to by the patient's husband who signed a written consent form consenting to whatever operation and the administration of whatever anesthetic the physician deemed necessary. The court held that the anesthetic was incidental to the operation and was necessary to perform the operation. The court found consent to be implied by the existence of the emergency. (*Gravis v. Physicians & Surgeons Hospital of Alice*, 1967)[119]

The typical factual situation in a consent-related battery case arises when the patient consents to a certain type of operation or anesthetic, but the physician performs or administers another. Liability for battery may also lie in cases where the *scope* of the consent was exceeded or disregarded by the physician.[120]

To many physicians, the law regarding consent and technical battery may seem harsh; its justification stems from judicial recognition of the inviolability of the human body. Whatever harshness may be inherent in the doctrine is further tempered by the fact that generally only nominal damages are awarded the patient and some courts have recently declined to award even those.[121] (See § 1.60, Damages.) Of course, where the battery results in injury, courts will award compensatory damages, and if the battery was willfully or wantonly committed, punitive damages may be awarded. At least one jurisdiction, Arizona, has passed a statute that eliminates battery as a legal cause of action which may be brought against a physician.[122] The statute was passed in 1976 and applies only to those cases arising out of injuries that have occurred after its effective date.[123]

In the usual case, in order to vindicate the patient-plaintiff's legal right to be free of undesired contact, only nominal damages are awarded for battery without proof of any harm.[124] This is due to the fact that battery is an intentional tort, as stated above, as opposed to the doctrine of informed consent which is an unintentional tort. In order to recover for an unintentional tort, the plaintiff must have suffered an injury caused by the tortious act. (See § 1.50, Causation.) Thus, while failure to obtain patient consent for a treatment procedure may constitute battery and entitle the patient to nominal damages, failure to obtain *informed* consent entitles the patient to damages only if such failure causes an injury.

Informed Consent: In addition to requiring that a patient's consent be obtained prior to administering treatment, the law imposes a requirement regarding the nature or quality of that consent. In order to be effective, the patient's consent must be an informed consent, one that is given after the patient has received a fair and reasonable explanation of the contemplated treatment or procedure.[125]

CASE ILLUSTRATION

The patient entered the hospital for a hysterectomy. The anesthesiologist visited the patient the evening prior to the operation. He gave her no physical examination but asked her what kind of anesthetic she wanted. She replied that her gynecologist had recommended a spinal to which the anesthesiologist replied, "Well, those are the best." He went on to state that he preferred to give spinals and the most one could get from them was a headache and "we have medicine for that now." The operation was performed and the patient suffered paralysis on the left side. Additionally, the patient suffered a problem with control of bladder and bowels. The court held that the anesthesiologist either knew or should have known, based on his duty to possess the requisite skill and knowledge of a medical practitioner, that spinal anesthesia carried more risks for the patient than mere headaches, and that the other risks were greater in severity. When the anesthesiologist told the patient that a headache was the only possible danger, he misinformed and misled her. The court held that the patient's consent to a spinal was not an informed consent and therefore a nullity. Though the court recognized that there did not have to be negligence in the administration of the spinal anesthesia to induce the damage the patient suffered, the anesthesiologist was found liable for failure to obtain an informed consent. (*Funke v. Fieldman*, 1973)[126]

The source of the doctrine is the patient's right to exercise control over his or her own body.[127] Some courts have emphasized the importance of the fiduciary relationship between doctor and patient as it affects the duty of disclosure.[128] The doctrine requires the physician to reveal to the patient the nature of the ailment, the nature of the proposed treatment, the probability of success of the contemplated therapy and its alternatives, and the risk of unfortunate consequences associated with such treatment.[129]

As a California court stated:

> . . . A physician violates his duty to his patient and subjects himself to liability if he withholds any facts which are necessary to form the basis of an intelligent consent by the patient to the proposed treatment. Likewise the physician may not minimize the known dangers of a procedure or operation in order to induce his patient's consent. At

§ 1.33   Consent and Informed Consent

the same time, the physician must place the welfare of his patient above all else and this very fact places him in a position in which he sometimes must choose between two alternative courses of action. One is to explain to the patient every risk attendant upon any surgical procedure or operation, no matter how remote; this may well result in alarming a patient who is already unduly apprehensive and who may as a result refuse to undertake surgery in which there is in fact minimal risk; it may also result in actually increasing the risks by reason of the physiological results of the apprehension itself. The other is to recognize that each patient presents a separate problem, that the patient's mental and emotional condition is important and in certain cases may be crucial, and that in discussing the element of risk a certain amount of discretion must be employed consistent with the full disclosure of facts necessary to an informed consent.[130]

This statement identifies aspects of the dilemma facing physicians who must make all disclosures conform to the dictates of the informed consent doctrine.

Two competing rules exist among the jurisdictions governing the standard by which a physician's duty to disclose is measured. Many courts use the professional standard of care analysis according to which the physician's duty to disclose is a matter of professional judgment. A breach of that duty is determined by what risks a "reasonable" i.e., ideal practitioner would disclose under similar circumstances.[131] Under this rule, required disclosure must be based on professional criteria. Thus, the physician's disclosure to the patient is determined by the medical standard of care established by the professional practice in that or similar communities, except for specialists, whose disclosure must comport with the standards of the specialty (nationally).

A growing number of courts use a lay standard of reasonableness in informed consent cases. The focus is not on what the physician thinks a patient should know, but what the patient should know or want to know in order to make an informed decision. The test for disclosure in these cases is whether or not the information is *material* to the patient's decision. By definition, "material risk" is one which the physician knows or ought to know would be significant to a reasonable person in the patient's position of deciding whether or not to submit to a particular medical treatment or procedure.[132] The physician's duty to disclose is therefore determined by reference to a patient-oriented standard of disclosure rather than a professional one.

Whenever a physician is shown to have a duty to disclose under either rule, the actual disclosure of attendant risks must be made so that the patient is truly informed. The Pennsylvania Supreme Court has stated that "[I]t will be no defense for a surgeon to prove that the patient had given his consent, if the consent was not given with a true understanding of the nature of the operation to be performed, the seriousness of it, and organs of the body involved, the disease or incapacity sought to be cured and the possible results."[133] Consequently, though the patient may sign a consent form prior to treatment, if the signature is obtained without proper disclosure a court may look beyond the document to consider whether the physician adequately informed the patient of the nature and possible consequences of the procedure, as well as its alternatives, and whether under all the circumstances the description was adequate to inform a reasonable person and render the consent valid.[134]

In most jurisdictions the physician is not held to an unlimited duty of disclosure. Courts have generally stated that so long as a disclosure is sufficient to assure informed consent, the duty to disclose is limited to disclosures that a reasonable medical practitioner would make under the same or similar circumstances: what constitutes a reasonable disclosure depends upon the facts and circumstances of each case.[135]

Exclusions and Exceptions: Inverting the general rule, physicians have no duty to disclose risks which are not generally disclosed as a matter of accepted professional practice in the locality or within the specialty.

Foremost among the list of generally recognized exceptions to the physician's duty of disclosure are those risks which are minor and/or remote.

Other exceptions arise where the:

1. Patient is already aware of risk
2. Existence of the risk is a matter of common knowledge (the patient's knowledge of that risk may be inferred)
3. Risk was not generally known to the medical community at the time the procedure was carried out
4. Risk exists only when the procedure is negligently or improperly performed
5. Patient expressly requests that he or she not be informed*

One recognized limitation to the duty to disclose is referred to as the *Therapeutic Privilege*. The courts recognize that complete disclosure may constitute a therapeutic detriment to the patient. The determination of the extent of disclosure in such a case is seen as involving medical judgment as to whether disclosure of possible risks may so adversely affect the patient as to jeopardize success of the proposed therapy, no matter how expertly performed.[136] Because this is recognized as a medical decision, expert testimony may be required to prove that the therapeutic privilege has been properly exercised. In any event it is generally the physician-defendant's burden to prove that the exercise of "therapeutic privilege" was justified.

---

*If the patient makes such a request, it must be noted in the patient's record. Otherwise, the physician will be unable to *show* that such a request was made and it will be the patient's word against the physician's (see § 4.47, Medical Records).

§ 1.33   Consent and Informed Consent   25

One federal court has recognized, for example, that the privilege may apply to disclosure of anesthesia risks to the patient in the delivery room. Most of these patients are in a state of high nervous tension when preparing for such a procedure and it might, in a particular case, be considered bad practice to warn such a patient that she might die or become paralyzed as a result of receiving a spinal anesthetic.[137]

Because the informed consent doctrine and its exceptions cause the appropriate extent of disclosure to vary from case to case, the courts have attempted to provide general guidelines which consider the risks involved. The physician need apprise the patient only of those risks inherent in the medical treatment to be instituted;[138] the physician is not liable for failing to warn of a danger posed by the improper performance* of an appropriate procedure.[139] If the statistical risk of an adverse result is high, courts have held that the patient should be informed, even the unduly apprehensive one.[140]

When the statistical risk of injury is low, but the severity of potential injury great, the patient should be informed of the risk.[141] Generally, however, when the statistical risk is low,[142] or the severity of the potential risk minor,[143] the physician may use his or her discretion to avoid inciting undue fear in the patient. Disclosure of risks is unnecessary** if the patient is already aware of them.[144]

Additional limitations on the duty to obtain informed consent include the emergency situation [145] discussed earlier, or cases in which the risks involved are obvious to the patient, relatively remote, or risks of which the physician cannot be expected to be aware.[146]

Where the patient is a minor or incompetent, a physician must always inform the parents or guardian of the risk involved since disclosure would not induce apprehension in the subject patient.[147]

Any plaintiff bringing an action in negligence must show that there was an injury. One court has stated: "On any view of a doctrine of informed consent, a plaintiff must prove not only that the undisclosed risk was material, but that it materialized."[148] Otherwise, the omission, however unpardonable, is legally without consequence. The risk must be harmful to the patient because negligence unrelated to injury is nonactionable. And, as is generally true in malpractice actions, there must be a causal relationship between the physician's failure in adequate communication of the risks, and damage to the patient.[149] (See § 1.50, Causation.)

A causal connection exists when, but only when, disclosure of the significant risks incidental to treatment would have resulted in a decision against it.[150] If the

---

*However, improper performance of the procedure, if due to negligence, may itself give rise to liability.

**While this position has been upheld, it should be understood in the context of the courts' requirement that physicians volunteer information needed for an intelligent decision whether the patient requests it or not. *Canterbury v. Spence*, 464 F.2d 772 (D.C. Cir. 1972).

patient would have submitted to the anesthesia despite knowledge of all risks, there is no complaint. The issue dealt with by the courts is whether causation is to be judged by a subjective test—what the *patient* would have done had adequate disclosure been made, or an objective test—what a *reasonable person* in the patient's position would have done.

Some courts use the subjective test by examining whether the particular patient would have agreed to the treatment if he or she had known of the danger which later ripened into injury.

CASE ILLUSTRATION

The female patient was admitted to the hospital for a tubal ligation. The anesthesiologist visited the patient on the evening prior to the operation for the purpose of assessing her as a candidate for spinal anesthesia. During the visit the anesthesiologist ascertained that that patient was in good health and that she had received spinal anesthesia during a surgical procedure performed nine years earlier with no ill effects. The anesthesiologist did not discuss the risks of spinal anesthesia with the patient as he felt that the patient was familiar with the procedure and her medical history did not indicate that the procedure was inappropriate. Spinal anesthesia was attempted but, due to difficulties encountered in administration (the anesthesiologist "hit bone" on two attempts to insert the needle eliciting paresthesia down the patient's back and in her legs) was abandoned in favor of general anesthesia. The patient sustained permanent nerve damage causing back and leg pain. The patient sued the anesthesiologist alleging that he had failed to obtain her informed consent. The court held for the anesthesiologist stating that insufficient evidence had been presented to show that the patient "would have declined spinal anesthesia had she been advised that nerve damage might result." (*Beauvais v. Notre Dame Hospital*, 1978)[151]

Perhaps the preferred approach today is the objective test. Courts have noted that a rule which ties the factual conclusion on causation to the credibility of the hindsight of a person seeking recovery after experiencing an undesirable result is unsatisfactory. When causation is explored at a postinjury trial with a professedly uninformed patient, the question whether he actually would have turned the treatment down if he had known the risks is purely hypothetical.[152] And the answer which the patient supplies hardly represents more than a guess, perhaps tinged by the circumstance that the uncommunicated hazard has in fact materialized. This subjective method of determining causation has been rejected because it places the physician in jeopardy of the patient's hindsight and bitterness. It places the factfinder in the position of deciding whether a speculative answer to a hypothetical question is to be credited. It calls for a subjective determination solely on the testimony of a patient-witness influenced by the occurrence of the undisclosed risk.[153]

Consequently, courts have attempted to resolve the causation issue objectively by reference to what a prudent person in the patient's position would have decided if suitably informed of all perils bearing significance.[154]

CASE ILLUSTRATION

The female patient entered the hospital for an elective bilateral mastectomy to remove pendulous breasts, which because of their size and weight were causing her severe discomfort and affecting her posture. The operation itself was performed without incident, but for two or three days before discharge, the patient suffered a slight fever and felt nauseous. She went home after a week in the hospital, still feeling weak. She was readmitted after two weeks and stayed a further 16 days until she felt better and was discharged. The patient sued the anesthesiologist, claiming that her difficulty arose from the use of halothane as an anesthetic. She claimed to have suffered from hepatitis, a risk associated with halothane of which the anesthesiologist conceded he had failed to inform her. The trial court held for the anesthesiologist, but the patient appealed the decision. The Court of Appeals stated that while a physician has a duty to inform the patient of attendant risks, where treatment is elective, as in this case, the right of informed choice is even more significant. Accordingly, the appellate court reversed the trial court and ordered a new trial. It ruled that the proper measure of the information furnished is the significance a reasonable person would have attached to the risks presented by the physician. (*Small v. Gifford Memorial Hospital*, 1975)[155]

§ 1.40 BREACH OF DUTY

As previously discussed, the legal significance of a duty is that of an obligation recognized by the law. The physician's duty to his patient is generally to provide the degree of care ordinarily exercised by physicians practicing in the same community or area of specialization. (See § 1.32, Standard of Care.) A breach of duty occurs when the physician's care fails to meet this standard.

In order for a patient-plaintiff to succeed on a negligence theory, he or she must first establish the standard of care to which the physician-defendant should be held, and second, show that the physician-defendant's care fell below the standard. This is generally an evidentiary task accomplished by examining the facts of the case which gave rise to the malpractice lawsuit.

CASE ILLUSTRATION

The urologist, who had been treating the patient for a severe urinary infection and gross hematuria for several weeks without a successful diagnosis, recommended that the patient undergo a cystoscopic examination. The patient elected to have the procedure done under a general rather than a local anesthetic to avoid as much pain as possible. The nurse-anesthetist administered succinylcholine di-chloride, or anectine, at 2:10 p.m. on the afternoon of the examination. The cystoscopic examination was completed and the anectine was discontinued at 2:25 p.m. The patient had not resumed normal nerve function or unassisted breathing by 3:00 p.m. so the nurse-anesthetist concluded he had experienced an adverse reaction to the anectine. The nurse-anesthetist continued to provide positive pressure ventilation and to monitor the patient's vital signs. At about 5:30 the urologist requested a general practitioner on the staff at the health care facility to supervise the patient so the urologist could leave for a nearby city. On arriving in the city, the urologist consulted an anesthesiologist who concurred in the diagnosis of an anectine reaction. At 9:00 p.m. the anesthesiologist advised the general practitioner and nurse-anesthetist that, in addition to continuing artificial respiration, precautionary x-rays of the patient's chest be made. At about 10:00 p.m., after being moved to the x-ray room, the patient suffered a cardiac arrest. His heart action was restored by external heart massage and an injection of adrenalin. Following this incident the urologist and the general practitioner conferred and agreed that the patient should be transferred to a hospital in the nearby city. The patient arrived by ambulance at the hospital at about 1:20 a.m. and died approximately ten minutes later after suffering another cardiac arrest. An autopsy was performed which disclosed that the patient was suffering from myocarditis which was subacute and diffuse. The patient's family sued the medical personnel involved, claiming that the following duties to the patient had been breached:

1. The urologist failed to examine the patient's medical record which revealed a reaction to a sulfa drug a few weeks prior to the examination.
2. The urologist failed to supervise properly the anesthesia administered by the nurse-anesthetist and should not have permitted her to select the drug to be used.
3. All medical staff personnel failed to render proper treatment after the patient did not regain normal breathing within the usual time the effect of the anectine was expected to wear off.

The court responded to each allegation as follows:

    1. The evidence shows that . . . [the patient's] regular physician, had given [the patient] a series of medical examinations including electrocardiograms

during the several days prior to the cystoscopic examination, and that there was no indication of any abnormality in his heart or cardiovascular system. The preponderance of the medical testimony shows there was no lack of good medical judgment in concluding decedent was capable of undergoing a general anesthesia.

2. [Expert] testimony . . . shows that after the supervising physician decides the patient is suited for a general anesthetic, it is customary to rely on the anesthetist to decide which drugs are most suited for the particular situation. There is no evidence of any improper selection or administration of drugs . . . [The patient's] expert . . . admitted the drugs and gases used were proper.

3. We find the evidence to show that [the urologist] was advised by [the nurse-anesthetist] at about 3:00 p.m. that she was concerned [the patient] had an anectine reaction as he had not regained nerve function or voluntary breathing as would have been expected. . . . [Expert] testimony . . . indicated it would have been the best medical judgment not to move [the patient] so long as it was believed he was merely experiencing an anectine reaction. The evidence shows that [the urologist] did consult with a specialist . . . after it appeared the reaction would be protracted. [The patient] was being prepared for x-rays to determine the condition of his chest when he suffered the cardiac arrest, which was the earliest time it could be determined that there was anything critical in his condition. He was then transferred to [the nearby city] as soon as his cardiac condition became sufficiently stabilized to permit the trip. [The patient's expert stated that a blood gas test should have been furnished at frequent intervals but the anesthesiologist testified that] "it was a very sophisticated, expensive procedure and was not generally used for patients requiring short periods of artificial respiration as is expected following an anectine reaction.

The court held in favor of the physician-defendants stating that the evidence failed to show any lack of knowledge or skill on their part or that their failure to exercise their best medical judgment was the cause of the patient's death. (*Brown v. Allen Sanitarium*, 1978)[156]

Courts often fail to distinguish between duty and the breach of duty in malpractice cases. This usually occurs when the parties to a case agree on case facts but disagree on the standards of care appropriate to the facts. For example, in a case where the patient-plaintiff claims he or she was given an overdose of a drug, the medical record may disclose that the patient, suffering from x, was treated by the physician-defendant, who ordered a certain dosage of y to be administered a certain number of times per day. Expert eyewitnesses will give testimony on what they believe the standard of care requires for treating a patient with problem x with drug y. The finder of fact (a judge or jury) will then define the limits of the proper standard of care before determining whether or not it has been breached. Thus, the question of appropriate standard can "swallow up" the question of whether the standard has been breached. A finding of negligence requires both: the determination of the standard of care and a determination that the acts of the physician-defendant breached that standard.

§ 1.50 CAUSATION

Another of the essential elements for any claim of negligence is proof of causation, i.e., that there be some reasonable connection between the act or omission of the physician-defendant and the injury which the plaintiff has suffered. In fact, it has been held that if causation cannot be shown, then it is immaterial whether the patient-plaintiff sustained any damage.[157] (See § 1.60, Damages.)

It is important for physicians to recognize that judges and attorneys view "causation" quite differently from physicians. For example, a physician viewing a patient's current medical problems must usually search for the basic or most immediate cause or causes of the disorder underlying those problems. Also, the physician strives to identify and understand all aspects of the patient's condition. In contrast, the goal of judges and attorneys involved in a malpractice suit is very specific—to determine whether a particular occurrence has caused a specific condition suffered by the patient. Concern is limited exclusively to whether the event in question has caused the condition. A second difference is in the criteria for causation. The legal requirement of establishing proximate cause generally is "probability," "50.1 percent," "more likely than not," or "reasonable medical certainty"—all of which are requirements far less demanding than the scientific proof sought by physicians.[158] Consequently, the word "causation" means one thing to most physicians and quite another thing to judges and attorneys.

§ 1.51 Legal Principles of Causation

The legal issue of causation may be broken down into two inquiries: (1) cause-in-fact and (2) proximate cause. The cause-in-fact inquiry is a question of fact which asks whether the conduct of the defendant caused the plaintiff's harm. The proximate cause inquiry involves the attempt by the courts to limit legal responsibility to those causes which are so closely connected with the result and of such significance that the law is justified in imposing liability. This involves a question which is often one of policy, i.e., setting boundaries to liability for the consequences of an act on the basis of a social idea of justice or policy.[159]

Two formulas have evolved for dealing with questions of cause-in-fact. First is the "but for" formula. This formula makes the plaintiff prove that his or her injury would not have occurred "but for" the negligence of the physician-defendant. Often, this favors the physician-defendant because the plaintiff will theoretically lose any case where the physician's wrongdoing was not the *sole* cause of the patient's injury. In a sense this formula absolves those defendants

§ 1.51   *Legal Principles of Causation*   31

whose wrongdoing coincided with other causes, e.g., an equipment failure or patient error in reporting history.[160]

The second formula used by the courts in determining cause-in-fact is whether the defendant's conduct was a "substantial factor" in bringing about the harm.[161] The "substantial factor" formula tends to favor the injured patient. It also protects our society's interest in holding wrongdoers responsible for the consequences of their actions. Additionally, it may work to answer the question of causation in situations where the "but for" rule fails. For example, when two causes that may have brought about an injury are present and either one of them, operating alone, might have been sufficient to cause the same result, the "but for" rule fails to do justice. When each of the causes has been a "substantial factor" in bringing about the injury liability may be found.[162]

Proof of Causation: In proving the existence of cause-in-fact it is important to consider the party on which the burden of proof is placed. Generally, the plaintiff bears the burden of proof that the tortious conduct of the defendant has caused harm to the plaintiff.[163] This means that in most suits for malpractice, the plaintiff must introduce evidence which offers a reasonable basis for the conclusion that the conduct of the physician was most likely a substantial factor in bringing about the plaintiff's injury.[164] Evidence must be presented to show that the patient's injury was more than probably caused by the physician's conduct; it is not sufficient to prove it was *possibly* caused by the physician's conduct.[165] A plaintiff has successfully borne the burden of proof when the evidence taken as a whole indicates that the defendant's negligence was the most plausible or likely cause of the occurrence and no other factor can as reasonably be ascribed as the cause.[166]

In certain circumstances the burden of proof may be placed on the defendant. For example, when the tortious conduct of two or more actors has combined to bring about harm to the plaintiff, and one or more of the actors seeks to limit his liability on the grounds that harm is apportionable among them, the burden of proof as to the apportionment is upon each actor. Also, when the conduct of two or more actors has been found to be negligent and it is proved that the injury to the plaintiff has been caused by only one of them, where there is uncertainty as to which one has caused it, the burden is upon each defendant to prove that he or she has not caused the harm.[167] Thus, when two or more physicians may have caused injury to a patient through negligent behavior, the burden of proof may be placed on them as to (1) what portion of the harm may have been caused by each and (2) whether or not the harm may have been caused solely by the other physician.

The question of which party bears the burden of proof becomes very important when the evidence introduced at the trial shows only that it is as equally probable that the defendant's conduct caused the plaintiff's harm as it is that his or her conduct did not cause the plaintiff's harm. In this situation, the court must direct a verdict for the party that did not have the burden of proof, since the party with the burden has failed to meet it.[168] Thus, when a patient alleges negligence on the part of a physician, and has the burden of proof, but can only introduce evidence that there is an equal chance that the physician did or did not cause the patient's injury, the court must decide in favor of the physician-defendant.

CASE ILLUSTRATION

The female patient underwent a hysterectomy and afterwards sustained a loss of feeling and mobility in her left arm. She offered medical testimony suggesting that she had suffered a brachial plexus injury to her left arm as a result of improper positioning of her arms during surgery. The physician-defendant at trial showed that the positioning of the patient was in accordance with the standard procedures for positioning and offered conflicting testimony showing that her symptoms were also compatible with the diagnosis of a small artery occlusion in the brain. About two years after the hysterectomy, the patient suffered additional cardiovascular problems. A transfemoral aortic angiogram showed significant blockage of the artery supplying her left arm in the left side of her brain. The jury found the defendant's theory of causation more persuasive, and therefore exonerated the physician. The appellate court affirmed this conclusion, stating that ample evidence was submitted to permit the jury to find that the patient did not suffer a brachial plexus injury or that if she did it was not the fault of the physician. (*Bertrand v. Aetna Casualty and Surety Company*, 1975)[169]

"Causation in fact" is a question of fact appropriately left for the laypersons of the jury. The jury, or judge in a nonjury trial, assesses the causal link by considering relevant evidence. Like any other fact, causation may be proved by direct or circumstantial evidence.[170] However, expert medical testimony is generally required to supply evidence of causation. The jury is not permitted to speculate whether different treatment would have yielded a different result in the absence of such testimony.[171]

Proximate Cause: Once the issue of cause-in-fact has been settled in favor of the plaintiff, the question remains whether the physician-defendant should be legally responsible for the harm he or she has caused. Inquiry at this point becomes essentially a question of whether the policy of the law will extend responsibility for conduct to consequences which have in fact occurred. The issue becomes whether the defendant owes any duty to the plaintiff, which includes protection against such consequences.[172] In other words, the foreseeability of the actual sustained injury is considered. The party charged with negligence is responsible for the consequences of the negligent act which a prudent person, acquainted with all existing

§ 1.51   *Legal Principles of Causation*   33

factual circumstances whether ascertainable by reasonable diligence or not, would have entertained as a reasonably possible outcome of the negligent act.[173] The legal determination of the proximity of the injury suffered to the deed alleged to have caused it is the realm of proximate causes.

The proximate cause of an injury must be the efficient cause setting in motion the chain of circumstances leading to the injury; if the negligence complained of merely furnished a condition by which the injury was possible and a subsequent independent act caused the injury, the existence of the produced condition is not the proximate cause of the injury.[174] The independent act or intervening cause will destroy the original causal connection alleged.

CASE ILLUSTRATION

The 42-year-old patient, while undergoing a hysterectomy under a general anesthetic, suffered a cardiac arrest about 15 minutes after the operation began. Emergency treatment was given and the heart resumed beating about one hour and 20 minutes later. An electrocardiogram was obtained about an hour after the arrest was detected and showed the type of arrest to be ventricular fibrillation. As soon as the arrest ended, the surgery was resumed. After the operation it was discovered the patient had suffered a transverse myelitis to her spinal cord at approximately the level of the eleventh thoracic vertebra, resulting in permanent paralysis below the waist. The patient brought suit claiming that the failure of the operating room personnel to act more expeditiously to end the patient's cardiac arrest caused her injuries. The patient submitted expert testimony that an earlier electrocardiogram would have led to the use of a defibrillator, that sodium bicarbonate should have been administered sooner to treat the acidosis that developed during cardiac arrest, and that the poor blood circulation resulting from these omissions precipitated the patient's paralysis. Other expert testimony was offered to the effect that some local phenomenon caused the poor circulation to the specific area of the spinal cord, such as a blood clot in the artery, plaque, or an anatomical configuration. Testimony was also offered that the patient's transverse myelitis was caused by an occlusion of the anterior spinal artery and could have occurred at any time during the arrest or shortly thereafter. Furthermore, since the patient suffered no permanent brain damage, it was unlikely that her blood was so poorly oxygenated during the arrest as to have injured the anterior spinal artery alone, the brain being more susceptible to injury under such conditions than the spine.

At trial, the jury found that the operating personnel were negligent in failing to obtain an electrocardiogram sooner and in failing to administer sodium bicarbonate sooner but declined to find that either failure was a proximate cause of the patient's injuries. Rather, the jury accepted the opinion of the physician's experts that the patient's injuries were due to an intervening cause. The appellate court held that since the jury's verdict could be supported by the evidence and that negligence cannot be imputed merely from unsatisfactory results, the lower court decision was proper and the physician-defendants were not liable. (*Hunter v. Robison*, 1972)[175]

§ 1.52 Res Ipsa Loquitur

If a patient suffers an injury under circumstances making it difficult to identify the cause, and if the injury is one which would not ordinarily have occurred without negligence, the law affords the patient a possible means of recovery: the doctrine of res ipsa loquitur, a Latin phrase which means "the thing speaks for itself."[176] Res ipsa loquitur permits the jury to draw logical conclusions from circumstantial evidence,[177] and negligence, like any other fact, may be proved by circumstantial evidence.[178]

The basic premise of res ipsa loquitur is that in certain fact situations the probability that the defendant was negligent "speaks for itself." In these cases the patient-plaintiff is relieved of the usual burden to prove a specific act or omission constituting negligence. The 1863 English case in which the doctrine was first applied provides an example of a situation in which, in the absence of contrary evidence, common sense says there *must* have been negligence.

CASE ILLUSTRATION

The plaintiff was walking down a street when he was hit and injured by a barrel of flour that rolled out of a warehouse window. The plaintiff sued the owner of the warehouse, but could not identify the specific negligent act which allowed the barrel to fall. In previous cases, the plaintiff's inability to produce such evidence would have required dismissal of his suit. The court, however, applied the doctrine of "res ipsa loquitur," holding that a barrel is so unlikely to fall out of a warehouse window in the absence of negligence that proof of a specific act of negligence is unnecessary. Instead, said the court, the facts surrounding the injury by themselves create an inference of negligence sufficient to allow recovery by the plaintiff. (*Byrne v. Boadle*, 1863)[179]

Courts and legal commentators have provided policy arguments supporting the use of res ipsa loquitur in appropriate cases. The doctrine has been described as providing a remedy to insure that the patient who is unexplainedly injured will not bear the full burden of the injury.[180] In the context of medical malpractice, it is argued that placing the risk of unexplained injuries on the physician-defendant could possibly result in better procedures and greater protection for the unconscious patient.[181]

The reluctance of physicians to testify against one another, identified by the courts as a so-called "conspiracy of silence," has given impetus to the use of res ipsa loquitur in medical malpractice suits.[182] No matter how lacking in skill or how negligent the physician-defendant might be, it has at times been almost impossible to find other physicians willing to provide adverse testimony in litigation based on the defendant's alleged negligence. Not only would the guilty person thereby escape from civil liability for the wrong committed, but his or her professional colleagues would take no steps to ensure that the same results would not occur again at the same hands. To overcome this problem and to aid patients who by reason of anesthesia or lack of medical knowledge cannot identify the source of their injury, the courts attempt to equalize the situation by placing on the physician the burden of explaining what occurred.[183]

The courts have justified the use of this circumstantial evidentiary doctrine in technical medical cases by recognizing that certain medical and surgical procedures have become so familiar that laymen as potential jury members often have sufficient common knowledge to determine that untoward results would not occur from such procedures if properly conducted. The majority of cases involve unfamiliar procedures, however, and in these the expert testimony of physicians using specialized knowledge is relied on to provide evidence that results would have been otherwise unless negligence had occurred.[184]

The application of res ipsa loquitur is appropriate to a case arising out of an anesthesia mishap. Application of the doctrine to malpractice cases generally has its primary justification in the fact that the patient-plaintiff was unconscious when the alleged negligent acts were taking place so he or she is unable to remember and specifically allege them.[185] The anesthesiologist is responsible for inducing such a state in the patient. Furthermore, the doctrine has been applied where the proven injury is not in the area of the body involved in the actual surgery, for example, where paralysis results from administration of spinal anesthesia during childbirth[186] or where a patient receives burns or trauma to parts of the body not in the immediate area of the operation.[187] The anesthesiologist's major concern is quite specifically the overall maintenance of the patient's body via the monitoring of blood pressure, pulse and respiration.[188]

Additionally, res ipsa loquitur has been used to establish liability in multiple defendant malpractice situations in some jurisdictions in light of the fact that hospitals conduct a highly integrated system of activities in which a number of individuals contribute to outcome. There may be, for example, preparation for surgery by nurses and interns who are hospital employees; administration of an anesthetic by a physician who may be a hospital employee, an employee of the operating surgeon, or an independent contractor; performance of an operation by a surgeon and an assistant who may be one of his or her employees, or both may be hospital employees or independent contractors; and presurgical care by the surgeon, hospital physician, or nurses. The number of those who care for the patient is not, the courts have found, a good reason for denying him or her all reasonable opportunity to recover for negligent harm. Where a patient receives unusual injuries while unconscious and in the course of medical treatment, courts have held that all those parties with any control over the patient's body or the instrumentality which might have caused injury, may properly be called upon to meet the inference of negligence raised by res ipsa loquitur by explaining their conduct.[189]

These arguments are tempered by additional considerations of the physician's position. Courts have recognized that to apply res ipsa loquitur in all cases with unexpected results would hamstring the development of medical science. Physicians would be reluctant to use new procedures, because if injury resulted, they could be found negligent. Courts have acknowledged their responsibility to determine the point at which the doctrine should apply in order to be fair to a patient who has sustained a result which would not occur without negligence, and to be fair to the physician if the result is one which could occur without negligence and without inviting the presumption of negligence.[190]

Thus, the doctrine can have no application in a malpractice suit which involves the merits of a diagnosis or of scientific treatment.[191] The physician is not required at his or her peril to explain why any particular diagnosis was not correct or why any particular scientific treatment did not produce the desired result. The doctrine has no application in an ordinary physician malpractice suit where the only complaint is that the desired result of an operation was not accomplished.[192]

Where the rule applies, the burden of proof* shifts from the plaintiff to the defendant, requiring the defendant to come forward and exculpate himself or herself from negligence.[193] (See § 1.20, Elements of Negligence.) In a majority of jurisdictions, res ipsa loquitur permits, but does not compel, the inference that the defendant was negligent,[194] leaving the jury to accept or reject the inference. A minority of jurisdictions, however, hold that res ipsa loquitur requires a finding of negligence unless the defendant offers evidence in rebuttal.[195]

When a plaintiff in a negligence case seeks to take advantage of the doctrine of res ipsa loquitur, courts require the plaintiff to demonstrate fully the situation in which it is applicable. This is in order to avoid a plaintiff's attempt to shift the burden of proof to the physician by merely asserting the doctrine itself. The doctrine is a rule of evidence and not one of substance of law. The general rule is that the negligence of the defendant is never presumed but must be established by proof. The cases to which res ipsa loquitur apply are not exceptions to this. Proof of

---

*Burden of proof refers to the duty of the plaintiff in a civil suit to prove, before the defendant is required to prove anything, that sufficient facts exist to merit the court's consideration of the complaint. Where res ipsa loquitur applies, the burden shifts to the defendant to prove otherwise.

negligence in these cases is made by circumstantial evidence. Most importantly, the proof of the injury and of the surrounding circumstances must establish that the only reasonable conclusion is that the injury occurred because of the negligence of the defendant.[196]

Applying the doctrine of res ipsa loquitur requires proving certain factual elements. Traditionally, these have been identified as follows: (1) the event or injury must be of a kind which ordinarily does not occur in the absence of someone's negligence; (2) it must be caused by an agency or instrumentality within the exclusive control of the defendant; (3) it must not have been due to any voluntary action or contribution on the part of the plaintiff; and (4) the evidence for the explanation of events causing harm must be more accessible to the defendant than to the plaintiff.[197]

Injury Caused by Negligence: Across jurisdictions, the first and nearly universal requirement for applying the doctrine of res ipsa loquitur is that an accident or injury must be of the kind which ordinarily or probably does not happen in the absence of negligence.[198] The facts shown by the patient-plaintiff regarding the injury must suggest that the negligence of the physician is the most plausible explanation for the injury,[199] particularly where the actual cause of the injury is a mystery.[200] It is not sufficient for the patient to show that the result of the operation was unusual and unexpected[201] or even fatal, because without an abnormal consequence no legal action in damages could be brought in the first place. For res ipsa loquitur to apply, the patient-plaintiff must show that in the process of the medical treatment some extraordinary or unusual event outside of the routine of such a procedure occurred, which unexplained, would appear to be negligence to the average man.[202]

Some courts require that the testimony support a finding that injuries such as the patient's are more likely the result of negligence than some other cause.[203] Other courts have stated that all possible explanations of the injury other than the defendant's negligence must be excluded.[204] It has also been held that when the record is abundantly clear that what occurred in the case could not have been prevented by any technique known to and recognized by the medical profession, the doctrine of res ipsa loquitur will not be applied.[205] The evidence must demonstrate at least a probability that the patient's mishap could not have occurred without negligence by the physician.[206] Some courts have imposed a corollary requirement that no direct evidence establishing a specific act of negligence as the only likely cause of the harm should exist. If such a specific act is the only explanation, it must be proved without the aid of the doctrine.[207]

Where a patient alleges negligence on the part of a physician-defendant, generally it must be proven by a preponderance or greater weight of the evidence. Res ipsa loquitur does not eliminate this burden.[208] It only modifies it somewhat to require a showing that the injury would not have occurred unless the defendant was negligent.

CASE ILLUSTRATION

The patient underwent knee surgery under general anesthesia. His vital signs were monitored and appeared normal during the entire anesthetic and surgical period. After the operation the patient was "coming around" sufficiently to be extubated in the operating room and was then removed to the recovery room. An hour and a half after the completion of the operation the patient was discovered to have suffered severe and permanent brain damage. The plaintiff sued the anesthesiologist and other hospital personnel asserting that res ipsa loquitur applied because, prior to the administration of anesthesia for the knee operation, the patient was in excellent health whereas after the operation he suffered severe and permanent brain damage, presumably due to an anoxic episode. Expert testimony was introduced on behalf of the anesthesiologist and the other defendants which maintained that the patient's failure to regain normal cerebral function was not caused by negligence on the part of the anesthesiologist or any other hospital personnel. This conclusion was based on the fact that all vital signs were normal during the crucial period; anoxia would have been reflected in blood pressure, pulse, respiration, or EKG if it had occurred. Furthermore, explanations for the patient's condition other than negligence existed, including a sudden heart attack, pulmonary embolism blocking the blood flow, shock causing the failure of peripheral blood circulation, or a lack of blood glucose causing brain cells to die. The court noted that res ipsa loquitur is a way of showing negligence in some unspecified way by excluding all possibilities other than the defendant's negligence, although not going far enough to show just what the defendant did or failed to do that was wrong. Since the patient failed to counter the testimony offered by the expert that the injury could have been a consequence of factors other than the defendant's negligence, the court held that res ipsa loquitur did not apply and that the anesthesiologist was not liable. (*Haas v. United States*, 1980)[209]

Requirements vary among the jurisdictions regarding the sort of evidence necessary to prove that the patient's injury was caused by negligence. Some require that there be expert medical testimony to that effect[210] unless the negligence is so grossly apparent that a lay jury would have no difficulty in recognizing it.[211] In some situations, expert testimony may be required to invoke the doctrine of res ipsa loquitur at all, since medical expertise may be needed to assist a lay jury when

§ 1.52 *Res Ipsa Loquitur* 39

the medical cause of an injury is not grossly apparent.[212] Some jurisdictions allow the introduction of expert medical testimony (apparently at the patient-plaintiff's option in appropriate cases) when such testimony may merely strengthen the inference that accidents of the kind in question do not commonly happen in the absence of negligence.[213] In situations where expert testimony is required, the plaintiff's failure to bring expert testimony linking the negligence of an anesthesiologist with his or her injuries would prevent the doctrine from being applied.[214] The expert opinion requirement has been held to apply only to such matters as are within the domain of medical science; matters within the common knowledge of mankind may be testified to by anyone familiar with the facts.[215]

Some jurisdictions require that to apply res ipsa loquitur it be a matter of common knowledge among lay or medical personnel or both that the patient's injury would not have occurred without negligence.[216] It is the general rule in Texas and some other jurisdictions that res ipsa loquitur never applies in medical malpractice cases except where the nature of the alleged malpractice and injuries are plainly within the common knowledge of laymen.[217] General examples given of common knowledge situations include the leaving of surgical instruments or foreign objects inside the body and the sustaining of an injury by a part of the body not involved in an operation.[218] Injuries such as damaged tissues due to extravasation of pentothal,[219] herniation of disk material,[220] and nerve damage sustained as a result of a spinal anesthesia[221] have been determined to be outside of the scope of lay common knowledge, and therefore not appropriate to lay determinations of negligence. Determinations of negligence are held to be within common knowledge when such determinations can be made in the light of past experience[222] or based on "common sense."[223]

In a New Jersey case, *Rothman v. Silber*,[224] the patient-plaintiff alleged that the administration of the anesthetic agent constituted the introduction of a foreign substance into the body. If accepted, such a theory may allow for the application of res ipsa loquitur, but in this case the allegation was made only for purposes of overcoming a statute of limitations problem. The court's response offers some clue as to how an attempt by a plaintiff to place such a case into this common knowledge category might be met. The court held that a drug was not to be considered a foreign substance since it is deliberately injected and intended to remain in the body and loses its identity quickly after injection or ingestion. The court concluded that recovery for negligent introduction of a drug must be predicated upon lack of care or skill in the selection or administration of the drug.

Probably the common knowledge situation most applicable to anesthesiology is that in which a sound and unaffected part of the body is injured or destroyed while the patient is unconscious and under the immediate and exclusive control of the physician-anesthesiologist[225] responsible for monitoring bodily functions during the surgical procedures. The courts recognize that if surgery or manipulation of one part of the human anatomy normally produces drastic symptoms in other areas unrelated to the site of the surgery or manipulation, the secondary effects might readily be proved a natural outcome.[226] These principles have been applied to cases in which a patient lost an eye as a result of a cough reflex allegedly caused by inadequate anesthesia during or following an operation for appendicitis;[227] a patient emerged from a hysterectomy with a paralyzed right arm;[228] and a patient lost the use of his right arm due to atrophy following an appendectomy.[229]

Where evidence is offered that the injury could have occurred as the result of other causes, the use of res ipsa loquitur has been questioned by the courts. Jurisdictions that do not require that the plaintiff exclude every possibility that the injury was caused by other than the defendant's negligence allow the jury to draw an inference of defendant negligence if the plaintiff produces sufficient evidence. This approach is supported by a concept stating that where reasonable parties differ on the balance of probabilities at fault, the court must leave the question to the jury.[230] Such an approach to the application of the doctrine has been referred to as "conditional res ipsa loquitur" by some courts.[231] Certain jurisdictions have further refined this requirement by holding that where two or more possible causes of the injury exist and the physician is responsible for only one of the causes, the several causes of the injury must be equally probable to preclude jury application of res ipsa loquitur.[232] In jurisdictions in which the doctrine is applied, the plaintiff is allowed to offer proof that specific acts of the defendant caused the injury and rely on res ipsa loquitur, unless the evidence for the specific acts fully explains the cause of the injury. If the specific proof is unpersuasive, the plaintiff may still rely on res ipsa loquitur.[233]

In practice, the fact that there may be multiple causes of a particular injury often results in the non-application of res ipsa loquitur. In *Merritt v. Deaconess Hospital*, the court found that the operating surgeon's actions, and not those of the anesthesiologist (the only party against whom the case was brought), were the most probable cause of injury and the doctrine was not applied.[234] In *Faris v. Doctor's Hospital, Inc.*, the patient-plaintiff attempted to utilize the doctrine of res ipsa loquitur to infer that negligence had caused vertebrae disk herniation in the patient's neck during abdominal surgery. The court held that res ipsa loquitur would not apply because: (1) extensive medical opinions showed that the plaintiff's condition was such that entirely natural acts (e.g., coughing, sneezing) could have caused it; and (2) that there was no evidence to support the allegation of negligent hyperextension of the plaintiff's neck or of this as the cause of the plaintiff's condition.[235]

If it can be shown that the injury which occurred is one which may ordinarily happen in the absence of negligence, res ipsa loquitur will not be applied.[236] This has been the holding in cases involving such injuries as cardiac arrest,[237] loss of feeling and mobility in a limb,[238] and spinal cord paralysis.[239] It has been recognized that these sequelae of anesthesia may occur in the absence of conduct amounting to negligence. They could easily be the result of the non-negligent conduct of the anesthesiologist or surgeon, taken together with pre-existing disease conditions and the stresses on normal body physiology, a factor in any surgical procedure. Often, the anesthetic agent itself could be the cause of the injury (e.g., toxic arachnoiditis or neuritis) in the absence of negligence.[240]

To summarize, where the patient-plaintiff can show that his or her injury was of the type that would only occur as the result of the defendant's negligence, the first element required by the doctrine of res ipsa loquitur to establish an inference of such negligence has been proved. This element is not satisfied in some jurisdictions if common knowledge would not permit such an inference, and in others, if expert testimony will not support it. Where causes other than negligence may be relied on to explain the injury, res ipsa loquitur will not apply unless the patient-plaintiff has produced sufficient evidence to permit an inference of negligence despite the existence of other explanations. In all cases, res ipsa loquitur is merely an evidentiary doctrine and it is the jury or court which makes the final decision of fact.

Defendant-controlled Instrumentality: Once the requirements of the first element of res ipsa loquitur have been met, the plaintiff must address the second element and show that the injury was caused by an agency or instrumentality within the exclusive control of the defendant.[241]

A minority of courts have interpreted this requirement as limiting the applicability of the doctrine. Where a number of people have control or partial control of the patient during surgery and thereafter, and where the patient's injury may have occurred by the act or omission of any of them, res ipsa loquitur has not been applied due to failure on the part of the patient to show the actual thing, instrument or occurrence causing the disability.[242] In cases where res ipsa loquitur has been applied against multiple defendants, usually all medical personnel present during the operation, the defendants have attacked such an application as an attempt to fix liability en masse. In an early case, *Ybarra v. Spangard,* such a defense was stated in two propositions: (1) that where there are several defendants, and there is a division of responsibility in the use of an instrumentality causing the injury, and the injury might have resulted from the separate acts of either one of two or more persons, res ipsa loquitur should not be used; and (2) that where there are several instrumentalities, and no showing is made as to which caused the injury or the particular defendant in control of it, the doctrine should not apply. The court responded by stating that every defendant who had custody of the plaintiff for any period had control of the instrumentality causing the injury, and thus assumes the burden of explanation. The test is one of right of control rather than actual control. As the plaintiff was rendered unconscious, it was unreasonable to insist that he identify one of them as committing the negligent act. Furthermore, the court stated it sufficient for the plaintiff to show that an injury resulted from an external force applied while he lay unconscious, since this is as clear a case of identification of the instrumentality as the plaintiff might ever be able to make.[243]

Most courts do not give this control requirement a strict literal interpretation, and the phrase "exclusive control" has been criticized as not, in all cases, an accurate expression of the principle. The principle requires that other responsible causes, including the conduct of the plaintiff and third persons, be sufficiently eliminated by the evidence. "Control" is afforded substantial flexibility by the courts. The defendant has the right or power of control, the opportunity to exercise it, and shares the duty and the responsibility of such control. Certain courts have commented that it would be far better, and much confusion avoided, if the idea of "control" was discarded altogether in favor of a statement that the apparent cause of an accident must be such that the defendant would be responsible for any negligence connected with it.[244]

This element has been afforded flexibility because the courts have recognized, particularly in the case of anesthesia, that an insensible passive recipient of treatment administered by other parties, who is injured in the course of that treatment, is hardly in a position to demonstrate each person's exclusive control. Consequently, it is sufficient to show that at the relevant time the instrumentality was not under the control of any person who was not a defendant or an employee of a defendant. It is further recognized that a plaintiff injured during a state of unconsciousness, in the absence of voluntary disclosure by the participants as to the precise cause of the injury, is at an evidentiary disadvantage which the courts attempt to remedy by use of the res ipsa loquitur doctrine.[245]

Where control of the injury-causing instrumentality can be shown to exist in someone other than the defendant, the patient-plaintiff will have failed to meet the second requirement.[246]

CASE ILLUSTRATION

The patient entered the hospital to have a vocal cord nodule removed by the surgeon. She was taken to the operating room and anesthetized by the anesthesiologist and surgery was performed. The patient, who had no previous history of neck pain or trauma, awoke with a fracture of the fourth cervical vertebra presumably caused by hyperextension of her head and neck during surgery. The patient required extensive treatment of her neck including physical therapy and additional surgery; she wore a neck brace for a year following the operation.

The patient sued the surgeon but failed to include the anesthesiologist. The trial court found in favor of the surgeon, denying the patient application

§ 1.52 Res Ipsa Loquitur 43

of the doctrine of res ipsa loquitur. The patient appealed and the appeals court upheld the verdict, reasoning that the patient's own expert witness had testified that the anesthesiologist may have hyperextended the patient's neck. Therefore, the instrumentality that caused the injury was not under the exclusive control of the named defendants. (*Spannaus v. Otolaryngology Clinic*, 1976)[247]

Often, for res ipsa loquitur to apply, the courts require that the instrumentality of the injury be established first. Furthermore, it has been held that a physician-defendant cannot be considered in full control of the instrumentalities involved when the patient has an allergic reaction to the anesthetic agent. Such a reaction is an element beyond the physician's control.[248]

Absence of Patient's Contributory Negligence and Accessibility of Evidence: The third factual requirement of res ipsa loquitur, that the patient's injury must not have been due to any voluntary action or contribution on the part of the patient, has not often been an issue in cases involving injury during anesthesia. Because the patient is unconscious in these cases, it has been recognized that it would be difficult for the patient to act in any manner that would contribute to his or her injury.[249] However, where a patient knowingly fails to disclose a prior adverse reaction to an anesthetic agent, it is conceivable that such a nondisclosure may be said to have contributed to a subsequent adverse reaction. In an early case, *Seneris v. Haas*, where the patient suffered paralysis after administration of spinal anesthesia, the physician asserted that the patient did not meet the third condition of res ipsa loquitur. The physician argued that another of the patient's physicians testified that she suffered from a "psychic overlay factor" prior to the operation and may have had a sensitivity to the anesthetic solution used which she had failed to disclose. The court rejected this assertion, however, because the patient proved that she had previously had an uneventful spinal anesthetic and was by expert medical testimony of the physician-defendant found to be non-allergic. The patient also proved that at the time of her admission to the hospital, she was a strong and healthy woman who suffered no disease in which a spinal anesthetic would be contraindicated.[250] This case indicates the probable lack of success that an anesthesiologist-defendant will meet in challenging the use of res ipsa loquitur on the basis of the third element.

The fourth factual requirement, that the evidence for explaining the events causing harm be more accessible to the physician than the patient,[251] has been minimally elucidated by the courts. Courts have noted that the mere fact that the patient was under anesthesia at the time of the injury would not automatically satisfy the fourth element,[252] nor does the fact that the patient may have received a local rather than a general anesthetic satisfy the fourth element. The courts recognize that the patient's lack of knowledge about the facts causing the injury might exist not only where he is totally unconscious, but also where he is partially unconscious and largely, if not entirely, unaware of what the medical personnel are doing.[253] However, if the patient can show that the injury-causing events are peculiarly within the knowledge of the physician-defendants and their employees and unavailable to the patient, then res ipsa loquitur may prevent the court from dismissing the suit.[254]

Most jurisdictions have not treated the third and fourth elements of res ipsa loquitur as having weight and importance equal to the first two.[255] The fourth, particularly, is often referred to as merely "another factor which some of the cases have considered in applying the doctrine."[256] In the event of an anesthesia-based injury, however, both elements will likely be relevant and easily proved by the plaintiff. Some commentators have stated that the situation should be otherwise, recognizing that

> since res ipsa loquitur alters what a defendant-physician would ordinarily be required to do in defending against a malpractice claim, equity requires that the *lack* of greater accessibility to evidence by the defendant-physician be considered. One need not be a physician to know that operative procedures, for example, are becoming more sophisticated and complicated, and there is necessarily greater reliance by physicians on the expertise of a growing number of fellow professionals. Consequently, a physician may well have no more personal knowledge of the circumstances immediately surrounding the injury than the plaintiff, and it may be unreasonable to assume that he has superior knowledge or access thereto in every situation. The physician may have superior knowledge of medical matters generally, and he may have voluntarily assumed a position of special trust and confidence to his patients; but it does not necessarily follow that the physician be prevented from effectively asserting good faith objection to the application of res ipsa loquitur where he has no greater access to explanatory evidence than does the patient.[257]

§ 1.60 DAMAGES

In order to succeed on a negligence cause of action against a physician the final element to be proved by the patient-plaintiff is damages. Generally, the concept of "damages" encompasses actual loss or damage to the interests of another resulting from the negligent acts of the physician.[258] Where such damages can be proved, the element encompasses a wide range of financial, physical or emotional injuries. The law has identified these various injuries by recognizing certain damage categories. This categorization is often imprecise and inconsistent since some of the categories tend to overlap or are not strictly adhered to by the courts. The more common categories include:

§ 1.60 *Damages* 45

1. *General Damages*—those that the law presumes to have accrued from the wrong complained of because they are the immediate, direct and proximate result, or those that necessarily result from the injury without reference to any special circumstance of the plaintiff,[259] such as generalized pain and suffering.

2. *Special Damages*—those which are the actual but not the necessary or inevitable result of the injury complained of and which in fact follow it as a natural and proximate consequence in the particular case,[260] e.g., the cost the patient might incur in hiring a visiting nurse as a result of the injury. Some typical items of special damage that the law regards as compensable are: (1) past and future medical, surgical, hospital and related costs; (2) past and future loss of income (wages, salary, profits); (3) the necessary hiring of a substitute; (4) in a death case, funeral expenses; and (5) unusual physical or mental consequences of the injury alleged, such as aggravation, through malpractice, of a preexisting condition,[261] or the cost and pain associated with additional operations made necessary by the physician's initial negligence.[262]

3. *Punitive/Exemplary Damages*—Generally, punitive damages are awarded to the plaintiff over and above his or her actual losses. These damages are intended to "punish" the physician where the wrong done was aggravated by circumstances of violence, oppression, malice, fraud or wanton and intentional conduct. In contrast, exemplary damages give the plaintiff more money than he or she would have been entitled to because the wrong suffered was aggravated. Most courts claim that punishment does not enter into the definition of exemplary damages.[263] Thus, the difference between these two damages is more semantic than real. Both give the plaintiff more money than he or she would otherwise be entitled to. The spirit behind each differs though—one is to "punish" the physician and the other is to reward the plaintiff for suffering more than he or she should have suffered. The sometimes imprecise use of these two concepts by various courts across the country has institutionalized the definitional and policy confusion surrounding them.

With the possible exception of exemplary damages, the purpose of a damage award is to compensate the plaintiff for the injury suffered in the only manner open to the law: payment of money damages.[264] Damages are measured by comparing the condition the plaintiff would have been in, had the defendant not been negligent with the plaintiff's impaired condition resulting from such negligence.[265] They are awarded to the extent that a plaintiff can be restored to the position he or she would have occupied had the injury not occurred.[266] Some courts hold that the person responsible must respond for all damages resulting directly from and as a natural consequence of the wrongful act according to common experience and in the usual course of events, whether the damages could or could not have been foreseen by that person.[267]

As items of general damages, the injured party may recover for both the physical injury and concomitant mental and emotional suffering sustained as a natural consequence of the wrongful act.[268]

The courts recognize the difficulty in objectively evaluating and presenting evidence of subjective pain. In some jurisdictions, in order to prevent self-serving testimony, no lay witness may express his opinion on the matter,[269] while other jurisdictions allow the injured party himself to testify to his own pain.[270]

Since an unconscious patient cannot experience pain and suffering, courts uniformly disallow such damages during periods of unconsciousness.[271] By similar reasoning an anesthetized patient should receive no compensation for unrealized pain. Of course, if the anesthesia is ineffective, a patient will realize some pain. This question of fact, regarding the efficacy of the anesthesia, is for the judge or jury to determine in the normal fashion, by weighing conflicting evidence.

CASE ILLUSTRATION

Prior to a cesarean section, an 18-year-old patient was preoxygenated for ten minutes and was then given a general anesthetic (50 percent oxygen and 50 percent cyclopropane) for two minutes as well as anectine to paralyze the muscles during the surgery. The anesthetist intubated the patient and reported that the chest was expanding and that breath sounds were heard, whereupon the obstetrician made the incision. The anesthetic was switched to ethylene and oxygen, and an anectine drip was started. Within a minute after delivery of the placenta, the assisting obstetrician observed and reported that the patient's blood had darkened. The anesthetist cut off the ethylene and switched to 100 percent oxygen, checked the chest expansion, the breath sounds and the anesthesia machine, checked the placement of the tube with a laryngoscope, then suctioned the tube and determined it to be free of obstructions. The blood continued to darken despite the administration of pure oxygen. The patient's uterus became flaccid and her pulse dropped rapidly. About this time the anesthetist noticed the bag was hard to squeeze, and he removed the tube and attempted to reinsert it. He was unable to do so because of excessive saliva in the patient's mouth and because she was not relaxed. Therefore he inserted a plastic airway and ventilated the patient by mask. The patient went into cardiac arrest whereupon the surgeons applied cardiac massage. The patient's blood brightened and she was resuscitated. The surgeons noticed a large amount of gas in her bowels and suctioned it out with a nasal gastric tube. The incision was closed. Later

§ 1.60   Damages   47

neurological examination revealed brain damage. The patient never regained consciousness and died eight days after surgery.

The patient's widower and newborn child sued the parties involved. At trial evidence was introduced that the endotracheal tube had been inserted into the esophagus, thus causing the damage. The plaintiffs sought to recover damages for the patient's pain and suffering, among other things, which the patient sustained after the cyclopropane wore off. She could not communicate that she was experiencing pain because her muscles were paralyzed. However, the plaintiffs asserted that the initial anesthesia would have been effective for about five minutes and, without additional anesthesia, the patient would have experienced pain until she became unconscious in perhaps ten or 15 minutes. The court held that such evidence of pain was too speculative to support an award. Other less speculative claims of damage, however, did produce an award for the patient-plaintiff. (*Aubert v. Charity Hospital of Louisiana*, 1978)[272]

The courts have also wrestled with the subjective aspect of general damages for emotional suffering and anguish, leaving the issue largely unsettled. Emotional damages such as anxiety and mental distress are usually recoverable when they can be shown to be a direct injury resulting from the physician-defendant's breach of duty. The courts have recognized that mental and emotional distress is just as "real" as physical pain and just as compensable.[273]

The courts note that medical knowledge of the relationship between emotional disturbance and physical injury has deepened, and that the existence of the relationship no longer seems open to serious challenge.[274] Moreover, not only justice but logic compels the conclusion that if a plaintiff is entitled to recover pecuniary losses for physical injury, he or she is also entitled to recover for the emotional harm caused by the same tortious act.[275] While this recognition allows some courts to award damages for emotional suffering where physical injury is also shown, it can serve to preclude recovery for negligent infliction of emotional distress in the absence of physical injury.[276]

Often a plaintiff will seek damages for emotional trauma when a physical injury is suffered by someone other than themselves with whom they have a close personal relationship, e.g., parents who witness injuries to their children.[277] Most jurisdictions require that such an injury must be a reasonably foreseeable consequence of the defendant's negligence[278] to limit what has been characterized as the otherwise potentially infinite liability which would follow every negligent act. The current test of foreseeability of emotional damages requires that factors like the following be taken into account: (1) was the plaintiff located near the scene of the accident, (2) did the shock stem from the direct emotional impact of the plaintiff's sensory and contemporaneous observance of the accident, and (3) were the plaintiff and the victim closely related.[279] Those jurisdictions which recognize the foreseeability element as essential to a recovery of emotional damages still impose certain restraints. The fear has been expressed that if foreseeability were the sole test, then once liability had been established it could potentially be applied almost limitlessly. It could extend to other children, fathers, grandparents, relatives or others *in loco parentis*, and even to sensitive caretakers or any other affected bystanders. Moreover, in any one accident, there might well be more than one person indirectly but seriously affected by the shock of injury or death to a child.[280]

Special damages often compensate the plaintiff for a future loss. The fact that such loss has not materialized at the time of trial is not an obstacle to recovery; however, such future loss must be shown to be reasonably certain to occur. An award for future suffering may not be based solely on speculations.[281] Earnings lost as the result of the injury suffered may be recovered as well as damages suffered due to the impairment of future earning capacity. With respect to diminished earning capacity, a Colorado court has held that the fact that the patient is earning more money than he or she did before the injury does not preclude recovery for such damages as long as the injury has actually resulted in some diminishment.[282] The plaintiff may also recover medical expenses that have been reasonably or necessarily incurred, or will, to a reasonable medical certainty, be incurred in the future because of additional medical, hospital or supportive expense occasioned by the injury.[283] Some jurisdictions have characterized this expense as "economic injury" which flows from negligent conduct.[284]

Other special damages often sought are those for loss of the services of the injured party by family members. When a spouse seeks such damages they are referred to as loss of consortium. (Consortium refers to the conjugal fellowship of husband and wife, and the right of each to the company, cooperation, affection and aid of the other in every conjugal relation.) Such damages are awarded if they can be shown to "flow from the tort."[285] Each spouse has a cause of action for loss of consortium caused by negligent or intentional injury to the other spouse by a third party. Some courts hold that special damages for a loss of consortium may only be awarded if a physical injury is suffered by the non-plaintiff spouse.[286] Where a wife is debilitated as the result of negligently performed treatment, any resulting injuries she sustains constitutes a direct tort on her, but not her husband. The actionable wrong against the husband is seen to be the interference with his marital rights, depriving him of his wife's services, society and companionship and requiring expenditures by him for her medical treatment and care.[287]

Jurisdictions vary in their treatment of a child's claim for loss of his or her parent's services. This issue was raised in a 1979 Washington case where a mother suffered a stroke as the result of an oral contraceptive prescription. She suffered significant permanent impairment, including loss of mobility and an inability to speak and carry on conversations in a normal manner. The court noted numerous considerations that weighed against granting children a right of action, including

§ 1.60 Damages 49

(1) the absence of any legally enforceable claim by a child to his parent's services, (2) the absence of precedent for such a holding, (3) the uncertainty and remoteness of the damages involved, (4) the possible overlap with the other parent's recovery for loss of consortium, (5) the potential multiplication of litigation, if such damages were allowed, (6) the possibility of settlements made with parents in the same suit being disrupted, (7) the danger of fabricated actions and, (8) the predicted resulting increase in insurance costs.[288] On the other hand, in a 1980 Texas case involving a mother who died during an elective operation to remove her gallbaldder, the court held that children may recover damages for the loss of their mother's services. In such cases, the court stated that juries may consider the care, maintenance, support, services, education and advice that the children would in reasonable probability have received from their mother.[289]

While punitive or exemplary damages are rarely awarded in malpractice actions, courts have noted that there is no rational justification for a separate rule or language applicable to the medical profession.[290] A leading authority defines punitive damages as "damages, other than compensatory or nominal damages, awarded against a person to punish him for his outrageous conduct." Outrageous conduct is further defined to include "acts done with a bad motive or with a reckless indifference to the interests of others.[291] Thus, acts of negligence alone are not a sufficient basis for awarding punitive damages.[292]

Where sufficient evidence exists for a jury to find a physician recklessly indifferent to a patient's interests, punitive damages may be awarded.

CASE ILLUSTRATION

The patient underwent elective renal arteriography which required the injection of a radiopaque dye into her blood vessels for the purpose of taking x-rays of her right kidney. The aim of the procedure was to determine whether the patient suffered from any tumors in her right kidney. It was ascertained that she did not. Within forty-eight hours of the operation, the patient became completely and irreversibly paralyzed from the waist down.

The patient sued the anesthesiologist, the surgeon and the company that manufactured the dye. Several theories were offered to explain the medical cause of the transfer of the dye, which was conceded to have neurotoxic properties, into the spinal cord. The plaintiff asserted that the transfer occurred because the injections of dye were continued despite a precipitous drop in the patient's blood pressure. The anesthesiologist had failed to inform the surgeon of the drop, which was recorded. If he had been informed, the surgeon testified that he would have halted the procedure. Furthermore, the anesthesiologist administered neosynephrine to raise the patient's blood pressure. Since the consequence of administering neosynephrine is to constrict the blood vessels, its injection was argued to cause the dye in effect to be squeezed into the patient's spinal cord. The anesthesiologist argued that the transfer occurred because of the volume, pressure, or frequency of the injections of the dye, which were matters in control of the surgeon. The plaintiff proved that the anesthesiologist left the operating room in the midst of the procedure to go to lunch, and the evidence, while in conflict as to whether a replacement was obtained, indicated that this had not been done. The court held that the plaintiff had presented a case that could be decided by a jury to constitute abandonment and that in such a case, punitive damages could be awarded. Therefore, the case was ordered to be retried. (*Medvecz v. Choi*, 1977)[293]

Establishing a monetary value for such subjective concepts as physical pain, emotional pain, suffering or loss of conjugal relations is a task generally left to a jury based on the evidence it has heard.[294] While courts have stated that damages may not be determined by mere speculation or guess,[295] calculations described as "a reasoned estimate of the damages sustained[296] or "the best estimate that can be made under the circumstances[297] have been held acceptable. The courts assert that calculations of this nature are not alien to the American judicial system and jurors are called upon to make similar determinations quite often.[298] Furthermore, such calculations are made by estate planners, insurance companies and sometimes by private parties as incident to support proceedings or matrimonial settlements.[299]

Imprecision in estimating a monetary value has not been allowed to constitute a barrier to the plaintiff's recovery.[300] There need only be a basis for reasonably ascertaining the amount of damages.[301] One court has expressed this consideration in the following strong language.

> [W]here a wrong itself is of such a nature as to preclude the computation of damages with precise exactitude, it would be a perversion of fundamental principles of justice to deny all relief to the injured party and thereby relieve the wrongdoer from making any amend for his act.[302]

Evidence offered as the basis of evaluation decisions may come from witnesses with an expertise in fields like economics. Experts may offer various methods of calculation. In a 1978 Louisiana case, an economics expert computed the value of a deceased mother's services as a housekeeper at the current hourly rate for cleaning and child care services. She included adjustments for increases attributable to productivity and rising living costs, and decreases attributable to periods of unemployment with a further deduction attributable to personal expenditures.[303] In a 1980 Texas case, an economics expert computed the economic value for the loss of moral guidance as equal to the annual salary of a school teacher, adjusted for inflation.[304]

§ 1.60 *Damages* 51

Once a jury makes a damage award, it is highly unlikely that its award will be altered by either the trial judge or a reviewing appellate court[305] unless the award shocks the court's conscience or is clearly erroneous.[306] Where a jury has not acted arbitrarily or capriciously, its decision as to the amount of damages will stand. Generally the courts do not recognize any hard and fast rule for determining maximum compensation,[307] though courts in some jurisdictions compare the award in a given case with other previously decided awards in cases involving fairly comparable injuries.[308]

Generally, courts impose an affirmative duty on the patient to lessen or mitigate the degree of damage he or she suffers. The patient cannot recover for damage that could be readily avoided without undue risk or expense, such as undergoing safe and simple treatment to correct the injury.[309] Nor may the patient aggravate or increase the injury by his or her own negligence[310] by failing to follow the physician's advice. On the other hand, a patient is not required to undergo a dangerous or serious operation that poses a threat to his or her life or that represents only one choice among several less radical treatments.[311] The patient is only required to undergo additional treatment to the extent that an ordinary and reasonable person would, under the same or similar circumstances, in accordance with sound medical practice.[312]

Finally, it is well established that in cases with multiple defendants the apportionment of damages must reflect the culpability of the various parties.[313] Thus, it is not the total number of defendants involved, but the number of directly and primarily liable parties which determines the number of pro-rata shares. In a 1980 Pennsylvania case where a hospital was found vicariously liable (see § 2.30, Vicarious Liability) for the direct negligence of a nurse-anesthetist, the court determined that direct negligence was attributed to the nurse-anesthetist and the surgeon. The surgeon was responsible for one half of the damage award and the nurse-anesthetist and hospital were responsible for the other half.[314]

NOTES

1. Continuing Medical Malpractice Insurance Crisis: Hearings before the Subcomm. on Health of the Comm. on Labor and Public Welfare, 94th Cong., 1st Sess. 154, 220 (1975-76).
2. Black's Law Dictionary 1111 (4th ed. 1978).
3. Ziemba v. Sternberg, 45 A.D.2d 230, 357 N.Y.S.2d 265 (1974).
4. Leighton v. Sargent, 27 N.H. 460, 59 Am. Dec. 388 (1853).
5. W. Prosser, Handbook of the Law of Torts 139 (4th ed. 1971).
6. Stewart v. Rudner, 349 Mich. 459, 84 N.W.2d 816 (1957).
7. Mich Comp. Laws Ann. § 556.132 (1967 & Supp. 1981-82).
8. National Association of Insurance Commissioners, 2 NAIC Malpractice Claims 3 (1978).

Notes: Chapter I

9. St. Paul Fire and Marine Insurance Company, Physician and Surgeon Professional Liability Countrywide Summary Report by Allegation (1978).
10. National Association of Insurance Commissioners, *supra* note 8, at 48.
11. Hirsch & White, *The Pathologic Anatomy of Medical Malpractice Claims*, 6 Legal Aspects of Med. Practice 26-28 (1978).
12. R. Dripps, J. Eckenhoff & L. Vandam, Introduction to Anesthesia 3 (5th ed. 1977) [hereinafter cited as Dripps].
13. Campbell, Weiss & Blanke, *Symposium—Deaths Due to Anesthesia*, 5 J. For. Sci. 501 (1960).
14. *See* Hirsch & White, *supra* note 11, at 32; Dripps, *supra* note 12, at 53.
15. Dripps, *supra* note 12, at 53.
16. Dripps, *supra* note 12, at 55.
17. *Id.* at 57.
18. Hersey, *The Defensive Practice of Medicine—Myth or Reality?*, Milbank Memorial Fund Quarterly, 69-97, January 1972.
19. H. Hirsch & E. White, *supra* note 11, at 32.
20. W. Prosser, *supra* note 5, at 143.
21. *Id.* at 149-50.
22. Yoshizawa v. Hewitt, 52 F.2d 411 (9th Cir. 1931); Boyce v. Brown, 51 Ariz. 416, 77 P.2d 455 (1938); Ales v. Ryan, 8 Cal. 2d 82, 64 P.2d 409 (1936); Rierce v. Patterson, 50 Cal. App. 2d . 486, 123 P.2d 544 (1942); Froid v. Knowles, 95 Colo. 223, 36 P.2d 156 (1934); Hudson v. Weiland, 150 Fla. 523, 8 So.2d 37 (1942); Merker v. Wood, 307 Ky. 331, 210 S.W.2d 946 (1948).
23. Childs v. Weis, 440 S.W.2d 104 (Tex. 1969); Kreisman v. Thomas, 12 Ariz. App. 215, 469 P.2d 107 (1970); Clark v. Smith, 494 S.W.2d 192 (Tex. 1973).
24. Restatement (Second) of Torts § 283 (1965).
25. Linhares v. Hall, 357 Mass. 290, 257 N.E.2d 429 (1970).
26. Robinson v. Wirts, 387 Pa. 291, 127 A.2d 706 (1956).
27. Lince v. Monson, 363 Mich. 135, 108 N.W.2d 845 (1961).
28. Alexandridis v. Jewett, 388 F.2d 829 (1st Cir. 1968).
29. Koury v. Follo, 272 N.C. 366, 158 S.E.2d 548 (1968).
30. *See, e.g.*, Tomer v. Am. Home Prod. Corp., 170 Conn. 681, 368 A.2d 35 (1976); Seaton v. Rosenberg, 573 S.W.2d 333 (Ky. 1978).
31. Childs v. Weis, *supra* note 23.
32. American Medical Association, *Principles of Medical Ethics*, VI in Current Opinions of the Judicial Council of the American Medical Association ix (1981) [hereinafter cited as AMA].
33. Manlove v. Wilmington Gen. Hosp., 53 Del. 338, 169 A.2d 18 (1965), *aff'd*, 54 Del. 15, 174 A.2d 135 (1961); Hurley v. Eddingfield, 156 Ind. 416, 59 N.E. 1058 (1901); Rice v. Rinaldo, 67 Ohio L. Abs. 183, 119 N.E.2d 657 (1951).
34. Travelers Ins. Co. v. Bergeron, 25 F.2d 680 (8th Cir. 1928), *cert. denied*, 278 U.S. 638 (1928); Findlay v. Board of Supervisors, 72 Ariz. 58, 230 P.2d 526 (1951); Kennedy v. Parrott, 243 N.C. 355, 90 S.E.2d 754 (1956); Hull v. Enid Gen. Hosp. Foundation, 194 Okla. 446, 152 P.2d 693 (1944).
35. Hammonds v. Aetna Cas. & Sur. Co., 237 F. Supp. 96 (N.D. Ohio 1965); Berkey v. Anderson, 1 Cal. App. 3d 790, 82 Cal. Rptr. 67 (1969); Adams v. Ison, 249 S.W.2d 791 (Ky. 1952).
36. Spencer v. West, 126 So.2d 423 (La. 1960).
37. Hankerson v. Thomas, 148 A.2d 583 (D.C. 1959).
38. McNamara v. Emmons, 36 Cal. App. 2d 199, 97 P.2d 503 (1939); Stewart v. Rudner, *supra* note 6.

Notes: Chapter I

39. Tunkl v. Regents of the Univ. of Cal., 60 Cal. 2d 92, 383 P.2d 441, 32 Cal. Rptr. 33 (1963); Olson v. Molzen, 558 S.W.2d 429 (Tenn. 1977).
40. James v. Holder, 34 A.D.2d 632, 309 N.Y.S.2d 385 (1970).
41. Restatement (Second) of Torts § 323 (1965).
42. *See generally*, W. Prosser, *supra* note 5, at 344.
43. Keene v. Wiggins, 69 Cal. App. 3d 308, 138 Cal. Rptr. 3 (1977).
44. Wilcox v. Salt Lake City Corp., 26 Utah 2d 78, 484 P.2d 1200 (1971); Rogers v. Horvath, 65 Mich. App. 644, 237 N.W.2d 595 (1976).
45. Johnston v. Sibley, 558 S.W.2d 135 (Tex. 1977).
46. Rainer v. Grossman, 31 Cal. App. 3d 539, 107 Cal. Rptr. 469 (1973); Oliver v. Brock, 342 So.2d 1 (Ala. 1977).
47. Ala. Code § 7-121(1) (1975 & Supp. 1980); Alaska Stat. § 08.64.365 (1977); Ariz. Rev. Stat. Ann. § 32-1471 (1976 & Supp. 1980-81); Ark. Stat. Ann. § 72-624 (1979); Cal. Bus. & Prof. Code § 2144 (West 1974 & Supp. 1981); Conn. Gen. Stat. Ann. § 52-557b (West Supp. 1981); Del. Code Ann. tit. 24, § 1767 (Supp. 1980); D.C. Code Encycl. § 2-142 (West Supp. 1978-79); Fla. Stat. § 768.13 (West 1976 & Supp. 1980); Ga. Code Ann. § 84-930 (Harrison 1979 & Supp. 1980); Hawaii Rev. Stat. § 663-1.5 (1976); Idaho Code § 5-330 (1979 & Supp. 1981); Ill. Ann. Stat. ch. 91, § 2a (Smith-Hurd 1978 & Supp. 1980-81); Ind. Code Ann. § 34-4-12-1 (Burns 1976); Iowa Code Ann. § 613.17 (West Supp. 1981-82); Kan. Stat. Ann. § 65-2891 (1980); La. Rev. Stat. Ann. § 9:2793 (West 1977 & Supp. 1981); Me. Rev. Stat. Ann. tit. 32, § 3151 (1980); Md. Health Code Ann. art. 43, § 149A (Supp. 1980); Mass Gen. Laws Ann. ch. 112, § 12B (1980); Mich. Comp. Laws Ann. § 691.1501 (Supp. 1981-82); Miss. Code Ann. § 88-93-5 (1972); Mont. Rev. Codes Ann. § 17-410 (1970 & Supp. 1977); Neb. Rev. Stat. § 25-1152 (1965); Nev. Rev. Stat. § 41.500 (1979); N.H. Rev. Stat. Ann. § 329:25 (1966 & Supp. 1979); N.J. Stat. Ann. § 2A:62A-1 (West Supp. 1981-82); N.M. Stat. Ann. § 12-12-3 (Supp. 1975); N.Y. Educ. Law § 6513 (McKinney 1972 & Supp. 1980-81); N.C. Gen. Stat. §§20-166, 8-95 (1975 & Supp. 1979); N.D. Cent. Code § 43-17.37 (1960 & Supp. 1977); Ohio Rev. Code Ann. § 2305.23 (Page 1980); Okla. Stat. Ann. tit. 76, § 5 (Supp. 1980-81); Or. Rev. Stat. § 30.800 (1979); 12 Pa. Cons. Stat. Ann. §§ 1641, 1642 (Purdon Supp. 1981-82); R.I. Gen. Laws § 5-37-14 (Supp. 1980); S.C. Code § 46-803 (Supp. 1980); Tenn. Code Ann. § 63-622 (1976); Tex. Rev. Civ. Stat. Ann. art. la (Vernon Supp. 1980-81); Utah Code Ann. § 58-12-23 (1974 & Supp. 1979); Vt. Stat. Ann. tit. 12, § 519 (Supp. 1980); Va. Code § 54-276.9 (1978); Wash. Rev. Code §§ 4.24.300, .310 (Supp. 1981); W. Va. Code § 55-7-15 (1981); Wis. Stat. Ann. § 147.17(7) (West Supp. 1980-81); Wyo. Stat. Ann. § 33.343 (1977).
48. D. Louisell & H. Williams, Medical Malpractice, § 21.35 (1980).
49. *See, e.g.*, Va. Code § 54-276.9 (1978).
50. *See, e.g.*, Ga. Code Ann. § 84-930 (Harrison 1979 & Supp. 1980); Md. Health Code Ann. art. 43, § 142A (Supp. 1980); Mich. Comp. Laws Ann. § 691.1501 (Supp. 1981-82).
51. *See, e.g.*, Ariz. Rev. Stat. Ann. § 32-1471 (1976); Conn. Gen. Stat. Ann. § 52-557b (West Supp. 1981); Mass. Gen. Laws Ann. ch. 112, § 12B (1980); N.Y. Educ. Law § 6527 (McKinney 1972 & Supp. 1980-81); Ohio Rev. Code Ann. § 2305.23 (Page 1980).
52. *See, e.g.*, Cal. Bus. & Prof. Code § 2144 (West 1974 & Supp. 1981); Conn. Gen. Stat. Ann. § 52-557b (West Supp. 1981); Mass Gen. Laws Ann. ch. 112, § 12B (1980).
53. *See, e.g.*, N.D. Cent. Code § 43-17.37 (1975 & Supp. 1977); N.H. Rev. Stat. Ann. § 329:25 (1966 & Supp. 1979); S.D. Comp. Laws Ann. § 20-9-3 (1979); Mass. Gen. Laws Ann. ch. 112, § 12B (1980).

Notes: Chapter I

54. *See, e.g.*, Mich. Comp. Laws Ann. § 691.1501 (Supp. 1981-82); N.Y. Educ. Law § 6527(10) (McKinney 1972 & Supp. 1980-81); 42 Pa. Cons. Stat. Ann. §§8331(a), (b) (Purdon Supp. 1981-82).
55. Ind. Code Ann. § 34-4-12-1 (Burns 1976).
56. McGulpin v. Bessemer, 241 Iowa 119, 43 N.W.2d 121 (1950).
57. Lee v. Dewbre, 362 S.W.2d 900 (Tex. Civ. App. 1962).
58. Ascher v. Guttierrez, 533 F.2d 1235 (D.C. Cir. 1976).
59. *Id.*
60. *Id.*
61. Medvecz v. Choi, 569 F.2d 1221 (3d Cir. 1977).
62. *See, e.g.*, Prack v. United States Fidelity & Guaranty Co., 1870 So.2d 170 (La. App. 1966); Alimchandani v. Goings, 39 Md. App. 353, 386 A.2d 789 (1978).
63. Lee v. Dewbre, *supra* note 57. *See also* AMA, *supra* note 32, at § 5.50.
62 Johnson v. Vaughn, 370 S.W.2d 591 (Ky. App. 1963).
65. Kenney v. Piedmont Hosp., 136 Ga. App. 660, 222 S.E.2d 162 (1975).
66. Howell v. Carpenter, 19 Mich. App. 233, 172 N.W.2d 549 (1969).
67. *In re* Culbertson's Will, 57 Misc. 2d 391, 292 N.Y.S.2d 806 (1968). *See also*, AMA, *supra* note 32, at § 5.70, p. 39.
68. W. Prosser, *supra* note 5, at 162.
69. Cullen & Larsen, Essentials of Anesthetic Practice 3-4 (1974).
70. Pederson v. Dumochel, 72 Wash. 2d 73, 431 P.2d 973 (1967).
71. Buras v. Aetna Cas. & Sur. Co., 263 So.2d 375 (La. Ct. App. 1972).
72. Webb v. Jorns, 488 S.W.2d 407 (Tex. 1973).
73. Pederson v. Dumochel, *supra* note 70.
74. Kronke v. Danielson, 108 Ariz. 400, 499 P.2d 156 (1972).
75. Tomer v. Am. Home Prod. Corp., *supra* note 30.
76. Christy v. Saliterman, 288 Minn. 144, 179 N.W.2d 288 (1970).
77. Kronke v. Danielson, *supra* note 74.
78. Wiggins v. Piver, 276 N.C. 134, 171 S.E.2d 393 (1970); Naccarato v. Grob, 384 Mich. 248, 180 N.W.2d 788 (1970).
79. Voegeli v. Lewis, 568 F.2d 89 (8th Cir. 1977); Hamilton v. Hardy, 549 P. 2d 1099 (Colo. App. 1976); Miller v. Raaen, 273 Minn. 109, 139 N.W.2d 877 (1966).
80. Cornfeldt v. Tongen, 262 N.W.2d 684 (Minn. 1977).
81. *Id.*
82. Chapman v. Argonaut-Southwest Ins. Co., 290 So.2d 779 (La. Ct. App. 1974).
83. *Id.*
84. *Id.*
85. Tomer v. Am. Home Prod. Corp., *supra* note 30.
86. Carlsen v. Javurek, 526 F.2d 202 (8th Cir. 1975).
87. Pry v. Jones, 253 Ark. 534, 487 S.W.2d 606 (1973).
88. Carlsen v. Javurek, *supra* note 86.
89. *Id.*
90. Cornfeldt v. Tongen, *supra* note 80.
91. Mueller v. Mueller, 88 S.D. 446, 221 N.W.2d 39 (1974); Lhotka v. Larson, 307 Minn. 121, 238 N.W.2d 870 (1976).
92. Sanzari v. Rosenfeld, 34 N.J. 128, 167 A.2d 625 (1961).
93. Mulder v. Parke Davis & Co., 288 Minn. 332, 181 N.W.2d 882 (1970).
94. Webb v. Jorns, 530 S.W.2d 847 (Tex. Civ. App. 1975).
95. Gridley v. Johnson, 476 S.W.2d 475 (Mo. 1972); Bivens v. Detroit Osteopathic Hosp., 77 Mich. App. 478, 258 N.W.2d 527 (1977).
96. Gridley v. Johnson, *supra* note 95.

Notes: Chapter I

97. Jones v. Bloom, 388 Mich. 98, 200 N.W.2d 196 (1972).
98. Lewandowski v. Preferred Risk Mut. Ins. Co., 33 Wis.2d 69, 146 N.W.2d 505 (1966).
99. Fed. R. Evid. 803(18).
100. W. Prosser, *supra* note 5, at 163. *See also*, Eastin v. Broomfield, 116 Ariz. 576, 570 P.2d 744 (1977).
101. Bryant v. Biggs, 331 Mich. 64, 49 N.W.2d 63 (1951).
102. Ferguson v. Gonyaw, 64 Mich. App. 685, 236 N.W.2d 543 (1975); Harris v. Bales, 459 S.W.2d 742 (Mo. App. 1970).
103. Drummond v. Hodges, 417 S.W.2d 740 (Tex. Civ. App. 1967).
104. Chumbler v. McClure, 505 F.2d 489 (6th Cir. 1974); Joy v. Chau, 377 N.E.2d 670 (Ind. 1978); Schreiber v. Cestari, 40 A.D.2d 1025, 338 N.Y.S.2d 972 (1972).
105. Broderick v. Gibbs, 296 N.E.2d 708 (Mass. 1973).
106. Hundley v. Saint Francis Hosp., 161 Cal. App. 2d 800, 327, P.2d 131 (1958); Beck v. Lovell, 361 So.2d 245 (La. App. 1978).
107. Gray v. Gunnagle, 423 Pa. 144, 223 A.2d 663 (1966).
108. Schloendorff v. Society of N.Y. Hosp., 211 N.Y. 125, 105 N.E. 92 (1914).
109. Black's Law Dictionary, *supra* note 2, at 147.
110. *Id.* at 193.
111. Mink v. University of Chicago, 460 F. Supp. 713 (N.D. Ill. 1978).
112. W. Prosser, *supra* note 5, at 35-36.
113. Mink v. University of Chicago, *supra* note 111 at 718.
114. Gravis v. Physicians & Surgeons Hosp., 415 S.W.2d 674 (Tex. 1967).
115. Patterson v. Van Wiel, 91 N.M. 100, 570 P.2d 931 (N.M. App. 1977).
116. Hall v. United States, 136 F. Supp. 187 (W.D. La. 1955).
117. *Id.*
118. Gravis v. Physicians & Surgeons Hosp., *supra* note 114.
119. *Id.*
120. *See, e.g.*, Rainer v. Buena Community Mem. Hosp., 18 Cal. App. 3d 240, 95 Cal. Rptr. 901 (1971); Cathemer v. Hunter, 27 Ariz. App. 780, 588 P.2d 975 (1977).
121. Lener v. Baron, 20 A.D.2d 814, 248 N.Y.S.2d 829 (1964).
122. Ariz. Rev. Stat. § 12-562B (1976 & Supp. 1980-81).
123. Cathemer v. Hunter, *supra* note 120.
124. W. Prosser, *supra* note 5, at 38.
125. Sard v. Hardy, 379 A.2d 1014, 1019 (Md. App. 1977).
126. Funke v. Fieldman, 212 Kan. 524, 512 P.2d 539 (1973).
127. Schloendorff v. Soc'y of N.Y. Hosp., *supra* note 108.
128. Miller v. Kennedy, 11 Wash. App. 272, 522 P.2d 852 (1974).
129. Natanson v. Kline, 186 Kan. 393, 350 P.2d 1093, 1106, *rehearing denied*, 187 Kan. 186, 354 P.2d 670 (1960); Sard v. Hardy, *supra* note 125.
130. Salgo v. Leland Stanford Jr. Univ. Bd. of Trustees, 154 Cal. App. 2d 560, 317 P.2d 170 (1957).
131. Tatro v. Lueken, 212 Kan. 606, 512 P.2d 529 (1972); Natanson v. Kline, *supra* note 129; Moore v. Underwood Mem. Hosp., 147 N.J. Super. 252, 371 A.2d 105 (1977); Gerety v. Demers, 92 N.M. 396, 589 P.2d 180 (1978).
132. Sard v. Hardy, *supra* note 125, *citing* Canterbury v. Spence, 464 F.2d 772, 785 (D.C. Cir.), *cert. denied*, 409 U.S. 1064 (1972); Fogal v. Genesee Hosp., 41 A.D.2d 468, 344 N.Y.S.2d 552 (1973); Wilkinson v. Vesey, 110 R.I. 606, 295 A.2d 676 (1972); Scaria v. St. Paul Fire & Marine Ins. Co., 68 Wis. 2d 1, 227 N.W.2d 647 (1975).
133. Gray v. Grunnagle, *supra* note 107.
134. Sauro v. Shea, 257 Pa. 66, 390 A.2d 259 (1978).
135. Tatro v. Lueken, *supra* note 131.

56 *Notes: Chapter I*

136. *See, e.g.,* Dunham v. Wright, 302 F. Supp. 1108 (M.D. Pa. 1969); Nishi v. Hartwell, 52 Hawaii 188, 473 P.2d 116 (1970); Carman v. Dippold, 63 Ill. App. 3d 419, 379 N.E.2d 1365 (1978); Sard v. Hardy, *supra* note 125.
137. Hall v. United States, *supra* note 116.
138. Patterson v. Van Wiel, *supra* note 115.
139. *See* Mallet v. Pirkey, 171 Colo. 271, 466 P.2d 466 (1969); Gates v. Jensen, 20 Wash. App. 81, 579 P.2d 374 (1978); Sawyer v. Methodist Hosp., 383 F. Supp. 563 (W.D. Tenn. 1974).
140. Mitchell v. Robinson, 334 S.W.2d 11 (Mo. 1960); Gray v. Grunnagle, *supra* note 107; Starnes v. Taylor, 272 N.C. 386, 158 S.E.2d 339 (1968).
141. Longmire v. Hoey, 512 S.W.2d 307 (Tenn. 1974).
142. Nishi v. Hartwell, *supra* note 136; Henderson v. Milobsky, 595 F.2d 654 (D.C. Cir. 1978); Martin v. Stratton, 515 P.2d 1366 (Okla. 1973).
143. Doerr v. Movius, 154 Mont. 346, 463 P.2d 477 (1970); Sawyer v. Methodist Hosp., *supra* note 139; Henderson v. Milobsky, *supra* note 142.
144. Stauffer v. Karabin, 30 Colo. App. 357, 492 P.2d 862 (1971); Platta v. Flatley, 68 Wis. 2d 47, 227 N.W.2d 898 (1975); Sard v. Hardy, *supra* note 125.
145. *See* Funke v. Fieldman, *supra* note 126.
146. Sard v. Hardy, *supra* note 125, at 1014.
147. Koury v. Follo, *supra* note 29.
148. Schroeder v. Lawrence, 372 Mass. 88, 359 N.E.2d 1301, 1303 (1977).
149. Cornfeldt v. Tongen, 295 N.W.2d 638 (Minn. 1980).
150. Karp v. Cooley, 349 F. Supp. 827 (S.D. Tex. 1972); Funke v. Fieldman, *supra* note 126.
151. Beauvais v. Notre Dame Hosp., 387 A.2d 689, 692 (R.I. 1978).
152. Scaria v. St. Paul Fire & Marine Ins. Co., *supra* note 132.
153. Canterbury v. Spence, *supra* note 132.
154. Funke v. Fieldman, *supra* note 126; Forney v. Memorial Hosp., 543 S.W.2d 705 (Tex. 1976).
155. Small v. Gifford Mem. Hosp., 349 A.2d 703 (Vt. 1975).
156. Brown v. Allen Sanitarium, Inc., 364 So.2d 661 (La. 1978).
157. Hunter v. Robison, 488 S.W.2d 555 (Tex. 1972).
158. Dawner & Sagall, *Medicolegal Causation: A Source of Professional Misunderstanding*, 3 Am. J.L. & Med. 303 (1977). Note, in some states, e.g. N.Y., a "substantial likelihood" (less than 50%) is enough.
159. W. Prosser, *supra* note 5, at 236-46.
160. *Id.* at 239.
161. Restatement (Second) of Torts § 431 (1964).
162. *See* W. Prosser, *supra* note 5, at 239.
163. Restatement (Second) of Torts § 433B(1) (1964).
164. Aubert v. Charity Hosp., 363 So.2d 1223 (La. 1978).
165. Beauvais v. Notre Dame Hosp., *supra* note 151; Cornfeldt v. Tongen, *supra* note 149; Aubert v. Charity Hosp, *supra* note 164; Holzberg v. Flower & Fifth Ave. Hosps., 39 A.D.2d 526, 330 N.Y.S.2d 682 (1972).
166. Aubert v. Charity Hosp., *supra* note 164.
167. Restatement (Second) of Torts § 433B(2)-(3) (1964).
168. W. Prosser, *supra* note 5, at 241.
169. Bertrand v. Aetna Cas. & Sur. Co., 306 So.2d 343 (La. App. 1975).
170. Aubert v. Charity Hosp., *supra* note 164.
171. Cornfeldt v. Tongen, *supra* note 149.
172. W. Prosser, *supra* note 5, at 244.

Notes: Chapter I

173. Sturm v. Green, 398 P.2d 799 (Okla. 1965).
174. *Id.*
175. Hunter v. Robison, 488 S.W.2d 555 (Tex. 1972).
176. Black's Law Dictionary, *supra* note 2 at 1471.
177. Weeks v. Latter Day Saints Hosp., 418 F.2d 1035 (10th Cir. 1969); Ewen v. Baton Rouge Gen. Hosp., 378 So.2d 172 (La. App. 1979); Haas v. United States, 492 F. Supp. 755 (D. Mass. 1980).
178. W. Prosser, *supra* note 5, at 212.
179. Byrne v. Boadle, 2 H. & C. 722, 159 Eng. Rep. 299 (1863).
180. Meisel, *The Expansion of Liability for Medical Accidents: From Negligence to Strict Liability by Way of Informed Consent*, 56 Neb. L. Rev. 51 (1979).
181. E. Thode, *The Unconscious Patient: Who Should Bear the Risk of Unexplained Injuries to a Healthy Part of His Body?*, 1969 Utah L. Rev. 11.
182. W. Prosser, *supra* note 5, at 223.
183. Salgo v. Leland Stanford Jr. Univ. Bd. of Trustees, *supra* note 130.
184. Faris v. Doctor's Hosp., Inc., 18 Ariz. App. 264, 501 P.2d 440 (1972); Haas v. United States, *supra* note 177.
185. Terhune v. Margaret Hague Maternity Hosp., 63 N.J. Super. 106, 164 A.2d 75 (1960); Ybarra v. Spangard, 25 Cal. 2d 486, 146 P.2d 982 (1944).
186. Mayor v. Dowsett, 240 Or. 196, 400 P.2d 234 (1965); Seneris v. Haas, 45 Cal. 2d 811, 291 P.2d 915 (1955).
187. Fogal v. Genesee Hosp., *supra* note 132; Wiles v. Myerly, 210 N.W.2d 619 (Iowa 1973).
188. V. Collins, Principles of Anesthesia 43-89 (1976).
189. Ybarra v. Spangard, *supra* note 185.
190. Salgo v. Leland Stanford Jr. Univ. Bd. of Trustees, *supra* note 130.
191. Stephenson v. Kaiser Foundation Hosp., 203 Cal. App. 631, 21 Cal. Rptr. 646 (1962).
192. Voss v. Bridwell, 188 Kan. 643, 364 P.2d 955 (1961); Funke v. Fieldman, *supra* note 126.
193. Ewen v. Baton Rouge Gen. Hosp., *supra* note 177.
194. *See, e.g.*, Cronin v. Hagan, 221 N.W.2d 748 (Iowa 1974); Beaudoin v. Watertown Mem. Hosp., 32 Wis. 2d 132, 145 N.W.2d 166 (1966).
195. Spidle v. Steward, 68 Ill. App. 3d 134, 24 Ill. Dec. 489, 385 N.E.2d 401 (1979); Bryant v. St. Paul Fire & Marine Ins. Co., 272 So. 2d 448 (La App. 1973).
196. Haas v. United States, *supra* note 177.
197. Haas v. United States, *supra* note 177; Kitto v. Gilbert, 39 Colo. App. 374, 570 P.2d 544 (1977); Warrick v. Giron, 290 N.W.2d 166 (Minn. 1980); Spannaus v. 0tolaryngology Clinic, 308 Minn. 334, 242 N.W.2d 594 (1976).
198. Haas v. United States, *supra* note 177; Faris v. Doctor's Hosp., Inc., *supra* note 184; McAdams v. Holden, 349 So.2d 900 (La. App. 1977); Merritt v. Deaconess Hosp., 48 Ohio Misc. 7, 357 N.E.2d 65 (1975); Jones v. Harrisburg Polyclinic Hosp., 487 Pa. 506, 410 A.2d 303 (1980).
199. McCann v. Baton Rouge Hosp., 276 So.2d 259 (La. 1973).
200. Quintal v. Laurel Grove Hosp., 62 Cal. 2d 154, 397 P.2d 161, 41 Cal. Rptr. 577 (1964).
201. Warrick v. Giron, *supra* note 197; Mayor v. Dowsett, *supra* note 186.
202. Sanders v. Smith, 200 Miss. 551, 27 So.2d 889 (1946).
203. Martin v. Stratton, *supra* note 142.
204. Haas v. United States, *supra* note 177.
205. Hughes v. Hastings, 469 S.W.2d 378 (Tenn. 1971).
206. Galbraith v. Busch, 267 N.Y. 230, 196 N.E. 36 (1935).

Notes: Chapter I

207. Kitto v. Gilbert, *supra* note 197.
208. Wiles v. Myerly, *supra* note 187.
209. Haas v. United States, *supra* note 177.
210. Pederson v. Dumochel, *supra* note 70.
211. Faris v. Doctor's Hosp., Inc., *supra* note 184.
212. Haas v. United States, *supra* note 177; Meritt v. Deaconess Hosp., *supra* note 198.
213. Mayor v. Dowsett, *supra* note 186.
214. Haas v. United States, *supra* note 177; Kitto v. Gilbert, *supra* note 197.
215. Voss v. Bridwell, *supra* note 192.
216. Salgo v. Leland Stanford Jr. Univ. Bd. of Trustees, *supra* note 130.
217. Miller v. Hardy, 546, S.W.2d 102 (Tex. 1978); Forney v. Mem. Hosp., *supra* note 154.
218. Forney v. Memorial Hosp., *supra* note 154.
219. Miller v. Raaen, *supra* note 79.
220. Faris v. Doctor's Hosp., Inc., *supra* note 184.
221. Quintal v. Laurel Grove Hosp., *supra* note 200.
222. Funke v. Fieldman, *supra* note 126.
223. Mayor v. Dowsett, *supra* note 186.
224. Rothman v. Silber, 90 N.J. Super. 22, 216 A.2d 18 (1966).
225. Voss v. Bridwell, *supra* note 192; Meadows v. Patterson, 21 Tenn. App. 283, 109 S.W.2d 417 (1937).
226. Horner v. N. Pac. Beneficial Ass'n Hosps., Inc., 62 Wash. 2d 351, 382 P.2d 518 (1963).
227. Meadows v. Patterson, *supra* note 225.
228. Horner v. N. Pac. Beneficial Ass'n Hosps., Inc., *supra* note 226.
229. Ybarra v. Spangard, *supra* note 185.
230. Younger v. Webster, 9 Wash. App. 87, 510 P.2d 1182 (1973).
231. Crawford v. County of Sacramento, 239 Cal. App. 2d 791, 49 Cal. Rptr. 115 (1966).
232. Cowlthorp v. Branford, 279 Or. 273, 567 P.2d 536 (1977).
233. Voss v. Bridwell, *supra* note 192.
234. Merritt v. Deaconess Hosp., *supra* note 198.
235. Faris v. Doctor's Hosp., Inc., *supra* note 184.
236. Ayers v. Parry, 192 F.2d 181 (3d Cir. 1951); McAdams v. Holden, *supra* note 198.
237. Crawford v. County of Sacramento, *supra* note 231; McAdams v. Holden, *supra* note 198; Webb v. Jorns, 473 S.W.2d 328, (Tex. Civ. App. 1971); Edelman v. Ziegler, 233 Cal. App. 2d 871, 44 Cal. Rptr. 114 (1965); Dunlap v. Marine, 242 Cal. App. 2d 162, 51 Cal. Rptr. 158 (1966).
238. Bertrand v. Aetna Cas. & Sur. Co., *supra* note 169.
239. Ayers v. Parry, *supra* note 236.
240. *Id*.
241. McAdams v. Holden, *supra* note 198; Hoven v. Kelble, 79 Wis. 2d 444, 256 N.W.2d 379 (1977).
242. Talbot v. Dr. W.H. Groves' Latter-Day Saints Hosp., Inc., 21 Utah 2d 73, 440 P.2d 872 (1968).
243. Ybarra v. Spangard, *supra* note 185.
244. Hoven v. Kelble, *supra* note 241.
245. Kitto v. Gilbert, *supra* note 197.
246. Spannaus v. Otolaryngology Clinic, *supra* note 197; Holzberg v. Flower & Fifth Ave. Hosps., *supra* note 165.
247. Spannaus v. Otolaryngology Clinic, *supra* note 197.
248. Mogensen v. Hicks, 253 Iowa 139, 110 N.W.2d 563 (1961).

Notes: Chapter I

249. Voss v. Bridwell, *supra* note 192.
250. Seneris v. Haas, *supra* note 186.
251. Voss v. Bridwell, *supra* note 192; McCann v. Baton Rouge Hosp., *supra* note 199; Faris v. Doctor's Hosp., Inc., *supra* note 184.
252. Faris v. Doctor's Hosp., Inc., *supra* note 184.
253. Clark v. Gibbons, 66 Cal. 2d 399, 426 P.2d 525, 58 Cal. Rptr. 125 (1967).
254. McCann v. Baton Rouge Hosp., *supra* note 199.
255. *See, e.g.*, Hoven v. Kelble, *supra* note 241; Seneris v. Haas, *supra* note 186.
256. Seneris v. Haas, *supra* note 186.
257. Note, *Res Ipsa Loquitur: A Case for Flexibility in Medical Malpractice*, 16 Wayne L. Rev. 1136, 1144 (1970).
258. W. Prosser, *supra* note 5, at 143.
259. Black's Law Dictionary, *supra*, 2 at 468.
260. *Id.* at 469.
261. J. Waltz & F. Inbau, Medical Jurisprudence 284 (1971).
262. Laws v. Harter, 534 S.W.2d 344 (Ky. 1978).
263. Black's Law Dictionary, *supra* note 2, at 467.
264. Frisnegger v. Gibson, 598 P.2d 574 (Mont. 1979).
265. Betancourt v. Gaylor, 136 N.J. Super. 69, 344 A.2d 336 (1975).
266. Stills v. Gratton, 55 Cal. App. 3d 698, 127 Cal. Rptr. 652 (1976).
267. *Id.*; Betancourt v. Gaylor, *supra* note 265.
268. Park v. Chessin, 60 A.D.2d 80, 400 N.Y.S.2d 110 (1977).
269. Beagle v. Vasold, 65 Cal. 2d 166, 417 P.2d 673, 53 Cal. Rptr. 129 (1966).
270. *See, e.g.*, Judd v. Rudolph, 222 N.W. 416 (Iowa 1928); Happy v. Waltz, 244 S.W.2d 380 (Mo. App. 1951).
271. Aubert v. Charity Hosp., *supra* note 164; Guiltinan v. Columbia Presbyterian Medical Center, 97 Misc 2d 137, 410 N.Y.S.2d 946 (1978).
272. Aubert v. Charity Hosp., *supra* note 164.
273. Berman v. Allan, 80 N.J. 421, 404 A.2d 8 (1979).
274. Friel v. Vineland Obstetrical & Gynecological Professional Ass'n, 166 N.J. 579, 400 A.2d 147 (1979).
275. Johnson v. State, 37 N.Y.2d 378, 334 N.E.2d 590, 372 N.Y.S.2d 638 (1975).
276. Molien v. Kaiser Foundation Hosp., 96 Cal. App. 3d 468, 158 Cal. Rptr. 107 (1979); Bishop v. Bryne, 265 F. Supp. 460 (S.D. W.Va. 1967).
277. *See* Friel v. Vineland Obstetrical & Gynecological Professional Ass'n, *supra* note 274.
278. Molien v. Kaiser Foundation Hosp., *supra* note 276.
279. Dillon v. Legg, 68 Cal. 2d 728, 441 P.2d 912, 69 Cal. Rptr. 72 (1968).
280. Tobin v. Grossman, 24 N.Y.2d 609, 249 N.E.2d 419, 301 N.Y.S.2d 554 (1969). *See also* Karlsons v. Guerinot, 57 A.D.2d 73, 394 N.Y.S.2d 933 (1977).
281. Frisnegger v. Gibson, *supra* note 264.
282. Kitto v. Gilbert, *supra* note 197.
283. Dumer v. Saint Michael's Hosp., 69 Wis. 2d 766, 233 N.W.2d 372 (1975).
284. Park v. Chessin, *supra* note 268.
285. *Id.*
286. Molien v. Kaiser Foundation Hosp., *supra* note 276.
287. Custodio v. Bauer, 251 Cal. App. 2d 303, 59 Cal. Rptr. 463 (1967).
288. Roth v. Bell, 24 Wash. App. 92, 600 P.2d 602 (1979).
289. Garza v. Berlanga, 598 S.W.2d 377 (Tex. Civ. App. 1980).
290. Noe v. Kaiser Foundation Hosp., 248 Or. 420, 435 P.2d 306 (1967).
291. Restatement (Second) of Torts § 908(i).

Notes: Chapter I

292. Medvecz v. Choi, *supra* note 61.
293. *Id.*
294. Kitto v. Gilbert, *supra* note 197; Frisnegger v. Gibson, *supra* note 264.
295. Berman v. Allan, *supra* note 273.
296. Karlsons v. Guerinot, *supra* note 280.
297. Betancourt v. Gaylor, *supra* note 265.
298. Karlsons v. Guerinot, *supra* note 280.
299. Rivera v. State, 94 Misc. 2d 157, 404 N.Y.S.2d 950 (1978).
300. Green v. Sudakin, 81 Mich. App. 545, 265.N.W.2d 411 (1978); Karlsons v. Guerinot, *supra* note 280; Betancourt v. Gaylor, *supra* note 265.
301. Green v. Sudakin, *supra* note 300; Aubert v. Charity Hosp., *supra* note 164.
302. Berman v. Allan, *supra* note 273.
303. Aubert v. Charity Hosp. of La., *supra* note 164.
304. Garza v. Berlanga, *supra* note 289.
305. Montgomery v. Stephan, 395 Mich. 33, 101 N.W.2d 227 (1960).
306. Penetrante v. United States, 604 F.2d 1248 (9th Cir. 1979).
307. Frisnegger v. Gibson, *supra* note 264.
308. Herbert v. Travelers Indem. Co., 239 So.2d 367 (La. App. 1970).
309. King v. St. Louis, 155 S.W.2d 557 (Mo. App. 1941); Frisnegger v. Gibson, *supra* note 264.
310. Blair v. Eblen, 46 S.W.2d 370 (Tex. Civ. App. 1970).
311. Dodds v. Stellar, 77 Cal. App. 2d 411, 175 P.2d 607 (1946).
312. Frisnegger v. Gibson, *supra* note 264.
313. Dublicki v. Maresco, 64 A.D.2d 645, 407 N.Y.S.2d 66 (1978).
314. Jones v. Harrisburg Polyclinic Hosp., 410 A.2d 303 (Pa. Super. 1980).

Chapter II

Other Theories of Liability

§ 2.10 INTRODUCTION

Legal theories other than negligence principles may expose a physician to liability for injuries arising from the course of his or her practice. In some jurisdictions, depending on the facts of the case, the courts may view the physician's conduct not as a breach of duty, but as the breach of a contract with the patient. (See § 2.20, Contract Theory.) Such a resolution by the courts, while rare, still occurs.

The physician may also be held legally responsible for the acts of health care personnel whom he or she directs or supervises. (See § 2.30, Vicarious Liability.) The specific nature of the relationship between the physician and these individuals has far-reaching legal consequences. The medical record prepared by the physician in treating the patient presents the potential for legal dispute over such questions as property and privacy rights with respect to the contents of the records. (See § 2.40, Liability Arising from Medical Records.) Finally, in rendering treatment, physicians typically prescribe drugs and use devices ranging from simple hypodermics to sophisticated C.A.T. scanners. These are governed by a complex body of law known as "products liability." (See § 2.50, Products Liability.)

To gain a full understanding of his or her liability potential, the physician should be familiar with these legal principles as well as those governing the malpractice cause of action based on negligence theory. The following chapter discusses these concepts.

§ 2.20 CONTRACT THEORY

Under early English law, the liability of a physician for failure to exercise professional skill and care was based on the notion that the physician's profession was a public, or common, calling, somewhat like that of an innkeeper or common carrier (trolley or train operators). Because of this common calling and because the public was served, special duties were imposed by law. The physician had to answer for mistakes because the physician undertook the care of the patient in the course of a public calling.[1]

Early American courts looked to English court decisions and legal values for precedential guidance and at first applied the same analysis. However, as the American law of contracts developed, American courts increasingly chose to analyze the physician's liability in terms of contract concepts.* Approximately a century and a half ago, negligence received distinct judicial recognition as a separate tort.[2] (See § 1.20, Elements of Negligence.) Today most malpractice actions are based on the legal theory of negligence; however, the status of the contract action as the basis for a malpractice suit remains unsettled, despite the arguments of its critics and various legislative attempts to limit its availability.

The law recognizes two types of contracts: *express* and *implied*.

A contract is express when the parties reach a specific agreement by written or spoken words. Thus, there are two kinds of express contracts: written and oral.

A contract is implied when parties (such as a physician and a patient) engage in activities creating mutual obligations (the physician accepts and treats the patient and the patient agrees to pay the physician) but no words of agreement are spoken or written. Accordingly, although an implied contract is not a true contract, it is a contract created by the court to do justice to the parties because of activities engaged in by the parties. After the court determines that an implied contract exists, it is the jury's role to decide what the terms of the contract are. This is also the function of the jury where dispute exists as to the terms of an express contract.[3]

The distinction between contract and negligence is important to understand, because the legal theory pursued by the patient-plaintiff affects various aspects of the suit, including the outcome in many cases. The basic theoretical difference between contract and negligence lies in the nature of the interest protected—negligence actions are intended to protect members of society from various kinds of harm, whereas contract actions are intended to protect the interests of specific individuals in having the specific promises made between them enforced and performed.

In negligence actions, the legal duties of conduct between individuals are based primarily on social policy, not necessarily the will, intention or promises made between the parties. Further, the duties involved may be owed to all individuals within the range of harm.

Contract actions protect the agreements made between limited and specifically identifiable parties. The duties are imposed because the parties to the contract have agreed to assume them by their words or deeds.

---

*A contract is a promissory agreement between two or more persons which creates a relation between the parties carrying certain rights and duties agreed to which are enforceable by law.

Courts tend to take a strict view of actions in contract, probably because negligence actions are available to the patient. Contract theory holds a certain disadvantage for patients, however, because in general there are more limits on the amount and type of damages that may be recovered. (See § 1.60, Damages.) The traditional rule in contract law has been that punitive damages are never awarded. Damages for mental suffering or anguish are rarely awarded.[4] Such damages have been allowed where the contract is closely related to the human body or human life and mental or emotional damages are inevitable or foreseeable if the contract is breached.[5]

On the other hand, contract theory provides certain advantages to patient-plaintiffs. Negligence theory is based on fault concepts, in that it identifies a standard of conduct the physician failed to meet. Contract theory asserts only that the physician failed to live up to his or her "part of the bargain." The result is that the patient has a less burdensome requirement of proof at trial under a contract theory than under a negligence theory.

Also, in many jurisdictions, there is a longer statute of limitations (see § 3.50, Statutes of Limitations) for contract actions than for tort actions, and patients will sometimes attempt to recover under a breach of contract theory after the statute of limitations for tort actions has run.[6] For example, in Michigan a patient has two years to sue for malpractice through negligence,[7] but a general statute governing contract actions allows a patient six years to bring a contract action.[8] However, the Michigan courts have rejected the general contract statute of limitations in certain malpractice cases in favor of a statute allowing only three years for actions to recover damages for injuries to persons and property.[9] At present, where a patient-plaintiff sues to recover damages for injury to persons or property on a claim arising out of an *implied* contract to treat, a three-year statute applies. If an action is brought on an express contract, the six-year statute applies.[10] In either case, the patient (in Michigan) has a greater period of time in which to sue under a contract theory than under a negligence theory.

Courts generally permit contract actions only if there is an express written or oral contract or promise between the parties.[11] Some examples of statements that might be construed as express promises include assertions that an operation is a "foolproof thing" or "perfectly safe."[12] Failure to achieve the promised result or to perform the promised service may give rise to liability.[13] Such express promises must be distinguished from therapeutic assurances of recovery which the courts recognize a physician must make to patients on many occasions without incurring liability. The courts recognized a delicate balance between the need for a therapeutic reassurance and the rights of individuals to enter into and enforce contracts.[14]

In many cases the courts will hold that the parties have not reached an express agreement. In these cases a patient may attempt to recover on the basis of an implied contract.[15] For instance, a patient may allege the breach of an implied contract to provide medical services in a professional manner or the breach of an implied contract to meet the standard of care of the profession. But many courts view this as a restatement of an action for negligence (a breach of duty or a failure to meet the standard of care); the courts usually hold that the standard for recovery for breach of an implied contract would therefore be that of recovery for breach of duty for negligence. Thus, they would apply the rules for the tort action rather than the contract action.[16]

Statutes in 25 states require actions for medical malpractice to be brought in tort and not in contract, and the courts in almost all the states do not permit malpractice actions to be brought on an implied contract theory.[17] However, some courts still recognize a need to have the contract action available for certain cases, for example, to control against the unprincipled promises of medical charlatans.[18] Some jurisdictions may not permit the patient to sue on a physician's express promise unless the patient has relied on that promise to his or her detriment. Proof of such reliance, however, is usually not difficult to make.

Another part of contract law which may be critical in an action against a physician is the doctrine of consideration. The doctrine of consideration requires that before a promise can be enforced, something of value, e.g. a money payment, must be given in exchange for that promise. Promises that are made as a gift or in a gratuitous spirit without any exchange by the other party may not be enforced if they are broken. Therefore, the law might require that a patient give or pay something specifically in exchange for a physician's promise.[19] However, the doctrine of consideration is quite malleable and is sometimes used to reach whatever result is desired. One court might hold the fee a patient paid to a physician was only for medical services and could not support a separate contract of a perfect result. Another court might hold that a single consideration, e.g. a promise to pay, could support several promises and reach a result favorable for the patient-plaintiff.

Some courts raise a further barrier to recovery by placing a special burden of proof upon the patient who alleges breach of a medical contract. These courts hold that there can be no recovery for breach of an alleged expressed warranty unless the existence of the warranty is shown by "clear proof," that is, by "clear and convincing evidence."[20] According to one court, the clear proof rule requires the judge or jury to consider specifically whether the physician made a statement which could have been reasonably interpreted by the patient as a promise that a given result or cure would be achieved.[21] If, under the circumstances of the case and in the context of the particular physician-patient relationship, no such statement can be found, there can be no liability for breach of warranty.

As of this writing, no anesthesiologist has been successfully sued for breach of contract in a reported case. Since anesthesiologists typically have less contact with patients than surgeons, for example, one might expect breach of contract actions against anesthesiologists to be quite rare. It is clear, however, that the theory of contractual liability is as applicable to anesthesiologists as it is to any

§ 2.30   *Vicarious Liability*   65

other medical practitioner. To avoid liability, the anesthesiologist must carefully guard against promising specific results to a patient. Like all medical practitioners, anesthesiologists must provide realistic and reasonably accurate assessments of what the patient should anticipate from a particular course of treatment.

§ 2.30 VICARIOUS LIABILITY

"Agency" describes the legal relationship created between two parties when the first party in some way authorizes the second party to act for or represent it. Vicarious liability refers to the legal responsibility thus assumed—within certain limits—by the first party for the actions of the second. In legal jargon, the doctrine is known as respondeat superior, a Latin phrase meaning "let the master answer."[22] The parties to an agency relationship are referred to as "principal" and "agent" or "master" and "servant."

Vicarious liability of the principal does not negate the liability of the agent. Rather, both agent and principal are liable for the negligence of the agent. Vicarious liability, therefore, broadens rather than shifts liability.

The essential elements of vicarious liability are well established. The agent is the individual who commits the allegedly negligent act. The principal is the person or organization allegedly responsible for the acts of the agent. Before a principal may be held liable for the acts of an agent, certain facts must be established. First, the existence of an agency relationship must be proved.[23] This usually hinges on the question of whether one party is subject to the control or right of control of the other. In certain other situations, the law recognizes the existence of the agency relationship based on the borrowed servant doctrine or the captain of the ship doctrine, legal concepts which are discussed below. Further, it must be shown that the agent was acting on the business of the principal, or at least for the principal's benefit, within the scope of the agent's duties.[24] If these facts can be proven, a principal may be held liable for the negligent act of his or her agent. This liability may be imposed even though the principal has in no way aided or encouraged the negligent act and may even have attempted to prevent it.[25]

Justification for vicarious liability is derived from the point of view of the victim of the agent's negligent act. When an agent is engaged in work for his or her principal, the profits of work generally go to the principal. If an individual harmed by the agent is limited to suing the agent, he or she may be effectively barred from recovery. To compensate the individual, a "deep pocket" must be found. Generally, the law recognizes that principals are able to compensate victims more fully, are better able to absorb the costs, and can insure themselves more easily. The cost of indemnifying can be included in the principal's costs of doing business and the principal will thus be motivated to select his or her agents with care. Vicarious liability serves to assure full recovery for injured persons and seeks to deter future acts of negligence.[26]

Historically, the search for a deep pocket to compensate for injuries related to medical care had to go beyond the hospital because of the concepts of governmental and charitable immunity. In many jurisdictions hospitals, which were either governmental or charitable institutions, were legally immune from lawsuits. Thus, vicarious liability could not have been imposed on the hospital for the negligence of its employees. Because of this immunity the physician who worked with the hospital employee was the only logical party left upon whom to impose liability.[27] Immunity for hospitals is currently being abandoned in many states.[28] Thus, some of the original impetus for imputing the liability of the hospital employee to the physician is disappearing. However, changes in the various rules of law do not occur concurrently, and an absolute statement of law with regard to vicarious liability in the medical care setting cannot be made.

In any event, the proof of the principal-agent relationship is a complex problem in medical malpractice cases because there are several ways in which the principal-agent relationship can arise in the health care setting. Part of the complexity arises from the concept of control as it applies to the interactions of the various medical personnel in providing health care. A scrub nurse, for example, is frequently under the control of the surgeon. An anesthesiologist, however, may not be under the surgeon's control. In some situations the lack of control is so obvious that the court will find no principal-agent relationship. Referrals by one physician to another illustrate such a situation. The referring physician is not subject to liability for any negligent acts of the physician to whom he or she referred the patient, unless the two physicians are partners or engaged in some other type of employment relationship. The recommended physician is independent and liable only for his or her own negligence.[29] It is important to note, however, that in some jurisdictions physicians have been held responsible for "negligent referrals"; this may be an emerging trend. Accordingly, physicians should use due care in making referrals.

An employer is frequently held vicariously liable for the negligence of an employee. The employee almost always acts on the business of the employer; equally common is the employer's right to control the employee. Thus, physicians in a professional service corporation are liable for the negligence of the corporation employees who fail to perform the duties owed by a physician to a patient, including clerical details necessary for competent medical treatment.[30]

CASE ILLUSTRATION

The patient fell on a piece of soap left on the bathroom floor, sustaining a herniated disk, which required two subsequent hospitalizations and a laminectomy. The patient-plaintiff sued the hospital on a respondeat superior

§ 2.30 Vicarious Liability 67

theory, and settled out of court for $10,000, the maximum the hospital was liable for by statute in the state where the incident took place. The plaintiff then sued the three floor nurses allegedly responsible for the unsafe condition. The nurses claimed the settlement with the hospital barred the plaintiff from suing them.

In rejecting the nurse's argument, the court stated, "[This] case presents the question as to whether [plaintiff is barred from bringing] separate suits against a master on the theory of respondeat superior and its servants based upon identical negligent act. . . . [A]lthough the act of negligence complained of is the same in each action, there are nevertheless two distinct and separate persons responsible to the plaintiff, the actual tortfeasor himself and the person vicariously liable for the tort." The court held that if the jury found the patient's damages to be in excess of $10,000, the nurses could be held responsible for the balance. (*McFadden v. Turner*, 1978)[31]

Vicarious liability may be imposed beyond the employee/employer setting. Under the borrowed servant doctrine, one party may be liable for the acts of an employee of another party if the negligent act occurs while the employee is under the first party's direction or control. Thus, a surgeon may be held liable for the negligence of a member of his surgical team, even though that member is employed by the hospital and not by the surgeon.[32]

There are two interpretations of the borrowed servant doctrine. The narrower of the two requires that the master actually exercise control over the borrowed servant at the time of the negligent act in order for the master to be vicariously liable.[33] It has been calculated that, as of 1974, 21 jurisdictions followed this interpretation of the borrowed servant doctrine. Where the master has actual control over the borrowed servant, it is necessary that such control be exercised with reasonable care.[34]

CASE ILLUSTRATION

The patient suffered a shoulder separation while playing football in a park near his home, and surgery was prescribed. The nurse-anesthetist anesthetized the patient and the surgeon draped him from head to toe, leaving an opening for the surgery. During the operation, the patient's blood pressure and pulse weakened and by the close of the operation he was not breathing. The surgeon left the operating room at that point, while the patient's breathing was totally assisted by the nurse anesthetist. She disconnected the anesthetic machine from the intubation tube and had the patient lifted from the operating table onto a cart. As the patient still had the endotracheal tube in his mouth, the nurse anesthetist gave him an excess of oxygen to build up the amount in his bloodstream. The endotracheal tube was removed and the patient was wheeled to the recovery room, 50 to 75 feet away. The nurse-anesthetist connected the patient to the Bennet resuscitating machine; however, his pulse could not be detected and despite resuscitative attempts by various physicians, the patient died.

The patient's widow sued the surgeon, the nurse-anesthetist and the hospital. Expert testimony was offered to the effect that the patient did not receive assisted ventilation early enough in the case. With respect to the surgeon's liability it was established that the surgeon, when assisted by an anesthetist, rather than an anesthesiologist, had the privilege of deciding what anesthetic agent would be used, was responsible for draping the patient and should have left the patient's face exposed to allow the anesthetist to monitor coloration, should not have left the operating room until the patient was breathing, or should not have permitted the patient to be moved until he was breathing. The court held that although a nurse is subject to hospital rules and may still be considered an employee of the hospital, where a surgeon has direct control over the nurse-anesthetist as this one did, yet fails to exercise it with reasonable care, he will be held liable. (*Foster v. Englewood Hospital Association*, 1974)[35]

This case focuses on the direct actions of the physician in preparing the patient for surgery and attending him and finds a lack of care evident. Thus, it is not entirely clear whether the physician is being held directly liable for his own negligence or vicariously liable for the negligence of the nurse-anesthetist. The facts of the case imply that the court is imposing liability under a combination of the two theories.

A majority of states adhere to a broader interpretation of the borrowed servant doctrine. Instead of actual control, the plaintiff need only show that the principal had the right to direct or control the agent.[36]

CASE ILLUSTRATION

The patient was operated on to correct a vascular circulatory problem. He came out of surgery with burns on his buttocks where a cautery machine electrode had been placed. The surgeon, the anesthesiologist, and the hospital were all found to be vicariously liable for the negligence of the surgical team.

The anesthesiologist appealed the judgment, claiming he was an independent contractor. The court rejected his argument, stating "[The anesthesiologist's] contention that there is no evidence he exercised any

§ 2.30   *Vicarious Liability*

direction, supervision, or control over any of the people involved in the operation is not tenable. The criterion . . . is not whether [the anesthesiologist] did in fact exercise such control but whether under the circumstances he had the right to exercise it. The . . . testimony constitutes substantial competent evidence [the anesthesiologist] was charged with the care of [the patient] and the duty to protect him from the time he put the patient under an anesthetic until he came out of the anesthetic in the recovery room. This included the duty to cope with whatever situations might arise during the course of the operation. If [the anesthesiologist] thus charged with the patient's care so neglected him as to allow the injury to occur, he would be liable for the negligence, if any, of those who became his temporary assistants while performing the duty owed by him to [the patient], regardless of whether he paid or employed them. [The anesthesiologist] was responsible for the activities of those performing his duty to the patient." (*Wiles v. Myerly*, 1973)[37]

Under the broader interpretation, the courts distinguish between the right to supervise a person and the right to control him or her. A supervisor may have considerable power over an agent, but a supervisor is not ultimately responsible[38] for the acts of the agent. Whether the test used is actual control or the right to control, the issue of control is a question of fact to be decided by the jury.[39]

It is not clear whether the borrowed servant doctrine broadens liability (by making three parties—the agent, the primary principal and the borrowing principal—all liable) or merely shifts vicarious liability from the primary principal to the borrowing principal. At least one court has held that, before a nurse-anesthetist may become a borrowed servant, he or she must become wholly subject to the control and direction of the physician and free from the control of the hospital.[40] Under this theory of the borrowed servant doctrine, an agent can have only one principal at a time. Thus, either the hospital or the physician, but not both, may be vicariously liable for the negligence of a hospital employee. Other courts, ruling that a nurse-anesthetist employed by a hospital may be acting as the agent of a physician and the hospital simultaneously, have held both physician and hospital vicariously liable for the negligence of the nurse-anesthetist.[41]

Some courts have followed this principle of simultaneous agency because it would be unrealistic and unfair to hold a physician liable under the borrowed servant theory for the negligence of a hospital's loaned employee while freeing the hospital from any vicarious liability for the employee's acts.[42]

In fact, most often a hospital employee who is temporarily lent to a physician continues to carry out hospital duties. The employee's work is then of mutual interest to both the physician and the hospital and is performed to achieve their common purpose. In determining the question of agency, the jury must consider whose work was being done, who had the right to control the work and the manner of doing it, and who received the benefit from the performance of the work.[43]

A hospital resident who is an employee of the hospital but who performs his or her services under the supervision of an independent physician is in a similar situation. Courts have consistently held that a hospital resident may be simultaneously the agent of the hospital and of another physician, although his or her employment is not joint.[44]

Respondeat superior and the borrowed servant doctrine are aspects of general agency law. Some jurisdictions have fashioned a very broad form of vicarious liability for medical malpractice cases only. Known as the captain of the ship doctrine, the surgeon or head of an operating team is seen as an analogue to the captain of a ship and the operating team to the ship's crew. As originally used in Pennsylvania, the phrase was merely meant to explain the operation of the borrowed servant doctrine in the hospital setting.[45] However, as the phrase was used in subsequent cases it emerged as an independent doctrine, whereby the issue of whether an agent had become a borrowed servant changed from a question of fact for the jury to decide to a question of law, allowing the court alone to impose liability.[46]

In one case, a surgeon was held liable for a negligent act of the operating room team that occurred outside the operating room and without the surgeon present.[47] A later case held a surgeon responsible for the negligence of a chief anesthesiologist occurring prior to surgery and of which the surgeon was not aware; in other words, the surgeon became vicariously liable for the negligence of an agent he had no right to control.[48] Thus, the doctrine imposed a form of strict liability on the surgeon for whatever negligence might occur in the course of the operation.

Many other courts have borrowed the phrase "captain of the ship." Some borrowed it soon after it was coined, when it was intended only as an analogy.[49] Others adopted it later as a doctrine of strict liability.[50] Still other courts expressly rejected this form of the doctrine.[51]

The doctrine's use has been continually criticized. In practice, "captain of the ship" is an attractive but imprecise metaphor. Critics observe that "its felicity leads to its lazy repetition; and repetition soon establishes it as a legal formula, indiscriminatingly used to express different and sometimes contradictory ideas."[52]

In a 1971 decision, Pennsylvania, the jurisdiction in which the doctrine originated, limited its strict liability construction. The Pennsylvania Supreme Court held that the term "captain of the ship" constitutes a simple analogy and that the jury must decide whether a master-servant relationship exists at the time of the negligent act.[53] However, other jurisdictions are not restricted to Pennsylvania's revised interpretation, and those that have adopted it may continue to apply the doctrine in its strictest sense.

§ 2.31 *Anesthesiologists*

Anesthesiologists, as physicians, are generally held personally liable for their own negligent acts. The anesthesiologist is regarded as an independent medical specialist, accountable to no person or entity other than the patient in terms of duties owed.

This was not always the case. When anesthesiology was emerging as a medical specialty in the 1950s, the agency status of the anesthesiologist was dependent on the jurisdiction in which the patient brought the lawsuit. Thus in 1955, the California Supreme Court held that whether a physician anesthesiologist was an agent of the hospital was a jury question;[54] whereas in 1956, an Appellate Court in Indiana held that an anesthesiologist, although clearly employed by the hospital, was independently liable for his own negligence.[55] At least one commentator has attributed the demise of the "captain of the ship" doctrine (see § 2.30, Vicarious Liability) to the advent of anesthesiology as a separate medical specialty.[56]

In some jurisdictions, the operating surgeon may still be held liable for the negligence of the anesthesiologist. In a 1978 Pennsylvania case, the court imposed such liability stating that "the surgeon has an obligation to monitor his patient regardless of what the anesthesiologist is doing and . . . has the right to cancel the procedure at any time. . . . The governing standard is the right of controlling the manner of performance of the work regardless of whether that control is actually exercised."[57]

In most cases, surgeons are not held vicariously liable for the negligence of anesthesiologists. Surgeons and anesthesiologists have independent areas of responsibility towards the patient and, normally, neither controls nor directs the activities of the other. As one court has noted, "it is recognized that anesthesiologists are virtually autonomous and the surgeon is not responsible for the anesthesiologist's independent procedures.[58]

CASE ILLUSTRATION

While undergoing a hemorrhoidectomy, the patient-plaintiff suffered an adverse reaction to the anesthetics being used; caudal epidural anesthesia was supplemented by intravenous injections of sodium pentothal. Her breathing stopped for a brief period. She was revived, surgery was completed, and she was placed in the hospital's intensive care unit. Six days later she suffered a relapse and lost consciousness for ten days. Resultant brain damage left the patient-plaintiff unable to walk, talk, or see.

The plaintiffs sued the hospital, the anesthesiologist and the surgeon.

The hospital and anesthesiologist settled out of court. The court held that, where the anesthesiologist had chosen and administered anesthesia independently of the surgeon, the surgeon could not be held vicariously liable for the anesthesiologist's negligence. To hold otherwise, ". . . would not only permit but command that a specialist in one field of medicine—surgery—must supervise the precise manner of performance by a practitioner in another specialized field—one in which ever increasing scientific knowledge demands greater and greater expertise." (*Marvulli v. Elshire*, 1972)[59]

Anesthesiologists, like other physicians, may also be held liable for the negligence of their agents. When the agent is not on the anesthesiologist's payroll, it is not always easy to prove that an agency relationship exists. Again, the test is actual control or right to control the servant. Under the borrowed servant doctrine, anesthesiologists have been held liable for the negligence of temporary assistants regardless of whether they were paid or employed by the anesthesiologist.[60]

Physicians may only delegate those duties to their agents which are within the agent's capabilities. Improper delegation of duties would constitute direct negligence by the physician.[61]

Anesthesiologists who head the hospital's department of anesthesiology and have teaching and supervisory duties with respect to staff anesthesiologists may be found vicariously liable for the negligence of anesthesiologists working under their supervision. Moreover, they may be held personally liable with the staff physician as joint tortfeasors when they sufficiently participate in the procedure.[62] However, in cases where no need for immediate supervision by the department head has been shown, and it cannot be proven that lack of supervision in a particular case was a legal cause of the injury suffered, the director of the anesthesiology department cannot be held liable for his or her failure to provide direct supervision in the operating room; he or she may assume that due to its education and training, the staff is competent to handle a particular assignment.[63]

Hospitals may be held liable for the negligent acts of their anesthesiologists under the doctrine of respondeat superior where sufficient evidence is presented to prove the existence of the agency relationship. That is, there is sufficient proof to show that the anesthesiologist was an agent of the hospital.

CASE ILLUSTRATION

A patient, allegedly harmed due to the negligence of an anesthesiologist, sued the anesthesiologist and the hospital. The hospital claimed that the anesthesiologist was an independent contractor and therefore it could not be held vicariously liable for his acts. The court rejected the hospital's argument and found the anesthesiologist to be an agent of the hospital. The court noted that the anesthesiologist had a written agreement with the hospital guaranteeing him 50 percent of the hospital's anesthesia work, that the anesthesiologist was not chosen by the surgeon or patient, and that the hospital supplied the anethesiologist's equipment. (*Garcia v. Tarrio*, 1980)[64]

§ 2.32 Nurse-Anesthetists

As a general rule, whether the hospital, surgeon or nurse-anesthetist is held liable for the negligence of a nurse-anesthetist depends on the facts of the case (Did the surgeon exercise control over the nurse-anesthetist? and if so, How extensive was that control?), and the legal jurisdiction (Michigan, Virginia, etc.) in which the issue is to be decided.

The traditional rule that the surgeon is responsible for everything that happens in the operating room,[65] including nurse-anesthetist errors, is changing in response to political influences and technological advances. As anesthetic practices, agents and equipment became more complex, and as physicians now recognize the medical specialty of anesthesiology, it made increasingly less sense to expect a general surgeon to meaningfully control the anesthetic process. The increasing technical burdens on the surgeon also make it unrealistic to expect him or her to do two jobs. The apparent demise of the captain of the ship doctrine is also prompting this change. (See § 2.30, Vicarious Liability.)

In response to these changes, the better rule may be to hold the hospital and not the surgeon responsible for the negligent acts of a nurse-anesthetist.[66]

As an agent of the hospital or the operating physician, the nurse-anesthetist is in a unique position. Because the anesthesia services the nurse-anesthetist provides demand a mastery of technical-professional skills and the use of independent judgment, standards applied to evaluate the conduct of the nurse-anesthetist should reflect the nurse-anesthetist's status as a skilled professional, responsible for his or her own acts. On the other hand, most nurse-anesthetists function as employees of hospitals, or, depending on the procedures utilized, as assisting surgical personnel subject to the supervision or control of the physician. From this perspective the status of the nurse-anesthetist dictates, under current law, that liability for his or her negligent acts may be imputed to the hospital or surgeon. Whether vicarious liability will be imputed to the hospital or surgeon in a case involving a nurse-anesthetist depends upon the facts of the case. (See § 2.30, Vicarious Liability.)

Court decisions have, in certain instances, recognized the independent status of the nurse-anesthetist. The courts have deferred to the judgment of the nurse-anesthetist in choosing between a number of accepted methods for the administration of anesthesia, just as they defer to the best judgment of a physician in choosing between appropriate methods of treatment.[67] (See § 1.32, Standard of Care.) More than one case decision has recognized the authority of the nurse-anesthetist to choose the anesthetic to be used, in the absence of any direct orders from the surgeon,[68] and the right of the surgeon to rely on the expertise of the nurse-anesthetist.[69]

CASE ILLUSTRATION

A seven-day-old patient underwent emergency surgery to correct an intestinal obstruction. It was necessary to keep the patient warm during the operation because of the tendency of a newborn child to lose body temperature rapidly, once rendered unconscious. The method used by the nurse-anesthetist consisted of a hot water bottle covered by an inverted flash pan with several layers of cotton on top. The circulating nurse filled the hot water bottle and the patient was placed on the prepared surface and covered by appropriate sheets. Although the surgery, which lasted two hours and ten minutes, corrected the blockage, the patient sustained a third degree burn on his backside, covering most of the surface area of his buttocks. The patient, through his parents, sued the hospital, the surgeon, and the nurse-anesthetist. The patient's evidence suggested that the hot water bottle was filled with excessively hot water, thus causing the burn. The court concluded that the evidence showed it was the nurse-anesthetist's responsibility to warm the patient; thus, the jury could determine she had been negligent. The court rejected imposing vicarious liability on the hospital for the nurse-anesthetist's negligence either on the basis of improper hiring, improper training or improperly assigning an anesthetist rather than an anesthesiologist to the case. Also the court refused to impute liability to the surgeon stating, "Absent some conduct or situation that should reasonably place the surgeon on notice of negligent procedure, the surgeon is entitled to rely on the expertise of the anesthetist." (*Starnes v. Charlotte-Mecklenburg Hospital Authority*, 1976)[70]

In this case, the court did not impose vicarious liability on the hospital because the hospital was a charitable institution. Although the law has since changed in the jurisdiction where the case was decided, at the time of the suit a charitable hospital was immune from liability unless it negligently selected or retained its employees or provided defective treatment equipment. The patient failed to prove either of these facts against the hospital. Thus it is not entirely accurate to infer from the case that recognition of the nurse-anesthetist as an independent professional will absolve the employing hospital from liability.

On the other hand, the *Starnes* decision suggests that imposing independent liability on the nurse-anesthetist is tenable. The court's reasoning about the vicarious liability of the surgeon bears this out. The case also hints that recognition

§ 2.32   *Nurse-Anesthetists*   75

of the professional status of the nurse-anesthetist may give rise to vicarious liability for the acts of his or her agent. In this case, it was a circulating nurse, rather than the nurse-anesthetist herself, who filled the water bottle.[71] That nurse-anesthetists are regarded as independent professionals is also borne out by the construction courts have given to statutes which regulate their practice. (See § 7.82, State Regulation.) For example, a Louisiana statute provides that a nurse-anesthetist who administers general anesthesia must do so under the supervision of a licensed physician.[72] This has been construed by a Louisiana court as not requiring the physician to direct the nurse-anesthetist in the selection and method of application of the anesthetic drug.[73]

Like any other agent, a nurse-anesthetist may be held liable for his or her own negligent act, regardless of whether some other party is held vicariously liable for the same act. Nurse-anesthetists are expected to exercise reasonable judgment based on their own knowledge and expertise and, at the same time, they are expected to follow the instructions of the physician in charge of the operation where standard practice requires this. A nurse-anesthetist who receives what he or she feels is an inappropriate instruction from a physician is faced with a predicament. If the physician's instruction is ignored and the patient is harmed, the nurse-anesthetist may be liable for not following the instruction.[74] On the other hand, if the nurse-anesthetist blindly follows the physician's instruction and, as a result, the patient is harmed, the nurse-anesthetist may be held liable for not exercising his or her professional judgment.[75]

The nurse-anesthetist can avoid legal liability and better serve patients by avoiding these two extreme courses of action. When a physician has ordered an anesthetic agent or procedure which the nurse-anesthetist feels is inappropriate due to the condition of the patient, the nurse-anesthetist should discuss the matter with the physician, pointing out why the order may be contraindicated by the condition of the patient. If the physician insists on the order, the nurse-anesthetist should record his or her objection to the order in the patient's medical record and, if circumstances permit, seek a second opinion from another physician.[76] In any event, a nurse-anesthetist does not necessarily become the agent of a physician merely because the physician instructs the anesthetist regarding work to be performed.

CASE ILLUSTRATION

The female patient was admitted to the hospital to deliver her baby. Prior to the delivery, the nurse-anesthetist inserted an airway and catheter into the patient's mouth and throat. During birth, the patient suffered damage to her teeth and mouth. The patient sued the obstetrician attempting to impute to him the liability of the nurse anesthetist. The court stated, "[The nurse-anesthetist] did not become the legal servant or agent of [the obstetrician] merely because she received instructions from him as to the work to be performed. . . . During the administration of the anesthesia and the dynamics of the childbirth we find nothing in the record whereby we can fairly say that [the obstetrician] undertook to exercise control over [the nurse-anesthetist]." (*Sesselman v. Muhlenberg Hospital*, 1973)[77]

Despite all of the foregoing, courts may still hold hospitals and physicians vicariously liable for the negligence of a nurse-anesthetist[78] under general vicarious liability principles or the borrowed servant doctrine. (See § 2.30, Vicarious Liability.)

The following case, recently decided, holds that any immunity a chief surgeon might have for the negligence of an assisting nurse-anesthetist does not exist as a matter of law, but must be justified by the facts.

CASE ILLUSTRATION

The patient underwent a laminectomy at the hospital to alleviate blocked vertebrae in her spine resulting from Klippel-Feil syndrome. The operating surgeon was aware that the patient suffered from spondylosis as well as Klippel-Feil syndrome and that her spinal cord might be compromised if the operation were performed with the patient in a sitting position. Consequently, the operating surgeon assisted the nurse-anesthetist in the patient's intubation by positioning the patient's head and torso. While the operating surgeon did not perform the actual insertion of the tube in the patient's trachea, he was present at all times during the intubation. As a result of the operation, the patient was rendered a paraplegic from the C-6 level down. The patient sued the operating surgeon. The court noted the role the surgeon played in assisting the anesthetist as well as the right he admitted he had to control the intubation. The court held that while the "captain of the ship" doctrine was not intended to be resurrected, the surgeon could be held liable. The court stated, ". . . [W]e seek only to ensure that where, in the operating room, a surgeon does control or realistically possesses the right to control events and procedures he does so with a high degree of care." (*Baird v. Sickler*, 1982)[79]

This case reveals the importance of the events that actually occur to determining whether liability for the acts of the nurse-anesthetist will be imposed on the operating surgeon. It also indicates that a key consideration in imposing liability is whether the operating surgeon has the right, in fact, to supervise or control the nurse-anesthetist. If the anesthesiology department of a hospital has written

§ 2.33 Hospitals

protocols assigning responsibility to various personnel for specific aspects of care, who supervises and who is responsible may well be stated in these protocols. Thus, the protocols themselves may serve as compelling evidence in a case like this one.

In summary, for the surgeon to become responsible for the nurse-anesthetist, it must be shown that the surgeon exercised control over the anesthetist in the same way he or she would over other assistants in the operating room.[80] Depending on the facts of the case, the anesthesiologist in charge of a hospital's department of anesthesiology may also be held vicariously liable for the negligence of a nurse-anesthetist.[81] In addition, the fact that statutes like the Louisiana statute exist indicates that nurse-anesthetists are still considered susceptible to supervision and control by physicians and by hospitals. This ruling serves to establish the agency relationship, which is a prerequisite to the imposition of vicarious liability. (See § 6.20, Regulation of Nurse-Anesthetists, and § 6.30, Regulating Competing Professions.)

§ 2.33 Hospitals

A hospital's liability is generally based upon either of two theories: (1) corporate negligence, or (2) respondeat superior.

Corporate negligence is based on a non-delegable duty of the hospital owed directly to the patient.[82] The duties of hospitals are many and differ from state to state. Examples of duties include: (1) the provision of safe premises for all hospital entries;[83] (2) the provision of properly trained personnel in the operating room (including an anesthetist);[84] (3) the provision of properly functioning (anesthesia) equipment;[85] (4) the use of reasonable care in the selection of staff physicians and other employees;[86] (5) the supervision of all personnel who practice medicine in the hospital;[87] (6) the careful investigation and review of the general competence of independent physicians who practice medicine in the hospital.[88]

Hospitals have been held directly negligent when breaching those duties to the patients.

CASE ILLUSTRATION

The patient-plaintiff was burned by a malfunctioning electric cauterizing machine. The patient-plaintiff sued the surgeon and the hospital. The court held that, where the surgeon cannot direct or control the machine's maintenance and cannot test it prior to surgery without contaminating himself or herself, the surgeon cannot be held liable for its malfunctioning. The court stated further that

> when technical equipment and the personnel to operate it are furnished by the hospital to the surgeon and injury is caused by malfunctioning equipment or negligent operators, [if] it is not shown that the surgeon was personally

> negligent or that the circumstances were such that it was practical for him to exercise direct supervision or control over the machine or its operation, *respondeat superior* liability does not attach to the surgeon.
>
> It may well be that the real basis for the application of *respondeat superior* is not control, but rather the negligent party's act of carrying forward the business of his principal. The motivating force may be the idea that the business should pay the cost of its negligent operation. . . . Such a basis for *respondeat superior* initially points toward the liability of both hospital and surgeon because the operator of the equipment is simultaneously carrying on the business of both employers. The hospital is in the business of furnishing the facilities and personnel to the surgeon, and the surgeon is using them to operate on his patient. Also, both hospital and surgeon are normally capable of satisfying any judgment against them and of spreading the cost of doing so. Therefore, there would be no choice between the two on that basis.
>
> However, there is a policy reason for making a choice between the two employers whose business is being conducted and, in doing so, to choose the hospital as the one who should be responsible. Although no negligence of [the] hospital may be pointed to in a specific case, any opportunities for prevention of like occurrences in the future primarily lie in the care with which equipment is maintained and with which personnel to operate it are selected and trained. These opportunities all lie within the realm of the hospital; therefore, it is proper to place the burden of defective equipment and negligent operators upon it. The responsibility to devise means to prevent future accidents should be placed upon those who best have it within their power to devise such means. (*May v. Broun*, 1972)[89]

Respondeat superior, on the other hand, is based on vicarious liability and applies only when an agency relationship exists between the hospital and the wrongdoer. Except for immunity still enjoyed by some governmental hospitals, hospitals in general are liable for their employees' negligence. Courts today usually make no distinction between various types of employees or kinds of acts when holding a hospital liable under respondeat superior. Responsibility for negligence of physician employees is the same as that for other employees.[90]

Traditionally, however, courts have made a distinction between the *medical* acts and *administrative* acts of their physician employees, holding hospitals vicariously liable for the physician's negligence only when they performed administrative acts. If negligence occurred in the performance of a medical act, the physician was solely liable. The rationale behind the distinction was the difficulty courts had in regarding as "servants" those with the status of physicians. Today this distinction has been abandoned.[91] A small minority of states, however, still adhere to the theory that hospitals can never be held vicariously liable for the medical acts of physicians.[92]

When applying the doctrine of respondeat superior to the hospital-physician relationship, courts do not frame the issue in terms of the traditional right of control, since this would require the plaintiff to show that the hospital had the right of control over the manner and details of the treatment rendered by the negligent physician, a charge impossible to prove. Rather, to prove the existence of a relationship the courts have accepted a showing that the negligent physician is either "salaried" by the hospital[93] or has some other significant relationship with the hospital.[94] Anesthesiologists often conduct their practice under various arrangements with hospitals. When an anesthesiologist is employed by a hospital on a fixed salary, he or she is undoubtedly in a master-servant relationship with the hospital. But even when he performs his services under a concession, or monopoly, to treat the hospital's patients, the arrangement may contain elements upon which the liability of the hospital can be predicated under respondeat superior.[95]

In a 1955 California case, the court held that an anesthesiologist not salaried by the hospital but performing his services there as one of a group of independently contracted anesthesiologists had such a significant relationship with the hospital that he was in fact a servant of the hospital. The hospital was thus held vicariously liable for the anesthesiologist's negligence. In this case, the court attached much weight to the injured plaintiff's reasonable impression that the anesthesiologist was an employee of the hospital.[96] When an independent specialist such as the one in this case has his or her office at a hospital, treats all patients there and serves no other hospital, the hospital in question may be held vicariously liable for the negligence of the specialist.[97]

§ 2.34 Joint Enterprise

The principles of vicarious liability provide a legal means to impose liability on a party ultimately responsible for a negligent act. A principal may be held liable for the agent's acts only if he or she controls or has the right to control these acts. But less clearly delineated hierarchies may exist, especially when professionals of equal stature (e.g., two physicians) work together. Under the principles of joint enterprise, parties engaging to treat a patient jointly may be held jointly liable for negligence.

To establish a joint enterprise, several factors must be shown. First, the participants must be engaged in a mutual undertaking for a common purpose. Second, each participant must have an equal right to direct and control the other participant.[98] If one participant possesses a superior right to control, vicarious liability theories come into play.

Generally, anesthesiologists and other doctors do not function as a joint enterprise. As one court noted, "today it is recognized that anesthesiologists are virtually autonomous and the surgeon is not responsible for the anesthesiologist's procedures."[99] If two anesthesiologists unite on a particular case, and neither can be said to possess a superior right to control, the joint enterprise theory may be appropriate.

§ 2.40 LIABILITY ARISING FROM MEDICAL RECORDS

The law has long recognized that the health care provider, physician, or hospital is the owner of the patient's medical record and has absolute rights to its possession. However, most states recognize the patient's right to a copy of his or her record.

Judicial decisions involving ownership of medical records have almost universally decided the issue on the basis of strict and narrow interpretations of the rules of personal property. Ownership resides in the health care provider who owns and possesses the physical material on which the information is written.[100] The fact that the patient has paid fees for service does not constitute an entitlement to any rights of ownership in, or possession of, the medical records. In arriving at this conclusion, the courts have noted that, generally speaking, a patient does not seek out a physician for the purpose of obtaining records for his or her personal use, but rather to acquire the physician's services. Although the patient may pay the costs involved in producing records, such as lab fees required for tests or x-rays, the records are supplied to the physician for use in connection with the treatment of the patient.[101]

When a physician acts as the employee of another, such as a hospital or clinic, in examining or treating patients or in making records, records usually become the property of the employer unless there is an agreement to the contrary.[102] However, the patient can acquire ownership or control by contractual agreement with the health care provider. Courts would enforce such an agreement.[103]

While the courts recognize that records are primarily the physician's own notes for purposes of review and study during the course of illness and treatment,[104] the physician has the duty to permit inspection of medical records. Although information must be given, physicians' records themselves need not be turned over to the patient.[105] The fiduciary nature of the physician-patient relationship places a duty on physicians to reveal to patients what in their best interests they should know, and that duty also extends to the hospital which is the repository of such information.[106] When a physician or hospital refuses to release information deemed harmful, the patients must decide whether to institute legal proceedings.[107]

The hospital's property right in the record is qualified by the patient's right to access. This qualification has been characterized as the splitting of the property interest between the hospital and the patient. The hospital has a right to the paper, tape, or film on which the record is stored. The patient's right is to the information contained therein.[108]

§ 2.40 Liability from Medical Records

The patient's right to know the contents of his or her record and the right to control who may have access to it are rights within the state's discretion to create and define.[109] State laws tend to vary in the extent to which the property rights of physicians or hospitals are qualified for the patient's benefit; Connecticut, Massachusetts, and Wisconsin have granted the patient or his or her authorized representative a direct right of access to the record.[110] The Connecticut statute allows access under any circumstances—the patient has a right to see the record merely to satisfy his or her curiosity.

Other states place limitations on the patient's right to access. California explicitly allows access to the attorney only, not the patient, prior to the filing of a lawsuit.[111] New Jersey allows access to parties involved in personal injury litigation.[112] Under Mississippi law, the patient must show "good cause" in order to see his or her records.[113] Louisiana provides only that the patient or the attorney is entitled to a "full report from the hospital," implying that the patient has no right to see the actual, physical documents that comprise the record.[114] Illinois grants the patient's physician or attorney the right to examine the patient's hospital records.[115] Although the existing statutes vary with the jurisdiction, those cited above are representative of the legislative patterns governing the subject.

The statutes generally make no distinction as to the nature of the medical records, with one exception: psychiatric records are generally not open to patients, even in states that give a patient otherwise unrestricted access.[116]

Where the right of access is not statutory, courts granting access to medical records have generally recognized that although the hospital clearly has a property right, the patient also clearly has an interest in certain information contained in the record.[117] One court has emphasized that the physician is required to disclose medical data to the patient or his representative on request and the patient need not obtain a court order to compel disclosure. In the court's words, "the patient need not engage in legal proceedings to attain a loftier status in his quest for information."[118] Even in states where courts have granted access, hospital policies may present a further barrier to the patient. In the absence of specific legislation, a patient may be forced to take court action to obtain access to his or her record.[119]

Legal commentators have advocated a broadening of the patient's right of access.[120] A patient's attorney may request access to the patient's record in preparation for trial. Such a request is subject to state laws governing discovery (see § 4.32, Subpoena) and the physician-patient privilege (see § 4.46, Physician-Patient Privilege).

Legal interests tangentially related to property may also be involved in a consideration of medical records. Because of the confidential nature of record contents, the improper release of such information may subject the physician to liability either for defamation or for invasion of privacy.

Defamation is an oral or written communication to a third party of false information respecting a living person which injures his or her reputation by diminishing the esteem, respect, or confidence in which the person is held or by exciting adverse or derogatory feelings against the person. Such a communication made orally constitutes slander; if written, such a communication constitutes libel.[121] Defamation suits brought against physicians for the release of medical information have been largely unsuccessful,[122] generally because of the available defenses. The truth of the publication when made will absolve a defamation defendant from liability. Also, statements published in judicial proceedings are protected.[123]

A patient may sue for invasion of privacy where information is published or disseminated to someone who has no legitimate interest in the information. The publication must unreasonably and seriously interfere in the subject's personal affairs, and exceed the limits of decent conduct and offend persons of ordinary sensibilities. The truth of the publication does not provide a defense in an invasion of privacy case.[124] For example, a court in 1930 enjoined a hospital from publishing photographs of a malformed, deceased child to protect the privacy of the parents.[125] If the information disclosed advances the legitimate interests of the disclosing party or others, a privacy suit will fail. A New York court has held that a physician's disclosure of a patient's condition to the patient's spouse does not violate the patient's privacy.[126] Others who might have legitimate interest in such information include insurance carriers, the patient's attorney, various governmental agencies such as state health departments, and bona fide research personnel.[127]

Cases for defamation and invasion of privacy may only be brought where information is released without the patient's consent. If consent is obtained, this generally constitutes a defense. Although defamation and privacy suits are rarely successful, in light of the patient's property rights in the record and potential recourse to suits, the physician is well-advised to confer with the patient and obtain consent before disclosing such information to third parties.

§ 2.50 PRODUCTS LIABILITY

Products liability is that body of law which deals with the liability of manufacturers and suppliers of products for harm caused by defects in their products.[128] Products liability law is a complex and rapidly changing area of law with substantial nonconformity among the states. Because anesthesiologists administer drugs and use mechanical devices, both of which fall under the rubric of "products," products liability law is of particular pertinence to the practice of anesthesiology.

A person injured by a defective product who decides to sue the manufacturer or seller may do so under a number of products liability theories. Listed in the order of their development, they are negligence, warranty, and strict liability in tort. Each theory has successively made it easier for the plaintiff to recover against the defendant. The later theories of products liability do not replace, but supplement, the preexisting theories.

A plaintiff need not select one theory of liability by which to sue, but may sue on the several theories at once, and need only succeed on one theory to collect damages. Succeeding on two or more theories does not entitle the plaintiff to multiple damages. If the plaintiff succeeds on any or all theories of liability, he or she is entitled to damages sufficient to compensate him or her for the injuries suffered.

Originally, a products liability plaintiff had to sue under a theory of negligence. This meant that the plaintiff had to establish that the defendant-manufacturer did not exercise reasonable care in the design, manufacture, testing or marketing of the product. Since the plaintiff usually had no idea at which stage of production the defect occurred, and since the witnesses to any act of negligence would generally be employees of the manufacturer, this proved to be a difficult burden of proof for the plaintiff to meet. Furthermore, to defend such a suit, a manufacturer could come into court with all sorts of photographs and film (showing, for example, a sparkling clean factory with employees dressed in white lab coats and white gloves) in order to disprove negligence in the manufacture of the product. Such evidence was usually quite damaging to the plaintiff's claim.[129] This difficulty diminished somewhat when a court could apply the doctrine of *res ipsa loquitur*, the Latin phrase meaning, "the thing speaks for itself."[130] The doctrine is applied in cases where it can be inferred from circumstantial evidence that someone who is difficult to identify specifically has been negligent, and the evidence of identity and facts surrounding the negligence are more accessible to the defendant than to the plaintiff. Under the doctrine, the burden of proof is placed upon the defendant to show the absence of negligence. (See § 1.52, Res Ipsa Loquitur.)

The negligence theory as modified by res ipsa loquitur still allowed manufacturers to escape liability for the harm caused by their defective products if they could show that their behavior met the standard of reasonable care. Some courts, dissatisfied with the negligence theory because it so often failed to effect recovery for deserving plaintiffs, looked for a theory that would hold manufacturers liable for harm produced by defects in their products despite the fact that they had exercised all reasonable care. This in effect would make manufacturers the insurers of the safety of their products. It was felt that such a policy would promote the highest care and safety and that manufacturers themselves could spread the cost of injuries caused by their products across the buying public by making the price of their products reflect the cost of injuries caused by those products. The courts subscribed to the views that by placing goods on the market manufacturers represented them as safe and suitable, and reputable merchants endorsed them by offering those goods. The courts turned to contract law, where parties to a contract are held strictly liable for failing to live up to the terms of their contracts. Where a contractual term amounts to a representation concerning the quality or character of the goods which are the subject of the contract, such a term constitutes a warranty.[131] Merchants could be held liable for damages caused by their products' failures to live up to their warranties.

The major problem with the warranty theory of products liability is that since it is a contract theory, the manufacturer may assert contract defenses. Historically, the most effective contract defense manufacturers have had is the requirement of privity of contract between the plaintiff and defendant. Privity of contract refers to the relationship existing between parties to a contract. If a manufacturer sells defective products to a retailer who in turn sells one of these to a person who is injured by the product, the injured person cannot sue the manufacturer because there was not privity of contract between them.

The courts gradually eliminated the requirement of privity of contract between plaintiff and defendant in products liability litigation. A 1916 case first recognized the role of car dealers as a mere conduit between the manufacturer and the buyer.[132] Today, even innocent bystanders injured by the use of a defective product may sue the manufacturer of the product.

Other contract defenses remain, however. A warranty must be relied on by the purchaser to be enforced against the warrantor. Also, a plaintiff who fails to notify the manufacturer within a reasonable time that his products are defective may be barred by statute from suing that manufacturer.[133] And manufacturers can place disclaimers or warnings on their products to avoid liability from breach of warranty. A warning may be as simple a statement as, "Cigarette smoking is dangerous to your health."

When applied to knowledgeable commercial parties of equal bargaining strengths, these rules of contract law make sense, but they make less sense when applied to consumers ignorant of commercial law who are offered products on a "take it or leave it" basis. Some courts have used a great deal of imagination to prevent these rules from barring injured consumers' suits. Extensive lengths of time between injury and manufacturer notification have been found to be reasonable. Disclaimers, e.g. "this product is sold without warranty, express or implied," have been attacked as not affording notice to the purchaser, or as amounting to unconscionable adhesion contracts, the enforcement of which would be contrary to public policy.

Recently, the courts have taken the more direct route to avoiding the problems of contract defenses via adopting a new theory of products liability.[134] Known as strict liability in tort,[135] this theory has spread to a majority of states and may soon replace the warranty theories. Basically strict liability is imposed on a manufacturer for injuries caused by a product which is unreasonably dangerous as marketed, whether or not it is manufactured exactly as intended, i.e. without a production or design defect. Thus, under this theory, which analyzes the defectiveness requirement for legal recovery in terms of the unreasonable danger of the product, such factors as the circumstances of marketing the product might con-

§ 2.50 Products Liability

stitute a defect. The defect might also be something extrinsic to the product itself. Consequently, courts have found drug products to be "unreasonably dangerous as marketed" when they are not accompanied by proper directions and warnings related to their use.[136]

In light of this standard, under strict liability, physicians should be aware of the manufacturers' instructions and warnings, not only to avoid misusing the products, but also to enable themselves to disclose possible hazards to their patients[137] and avoid charges of lack of informed consent. (See § 1.33, Consent and Informed Consent.) Manufacturer instruction and warnings are playing an increasingly important role in defining the physician's standard of care. Originally, manufacturer instructions and warnings were no more authoritative than any medical textbook and inadmissible in court as direct evidence, but today the FDA requires and approves manufacturer instructions and warnings.[138] Some courts define a physician's deviation from these "standards" as prima facie negligence.[139] (See § 1.32, Standard of Care.)

The continued existence of multiple products liability theories is due to several factors. Some attorneys, more familiar and comfortable with the negligence cause of action, plead it as a back-up theory. Also, juries tend to return greater verdicts when the manufacturer has been shown to be negligent. The strict liability in tort theory may not always be available to plaintiffs even in states which have recognized it. The statute of limitations is longer for bringing suits based on contract law than tort law, so that only warranty theories may be available to the plaintiff. (See § 3.50, Statute of Limitations.)

Regardless of what theories the plaintiff chooses to use, he or she must meet essentially the same burden of proof. The plaintiff must show (1) that the product was defective, unreasonably dangerous, or somehow foreseeably deleterious to the plaintiff at the time it left the defendant's hands; (2) that the plaintiff was injured or suffered damages; and that (3) the defect or danger was the proximate cause of the injury or damage.[140]

Depending on which theory of liability is used, different defenses are available to the defendant. Under the negligence theory, the defendant may submit evidence that his or her conduct has met a standard of reasonable care. Under warranty theories, the defendant may use contract defenses. Under strict liability in tort, the defendant may defend the suit by proving that the product was altered or damaged after it left the defendant's hands, put to an unintended use by the user which was unforeseeable to the manufacturer, or used negligently at the time of injury.[141]

A patient who has suffered injury through the use of a medical product in the course of treatment may sue the manufacturer and supplier of the medical product involved as well as the physician or hospital. Other potential plaintiffs include the buyer or user or consumer of the product, as well as innocent bystanders and anyone else foreseeably harmed by the defective product. Potential defendants consist of the manufacturer, including the maker of any defective part of a product and the assembler of the product, as well as the packager, wholesaler, and retailer. Generally, products liability principles impose liability only on the manufacturers and the suppliers of the product; physician and hospital liability is predicated on malpractice negligence principles.[142] Because of the two different legal theories at play, attempts will be made to shift the onus of liability. Thus, the manufacturer may defend the products liability claim by asserting that the patient's harm was caused by negligent storage or maintenance on the part of the hospital or negligent use by the physician. Likewise, the physician and the hospital may attempt to exculpate themselves from the charge of negligence by establishing that the medical product was defective when it arrived from the manufacturer. In this type of case, all parties should engage independent legal counsel.

CASE ILLUSTRATION

A surgical suturing needle broke in the patient's vaginal cuff during surgery, and the surgeon was unable to locate the broken fragment to remove it. The patient-plaintiff sued the manufacturer of the needle, the distributor of the needle, the hospital, and the surgeon. The manufacturer and distributor claimed that the needle broke as a result of improper use by the surgeon, who was pushing rather than pulling the needle through tissue when it broke. The surgeon and hospital claimed that it was ordinary practice to use surgical needles in this fashion, and that the needle was defective as a result of the crimping done by the manufacturer to hold the suture material in place. The court found that the method used of drilling a hole in the needle into which the suture material is inserted and then crimped tended to weaken the needle and constituted a defect in manufacturing. The court also held that the needle had been used as intended, because it arose from the use for which the needle was both manufactured and sold. The court found the manufacturer and distributor liable, and the surgeon and hospital not liable. (*Ethicon, Inc. v. Parten*, 1975)[143]

In light of all this, it is important to consider what makes a given product defective. The nature of the defect itself may affect the appropriate products liability theory on which to base a suit.

A defective product has been defined as any product which does not meet the reasonable expectations of the ordinary consumer as to its safety.[144] Not all products which cause injuries may be considered defective. Some products are unavoidably unsafe; that is, their dangerous aspect is inherent in a useful or desirable feature of the product. Knives, autos and chainsaws are examples of such products. Unavoidably unsafe products may still be defective. In such cases, plaintiffs must proceed against the manufacturers of such products on a negligence

§ 2.50　　　　　　　　　　　　*Products Liability*　　　　　　　　　　　　87

theory. Other products will harm only the allergic, susceptible, or idiosyncratic consumer. Here, the manufacturer's duty to warn consumers of the potential hazard which their products represent may depend on the number of people affected and the magnitude of the harm which they face.[145]

A product need not be incorrectly manufactured in order to be defective. A product may be defective in design. Generally, a plaintiff charging a manufacturer with defective design must proceed on a negligence theory. A product includes the container or package in which the product is sold. Therefore, the plaintiff need not worry whether a bottle of soda pop, for example, exploded because the soda pop was overcharged or because the bottle was flawed. In either case, the bottle together with the soda pop constitute a single defective product.[146] Thus, a product may be defective due to improper design or manufacture, testing, or packaging, or faulty instructions for use or inadequate warnings of dangerous properties of the product.

Medical products comprise a huge and diverse class of items, many of which are capable of harming patients. Cases have been brought to recover for injuries resulting from the use of such products as catheters,[147] thermometers,[148] surgical needles,[149] hospital beds,[150] cauterizers,[151] anesthesia,[152] and heart-lung[153] machines, aspirin,[154] antibiotics,[155] halothane,[156] and polio vaccine.[157] With over 10,000 types of medical devices,[158] and a myriad of different drugs in use, the field of medical products liability is broad and diverse.

Whether something is a medical product is not always clear. X-rays have been found to be products,[159] while blood used for transfusions has been classified as a service not a product by most courts[160] and legislatures.[161] The classifications make sense when viewed as a way for the courts to define the allowable theories of liability not the physical distinctions. X-ray machines are controllable and their short-term effects on humans are generally understood. Therefore, courts have classified x-rays as products, allowing injured plaintiffs to proceed on a strict liability theory. By contrast, blood banks and hospitals have an uncertain source of blood with no efficient way to detect blood-borne hepatitis. Therefore, the courts have held that plaintiffs must proceed on a theory of negligence in these cases. A public policy favoring the ready availability of blood may explain this favored treatment.

Some manufacturers have attempted to defend medical products liability cases by claiming that patients do not purchase, use or consume the product and, therefore, may not sue them as consumers. Courts have rejected this argument and have held that patients are consumers of the medical products used in their care and treatment.[162]

Patients have attempted to hold hospitals[163] and their physicians[164] strictly liable for medical product defects on the theory that the hospital or physician is the retailer of the product. Courts have rejected this theory, realizing that physicians and hospitals provide services and that the medical products used are incidental to those services. Thus, manufacturers are held to a higher standard of care than physicians or hospitals. Because patients are unique and sometimes unpredictable, physicians must often balance risks in treating patients, and there is no certainty of results.

Again, medical products can be categorized as drugs or devices. This is a useful distinction because the issues involved in defective drug cases are generally different from issues which arise in cases involving defective devices.

§ 2.51 Defective Devices

In recent years, there has been a biomedical engineering explosion. Today, over 1,100 manufacturers produce approximately 12,000 types of medical devices, ranging in complexity from gauze and scalpels to heart-lung machines and C.A.T. scanners. It has been estimated that defects in these devices cause over 1,000 injuries per year.[165]

Medical devices can be sub-divided into two classes, internal implants and external equipment. Implants are those devices inserted or grafted into the body. Defective implants are rare, but when they do occur, they cause serious problems. The most common implant-related problems include chemical reactions with the body and failure of the implant due to wear, problems compounded by the impossibility of easily examining and replacing implants.[166]

Equipment-related injuries, including defects, improper maintenance and improper use, account for 11 percent of all medical malpractice cases, according to the National Association of Insurance Commissioner's recent report.[167] Of these, 43 percent involve surgical equipment and materials, and 16 percent involve anesthesia equipment. As a class, equipment-related injuries have the highest average indemnity—$42,000. Equipment-related cases involving anesthesia equipment have an average indemnity of $82,000.[168] While relatively rare, these injuries are among the most serious.

When a patient is injured by a relatively simple piece of equipment, e.g. a needle, the issue that usually arises is whether the device was defective when received by the hospital or was used incorrectly by a member of the hospital staff.

CASE ILLUSTRATION

While the patient was in the hospital, it became necessary to give her fluids intravenously. To accomplish this, a registered nurse used a Bardic-Deseret intracath which had been assembled by Deseret Pharmaceutical Company (the manufacturer) and distributed by C.R. Bard, Inc. As the needle of the intracath was being extracted, a portion of the catheter broke off in the patient's vein and was carried through the venous system until it lodged in the right atrium of her heart causing serious injury that necessitated open

§ 2.51　　　　　　　　　*Defective Devices*　　　　　　　　　89

heart surgery. The administering nurse had not followed prescribed procedure in inserting the intracath. The intracath unit consists of a needle through which a plastic catheter is inserted into the vein, once the needle punctures the skin and protrudes into the vein. Once the catheter has been threaded into the vein, the needle is extracted so that only the catheter is left in the patient's arm. At this point, the catheter is connected to a tube from a bottle of solution which allows the fluid to flow through the catheter directly into the vein. The administering nurse attached the tube from the bottle prior to extracting the needle from the patient's vein. At trial, the manufacturer denied the device was defective and alleged that the distributor had failed to include proper instructions and, if there was a defect in the device, it was caused by the distributor's mishandling of the item. Furthermore, the manufacturer claimed that the injury was a result of the nurse's negligence. The jury found that the intracath as manufactured was not reasonably fit for its intended use and that this was the proximate cause of the patient's injuries. As to the nurse, the jury agreed that she had been negligent in her use of the product, but found that such negligence was not the proximate cause of the patient's injuries. The distributor had been dismissed due to failure on the part of the manufacturer to introduce evidence supporting its allegations. The decision was upheld on appeal. (*Vergott v. Deseret Pharmaceutical Co., Inc.*, 1972)[169]

A finding that the medical device is defective does not always exculpate the hospital and physician. The duty to select the proper device for the job includes the duty to inspect the device for defects before it is used.[170] Physicians need only discover patent defects, while hospitals must discover less obvious ones, especially if the hospital maintains and services the device.[171] Once the device is known or suspected to be defective, the hospital or physician may not continue to use the device without risking liability.

CASE ILLUSTRATION

The infant-patient was admitted to the hospital suffering from tonsillitis and an ear infection. Surgery was performed to remove the patient's tonsils and adenoids and to perform a myringotomy on his infected ear. During the surgery, the patient's blood darkened twice and his heart stopped for two and a half minutes. After surgery, the patient was given intravenous fluids and medication, and his body temperature was ordered to be reduced to 90° through hypothermia. The telethermometer attached to the hypothermia machine used to treat the patient was known to be inaccurate, but the intensive care unit staff relied on it. The patient's temperature rise was undetected, and was followed by grand mal convulsions, leaving the patient with permanent severe brain damage.

The patient sued the surgeon, the anesthesiologist association, and the hospital. The surgeon and anesthesiologist association settled out of court. The court held the hospital liable for several reasons. First, the court found the hospital vicariously liable for the failure of its staff to check the accuracy of the patient's temperature in light of their knowledge of the inaccurate telethermometer. Furthermore, the hospital was liable for the use of equipment known to be defective in caring for the patient. (*Rose v. Hakim*, 1971)[172]

Medical-legal commentators have suggested that when a physician knows or suspects that a piece of equipment is defective he or she should notify the appropriate department head in writing and make a recommendation for necessary maintenance or replacement.[173]

Complex medical machines, such as anesthesia machines, may injure a patient because of improper maintenance as well as defective manufacture or improper use. Courts have recognized that the physician has limited time and ability to check the machines he or she uses in hospitals and for this reason the courts generally hold hospitals responsible for the maintenance of their machines.[174]

Hospitals can protect themselves from charges of negligent maintenance by contracting with the equipment manufacturer to maintain the equipment.[175] When neither the hospital nor the manufacturer assures that the equipment functions properly, both may be held liable.[176]

Occasionally, a medical device will be properly built, maintained, and used, but will injure a patient because a manufacturer has failed to instruct the user in its use or failed to warn of the machine's limitations.

CASE ILLUSTRATION

The patient fractured his ribs and pelvis in a fall. While hospitalized in traction, one physician prescribed Dextran for a fat embolism and another physician ordered a blood sugar test taken. The blood sugar machine read the Dextran as sugar due to its use of sulphuric acid, which breaks down the Dextran molecules into sugars, and gave a reading of 2,000 mg. Despite the abnormally high reading in an apparently healthy patient and the absence of sugar in the patient's urine, the second physician repeatedly ordered insulin injections and blood tests until the patient went into a hypoglycemic coma and died.

The deceased's estate sued the physicians, the hospital, and the

§ 2.52   *Defective Drugs*   91

manufacturer of the blood sugar machine. The court found the manufacturer liable for failing to list Dextran as a possible source of error in the machine's manual, and found that the chain of causation was not broken by any intervening negligence of the physician. (*Kincl v. Hycel*, 1977)[177]

Thus, a medical product is defective if the manufacturer fails to instruct the user or warn of potential hazards, and the manufacturer may be held liable for injuries in such a case.

§ 2.52 Defective Drugs

Since the development of the first sulfa drugs, there has been an exponential growth in the number of drugs available to physicians.[178] With several drugs appropriate for many problems and many drugs useful in a range of applications, selecting the right drug and dosage for the particular patient's problem has become a difficult task. It has been reported that in 1973, 10 percent of all medical malpractice cases involved drug-related malpractice.[179] Products liability cases involving drugs can be expected to grow with the number of drugs available.

There are few reported cases of impure drugs. Thanks in part to government-mandated manufacturing and testing requirements, the American pharmaceutical industry has an enviable record of safety. In order to find a reported case involving an injury resulting from the use of impure anesthetic, one must go back to 1918, where a Minnesota court held that the manufacturer had negligently sold ether contaminated with aldehydes.[180]

Occasionally the government determines a drug safe for marketing then later pulls the drug from the market when dangerous side effects are discovered. Examples are quadrigen[181] and MER/29.[182] Most drug products liability cases, however, involve drugs rendered defective due to incomplete or inaccurate manufacturers' warnings and recommendations for usage. FDA regulations require that drug manufacturers include inserts with their products, listing uses, doses, contraindications, side effects, and hazards.[183] Generally, a patient injured by a drug will sue both his or her physician and the drug manufacturer. The issue will be whether the manufacturer reasonably informed the medical community of the hazards associated with the product.

CASE ILLUSTRATION

The patient was admitted to the hospital suffering from phlebitis. Her physician, who had earlier confirmed her suspicions that she was pregnant, prescribed dicumarol, an anticoagulant which crosses the placental barrier. The patient received dicumarol while in the hospital and later as an outpatient. The patient's child was subsequently born with severe and irreparable birth defects including brain damage and partial paralysis.

The patient sued two hospitals and four physicians for medical malpractice and three pharmaceutical manufacturers on theories of products liability, alleging that the birth defects resulted from bleeding in the fetal brain caused by her ingestion of dicumarol. The physicians claimed that they had not been adequately warned by the drug manufacturers of the dangers of dicumarol to pregnant women. The drug manufacturers claimed their package inserts provided adequate warning and that the physicians caused the harm to the patient's child by disregarding the inserts and failing to consult available reference material on dicumarol before prescribing it.

The court, noting that the Physician's Desk Reference for 1972 contained no warning and that druggists often discard package inserts before they can be read by physicians, held that the drug manufacturers had not adequately warned the medical profession of the dangers of dicumarol. No "Dear Doctor" letters had been sent, nor had any warnings been published. Furthermore, the physicians' failure to search the literature for warnings was not an intervening cause of the harm because it was foreseeable to the manufacturers. (*Baker v. St. Agnes Hospital*, 1979)[184]

Manufacturers have a duty to update their warnings, but a change in warning does not necessarily constitute evidence that the prior warning was inadequate. The warnings are to be judged on the basis of the information available to the manufacturer at the time the warning is made.[185]

Some drugs pose a threat to only a small number of allergic or hypersensitive people. Unlike other manufacturers, drug manufacturers are required to warn of extremely rare adverse reactions. One drug company has been held liable for failing to warn that its oral polio vaccine may induce polio in as few as one in three million persons.[186]

Halothane is a good example of the courts' strict enforcement of the drug manufacturers' duty to warn. (See § 10.31, Halothane.) Halothane was introduced in the United States in 1958. Its advantage is that it is an inflammable anesthetic which is easy to use and control without inducing cardio-vascular irritation. Studies on animals and humans had shown no hepatic damage. However, isolated reports of massive hepatic necrosis led to a National Halothane Study in 1963.[187] The study concluded that halothane is generally as safe or safer than other anesthetics, but should not be administered to patients with known liver or biliary tract diseases. The study also suggested that administering halothane sensitized some patients, causing unexplained fever after surgery, and it should not be administered again to these persons.[188]

§ 2.52 *Defective Drugs* 93

CASE ILLUSTRATION

A patient with a fracture of the right ankle underwent an operation under halothane, and ran a fever afterwards. Eleven days later, the patient had a second operation under halothane. The patient developed a high fever, became jaundiced, went into a coma, and died due to liver damage, allegedly caused by a hypersensitive reaction to halothane.

The patient's wife sued the physicians and manufacturer. The court held that where the manufacturer knew or should know that a product may cause serious injury to users but does not warn of the potentially injurious effects either through negligence or because of concern that sales of the product would be reduced, the fact that an appreciable number of users would not be affected would not excuse the manufacturer. The manufacturer is obligated to warn in cases where the drug may affect only a small number of idiosyncratic or hypersensitive users. (*Tomer v. American Home Products*, 1976)[189]

Most courts have held that the drug manufacturer has a duty to warn the physician, and not the patient.[190] The drug manufacturer need not interfere in the physician-patient relationship. The physician will exercise his or her discretion and convey to the patient whatever information he or she believes the patient should have, consistent with the physician's duty to inform.

Occasionally, courts require the manufacturer to warn the patient directly as in the case of a drug dispensed in a mass immunization campaign[191] or drugs sold over-the-counter.

CASE ILLUSTRATION

The patient, suffering from arthritis for fourteen months, took six to eight Anacin tablets per day pursuant to a recommendation of the product's label not to exceed a dosage of eight tablets per day. He developed gastrointestinal hemorrhaging and sued the manufacturer for providing an inadequate warning of inherent danger. The box suggested consulting a physician for use of more than ten days' duration. The patient did consult a physician who told him that if the Anacin tablets ameliorated his pain, he should continue to use them. The court held that a manufacturer's duty to warn public consumers of risk arising from prolonged use of an over-the-counter drug cannot be discharged merely by instructing the user to consult his physician. Further, the patient's consultation with his physician, even if the physician acted negligently, did not exculpate the manufacturer. (*Torsiello v. Whitehall Labs*, 1979)[192]

When a consumer uses a drug without a physician's supervision, the manufacturer may have a duty to warn the consumer of the drug's dangers.

A drug manufacturer's failure to warn of a drug's danger, however, does not free the physician from liability. As in cases dealing with medical products,[193] if a physician or hospital staff member is aware of the product's defect, he or she cannot use the product without risking liability.[194] Furthermore, a physician's deviation from a drug manufacturer's recommendation may constitute evidence of negligence if expert testimony indicates the deviation was the cause of the patient's injury.[195] An increasing number of courts have held that where a drug manufacturer's recommendations are clear and explicit, deviations from them may constitute a breach of the physician's duty to meet a standard of reasonable care.[196] (See § 1.32, Standard of Care.)

Finally, it now appears that a drug manufacturer has a duty not only to warn physicians of the dangers associated with their drug, but also a duty not to "water down" the warning by over-promoting the drug.[197] Thus, manufacturers must do more than follow the FDA's regulations regarding drug warnings. Manufacturers must also take steps to assure that physicians do not misuse their products.

NOTES

1. Leighton v. Sargent, 27 N.H. 460, 59 Am. Dec. 388 (1853).
2. W. Prosser, Handbook of the Law of Torts 139 (4th ed. 1971).
3. Guilmet v. Campbell, 385 Mich. 57, 188 N.W.2d 601 (1971); Tschirhart v. Pethtel, 61 Mich. App. 581, 233 N.W.2d 93 (1975), *appeal denied*, 395 Mich. 774 (1976).
4. Karlsons v. Guerinot, 57 A.D.2d 73, 394 N.Y.S.2d 933 (1977); Sullivan v. O'Connor, 363 Mass 579, 583, 296 N.E. 2d 183, 186 (1973).
5. Green v. Sudakin, 81 Mich. App. 545, 265 N.W.2d 411, *appeal denied*, 403 Mich. 855 (1978); Stewart v. Rudner, 349 Mich. 459, 84 N.W.2d 816 (1957).
6. Woodbury, *Physicians and Surgeons—Sullivan v. O'Connor, A Liberal View of the Contractual Liability of Physicians and Surgeons*, 54 N.C.L. Rev. 885, 887 (1976).
7. Mich. Comp. Laws Ann. § 600.5805(3) (1968 & Supp. 1981-82).
8. Mich. Comp. Laws Ann. § 600.5807(8) (1968).
9. Mich. Comp. Laws Ann. § 600.5805(7) (1968 & Supp. 1981-82).
10. Rach v. Wise, 46 Mich. App. 729, 208 N.W.2d 570, *appeal denied*, 390 Mich. 778 (1973); Kelleher v. Mills, 70 Mich. App. 360, 245 N.W.2d 749 (1976).
11. Liebler v. Our Lady of Victory Hosp., 43 A.D.3d 898, 351 N.Y.S.2d 480 (1974); Bishop v. Byrne, 265 F. Supp. 460 (S.D.W.Va. 1967).
12. Hockworth v. Hart, 474 S.W.2d 377 (Ky. App. 1971); Johnston v. Rodis, 251 F.2d 917, 918 (D.C. Cir. 1958).
13. Foran v. Carangelo, 153 Conn. 356, 216 A.2d 638 (1966).
14. Woodbury, *supra* note 6 at 889.

Notes: Chapter II

15. Alexandridis v. Jewett, 388 F.2d 829 (1st Cir. 1968).
16. Grewe v. Mt. Clemens Gen. Hosp., 404 Mich. 240, 273 N.W.2d 429 (1978).
17. Comment, *The Implied Contract Theory of Malpractice Recovery*, 6 Willamette L.J. 275 (1970).
18. Sullivan v. O'Conner, *supra* note 4.
19. Clegg v. Chase, 391 N.Y.S.2d 966 (1977).
20. Sard v. Hardy, 379 A.2d 1014 (Md. App. 1977); Clevenger v. Haling, 394 N.E.2d 1119 (Mass. 1979).
21. Clevenger v. Haling, *supra* note 20.
22. Black's Law Dictionary 1475 (4th ed. 1978).
23. Sturm v. Green, 398 P.2d 799 (Okla. 1965).
24. Voss v. Bridwell, 188 Kan. 643, 364 P.2d 955 (1961); Whitfield v. Whittaker Mem. Hosp., 210 Va. 176, 169 S.E.2d 563 (1969); Restatement (Second) of Agency § 220(1) (1958).
25. W. Prosser, *supra* note 2, at 568.
26. Leeper, *Texas Labels Captain of the Ship Doctrine: "False Rule of Agency,"* 14 Wake Forest L. Rev. 319 (1978); Note, *Separation of Responsibility in the Operating Room: The Borrowed Servant, The Captain of the Ship and the Scope of Surgeon's Vicarious Liability*, 49 Notre Dame L. Rev. 933 (1974).
27. Leeper, *supra* note 26; Comment, *The Hospital's Responsibility for its Medical Staff: Prospects for Corporate Negligence in California*, 8 Pac. L.J. 141 (1977).
28. R. Goodman & L. Goldsmith, Modern Hospital Liability: Law and Tactics 368, 371 (1972).
29. Llera v. Wisner, 171 Mont. 254, 557 P.2d 805 (1976).
30. Boyd v. Badenhauser, 556 S.W.2d 896 (Ky. 1977).
31. McFadden v. Turner, 159 N.J. Super. 360, 388 A.2d 244 (1978).
32. Whitfield v. Whittaker Mem. Hosp., *supra* note 24.
33. Synnott v. Midway Hosp., 287 Minn. 270, 178 N.W.2d 211 (1970); Sesselman v. Muhlenberg Hosp., 124 N.J. Super. 285, 306 A.2d 474 (1973); Martin v. Perth Amboy Gen. Hosp., 104 N.J. Super. 335, 250 A.2d 40 (1969).
34. Foster v. Englewood Hosp. Ass'n, 19 Ill. App. 3d 1055, 313 N.E.2d 255 (1974).
35. *Id.*
36. Wiles v. Myerly, 210 N.W.2d 619 (Iowa 1973); Voss v. Bridwell, *supra* note 24; Whitfield v. Whittaker Mem. Hosp., *supra* note 24.
37. Wiles v. Myerly, *supra* note 36.
38. Voss v. Bridwell, *supra* note 24.
39. Grubb v. Albert Einstein Medical Center, 255 Pa. Super. Ct. 381, 387 A.2d 480 (1978); Whitfield v. Whittaker Mem. Hosp., *supra* note 24.
40. Foster v. Englewood Hosp. Ass'n, *supra* note 34.
41. Willinger v. Mercy Catholic Medical Center, 241 Pa. Super. Ct. 456, 362 A.2d 280 (1976).
42. Dickerson v. American Sugar Refining Co., 211 F.2d 200 (3d Cir. 1954).
43. Collins v. Hand, 431 Pa. 378, 246 A.2d 398 (1968); Grubb v. Albert Einstein Medical Center, *supra* note 39.
44. Tonsic v. Wagner, 458 Pa. 246, 329 A.2d 497 (1974); Yorston v. Pennell, 397 Pa. 28, 153 A.2d 255 (1959).
45. McConnell v. Williams, 261 Pa. 355, 65 A.2d 243 (1949).
46. Young, *Separation of Responsibility in the Operating Room: The Borrowed Servant, the Captain of the Ship, and the Scope of Surgeons' Vicarious Liability*, 49 Notre Dame L. Rev. 933 (1974).
47. Yorston v. Pennell, *supra* note 44.

48. Rockwell v. Stone, 404 Pa. 574, 173 A.2d 54 (1961).
49. Minogue v. Rutland Hosp., 119 Vt. 336, 125 A.2d 798 (1956).
50. Harle v. Krchnak, 422 S.W.2d 810 (Tex. Civ. App. 1967).
51. Foster v. Englewood Hosp. Ass'n, *supra* note 34; Sesselman v. Muhlenberg Hosp., *supra* note 33; Sparger v. Worley Hosp., Inc., 547 S.W.2d 582 (Tex. 1977).
52. Sparger v. Worley Hosp., Inc., *supra* note 51.
53. Thomas v. Hutchinson, 442 Pa. 118, 275 A.2d 23 (1971).
54. Seneris v. Haas, 45 Cal.2d 811, 291 P.2d 915 (1955).
55. Huber v. Protestant Deaconess Hosp. Ass'n, 127 Ind. App. 565, 133 N.E.2d 864 (1956).
56. D. Louisell & H. Williams, Medical Malpractice 498 (1980).
57. Schneider v. Albert Einstein Medical Center, 257 Pa. Super. Ct. 348, 390 A.2d 1271 (1978).
58. Spannaus v. Otolaryngology Clinic, 308 Minn. 334, 242 N.W.2d 594 (1976).
59. Marvulli v. Elshire, 27 Cal. App. 3d 180, 103 Cal. Rptr. 461 (1972).
60. Wiles v. Myerly, *supra* note 36.
61. Stahlin v. Hilton Hotels Corp., 484 F. 2d 580 (7th Cir. 1973).
62. Schneider v. Albert Einstein Medical Center, *supra* note 57.
63. Aubert v. Charity Hosp., 363 So.2d 1223 (La. 1978).
64. Garcia v. Tarrio, 380 So.2d 1068 (Fla. 1980).
65. Schloendorff v. Society of New York Hospital, 211 N.Y. 125, 105 N.E. 92 (1914).
66. Abbe v. Woman's Hospital Association, 35 Mich. App. 429, 192 N.W.2d 691 (1971); May v. Broun, 261 Ore. 28, 492 P.2d 776 (1972).
67. Forney v. Memorial Hosp., 543 S.W.2d 705 (Tex. 1976).
68. Carlsen v. Javurek, 526 F.2d 202 (8th Cir. 1975); Brown v. Allen Sanitarium, Inc., 364 So.2d 661 (La. 1978); Forney v. Mem. Hosp. *supra* note 67.
69. Starnes v. Charlotte-Mecklenburg Hosp. Auth., 28 N.C. App. 418, 221 S.E.2d 733 (1976).
70. *Id.*
71. *Id.*
72. La. Rev. Stat. Ann. § 37.930 (West 1977 & Supp. 1981).
73. Brown v. Allen Sanitarium, Inc., *supra* note 68.
74. Carlsen v. Javurek, *supra* note 68.
75. Norton v. Argonaut Ins. Co., 144 So.2d 249 (La. App. 1962).
76. Kucera, *Individual Accountability*, J. Am. A. Nurse Anesthetists 630 (Dec. 1978).
77. Sesselman v. Muhlenberg Hosp., *supra* note 33.
78. Willinger v. Mercy Catholic Medical Center, 241 Pa. Super. Ct. 456, 362 A.2d 280 (1976).
79. Baird v. Sickler, 69 Ohio St.2d 652, 433 N.E.2d 593 (1982).
80. Webb v. Jorns, 488 S.W.2d 407 (Tex. 1973).
81. Willinger v. Mercy Catholic Medical Center, *supra* note 78.
82. Southwick, *The Hospital's New Responsibility*, 17 Clev. Mar. L. Rev. 146 (1968).
83. Pullins v. Fentress County Gen. Hosp., 594 S.W.2d 663 (Tenn. 1979).
84. Pederson v. Dumouchel, 72 Wash. 2d 73, 431 P.2d 973 (1967).
85. Garcia v. Memorial Hosp., 557 S.W.2d 859 (Tex. 1977); May v. Broun, *supra* note 66.
86. Mitchell County Hosp. Auth. v. Joiner, 229 Ga. 140, 189 S.E.2d 412 (1972).
87. Tucson Medical Center, Inc. v. Miseuch, 113 Ariz. 34, 545 P.2d 958 (1976); Darling v. Charleston Memorial Hosp., 33 Ill. 2d 326, 211 N.E.2d 253 (1965); J. Cunningham, *The Hospital-Physician Relationship: Hospital Responsibility for Malprac-*

Notes: Chapter II

tice of Physicians, 50 Wash. L. Rev. 385 412-13 (1975).
88. Mitchell County Hosp. Auth. v. Joiner, *supra* note 86.
89. May v. Broun, *supra* note 66.
90. Hiatt v. Groce, 215 Kan. 14, 523 P.2d 320 (1974); Ulmer v. Baton Rouge Gen. Hosp. 361 So.2d 1238 (La. 1978); Aubert v. Charity Hosp., *supra* note 63.
91. Bing v. Thunig, 2 N.Y.2d 656, 143 N.E.2d 3 (1957).
92. Rabon v. Rowan Mem. Hosp., 152 S.E.2d 485 (1967).
93. Seneris v. Haas, *supra* note 54.
94. Ider v. Stewart, 148 Mont. 117, 417 P.2d 476 (1966).
95. Seneris v. Haas, *supra* note 54; Grewe v. Mt. Clemens Gen. Hosp., *supra* note 16; Arthur v. St. Peters Hosp., 189 N.J. 575, 405 A.2d 443 (1979).
96. Seneris v. Haas, *supra* note 54.
97. Ider v. Stewart, *supra* note 94.
98. Spannaus v. Otolaryngology Clinic, *supra* note 58.
99. *Id*.
100. Hirsch, *Difficulties the Attorney Encounters in Procuring Medical Documents*, 10 Forum 361 (Fall, 1974).
101. *In re* Culbertson's Will, 57 Misc. 2d 391, 292 N.Y.S.2d 806 (1968).
102. Hirsch, *supra* note 100, at 362.
103. *Id*. at 363.
104. Gotkin v. Miller, 514 F.2d 125 (2d Cir. 1975); Cannell v. Medical & Surgical Clinic, 21 Ill. App. 3d 383, 315 N.E.2d 278 (1974); *In re* Culbertson's Will, *supra* note 101.
105. Emmett v. Eastern Dispensary & Cas. Hosp., 396 F.2d 931 (D.C. Cir. 1967); Cannell v. Medical & Surgical Clinic, *supra* note 104.
106. *Id*.
107. Pyramid Life Ins. Co. v. Masonic Hosp. Ass'n. 191 F. Supp. 51, (W.D. Okla. 1961).
108. Rabens v. Jackson Park Hosp. Foundation, 41 Ill. App. 3d 113, 351 N.E.2d 276 (1976); Gaertner v. State of Michigan, 385 Mich. 49, 187 N.W.2d 429 (1971).
109. Felch, *Access to Medical & Psychiatric Records: Proposed Legislation*, 40 Albany L. Rev. 580, 597 (1976).
110. Conn. Gen. Stat. Ann. §§4-104, 105 (West 1969); Mass. Gen. Laws Ann. ch. 111, § 70 (1971); Wis. Stat. Ann. § 269.57 (West Supp. 1975-76).
111. Cal. Evid. Code § 1158 (West Supp. 1981).
112. N.J. Rev. Stat. Ann. §§ 2A:82-41 to 45 (West 1976 & Supp. 1981-82).
113. Miss. Code Ann. § 41-9-65 (1977).
114. La. Rev. Stat. Ann. § 40:2014.1 (West 1977).
115. Ill. Ann. Stat. ch. 51, § 71 (Smith-Hurd 1977).
116. Hayes, *The Patient's Right of Access to His Hospital & Medical Records*, X Scalpel and Quill, No. 4 (December, 1976), reprinted in 24 Med. Trial Tech. Q. 295 (Winter, 1978).
117. *Id*.
118. Emmett v. Eastern Dispensary & Cas. Hosp., *supra* note 105, Cannell v. Medical & Surgical Clinic, *supra* note 104.
119. Hayes, *supra* note 116.
120. Grayson, *How State Medical Access Laws are Working*, 8 Hosp. Med. Staff 10 (September, 1979).
121. W. Prosser, *supra* note 2, at 737-51.
122. *See*, *e.g.*, Klinge v. Lutheran Medical Center, 518 S.W.2d 157 (Mo. App. 1974); Quarles v. Sutherland, 215 Tenn. 651, 389 S.W.2d 249 (1965).
123. A. Southwick, The Law of Hospital and Health Care Administration 317-21 (1978).

Notes: Chapter II

124. *Id.* at 321-31.
125. Bazemore v. Savannah Hosp., 171 Ga. 257, 155 S.E. 194 (1930); for a general discussion, *see,* W. Prosser, *supra* note 2, at 802-18.
126. Curry v. Corn, 52 Misc. 2d 1035, 277 N.Y.S.2d 470 (1966).
127. A. Southwick, *supra* note 123, at 327.
128. *See* W. Prosser, *supra* note 2, at 641 *et seq.*
129. Morris, *The Legal Theories of Products Liability: Negligence, Warranty and Strict Liability,* in New Developments in Law/Medicine 95 (G. Morris & M. Norton eds. 1974).
130. Black's Law Dictionary *supra* note 22, at 1470.
131. *Id.* at 1757.
132. MacPherson v. Buick Motor Co., 217 N.Y. 382, 111 N.E. 1050, 138 N.Y.S. 224 (1916).
133. U. C. C. § 2-607(3)(a).
134. Greenman v. Yuba Power Prod., 59 Cal. 2d 57, 377 P. 2d 897, 27 Cal. Rptr. 697 (1963).
135. Restatement (Second) of Torts § 402A (1965 & Cum. Supp. 1978).
136. Reyes v. Wyeth Laboratories, 498 F.2d 1264 (5th Cir. 1974); Tomer v. Am. Home Prod. Corp., 170 Conn. 681, 368A. 2d 35 (1976).
137. *See, e.g.,* Vergott v. Deseret Pharmaceutical Co., Inc., 463 F.2d 12 (5th Cir. 1972).
138. Note, *Package Inserts for Prescription Drugs as Evidence in Medical Malpractice Suits,* 44 U. Chi. L. Rev. 398 (1977).
139. Mueller v. Mueller, 88 S.D. 446, 221 N.W.2d 39 (1974).
140. Gravis v. Parke-Davis & Co., 502 S.W.2d 863 (Tex. App. 1973).
141. Ethicon, Inc. v. Parten, 520 S.W.2d 527 (Tex. App. 1975).
142. Putensen v. Clay Adams, 12 Cal. App. 3d 1062, 91 Cal. Rptr. 319 (1970).
143. Ethicon, Inc. v. Parten, *supra* note 141.
144. W. Prosser, *supra* note 2, at 659.
145. Reyes v. Wyeth Laboratories, *supra* note 136.
146. W. Prosser, *supra* note 2, at 659.
147. Vergott v. Deseret Pharmaceutical Co., Inc., *supra* note 137.
148. Rose v. Hakim, 335 F. Supp. 1221 (D.D.C. 1971).
149. Ethicon, Inc. v. Parten, *supra* note 141.
150. Mattair v. St. Joseph's Hosp., 141 Ga. App. 597, 234 S.E.2d 537 (1977).
151. May v. Broun, *supra* note 66.
152. North Miami Gen. Hosp., Inc. v. Air Prod. & Chem., Inc., 216 So.2d 793 (Fla. App. 1968); Patel v. Albany Medical Center Hosp., 101 Misc. 2d 457, 421 N.Y.S.2d 182 (1978).
153. Ardoin v. Hartford Accident & Indem. Co., 350 So.2d 205 (La. App. 1977).
154. Torsiello v. Whitehall Laboratories, 165 N.J. Super. 311, 398 A.2d 132 (1979).
155. Incollingo v. Ewing, 444 Pa. 263, 299, 282 A.2d 206 (1971).
156. Tomer v. Am. Home Prod. Corp., 170 Conn. 681, 368 A.2d 35 (1976).
157. Givens v. Lederle, 556 F.2d 1341 (5th Cir. 1977); Davis v. Wyeth Labs, Inc., 399 F.2d 121 (9th Cir. 1968).
158. Morris, *Defective Devices-Who's Liable?,* 8 Hospital Med. Staff 2 (May, 1979).
159. Dubin v. Michael Reese Hosp. & Medical Center, 74 Ill. App. 3d 932, 393 N.E.2d 588 (1979).
160. McDonald v. Sacramental Medical Foundation Blood Bank, 62 Cal. App. 3d 866, 133 Cal. Rptr. 444 (1976); Perlmutter v. Beth David Hosp., 308 N.Y. 100, 123 N.E.2d 792 (1954).

Notes: Chapter II

161. *See, e.g.*, Idaho Code § 39-3702 (1977); N.D. Cent. Code § 41-02-33 (3d) (Supp. 1979); S.C. Code § 44-43-10 (1977).
162. Carmichael v. Reitz, 17 Cal. App. 3d 958, 95 Cal. Rptr. 381 (1971); Ethicon, Inc. v. Parten, *supra* note 141.
163. Vergott v. Deseret Pharmaceutical Co., Inc., *supra* note 137.
164. Carmichael v. Reitz, *supra* note 162.
165. Morris, *supra* note 158.
166. *Id.*
167. National Association of Insurance Commissioners, 1 NAIC Malpractice Claims 2 (1978).
168. *Id.*
169. Vergott v. Deseret Pharmaceutical Co., Inc., *supra* note 137.
170. Marcus, *Safe Equipment: A Matter of Selection and Detection*, 8 Hospital Med. Staff 14 (May, 1979).
171. Morris, *supra* note 158, at 4.
172. Rose v. Hakim, *supra* note 148.
173. Marcus, *supra* note 170 at 17.
174. May v. Broun, *supra* note 66.
175. North Miami Gen. Hosp., Inc., v. Air Prod. & Chem., Inc., *supra* note 152.
176. Ardoin v. Hartford Accident & Indem. Co., *supra* note 153.
177. Kincl v. Hycel, Inc., 56 Ill. App. 3d 772, 372 N.E.2d 385 (1977).
178. Note, *supra* note 138.
179. Department of Health, Education and Welfare, *Report of the Secretary's Commission on Medical Malpractice*, Publ. No. (05) 73-89 (Jan. 16, 1973).
180. Moehlenbrock v. Parke-Davis & Co., 141 Minn. 154, 169 N.W. 541 (1918).
181. Parke-Davis & Co. v. Stromsodt, 411 F.2d 1390 (8th Cir. 1969).
182. Roginsky v. Richardson-Merrell, Inc., 378 F.2d 832 (2d Cir. 1967).
183. Note, *supra* note 138.
184. Baker v. St. Agnes Hosp., 70 A.D.2d 400, 421 N.Y.S.2d 81 (1979).
185. Smith v. E. R. Squibb & Sons, Inc., 405 Mich. 79, 273 N.W.2d 476 (1979); Tomer v. Am. Home Prod. Corp., *supra* note 156.
186. Givens v. Lederle, *supra* note 157.
187. *Summary of the National Halothane Study*, 197 J.A.M.A. 121 (Sept. 5, 1966).
188. *Id.*
189. Tomer v. Am. Home Prod. Corp., *supra* note 156.
190. Carmichael v. Reitz, *supra* note 162; Gravis v. Parke-Davis & Co., *supra* note 140.
191. Davis v. Wyeth Labs, Inc., *supra* note 157.
192. Torsiello v. Whitehall Laboratories, *supra* note 154.
193. Rose v. Hakim, *supra* note 148.
194. Mulder v. Parke-Davis & Co., 288 Minn. 332, 181 N.W.2d 882 (1970).
195. *Id.*
196. Lhotka v. Larson, 307 Minn. 121, 238 N.W.2d 870 (1976).
197. Salmon v. Parke-Davis & Co., 520 F.2d 1359 (4th Cir. 1975); Stevens v. Parke-Davis & Co., 9 Cal. 3d 51, 507 P.2d 653 (1973); Whitley v. Cubberly, 24 N.C. App. 204, 210 S.E.2d 289 (1974).

Chapter III

Defenses

§ 3.10 INTRODUCTION

When a patient sues a physician for malpractice, the law gives the physician certain defenses. (See Table 3.1.) Generally, the patient-plaintiff has the burden of proving the allegations made against the physician-defendant; and the jury is told that the defendant must prevail unless the patient-plaintiff proves by a preponderance of the evidence each element of his or her claim. (See § 1.20, Elements of Negligence.)

If the plaintiff succeeds in proving a case, the physician-defendant must defend the action. The most common defense is to deny the elements of the patient-plaintiff's claim. Thus, the physician-defendant may prove that he or she exercised ordinary skill and reasonable care (see § 1.30, Duty; § 1.40, Breach of Duty); that he or she did not cause the patient's injury (see § 1.50, Causation); that the patient suffered no injury (see § 1.60, Damages); or all or any combination of these defenses.

The physician has additional defenses to malpractice which fall into one of two categories: substantive and procedural defenses.

Substantive, or affirmative, defenses, as lawyers call them, refer to the facts or merits of the lawsuit. They include contributory or comparative negligence and assumption of risk. Each of these defenses looks to the actions or inactions of the patient-plaintiff. Procedural defenses on the other hand refer to some requirement of the legal process which the patient-plaintiff has not met and, consequently, this bars the plaintiff from recovering against the physician. Procedural defenses include statutes of limitation, res judicata, and release from liability agreements. Each of these defenses is discussed in Table 3.1.

§ 3.20 CONTRIBUTORY NEGLIGENCE

Contributory negligence has been defined as

> conduct on the part of the plaintiff, contributing as a legal cause to the harm he has

§ 3.20   *Contributory Negligence*   101

suffered, which falls below the standard to which he is required to conform for his own protection. . . . although the defendant has violated his duty, has been negligent, and would otherwise be liable, the plaintiff is denied recovery because his own conduct disentitles him to maintain the action. In the eyes of the law both parties are at fault; and the defense is one of the plaintiff's disability, rather than the defendant's innocence.[1]

Basically, the contributory negligence of the patient-plaintiff must be a proximate cause of the injury suffered. (See § 1.50, Causation.) In a medical malpractice action, the patient's negligence, to constitute a bar to liability, must have been an active and efficient contributing cause of the injury. It must have been simultaneous and cooperating with the actions of the defendant. Furthermore, it must have entered into the creation of the cause of action and have been an element in the transaction that constituted it.[2]

The defense of contributory negligence has been recognized in cases where the patient has failed to follow the physician's or nurse's instruction,[3] refused suggested treatment, or given the doctor false, incomplete or misleading information concerning symptoms or medical history.[4] The question of whether a patient's actions were contributorily negligent is a question for the jury.

TABLE 3.1   Physician Defenses

Incomplete Tort Defenses	Substantive Defenses	Procedural Defenses
1. Duty?	1. Contributory negligence*	1. Statute of limitations
2. Breach of duty?	2. Comparative negligence**	2. Release forms
3. Damage?	3. Assumption of risk[†]	
4. Proximate cause?	4. Standard of care options[††]	
	a. Best judgment rule	
	b. Respectable minority	
	c. Different schools	

*Both parties considered to be at fault; physician must prove the patient's contribution. Recovery by patient is all-or-none. None if patient is found contributorily negligent.

**Responsibility for damage is apportioned between patient and physician according to percent of wrongdoing.

[†]Once patient is informed of the risks and authorizes the treatment, the patient is held to have assumed the risk.

[††]If the physician complies with the (an) acceptable standard of care, the physician can claim to have used his or her *best judgment*. If there is more than one standard of care, compliance with a *respectable minority* standard is OK. And where physicians from *different schools* (e.g., M.D., D.O., chiropractic) follow the standards of their schools, and the standards between the schools are different, they will be judged according to their school's standard and not that of another.

CASE ILLUSTRATION

During the course of a breast biopsy, the patient suffered a cardiac arrest. Massive and irreversible brain damage was sustained as a result of the cardiac arrest. Prior to the biopsy, the patient had been taking nitroglycerine for chest pain and the drug Lasix, a potent diuretic used primarily in the treatment of heart disease. The patient had failed to inform either the surgeon or the anesthesiologist of these facts, although the patient did inform a floor nurse that she was using Lasix which was listed in the nurse's notes. The patient and her husband brought suit, naming the surgeon, the anesthesiologist and the hospital as defendants. The court noted that Lasix can deplete the body's store of potassium and that a low level of potassium increases the risk of cardiac arrest during anesthesia. In the event of cardiac arrest, a low potassium level can interfere with the restoration of normal heart function. With respect to the defense raised by the defendants that the patient was contributorily negligent in failing to give a complete history, the court made the general statement that contributory negligence on the part of a patient in relating medical history is directly related to the care taken by the physician and nurses in obtaining the history. The patient is considered contributorily negligent if a reasonably prudent person would know that the history was false and misleading. When the physicians or nurses are negligent in obtaining the history, the patient is contributorily negligent only if he knows the physician is unaware of a condition which imposes a risk of danger to the patient and his failure to inform the physician of the condition under the circumstances. With regard to the facts of the case at hand, the court stated that the patient had a duty to exercise ordinary care for her own safety in giving her medical history and that this duty was influenced by whether the questions asked by the surgeon and anesthesiologist were sufficient to apprise her of the necessity of communicating particular aspects of her medical history. Evidence was entered that both the surgeon and anesthesiologist asked the patient whether she suffered from heart disease and whether she was under any medication, to which she responded in the negative. The court held that the evidence supported a finding that the patient's failure to give a true history to the physicians was a substantial factor in the cardiac arrest during surgery and the defendants were absolved from liability. (*Mackey v. Greenview Hospital*, 1979)[5]

Occasions could also arise when the patient would be contributorily negligent in submitting to the suggested treatment rather than refusing it, e.g., allowing a drunken doctor to give an injection and sustaining injury as a result.[6] However, patient negligence prior to the defendant's alleged negligence will not bar a claim by a patient. The physician's negligence occurs in treating only the patient's presenting condition at the time of treatment.[7]

A defense of contributory negligence may not be available if the patient's state of mind or health may be understood to render the patient irresponsible for such negligence. The defense may also be rejected when a patient is mentally ill,[8] semi-conscious,[9] heavily sedated,[10] or a victim of the aging process.[11]

Contributory negligence does bar all recovery by the patient-plaintiff. This is true regardless of the extent of the plaintiff's negligence. It is a well-established rule that a patient is required to exercise the ordinary prudence that is expected of a person in such circumstances,[12] and contributory negligence has long been recognized as a valid complete defense to an action for damages arising out of medical malpractice.[13] It is an affirmative defense. This means that the burden is on the physician-defendant to prove it.[14] If the physician fails to prove that the patient was contributorily negligent, the patient's claim will not be barred.[15]

Both courts and commentators have emphasized that the availability of a contributory negligence defense in a malpractice case is limited because of the disparity of medical knowledge between patient and physician and because of the patient's right to rely on the physician's knowledge and skill in the course of medical treatment. It has been held that a patient does not contribute to negligence by following a physician's instructions or failing to consult another physician when there is no reason to believe his or her pain is the result of physician negligence. Nor does the patient contribute to negligence by refusing to submit to a second procedure that is intended to correct the result of the physician's initial negligent treatment.[16]

From a strategic standpoint, a defense of contributory negligence probably should not be raised in every case in which a plaintiff has done something which aggravates his or her own injury. The wisdom of invoking contributory negligence may involve more delicate considerations in malpractice cases than in the general run of tort cases. A jury naturally may resent the attempt of a professional to offset a particularly egregious error with a relatively minor error of a sick patient. Possibly, too, the word "contributory" may in some malpractice cases connote, more than it does generally in tort cases, i.e., an admission that the defendant was negligent in the first place. It may be wise, depending on the facts, for the defendant to rely on the defense that the plaintiff's negligence was the sole cause of the injury, not contributory negligence.[17] This is a question that the physician's attorney must decide based on the facts of the case as well as the attorney's personal style and legal theory preferences.

§ 3.30 COMPARATIVE NEGLIGENCE

The doctrine of comparative negligence relieves the plaintiff from the hardship often imposed by the doctrine of contributory negligence. In contrast to the contributory negligence rule that negligence by the plaintiff totally bars his or her action, comparative negligence "compares" the wrongdoing of the parties so that damages are divided between the defendant and plaintiff in proportion to their fault for the injury.[18] For example, in a case where the patient suffers $10,000 damage the jury may find that the physician was responsible for 70 percent of the injury and the patient for 30 percent. The physician would be held liable for 70 percent of the damage, i.e. $7,000, which the patient would receive. In a jurisdiction adhering to the contributory negligence doctrine, the finding that the patient's own negligence was a partial cause of the injury would bar the action and the plaintiff would get nothing.[19]

As the example shows, the doctrines of contributory negligence and comparative negligence are incompatible. All jurisdictions use one or the other of the rules; none use both. Primarily because the contributory negligence rule totally denies recovery to plaintiffs only nominally at fault, an increasing number of jurisdictions are adopting the comparative negligence rule.

The obstacle to adopting comparative negligence is the rigid precedent of case law recognizing contributory negligence.[20] As of 1978, legislatures in 26 jurisdictions circumvented their courts' adherence to precedent by passing comparative negligence statutes.[21] In still other jurisdictions, the courts are reversing themselves and adopting the comparative negligence doctrine.[22] Application of the rule in those jurisdictions that have adopted it is not uniform among the jurisdictions. The courts disagree on whether or not a plaintiff who is equally or more at fault than the defendant can still recover damages. In other words, if the plaintiff is 50 percent or more at fault for the injury, can he or she recover? Some jurisdictions permit recovery in this situation; others do not. A compromise approach adopted by still other states permits recovery if the plaintiff's fault is 50 percent or less, but not if it is more.[23] The Minnesota Supreme Court has held that a patient could not be equally negligent with a physician because the subject matter of the negligence, where it involves the interpretation of medical matters, is an area in which the physician owes a greater duty to patients than patients do to themselves.[24]

Comparative negligence may have particular application in malpractice cases when the patient negligently fails to follow the physician's advice on self-care. In such cases, however, the courts will take into consideration the disparity in medical knowledge between patient and physician. Thus, if the physician, out of negligence, fails to give the patient adequate advice on the implications of the patient's condition, the patient's liability for injuries caused by improper self-care will be correspondingly lessened.[25] In such circumstances, damages are reduced to the degree that the plaintiff's negligence increases the extent of his or her injury.[26] Where the fault of the patient was subsequent to the fault of the physician and only served to aggravate the injury, only the amount of damages recoverable by the patient is affected.[27]

§ 3.40 ASSUMPTION OF RISK

The doctrine of assumption of risk recognizes generally that, if a patient has full knowledge of an open and visible condition, appreciates the dangers incident to that condition, and voluntarily acts with reference to that condition, the patient assumes or absorbs the risks of the attendant dangers. It is a matter of the patient's full knowledge and intelligent acquiescence.[28]

A physician must prove two basic elements to succeed with a defense of assumption of risk:

1. The patient-plaintiff must have known of the danger.
2. The patient-plaintiff must have voluntary exposure to the known danger.[29]

In a malpractice case the doctrine may apply in two ways, medical and nonmedical. Nonmedical risks are those that a patient, through common sense or experience, can appreciate without medical information. If a patient appreciates such a nonmedical risk and acts despite the existence of the risk, the patient cannot recover for injury resulting from the actualization of the potential risk. One commentator has asserted that the defense is more likely to be raised in cases involving questions other than those that are purely medical. Under a true application of the doctrine, a patient's assumption of risk would be difficult to assert successfully because a patient's medical knowledge usually is not adequate enough for him or her to realize that he or she is being treated negligently.[30]

CASE ILLUSTRATION

An elderly patient fell and injured herself in the physician's dressing room. The patient alleged that the physician was negligent in failing to have a nurse assist her in disrobing. The physician argued that the patient was offered assistance by his nurse, but the patient had refused to allow the nurse in the dressing room or to assist her and thereby assumed any risk involved. The court rejected the plaintiff's claim that the physician failed to meet the standard of care because no expert testimony was offered. The court affirmed the jury verdict for the defendant, accepting the defense of assumption of risk. (*Levett v. Etkind*, 1969)[31]

Medical risks are tied into the doctrine of informed consent (see § 1.33, Consent and Informed Consent). Specifically, if the physician has fulfilled the duty of informing the patient of risks and expected results of a treatment, then the patient's consent is informed and the patient has assumed the risks of the treatment. If the patient knows and comprehends the danger, yet voluntarily exposes himself or herself to it, the patient is deemed to have assumed the risk and is precluded from recovering for a resulting injury.[32] However, the patient is never held to assume the risk of negligent or improper treatment.[33]

The courts recognize that it is not the patient's duty to set his or her judgment against that of the physician, an expert in medicine. The physician-patient relationship assumes trust and confidence and that the patient has a right to rely on the professional skill of the physician.[34] Thus, in medical malpractice actions asserting patient assumption of risk is generally not a feasible defense. The superior knowledge and expertise of the physician in medical matters and the limited ability of the patient to comprehend the risk and dangers of certain treatments serve to undermine the effective use of this defense. The defense usually arises in exceptional circumstances—for example, when a patient is specifically warned of the risk and refuses to follow, or ignores, the physician's instructions.

§ 3.50 STATUTE OF LIMITATIONS

A person who has been intentionally or negligently injured by another must sue within a specified period after the injury occurred or the law will not permit the suit to be brought at all. The period within which the suit must be brought is specified by a "statute of limitations" and varies according to the nature of the right asserted by the plaintiff. Contract actions, for example, typically may be brought within six years of the date of breach (see § 2.20, Contract Theory), while a limitations period of only two to three years may be applicable in cases of malpractice. There is, however, a great variation in the statutes of limitations enforced in the various states, and nowhere is this more true than with respect to statutes governing medical malpractice actions. (See Table 3.2.) It is therefore necessary to set forth the basic rules that apply to such actions (although not all states follow all of the rules), and to remind physicians that they would be well-advised to consult an attorney familar with the particular laws of the state in which they practice. Nonetheless, certain basic rules apply.

The most restrictive rule, still followed in a number of jurisdictions, might be described as the "date of injury" rule. Under such statutes, the patient's right to bring suit accrues on the date of the alleged negligent act or omission, at which time a limitations period also begins to run.[35] However, because an injury caused by malpractice may not become apparent until many years after the date of treatment, it is quite possible under the date of injury rule for the patient to lose the right to sue before he or she is even aware of the injury.[36]

To avoid this difficulty, an increasing number of states today adhere to what is known as the "discovery rule." In general, the discovery rule postpones the start

TABLE 3.2* Statutes of Limitation for Malpractice, Contract and Wrongful Death** by Jurisdiction

State	Malpractice	Contract**	Wrongful Death[†]
Alabama	2 years after date of injury or 6 months after discovery of injury but within 4 years of date of injury	Same	2 years after death
Alaska	2 years	6 years	2 years after death
Arizona	3 years after date of injury or discovery	3 years	2 years after death
Arkansas	2 years after date of injury	Same	3 years after death
California	3 years after date of injury or 1 year after discovery but within 4 years of date of injury	2 years	3 years after death
Colorado	2 years after discovery but within 5 years of date of injury	Same	2 years after act resulting in death
Connecticut	1 year after date of injury or 1 year after discovery of injury but within 3 years of date of injury	3 years	1 year after act resulting in death or 1 year after discovery but within 3 years of act
Delaware	2 years after date of injury or upon discovery within 3 years of date of injury	3 years	2 years after death
District of Columbia	3 years	3 years	1 year after death
Florida	2 years after date of injury or 2 years after discovery but within 4 years of date of injury	3 years	2 years after death
Georgia	2 years after date of injury or 1 year after discovery	Same	2 years after death
Hawaii	2 years after discovery of injury but within 6 years of date of injury	6 years	Same as malpractice
Idaho	2 years after date of injury or 2 years after discovery of injury	4 years	2 years
Illinois	2 years after discovery but within 4 years of date of injury	5 years	Same as malpractice
Indiana	2 years after date of injury	Same	2 years after death
Iowa	2 years after discovery but within 6 years after date of injury	Same	Same as malpractice

Continued

*This table attempts to compare statutory limitations periods pertinent to malpractice actions and offers only a distillation of statutory meaning. Specific statutory language should be consulted for a particular case.

**Where the malpractice statute specifies a limitations period applicable to contracts, the word "same" appears in the contracts column. Where a different statute applies to contracts, the period is given even if, coincidentally, the period is the same.

[†]At Common Law the death of a human being could not be complained of as an injury in a civil court. Wrongful death statutes operate to abrogate this common law rule and provide a course of action for the survivor-beneficiaries.

TABLE 3.2* Continued

State	Malpractice	Contract**	Wrongful Death[†]
Kansas	2 years after date of injury or upon discovery but within 4 years after date of injury	3 years	2 years after death
Kentucky	1 year after date of injury	5 years	Same as malpractice
Louisiana	1 year after date of injury or 1 year after discovery but within three years after date of injury	Same	Same as malpractice
Maine	2 years after date of injury	6 years	2 years after death
Maryland	5 years after date of injury or 3 years after discovery, whichever is shorter	Same	2 years after death
Massachusetts	3 years after date of injury	Same	1 year after death
Michigan	2 years after discontinuing treatment or 6 months after discovery	6 years/3 years implied contract	Same as malpractice
Minnesota	2 years after date of injury	Same	3 years after act resulting in death
Mississippi	2 years after date of injury or discovery	3 years	Same as malpractice
Missouri	2 years after date of injury or 2 years after discovery but within 10 years of date of injury	5 years	2 years after death
Montana	3 years after date of injury	5 years	3 years after death
Nebraska	2 years after date of injury or 1 year after discovery but within 6 years after date of injury	Same	2 years after death
Nevada	4 years after date of injury or 2 years after discovery	4 years	Same as malpractice
New Hampshire	2 years after date of injury or discovery	6 years	2 years after death
New Jersey	2 years after date of injury or discovery	Same	2 years after death
New Mexico	3 years after date of injury	4 years	3 years after death
New York	2-1/2 years after date of injury or 1 year after discovery of foreign object	6 years	2 years after death
North Carolina	3 years after date of injury or 1 year after discovery but within 4 years after date of injury or within 10 years after date of injury if foreign object is discovered	3 years	2 years after death
North Dakota	2 years after date of injury or discovery plus 6 months for fraudulent concealment	6 years	2 years after death
Ohio	1 year after date of injury or discovery but within 4 years of date of injury or termination of physician-patient relationship	6 years	2 years after death
Oklahoma	2 years after discovery but within 3 years of date of injury (damages limited after 3 years)	Same	Same as malpractice
Oregon	2 years after discovery but within 5 years of date of injury	6 years	3 years after death
Pennsylvania	2 years after date of injury	6 years	1 year after death
Rhode Island	2 years after date of injury or 1 year after discovery	6 years	2 years after death

TABLE 3.2* Continued

State	Malpractice	Contract**	Wrongful Death†
South Carolina	6 years	6 years	6 years after death
South Dakota	3 years after date of injury	Same	3 years after death
Tennessee	1 year after date of injury or 1 year after discovery but within 3 years of date of injury	6 years	1 year after act resulting in death
Texas	2 years after date of injury or discovery	2 years	Same as malpractice
Utah	2 years after discovery but within 4 years after date of injury	Same	2 years after death
Vermont	3 years after date of injury or discovery	6 years	2 years after death
Virginia	2 years after date of injury or discovery if injury is fraudulently concealed	3 years	2 years after death
Washington	3 years after date of injury or 1 year after discovery but within 8 years of date of injury	3 years	Same as malpractice
West Virginia	2 years after date of injury or discovery if injury is fraudulently concealed	5 years	2 years after death
Wisconsin	3 years after date of injury	Same	3 years after death
Wyoming	2 years after date of injury or 2 years after discovery	8 years	2 years after death

of the limitations period until the patient knows, or in the exercise of reasonable diligence should know, of his or her injury.[37] Lack of knowledge of the extent of the injury, however, does not postpone the beginning of the limitations period. Instead, the period begins to run as soon as the patient is, or should be, aware of any injury at all and its possible connection to malpractice.[38]

In determining at what point a patient should have discovered a cause of action for malpractice, the patient's experience, background, and medical skills may be taken into account. Thus, a court may impute knowledge of injury to a health care professional if, under the circumstances, the professional's special training should have revealed the injury to him or her, even if the available facts would not have indicated to the typical patient that anything was amiss.[39]

Determining whether or not a patient has exercised reasonable diligence to discover an injury is also a matter decided by the facts of a particular case. However, it has been held that a patient has exercised reasonable diligence if he or she has relied on repeated assurances of recovery made by the treating physician when there is no apparent reason to disbelieve the physician.[40]

Having stated the rule generally, it should be noted that some diversity of opinion exists regarding just what must be discovered for the limitations period to begin. A majority of jurisdictions following the rule hold that it is the patient's discovery of the injury which is relevant.[41] A minority, however, count the limitations period from the date on which the patient either discovers, or through reasonable diligence should have discovered, the specific acts or omissions of the physician which are alleged to constitute malpractice.[42]

Certain other doctrines, independent of the date of injury and discovery rules, may "toll" or postpone the running of the statute. Many states hold that the statute does not begin to run, regardless of the date of malpractice or the status of the patient's knowledge, until the physician-patient relationship terminates.[43] This relationship is a purely personal one. Thus, the statute begins to run as soon as the physician has performed his or her last services for a particular patient. This is true even when the patient relies on the physician's referral to another physician or continues to use, without the physician's knowledge, a drug the physician prescribed.[44] Some states, in refinement of this rule, follow a doctrine known as the "continuous treatment" doctrine. In these states, the mere continuity of a professional relationship between a particular physician and patient does not toll the statute. Instead, the statute is suspended only as long as the patient continues to be treated by the allegedly negligent physician for the same condition or a condition related to the one that occasioned the alleged act of malpractice.[45] However, most courts following the continuous treatment doctrine hold that the statute begins to run as soon as the patient discovers, or should have discovered, the injury and its connection to the negligent act.[46] Other courts may not make this exception.[47]

A physician's fraudulent concealment of the results of malpractice will also toll the statute. Thus, a physician's repeated and knowingly false assurances of recovery or absence of injury will suspend the statute, even though in the absence of such assurances the patient would be charged with actual or imputed knowledge of injury.[48] Most courts hold that the physician's actual knowledge of a wrong done the patient is essential to a finding of fraudulent concealment in a malpractice action.[49] The courts disagree, however, as to whether an affirmative act on the part of the physician is necessary for such a finding. Some jurisdictions will not find fraudulent concealment unless the physician makes knowingly false statements to the patient;[50] others consider it sufficient that the physician failed to disclose relevant information in his or her possession.[51] Disagreement also exists on whether the statute begins to run on the date the patient actually discovers the fraud,[52] or on the date he or she should have discovered it.[53]

Still other circumstances may toll an otherwise applicable statute of limitations. Some states have case decisions or statutes that say the statute cannot run against an individual who was disabled by mental incapacity[54] or infancy (any age below the age of majority)[55] at the time his or her cause of action accrued, and was therefore unable to bring an action on his or her own behalf. The statute does not begin to run against that individual until the disability is removed by either recovery of mental capacity[56] or attainment of the age of majority.[57] Most state statutes require that actions be brought within a specified period after the removal of the disability.

An action may be brought on behalf of the incompetent by either a parent or a guardian; and these actions may also be used to recompense the parent or guardian for expenses paid in consequence of the incompetent's injury. However, a parent or guardian's failure to seek recovery for the individual's personal losses within the statutory period does not remove the incompetent's right to recover his or her own damages.[58] To toll the statute, the disability must exist at the time the cause of action accrues. A disability acquired subsequent to the accrual of the cause of action (as, for example, mental incapacity suffered after an act of malpractice has been discovered) will not toll the statute.[59] An exception may be made, however, if the injury for which recovery is sought caused the disability.[60]

In the event that a foreign object is mistakenly left in a patient's body by the physician, a foreign object rule will be applied in some states. Under this rule, the statute is suspended until the patient either discovers or should have discovered the presence of the object.[61] Although virtually the same as the discovery rule, the foreign object rule may be applied in jurisdictions that do not follow a discovery rule in other types of malpractice cases.[62] Most commonly, the rule is applied in situations where the object involved (e.g., a sponge or forceps) was clearly not intended to remain inside the patient's body.[63] A few jurisdictions, however, have applied the rule in cases where the object involved was intentionally inserted in the patient's body but later broke or deteriorated.[64] The foreign object rule has not been successfully applied in cases of anesthesiological malpractice.

CASE ILLUSTRATION

After giving birth to her third child, plaintiff suffered sciatic type pain and stiffening in her right side for a period of five months. After the two-year statute of limitations applicable to medical malpractice actions had expired, plaintiff and her husband brought suit against the attending anesthesiologist, alleging negligence in the administration of saddle block anesthesia. The plaintiff sought to avoid the statutory problem by arguing that the administration of the anesthesia amounted to the introduction of a foreign object into her body, thus suspending the statute until she discovered the anesthesia to be the cause of her injury. Although recognizing the foreign object rule, the court rejected the plaintiff's argument, and held her suit barred by the two-year statute of limitations. The court indicated that the foreign object rule was intended to apply only to objects unintentionally inserted which retain their identity over time. In contrast, noted the court, an anesthetic is intentionally injected and does not retain its identity in the body after passage of time. (*Rothman v. Silber*, 1966)[65]

This case, however, does not necessarily represent a universal rule. At least one other court has indicated that it would apply the foreign object rule in a case involving alleged anesthesiological malpractice, should such a case arise.[66]

In a majority of jurisdictions any action brought by the survivors of a patient who dies as a consequence of malpractice will be subject to the statutory period applicable in wrongful death actions and not to the period otherwise used in malpractice cases.[67] (See Table 3.2.) A wrongful death action allows the survivors of a person wrongfully killed or fatally injured to recover, on their own behalf, the net economic benefit they would have received from the decedent had he or she lived. Some jurisdictions also permit survivors to recover damages for loss of society and companionship in wrongful death actions, particularly when a child dies and the traditional measure of damages would lead to no recovery at all.[68] The statutory period for wrongful death actions begins to run on the date of death, not on the date of injury leading to death.[69] In some states, however, the death of the patient does not by itself affect the statutory period. In those states the survivors' action will be subject to the period generally used in malpractice cases.[70]

§ 3.60 RES JUDICATA AND COLLATERAL ESTOPPEL

To promote legal efficiency, economy and fairness, legal doctrines exist which preclude a party from relitigating a claim or an issue he or she previously litigated to a final conclusion. Known as res judicata and collateral estoppel, these doctrines may in appropriate circumstances be pleaded as a special defense in malpractice cases. These two rules of law are quite distinct and should not be confused.

The doctrine of res judicata states that a valid, final judgment rendered on the merits of the case constitutes an absolute bar to subsequent relitigation between the same parties, or those in privity* with them.[71] As might be expected, difficult problems can arise in individual cases when a plea of res judicata is interposed. Was the original decision based "on the merits" of the case? Did privity exist between the party sought to be precluded and one of the parties to the original suit? Is the present litigation based upon the same claim or demand as the original? For purposes of malpractice, the most important question raised by a plea of res judicata is the latter, and only that question will be given detailed consideration here.

Suppose, for example, a physician negligently uses a drug that causes injury to a patient's sight and hearing. The patient recovers damages for the injury to his sight in a malpractice action, but does not plead injury to his hearing. Next, in a separate action, the patient seeks to recover for his hearing loss. Can he do so? No. Res judicata precludes relitigation not only of claims actually decided in an earlier

---

*Privity refers to a special relationship between parties that the law recognizes because the transactions between them generate mutual or successive rights or interests in the subject matter of the transaction.

action but also of claims that *should* have been determined in the earlier action.[72] Because the patient's claim for hearing loss arose out of the same negligent act as did his earlier claim for loss of sight, both actions involved the same claim and should have appeared in a single suit. Failing to plead them as one, the patient is precluded from subsequently raising the hearing claim. Suppose in the second action the patient does not plead that the physician negligently injured his hearing, but that the physician breached a warranty that the drug would not injure his health. Does the second theory get the patient past the bar of res judicata? No. The fact that the physician's act can be variously characterized does not defeat the identity of the claims.[73]

In contrast, collateral estoppel applies to issues of fact, not to claims. The doctrine states that where a question of fact essential to a judgment was litigated and determined by valid and final judgment, the issue cannot again be litigated between the same parties in any future lawsuit.[74] Thus collateral estoppel unlike res judicata cannot be used to preclude litigation of matters which have not already been litigated.[75]

The effect of collateral estoppel might best be seen through a continuation of the example above. Suppose the physician, having been found negligent in the patient's action for loss of sight, brings an action against a patient to recover overdue payments. The patient pleads in defense that he owes no debt because the treatment was negligent. Need the patient once again prove the physician's negligence? No. Because the earlier finding of negligence was actually litigated and necessary to the judgment (the physician could not have been held liable had he not been found negligent), the physician will be collaterally estopped from relitigating the issue of his negligence. The patient need not prove the physician's negligence again.

A question of some importance to law today is whether collateral estoppel may be invoked by someone who is neither a party to the original action nor in privity with someone who was. For example, if patient A successfully recovers from physician B on grounds that B was negligent in administering a certain drug, can patient C, who had the same condition as A and received the same drug from B, recover from B *solely* on the basis of the earlier judgment? Patient C may indeed be able to do so. The U.S. Supreme Court has recently indicated that such "offensive use of collateral estoppel," i.e., where the plaintiff seeks to foreclose the defendant from litigating an issue litigated unsuccessfully in a prior suit or action, is generally permissible.[76] In deciding whether special circumstances barring the use of offensive collateral estoppel exist, wide discretion is left in the hands of the trial judge.[77]

Defensive use of collateral estoppel occurs when a defendant seeks to prevent a plaintiff from asserting a claim the plaintiff has previously litigated and lost against another defendant. Thus, if physician B is specifically found to have been not negligent in giving a certain drug to patient A, A will be collaterally estopped in attempting to prove physician C's negligence, if C gave A the same drug under the same conditions. Such defensive use of collateral estoppel is widely accepted.[78]

A basic point to remember in all questions of collateral estoppel is that a party uninvolved in the earlier action, whether in person or through privity, can *never* be collaterally estopped. As seen above, however, such a person may be able to *assert* collateral estoppel against a person who was involved in the earlier action.

§ 3.70 RELEASE FROM LIABILITY FORMS

Generally, individuals may not contract against the effects of their own negligence, and agreements attempting that are invalid. This is particularly true in cases where public policy requires that the duties involved be performed non-negligently, and where the party releasing rights holds a weaker bargaining position. It is thus established by courts that have passed on the question, that a physician may not, in advance, relieve himself of liability for malpractice.[79] In other words, a contract between patient and physician signed prior to treatment in which the patient releases his right to recover damages in the event of malpractice is invalid and will not be enforced.[80] For an example of such a voidable release, see Appendix F.

Release of liability forms may be effective, however, if signed before the performance of an experimental and inherently dangerous surgical procedure or course of treatment. In such cases, parties may validly contract to exempt medical practitioners from liability for injuries that may arise as consequences of the non-negligent, proper performance of the procedure. For example, an experimental procedure, because of its inherent dangers, constitutes a departure from customary and accepted practice and is thus a target for malpractice even when performed in a non-negligent manner. A release of liability form will render the procedure unactionable. Such an agreement will not, however, exempt the physicians involved from liability for any adverse consequences resulting from the negligent performance of such a procedure.[81]

After malpractice has occurred, patients may validly release their rights to recover in a lawsuit in return for a specified consideration.

CASE ILLUSTRATION

A patient became seriously incapacitated during surgery at which the physician-defendant served as anesthesiologist. The patient and his wife filed suit against the anesthesiologist, alleging negligence. In consideration of the

§ 3.70   *Release from Liability Forms*   115

sum of $400,000, the wife individually, as guardian of her incapacitated husband, and as representative of the couple's children, dismissed the suit and agreed not to sue the anesthesiologist for any present or future claims arising from the alleged acts of negligence. The patient subsequently died, and his estate filed a wrongful death action against the anesthesiologist on behalf of the children. An entry of judgment for the anesthesiologist was upheld on the ground that the covenant not to sue executed by the wife in her capacity as representative of the children constituted a bar to the subsequent action. *(Hutton v. Davis, 1976)*[82]

For a release to be valid, the person giving it must be competent.[83] The release must not be obtained by fraud,[84] misrepresentation,[85] or duress.[86] A physician's knowingly false statements of absence of injury or probable recovery will invalidate a release if the patient entered into the agreement on the basis of those assurances. Mutual mistake will also constitute sufficient grounds to set aside a release.[87] If, for example, both physician and patient believed at the time they executed the agreement that the patient's injuries were minor, but time reveals the injuries as serious, the release signed by the patient will not prevent a malpractice action.

NOTES

1. W. Prosser, Handbook of the Law of Torts 416-17 (4th ed. 1971).
2. Bird v. Pritchard, 33 Ohio App. 2d 31, 291 N.E.2d 769 (1973).
3. Heller v. Medine, 50 App. Div. 2d 831, 377 N.Y.S.2d 100 (1975).
4. Martineau v. Nelson, 311 Minn. 92, 247 N.W.2d 409 (Minn. 1976).
5. Mackey v. Greenview Hosp., Inc., 587 S.W.2d 249 (Ky. App. 1979).
6. Kimbal, *Contributory Negligence as a Defense to Medical Malpractice in California*, 8 U. S. F. L. Rev. 386 (1973), *citing*, Champs v. Stone, 74 Ohio App. 344, 48 N.E.2d 803 (1944).
7. Sendejar v. Alice Physicians & Surgeons Hosp., 555 S.W.2d 879 (Tex. 1977).
8. Young v. State, 92 Misc. 2d 795, 401 N.Y.S.2d 955 (1978); Bennett v. State, 49 Misc. 2d 306, 299 N.Y.S.2d 288 (1969).
9. Bess Ambulance Inc. v. Boll, 208 So.2d 308 (Fla. App. 1968).
10. Southeastern Ky. Baptist Hosp. v. Bruce, 539 S.W.2d 286 (Ky. 1976); Warner v. Kiowa County Hosp. Auth., 551 P.2d 1179 (Okla. 1976).
11. Clark v. Piedmont Hosp., Inc., 117 Ga. App. 875, 162 S.E.2d 468 (1968).
12. Johnson v. United States, 271 F. Supp. 205 (W.D. Ark. 1967).
13. Musachia v. Rosman, 190 So.2d 47 (Fla. App. 1967).
14. W. Prosser, *supra* note 1, at 416.
15. Wells v. Women's Hosp. Foundation, 286 So.2d 439, *writ denied*, 288 So.2d 646 (La. App. 1973).

Notes: Chapter III

16. Martineau v. Nelson, *supra* note 4.
17. D. Louisell & H. Williams, Medical Malpractice, § 9.03, at 249-50.
18. W. Prosser, *supra* note 1, at 417.
19. *Id.* at 436.
20. Mackey v. Greenview Hosp., Inc., *supra* note 5.
21. Ark. Stat. Ann. §§ 27-1763 to 1765 (1979); Colo. Rev. Stat. Ann. § 13-21-111 (Bradford Supp. 1980); Conn. Gen. Stat. Ann. §§ 52-572h (West Supp. 1981); Ga. Code Ann. §§ 94-703, 105-603 (Harrison 1968 & Supp. 1980); Hawaii Rev. Stat. § 663-31 (1976); Idaho Code Ann. §§ 6-801 to 806 (1979); Kan. Stat. Ann. §§ 60-258a to 258b (1976); Mass. Gen. Laws Ann. ch. 231, § 85 (Supp. 1980); Minn. Stat. Ann. § 604.01 (West Supp. 1981); Miss. Code Ann. § 11-7-15 (1972); Mont. Rev. Codes Ann. §§ 58-607.1, .2 (1970 & Supp. 1977); Neb. Rev. Stat. § 25-1151 (1965); Nev. Rev. Stat. § 41.141 (1979); N.H. Rev. Stat. Ann. § 507:7-a (Supp. 1979); N.J. Stat. Ann. §§ 2A:15-5.1 to 5.3 (West Supp. 1981-82); N.Y. Civ. Prac. Law §§ 1411-13 (McKinney 1976); N.D. Cent. Code § 9-10-07 (1975); Okla. Stat. Ann. tit. 23, §§ 13, 14 (West Supp. 1980-81); Or. Rev. Stat. §§ 18.470-.510 (1979); R.I. Gen. Laws Ann. §§ 9-20-4, 4.1 (Supp. 1980); S.D. Comp. Laws § 20-9-2 (1979); Tex. Civ. Code Ann. art. 2212a, §§ 1, 2 (Vernon Supp. 1980-81); Utah Code Ann. §§ 78-27-37 to 43 (1977); Vt. Stat. Ann. tit. 12, § 1036 (Supp. 1980); Wash. Rev. Code Ann. § 4.22.010 (Supp. 1981); Wyo. Stat. Ann. § 1-1-109 (1980).
22. *See, e.g.*, Kaatz v. State, 540 P.2d 1037 (Alaska 1975); Nga Li v. Yellow Cab Co., 13 Cal. 3d 804, 532 P.2d 1226, 119 Cal. Rptr. 858 (1975); Placek v. City of Sterling Heights, 405 Mich. 638, 275 N.W.2d 511 (1979).
23. Miller v. Trinity Medical Center, 260 N.W.2d 4 (N.D. 1977).
24. Martineau v. Nelson, *supra* note 4.
25. *Id.*
26. Heller v. Medine, *supra* note 3.
27. Bird v. Pritchard, *supra* note 2.
28. Mainfort v. Giannestras, 49 Ohio Op. 440, 111 N.E.2d 692 (1951); Morrison v. MacNamara, 407 A.2d 555 (D.C. App. 1979).
29. Morrison v. MacNamara, *supra* note 28.
30. D. Harney, Medical Malpractice 243 (1973).
31. Levett v. Etkind, 158 Conn. 567, 265 A.2d 70 (1969).
32. Munson v. Bishop Clarkson Mem. Hosp., 186 Neb. 778, 186 N.W.2d 492 (1971).
33. Mainfort v. Giannestras, *supra* note 28.
34. Los Alamos Medical Center v. Coe, 58 N.M. 686, 275 P.2d 175 (1954).
35. Cook v. Soltman, 96 Idaho 187, 525 P.2d 969 (1974); Olson v. St. Croix Valley Mem. Hosp., 55 Wis. 2d 628, 201 N.W.2d 63 (1972).
36. Peterson v. Roloff, 57 Wis. 2d 1, 203 N.W.2d 699 (1973).
37. Owens v. White, 380 F.2d 310 (9th Cir. 1967).
38. Hulver v. United States, 562 F.2d 1132 (8th Cir. 1977).
39. Jones v. Sugar, 18 Md. App. 99, 305 A.2d 219 (1973).
40. Toman v. Creighton Mem. St. Joseph's Hosp., 191 Neb. 751, 217 N.W.2d 484 (1974).
41. Anguiano v. St. James Hosp., 51 Ill App. 3d 229, 366 N.E.2d 930 (1977).
42. Kelleher v. Mills, 70 Mich. App. 360, 245 N.W.2d 749 (1976).
43. Shrewsbury v. Smith, 511 F.2d 1058 (6th Cir. 1975).
44. Millbaugh v. Gilmore, 30 Ohio St. 2d 319, 285 N.E.2d 19 (1972).
45. Tod v. Boutelle, 91 Misc. 2d 464, 398 N.Y.S.2d 128 (1977).
46. Lopez v. Swyer, 15 N.J. Super. 237, 279 A.2d 116 (1971).
47. Hundley v. St. Francis Hosp. 161 Cal. App. 2d 800, 327 P.2d 131 (1958).

48. Swope v. Printz, 468 S.W.2d 34 (Mo. 1968).
49. Turner v. Rust, 385 S.W.2d 175 (Ky. App. 1964).
50. Layton v. Allen, 246 A.2d 794 (Del. 1968).
51. Kauchick v. Williams, 435 S.W.2d 342 (Mo. 1968).
52. Seitz v. Jones, 370 P.2d 300 (Okla. 1961).
53. Crawford v. McDonald, 125 Ga. App. 289, 187 S.E.2d 542 (1972).
54. Lacy v. Ferrence, 222 Ga. 635, 151 S.E.2d 763 (1966).
55. Barnum v. Martin, 135 Ga. App. 712, 219 S.E.2d 341 (1975); Mich. Comp. Laws Ann. § 600.5851 (1968 & Supp. 1981-82).
56. Seymour v. Lofgreen, 209 Kan. 72, 495 P.2d 969 (1972).
57. Canterbury v. Spence, 464 F.2d 772 (D.C. Cir.), *cert. denied*, 409 U.S. 1064 (1972).
58. Bergstreser v. Mitchell, 448 F. Supp. 10 (E.D. Mo. 1977).
59. Hogan v. Stumper, 257 Md. 520, 263 A.2d 571 (1970).
60. Chartener v. Kice, 270 F. Supp. 432 (E.D.N.Y. 1967).
61. Flanagan v. Mount Eden Gen. Hosp., 24 N.Y.2d 427, 248 N.E.2d 871, 301 N.Y.S.2d 23 (1969).
62. Stoner v. Carr, 97 Idaho 641, 550 P.2d 259 (1976).
63. Billings v. Sisters of Mercy, 86 Idaho 485, 389 P.2d 224 (1964).
64. Murphy v. St. Charles Hosp., 35 A.D.2d 64, 312 N.Y.S.2d 978 (1974).
65. Rothman v. Silber, 90 N.J. Super. 22, 216 A.2d 18 (1966).
66. Prince v. Trustees of Univ. of Penn., 282 F. Supp. 832 (E.D. Pa. 1968).
67. Lambert v. Michel, 364 So.2d 248 (La. App. 1978).
68. Selders v. Armertrout, 90 Neb. 275, 207 N.W.2d 686 (1973).
69. Smith v. McComb Infirmary Ass'n, 196 So.2d 91 (Miss. 1967).
70. Weiss v. Bigman, 84 Mich. App. 487, 270 N.W.2d 5 (1978).
71. Saylor v. Lindsley, 391 F.2d 965 (2d Cir. 1968).
72. Tutt v. Doby, 459 F.2d 1195 (D.C. Cir. 1972).
73. Fassas v. First Bank & Trust Co., 353 Mass. 628, 233 N.E.2d 924 (1968).
74. Sanders v. State, 242 So.2d 412 (Miss. 1970).
75. Adzigian v. Harron, 297 F. Supp. 1317 (E.D. Pa. 1969).
76. Parklane Hosiery Co. v. Shore, 439 U.S. 322, 99 S. Ct. 645 (1979).
77. *Id.*
78. *Id.*
79. Belshaw v. Fernstein, 258 Cal. App. 2d 771, 65 Cal Rptr. 788 (1968).
80. Olsen v. Molzen, 558 S.W.2d 429 (Tenn. 1977).
81. Colton v. New York Hosp., 98 Misc. 2d 957, 414 N.Y.S.2d 866 (1979).
82. Hutton v. Davis, 26 Ariz. App. 215, 547 P.2d 486 (1976).
83. Fleming v. Ponziani, 24 N.Y.2d 105, 247 N.E.2d 114, 299 N.Y.S.2d 134 (1969).
84. Brady v. Johnson, 512 S.W.2d 359 (Tex. Civ. App. 1974).
85. Hendricks v. Simper, 24 Ariz. App. 415, 539 P.2d 529 (1975).
86. Hylton v. Phillips, 270 Or. 760, 529 P.2d 906 (1974).
87. Central of Georgia Ry. Co. v. Ramsey, 275 Ala. 7, 151 So.2d 725 (1962).

Chapter IV

The Lawsuit in Court

§ 4.10 INTRODUCTION

When patients feel they have suffered an injury due to physician malpractice, they may retain legal counsel to investigate the treatment received to determine whether a lawsuit alleging malpractice against the physician should be filed. The purpose of such lawsuits is to recover money damages (see § 1.60, Damages) from the physician for the injury caused by the alleged medical malpractice.

Although the courtroom, the suit, and the attendant proceedings are primarily the responsibility of the physician's attorney,[*] physicians should familiarize themselves with the mechanics of malpractice suits and court proceedings. This chapter attempts to provide a general background helpful to the physician confronted with a malpractice suit. References to the Federal Rules will indicate the procedure followed in a majority of courts.[**]

§ 4.20 PLEADINGS

Pleadings—the patient's complaint, and the physician's answer—are the first official documents filed in a lawsuit. Essentially, pleadings are the mechanisms used to define legal and factual issues of a lawsuit. Effectively used, pleadings may eliminate irrelevant and uncontested claims at the outset of the suit. By the close of pleadings, a reasonably accurate blueprint of the issues to be argued at trial is

---

[*]Usually the attorney representing the physician is chosen and paid for by the physician's malpractice insurance carrier. Increasingly, however, physicians are retaining personal counsel to work with counsel provided by the insurance company to insure that their personal interests are protected in the event that their interests and those of the insurance company diverge.

[**]The Federal Rules of Civil Procedure, first adopted in 1938, govern procedure in all federal courts. About half the states have adopted these rules virtually unchanged, and all the others have revised their procedure under the Rules' influence. *See* C. Wright, Law of Federal Courts 294 (3d ed. 1976).

§ 4.21 The Patient's Complaint

For the patient-plaintiff's attorney, the first step in bringing a legal action against a physician-defendant is drafting and filing a complaint. The basic purpose of the complaint is to state pertinent information. Under the Federal Rules, the essential concern is whether the complaint reveals enough information to allow the physician to understand the reason for the suit and to respond. The usual standard is that the patient-plaintiff must present a claim showing that he or she is entitled to some relief.[1] The Federal Rule system is called notice pleading because the emphasis is on affording sufficient notice of the suit to the defendant; notice pleading generally avoids elaborate rules. (See Appendix G for sample complaint.)

Some states require fact pleading, which requires that the patient state the essential facts of the case with enough specificity to alert the physician to what the patient proposes to prove in court. This requirement is designed to give the physician (and the attorney) the information necessary to prepare a defense quite early in the suit. Under notice pleading, the physician would have access to this information in the discovery phase, which occurs after the pleadings. (See § 4.30, Discovery.)

§ 4.22 The Physician's Answer

After the plaintiff's complaint has been filed, the physician will have a specified time within which to file an answer. Under the Federal Rules,[2] the physician must respond within 20 days. Some states, for example California,[3] allow a longer period (30 days), while others, like Washington,[4] have a significantly shorter requirement (10 days). (See Appendix H for sample answer.)

In the answer, the defendant takes issue with the plaintiff and the plaintiff's assertions of fact and law. The defendant may admit certain factual allegations set forth in the plaintiff's complaint (yes, the physician-defendant did treat the patient-plaintiff) and deny others (no, the actions of the physician-defendant were not negligent). As a general rule, a defendant's failure to deny a fact presented in the complaint constitutes an admission of that fact. The physician's attorney is responsible for responding appropriately to the plaintiff's complaint.

Denials of the facts set forth in the complaint constitute negative defenses. Affirmative defenses should also be raised. These are claims that there are other factual circumstances which, if proven, would exonerate the defendant even though the facts as alleged by the complaint are true. For instance, a physician may assert that the patient-plaintiff assumed the risk of injury when he or she consented to the treatment proposed by the physician with full knowledge of the attendant risk of injury. (See Chapter III, Defenses.)

§ 4.30 DISCOVERY

Following, or sometimes during, the pleadings stage, the parties may begin discovery. The discovery process entails just what its name implies: the discovery of facts and evidence relevant to the upcoming trial. The American legal system provides a number of mechanisms to achieve this goal, including depositions, written interrogatories, subpoenas for the production of documents and things, and physical examinations.

The avowed purpose of discovery is straightforward: to simplify and clarify the issues and to allow for the gathering of accurate information in advance of trial. Courts tend to construe discovery requests liberally in order to enable the parties to identify the true facts and circumstances of the case. Liberal discovery serves several purposes. First, it enables the parties to gather all of the relevant facts and evidence so that each can present the best possible case at trial. Second, it is hoped that the discovery process will minimize the chance that one party's ignorance of key facts or an opponent's surprise presentation of unknown evidence will defeat the truth-finding goal of the trial court. Full and open disclosure of the facts also encourages settlements where appropriate. If discovery indicates that one party is likely to prevail at trial, a settlement may save both the court and the parties the additional time, effort, and expense of a trial.[5]

Another, albeit illegitimate, use of discovery may be the harassment of an opponent. Each party is given wide latitude in determining the extent of discovery necessary; abuse of that discretion can subject an opponent to great expenditures of time and money. For example, one party may flood an opponent with hundreds of far-reaching written interrogatories (see § 4.33, Written Interrogatories) in the chance hope of discovering something important ("a fishing expedition") while at the same time subjecting the opponent to great effort and cost.

§ 4.31 Depositions

A primary discovery mechanism is the deposition, a record of the sworn testimony of a party or a witness taken before an authorized individual who is usually an officer of the court.[6] Generally, depositions may be taken after the commencement of an action in any court, and all parties and attorneys have the right to be present to examine and cross-examine the witness. In malpractice suits, depositions usually take place in either the physician's or lawyer's office. A court reporter takes down the witness's testimony after swearing in the witness. They also develop evidence for use at trial: when a witness will be unable to appear at trial, the deposition serves as a means of preserving the witness's testimony.[7] Such testimony is entitled to the same consideration by the finder of fact (judge or jury) as testimony given in open court.[8] Also, deposition testimony can be used to impeach the testimony of a witness who actually appears at trial offering testimony contradicting his or her

§ 4.31 Depositions

prior deposition testimony.[9] Primarily, the deposition enables a party to discover and preserve evidentiary information.[10]

Under the Federal Rules there are, however, three basic limitations to the scope of examination.[11]

1. The information must be non-privileged. (See § 4.46, Physician-Patient Privilege.)
2. The information must be admissible under the rules of evidence or reasonably calculated to lead to discovery of admissible evidence.
3. The information must be relevant to the subject matter involved in the pending action.

If a witness bases a refusal to answer on one of these limitations, the court may order the witness to answer.[12] If the refusal was without justification, the refusing party may be required to pay the expenses incurred by the examining party in obtaining the court order to answer and the deposition will be resumed.[13] In general, witnesses should not refuse to answer for insubstantial reasons, and then, only on instruction from their attorney.

Deposition of Experts: Under the Federal Rules defining expert deposition, a litigant can discover certain facts known and opinions held by experts the other party intends to call as witnesses and, under certain circumstances, the experts the party has retained in anticipation of or preparation for the suit.[14] Each party can require the other to identify, in written interrogatories (see § 4.33, Written Interrogatories), each expert witness they intend to use, the substance of the facts on which forthcoming expert testimony will be based, and a summary of the expert opinions. The court may also allow further discovery of expert witnesses by other means, e.g., oral deposition.[15] For an expert retained in anticipation of or preparation for a suit, but not as a potential witness, the opposing party may discover the expert's facts and opinions only upon showing that it would be impracticable to obtain facts and opinions on the same subject by other means.[16]

In malpractice suits in which the mental or physical condition of the patient is an issue, the physician may request a court order to require the patient to submit to a physical or mental examination.[17] If the court orders the examination, the patient can obtain by discovery the detailed written report of the examining physician, including findings, test results, diagnosis, and conclusions.[18] The party requesting discovery in these situations must pay the expert a reasonable fee for time spent responding to the discovery request "unless manifest injustice would result."[19] In some cases the discovering party must also pay a portion of the fees and expenses the other party incurred in obtaining facts and opinions from the expert.[20]

The federal discovery rules concerning experts attempt to facilitate the presentation and clarification of issues at trial while guarding against the danger that one party will unfairly use the other party's experts to prepare his or her own case.

Some states allow pretrial discovery of experts only at the trial court's discretion.[21] The judge may require the deposing party to pay the expert a reasonable fee for the time involved.[22] In at least one state, Michigan, the state appellate court has ruled that a physician has a property right in his or her professional opinion and need not divulge it even under subpoena.[23]

§ 4.32 *Subpoena*

A subpoena is an order issued under the seal of the court which commands the individual to attend and give testimony at the time and the place specified.[24] Physicians may resent having to appear in response to a subpoena; some feel a written statement should suffice. However, the adversarial structure of the American legal system places a great premium on the face-to-face confrontation of witnesses and the right of cross-examination. This is reflected in the fact that failure to obey a subpoena may subject the subpoenaed individual to a contempt of court citation or other consequences.*

If the physician is subpoenaed on behalf of the party opposing his or her patient, the physician should inform the patient and the patient's attorney. If the state in which the suit is filed honors the physician-patient privilege, the patient's attorney may want to quash the subpoena.

WARNING: Unless counsel advises otherwise, subpoenas are to be taken seriously.

§ 4.33 *Written Interrogatories*

Written interrogatories are similar to depositions in purpose and scope. Parties may use written interrogatories, like depositions, to take the testimony of any person, including another party, in order to discover information or to use the written information as evidence in the action.[25] Written interrogatories are basically what the name implies. The discovering party drafts a list of written questions which is sent to the opposing party or witness who returns written answers to the discovering party.

---

*Individuals found to be in contempt of court may be ordered to appear again, fined, or jailed until they comply with the court's order. "Other consequences," where the noncomplying person is a party to the action, include: staying of all further proceedings until the party complies; striking all or part of that party's pleadings; considering the matter which the order dealt with to be established in favor of the party obtaining the order; requiring the disobedient party to pay all reasonable expenses, including attorney's fees, caused by the failure. (*See* Fed. R. Civ. P.37(b).)

§ 4.34 *Production of Documents and Things*

Discovery procedures also give a party the right to inspect relevant documents and tangible objects that may be held by or in the possession of an opposing party or witness.[26] If the opposing party refuses to deliver the materials voluntarily upon request, the discovering party may seek a court order compelling inspection.[27] Generally, the same rules apply to court orders compelling inspection as to orders (subpoenas) compelling depositions.[*] For example, if a state has a statute establishing the physician-patient privilege, a patient may assert the privilege to withhold certain information from the physician-defendant. Under the privilege, the patient could prevent the physician-defendant from inspecting medical records and from directly questioning (by deposition) the patient's other physicians about the injury at issue in the case. (See § 1.31, Physician-Patient Relationship.)

The Work Product Exception: Under the generally recognized work product exception, a party may not ordinarily obtain documents, or work products, prepared in anticipation of litigation or for trial by or for the party. This exception includes work products of the party's attorney, consultant, insurer, or agent. However, if the discovering party can show a substantial need for the materials and that he or she cannot obtain the equivalent of the materials without undue hardship, the court, under the Federal Rules, may order discovery of the requested work products. The Federal Rules also require the court, when ordering discovery, to protect against disclosure of the mental impressions, opinions, or legal theories of an attorney concerning the case.[28]

§ 4.35 *Physical Examinations*

Under the Federal Rules, a physician-defendant may request the court to require the plaintiff to submit to a physical examination by a physician in order to ascertain the nature, extent, and permanence of any alleged injuries. The decision, however, lies within the discretion of the trial court.[29] To obtain the order, the physician must show that the patient's physical condition is in contention and that the physician has "good cause" to request an examination. Should the trial court order an examination, the plaintiff may have the right to have his or her own physician and attorney present at the examination. If the patient refuses to comply with the court order, he or she may suffer the same consequences as failing to comply with orders to appear for depositions (subpoenas) or to produce documents.

---

[*]A subpoena duces tecum is similar to a regular subpoena except that its object is the deliverance of documents and tangible objects.

§ 4.36 Protective Orders

Under the Federal Rules, a party may request the court to issue a protective order forbidding or modifying the opposing party's right to discovery of certain matters.[30] The requesting party must show a substantial reason for this limitation, such as protection from annoyance, embarrassment, oppression, or undue expense.

§ 4.40 EVIDENCE AND WITNESSES

In bringing an action for medical malpractice, the patient-plaintiff has the burden of proving by a preponderance of the evidence that the physician violated the requisite standard of care. This is the general standard for all negligence cases in which a plaintiff alleges that a defendant breached a standard of care and that the breach caused the plaintiff harm. Most malpractice cases come under negligence law. (See § 1.20, Elements of Negligence.)

In some jurisdictions, where the doctrine of res ipsa loquitur is recognized (see § 1.52, Res Ipsa Loquitur), the burden of proof may shift to the physician-defendant. In either situation, the physician's testimony, medical records, and other materials prepared by the physician in the course of treating the patient may be pertinent to the trial of the case and therefore essential to meeting the burden of proof. Specific legal rules governing the admissibility, presentation and availability of these items of evidence may affect the outcome of the lawsuit.

§ 4.41 Expert Testimony

As a general rule of evidence, the testimony of the non-expert witness at a trial is limited to facts and circumstances within the witness's own observation, knowledge, or recollection. This basic rule limits the witness's testimony to those facts directly perceived by the witness, as distinguished from opinions, inferences, impressions, or conclusions. The trier of fact, whether judge or jury, must draw conclusions based on the factual testimony of the witness.

Sometimes, however, the judge or the jury may not be able to derive valid conclusions from factual testimony if that testimony is of a technical nature and involves a subject beyond the comprehension of a lay person unschooled in the subject. This is the case with complex medical issues. In these situations, the layperson is not equipped by common knowledge and experience to reach accurate judgments; he or she needs the assistance of expert testimony to reach considered judgments. If the court determines that specialized knowledge will assist the trier of fact in understanding the evidence or in determining the issues of the case, a witness qualified as an expert may testify by giving factual information or an opinion on the subject.[31]

As a general rule, expert testimony is also essential to support a patient's cause of action for malpractice.[32] Often, expert testimony is a prerequisite to the patient's right to recover for the alleged malpractice of either a physician or a hospital.[33] Expert testimony is necessary to establish both the appropriate standard of care and the physician-defendant's violation of that standard.[34] (See § 1.32, Standard of Care.) This requirement for expert testimony is predicated on the belief that in cases involving professional service, the layperson is not equipped by common knowledge and experience to judge the skill and competence of that service nor to determine whether it conforms with the appropriate standard of medical practice.

The Expert's Qualifications: Whether or not a witness qualifies as an expert is a determination left to the discretion of the trial court judge.[35] In most jurisdictions a witness may be classified as an expert on the basis of knowledge, skill, experience, training, or education.[36] There is, however, no presumption that a witness is competent to qualify as an expert; therefore, the party offering the witness must show that the witness has the necessary qualifications.

As a general rule, any licensed physician is considered to be a medical expert. References to membership in medical societies, appointments, published books or articles, or honors and recognitions, however, may have bearing on the *weight* the trier of fact will give the expert testimony.

Expert Witness Fees: It is ethical and legal for physicians to accept compensation for their services as expert witnesses. Fees based on an hourly or daily compensation basis are usually permissible.

The exception to this general rule is the contingent-fee arrangement, in which the physician-witness's fee depends on the outcome of the litigation. This arrangement is unethical because it undermines the physician's impartiality and distorts the truth-finding process of the trial. Contingent fees are also likely to detract from a witness's professional credibility and to cast great doubt on the reliability and veracity of his or her testimony. Expert witnesses may legitimately be cross-examined as to their interest in the case and may be asked if the fee payment depends on the outcome of the case.[37] Expert witnesses should be frank in their responses and not attempt to hide the facts surrounding their compensation.

Preparation for Trial: Preparation for the trial is imperative. Examination of the injured party, preparation of a medical report, and a review of the relevant technical literature may all be necessary to assure informed and effective testimony at trial. This preparation also diminishes the potential for embarrassment when the predictable cross-examination comes.

Before the trial, the expert witness should meet with the attorney for the party who has asked him or her to testify. Such meetings are completely legitimate and are vital to an effective presentation of the expert's testimony at trial. Attorneys should not tell their experts what their opinions should be, and expert witnesses should not change their testimony to satisfy the attorney. It is proper, however, for attorneys to ask that answers be responsive to the questions asked and that expert witnesses not volunteer answers where no question has been asked.

The Expert Witness and the Witness Stand: Generally, under the rules of evidence and courtroom procedure there are two types of witness interrogation: direct examination and cross-examination. There are defined limits to the proper nature and scope of questions for each type of interrogation.

Direct examination takes place when one side calls an individual to the witness stand. Questions asked under direct examination may be specific or general, calling for a freer narrative, but should not be leading. A leading question is one that strongly suggests a specific answer to the witness. Attorneys are not ordinarily allowed to use leading questions on direct examination, except under the discretionary approval of the trial judge.[38]

After direct examination by the attorney who called the witness to the stand, opposing counsel cross-examines the same witness. The rules governing cross-examination are less restrictive than those for direct examination and generally allow leading questions.[39] However, the examining attorney must usually restrict questions to the subject matter of the direct examination and to matters relating to the credibility of the witness.[40]

The trial judge plays an important role in supervising the proceedings. The Federal Rules of Evidence explicitly require the judge to exercise reasonable control over the interrogation of the witnesses to make the interrogation an effective tool in a search for truth and to protect witnesses from harassment or undue embarrassment.[41]

Direct Examination: During the trial, expert witnesses are called to the stand by the attorney for the party who has engaged their services. Through direct examination, the attorney questions the expert in order to present the expert's knowledge and opinion to the trier of fact. This is a relatively straightforward process and if the attorney and expert are properly prepared, the expert will be familiar with the questions and will give answers consistent with those given in the past (i.e., at deposition or in preparation for trial).

Experts may relate their findings and opinions or respond to hypothetical questions relevant to the medical issues in the case. (See § 4.43, Hypothetical Question and Opinion Testimony.)

Cross-Examination: Following direct examination, the counsel for the opposing party will cross-examine the expert witness. This is likely to be the most

§ 4.41   Expert Testimony   127

trying time for the expert witness.

The purpose of cross-examination is to test the expert, the expert's testimony, or the basis of the expert's testimony. In theory this testing process is the adversary system's mechanism for finding the truth. Too often, however, truth gets lost in the testing, and legitimate experts with legitimate opinions feel confounded and attacked. A cross-examining attorney may employ a number of unpleasant techniques in his or her attempt to establish that the witness's knowledge is inadequate or unsound or that the witness is partisan. In this respect the attorney is motivated by his or her ethical duty to employ all available legal means in representing the client's interest in court.[42]

Experts should be prepared for bullying, rude, and rough cross-examinations. They may have to contend with shouting and finger-pointing. Some attorneys choose less harsh tactics, such as questions intended to disturb the witness. Questions about the compensation to be received for testifying are traditional. Cross-examining counsel may pose a series of questions necessitating the recall of picayune medical facts that the expert has had no need to recall since medical school. The attorney may ask the expert a long series of questions requiring an affirmative answer, thus giving the impression of agreement with the opposing party.

In response to such techniques, expert witnesses should remain as calm as possible, answering the questions as honestly as possible. This may be difficult, because courtroom procedure may be abused by skillful attorneys to obfuscate the truth rather than reveal it. These problems are the object of raging debate, but for the present they are the unpleasant realities of the adversarial system of justice. The best way to counter these difficulties is to anticipate them through pre-trial preparation and open communication between the expert witness and counsel for the party who engaged the expert's services.

General Guidelines for the Expert Witness in Court: The law department of the American Medical Association has formulated a useful guide for the physician preparing for an appearance in court.[43] The rules are as follows:

1. *Do* take the role of the medical witness seriously. The courtroom is a place in which all present are engaged in the serious work of endeavoring to administer justice. The role of the medical witness is a key one in this endeavor.

2. *Don't* agree to or accept compensation for your services contingent upon the outcome of litigation. This practice is unethical and its disclosure would be apt to destroy the value of your testimony.

3. *Do* insist on preparation for your testimony in consultation with the attorney for the party who called you as a witness. He should advise you

on what to expect on cross-examination. You have a right to consult with the party and his attorney about the case, so don't be embarrassed if asked about such consultations.

4. *Don't* act as an advocate or partisan in the trial of the case. If the attorney for the party who calls you as a witness needs the advice or guidance of a doctor during the trial, let him employ another doctor. Disclosure of partnership of a witness strongly tends to discredit his testimony.

5. *Do* be as thorough as is reasonably necessary under the circumstances in examining a party in preparation for trial. Exhaustion of all possible tests and procedures may not be required, but be prepared to justify any omission.

6. *Don't* exaggerate. Any attempt to puff up your qualifications or to elaborate the extent of the examination you have made is apt to expose you to embarrassment.

7. *Do* inform the attorney for the party who calls you as a witness of all unfavorable information developed by your examination of the party as well as the favorable information.

8. *Don't* try to bluff. If you don't know the answer to a question, don't guess. If you guess wrong, you may be falling into a trap.

9. *Do* be frank about financial arrangements with the party who called you as a witness, with respect to your compensation for both treatment given and services in connection with the litigation.

10. *Don't* regard it as an admission of ignorance to indicate that your opinion is not absolutely conclusive or that you don't have the answer to a particular question. Honesty may frequently require testimony of this nature.

11. *Do* answer all questions honestly and frankly. Any display of embarrassment or reluctance to answer will tend to discredit your testimony.

12. *Don't* use technical terminology which will not be understood by the jury, the attorney, or the judge. If technical terms are unavoidable, explain them as best you can in the language of the layperson.

13. *Do* be willing to disagree with so-called authorities if you are convinced they are wrong. If you have sound reasons for disagreement, the contrary opinion of authorities will not necessarily discredit you.

14. *Don't* be smug. A jury is quite likely to react adversely to an attitude of this nature. A modest attitude on the part of the witness is apt to elicit a more favorable response. Leave it to the attorney to bring out your special qualifications.

15. *Do* be courteous no matter what the provocation. If a cross-examining

attorney is discourteous to you, this is apt to win sympathy for you from the jury provided you don't descend to the same level.

16. *Don't* lose your temper. If a cross-examining attorney can provoke you to a display of anger or sarcasm, he has already substantially succeeded in discrediting your testimony.

17. *Do* pause briefly before answering a question asked on cross-examination, to give the other attorney an opportunity to object to the question if he so desires. Taking a moment for deliberation before answering a question does not indicate uncertainty or embarrassment.

18. *Don't* allow yourself to be forced into a flat yes or no answer if a qualified answer is required. You have a right to explain or qualify if that is necessary for a truthful answer.

§ 4.42 Court-appointed Experts

As a way of mediating conflict in expert testimony, the trial judge may, at his or her discretion, appoint an independent medical expert to testify.[44] In some cases this may add much to the truth-seeking process because it provides a neutral party in a potentially confusing and divided situation. In addition, physicians are often more willing to testify as an officer of the court than as a partisan witness in a dispute.

If the court decides that an independent expert is needed, it may appoint an expert on its own or ask the opposing parties to nominate mutually agreeable candidates. Court-appointed experts are subject to deposition and cross-examination by both parties.

§ 4.43 Hypothetical Question and Opinion Testimony

As a general rule, witnesses qualified as experts may testify in the form of opinion. The hypothetical question is one of the standard means of eliciting opinion testimony. Basically, a hypothetical question is one that asks for an opinion on the basis of a set of assumed facts.

At one time, physicians who had not treated the patient-plaintiff could not give testimony regarding that patient's treatment, diagnosis or prognosis because they did not have first-hand knowledge. To skirt this problem the law created a legal fiction—the hypothetical question. This fiction allows the attorney seeking the opinion to state a series of hypothetical facts that the expert is then expected to assume are true. The expert may then state opinions based on those hypothetical facts. Of course, in practice, the facts stated in the hypothetical question mirror the facts of the case under consideration.

A few states and the Federal Rules of Evidence have significantly liberalized the restrictions on expert testimony.[45] In those states, and in federal courts, much of the original rationale for the use of hypothetical questions is gone. However, attorneys still commonly employ hypothetical questions under both the liberalized and the more traditional rules. For these reasons, physicians should have an understanding of this interrogation technique.

Once the court has qualified a witness as an "expert," the examining attorney may ask hypothetical questions. In many states, the expert may stay in the courtroom during the taking of other testimony. Then, when the expert testifies, the examining attorney can simplify the hypothetical question by asking the expert to assume the truth of the previous testimony,[46] or some specified part(s) of it. The expert will be asked to base his or her opinion(s) on those assumptions. When not grounded on other testimony in the case, hypothetical questions should contain all of the relevant facts to be assumed by the expert witness and should be complete enough to allow the expert to form an opinion. Hypothetical questions do not need to include all of the facts in the case, but the facts assumed must be supported by evidence in the case.[47] The hypothetical question must include all of the facts on which the answer is based.[48] Some states require that the question include all material facts,[49] but the more widely prevailing view rejects that requirement.[50] Where the facts are in dispute, the attorney posing the hypothetical question may base it on testimony supporting his or her client's theory of the case, although contradictory testimony may be called to the expert's attention by varying the hypothesis on cross-examination.[51] Although facts assumed in the hypothetical question do not have to be in evidence at the time the question is posed, the examining counsel must give assurances that they will be presented before the close of trial.[52] However, on cross-examination, the examining attorney may often use hypothetical questions to test the expert's skill and knowledge even though the questions are not based on evidence in the case.[53]

Hypothetical questions are difficult for attorneys to frame, for courts to rule upon, and for juries to understand.[54] Hypothetical questions, "misused by the clumsy and abused by the clever, [have] in practice led to intolerable obstruction(s) of truth."[55] As one critic put it, a hypothetical question is "perhaps the most abominable form of evidence that was ever allowed to choke the mind of a juror or throttle his intelligence."[56] The primary difficulty is with hypothetical questions not based on facts in evidence. Because these questions need not include all the facts in a case, those facts that are assumed as part of the hypothesis must somehow be drawn from the evidence; in complex trials, attorneys may, if they are not extremely careful, forget which facts are in evidence and which facts are not. In all of this the trial court has, and needs, considerable discretion in passing on the propriety of hypothetical questions.[57]

§ 4.44 *Textbooks*

If the authors of medical textbooks or scholarly articles are not available for cross-examination in a trial, many state courts will not admit statements or extracts as independent evidence bearing on a medical issue in the case.[58] The Federal Rules of Evidence are more liberal than this traditional rule; in federal courts attorneys may read authoritative textbook materials into evidence.[59]

Most courts permit attorneys to use learned materials in cross-examination when the witness has already relied on a particular treatise and the cross-examining attorney is attempting to show that the material does not, in fact, support the witness's position.[60] A number of courts also permit cross-examination from learned works other than the one the witness has used to support his or her opinion. In these cases, once a witness cites a particular treatise as support for a medical opinion, the opposing attorney may use other established works to undermine the credibility of the witness's testimony.[61] A third group allows the cross-examiner to interrogate the witness from treatises the witness has recognized as authoritative in the field, regardless of whether the witness has based his or her opinion on the work in question.[62] A number of courts also allow attorneys on cross-examination to test the witness's competency or qualifications by using textbooks, whether or not he or she has relied on or recognized the authority of the text.[63] As with many questions of evidence and trial procedure, the judge generally has broad discretion in controlling the extent to which attorneys may use medical texts as tools for cross-examination.[64]

Although the majority of states allow the introduction of professional literature only under the limited circumstances described above, there are strong arguments for relaxing the rules and allowing plaintiffs and defendants to introduce treatises and texts as substantive evidence on issues of medical practice in the case.[65] Actually, the testimony of experts is often based on information from the professional literature. Allowing the literature into evidence directly could improve the quality of information available to judges and juries. In addition, the judicial emphasis on trustworthiness of evidence would be amply satisfied by the author's desire to write a text respected within the profession.

§ 4.45 *Adverse Witness Provisions*

In malpractice actions, problems arise when counsel for the physician-defendant chooses not to call the physician-defendant to the stand. Under the normal rules of evidence, if the plaintiff's counsel wants to question the defendant on the witness stand, he or she must call the physician as an ordinary witness and is therefore limited by the rules of direct examination. This puts the plaintiff's counsel in a position of less advantage than if he or she could question the physician-defendant according to the more liberal rules of cross-examination.

To combat the problem posed by the strict application of the rules of evidence, many states have adverse witness provisions in state statutes or practice rules. Adverse witness rules enable either party in a lawsuit to call the opposing party (or an employee or agent of the opposing party) to the witness stand and to engage in cross-examination.[66] If the plaintiff is permitted to use the testimony of a physician-defendant as the basis for establishing the fact of malpractice, as some courts allow,[67] the adverse witness rule is a very helpful tool for the plaintiff.

§ 4.46 Physician-Patient Privilege

The physician-patient relationship may be described as fiduciary* in nature. (See § 1.31, Physician-Patient Relationship.) Consequently, the American Medical Association advises that the physician should safeguard patient confidences within the constraints of the law,[68] and the law recognizes the legally enforceable duty of the physician to maintain the confidentiality of information obtained during the course of a physician-patient relationship.[69] In legal parlance, physician-patient information exchange is viewed as privileged communication: the privileged privacy of such information is recognized by the law to assure that a patient may speak freely with the physician so that the physician will have sufficient information on which he or she can make treatment decisions. Even though recognized by the law, the physician-patient privilege is given limited application, particularly when the privileged information constitutes evidence in the litigation of a case.

The physician-patient privilege is a creature of state legislation.[70] In states without such a statute, physician-patient communications are not protected; where such statutes exist, they have been held to extend to information contained in the patient's hospital record.[71] In many of the states that have privilege statutes, a physician ordinarily cannot give in evidence in a court of law any information acquired in the discharge of professional duties. Because the privilege is said to belong to the patient, only the patient may waive or give up the privilege.[72] Patients may waive the privilege by failure to object to taking testimony on information protected under it. Thus, by inaction or inadvertance, patients may lose the statute's protection.

Some states have laws that require automatic waiver when the patient brings an action for personal injuries (such as those resulting from a car accident) or where the patient's physical or mental condition is at issue.[73] Several state courts have held that, under these laws, the patient waives the privilege for discovery proceedings as well.[74] (See § 4.30, Discovery.) As a result, before the trial a physician-defendant may obtain information regarding medical examinations by other physicians concerning the injury or condition at issue in the case. Other states have statutes providing that the patient necessarily gives up the privilege by offering himself or any physician as a witness in his behalf in a suit involving

---

*A fiduciary relationship involves both formal and informal relationships where a person or institution is placed in a position of trust or confidence by another.

§ 4.47   *Medical Records*   133

personal injuries.[75] Some state courts have decided that, under these statutes, merely beginning a lawsuit involving a patient's physical condition does not mean automatic loss of the privilege.[76] In Michigan, for example, a patient suing for injuries may prevent the deposition of a physician on the basis of the physician-patient privilege, but the patient may not then use that physician as a witness. On the other hand, the patient may give up the privilege, allow the deposition, and use the physician as a witness.[77]

In the absence of a statute specifically governing the conditions of waiver, some state courts have held that the commencement of a personal injury suit, including malpractice, operates to end the privilege for the injuries at issue, both at trial and in discovery.[78] In other states, the courts have found that, in the absence of a specific statute defining conditions of waiver, beginning a suit involving the patient's physical condition does not necessarily operate automatically to cut off the patient's right to insist on the physician-patient privilege.[79] These courts have refused to permit the defendant to discover the patient's medical evidence prior to trial.

In states that have a statute creating the physician-patient privilege, a physician's breach of the privilege may result in legal liability. For example, if a physician wrongfully discloses information regarding a patient's medical condition, such as venereal disease, the patient may sue the physician for damages on a defamation theory. (See § 2.40, Liability Arising from Medical Records.) Generally, privileged information must not be disclosed without the patient's consent unless public interest or the patient's own interests require it.[80] Thus physicians have not been held liable for disclosing information to insurers[81] or to a third party where the communication discloses a danger to the third party.[82] Physicians should consult an attorney to determine whether their state has a privilege statute and scrupulously protect the confidences of their patients.

§ 4.47 *Medical Records*

Information in the patient's medical record is subject to laws protecting its confidentiality (see § 4.46, Physician-Patient Privilege), defining the property rights of those with an interest in it, (see § 2.40, Liability Arising from Medical Records) and governing its admissibility as evidence in a court of law. Where such information is not privileged, the medical record that contains it is admissible in evidence, subject to the following legal considerations.

In order to assure that the trier of fact, usually the jury, hears both sides of a controversy, the law requires that each party have the opportunity to place a witness under oath, cross-examine the witness, and allow the trier of fact to observe the witness's demeanor on the witness stand. A medical record fails to meet these requirements. Statements on the record are not subject to cross-examination and may be viewed as hearsay* which cannot be introduced into evidence. However, business records—records made in the regular course of business activity—are admissible as an exception to the hearsay rule in most jurisdictions, and medical records have been recognized as business records by most courts.

The inconvenience or impossibility of introducing certain records into evidence has led to legislation such as the Uniform Business Records Act. In a 1978 decision, a Pennsylvania court considered the admission into evidence of hospital or medical records. The court stated that hospital or medical reports are admissible as business records pursuant to the Uniform Business Records Act if the report meets the following criteria: (1) it is made contemporaneously with the events it purports to relate; (2) at the time it was prepared it was impossible to anticipate reasons for making a false entry into it; (3) the person responsible for the statements contained in the report is known.[83]

§ 4.50 COUNTERSUITS

Physician countersuits against patients or their attorneys are among the most controversial responses to the recent "medical malpractice crisis." In these suits, the physician-defendant in a medical malpractice case sues the patient-plaintiff or the plaintiff's attorney, or both, after the defendant has won a jury verdict or the trial court has dismissed the case for the plaintiff's failure to state a cause of action.[84]

Physician-defendant countersuits may be based on a number of legal theories, including defamation** (the physician claims the patient's wrongful suit injured the physician's reputation or character); malicious prosecution (the patient allegedly filed suit only to torment the physician and without any reasonable basis in fact to support the claim); and abuse of process (the patient or patient's attorney is alleged to have used the courts for a wrongful purpose).

In one of the first successful abuse of process cases, the Supreme Court of Nevada noted that in order to prevail against the attorney or the patient, the physician must prove an ulterior purpose for bringing the suit and a willful act in

---

*Hearsay is defined as evidence not proceeding from the witness's personal knowledge but from the repetition of what others were heard to say. It is inadmissible because its veracity is dependent upon the veracity of persons not subject to examination.

**Generally, an attorney is absolutely privileged to make defamatory remarks concerning another in communications preliminary to or during the course of a judicial proceeding or as a part of a judicial proceeding in which he or she participates as counsel as long as the remarks have some relation to the proceedings. Bull v. McCuskey, 615 P.2d 957, 961 (Nev. 1980)

§ 4.50 Countersuits 135

the use of process not proper in the regular conduct of the proceeding.[85] Damages recoverable in this type of action include compensation for fears, anxiety, mental and emotional distress, injury to reputation, and inconvenience.[86]

The policy of American jurisprudence tends to protect patients, because the founding fathers highly valued the individual's right to have disputes heard in courts of law. Accordingly, American courts are reluctant to allow countersuits. They fear that recognizing such suits will frighten patient-plaintiffs out of exercising their constitutional right to have disputes heard in court. The counterbalancing policy of protecting physician-defendants from unwarranted suits has traditionally been valued less. However, where the intent or motivation of either the patient or the patient's attorney can be shown to be malicious (for example, where it can be shown that the patient, because of spite, hate, or ill-will, disregards the rights and interests of the physician), courts may find in favor of the physician. The problem the physician confronts is one of proof. For example, unless the patient has gone on record, either in writing or orally before reliable witnesses, it is difficult to prove that the patient's reason for filing suit was motivated by malice. Complicating the problem even further are attorney defenses that they owe no duty to the opposing parties, and that their first duty is to advocate zealously the interests of their clients (i.e., the patients). At least one state court has adopted this rationale.[87]

Although countersuits are attractive to many physicians, the likelihood of bringing a successful countersuit today is not great. Further, few attorneys will file countersuits on behalf of physicians on a contingent fee basis because no countersuit has yet been won and affirmed at the appellate level. Accordingly, physicians desiring to bring countersuits against patients or their attorneys are usually required to pay substantial retainers, which tends to discourage such actions. It is possible, however, that physician countersuits may be more successful with the emergence of legal standards of care applicable to plantiffs' malpractice attorneys.

NOTES

1. Fed. R. Civ. P. 8.
2. Fed. R. Civ. P. 12.
3. Cal. Civ. Proc. Code § 412.20 (West 1977).
4. Wash. Rev. Code § 4.28.060 (1974).
5. *See generally* Green, Basic Civil Procedure, ch. 6 (1979); James & Hazard, Civil Procedure § 6.2 (1977).
6. Fed. R. Civ. P. 29(c), (f).
7. *Id.* at 32(a)(3).
8. *Id.* at 32(a).
9. *Id.* at 32(a)(1).
10. *Id.* at 26(a).
11. *Id.* at 26(b)(1).

12. *Id.* at 37(a).
13. *Id.* at 37(a)(4).
14. *Id.* at 26(b)(4).
15. *Id.* at 26(b)(4)(A).
16. *Id.* at 26(b)(4)(B).
17. *Id.* at 35(a).
18. *Id.* at 35(b).
19. *Id.* at 26(a)(4)(C)(i).
20. *Id.* at 26(a)(4)(C)(ii).
21. Dow Chemical Co. v. Superior Court, 2 Cal. App. 3d 1, 82 Cal. Rptr. 288 (1969); Klabunde v. Stanley, 16 Mich. App. 490, 168 N.W.2d 250 (1969), *rev'd on other grounds*, 384 Mich. 276, 181 N.W.2d 918 (1970).
22. *See, e.g.*, J. Honigman & C. Hawkins, Michigan Court Rules Annotated, Rules 302.1, 306.2 (2d ed. 1963); State *ex rel.* Reynolds v. Circuit Court, 15 Wis. 2d 311, 112 N.W.2d 686 (1961), *rehearing denied*, 113 N.W.2d 537.
23. Klabunde v. Stanley, *supra* note 21.
24. Fed. R. Civ. P. 45.
25. *Id.* at 33.
26. *Id.* at 34.
27. *Id.* at 37(a).
28. *Id.* at 26(b).
29. *Id.* at 35(a).
30. *Id.* at 26(c).
31. *See, e.g.*, Har-Pen Truck Lines, Inc. v. Mills, 378 F.2d 705 (5th Cir. 1967); Pennsylvania Threshermen & Farmers Mut. Ins. Co. v. Messenger, 181 Md. 295, 29 A.2d 653 (1943); Swartley v. Seattle School Dist. No. 1, 70 Wash. 2d 17, 421 P.2d 1009 (1966); Fed. R. Evid. 702.
32. *See, e.g.*, Stephenson v. Kaiser Foundation Hosp., 203 Cal. App. 2d 631, 21 Cal Rptr. 646 (1962); Dimitrijevic v. Chicago Wesley Mem. Hosp., 92 Ill. App. 2d 251, 236 N.E.2d 309 (1968); Morgan v. State, 40 A.D.2d 891, 337 N.Y.S.2d 536 (1972), *aff'd*, 34 N.Y.2d 709, 313 N.E.2d 340, 356 N.Y.S.2d 860, *cert. denied*, 419 U.S.1013 (1974).
33. *Id.*; Thomas v. Corso, 265 Md. 84, 288 A.2d 379 (1972); Bivens v. Detroit Osteopathic Hosp., 77 Mich. App. 478, 258 N.W.2d 527 (1977).
34. *See, e.g.*, Norden v. Hartman, 134 Cal. App. 2d 333, 285 P.2d 977 (1955); Lince v. Monson, 363 Mich. 135, 108 N.W.2d 845 (1961); Williams v. Chamberlain, 316 S.W.2d 505 (Mo. 1958).
35. *See, e.g.*, Fed. R. Evid. 104(a), 403, 702; Bronaugh v. Harding Hosp., Inc., 12 Ohio App. 2d 110, 231 N.E.2d 487 (1967).
36. *See, e.g.*, Fed. R. Evid. 702; Mich. R. Evid. 702.
37. *See, e.g.*, Fed. R. Evid. 611(b); 3A Wigmore, Evidence § 961 n. 2 (Chadbourn rev. 1970).
38. McCormick's Handbook of the Law of Evidence § 6 (2d ed. 1972); Fed. R. Evid. 611(c).
39. 3A Wigmore, *supra* note 37 at § 773; Fed. R. Evid. 611(c).
40. 6 Wigmore, Evidence §§ 1886-91 (3d ed. 1940); Fed. R. Evid. 611(b).
41. Fed. R. Evid. 611(a).
42. A.B.A. Code of Professional Responsibility, Canon 7.
43. Law Department of the American Medical Association, *Do's and Don't's for the Medical Witness*, Proceedings Medical-Legal Symposium, Miami Beach, Florida 277-79 (November 8-9, 1963).

44. *See, e.g.*, Hunt v. State, 248 Ala. 217, 27 So.2d 186 (1946); Citizens' Bank v. Castro, 105 Cal. App. 284, 287 P. 559 (1930); Fed. R. Evid. 706; Mich. R. Evid. 706.
45. *See, e.g.*, Mich. R. Evid. 703 (based on Fed. R. Evid. 703); Rabata v. Dohner, 45 Wis. 2d 111, 172 N.W.2d 409 (1969); Kan. Civ. Pro. Code Ann. § 60-456 (Vernon 1977); N.J.R. Evid. 57, 58; N.Y. Civ. Prac. Law § 4515 (McKinney 1976).
46. 2 Wigmore, Evidence § 681 (3d ed. 1940).
47. Barnett v. State Workmen's Compensation Comm'r, 153 Va. 796, 172 S.E.2d 698 (1970); Nisbet v. Medaglia, 356 Mass. 580, 254 N.E.2d 782 (1970).
48. *In re* Cottrell's Estate, 235 Mich. 627, 209 N.W. 842 (1928).
49. Stumpf v. State Farm Mut. Auto. Ins. Co., 252 Md. 696, 251 A.2d 362 (1969); Leitch v. Getz, 275 Mich. 645, 267 N.W. 581 (1936); Ames & Webb, Inc. v. Commercial Laundry Co., Inc., 204 Va. 616, 133 S.E.2d 547 (1963).
50. Virginia Beach Bus Line v. Campbell, 73 F.2d 97 (4th Cir. 1934); Pickett v. Kyger, 151 Mont. 87, 439 P.2d 57 (1968); Gordon v. State Farm Life Ins. Co., 415 Pa. 256, 203 A.2d 320 (1964).
51. *In re* McCord, 243 Mich. 309, 220 N.W. 710 (1928).
52. Gibson v. Healy Bros. & Co., 109 Ill. App. 2d 342, 248 N.E.2d 771 (1969); Barretto v. Akau, 51 Hawaii 383, 463 P.2d 917 (1969).
53. Randall v. Goodrich-Gamble Co., 244 Minn. 401, 70 N.W.2d 261 (1955); Seibert v. Ritchie, 173 Wash. 27, 21 P.2d 272 (1933); 2 Wigmore, *supra* note 46, at § 684.
54. Honigman, *The Hypothetical Question Meets its Answer*, 36 Mich. S.B.J. 12 (Nov., 1957).
55. 2 Wigmore, *supra* note 46, at § 686.
56. Wellman, The Art of Cross-Examination 103 (4th ed. 1963).
57. *In re* Stephen's Estate, 244 Mich. 547, 222 N.W. 128 (1928).
58. *See, e.g.*, Salgo v. Leland Stanford Jr. Univ. Bd. of Trustees, 154 Cal. App. 2d 560, 317 P.2d 170 (1957); Noland v. Dillon, 261 Md. 516, 276 A.2d 36 (1971); O'Connell v. Williams, 17 Misc. 2d 296, 181 N.Y.S.2d 434 (1958).
59. Fed. R. Evid. 803(18).
60. *See, e.g.*, Hope v. Arrowhead & Puritas Waters, Inc., 174 Cal. App. 2d 222, 344 P.2d 428 (1959); Darlington v. Charleston Community Mem. Hosp., 50 Ill. App. 2d 253, 200 N.E.2d 149 (1964); Myers v. St. Francis Hosp., 91 N.J. Super. 377, 220 A.2d 693 (1966).
61. *See, e.g.*, Briggs v. Chicago Great W. Ry. Co., 238 Minn. 472, 57 N.W.2d 572 (1953); Farmers Union Federated Co-Op Shipping Ass'n v. McChesney, 251 F.2d 441 (8th Cir. 1958); Bruins v. Brandon Canning Co., 216 Wis. 387, 257 N.W. 35 (1934).
62. *See, e.g.*, Kaplan v. Mashkin Freight Lines, Inc., 146 Conn. 327, 150 A.2d 602 (1959); St. Petersburg v. Ferguson, 193 So.2d 648 (Fla. App. 1966); Jones v. Bloom, 388 Mich. 98, 200 N.W.2d 196 (1972).
63. *E.g.*, Superior Ice & Coal Co. v. Belger Cartage Serv., Inc., 337 S.W.2d 897 (Mo. 1960); Iverson v. Lancaster, 158 N.W.2d 507 (N.D. 1968); Gravis v. Physicians & Surgeons Hosp., 415 S.W.2d 674 (Tex. Civ. App. 1967), *Rev'd on other grounds*, 427 S.W.2d 310 (Tex. 1968).
64. *E.g.*, Darlington v. Charleston Community Mem. Hosp., *supra* note 60; Callaway v. Mountain State Mut. Cas. Co., 70 N.M. 337, 373 P.2d 827 (1962); Sutkowski v. Prosperity Co., 7 A.D.2d 660, 170 N.Y.S.2d 166 (1958).
65. See 6 Wigmore, *supra* note 40, at §§ 1690-92.
66. *See, e.g.*, Libby v. Conway, 192 Cal. App. 2d 865, 13 Cal. Rptr. 830 (1961); Loggin v. Morgenstern, 60 So.2d 732 (Fla. 1952); Argo v. Goodstein, 438 Pa. 468, 265 A.2d 783 (1970); Fed. R. Evid. 611(b).
67. *See, e.g.*, Daggett v. Atchison, Topeka & Santa Fe Ry. Co., 48 Cal.2d 655, 313 P.2d

557 (1957); Ferguson v. Gonyaw, 64 Mich. App. 685, 236 N.W.2d 543 (1975), *appeal denied*, 396 Mich. 817 (1976).
68. American Medical Association, *Principles of Medical Ethics*, § IV in Current Opinions of the Judicial Council of the American Medical Association (1981).
69. Horne v. Patton, 291 Ala. 701, 287 So.2d 824 (1974).
70. *See, e.g.*, Cal. Civ. Proc. Code § 1181 (West 1977); Cal. Penal Code § 1321; Cal. Evid. Code § 990-95 (West Supp. 1967); N.Y. Civ. Prac. Law §§ 352,354 (McKinney 1976); Ohio Rev. Code § 2317.02 (Page 1980).
71. State v. Bedel, 193 N.W.2d 121 (Iowa 1971).
72. *See, e.g.*, Koump v. Smith, 25 N.Y.2d 287, 250 N.E.2d 857, 303 N.Y.S.2d 858 (1969); Sagmiller v. Carlsen, 219 N.W.2d 885 (N.D. 1974).
73. *See, e.g.*, Cal. Evid. Code § 996 (West 1977).
74. *See, e.g.*, Hall v. Superior Court, 20 Cal. App. 2d 652, 97 Cal. Rptr. 879 (1937); Lind v. Canada Dry Corp., 283 F. Supp. 861 (D. Minn. 1968) (applying Minn. law).
75. *See, e.g.*, Mich. Comp. Laws Ann. § 600.2157 (1968).
76. *See, e.g.*, Hardy v. Riser, 309 F. Supp. 1234 (N.D. Miss. 1970) (applying Miss. law); D. v. D., 108 N.J. Super. 149, 260 A.2d 255 (1969); Avery v. Nelson, 455 P.2d 75 (Okla. 1969).
77. Roe v. Cherry-Burrell Corp., 28 Mich. App. 42, 184 N.W.2d 350 (1970).
78. *E.g.*, Trans-World Investments v. Drobny, 554 P.2d 1148 (Alaska 1976); State *ex rel.* McNutt v. Keet, 432 S.W.2d 597 (Mo. 1968); Koump v. Smith, *supra* note 72.
79. *E.g.*, Bower v. Murphy, 247 Ark. 238, 444 S.W.2d 883 (1969); State *ex rel.* Lambdin v. Brenton, 21 Ohio St. 2d 21, 254 N.E.2d 681 (1970); Phipps v. Sasser, 74 Wash. 2d 439, 445 P.2d 624 (1968).
80. Horne v. Patton, *supra* note 69.
81. Conyers v. Massa, 512 P.2d 283 (Colo. App. 1973).
82. Tarasoff v. Regents of Univ. of California, 13 Cal. 3d 177, 529 P.2d 553, 118 Cal. Rptr. 129 (1974).
83. Sauro v. Shea, 257 Pa. 66, 390 A.2d 259 (1978).
84. Cavanaugh, *Countersuit: A Viable Alternative for the Wrongfully Sued Physician?*, 19 Washburn L. J. 450 (1980); Higgs, *Physicians' Countersuits—A Solution to the Malpractice Dilemma?*, 28 Drake L. Rev. 81 (1978-79); Birnbaum, *Physicians Counterattack: Liability of Lawyers for Instituting Unjustified Medical Malpractice Actions*, 45 Fordham L. Rev. 1003 (1977). *See also*, Kerr, *The Countersuit: The Situation in Michigan Today*, Mich. Med. 432 (August, 1978). *See also, infra* note 87.
85. Bull v. McCuskey, 615 P.2d 957 (Nev. 1980).
86. *Id*.
87. Friedman v. Dozorc, 412 Mich. 1, 312 N.W.2d 585 (1981).

Part II
Regulation

Chapter V

Governmental Regulation

§ 5.10 INTRODUCTION

In the general legal sense, regulation involves the application of certain standards of conduct to a field of activity, such as the practice of medicine. Malpractice litigation constitutes one form of regulation in that it applies a standard of care (see § 1.32, Standard of Care) to a physician's conduct in a given case. However, as a regulatory mechanism, malpractice litigation itself is not sufficient to ensure a desirable level of quality in the provision of health care services. Litigation fails to identify the general standards of minimum competence that a health care practitioner must possess before engaging in practice; it focuses instead on a specific standard applicable to the specific case being litigated. While litigation may provide a remedy for the individual who institutes a lawsuit, it does nothing to guarantee that others will not suffer the same injuries in the future at the same hands. Nor can litigation ensure that physicians are continually exposed and educated to new methods of treatment for the benefit of their patients.

Governmental regulation is intended to deal with these concerns by defining minimum levels of competence, requiring that these levels be met by practitioners, and enforcing such requirements. Other than questions of competency, sweeping issues which are peculiar to the practice of medicine may be resolved by regulation where a case-by-case resolution is inadequate. Generally, where a problem permeates a field, regulation is viewed as the answer; for example, legislation establishing Professional Standards Review Organizations has been one regulatory solution to the problem of rising health care costs.

Regulation of the health care field originates from a variety of quarters. Government regulation is perhaps the most familiar. As an exercise of its "police power" to protect the public health, safety, and welfare, the government, both state and federal, is empowered to regulate the health care professions.[1] States achieve this objective through licensure laws as well as specific public health provisions. Federal regulation generally encompasses broad issues such as the distribution of drugs or controlled substances, and the control of the cost of health care.

Often the government looks to the profession for guidance in defining the standards to impose or identifying the areas of professional activity that require scrutiny. Certification standards are derived from professional associations (see § 6.10, Specialty Certification in Anesthesiology). This is a time-worn mode of regulation in America: in the early 1800s, states empowered local medical societies to examine and license prospective physicians; unlicensed physicians were prohibited from collecting fees through court process or were fined for unauthorized practice.[2] Furthermore, the serious medical professional has traditionally shown an interest in legitimatizing his or her profession by delineating standards of quality professional service.

Another source of physician regulation is the hospital (see Chapter VII, Hospital Regulation). Not only is the hospital itself subject to government regulation, hospital bylaws generally define and regulate the scope and extent of the hospital practice of physicians on the medical staff. To maintain accreditation, most hospitals must provide certain specified facilities, staffing them with professionals of specified qualifications (see § 7.70, Regulation of the Hospital).

Regulation focuses generally on the practice of medicine. Very little regulation exists that is pertinent to a single specialty, although instances exist in varying degrees from specialty to specialty. For example, the anesthesiologist is subject to few governmental regulations dealing solely with the practice of anesthesiology, whereas obstetricians and gynecologists may be subject to governmental strictures regarding such topical aspects of their practice as abortion, contraception, sterilization, and fetal research. Members of both specialties are subject to specific standards imposed by their respective professional societies.

The following chapter reviews governmental regulation on both the state and federal level. Some regulatory schemes are engaged in only by the state; others only by the federal government; still others are engaged in by both. Licensure, an example of state regulation, the Professional Standards Review Organization, a federal regulatory mechanism, and both state and federal Controlled Substances law are examined in the pages ahead.

§ 5.20 STATE LICENSURE

Licensure is a process by which government grants permission to individuals who have obtained a specified minimum degree of competence to engage in a given profession. This minimum degree of competence is achieved by satisfying a variety of expressed conditions. Traditionally these include such things as academic qualifications, training and experience, passing a licensure examination, and miscellaneous personal qualifications. Thus, licensure provides barriers to entry into the profession and serves to ensure an acceptable level of quality services.[3]

As an exercise of its police power to protect the public health, safety, and

§ 5.20 *State Licensure* 143

welfare, the state is empowered to regulate the practice of medicine.[4] The practice of medicine is viewed as a privilege granted by the state rather than as an individual right.[5] The state may not exercise its police power in an arbitrary or capricious manner and legislation regulating the practice of medicine must bear a reasonable relation to the state's legitimate interest in protecting the public from incompetent practitioners.[6] The rationale underlying the state's interest is that the state, as opposed to the individual, is considered in a better position to safeguard the patient's interests in evaluating a physician's competence.

To fulfill their regulatory functions, states have delegated the responsibility for establishing the qualifications, conditions and requirements of medical licensure to medical licensing boards. Some states have departments which regulate and license all professions and include medical licensing boards within them.[7] For example, the general licensing board is the Department of Regulatory Agencies in Colorado, the Department of Professional and Occupational Regulation in Florida, the Department of Registration and Education in Illinois, the Division of Registration in Massachusetts, the Department of Licensing and Registration in Michigan, and the Department of Registration and Licensing in Wisconsin. Alternatively, the Boards may be independent state bodies or included within another state agency. For example, the licensing board is included in the Department of Consumer Affairs in California, the Department of Health in Maryland, the Department of Education in New York, and the Department of State in Pennsylvania. Generally, the organization of these governmental bodies, usually called Boards of Medical Examiners, is similar across the United States. Most states combine licensing and disciplinary functions in one Board.[8] Some states, however, provide for a separate entity to conduct or assist conducting Board disciplinary proceedings.[9] State statutes delegate a broad range of powers and duties to the licensing boards. These powers and duties generally include: examination of applicants, issuance of licenses, definition of standards of practice, enforcement of licensing laws, and approval of educational programs and/or recognition of accrediting agencies.[10]

The number and qualification requirements of members of the state medical boards vary slightly. The majority of states have fewer than 10 members,[11] while others range between four[12] (Alabama) and 20[13] members (New York). Physicians comprise a majority of the membership of state licensing boards in every state. In several states, where the board regulates other health care professionals in addition to physicians,[14] board membership includes representatives of other professions. For example, the New Jersey Board, which regulates physicians as well as chiropractors, consists of ten physicians, one chiropractor, one podiatrist, one bioanalyst, one laboratory director, one representative from the state executive department, and one public member.[15]

A number of states regulate different types of physicians under one board.[16] For example, the Massachusetts Board of Registration and Discipline in Medicine regulates M.D.s as well as "other professionals" such as osteopathic physicians and chiropractors.[17] A sizable minority of states provide for public membership of the Board.[18] For example, the Connecticut Medical Examining Board requires membership of two persons unconnected with medicine.[19]

In the majority of states, the state medical society plays an important role in the selection of board members. This role varies from direct selection of members by the state medical society[20] to submission of a list from which the Governor or appointing person is either required[21] or encouraged to select board members.[22] It has been recommended that the system of mandatory selection of members from lists submitted by the medical society be replaced by a system of selection of appointees based on appropriate standards developed by the legislature.[23] In fact, few states specify minimum qualifications for board membership. Some require active practice in the state for a specified number of years.[24] Residency may also be a requirement.[25] Other less common requirements include representation from different congressional districts,[26] graduation from a recognized medical college,[27] and representation from hospital staffs.[28]

Some states require representation from medical school faculties[29] while others prohibit such representation.[30] The presence of faculty members is thought to add distinguished professionals knowledgeable about current advances in medicine and practice, and medical training and competence measurement.[31]

The majority of state boards of medical examiners are funded from legislative appropriations from state treasuries; all other states rely on licensure and registration fees generated by the board. The source of funding has a bearing on both the amount of money with which a board can operate, and the degree of political control exercised by the state over the board itself.[32]

§ 5.21 Requirements

The basic requirements a physician must meet to obtain a state license vary by state and are specified in the state medical practice laws. Many states allow the state licensing authority (Board) to define specific licensure standards in rules. Four types of qualifications are generally used to determine initial competence for licensing as a physician: academic and educational background, postgraduate training and experience, passing a licensure examination, and moral and personal fitness.[33]

Education and Postgraduate Training: All states require graduation from an approved medical school as a condition for licensure as a medical doctor (M.D.),[34] and graduation from an approved college of osteopathic medicine as a condition for licensure as a doctor of osteopathic medicine (D.O.).[35] Thirty-six jurisdictions now have a one year postgraduate "experience" requirement (formerly referred to as "internship") for M.D.s.[36] Thirty-four states have a similar requirement for D.O.s.[37]

Twelve states still require a basic science certificate as a prerequisite to

§ 5.21   *Requirements*   145

licensure, although the tendency is to eliminate this requirement since basic science is included in all medical curricula.[38]

California imposes its educational requirements in great detail.[39] The statute provides that an applicant for a license must submit an official transcript showing that minimum course requirements were met[40] and that he or she has completed at least two years of preprofessional post-secondary education which includes the subjects of physics, chemistry, and biology. If one of these was not taken, the applicant must take it at an approved institution prior to taking the licensing examination. The applicant must also have completed four years of study at an approved medical school.[41] Finally, the statute specifies areas of study required of the medical school curriculum, such as anatomy, anesthesiology, geriatric medicine, and pharmacology. There are approximately 15 such required subjects. California, like other states, also requires a one-year postgraduate training period at an approved hospital.[42] It also provides that an applicant rejected by the Division of Licensing for admission to the examination may sue in state court to compel admittance or for any other appropriate relief.[43]

Examinations: Generally, states impose a written examination requirement for both M.D.s and D.O.s. Some states also have oral examinations[44] or require practical examinations[45] for licensure of M.D.s. A few states require oral examination[46] or practical examination of D.O.s.[47]

In most states boards of medical examiners do not devise their own examinations, but use examinations prepared by national organizations. For example, 27 states and the District of Columbia accept successful completion of the National Board of Medical Examiners' examination in lieu of the state examination for M.D.s.[48] Twenty-nine states accept the examination prepared by the National Board of Examiners for Osteopathic Physicians and Surgeons rather than a state examination.[49]

Many states specify the subject matter of licensure examinations.[50] Most require a 75 percent proficiency performance on the examination for M.D.s;[51] several also require 75 percent proficiency for D.O.s.[52]

At least six states limit the number of times an applicant for M.D. licensure may be reexamined,[53] while only three states limit reexamination of an applicant for D.O. licensure.[54] In some of these states, the limitation is applied only to applicants who have not sought further education since the previously failed examination.

Personal Qualifications: Most states have miscellaneous licensure requirements addressing personal qualifications such as age, citizenship and character. Some states require an applicant to be 21[55] or 18[56] years of age to be licensed as an M.D. Some states enforce a minimum age of 21 for licensure as a D.O.,[57] and a few a minimum age of 18.[58]

About half the states require that the applicant be a U.S. citizen or declare an intent to be a U.S. citizen as a condition of licensure as an M.D.[59] Slightly less than half have a similar requirement for D.O.s.[60] Similar requirements for lawyers and engineers have been found unconstitutional by the U.S. Supreme Court.[61]

Many states and the District of Columbia require evidence of the applicant's good character as a condition of licensure as an M.D. or D.O.[62] Only a few states, however, actually define what is meant by "good moral character." The law of Michigan, one jurisdiction which does define the term, states that good moral character is a propensity on the part of the person to serve the public in the licensed area in a fair, honest, and open manner.[63]

Foreign Trained Physicians: One response to the perceived shortage of physicians in the mid-1960s was to give physicians occupational preference in immigration policy.[64] Between 1963 and 1973 approximately 65 percent of the net increase in the U.S. physician-to-population ratio was attributable to physicians trained in foreign countries.[65] In 1972, Foreign Medical Graduates (FMGs) accounted for 46 percent of new licensees, and in 1974 FMGs occupied 29 percent of total filled residencies.[66]

The rapid increase in the number of FMGs in the U.S. raised questions about the overall quality of care provided. Particular concerns were voiced about the relatively poor performance of FMGs on licensure and credentialing examinations and the quality of their training vis-à-vis that of U.S. trained physicians. These concerns led Congress to declare a restriction on the granting of visas to FMGs since by 1973 the physician shortage seemed to have abated. Subsequently, the date of these restrictions was postponed to 1978.[67]

Some states also took action to assure the quality of care rendered by FMGs. Many states license physicians educated in foreign medical facilities as M.D.s.[68] Only a few states have some special licensure requirements for foreign trained osteopaths.[69] Several states place conditions on the professional education of foreign trained M.D.s. For example, California and Maryland require that the professional education of foreign trained M.D.s be substantially equivalent to that of U.S. trained M.D.s.[70] Florida provides for waiver of formal education requirements if the foreign trained M.D. applicant is eligible or certified as a specialist.[71] About 30 states may accept certification by the Educational Council for Foreign Medical Graduates (ECFMG) in lieu of or in addition to other requirements.[72]

States may also impose other requirements. Michigan, for example, requires that an applicant for licensure in any health profession, including M.D., have a working knowledge of the English language.[73] This requirement responds to the claim that language barriers and the cultural differences of FMGs may prevent them from providing good medical care.[74]

At least one study has attempted to determine the relationship between medical education and performance (as measured by technical performance and utilization of medical care resources) in offices and hospitals. According to the results, the differences in training among various medical schools did not have a significant effect except for specialists who were practicing in their own specialty. This study offered no evidence that U.S. medical graduates provide higher overall quality care than FMGs.[75]

In the last 20 years of FMG entry, many states and many facilities, such as those dependent on unaffiliated graduate medical education programs and state mental institutions, have developed a considerable dependency on FMG-delivered medical care. Studies have shown that hospital-based, as well as office-based, FMGs serve certain socioeconomic groups which otherwise might not find medical care readily available.[76]

With the exception of language problems and cultural differences, American graduates of foreign medical schools are likely to encounter the same difficulties meeting U.S. licensure and certification requirements as FMGs. U.S. graduates of foreign medical schools are also likely to confront stiff competition for graduate positions in the United States.[77]

In 1972, about 500 U.S. citizens went abroad to study medicine. The American Association of Medical Colleges predicts that only about 200 of these will eventually receive licensure to practice in the United States.[78] Less than 10 states have separate licensing provisions for U.S. citizens trained abroad as M.D.s,[79] while no state makes such provision for D.O. applicants.[80] About one third of the states do not classify Canadians as FMGs for purposes of M.D. licensure.[81]

Reciprocity and Endorsement: As with the procedures for obtaining a license and relicensure, the requirements for reciprocity and endorsement vary from state to state. In many states licensure by endorsement is a discretionary matter within the purview of the applicable administrative agency.[82] In New Jersey, for instance, a physician who has been examined by the licensing board of another state or who has taken the National Board of Medical Examiners' examination successfully may be granted a license to practice without further examination upon payment of a fee.[83] Some states require that the examination originally taken by the physician be of the same quality as its own and that the applicant's state extend the same privilege to its citizens.[84] Florida further requires that the applicant practice medicine for one year within three years of receiving the Florida license, or lose the license.[85]

In a number of states, successful completion of the National Board of Medical Examiners' examination is used as a benchmark in licensing out-of-state physicians. California, however, requires that the standard of the National Board examination be substantially the same as California's at the time the diplomate certificate was issued.[86] Furthermore, an oral examination is not deemed equivalent to a written examination for licensure, and the California Division of

Licensing will not issue a reciprocity certificate to a physician until he or she takes a comprehensive oral and clinical examination administered by the Division.[87]

§ 5.22 Relicensure and Continuing Medical Education

Some states have combined procedures for relicensure with provisions requiring continuing education.[88] Michigan requires anyone seeking to renew a license to complete coursework of not less than 150 hours during the three years immediately preceding his or her application. Such education must be in subjects related to the practice of medicine. Michigan further requires evidence of continuing competence to demonstrate that the licensee continues to meet the educational and practice standards of the profession.[89] Ohio, on the other hand, deals with compulsory continuing education in the context of a suspended or revoked license.[90] The state medical board may, at its discretion, require additional training and re-examination as a condition of reinstatement of the physician's license.[91] Similarly, the Florida statute, requiring additional education, applies only to renewal of inactive licenses.[92] Illinois is currently in the process of developing and evaluating a compulsory continuing education program.[93]

The procedures for relicensure vary by state, depending on the circumstances. If relicensure is merely renewal, the statutes tend to provide a period of time (California—five years,[94] Florida—one year[95]) within which the license may be renewed as a matter of form. The physician need only apply and pay a late penalty fee. If, however, the license is not renewed within that time the physician may be required to take 12 hours of coursework for each year the license was inactive, or to take and pass the examination for initial licensure or otherwise establish that he or she is qualified to practice.[96]

A suspended or revoked license is more difficult to renew, although there is again great variance from jurisdiction to jurisdiction. Under California law, the physician may not petition for reinstatement for at least one year after the date of the disciplinary action. The petition must be accompanied by a minimum of two verified recommendations from physicians with personal knowledge of the petitioner's activities after the disciplinary action was imposed. Further, the administrative body hearing the case may impose whatever restrictions or terms it deems necessary.[97] At the other end of the requirement spectrum are states such as New Jersey which provide that the physician may at the discretion of the examining board be relicensed at any time without an examination.[98] In Ohio, the Board may require an examination, either oral or written or both, as well as additional training.[99] Texas law provides for a one-year waiting period before application can be made; but reinstatement is otherwise discretionary with the Board of Medical Examiners.[100] Virginia has only a three-month waiting period.[101]

Some states provide for reinstating the license of a physician who has been found mentally incompetent.[102] In Illinois, a judgment by a state court operates as a

§ 5.23   *Disciplinary Proceedings*   149

suspension of his or her license. The physician may resume practice only when the state medical board confirms a court finding that the physician has recovered and should be permitted to resume practice.[103]

§ 5.23 Disciplinary Proceedings

The Due Process Clause of the Fourteenth Amendment to the U.S. Constitution protects individuals from the deprivation of property by state governments without due process of law. Many early legal decisions recognized the right to practice medicine as a valuable property right which is entitled to be protected and secured.[104] Consequently, medical licensure boards, as agents of state governments, are required to exercise fundamental fairness in disciplinary proceedings. The U.S. Supreme Court has recently held that while the federal Constitution does not guarantee the unrestricted right to engage in a business or to conduct it at pleasure, a person may not be excluded from a legitimate occupation without due process.[105]

Procedural Aspects: The type of procedural protections required by due process depends on factors such as the interests of the parties involved, the gravity and potential impact of the decision, the nature of the proceeding, the importance of the particular procedure in assuring the decision's validity and the possible burden on that proceeding.[106]

If the determinations of medical associations, specialty boards, hospitals and other non-governmental bodies take on the character of "state action" (see § 7.90, Medical Staff Privileges), they are subject to due process constraints. Often the disciplinary decisions of these bodies have major and far-reaching impacts on a professional's career.

Most procedural requirements for disciplinary proceedings have evolved from two essential constitutional mandates: (1) that adequate notice be given that the disciplinary action will take place and (2) that the party disciplined be given the opportunity to be heard.[107] Other aspects of due process have been provided by state statute or imposed by court decision. Many states have adopted legislation modeled after the Model State Administrative Procedures Act.[108] Model Act Standards include requirements for contents of the notice of hearing, hearing procedures, and criteria for judicial review of administrative decisions. These procedures apply in contested cases involving the grant, denial, renewal, revocation, or suspension of a license.

Notice: Due process requires that proper notice be given to afford the physician an opportunity to meet the charges against him or her. Due process is satisfied if the licensee has reasonable notice of the hearing and a reasonable opportunity to be heard and to present his or her claim or defense (within the context of the nature of the proceeding and the character of the right that may be affected by it).[109] The statement of charges or complaint must be specific enough to enable the accused to prepare a defense, although the exact statutory language under which the charges are brought need not be used.[110] Some courts have held that the notice requirement embraces not only accusations against the licensee, but the disciplinary action contemplated as well.[111] An Illinois court has held that the Constitution requires that the accused be personally notified.[112] Conducting the hearing on unreasonably short notice (i.e., two days) violates due process.[113] Unless statutorily required, the notice need not specify the right of the accused to be represented by an attorney.[114]

Requirements for response to the notice of charges vary among states. Some states require a written answer prior to the hearing.[115] Other states make the opportunity to respond optional.[116]

Hearing: A full, fair, and impartial hearing before an appropriate administrative body or tribunal is a minimum requirement of due process in most cases.[117] Although the tribunal is required to be impartial, it may handle both the investigative and adjudicative aspects of a disciplinary hearing. The honesty and integrity of the tribunal members is presumed; therefore, the burden of proving tribunal bias is on the person alleging its existence.[118] To disqualify the tribunal, bias must be of a personal nature leading to a substantially preconceived resolution of the issues. It then becomes a matter for review by a court.[119] Findings of bias have occurred when a specific medical or professional society has unduly influenced the disciplinary process or the board.[120] In cases in which the results appear fair and based on the record,[121] general bias claims against individual board members or the board as a whole have been unsuccessful. Although the notice of the hearing need not include notification of the right to counsel,[122] a physician is entitled to be represented by legal counsel at the hearing.

The person charged is also entitled to be an active participant in the hearing. This participation includes testifying on his or her own behalf, presenting, challenging and confronting witnesses.[123] The credibility of witnesses is for the board to determine.[124]

Evidence in support of the complaint is heard before the accused presents his or her evidence. If no evidence is offered to support the complaint, it should be dismissed, sparing the accused the necessity of presenting evidence.[125] Although evidence presented at hearings must meet some minimum standards of reliability, authenticity, and fairness, it need not conform to the strict rules of evidence observed in judicial proceedings. Generally, hearsay testimony unsupported by other corroborative evidence will not be admissible in an administrative hearing.[126] Evidence obtained through unconstitutional means is also not permitted at an administrative hearing.[127] One court has extended the protection of the physician-patient privilege to the administrative hearing in order to prevent the disclosure of confidential information acquired while treating a patient who has not waived the

§ 5.23   *Disciplinary Proceedings*   151

privilege.[128] However, transcripts from prior related judicial proceedings may be admitted as evidence.[129]

A board's action may be predicated on a physician's guilty plea to criminal charges arising from the same facts as those before the tribunal.[130] Revocation of a physician's license for conduct that resulted in a felony conviction does not violate due process. Double jeopardy does not apply since a licensure action is administrative and not criminal in nature.[131]

After the hearing, the board must publish a statement of its findings. Normally this will include an evaluation of the evidence presented, findings of fact, a statement of offenses committed, if any, and the assignment of a penalty.[132] An order of the board which is not sufficiently specific may be reversed on appeal.[133] Generally the reviewing court will not alter an order of the board that is supported by "substantial evidence."[134] The record of the hearing must contain the factual basis from which the board makes its conclusion regarding the complaint.[135]

Judicial Review: Generally, state statutes provide for some type of review of administrative decisions by the state court.[136] The case must meet three criteria before it may be reviewed by a court of law: jurisdiction, justiciability, and exhaustion of administrative remedies. Jurisdiction is the power of the court to recognize and decide an issue. Federal courts, for example, generally do not have jurisdiction to intervene in state medical board proceedings.[137]

Justiciability refers to the existence of an actual claim or dispute which requires a solution. Thus, a case may be dismissed as moot if the outcome of the decision would no longer have an effect on the parties owing to a change in circumstances following the dispute.[138] Such a case is not justiciable.

Exhaustion of administrative remedies requires that a party allow the board to review and enter a final order in a case before seeking judicial review. For example, a physician must petition the board for restoration of a suspended license before requesting a court order to require the board to restore it.[139]

The board's order will be terminated by the reviewing court in cases where the board cannot successfully defend its ruling.[140]

In some cases a physician may appeal to a court before the board has entered a final order. This is done where no other course of procedure is available and judicial review is necessary to preserve the fairness of the board proceedings. For example, judicial review has been allowed prior to the final administrative determination of a board ruling that had denied the accused physician's request for subpoenas to compel disclosure of certain documents prior to the hearing.[141]

Ex Parte Actions: In some states the board is empowered to suspend a physician's license temporarily without a formal hearing. Generally this power is limited to cases in which the public health, safety, or welfare requires emergency action.[142] Action taken on this basis is referred to as *ex parte* action.

Some courts have allowed the board to revoke a license without a hearing when the physician has been convicted of or has pleaded guilty to a felony,[143] or has violated certain federal or state narcotic laws.[144]

State statutes may provide for automatic suspension of a license based on a formal adjudication of the licensee's mental incompetence.[145]

Grounds: Grounds for instituting a disciplinary action against a physician are usually specified by state statute. These grounds may be specific offenses, such as criminal conduct, or may be generic offenses not specifically included in the statute but falling under a more general heading such as unprofessional conduct.

A statutory offense must be specific enough to inform the licensee of the actions it prohibits. Statutes which are not sufficiently specific may be attacked in court as unconstitutionally vague.[146]

Unprofessional conduct is a ground for disciplinary action in all states.[147] Most states specify the types of conduct included within this category. For example, the Michigan statute provides:

> Unprofessional conduct, consisting of any of the following:
>
> (a) Misrepresentation to a consumer or patient or in obtaining or attempting to obtain third party reimbursement in the course of professional practice.
>
> (b) Betrayal of a professional confidence.
>
> (c) Promotion for personal gain of an unnecessary drug, device, treatment, procedure, or service, or directing or requiring an individual to purchase or secure a drug, device, treatment, procedure, or service from another person, place, facility, or business in which the licensee has a financial interest.[148]

Texas gives a general definition of unprofessional conduct and then includes specific examples:

> Unprofessional or dishonorable conduct which is likely to deceive or defraud the public. Unprofessional or dishonorable conduct shall include, but shall not be limited to, the following acts:
>
> (a) The commission of any act which is a violation of the Penal Code of Texas when such act is connected with the physician's practice of medicine. A complaint, indictment, or conviction of a Penal Code violation shall not be necessary for the enforcement of this provision. Proof of the commission of the act while in the practice of medicine or under the guise of the practice of medicine shall be sufficient for action by the Board under this section.
>
> (b) Failure to keep complete and accurate records of purchases and disposals of drugs listed in [another section of the statute], or of narcotic drugs. A physician shall keep records of his purchases and disposals of the aforesaid drugs to include, but not be limited to, date of purchase, sale or disposal of such drugs by the doctor, the name and address of the person receiving the drugs and reason for disposing of or dispensing the drugs to such person. A failure to keep such records shall be

§ 5.23 *Disciplinary Proceedings* 153

grounds for revoking, cancelling, suspending or probating the license of any practitioner of medicine.

(c) Writing prescriptions for or dispensing to a person known to be an habitual user of narcotic drugs or dangerous drugs, or to a person who the doctor should have known was an habitual user of narcotic or dangerous drugs. This provision shall not apply to those persons being treated by the physician for their narcotic use after the physician notifies the Texas State Board of Medical Examiners in writing of the name and address of such person being so treated.

(d) The writing of false or fictitious prescriptions for narcotic drugs or dangerous drugs listed in [another section of the statute].

(e) Prescribing or administering a drug or treatment which is nontherapeutic in nature or nontherapeutic in the manner such drug or treatment is administered or prescribed.[149]

Statutory language which is vague, such as "unprofessional," "unlawful," or "unethical" conduct, has been justified when it has been adequately defined by subsequent judicial decisions.[150] For example, a physician was found to have committed acts of unprofessional conduct after he disclosed to medical board investigators that he had sold examination questions and answers to medical licensure candidates.[151] Child molesting[152] and violation of a civil statute prohibiting office abortions[153] have also been found to constitute "unprofessional conduct." Depending upon the facts involved, courts will not allow semantics to prevent an appropriate revocation.

CASE ILLUSTRATION

Two osteopathic physicians were charged with knowingly and intentionally making excessive and unwarranted charges to public funds under Medicare claims as medical providers. The physicians contended that their conduct did not constitute grounds for license revocation since the petition charging them alleged "unethical" conduct while the statute covered "immoral, unprofessional or dishonorable" conduct. The court found little substantial difference in the terms and held that the charges warranted revocation. (*Kansas Board of Healing Arts v. Seasholtz*, 1972)[154]

"Professional incompetence" has recently become a ground for disciplinary action outside of the general "unprofessional conduct" ground. Revocation of a physician's license must be supported by evidence of specific acts or a course of conduct showing incompetency.[155] Courts have been less willing to allow the board's broad discretion in the use of this charge.

CASE ILLUSTRATION

The board alleged that the physician had incorrectly diagnosed the cases of seven patients as gonorrhea and consequently had given them the wrong treatment. They charged her with unprofessional conduct in making "misleading, deceptive, or fraudulent representations and with engaging in unethical . . . conduct." The court reversed the board's suspension of the physician's license finding that the physician was only guilty of faulty diagnoses resulting from the use of a less preferred test. The test conformed to minimum standards of practice even though it was not the most accurate and currently acceptable method. The court concluded that incorrect diagnoses alone do not constitute medical incompetence unless they result from failure to conform to minimal standards of practice. (*Gentry v. Dept. of Professional and Occupational Regulation, 1974*)[156]

The generic term "immoral conduct" includes cases of sexual impropriety. Courts have split on whether the immoral conduct must be related to the physician's practice.[157] For example, in a case in which a physician had been charged with moral turpitude for making a homosexual gesture to a police officer in a public restroom, the court agreed with the physician that the issue was whether the claimed conduct would adversely affect future patients. However, the court sustained the board's action (probation) since their expertise placed board members in a better position to assess the likelihood of danger to patients.[158]

The category "unlawful conduct" includes convictions for specific offenses, conduct meriting, though for some reason not eliciting, criminal prosecution,[159] and acts for which the physician has been acquitted.[160] Disciplinary action may be imposed for unlawful conduct even though the law has not established guilt.[161] Physicians have unsuccessfully challenged disciplinary actions for unlawful conduct using equal protection arguments, claiming that additional sanctions are imposed on physicians without valid reason for distinguishing them from other persons who commit the same crimes.[162]

The majority of statutes also include specific grounds for disciplinary action. In Michigan, for example, the following list of grounds for disciplinary action includes several specific offenses:

    I. A. A violation of a general duty, consisting of negligence or failure to exercise due care, including negligent delegation to or supervision of employees or other individuals, whether or not injury results, or any conduct, practice, or condition which impairs, or may impair, the ability to safely and skillfully practice the health profession.
       B. Personal disqualifications, consisting of any of the following:
          i. Incompetence.
          ii. Substance abuse as defined by statute.

iii. Mental or physical inability reasonably related to and adversely affecting the licensee's or applicant's ability to practice in a safe and competent manner.
iv. Declaration of mental incompetence by a court of competent jurisdiction.
v. Conviction of a misdemeanor or felony reasonably related to and adversely affecting the licensee's or applicant's ability to practice in a safe and competent manner. A certified copy of the court record is conclusive evidence as to the conviction.

C. Prohibited acts, consisting of any of the following:
i. Fraud or deceit in obtaining a license.
ii. Permitting the license to be used by an unauthorized person.
iii. Practice outside the scope of a license.
iv. Obtaining, possessing, or attempting to obtain or possess a controlled substance without lawful authority; or selling, prescribing, giving away, or administering drugs for other than lawful diagnostic or therapeutic purposes.

D. Unethical business practices, consisting of any of the following:
i. False or misleading advertising.
ii. Dividing fees for referral patients or accepting kickbacks on medical or surgical services, appliances, or medications purchased by or in behalf of patients.
iii. Fraud or deceit in obtaining or attempting to obtain third-party reimbursement.

E. Unprofessional conduct, consisting of any of the following:
i. Misrepresentation to a consumer or patient or in obtaining or attempting to obtain third party reimbursement in the course of professional practice.
ii. Betrayal of a professional confidence.
iii. Promotion for personal gain of an unnecessary drug, device, treatment, procedure, or service, or directing or requiring an individual to purchase or secure a drug, device, treatment, procedure, or service from another person, place, facility, or business in which the licensee has a financial interest.

F. Failure to report a change of name or address within 30 days after it occurs.

G. A violation, or aiding or abetting in a violation, of the state licensing law.

H. Failure to comply with a subpoena issued pursuant to law.

I. Failure to pay an installment of an assessment levied pursuant to law within 60 days after notice by the appropriate board.

II. A. Failure or refusal to submit to an examination which a board is authorized to require after reasonable notice and opportunity, constitutes a ground for suspension of a license until the examination is taken.

B. Additional grounds for disciplinary action may be found in the law dealing with a specific health profession.[163]

Sanctions: Until recently only two options were available to most boards when a licensee was found to have violated a medical practice act—revocation or suspension of the license and reprimand or censure.[164] In many cases the former sanctions were considered too severe while the latter were too lenient.

Many states now allow their boards to impose sanctions which are differentiated according to the severity of the offense. Generally, where the charge is supported by substantial evidence, the choice of sanction authorized by statute is a matter within a board's discretion,[165] if supported by a preponderance of the evidence.[166]

CASE ILLUSTRATION

A physician without previous disciplinary actions against him was found to have prescribed Desoxyn, a controlled substance, to known drug addicts without conducting physical examinations. The prescriptions were not issued for monetary gain. The state board charged him with negligence or incompetence on more than one occasion. The hearing panel recommended that the physician's license be revoked but that such revocation be stayed and that the physician be placed on probation for two years. The board elected to revoke the physician's license in lieu of probation. The physician appealed this decision as too harsh in light of his prior record. The court of appeals sustained the board's action finding that revocation of the physician's license to practice medicine was not excessive in view of the evidence and was within the board's authority. *(Widlitz v. Bd. of Regents,* 1980)[167]

Evidence relied on to impose sanctions on a physician, including the revocation of a license to practice medicine, need not be provided by expert testimony where the hearing body is composed of medical experts. Such a panel is recognized as qualified to exercise medical judgment to determine the propriety of the sanction imposed.

The sanctions usually available to a board are: reprimand, probation, required re-training or rehabilitation, limitation on practice, suspension, revocation, and fines. Censure or reprimand is the least intrusive sanction since it allows the physician to continue to practice without affecting the scope of his or her license, whereas probation and re-training or rehabilitation requirements allow the board to monitor certain of the physician's professional activities. These sanctions also allow the board to use its power for rehabilitative rather than strictly punitive purposes.[168] Thus, in a California decision, where the board suspended a physician's license for one year unless the physician could pass an oral clinical examination in the management of fluid and electrolyte imbalances, the court held that such a penalty was valid.[169]

In conjunction with probation or re-training, or as a separate action, the board may limit the physician's license. Michigan defines a "limited license" as a "license to which restrictions or conditions, or both, as to scope of practice, place of practice, supervision of practice, duration of licensed status, or type or condition of patient or client served are imposed by the board."[170] This type of authority allows the board to tailor the sanction to the particular licensee and circumstances.

Some states require the board to impose a mandatory sanction for certain offenses. This type of mandatory sanction removes a significant amount of the board's discretionary power when dealing with more serious offenses. For example, Iowa requires the board to revoke or suspend a license when the licensee is found guilty of any of a series of offenses, including incompetence in the practice of his or her profession.[171]

§ 5.30 PROFESSIONAL STANDARDS REVIEW ORGANIZATIONS

Professional Standards Review Organizations (PSROs) were created in 1972 by an amendment to the Social Security Act. The PSRO program empowers these review organizations to evaluate both the quality of care provided to patients and the medical necessity of admissions and continued stay at acute-level-of-care hospitals. The program applies only to patients whose bills are paid through federal reimbursement programs (Medicare, Medicaid, and Maternal and Child Health).[172]

Although critics have attacked the PSRO program from the onset and although there have been recent funding cuts, the PSRO program or something like it under a different name* will probably continue into the foreseeable future. Changes in the PSRO system will probably include state funding contributions as well as the consolidation of PSRO areas on a statewide, as opposed to regional, basis. At the present time, however, the PSRO Act is as described below.

---

*Minnesota Senator Durenberger has submitted a PSRO replacement bill: Utilization and Quality Control Peer Review Act of 1982, S.2142, 97th Cong. 2d Sess. (1982).

Purpose: According to the legislative history and the Act itself, PSROs were created to control both the cost and the quality of the medical care received by patients whose bills are paid through federal reimbursement programs. The purpose of the Act is stated explicitly:

> In order to promote the effective, efficient, and economical delivery of health care services of proper quality for which payment may be made [by Medicare or Medicaid] . . . and in recognition of the interest of patients, the public, practitioners, and providers in improved health care services, it is the purpose of this part to assure . . . that the services for which payment may be made . . . will conform to appropriate professional standards for the provision of health care and that payment for such services will be made—(1) only when, and to the extent, medically necessary; (2) in the case of services provided by hospital or health care facility . . . only when . . . such services cannot, consistent with professionally recognized health care standards, effectively be provided on an out-patient basis or more economically. . . .[173]

Organization: In order to become a PSRO, a local organization must apply to, and be approved by, the Secretary of Health and Human Services.* Initially, the Secretary makes a determination of the organization's expertise. For an organization to be considered qualified to become a PSRO, it must be:

1. a nonprofit or part of a nonprofit organization
2. composed of M.D.s and/or D.O.s representative of the area's physicians
3. composed of a substantial proportion of all physicians in the area
4. organized so that all necessary professional competencies will be available to review all types of health care services for which the PSRO has review responsibilities
5. voluntary and not limited to dues-paying members of the local or state medical society or association
6. nondiscriminatory internally against any member with respect to eligibility to review or to serve as an officer of the PSRO.

The Secretary may determine that any "public, nonprofit, or other" agency or organization may qualify as a PSRO, provided that there is no organization in the area which meets the conditions specified above.[174]

The procedure for becoming a PSRO is comprised of three stages: the planning stage, the conditional stage (where the Secretary has approved the organization), and the fully operational stage. The progression to fully operational status usually requires a four-year period. Before designating an organization as a

---

*Formerly the Department of Health, Education and Welfare.

§ 5.30 PSROs 159

conditional PSRO, the Secretary must inform the physicians practicing in the PSRO area of his or her intent to enter into the PSRO agreement with the organization. If ten percent of these physicians object, then a poll must be conducted to determine whether 50 percent of the physicians in the area acquiesce in the choice. This assures that the organization is sufficiently representative of the physicians in the area to serve as a PSRO.[175] If more than 50 percent of the physicians oppose the choice, the Secretary is prohibited from designating that organization as a PSRO, and a substitute must be found.

Duties and Functions: Each PSRO is responsible for reviewing the activities of physicians and other health care providers in the provision of health care services for which payment may be made under the Act. The purpose of this review is to determine medical necessity, quality, and appropriateness of such services. The PSRO may conduct preadmission screening of elective admissions or of other health care which consists of extended or costly services to determine if such admission or service will meet the above criteria. Other duties and functions of PSROs can be summarized as follows:

1. Each PSRO must periodically determine and publish a classification of cases according to type of health care, diagnosis, and other criteria relevant to providing health care services.
2. Each PSRO should perform periodic evaluations of services received by and provided to patients.
3. For any service paid by federal reimbursement programs, each PSRO must ascertain whether this service was medically necessary.
4. Each PSRO is expected to determine whether the services provided meet professionally recognized standards of health care.
5. Each PSRO must determine whether services or items proposed for inpatient cases could, consistent with the provision of appropriate medical care, be provided more effectively or economically in an inpatient facility of a different type, or on an outpatient basis.
6. Each PSRO must keep and maintain the forms the Secretary of Health and Human Services may require and permit his or her access to and use of any such records on request.
7. Each PSRO is to encourage all physicians in the area served to participate as reviewers by rotating physician membership of review committees on an extensive and continuing basis.[176]

Peer Review: PSROs accomplish their duties and functions through a system of peer review. To identify instances of misutilization of health care services or delivery of substandard care, PSROs adopt standards of health care, diagnosis, and treatment. These standards are the primary tools in review activities. (See Appendix B, California Anesthesia Service Regulations.)

Utilization Review: Utilization review is one type of peer review which evaluates the necessity of admission and continued confinement in acute care hospitals. Within one working day of admission to the hospital, the necessity of the admission is evaluated by a non-physician review coordinator. The criteria used are predetermined according to local standards approved by the area PSRO. Federal regulations allow a PSRO, where it is appropriate, to certify an admission for an entire hospital stay because of accumulated information and prior experience with the patient or the particular illness.[177] Such a procedure alleviates the need for constant PSRO review of the case. These admissions generally occur after a PSRO has developed a substantial data base from which normative standards emerge. Patients grouped by diagnosis, by hospital department, or by physician may be eliminated from review if there is documented evidence that the average length of stay is appropriate, that mortality and morbidity are low, that there are few inappropriate admissions and continued stays, and that periodic retrospective review will occur. Within two working days of the time of admission, admissions are to be reviewed by non-physician review coordinators according to criteria adopted by physicians within each PSRO area. If an admission is not approved by the non-physician, a physician-advisor is consulted, who then makes the medical decision whether justification exists for admission. If the admission is deemed unnecessary, payment to the hospital and the physician may be denied.[178]

Continued stay review is done on a cyclic or periodic review basis. Each case is reviewed every 72 hours as long as the patient stays in the hospital.[179] If the non-physician cannot find criteria which would justify continued stay, then the physician-advisor is consulted, and termination of benefits may occur. Whenever the physician-advisor determines that admission or continued stay is not justified, consultation with the attending physician must occur within 24 hours. If the physician-advisor and the attending physician cannot agree, a second physician-advisor is consulted. Majority vote then determines whether or not a "cease benefits" letter is issued. Even if the letter is issued, discharge of the patient is not required. However, the "cease benefits" letter indicates to the patient, the attending physician, and the hospital that the third-party payer will not be responsible for hospital charges incurred after 24 hours. The patient, attending physician, or hospital may appeal the cessation of benefits decision.

Quality Review Studies: PSROs also carry out quality review studies (formerly called medical care evaluation studies), which are detailed peer reviews of the quality of care given to patient groups (e.g., categories of care reviewed include diagnosis, operation, or therapy). Initially, local physicians, usually at the hospital level, develop review criteria using guidelines provided by national groups or organizations. The first level of review is performed by analysts who apply the predetermined criteria to individual medical records. If information in a record indicates that the criteria have not been satisfied, then the record receives a second level of review conducted by physicians who consider individual patient variations in order to determine if there is a problem in the quality of care. In this manner, the bulk of records can be screened rapidly and physician time can be limited to those cases requiring medical judgment. The final portion of the quality review study consists of recommending solutions to the hospital director of quality assurance, the administrator, and the board of trustees for any problems uncovered, and conducting a proper follow-up to see that changes have occurred which will result in better quality patient care.[180]

Profile Analysis: The PSRO law requires that PSROs develop and analyze profiles of hospital data. These profiles are statistical reports produced by the PSRO through the aggregation of available patient care data. Profiles must be regularly reviewed to determine whether the care and services ordered or rendered are consistent with necessity, quality, and appropriateness criteria.[181] If aberrant patterns of care appear, the corrective changes will be demanded before the major sanction of withholding reimbursement is instituted.

For the above three types of peer review, the evaluations can be either concurrent or retrospective. Generally, utilization reviews are performed concurrently, and are divided into admission certification and continued stay review. Quality review studies combine elements of concurrent and retrospective review.

Furthermore, the procedures followed in utilization review and quality review studies provide the most efficient use of physician manpower. The procedures allow PSROs to channel physician input into the cases where it is needed most, by allowing the initial screening to be performed by non-physicians.

Appeal Procedures: The initial PSRO decision as to whether a physician or hospital should be reimbursed is not necessarily final. An appeal procedure exists. The dissatisfied claimant (patient, physician, or hospital) is entitled to have his or her case reconsidered by a local PSRO, the state Professional Standard Review Council, and ultimately by the Secretary of Health and Human Services.[182] When a PSRO disapproves a claim, the hospital, the physician, or both, may bear the financial loss. Medicare and Medicaid patients are usually immune from creditor actions for PSRO-disapproved services. However, PSROs rarely disapprove provider or physician claims for services rendered. A provider who consistently and flagrantly violates the PSRO standards may be subject to stiffer sanctions. The Secretary "may exclude . . . such practitioner or provider from eligibility to provide such services on a reimbursable basis." However, before a final decision is made, the practitioner is entitled to a hearing before the Secretary and judicial review.[183]

Associated Agencies: A number of agencies associated with PSROs facilitate their effective performance. One of these is the National Professional Standards Review Council, composed of 11 physicians recommended by various groups. Its purposes are to advise the Secretary, assist the statewide councils, evaluate the effectiveness of statewide councils, and arrange studies that will facilitate the purposes of the PSRO Act.

Currently, there are 203 PSRO areas in the United States. Each state is subdivided into PSRO regions as required by the PSRO Act and regulations.[184] Michigan, for instance, has 10 PSRO areas.[185] When there are three or more PSROs located in a single state, a statewide Professional Standards Review Council will be formed. The purposes of this Statewide Review Council are to coordinate the PSROs' activities and to exchange data, assist in evaluating PSRO performance, and assist in finding replacements for disenfranchised PSROs. The members of this Council are appointed by the Secretary according to the following criteria:

1. One representative from and designated by each PSRO
2. Two physicians designated by the state medical society
3. Two physicians designated by the state hospital association
4. Four public members.[186]

The AMA interacts with PSROs by promulgating some of the standards used in PSRO reviews. These standards may be modified at the local level. The American Association of PSROs (AAPSRO) has also promulgated updated standards.

Immunity: Although the government's desire to hold down costs and the medical profession's desire to improve the quality of medical care are not mutually exclusive, problems often arise. One problem involves immunity from liability for a physician who discloses a patient's health record. The framers of the PSRO Act anticipated this problem and adopted a section that severely limits the liability of those contributing information to PSROs and those analyzing this information.[187] The person providing such information is immune from liability (civil or criminal) unless the information is unrelated to a PSRO activity or the person providing the information knows or has reason to know that the information is false. Since many physicians fear that peer review procedures could prompt defamation suits by their colleagues, some states have enacted statutes providing immunity for those working for or providing information to peer review committees.[188] The purpose of these statutes is to prevent physicians from practicing defensive medicine.

A malpractice immunity section was written into the Act to shield physicians from malpractice claims for actions which comply with established standards of care and treatment.[189] This immunity is effective only if the physician acts in the exercise of his or her function as a provider of health services, and exercises due care. In practice, this provision has never been successfully employed as a defense by a physician-defendant in a malpractice case.[190]

The chief complaint of consumer critics is that physicians are appointed to watch over themselves. They question whether physicians will criticize their colleagues. Although some physicians also complain about PSROs, most see them as a necessary evil. As the head of one Michigan PSRO aptly put it, "We feel the PSRO program is distasteful at times but is workable and is a lot better than what might have happened to us and our patients."[191]

§ 5.40 STATE AND FEDERAL CONTROLLED SUBSTANCES ACTS

The Federal Controlled Substances Act (FCSA) was enacted by Congress in 1970 to control drug abuse and related matters. The purpose of the act is to create a closed system for the distribution of dangerous drugs in order to prevent the diversion of these drugs from the legitimate distribution chain.[192] This is accomplished by classifying dangerous drugs according to a schedule of controlled substances,[193] registering drug manufacturers, wholesalers, retailers, and others,[194] and requiring that records be kept of the transactions of nearly all the dangerous drugs in the system.[195] Civil and criminal penalties are prescribed for violations of the act.[196]

Although the FCSA is primarily concerned with drug manufacturers, wholesalers, and retailers, it affects physicians as well. Every physician who administers, prescribes, or dispenses any of the drugs listed in the Act must be registered annually with the Department of Justice, Bureau of Narcotics and Dangerous Drugs. Distinctions are made between the statutory definitions of "administer," "prescribe," and "dispense." To "administer" means to apply a controlled substance directly to the body of a patient. This is done by the practitioner or, in his or her presence, by authorized agent, by injection, inhalation, ingestion, or other means.[197] To "dispense" means to deliver a controlled substance to an ultimate user, and includes the prescribing, administering, and packaging or compounding necessary to prepare the substance for delivery.[198] To "prescribe" means to issue a prescription.[199]

Since many drugs used regularly in anesthesiology are classified as controlled substances,* the act applies to anesthesiologists, and they must register with the Attorney General in accordance with the rules and regulations promulgated by him.[200] This registration may be suspended or revoked by the Attorney General upon findings that the registrant:

1. Has materially falsified any application filed pursuant to or required by the FCSA
2. Has been convicted of a felony under the FCSA or any other law of the

---

*E.g., Secobarbital appears in Schedule 3.

[U.S.], or of any state, relating to any substance defined in the FCSA as a controlled substance

3. Has had his state license or registration suspended, revoked, or denied by competent state authority and is no longer authorized by state law to engage in the manufacturing, distribution, or dispensing of controlled substances[201]

In addition to the Federal Controlled Substances Act, physicians, including anesthesiologists, must comply with their state's laws dealing with dangerous drugs. Most states[202] have adopted a form of the Uniform Controlled Substances Act (UCSA) which was drafted as a model state law by the National Conference of Commissioners on Uniform State Laws in 1970 and recommended for adoption in all states.[203] The purpose of the model state UCSA, like the Federal Act, was to assure continued free movement of controlled substances between states while preventing the diversion of these drugs from legitimate uses.[204] By adopting the UCSA, states are assured of having a set of drug laws which are similar to the laws of other states and complement federal drug laws. Thus, the UCSA closely parallels the FCSA in terms of definitions, drug classification, registration, and record-keeping requirements.

The UCSA requires any person who manufactures, distributes, dispenses or prescribes a controlled substance to obtain an annual license issued by the state Board of Pharmacy or its designated or established authority.[205] Thus, physicians must obtain a license pursuant to the act. Reasonable fees may be charged for the license.[206]

The FCSA and UCSA place controlled substances into five schedules (see Appendix A). Substances placed in Schedule 1 have a high potential for abuse and no accepted medical use in treatment (in the United States) or lack accepted safety for use in treatment under medical supervision.[207]

Substances placed in Schedule 2 have a high potential for abuse and may lead to severe psychological or physical dependence; these have a currently accepted medical use with severe restrictions.[208] Substances with less potential for abuse, whose abuse may lead to moderate or low physical dependence or high psychological dependence, and which have currently accepted medical use, are placed in Schedule 3.[209] Substances are placed in Schedule 4 if, relative to Schedule 3 substances, they have a low potential for abuse which may lead to limited physical dependence or psychological dependence and have a currently accepted medical use.[210] Schedule 5 substances have a lower potential for abuse and a currently accepted medical use.[211] Many drugs used by anesthesiologists are classified as controlled substances. Some strong analgesics having morphine as a prototype are included in Schedule 2 or, depending on their chemical makeup, in Schedule 3. Other drugs which are placed in Schedule 3 are the barbiturates, including secobarbital and pentobarbital. The general anesthetic methohexital has been placed in Schedule 4, along with the following sedatives and hypnotics, which may be used as adjuncts to anesthesia: chlordiazepoxide, diazepam, and meprobamate.

A license issued under the UCSA allows physicians to dispense or prescribe drugs in Schedules 2, 3, 4, and 5. However, the issuance of a license does not authorize a physician to dispense, manufacture, distribute, or prescribe a controlled substance if such activities are not for legitimate and professionally recognized therapeutic, scientific, or industrial purposes, or are not in the scope of practice of a practitioner licensee.[212]

A license to manufacture, distribute, prescribe, or dispense a controlled substance may be denied, suspended, or revoked by the administrator of the Board of Pharmacy upon a finding that an applicant for licensure or a licensee:

1. Furnished false or fraudulent material information in an application for a license to distribute controlled substances
2. Was convicted of a felony under a state or federal law relating to a controlled substance
3. Has had his or her federal registration to manufacture, distribute, or dispense controlled substances surrendered, suspended, or revoked
4. Promoted a controlled substance to the general public
5. Is not a practitioner, manufacturer, or distributor
6. Has not maintained effective controls against diversion of controlled substances to other than legitimate and professionally recognized therapeutic, scientific, or industrial uses
7. Is not in compliance with applicable federal, state, and local laws
8. Manufactured, distributed, or dispensed a controlled substance for other than legitimate or professionally recognized therapeutic, scientific, or industrial purposes or is outside the scope of practice of the practitioner-licensee or applicant
9. Violated or attempted to violate, directly or indirectly, assisted in or aided the violation of, or conspired to violate any of the rules regulating controlled substances[213]

The administrator of the Board of Pharmacy may limit license revocation or suspension to the particular controlled substance for which grounds for revocation or suspension exist.[214]

If a license is suspended or revoked, all controlled substances owned or possessed by the licensee at the time of suspension or effective date of revocation may be placed under seal or seized at the discretion of the administrator. When a revocation order becomes final, all controlled substances may be forfeited to the state.[215]

Required Records: Under the USCA any person licensed to handle controlled substances must keep records and maintain inventories in conformance with the recordkeeping and inventory requirements of federal law and with any additional rules the administrator promulgates, unless exempted from those rules.[216]

Order Forms: A controlled substance in Schedules 1 and 2 can be distributed by a licensee to another licensee only pursuant to an order form. Compliance with the federal laws respecting order forms is deemed compliance with this requirement.[217]

The UCSA regulates the prescription of controlled substances as follows:

1. Except when dispensed directly by a practitioner, other than a pharmacy, to an ultimate user, no controlled substance in Schedule 2 may be dispensed without the written prescription of a practitioner.

2. In emergency situations, as defined by rule of the appropriate person or agency, Schedule 2 drugs may be dispensed upon oral prescription of a practitioner, reduced promptly to writing and filed by the pharmacy. Prescriptions shall be retained in conformity with the law. No prescription for a Schedule 2 substance may be refilled.

3. Except when dispensed directly by a practitioner, other than a pharmacy, to an ultimate user, a controlled substance included in Schedule 3 or 4, which is a prescription drug as determined under appropriate state or federal statute, shall not be dispensed without a written or oral prescription of a practitioner. The prescription shall not be filled or refilled more than six months after the date thereof or be refilled more than five times, unless renewed by the practitioner.

4. A controlled substance included in Schedule 5 shall not be distributed or dispensed other than for a medical purpose.[218]

The model Uniform Controlled Substances Act defines offenses which violate the act, but allows each state to set its own penalties.[219] These penalties vary widely, in both form and substance. New York has enacted a separate article to deal with controlled substances offenses.[220] At least one state and many localities have decriminalized the possession and/or sale of marijuana.[221]

Despite the goal of uniformity, other areas of state-controlled substance laws vary widely. Five states (Alaska, Colorado, Maine, New Hampshire, Vermont) and the District of Columbia have so far failed to enact any form of the UCSA.

§ 5.40   *Controlled Substances Acts*   167

Three of these states and the District of Columbia have retained and updated the old Uniform Narcotics Drug Act.[222] Two other states have enacted their own drug acts, which differ materially from the UCSA.[223]

Even among states which have adopted the UCSA, significant differences exist. A few states require triplicate prescriptions for Schedule 2 drugs while most states do not.[224] Some states prohibit dispensing samples of all controlled substances. Provisions regulating medical research with controlled substances vary greatly.[225] At least one state has inserted a generic drug law in its Controlled Substances Act.[226] A number of states are beginning to transfer drugs from one schedule to another and add drugs to schedules, and one state has introduced a Schedule 6 containing all prescription drugs not covered in Schedules 1–5.[227] These differences among states require that physicians become familiar with and keep abreast of changes in their particular state's controlled substances laws.

NOTES

1. Dent v. W. Va., 129 U.S. 114 (1888).
2. L. Friedman, A History of American Law 163 (1973).
3. U.S. Dept. Health, Education & Welfare, Report on Licensure and Related Personnel Credentialing, 54-55 (DHEW Pub. No. HMS 72-11) (1971).
4. Dent v. W. Va., *supra* note 1.
5. *Id.*
6. *In re* Griffiths, 413 U.S. 717 (1973); Adams v. Tanner, 244 U.S. 590 (1916).
7. U.S. Dept. Health, Education & Welfare, Report on Medical Disciplinary Procedures 57 (1978) [hereinafter cited as DHEW].
8. American Medical Association, 5 State Health Legis. Rep. 2 (Sept. 1977) [hereinafter cited as AMA].
9. *See, e.g.,* Cal. Bus. & Prof. Code § 2323 West (1974 & Supp. 1981); Ill. Ann. Stat. ch. 111, § 4435 (Smith-Hurd 1978 & Supp.1980-81); Md. Health Code Ann. art. 43, § 120 (Supp. 1980); N.Y. Educ. Law § 230 (McKinney Supp. 1981).
10. Dept. of Health, Education & Welfare, Public Health Soc., Health Resources Admin., State Regulation of Health Manpower 2 (DHEW Pub. No. HRA 77-49) (1976).
11. *Id.*
12. Ala. Code § 34-24-1 (1977).
13. N.Y. Educ. Law § 230 (McKinney Supp. 1981).
14. *See, e.g.,* Ill. Ann. Stat. ch. 111, § 4435 (Smith-Hurd 1978 & Supp. 1980-81); Ind. Code Ann. § 25-22.5-2-6 (Burns 1976); Va. Code § 54-282 (1978).
15. N.J. Stat. Ann. § 45:9-1 (West 1978 & Supp. 1981-82).
16. *See, e.g.,* Cal. Bus. & Prof. Code §§ 2000-22 (West 1974 & Supp. 1981); Ga. Code Ann. §§ 84-901 *et seq.* (1979 & Supp. 1980); Ill. Ann. Stat. ch. 111, §§ 4401 *et seq.* (Smith-Hurd 1978 & Supp. 1980-81); Ky. Rev. Stat. Ann. § 311.565 (Baldwin 1977); Md. Health Code Ann. art. 43, § 121 (Supp. 1980); Tenn. Code Ann. § 63-608 (1976).
17. Mass. Gen. Laws Ann. ch. 13, §§ 8 *et seq.* (West 1980).
18. *See, e.g.,* Ariz. Rev. Stat. Ann. § 32.1402 (1976); Cal. Bus. & Prof. Code § 2001

Notes: Chapter V

(West 1974 & Supp. 1981); Fla. Stat. Ann. § 458.307 (West Supp. 1980); Iowa Code Ann. § 147.14 (West Supp. 1981-82); Wash. Rev. Code Ann. § 18.72.040 (1978).
19. Conn. Gen. Stat. Ann. § 20-8(a) (West Supp. 1981).
20. *See, e.g.*, Md. Health Code Ann. art. 43, § 120 (Supp. 1980); N.C. Gen. Stat. § 90-3 (1975 & Supp. 1979).
21. *See, e.g.*, Del. Code Ann. tit. 24, § 1710 (Supp. 1980); Ga. Code Ann. § 84-903 (1979 & Supp. 1980); Neb. Rev. Stat. §71-117 (1971); Okla. Stat. Ann. tit. 59, § 482 (1971).
22. *See, e.g.*, Ariz. Rev. Stat. Ann. § 32-1402 (1976); Colo. Rev. Stat. § 12-36-103 (Supp. 1980); N.Y. Educ. Law § 230 (McKinney Supp. 1981); Va. Code § 54-284 (1978).
23. DHEW, *supra* note 7, at 60.
24. *See, e.g.*, Ariz. Rev. Stat. Ann. § 32-1402 (1976); Fla. Stat. Ann. § 458-307 (West Supp. 1980); Ga. Code Ann. § 84-902 (1979 & Supp. 1980); Miss. Code Ann. § 73-43-3 (Supp. 1980).
25. *See, e.g.*, Fla. Stat. Ann. § 458.307 (West Supp. 1980); Ga. Code Ann. § 84-902 (1979 & Supp. 1980); Ill. Ann. Stat. ch. 111, § 4435 (Smith-Hurd 1978 & Supp. 1980-1981); Wis. Stat. Ann. § 15-405(7) (West Supp. 1980-81).
26. *See, e.g.*, Del. Code Ann. tit. 24, § 1710 (1975 & Supp. 1980); Ga. Code Ann. § 84-902 (1979 & Supp. 1980); Wash. Rev. Code Ann. § 18-72-040 (1978).
27. *See, e.g.*, Ind. Code Ann. § 25-22.5-2-1 (Burns 1976).
28. *See, e.g.*, Conn. Gen. Stat. Ann.§ 20-8(a) (West Supp. 1981).
29. *See, e.g.*, Cal. Bus. & Prof. Code § 2007 (West 1974 & Supp. 1981); Neb. Rev. Stat. § 71-115 (1971).
30. *See, e.g.*, Fla. Stat. Ann. § 458.307 (West Supp. 1980); Iowa Code Ann. § 147.14 (West Supp. 1981-82).
31. DHEW, *supra* note 7, at 60.
32. AMA, *supra* note 8, at 18.
33. Dept. Health, Education & Welfare Public Health Service, Health Resources Admin., State Regulation of Health Manpower 3 (DHEW Pub. No. (HRA) 77-49) (1977) [herein after cited as DHEW State Regulation].
34. *Id.* at 157.
35. *Id.* at 171.
36. *Id.* at 157; *See, e.g.*, Ala. Code 34-24-70 (1977); Ariz. Rev. Stat. Ann. § 32-1423 (1976); Conn. Gen. Stat. Ann. § 20-10 (West Supp. 1981); Mich. Comp. Laws Ann. § 333.17031 (1980); Ill. Ann. Stat. ch. 111, § 4411 (Smith-Hurd 1978 & Supp. 1980-81).
37. DHEW State Regulation, *supra* note 33, at 171; Fla. Sta. Ann. § 459.006 (West Supp. 1980); Ill. Ann. Stat. ch. 111, § 4411 (Smith-Hurd 1978 & Supp. 1980-81); N.J. Stat. Ann. § 45.9-14.1 (West 1978 & Supp. 1981-82).
38. *See, e.g.*, Ala. Code § 34-23-23 (1977); Colo. Rev. Stat. § 12-36-107 (supp. 1980); Tenn. Code Ann. § 63-611 (1976).
39. Cal. Bus. & Prof. Code §§ 2080-89 (West Supp. 1981).
40. *Id.* at § 2082.
41. *Id.* at § 2089.
42. *Id.* at § 2096.
43. *Id.* at § 2087.
44. *See, e.g.*, Alaska Stat. § 08.64.220 (1977); Cal. Bus. & Prof. Code § 2281 (West Supp. 1981); Tenn. Code Ann. § 63-611 (1976); Wyo. Stat. § 33-26-112 (1969).
45. *See, e.g.*, Ariz. Rev. Stat. Ann. § 32-1428 (1976); Cal. Bus. & Prof. Code § 2281

Notes: Chapter V   169

(West Supp. 1981); N.J. Stat. Ann. § 45:9-15 (West 1978 & Supp. 1981-82).
46. *See, e.g.*, Alaska Stat. § 08.64.220 (1977); Cal. Bus. & Prof. Code § 2281 (West Supp. 1981); Iowa Code Ann. § 147.34 (West Supp. 1981-82); W. Va. Code § 30-14-5 (1980); Wyo. Stat. § 33-26-112 (1969).
47. *See, e.g.*, Cal. Bus. & Prof. Code § 2281 (West Supp. 1981); Iowa Code Ann. § 147.34 (West 1981-82); Mont. Rev. Codes Ann. § 37-5-302 (Supp. 1977); N.J. Stat. Ann. § 45.9-14.1 (West 1978 & Supp. 1981-82); Va. Code § 54-300.1 (1977 & Supp. 1980).
48. *See, e.g.*, Cal. Bus. & Prof. Code §§ 2194, 2288 (West Supp. 1981); Fla. Stat. Ann. §§ 458.09, .051 (West Supp. 1980); Mass. Gen. Laws Ann. ch. 112, §§ 2, 2A (1980); Ohio Rev. Code Ann. § 4731.13 (Page 1977); Rules of Ohio St. Med. Bd. MB-3-14; Tenn. Code Ann. §§ 63-611, 615 (1976).
49. *See, e.g.*, Ariz. Rev. Stat. § 32-1822 (1976); Cal. Bus. & Prof. Code § 2194 (West Supp. 1981); Fla. Stat. Ann. § 459.007 (West Supp. 1980); Minn. Stat. Ann. § 147.02 (West Supp. 1981); N.J. Stat. Ann. § 45.9-13 (West 1978 & Supp. 1981-82).
50. *See, e.g.*, Ariz. Rev. Stat. Ann. § 32-1428(c) (1976); Cal. Bus. & Prof. Code § 2288 (West Supp. 1981); Conn; Gen. Stat. Ann. § 20-18(a) (West Supp. 1981) (specified subjects for D.O.s but not for M.D.s); Mass. Gen. Laws Ann. ch. 112, § 3 (West 1980); Tenn. Code Ann. § 63-611 (1976).
51. *See, e.g.*, Ariz. Rev. Stat Ann. § 32-1428 (1976); Fla. Stat. Ann.§ 459.007 (West Supp. 1980); Ky. Rev. Stat. Ann. § 311.570 (Baldwin Supp. 1980); Minn. Stat. Ann. § 147.02 (West Supp. 1981); Or. Rev. Stat. § 677.110 (1979); S.D. Comp. Laws Ann. § 36-4-17 (1977).
52. *See, e.g.*, Colo. Rev. Stat. Ann. § 12-36-113 (Supp. 1980); Ky. Rev. Stat. Ann. § 311.570 (Supp. 1980).
53. *See, e.g.*, Ala. Code § 34-24-72 (1977); Idaho Code § 54-1810 (1979); Ind. Code Ann. § 25-22.5-4-2 (Burns 1980); N.H. Rev. Stat. Ann. § 329:13 (1966 & Supp. 1979); Vt. Stat. Ann. tit. 26, § 1394 (Supp. 1980).
54. Ala. Code § 34-24-72 (1977); Ind. Code Ann. § 25-22.5-4-2 (Burns 1980); Mont. Rev. Codes Ann. § 37-5-301 (Supp. 1977).
55. *See, e.g.*, Colo. Rev. Stat. Ann. § 12-36-107 (Supp. 1980); N.J. Stat. Ann. § 45:9-6 (West 1978 & Supp. 1981-82).
56. *See, e.g.*, Conn. Gen. Stat. Ann. § 20-10 (West Supp. 1981); Ky. Rev. Stat. Ann. § 311.570 (Baldwin 1977); Ohio Rev. Code Ann. § 4731.08 (Page 1977.).
57. *See, e.g.*, N.J. Stat. Ann. § 45:9-6 (West 1978 & Supp. 1981-82).
58. *See, e.g.*, Conn. Gen. Stat. Ann. § 20-10 (West Supp. 1981); Ky. Rev. Stat. Ann. § 311.570 (Baldwin 1977); Ohio Rev. Code Ann. § 4731.08 (Page 1977).
59. *See, e.g.*, Ariz. Rev. Stat. Ann. § 32-1423 (1976); Ill. Ann. Stat. ch. 111, § 4410 (Smith-Hurd 1978 & Supp. 1980-81); Mo. Ann. Stat. § 334.031 (Vernon 1966); N.Y. Educ. Law § 6524 (McKinney 1972 & Supp. 1980-81).
60. *See, e.g.*, Alaska Stat. § 08.64.205 (1977); Ill. Ann. Stat. ch. 111, § 4410 (Smith-Hurd 1978 & Supp. 1980-81); Mo. Ann. Stat. § 334.031 (Vernon 1966); N.J. Stat. Ann. § 45.9-14.1 (West 1978 & Supp. 1981-82).
61. *See, In re* Griffiths, *supra* note 6; Examining Bd. v. DeOtero, 426 U.S. 572 (1976).
62. *See, e.g.*, Cal. Bus. & Prof. Code § 2168 (West Supp. 1981); Fla. Stat. Ann. § 458.313 (West Supp. 1980); Ill. Ann. Stat. ch. 111, § 4410 (Smith-Hurd 1978 & Supp. 1980-81); Md. Health Code Ann. § 123 (Supp. 1980); N.Y. Educ. Law § 6524 (McKinney 1972 & Supp. 1980-81); Va. Code § 54-305 (1980).
63. Mich. Comp. Laws Ann. § 338.41(1) (Supp. 1981-82).
64. Dept. Health, Education & Welfare, A Report to the President and Congress on the

Status of Health Professions Personnel in the United States, DHEW Publication No. (HRA) 79-93, IV-7 (1978) [hereinafter cited as DHEW Health Professions].
65. *Id.* at IV-8.
66. *Id.* at IV-49.
67. *Id.* at IV-8.
68. DHEW State Regulation, *supra* note 33, at 165-6.
69. *Id.*
70. Cal. Bus. & Prof. Code § 2101 (West Supp. 1981).
71. Fla. Stat. Ann. § 458.05(3) (West Supp. 1980).
72. *See, e.g.*, Ariz. Rev. Stat. Ann. § 32-1424 (1976); Fla. Stat. Ann. § 458.05 (West Supp. 1980); Ohio Rev. Code Ann. § 4731.09 (Page 1977); Wis. Stat. Ann. § 448.03 (West Supp. 1980-81).
73. Mich. Comp. Laws Ann. § 333.16174 (1980).
74. S. Rhee, *U.S. Medical Graduates vs. Foreign Medical Graduates*, 15 Med. Care 568 (1977).
75. *Id.*
76. DHEW Health Professions, *supra* note 64, at IV-9.
77. Association of American Medical Colleges, Medical School Admission Requirements 1979-80 (29th ed. 1978).
78. D. Simmons, The Medical School Game 61-4 (1975).
79. Ariz. Rev. Stat. Ann. § 32-1421 (1976); Ill. Ann. Stat. ch. 111, § 4411(1)(d) (Smith-Hurd 1978 & Supp. 1980-81); Md. Health Code art. 43, § 123(A) (Supp. 1980).
80. DHEW State Regulation, *supra* note 33, at 171.
81. *Id., See, e.g.*, Ariz. Rev. Stat. Ann. § 32-1423 (1976); Del. Code Ann. tit. 24, § 1733(C) (Supp. 1980); Fla. Stat. Ann. § 458.05(3) (West Supp. 1980).
82. Fla. Stat. Ann. § 425.00 (West Supp. 1980); N.J. Stat. Ann. § 45:9-13 (West 1978 & Supp. 1981-82); Ohio Rev. Code Ann. § 4731.29 (Page 1977); Tex. Health & Safety Code Ann. art. 4498a (Vernon 1976); Va. Code § 54-311.2 (1978).
83. N.J. Stat. Ann. § 45:9-13 (West 1978 & Supp. 1981-82).
84. Cal. Bus. & Prof. Code § 2140 (West Supp. 1981); Ill. Ann. Stat. ch. 111, § 425 (Smith-Hurd 1978 & Supp. 1980-81); 63 Pa. Cons. Stat. Ann. §§ 421.1-18 (Purdon Supp. 1981-82); Tex. Health Code Ann. art. 4498a (Vernon 1976).
85. Fla. Stat. Ann. § 458.313 (West Supp. 1980); *See also* N.J. Stat. Ann. § 45:9-13 (West 1978 & Supp. 1981-82); 63 Pa. Cons. Stat. Ann. §421.1-18 (Purdon Supp. 1981-82).
86. Cal. Bus. & Prof. Code § 2135, 2136 (West Supp. 1981).
87. *Id.* at § 136.
88. Fla. Stat. Ann. §458.419 (West Supp. 1980); Mich. Comp. Laws Ann.§ 333.17033 (1980); Ohio Rev. Code Ann. § 4731.222 (Page 1977).
89. Mich. Comp. Laws Ann. § 333.17033 (1980).
90. Ohio Rev. Code Ann. § 4731.222 (Page 1977).
91. *Id.*
92. Fla. Stat. Ann. § 458.319 (West Supp. 1980).
93. Ill. Ann. Stat. ch. 111, § 4412 (Smith-Hurd 1978 & Supp. 1980-81).
94. Cal. Bus. & Prof. Code § 2428 (West Supp. 1981).
95. Fla. Stat. Ann. § 458.319 (West Supp. 1980).
96. Cal. Bus. & Prof. Code § 2428 (West Supp. 1981); Ohio Rev. Code Ann. § 4731.222 (Page 1977); Tex. Health Code Ann. art. 4498a (Vernon 1976).
97. Cal. Bus. & Prof. Code § 2428 (West Supp. 1981).
98. N.J. Stat. Ann. § 45:9-16 (West 1978 & Supp. 1981-82); Ill. Ann. Stat. ch. 111, § 4412 (Smith-Hurd 1978 & Supp. 1980-81); Mich. Comp. Laws Ann. § 333.17088 (1980).

Notes: Chapter V

99. Ohio Rev. Code Ann. § 4731.222 (Page 1977).
100. Tex. Pub. Health Code Ann. art. 4506 (Vernon 1976).
101. Va. Code § 54-321 (1978).
102. Ill. Ann. Stat. ch. 111, § 412 (Smith-Hurd 1978 & Supp. 1980-81); Ohio Rev. Code Ann. § 4731.221 (Page 1978); 63 Pa. Cons. Stat. Ann. art. 410 (Purdon Supp. 1981-82).
103. Ill. Ann. Stat. ch. 111, § 412 (Smith-Hurd 1978 & Supp. 1980-81).
104. *See, e.g.*, Hewitt v. State Medical Examiners, 148 Cal. 590, 84 P. 39 (1906); Hughes v. State Bd. of Medical Examiners, 162 Ga. 246, 134 S.E. 42 (1926); Lawrence v. Biry, 239 Mass. 424, 132 N.E. 174 (1921).
105. *In re* Ruffalo, 390 U.S. 544 (1968).
106. *See, e.g.*, Morrissey v. Bruner, 408 U.S. 471 (1972); Goldberg v. Kelly, 397 U.S. 254 (1970).
107. Missouri *ex rel.* Hurwitz v. North, 271 U.S. 40 (1925).
108. *See, e.g.*, Mich. Comp. Laws Ann. §§ 24.201-.315 (Cum. Supp. 1967-81).
109. Missouri *ex rel.* Hurwitz, *supra* note 107.
110. Kansas State Bd. of Healing Arts v. Foote, 200 Kan. 447, 436 P.2d 828 (1968).
111. Bd. of Medical Examiners v. Schutzbank, 94 Ariz. 281, 383 P.2d 192 (1963).
112. Bruni v. Dep't of Registration & Educ., 8 Ill. App. 3d 321, 290 N.E.2d 295 (1972).
113. Colorado State Bd. of Medical Examiners v. Palmer, 57 Colo. 40, 400 P.2d 914 (1965).
114. Bills v. Weaver, 25 Ariz. App. 473, 544 P.2d 690 (1976).
115. *See, e.g.*, Ga. Code Ann. § 88-1912 (1979).
116. *See, e.g.*, Alaska Sta. § 08.64.330 (1977).
117. *In re* Ruffalo, *supra* note 105.
118. Withrow v. Larkin, 368 F. Supp. 796 (E.D. Wis. 1973), *rev'd*, 421 U.S. 35 (1975.).
119. *See, e.g., Id.*; Gibson v. Berryhill, 411 U.S. 564 (1973).
120. *See, e.g.*, LeBow v. Optometry Examining Bd., 52 Wis. 2d 569, 191 N.W.2d 47 (1971); Blanchard v. Mich. Bd. of Examiners in Optometry, 40 Mich. App. 320, 198 N.W.2d 804 (1972).
121. *See, e.g.*, Petrucci v. Bd. of Medical Examiners, 45 Cal. App. 3d 83, 117 Cal. Rptr. 735 (1975); Clark v. Mich. Bd. of Registration, 367 Mich. 343, 116 N.W.2d 797 (1962).
122. Bills v. Weaver, *supra* note 114; Miller v. Bd. of Regents, 30 A.D.2d 994, 294 N.Y.S.2d 29 (1968).
123. *See, e.g.*, Sos v. Bd. of Regents, 19 N.Y.2d 990, 228 N.E.2d 814, 281 N.Y.S.2d 831 (1976); D'Aloris v. Allen, 31 A.D.2d 983, 297 N.Y.S.2d 826 (1969).
124. Glaskow v. Allen, 27 A.D.2d 625, 275 N.Y.S.2d 994 (1966).
125. Smith, *Due Process in the Disciplinary Hearing*, 208 J.A.M.A. 2229, 2230 (1969).
126. *See, e.g.*, Sunseri v. State Bd. of Medical Examiners, 224 Cal. App. 2d 309, 36 Cal. Rptr. 553 (1964); Stammer v. Bd. of Regents, 287 N.Y. 359, 39 N.E.2d 913 (1942); Korndorfter v. Texas State Bd. of Medical Examiners, 448 S.W.2d 819 (Tex. Civ. App. 1969).
127. *See, e.g.*, Sunseri v. State Bd. of Medical Examiners, *supra* note 126; Pepe v. Bd. of Regents, 31 A.D.2d 582, 295 N.Y.S.2d 209 (N.Y. 1968); Elder v. Bd. of Medical Examiners, 241 Cal. App. 2d 246, 50 Cal. Rptr. 304 (1966), *cert. denied*, 385 U.S. 1001 (1967).
128. Davis v. Bd. of Medical Examiners, 108 Cal. App. 2d 346, 239 P.2d 78 (1951).
129. Elder v. Bd. of Medical Examiners, *supra* note 127.
130. Mascitelli v. Bd. of Regents, 32 A.D.2d 701, 299 N.Y.S.2d 1002 (1969).
131. Younge v. State Bd. of Registration for the Healing Arts, 451 S.W.2d 348 (Mo. 1969),

Notes: Chapter V

      cert. denied, 397 U.S. 922 (1970).
132. Vodicka, *Medical Discipline Part VIII, Procedural Matters*, 235 J.A.M.A. 1051, 1052 (1976).
133. Gentry v. State Bd. of Medical Examiners, 283 So.2d 386 (Fla. App. 1973).
134. Martinez v. Tex. State Bd. of Medical Examiners, 476 S.W.2d 400 (Tex. Civ. App. 1972).
135. Hake v. Arkansas State Medical Bd., 237 Ark. 506, 374 S.W.2d 173 (1964).
136. American Medical Association, Disciplinary Digest: Court Decisions in Regard to Disciplinary Actions by State Boards of Medical Examiners 44 (1967).
137. Prosch v. Baxley, 345 F. Supp. 1063 (M.D. Ala. 1972); Geiger v. Jenkins, 316 F. Supp. 370 (N.D. Ga. 1970).
138. *See, e.g.*, Margoles v. Iowa State Bd. of Medical Examiners, 260 Iowa, 846, 151 N.W.2d 457 (1967).
139. Bryant v. State Bd. of Medical Examiners, 292 So.2d 36 (Fla. App. 1974).
140. *See, e.g.*, Tex. State Bd. of Medical Examiners v. Haney, 472 S.W.2d 550 (Tex. Civ. App. 1971).
141. Shively v. Stewart, 65 Cal. 2d 475, 421 P.2d 65, 55 Cal. Rptr. 217 (1966).
142. *See, e.g.*, Mich. Comp. Laws Ann. § 333.16233 (1980).
143. *See, e.g.*, Mascitelli v. Bd. of Regents, *supra* note 130.
144. *See, e.g.*, N.J. Stat. Ann. § 45:9-16 (West 1978 & Supp. 1981-82).
145. *See, e.g.*, Ill. Ann. Stat. ch. 111, § 4433 (Smith-Hurd 1978 & Supp. 1980-81); Ohio Rev. Code Ann. § 4731.22.1 (Page 1977); 63 Pa. Cons. Stat. Ann. § 421.14 (Purdon Supp. 1981-82).
146. *See, e.g.*, Czana v. Bd. of Medical Supervisors, 25 App. D.C. 443 (1925); *In re* Van Hyning, 257 Mich. 146, 241 N.W. 207 (1932).
147. Vodicka, *Medical Discipline Part VI: The Offenses*, 235 J.A.M.A. 302 (1976).
148. Mich. Comp. Laws Ann. § 333.16221(e) (1980).
149. Tex. Civ. Code Ann. art 4505(4) (Vernon Supp. 1980-81).
150. *See, e.g.*, Kudish v. Bd. of Regents, 356 Mass. 98, 248 N.E.2d 264 (1969); Sanchick v. State Bd. of Optometry, 342 Mich. 555, 70 N.W.2d 757 (1955).
151. Pepe v. Bd. of Regents, *supra* note 127.
152. Cadilla v. Bd. of Medical Examiners, 26 Cal. App. 3d 961, 103 Cal. Rptr. 455 (1972).
153. Martinez v. Tex. State Bd. of Medical Examiners, *supra* note 134.
154. Kansas Bd. of Healing Arts v. Seasholtz, 210 Kan. 694, 504 P.2d 576 (1972).
155. Hawkins v. Bd. of Medical Examiners, 542 P.2d 152 (Or. App. 1975).
156. Gentry v. Dep't of Prof. & Occupational Reg., 283 So.2d 95 (Fla. App. 1974).
157. *See, e.g.*, Prosch v. Baxby, 345 F. Supp. 1063 (M.D. Ala. 1972); Margoles v. Wisconsin Bd. of Medical Examiners, 47 Wis. 2d 499, 177 N.W.2d 353 (1970).
158. McLaughlin v. Bd. of Medical Examiners, 35 Cal. App. 3d 1010, 111 Cal. Rptr. 353 (1973).
159. Geiger v. Jenkins, *supra* note 137, Strance v. New Mexico Bd. of Medical Examiners, 83 N.M. 15, 487 P.2d 1085 (1971).
160. Younge v. State Bd. of Regents, *supra* note 131.
161. *See, e.g.*, Strance v. New Mexico Bd. of Medical Examiners, *supra* note 159; *Id*.
162. Weissbuck v. Bd. of Medical Examiners, 41 Cal. App. 3d 924, 116 Cal. Rptr. 479 (1974).
163. Mich. Comp. Laws Ann. §§ 333.16221, 16224 (1980).
164. F. Grad & N. Marti, Study of Medical Disciplinary Procedures, Legislative Drafting Research Fund 42 (1978).
165. *See, e.g.*, Windham v. Bd. of Medical Quality Assurance, 104 Cal. App. 3d 461, 163

Notes: Chapter V

Cal. Rptr. 566 (1980); Rear v. Bd. of Regents, 24 A.D.2d 1054, 265 N.Y.S.2d 421 (1965).
166. Ferguson v. Hamrick, 388 So.2d 981 (Ala. 1980).
167. Wirlitz v. Bd. of Regents, 77 A.D.2d 690, 429 N.Y.S.2d 794 (1980).
168. American Medical Association, Legislative Dep't, *A Report on Medical Discipline Legislation*, 5 State Health Legis. Rep. 16 (Sept., 1977) [hereinafter cited as AMA Legis. Rep.].
169. Gore v. Bd. of Medical Quality Assurance, 110 Cal. App. 3d 184, 167 Cal. Rptr. 881 (1980).
170. Mich. Comp. Laws Ann. § 333.16106 (1980).
171. AMA Legis. Rep., *supra* note 168.
172. 42 U.S.C. § 1320c (1974 & Cum. Supp. 1975-80).
173. *Id*.
174. 42 U.S.C. §§ 1320c-1(b), (c) (1974 & Cum. Supp. 1975-80).
175. J. Blum, P. Gertrran & J. Rabinow, PSROs and the Law 19 (1977) [hereinafter cited as J. Blum, *et al*.].
176. 42 U.S.C. § 1320c-4 (1974 & Cum. Supp. 1975-80).
177. 42 C.F.R. §§ 466.10, .15.
178. 42 C.F.R. § 463.15.
179. *Id*.
180. Michigan Area VII PSRO, The Role of the Physician in the PSRO Program 6 (1979).
181. 42 U.S.C. § 1320c-4 (1974 & Cum. Supp. 1980); 42 C.F.R. § 466.19.
182. 42 U.S.C. § 1320c-8 (1974 & Cum. Supp. 1975-80).
183. Blue Cross and Blue Shield, *PSRO*, 2d Q. Perspective 19-27 (1973).
184. 42 C.F.R. § 460.26.
185. Barsch, *MSMS Works with PSROs to Create Best Possible Peer Review System*, 78 Mich. Med. 1 (Jan., 1979).
186. 42 U.S.C. § 1320c-11 (1974 & Cum. Supp. 1975–80).
187. 42 U.S.C. § 1320 16(A) (1974 & Cum. Supp. 1975–80).
188. *See, e.g.*, Mich. Comp. Laws Ann. § 145.61(5).
189. 42 U.S.C. § 1320c-16(c) (1974 & Cum. Supp. 1975-80), cited in Simmons & Ball, *PSRO and the Dissolution of the Malpractice Suit*, 6 U. Tol. L. Rev. 739, 741 (1975).
190. *Id*.
191. Barsch, *supra* note 185.
192. 21 U.S.C. § 801 (1977).
193. *Id*. at §§ 812-20.
194. *Id*. at §§ 822-24.
195. *Id*. at § 827.
196. *Id*. at §§ 841-66.
197. *Id*. at § 802(2).
198. *Id*. at § 802(10).
199. *Id*. at § 802.
200. *Id*. at § 822.
201. *Id*. at § 824.
202. Ala. Code §§ 20-2-2 to -93 (Supp. 1980); Ariz. Rev. Stat. Ann. §§ 36-2501 to- 2553 (Supp. 1980-81); Cal. Health & Safety Code, §§ 11000-651 (West 1974 & Supp. 1981); Conn. Gen. Stat. Ann. §§ 19-443 to- 504j (West 1977 & Supp. 1981); Del. Code Ann. tit. 16, §§ 4701-78 (Supp. 1980); Fla. Stat. Ann. §§ 893.01 to .15 (West 1976 & Supp. 1981); Ga. Code Ann. §§ 79A-801 to -834, -9917 (Supp. 1980); Hawaii Rev. Stat. §§ 329-1 to -58 (Supp. 1980); Idaho Code §§ 37-2701 to -2751 (Supp.

1981); Ill. Ann. Stat. ch. 56 ½, §§ 1100-1603 (Smith-Hurd 1978 & Supp. 1980-81); Ind. Code Ann. §§ 16-1-28-1 to 31-10 (Burns 1973 & Supp. 1980); Iowa Code Ann. §§ 204.101 to .602 (West Supp. 1981-82); Kan. Stat. Ann. §§ 65-4101 to -4140 (1980); Ky. Rev. Stat. §§ 218A.010 to .990 (Supp. 1980); La. Rev. Stat. Ann. §§ 40.961 to .995 (West Supp. 1981); Md. Code Ann. art. 27, §§ 276 to 302 (1976 & Supp. 1980); Mass. Gen. Laws Ann. ch. 94C, §§ 1-48 (West 1975 & Supp. 1980); Mich. Comp. Laws Ann. §§ 333.7101 to .7545 (1980); Minn. Stat. Ann. §§ 152.01 to .20 (West Supp. 1981); Miss. Code Ann. §§ 41-29-101 to -175 (1973); Mo. Rev. Stat. §§ 195.010 to .320 (Supp. 1981); Mont. Rev. Codes Ann. §§ 54-301 to -327 (Supp. 1977); Neb. Rev. Stat. §§ 28-4,115 to 142 (1965); Nev. Rev. Stat. §§ 453.011 to .361 (1979); N.J. Stat. Ann. §§ 24:21-1 to -45 (West Supp. 1981-82); N.M. Stat. Ann. §§ 54-11-1 to -39 (Supp. 1975); N.Y. Pub. Health Law §§ 3300-96 (McKinney 1971 & Supp. 1980-81); N.C. Gen. Stat. §§ 90-86 to -113.8 (1975 & Supp. 1979); N.D. Cent. Code §§ 1903.1-01 to -43 (Supp. 1977); Ohio Rev. Code Ann. §§ 3719.01 to .99 (Page 1980); Okla. Stat. Ann. tit. 63, §§ 2-101 to -610 (West Supp. 1980-81); Or. Rev. Stat. §§ 475.005 to .285, .992 to .995 (1979); 35 Pa. Cons. Stat. Ann. §§ 780-101 to -144 (Purdon 1977 & Supp. 1981-82); R.I. Gen. Laws §§ 21-28-1.01 to -6.02 (Supp. 1980); S.C. Code §§ 44-53-110 to -580 (Supp. 1980); S.D. Comp. Laws Ann. §§ 39-17-44 to -155 (1977); Tenn. Code Ann. §§ 52-1408 to -1450 (1977); Tex. Rev. Civ. Stat. Ann. art. 4476-15 (Vernon 1976 & Supp. 1980-81); Utah Code Ann. §§ 58-37-1 to -19 (1974 & Supp. 1979); Va. Code §§ 54-524.1 *et seq.* (1978); Wash. Rev. Code §§ 69.50.101 to .608 (1962 & Supp. 1981); W. Va. Code §§ 60A-1-101 to -6-605 (1977 & Supp. 1980); Wis. Stat. Ann. §§ 161.001 to .62 (West Supp. 1980-81); Wyo. Stat. Ann. §§ 35-7-1001 to -1055 (West 1971).

203. *Commissioner's Prefatory Note*, Uniform Controlled Substances Act (U.L.A.) 188 (1979).
204. *Id.*
205. Uniform Controlled Substances Act (U.L.A.) § 302(a).
206. *Id.* at § 301.
207. *Id.* at § 203.
208. *Id.* at § 205.
209. *Id.* at § 207.
210. *Id.* at § 209.
211. *Id.* at § 211.
212. *Id.* at § 302(b).
213. *Id.* at § 303(a).
214. *Id.* at § 304(b).
215. *Id.* at § 304(c).
216. *Id.* at § 306.
217. *Id.* at § 307.
218. *Id.* at § 308.
219. *Id.* at Introduction.
220. N.Y. Penal Law §§ 220.00-.60 (McKinney 1980).
221. *See, e.g.*, Alaska.
222. Alaska Stat. §§ 17.10.010 to .240 (1977); Colo. Rev. Stat. §§ 12-22-301 to -323 (1973); D.C. Code Encycl. §§ 33-401 to -425 (West Supp. 1978-79); Me. Rev. Stat. Ann. §§ 2361-80 (1980).
223. N.H. Rev. Stat. Ann. § 318-13:1 to 13:30 (Supp. 1979); Vt. Stat. Ann. tit. 18, §§ 4201-25 (1968 & Supp. 1980).
224. David, *Interplay of Federal and State Regulatory Programs on the Distribution of*

Pharmaceuticals—The Legislative Aspects, 29 Food Drug Comm. L.S. 449,453 (1974).
225. *Id.* at 454.
226. Mich. Comp. Laws Ann. § 333.17755(3) (1980).
227. David, *supra* note 224, at 454.

Chapter VI

Professional Regulation

§ 6.10 SPECIALTY CERTIFICATION IN ANESTHESIOLOGY

Specialty board certification is not required for a physician to practice medicine, or even to practice a particular specialty. It has developed as a voluntary procedure out of the efforts of the medical profession to improve the quality of graduate medical education: specialty examinations are viewed as a means of differentiating the qualified from the unqualified physician for the purpose of peer recognition.[1] By 1975, 46 percent of all physicians not in training included in the national registry of physicians maintained by the AMA were diplomates of a specialty board.[2]

Unlike state licensure of the general practice of medicine, medical specialization is supervised by independent specialty boards which are private, nonprofit organizations which do not exercise any governmental authority. The number of members of a board ranges from 10 to nearly 40 members. All boards are composed entirely of physicians—none have any public or allied health field members.[3] As such, specialty boards can be seen as a mechanism of physician self-regulation.[4] They view themselves principally as organizations functioning to assess a physician's competence and knowledge at the time of entrance into a specialty.[5] By issuing certificates to candidates, the boards play an important role in evaluating a physician's competence as a specialist. By revoking certificates and developing re-certification programs, they begin to play a role in maintaining physician competence.[6] At this point, all 23 primary and conjoint specialty boards endorse the principle of re-certification.[7] As of July 1980, nine boards had received American Board of Medical Specialties approval of their re-certification proposals, five had completed one cycle, and three proposals were pending consideration.[8]

Board recognition gives a physician both privileges and liabilities. The public and professional recognition he or she receives as a specialist leads to increased patient referrals, but certification has also subjected physicians to more stringent standards of practice. The current trend in medical malpractice cases is to hold defendant specialists to the medical standards recognized in the specialty nationally.[9] (See § 1.32, Standard of Care.)

§ 6.10　　　　　　　　　*Specialty Certification*　　　　　　　　　177

Postgraduate Programs: To be eligible for certification in anesthesiology, a candidate must have successfully completed a postgraduate program in anesthesiology, hold a current and unrestricted license to practice medicine, have a Certificate of Clinical Competence obtained after completing 24 months of clinical anesthesia, and have completed all examination requirements of the American Board of Anesthesiology.[10] Postgraduate programs in anesthesiology are evaluated and reviewed by the Residency Review Committee for Anesthesiology of the American Board of Anesthesiology, the certifying board for the specialty. The Committee is composed of equal numbers of representatives of the American Board of Anesthesiology and of the Council on Medical Education of the American Medical Association. The Secretary of the Committee, through whom all correspondence must be channeled, is a member of the staff of the Council of Medical Education who serves ex officio. The Committee meets twice yearly to act on matters under its cognizance.[11]

Approved training programs are reviewed every three years by submission of data on forms supplied by the Council on Medical Education and inspection by a field representative assigned by the Council. These data are then reviewed by the Residency Review Committee, which may then assign an inspection by a Diplomate of the American Board of Anesthesiology. After all the program material has been received and reviewed, the Committee takes action to continue full approval, to place the program on probation, or to disapprove the program. Approval is withdrawn whenever the training program no longer meets the requirements outlined in the Council on Medical Education's "Essentials of Approved Residencies," or if there are no residents enrolled in the program for two consecutive years. When approval has been withdrawn, reinstatement can be effected *only* by following the procedures applicable to applications for approval of new programs.

The Residency Review Committee has stated that the primary purpose of a residency training program in anesthesiology is to train physicians who will be competent practitioners of the specialty. To this end, the Committee requires an institution seeking approval of a training program to demonstrate that it possesses the resources, material, and personnel to inculcate at least three criteria of competence in its residents:

1. Technical facility: facility in providing all technical services likely to be required in the practice of the specialty
2. Medical judgment: ready availability of mature medical judgment applicable to the solution of medical problems associated with a patient's care as they arise in the practice of the specialty
3. Scholarship: the talent, training and habits of study necessary for evaluating and applying new knowledge

To determine whether or not a training program meets these standards, consideration will be given to the number and caliber of the staff, the quality of basic science orientation, and the relationship of the program to other medical services. The method employed in the selection of residents is important.

The Committee will approve only programs adjudged to have the educational resources to provide four years of training in the specialty referred to as the Continuum of Education in Anesthesiology. Twelve months of the continuum must be devoted to clinical training other than clinical anesthesia and is referred to as Clinical Base. Twenty-four months must be devoted to approved residency training in clinical anesthesia, referred to as Clinical Anesthesia. At least 20 of the 24 months of Clinical Anesthesia must be concerned with the management of procedures for rendering patients insensible to pain during operative, obstetrical and certain other medical procedures and with life function support under the stress of surgical manipulations and anesthesia. In the 12 remaining months of the continuum, the resident must complete a curriculum designed by the program director in consultation with the resident. This 12-month period is the Specialized Year. The Specialized Year may be replaced by alternate pathways for which the resident must seek credit on an individual basis. The Board considers the following options as acceptable, subject to approval:

1. Two years of practice in the field of anesthesiology following completion of the Clinical Base and Clinical Anesthesia
2. Accredited years of training in a medical specialty related to anesthesiology
3. A Ph.D. degree in a scientific discipline related to anesthesiology[12]

The anesthesiology program at The University of Michigan provides an example of an approved program. In accordance with policies of the American Board of Anesthesiology, the Continuum of Education consists of four years of postdoctoral training, including 12 months devoted to training in areas other than anesthesia (Clinical Base), plus 24 months of training in anesthesiology (Clinical Anesthesia). The fourth and final Specialized Year is offered for those residents interested in pursuing additional training in either clinical anesthesiology or research. The program is flexible and tailored to the house officer's specific interests and needs. Training may be taken within the department, in a basic science department at The University of Michigan, or in another institution. Specific clinical rotations are available during the Specialized Year.

During the Clinical Base year, residents spend four months on anesthesia and a minimum of four months in ward medicine. The remainder of that year is spent in electives such as emergency room, endocrinology, cardiology, coronary care unit, renal service, pain clinic, pulmonary medicine, neonatal unit, thoracic-surgery, and intensive care unit. The two years of Clinical Anesthesia are devoted to learning the skills and reasoning which are necessary for competence in the practice of clinical anesthesiology. Because the resident spends four months on anesthesia during the first postgraduate year, four months of additional electives are taken during the second or third postgraduate year.[13]

Institutions that cannot provide an acceptable program intramurally may qualify for program approval by integrating with other institutions. An integrated program is one which:

1. Utilizes the facilities of more than one hospital
2. Is under the direction of a single Program Director, who appoints all of the residents, and is responsible for their training (even though the supervision of the residents may be assigned by the Program Director to a Chief of Service at the hospitals involved)
3. Offers a didactic program and training in the basic sciences involving all residents

The Residency Review Committee also allows some programs to affiliate with other institutions that offer appropriate training and experience, e.g., in pediatric anesthesia, which may not be available in the hospital or hospitals involved in the approved program. Approval of such affiliation is within the discretion of the Program Director, and rotations to affiliated hospitals may be made without formal approval by the Committee. However, such affiliations will not be recognized by the Committee as a means of qualifying programs.

Certain hospitals have unusual facilities and clinical material for offering specialized training in anesthesiology after residents have completed at least two years of clinical training in another program in anesthesiology: these hospitals are eligible for approval for one year of specialized clinical training. To qualify for this category of approved training, a hospital must demonstrate that it offers an educational experience which is substantially different from, and not generally available in, the first two years of clinical training. The one-year program must be highly specialized and at the third-year level, and must be offered only to residents who have had two years of clinical training in an approved program. The Residency Review Committee's general guidelines designed to ensure competency in the field apply also to such one-year programs.

The Committee has established the following standards for use in the evaluation of residency training programs.

Faculty: The most important element in the staffing of a training program is the genuine interest of the faculty in the instruction of residents in all aspects of anesthesiology. Programs in which the residency is maintained primarily to satisfy the needs of the clinical workload will not be looked upon favorably. The faculty should be composed of physicians with diversified interests and capabilities, including the clinical management of anesthesia, the basic sciences, general medicine, and research. The faculty should be sufficient in number to provide each resident with direct supervision at all times; a program in which there is only one functioning faculty member will not be approved. The director must not only be capable of administering the program in an efficient manner but must have the full authority to do so.

Clinical Material: A sufficient variety of anesthetic problems must be available to the resident to provide instruction and experience in anesthetic management of patients undergoing thoracic, cardiovascular, pediatric, neurosurgical, and obstetrical procedures, as well as in problems arising from all other types of surgical cases. The resident must participate directly in the administration and conduct of anesthesia in cases assigned to him; instruction and experience gained from observation is of limited value.

It is essential that the resident be instructed and given experience in all accepted methods of anesthesia. It is undesirable for residents to be exposed only to limited types of anesthetic procedures regardless of the standard practice in the community.

In addition to the clinical care of surgical patients, the program must provide instruction and experience in related fields. This includes not only assignment in the operating theater but also in the postanesthesia room, intensive care unit, and emergency room. Because personal identification of physician with patient is important, the resident should receive instruction and experience in the preoperative evaluation and preparation of the patient, and play a role in the care of patients in the postoperative period.

Didactic Program: All programs must include regularly scheduled teaching sessions, and residents must be freed from clinical responsibilities to attend them. The resident must have ready access to an up-to-date library and must be given sufficient time for study. The program must provide instruction in the following general areas:

1. The Basic Sciences as they pertain to anesthesiology, including physiology, pharmacology, anatomy, biochemistry, and physics. Instruction should be broad enough to provide a thorough understanding of the processes of respiration and circulation, kidney function, liver function, and the like.
2. General Medicine: Instruction in this area should emphasize the importance of fundamental aspects of various disorders of the patients. The resident should know how these disorders affect the patient and what impact therapy may have in order to adjust appropriately his or her management of anesthesia.
3. Technical: Instruction should be provided in such areas as fire and explosion hazards, the physics and mechanics of equipment employed, and the fields of inhalation therapy and intensive care.

In communities in which didactic programs of several residencies are combined, the staff of each approved program must actively and consistently participate in the combined effort and be capable of providing an adequate program if viewed independently.

After graduating from an accredited medical school and having obtained a license to practice medicine, and having completed three of the four-year postgraduate continuing education requirements, the applicant may enter the examination system of the American Board of Anesthesiology. Additionally, the applicant must have obtained a certificate of clinical competence. This certificate is conferred by the applicant's residency training program upon an evaluation indicating that the applicant has demonstrated satisfactory clinical competence commensurate with 18 or 24 months of clinical anesthesia training. The Board requires that each training program file these certificates in December and June on behalf of each resident who has spent any portion of the prior six months in clinical anesthesia training. When accepted by the Board for examination purposes, each applicant becomes a candidate and must pass a written examination as well as an oral examination which is given at least six months after the written examination. Candidates are allowed only three opportunities to pass each examination. The intent of the Board is that its certification reflect evidence of qualification as a physician and as a specialist and consultant in anesthesiology. Procedures created by the Board which are required for certification are intended to determine the attainments of the applicant.[14]

The Committee on Postdoctoral Training of the American Osteopathic Association (AOA) evaluates and recommends for approval all qualified osteopathic internship and residency programs. Final approval comes from the AOA Board of Trustees. A department of anesthesiology that desires approval for a residency must have a program director who is certified in anesthesiology by the American Osteopathic Association and associate anesthesiologists who are either board eligible or certified, and the hospital must have a sufficient number of anesthesiologists for its surgical-obstetrical volume. Departments must be composed of two or more members to be eligible for residency program approval.[15]

The AOA requires that all hospital staff members cooperate in a full program of coordinated teaching. The hospital must provide in-hospital supplementary education as well as outside experiences for its residents. It is also required to maintain a complete library of texts, journals, and tapes, and to supply the modern equipment required for the administration of all commonly used anesthetics as well as adequate safety equipment.

The educational standards of the AOA require that members of the department set aside time for formal teaching. In organizing the program, those responsible for education must allow the resident time for careful evaluation of patients, for study, and for preparation of scientific papers. Each resident must be given supervised responsibility. Individualized instruction should be modified to meet the needs and ability of each resident. The basic sciences must be taught as they apply to anesthesiology. If the hospital cannot provide weekly lectures in the basic sciences, the resident should attend an institution where such formal lectures are presented. Residents are required to be well-informed in osteopathic philosophy and evaluation of patients, and they must be thoroughly grounded in the code of ethics of the AOA.

The AOA recommends that if a department of anesthesiology cannot provide instruction and experience in any accepted anesthetic technique in current use, the program director should arrange for the resident to attend an institution where the technique or procedure is used. For instance, in hospitals where surgical procedures are not sufficiently varied to offer the resident practice in all types of anesthetic procedures, the program director should arrange for the residents to become acquainted with and to participate in the procedures at other institutions during the second year of residency training. However, no more than six months of a two-year osteopathic residency may be spent outside the parent institution.

The resident is required to have observed, assisted, and administered per year a total of no fewer than 500 and no greater than 800 anesthetics in surgery and obstetrics combined, under the supervision of the program director or his or her designates. The resident should become proficient in the examination and evaluation of patients and acquire a thorough working knowledge of premedication pharmacology and postanesthetic care. To enable the resident to distinguish a normal chest x-ray from an abnormal one, a radiology program of at least two weeks duration must be arranged with that department. The resident is also required to attend the monthly meetings of the department of anesthesiology and to submit a weekly or monthly written report to the program director. This report is essentially a log of all the residence- and anesthesiology-related experiences for the period. At the end of the month, the resident must submit to the program director a data sheet which satisfies the residency requirements. Each year the resident must prepare at least one scientific paper on a subject agreed upon with the program director. After this paper has been reviewed, it becomes an integral part of the resident's records.[16]

§ 6.20 REGULATION OF NURSE-ANESTHETISTS

Anesthesia care in the United States is currently provided by anesthesiologists, physicians with additional but less than complete training in anesthesia, and nurse-anesthetists. Often, anesthesiologists work together with nurse-anesthetists as a team providing anesthesia services. Because of the shortage and poor geographical distribution of anesthesiologists, however, anesthesia care in many hospitals may be provided by a team composed of a responsible physician and a nurse-anesthetist.

As providers of anesthesia care, nurse-anesthetists are governed by professional as well as governmental regulation. The dynamics of their interactions with anesthesiologists and other members of the health care team are also defined and limited by these regulations.

The American Association of Nurse-Anesthetists (AANA), the professional organization which sets standards for the practice of nurse anesthesia, was founded in 1931 and currently consists of about 23,000 Certified Registered Nurse-Anesthetists (CRNAs).[17] The AANA has two basic goals: first, to assure the continued existence of high quality, professionally competent schools of nurse-anesthesia and second, to enhance and further develop the clinical skills of individual nurse-anesthetists to assure the delivery of excellent anesthesia care.[18]

> *Initial Certification:* In order to become a CRNA a person must:
>
> 1. Graduate from an approved school of nursing and hold a current license as a registered nurse from a state licensing authority
> 2. Graduate from an approved program of nurse anesthesia accredited by the Council on Accreditation of Nurse Anesthesia Educational Programs/Schools or its predecessor
> 3. Demonstrate individual competency by passing a qualifying examination which confers eligibility for certification by the Council on Certification of Nurse-Anesthetists or its predecessor[19]

Recertification: A CRNA must be recertified every two years by the Council on Recertification of Nurse-Anesthetists of the AANA. To be eligible for recertification an applicant must:

> 1. Have been granted initial certification as specified above
> 2. Document current licensure as a professional registered nurse and have complied with state requirements for earning and maintaining licensure as a registered nurse
> 3. Document full- or continual part-time employment in the clinical practice of anesthesia, or the administrative practice of anesthesia, under the public or private auspices as an administrator, educator, or the like
> 4. Document having met the requirement for 40 hours of mandatory continuing education in the current AANA continuing education program[20]

Standards of Practice: The AANA has published standards which are intended as a general guide for the rendering of optimal anesthesia care rather than as fixed criteria. Practice in each local setting will depend on factors such as requirements or limitations imposed by state law, the sophistication, quality and availability of anesthesia equipment within the institution, the degree of medical specialization and the availability of anesthesia personnel within the community. Generally, these standards are intended by the AANA as guides for the formulation of local or regional level criteria. They are also intended to reflect the rights of those receiving anesthesia care. The specific intent is to:

1. Assist the profession in evaluating the quality of care provided by its practitioners
2. Provide a common base for practitioners to coordinate care and unify their efforts in the development of a quality practice
3. Assist the employers to understand what to expect from the practitioner
4. Support and preserve the basic rights of the patient[21]

Each of the AANA's Standards are accompanied by an Association "interpretation" which explains the Association's view of what each standard means. The Standards and Interpretations are:

Standard I: The patient shall receive a thorough and complete preanesthetic assessment.

Interpretation: The responsibility of a nurse-anesthetist begins before the actual administration of the anesthesia. The nurse-anesthetist has an obligation to determine that an appropriate preanesthesia examination has been made by a physician, relevant tests have been completed and a thorough assessment of the patient has been performed.

Standard II: An anesthetic care plan is formulated based on current knowledge, concepts, and scientific principles.

Interpretation: The plan of care is developed in a systematic manner based upon assessment, interpretation, anticipated procedure, and essential equipment, and coordinated with appropriate health care providers.

Standard III: Anesthesia management includes administering anesthetic agents and adjunctive therapeutics, monitoring physiological responses, taking corrective action to maintain or stabilize the patient's condition, and providing resuscitative care.

Interpretation: The nurse-anesthetist shall induce and maintain anesthesia at required levels as well as manage any untoward reactions which may develop. The nurse-anesthetist must monitor, chart, and report the patient's vital signs and other appropriate indicators as well as provide resuscitative care that includes fluid therapy, maintenance of airway and providing assisted and controlled ventilation.

The practice of the nurse-anesthetist is governed by the policies, rules and regulations as established by the health care institution in which the anesthesia care is being provided.

Standard IV: The nurse-anesthetist is responsible for the prompt, complete and accurate recording of pertinent information on the patient's records.

Interpretation: Accurate recording facilitates comprehensive patient care, provides information for retrospective review and research data, and establishes a medical-legal record.

Standard V: The nurse-anesthetist shall terminate anesthesia, determine adequacy of physiological status and report pertinent data to appropriate personnel.

Interpretation: The nurse-anesthetist is responsible for terminating anesthesia and remaining with the patient until it is safe to transfer responsibility for care to appropriate personnel. The nurse-anesthetist accurately reports on the condition of the patient to persons having need of such information.

Standard VI: The patient shall receive postanesthesia care by designated personnel.

Interpretation: The nurse-anesthetist remains with the patient as long as necessary to stabilize the patient's condition and reports all essential data regarding the emergence from anesthesia to the personnel in charge of postanesthesia care.

Standard VII: Appropriate safety precautions shall be taken to insure the safe administration of anesthesia care.

Interpretation: Safety precautions and controls, as established within the institution, shall be strictly adhered to, so as to minimize the hazards of electricity, fire and explosion in areas where anesthesia care is provided. Anesthetic apparatus shall be inspected and tested by the nurse-anesthetist before use. The nurse-anesthetist shall check the readiness, availability, cleanliness, and working conditions of all equipment to be utilized in the administration of the anesthesia care.

Standard VIII: Nurse anesthesia practice is reviewed and evaluated to assure quality care.

Interpretation: The nurse-anesthetist shall participate in the periodic review and evaluation of the quality and appropriateness of the anesthesia care. Review and evaluation shall be performed in conformity with the institution's quality assurance program.

Standard IX: The nurse-anesthetist shall maintain optimal anesthesia practice based on a continuous process of review and evaluation of scientific theory, research findings and current practice.

Interpretation: The nurse-anesthetist shall incorporate into practice the generally accepted new techniques and knowledge which have been acquired through continuing education. The nurse-anesthetist shall be involved in research as investigators, care providers to research subjects, or users of research for the advancement of the profession.

Standard X: The nurse-anesthetist supports and preserves the basic rights of patients for privacy, independence of expression, decision, and action.

Interpretation: The nurse-anesthetist respects and maintains the basic rights of patients, demonstrating concern for personal dignity and human relationships.[22]

Guidelines for Practice: In June 1980, the AANA established guidelines for the practice of nurse anesthesia which are intended to complement the standards outlined above. The guidelines recognize that when carrying out functions of an anesthetic nature, the nurse-anesthetist may practice independently, interdependently, or dependently, according to his or her expertise, state statutes, and institutional policy. In response to the need for a definitive statement on the permissible scope of nurse anesthesia practice, the AANA developed the following guidelines reflecting its position:[23]

>The institutional guidelines shall authorize the nurse-anesthetist to perform procedures which include, but are not limited to:
>
>(a) Preanesthetic evaluation of the patient;
>
>(b) Selection of anesthetic agent and technique with an appropriate concurrence;
>
>(c) Induction and maintenance of anesthesia and management of pain relief;
>
>(d) Performance of supportive life functions, including intratracheal intubation, management of blood, fluid, and electrolyte loss and replacement in maintenance of cardiovascular and respiratory functions;
>
>(e) Recognition of abnormal patient response to anesthesia or to any adjunctive medication or other form of therapy, and taking corrective action including the requesting of consultation whenever necessary;
>
>(f) Provision of professional observation and resuscitative care and requesting consultation whenever appropriate during the postoperative period;
>
>(g) Additional acts which the supervising physician and nurse agree are within his skills and which are appropriate to his specialty.
>
>Additionally, the specifics of the working relationships and changes in the function and scope of practice should be identified. Individual privileges may be expanded, modified, or revoked depending on ability and experience, and should be reviewed biennially.
>
>These individual privileges may include but not be limited to the following medically delegable acts:
>
>— Obtaining a complete health history including psychosocial as well as biophysical aspects;

- Conducting a complete physical screening assessment utilizing techniques of observation, inspection, auscultation, palpitation, and percussion as well as proper use of instruments to aid in the evaluation;
- Selecting and administering preanesthetic medication according to established protocol;
- Requesting and evaluating pertinent laboratory studies, pulmonary function studies, including blood gases, respiratory therapy, and other appropriate studies under established protocol;
- Inserting intravenous catheters, including central venous pressure catheters by basilic vein, external jugular vein, internal jugular vein, subclavian vein or other recognized routes of administration;
- Inserting Swan-Ganz catheters;
- Inserting arterial catheters, and performing arterial puncture for blood gases;
- Utilizing all current techniques in monitoring;
- Performing regional anesthetic, therapeutic, and diagnostic techniques including, but not limited to spinal, epidural, caudal, brachial plexus, transtracheal, superior laryngeal, femoral sciatic, and retrobulbar blocks;
- Selecting and administering anesthetic techniques, medications and adjunct drugs appropriate to the individual patient within established protocols;
- Performing intratracheal intubation and extubation;
- Identifying and managing emergency situations including assessment of adequacy of recovery or antagonism of muscle relaxants, narcotics, and other agents, and implementing appropriate management techniques;
- Recognizing abnormal patient response to anesthesia or to adjunctive medication and implementing corrective action;
- Managing fluid, blood, and electrolyte therapy within a medical care plan;
- Initiating and modifying therapies, including drug and pain therapy, within established protocols;
- Discharging patient from the recovery room according to established protocols;
- Participating in cardiopulmonary resuscitation and instituting cardiopulmonary resuscitation in absence of a physician according to established protocols;
- Providing consultation, management, and implementation of respiratory and ventilatory care;
- Keeping aware of current techniques appropriate to the conduct of anesthesia and implementing these techniques within established protocols.

The Council on Nurse Anesthesia Practice of the AANA has stated that regional anesthesia may be administered by a nurse-anesthetist provided:

1. The nurse-anesthetist has received education and training in the administration of regional anesthetics.

2. There are no existing statutory or regulatory preclusions to a physician delegating the performance of regional anesthesia to a nurse-anesthetist.

In the belief that the overall risks of regional blocks are no greater than those imposed by general anesthesia, the Council states that the performance of a regional block, as an acquired motor skill, can be accomplished by anyone who is properly trained. Evidence of fitness to perform this function can be shown by fulfilling didactic and clinical curriculum requirements as well as by performance of a given number of the more common blocks. Beyond this, the scope and extent of training needed by an individual would be difficult to define.[24]

The AANA has carefully defined the responsibilities of the nurse-anesthetist in light of the realities of practice,[25] and, in joint efforts with the American Society of Anesthesiologists (ASA), has sought to identify the ideal working relationship between the two professions in light of the patient's best interests.[26] The AANA contends that anesthesia care does not fall exclusively within either the practice of medicine or the practice of nursing. The process is comprised of practice components from both fields. In light of this, the AANA considers the anesthesia care team which contains an anesthesiologist and a nurse-anesthetist to constitute the ideal model for the provision of anesthesia care. The AANA further asserts that at a minimum all hospitals should provide access to at least one anesthesiologist for medical consultation.[27]

The AANA recognizes also that registered nurses are independently licensed and legally liable for the adequacy of their performance of both nursing functions and medically delegated functions. The nurse-anesthetist, therefore, must be capable of making judgments as to the appropriateness of his or her service and its probable effect on the patient, as well as the appropriateness of the medical direction. Pursuant to this, the AANA directs that if a nurse-anesthetist believes the medical direction for a particular patient is inappropriate, he or she should consult the responsible physician for more appropriate direction. If reasonable doubt continues to exist, the nurse-anesthetist may withdraw from rendering the service, providing the well-being of the patient is not jeopardized. The AANA also recommends that a protocol be developed in those facilities where non-anesthesiologist physicians are responsible for medical direction and that this protocol define the requirements for practice which should be developed and adopted in concert with the members of the anesthesia care team.[28]

In 1972, the American Society of Anesthesiologists and the American Association of Nurse-Anesthetists issued a joint statement concerning qualifications of individuals administering anesthetics. The statement recognizes the contributions of both nurses and physicians to anesthesia care and resolves that the principles outlined by the organizations be used by their respective memberships as criteria for determining qualifications of individuals administering anesthetics.[29]

The American Society of Anesthesiologists (ASA) recognizes the personal provision of anesthesia services by an anesthesiologist as a desirable primary goal. However, with respect to nurse-anesthetists, it also acknowledges that the establishment of an acceptable environment within which medical direction of the anesthesia health care team may be carried out is a proper concern for providing better anesthesia care for more patients.[30]

The ASA believes that the anesthesiologist should assume responsibility for the medical direction of the anesthesia team so that all patients receive professional service. Professional service occurs when anesthesia care is rendered solely by the anesthesiologist or with other members of the team under his or her immediate and personal direction. Under ASA guidelines, direction must be in such "numerical and geographic relationship as to make possible the continuous exercise of the medical judgment of the anesthesiologist throughout the administration of anesthesia." This relationship depends on the experience and skill of the team members. The anesthesiologist must not be personally administering an anesthetic while supervising an anesthesia team.[31]

Services provided by a physician who is assisted by a non-physician are regarded as supplied by the anesthesiologist. Such medical direction itself is a professional service. (See § 2.30, Vicarious Liability.) The anesthesiologist's responsibilities should include:

1. Preanesthetic evaluation of the patient
2. Prescription of the anesthesia plan
3. Personal participation in the most demanding procedures in this plan, especially those of induction and emergence
4. Following the course of anesthesia administration at frequent intervals
5. Remaining physically available for the immediate diagnosis and treatment of emergencies
6. Providing indicated postanesthesia care

The conduct of nurse-anesthetists is further regulated by hospitals in compliance with standards promulgated by the Joint Commission on the Accreditation of Hospitals (see § 7.81, JCAH Standards) and by state governments. State regulation of nurse-anesthetists takes three basic forms. The first form allows the inclusion of additional acts within the scope of practice of nursing as authorized by the board of nursing. For example, Colorado gives the board of nursing power to:

> Adopt and revise standards in the form of rules and regulations for practice and patient care for professional nurses, including the determination of when the performance of additional acts under emergency or other conditions requiring education and training as recognized by the medical and nursing professions are proper to be

performed by professional nurses within such conditions as are authorized by the board.[32]

The form allows the board of nursing to specify conditions, such as type of supervision, and education or training requirements for the performance of additional acts which may include the administration of anesthesia.

The second form involves recognition of the nurse-anesthetist either directly or as a type of expanded function nurse, i.e., nurse practitioner.

Several states now license or certify nurse-anesthetists.[33] In Louisiana, a nurse-anesthetist must be an R.N., certified by a nationally recognized certifying agency as a nurse-anesthetist, and work under the direct supervision of a licensed physician or dentist.[34] Michigan provides for the specialty certification of nurse-anesthetists who are registered professional nurses with advanced training beyond that required for initial nurse licensure and who demonstrate competence in the field through examination or another evaluative process.[35] The Pennsylvania Board of Nurse Examiners takes a different approach by recognizing certification by the American Association of Nurse-Anesthetists as follows:

> The administration of anesthesia is a proper function of a registered nurse and is a function regulated by this section; such function shall not be performed unless all of the following provisions are met:
>
> 1. The registered nurse has successfully completed the educational program of a school for nurse-anesthetists accredited by the American Association of Nurse-Anesthetists.
>
> 2. The registered nurse is certified as a Registered Nurse-Anesthetist by the American Association of Nurse-Anesthetists within one year following completion of the education program.
>
> 3. The registered nurse administers such anesthesia under the direction of and in the presence of a licensed physician or dentist.*[36]

Massachusetts includes nurse-anesthetists in the category of nurses practicing in expanded roles and prohibits practice in these expanded roles without Board authorization.[37] Authorization to practice as a nurse-anesthetist requires formal education as a nurse-anesthetist and current certification by the national accreditation body.[38] In Massachusetts the nurse-anesthetist may perform the following functions consistent with guidelines which may authorize the provision of anesthesia only under the medical direction of a specially qualified physician as a member of an anesthesia care team:[39]

---

*A Pennsylvania court has strictly construed this provision holding that the provision has been willfully violated even though a physician is present at the time anesthesia is administered if the nurse has administered the anesthesia without the physician's direction or awareness. *McCarl v. State Board of Nurse Examiners*, 396 A.2d 866 (1979).

§ 6.30 *Competing Professions* *191*

1. Performing an immediate preoperative patient evaluation;
2. Selecting an anesthetic agent;
3. Including and maintaining anesthesia and managing intraoperative pain relief;
4. Supporting life functions during the induction and period of anesthesia, including intratracheal intubation, monitoring of blood loss and replacement and electrolytes, and the maintenance of cardiovascular and respiratory function;
5. Recognizing abnormal patient responses to anesthesia or to any adjunctive medication or other form of therapy and taking corrective action;
6. Providing professional observation and resuscitative care during the immediate postoperative periods and until a patient has regained control of his vital functions; and
7. Such other additional professional activities as authorized by the guidelines under which a particular nurse-anesthetist practices.[40]

Oregon defines "nurse practitioner" as a registered nurse certified by the board of nursing as qualified to practice in an expanded specialty role within the practice of nursing.[41] Similarly, Kentucky defines an "advanced registered nurse practitioner" as one certified to engage in advanced registered nursing practice including nurse anesthesia.[42] The third form of nurse-anesthetist regulation is indirect. Some states have included provisions related to anesthesia services in their hospital regulations. Some of these provisions may relate directly to nurse-anesthetists, recognizing their increasing significance as part of the hospital operating team. For example, California provides that "anesthesia care shall be provided by physicians or dentists with anesthesia privileges, nurse-anesthetists, or appropriately supervised trainees in an approved educational program."[43] Illinois requires that "postanesthetic follow-up visits shall be made within 24 hours after the operation, by the anesthesiologist, nurse-anesthetist or responsible physician who shall note and record any postoperative abnormalities or complications from anesthesia."[44]

§ 6.30 REGULATING COMPETING PROFESSIONS

The provision of anesthesia care by nurse-anesthetists may pose a dilemma for anesthesiologists and surgeons. The American Society of Anesthesiologists clearly states that the provision of anesthesia care by physician anesthesiologists is the practice of medicine, not a service function. Nurse-anesthetists cannot, therefore, provide an identical level of care without "practicing medicine," and no regulatory agency is willing to recognize the practice of medicine by any person other than a duly licensed physician. The dilemma is how to allow nurses to provide anesthesia care while recognizing that such care is the practice of medicine.

In order to understand how this dilemma developed, it is necessary to gain some historical perspective on the development of anesthesia in the United States. In the mid-19th century, the major use of nitrous oxide and ether was for public entertainment in the form of "ether frolics" and "laughing gas" demonstrations. The surgery of that period was quite literally a life-or-death proposition. Mortality was high not only from the stress of surgery on awake patients, but also from the extremely high infection rate. The use of ether for surgical anesthesia by Morton in 1846 made the decision to operate somewhat easier on the surgeon's conscience, but the so-called "Golden Era" of surgery had to await the development of aseptic techniques. During this era, anesthesia was provided by the burliest intern or medical student available. If medical students were not available, then the clerk or porter would do. Physicians were not interested in providing anesthesia care because this service placed them in a subordinate position to the surgeon, paid poorly, and was considered to be an unsavory task because of the ethically questionable practices of pioneer anesthetists. Thus, by the turn of the century there was an increasing demand for the provision of anesthesia and very few physicians willing to provide this care.

Surgeons were discovering that the administration of anesthetics was a risky business and that trained people devoted solely to the care of the anesthetized patient were needed. These same surgeons recognized that this need could be met by specially trained nurses who worked exclusively for them and under their supervision. Thus, nurses became anesthetists largely by default. This practice, however, was not without controversy, even at its inception.

References to the medicolegal aspects of nurse anesthesia practice can be found dating back to 1894.[45] The issue of whether or not nurses could deliver anesthesia was tested in the courts in a 1934 suit brought by physician-anesthesiologists and the Anesthesia Section of the Los Angeles County Medical Association against Dagmar Nelson and St. Vincent's Hospital.[46]

The California physicians contended that the provision of anesthesia involved the administration of drugs and that observing the signs of anesthesia and acting on those observations constituted diagnosis. They further contended that the surgeon, separated from the anesthetist by a screen, could in no way supervise the administration of anesthesia. The defense contended that giving drugs upon direct or understood instruction of the physicians was a recognized nursing practice and that recognizing and reporting changes in the patient's condition, and acting accordingly under the direct or understood supervision of a physician, was within the province of nursing. The defense further contended that nursing education gave instruction in the administration of anesthesia and in the recognition of the signs and stages of anesthesia, and that it was an established practice within the law for registered nurses to give anesthesia as a nursing duty. The California Supreme Court, in finding for the defense, ruled that everything done by the nurse in administering anesthesia is done under the immediate direction and supervision of the operating surgeon and that this method seemed to be a uniform practice in operating rooms. The Court noted that nurse-anesthetists were only carrying out the orders of the physicians to whose authority they were subject, and that the surgeon had the duty to direct the nurse's actions during the operation.

The successful defense of this case was predicated on a history of successful anesthetic administration by nurses and a customary practice in effect at the time. It did not establish nurse-anesthetists as independent practitioners, but, rather, tied them to the operating surgeon or other physicians whose orders they carried out. The only way to avoid the question of diagnosis was to report the patient's condition to the physician who would make the diagnosis and prescribe treatment.

The practice of medicine and surgery has changed considerably since 1936. Surgeons today are not trained in the administration of anesthetics. Surgery of ever-increasing complexity is being performed on patients with complex medical management problems. The choices of anesthetics are not limited to ether or nitrous oxide and the sophistication of monitoring techniques requires increasing diagnostic skills. Certainly, the level of nurse-anesthetist training has increased with the increasing demands; however, some anesthesiologists are concerned about defining the limits of nurse anesthesia practice and the degree of supervision which is appropriate. Many surgeons are not aware that they may be liable for the provision of anesthesia where there is no supervising anesthesiologist. On the other hand, it is difficult to conceive of how nurse-anesthetists can be held independently liable for their actions without recognizing that they are practicing medicine rather than nursing.

In practice, there has been considerable expansion of the original mandate for nurse-anesthetists. Increasing demands are made on nurse-anesthetists to diagnose, initiate treatment and make decisions which might be only within the legal province of the physician. The guidelines of the AANA appear to allow nurse-anesthetists to perform histories and physical exams, determine pre-medications, request and interpret laboratory tests, choose the anesthetic plan, select and implement monitoring, including invasive cardiac monitoring, perform all types of regional anesthesia, discharge patients from the recovery room, and even consult on respiratory care. Upon careful reading, however, these functions are limited by statements such as "according to protocols" and "within a medical care plan." The problem is that such protocols and plans often do not exist.

Furthermore, while the use of protocols and plans may be useful for routine uncomplicated cases, it is impossible to provide such a "cookbook" approach for more difficult cases or to plan for all eventualities. Differences of opinion will always exist when more than one profession is involved in the management of anesthesia care. From a legal standpoint, there is little doubt that where such differences of opinion exist, the nurse-anesthetist must either yield to the opinion of the responsible physician or withdraw from the case. The latter alternative, however, may imperil the nurse's employment, as this situation puts the nurse-anesthetist in a very awkward political position.

The practice of nurse anesthesia has firm historical roots in the United States. Nurses have played a vital role in the development of anesthetic practice and in the provision of anesthesia care. Given the long tradition of nurse anesthesia, it is difficult to argue that the provision of anesthesia care by specially trained nurses is unsafe. Yet, the practice of surgery and hence anesthesia has changed dramatically since 1936. The issue is one of supervision. Who is qualified to act in the supervising role and what constitutes adequate supervision? How does one recognize the special training and qualifications of nurse-anesthetists and allow them the judgmental and discretionary powers rightfully afforded professionals without impinging on medical practice acts which limit the prescribing and diagnostic roles of non-physicians?

To date, these issues have not been satisfactorily resolved by legislatures, courts, or by mutual agreement between physicians and nurses. Further complicating this problem is the geographic variability in how physicians and nurses interact to provide anesthesia. There are, however, increasing demands for standardization by practitioners, hospitals and third-party carriers.

In sum, territorial problems between anesthesiologists and nurse-anesthetists will continue until (1) a mechanism for solving such disputes is established; (2) territorial agreements, including ratios of CRNAs to supervising anesthesiologists, are negotiated and endorsed; (3) geographical standardization is achieved; and (4) third-party carriers remove the financial incentives which foster the abuse of CRNA labor by provider institutions. The problems identified in this section are not amenable to easy remedy. Additional issues, such as the available supply of anesthesiologists and the costs associated with the care they provide, suggest that these conflicts will be with us for years to come. Solutions must be found, however, as quality patient care and peace between the professions are the values at issue.

NOTES

1. U.S. Dep't Health, Education & Welfare, Report on Medical Disciplinary Procedures 81-96 (1978) [hereinafter cited as DHEW Disciplinary Procedures].
2. American Board of Medical Specialties (ABMS), Annual Report 22 (1975-76).
3. DHEW Disciplinary Procedures, *supra* note 1.
4. *Id.*
5. DHEW Disciplinary Procedures, *supra* note 1, at 83-4.
6. *Id.* at 82-3.
7. American Board of Medical Specialties (ABMS), Annual Report and Reference Handbook 20 (1980).
8. *Id.* at 22.
9. *See, e.g.*, Naccarato v. Grob, 384 Mich. 248, 180 N.W.2d 788 (1970).
10. American Board of Anesthesiology, Booklet of Information 5 (1980).
11. Residency Review Committee for Anesthesiology, Guide for Residency Programs in Anesthesiology (1981).

Notes: Chapter VI

12. American Board of Anesthesiology, *supra* note 10, at 5-8.
13. University of Michigan Hospital, Department of Anesthesiology, Letter to Prospective Residents, detailing the Anesthesia program at that institution as of 1981, p. 1-2.
14. American Board of Anesthesiology, *supra* note 10, at 7.
15. American Osteopathic Association, Osteopathic Post-Doctoral Training Programs (Oct., 1980).
16. American Osteopathic College of Anesthesiologists and American Osteopathic Association, Standards for Residency Training Programs in Anesthesiology (1980).
17. American Association of Nurse Anesthetists (AANA), Guidelines for the Practice of the Certified Registered Nurse Anesthetist 1 (1980) [hereinafter cited as AANA Guidelines].
18. American Association of Nurse Anesthetists (AANA), Standards for Nurse Anesthesia Practice (1981) [hereinafter cited as AANA Standards].
19. AANA Guidelines, *supra* note 17.
20. Smith, *New Council on Recertification: What It Will Mean To You*, AANA News Bull. 7 (Nov., 1978).
21. AANA Standards, *supra* note 18, at 2.
22. *Id.* at 2-4.
23. AANA Guidelines, *supra* note 17, at 1, 2.
24. American Association of Nurse Anesthetists, Council on Nurse Anesthesia Practice, Policy Statement on Regional Anesthesia (May, 1978).
25. American Association of Nurse Anesthetists, Statement of Policy on the Provision of Anesthesia Services (May, 1978).
26. American Society of Anesthesiologists and the American Association of Nurse Anesthetists, Joint Statement Concerning Qualifications of Individuals Administering Anesthetics (January, 1972) [hereinafter cited as Joint Statement].
27. AANA Guidelines, *supra* note 17.
28. *Id.*
29. Joint Statement, *supra* note 26.
30. American Society of Anesthesiologists, *Guidelines to the Ethical Practice of Anesthesiology: The Anesthesiologists's Relationship to Nurse Anesthetists, and Other Non-Physician Personnel*, in American Society of Anesthesiologists Directory of Members C, 424 (46th ed. 1981).
31. *Id.*
32. Colo. Rev. Stat. § 12-38-209(1)(c) (1978); *See* Ariz. Rev. Stat. Ann. § 32-1602 (Supp. 1980).
33. *See, e.g.*, Ark. Stat. Ann. § 72-745 (1979).
34. La. Dept. of Health and Human Resources Bd. of Nursing Rules § R.N. 3.043 (1981).
35. Mich. Comp. Laws Ann. § 333.17210 (1980).
36. 49 Pa. Code § 21.17 (Nov. 1980).
37. 244 Code Mass. Reg. §§ 4.11(4), 4.12(1) (1979).
38. *Id.* at §4.13(4).
39. *Id.* at § 4.24(4).
40. *Id.* at § 4.25(4).
41. Or. Rev. Stat. § 678.010(4) (1979).
42. Ky. Rev. Stat. § 314.011(6) (Supp. 1980).
43. Cal. Admin. Code tit. 22, § 70235(b) (1979).
44. Ill. Admin. Code, Hospitals, Part XI Anesthesia Services § 11-1.12 (1980).
45. V. Thatcher, History of Anesthesia with emphasis on the Nurse Specialist (1953).
46. Chalmers-Francis v. Nelson, 6 Cal. 2d 402, 57 P.2d 1312 (1936); *also see*, Frank v. South, 175 Ky. 416, 194 S.W. 375, (1917).

Chapter VII

Hospital Regulation

§ 7.10 INTRODUCTION

This chapter focuses on the physician's perspective on his or her relationship with the hospital and addresses only those legal problems arising from the physician-hospital interface; other legal issues and problems pertinent to hospital activity are not addressed.

The hospital administrative structure is examined briefly in this chapter along with the legal requirements imposed on the hospital and its physicians in providing various services and procedures. Emphasis has been given to the legal aspects of granting, denying, or revoking hospital privileges and the procedural safeguards to which a physician is entitled in such a situation. It is this area that generates most of the conflict between physicians and hospitals.

As hospitals apply objective standards to the evaluation of physician performance, as the number of physicians increases, as cost-containment becomes a more highly valued goal, and as physicians continue to assert their rights through the legal system, the likelihood of conflict increases. Accordingly, if predictions are accurate, the interface of physician and hospital will probably generate more legal conflict than any other in the field of medical jurisprudence, with the exception of the physician-patient interface. Because the quality of patient care will be affected by these conflicts, it is important that hospitals, their leaders, physicians, and other involved parties anticipate these problems, engage in preventive measures where appropriate, and seek nonconfrontational resolutions.

§ 7.20 ORIGIN AND DEVELOPMENT

The first hospitals were small, overcrowded, underequipped places for the sick to die. Treatment afforded the sick in these hospitals was rarely given in an effort to cure. The earliest American hospital(s) appeared in the fifteenth century during the reign of Montezuma, the last Aztec ruler of old Mexico.[1] Following that, hospitals did not begin to appear in the United States and Canada until the seventeenth and

§ 7.30 Types of Hospitals 197

eighteenth centuries.[2] Many were still small, overcrowded, understaffed, and usually cared for the sick and the poor.

As society changed, so did the concept of hospitals. The growth of organized government brought a corresponding increase in government regulation and government responsibility for the public's health, safety and welfare. Factors such as health insurance, corporate law, taxation, the development of medical specialties, new concepts of liability, new professionals, and new levels of medical technology influenced the structure and development of hospitals. These factors shifted the focus of hospitals from the acceptance of death to the preservation of life, i.e., the treatment and discharge of admitted patients.

§ 7.30 TYPES OF HOSPITALS

Hospitals can be classified in a number of ways: by type of control, type of service(s), length of patient stay, or size and institutional purpose, to suggest a few.[3] The most general and perhaps most useful distinction to be made from the standpoint of hospital law is the distinction between public and private hospitals.

Public hospitals are established by a governmental unit. They are always organized as nonprofit institutions but they may limit services to a specified type of patient, e.g., the mentally ill or retarded, tuberculosis patients, or the elderly. Some are associated with universities as "teaching hospitals." Public hospitals are exempt from property, income and sales taxes.[4]

While it may be stated generally that a nonemergency patient has no legal right to be admitted to a hospital,[5] if a patient is eligible, the public hospital must admit the patient. The key to the right of the patient to admission is eligibility. Eligibility for admission to a public hospital may be determined by the purpose for which the hospital was established, which is generally specified in the statute creating the public hospital, or by the purpose defined by the governing board and administration of the hospital. Stated purposes may limit the type of patient the hospital treats by disease, as illustrated above, or other reasonable criteria.[6] However, statutes which require residency in the geographic area in which the hospital is located as a prerequisite to admission have been found unconstitutional by the U.S. Supreme Court.[7] In addition to federal and state civil rights laws prohibiting discrimination, many state licensing laws provide that to qualify for a license, a public hospital must comply in all phases of its operation with state and federal laws prohibiting discrimination.[8] Other states have inserted prohibitions against discriminatory practices in regulations pertaining to tax exempt status.[9] Racial discrimination would jeopardize the hospital's funding under both the Medicare and Hill-Burton programs.[10]

In general, all licensed physicians have privileges to treat patients in public hospitals subject to the rules and regulations of the hospital. According to the law in most states, a publicly owned hospital must have clearly stated reasonable rules regarding staff appointments and fair procedures pertaining to enforcement of those rules. A physician who applies for membership on the medical staff of a public hospital must be judged in the light of his training, experience, clerical and professional competence, ethical attitudes and ability to function effectively with patients and colleagues. The general rule is that public hospitals are under a duty not to act arbitrarily, capriciously or unreasonably in granting, withholding or restricting medical staff privileges. Each application must be decided upon in view of the merits and the facts of the particular situation.[11]

The Joint Commission on Accreditation of Hospitals (JCAH) further clarifies the general rule by requiring that professional and ethical criteria rather than criteria lacking professional justification, such as sex, race, creed, or national origin be used as the basis for granting medical staff membership.[12] (See § 7.71, Joint Commission on the Accreditation of Hospitals.)

The Fourteenth Amendment to the U.S. Constitution provides that " . . . no state [shall] deprive any person of life, liberty, or property, without due process of law; nor deny to any person . . . the equal protection of the laws." In order for these due process and equal protection constraints to apply there must be a finding of state action.* Where state action can be established, a hospital must extend both substantive and procedural due process as well as equal protection to a physician in admission to the hospital staff, discharge from the hospital staff, or reduction of staff privileges.[13] (See § 7.90, Medical Staff Privileges.)

Although the operation of a public or governmental hospital may be found to involve state action for purposes of the Fourteenth Amendment, it is not necessarily a governmental function for purposes of governmental immunity from tort liability. For example, the Supreme Court of Michigan has ruled that the defense of governmental immunity from liability in tort may no longer be used by governmental hospitals. The court concluded that the day-to-day operation of the hospital did not constitute a "governmental function" within the meaning of the statute granting immunity to governmental agencies in the exercise or discharge of such a function.[14]

Governmental immunity from liability in tort is still recognized to some extent in 20 states.[15] Some states limit the application of governmental immunity to claims brought by nonpaying patients.[16] Other states limit liability to the extent of the defendant hospital's insurance.[17] Several states enforce full liability of govern-

---

*State action is a legal concept used to analyze facts and circumstances under which an institution derives support from or relies upon the government to such an extent so as to justify classification of the actions of the institution as state action. Government ownership is one indication of state action, but a non-government owned institution may be held to be engaging in state action depending on the extent of its nexus with government or even the "public" nature of its activities.

§ 7.30 *Types of Hospitals* 199

mental units,[18] while no state continues to uphold full immunity for all governmental subdivisions.[19]

Private hospitals may be classified as either profit or nonprofit. The profit classification applies to those hospitals, also referred to as proprietary, owned generally by an individual or corporation and organized for the purpose of making profit. The profit hospital is subject to the same rules, laws and regulations as any other business operated for profit.[20] The nonprofit private hospital, also referred to as voluntary, is generally owned by a benevolent or nonprofit association or corporation, such as a church or other religious organization, and is organized not for the purpose of making a profit but for achieving public interest related goals. The most common example is the charitable hospital which provides care to all who seek it without regard to ability to pay for such care.[21]

The state regulates private hospitals under its police power, i.e., the broad power of the state to provide for the general health and welfare of the people. This power includes the power to license hospitals, to certify their eligibility for participation in state and federal programs, and to administer a Certificate of Need program. (See § 7.70, Regulation of the Hospital.) The Federal government regulates private hospitals indirectly through funding.

Like public hospitals, private nonprofit hospitals (generally charitable in nature) are exempt from property, income and sales taxes.[22] They are, however, supported by private funds including gifts, benefits, and fees for services rather than by taxes.

Unlike public hospitals, private hospitals are not required to admit all nonemergency patients who apply and are eligible for admission, although, once admitted, the hospital is required to exercise the appropriate standard of care in treating these patients.[23]

Since private hospitals are not generally considered agents of the state, they are not subject to the stringent requirements of the Equal Protection and Due Process clauses of the Fourteenth Amendment and are therefore free to regulate patient admissions and admissions or discharges from the medical staff by their own by-laws. Numerous cases, however, have attempted to apply the Due Process and Equal Protection clauses of the Fourteenth Amendment to private hospitals by showing government involvement through licensing, Hill-Burton assistance and other governmental links.[24] Most federal circuit courts hold these levels of involvement with the state insufficient to invoke the requirements of the Fourteenth Amendment.[25] The Fourth Circuit Court of Appeals, however, has held that the defendant hospital's receipt of substantial amounts of federal funds entitles physicians seeking staff privileges to the equal protection of the law.[26] The requirement of "state action" or governmental function in order to impose due process requirements may gradually give way to the conclusion that due process is also grounded in public policy and common law and therefore applies to private hospitals, regardless of the applicability of the Fourteenth Amendment.[27]

In addition, the federal regulations that apply to hospitals participating in the Medicare program,[28] the standards of the Joint Commission on the Accreditation of Hospitals (JCAH),[29] and a number of state court decisions have imposed requirements on private hospitals similar to those imposed on public hospitals by the federal Constitution. Therefore, the freedom that private hospitals once had in determining membership on the medical staff has been constrained by notice and hearing requirements similar to those imposed on public hospitals. (See § 7.90, Medical Staff Privileges.)

Although private hospitals are not exempt from tort liability on the basis of governmental immunity, some states still uphold the doctrine of charitable immunity in limited circumstances. Some states limit the charitable institution's liability to damages for injuries occurring as a result of the negligence of an employee negligently selected or retained by an agent of the hospital.[30] Other states limit a charitable hospital's liability to paying patients,[31] or to the extent of the institution's insurance.[32] Most jurisdictions, however, have abolished the doctrine of charitable immunity altogether.[33]

§ 7.40 LEGAL BASES FOR HOSPITAL OPERATION

Hospital operations are regulated externally by means of state incorporation statutes, federal and state licensing and certification laws, and the JCAH requirements. Internally, hospitals are regulated to a large extent by their own by-laws. Generally, the organization of a hospital is determined by its corporate or noncorporate, profit or nonprofit status.

§ 7.41 Corporations

Although a hospital may be formed as an association or even a partnership, most hospitals are organized as corporations. In states which have no separate statute regulating incorporation of nonprofit organizations, hospitals may incorporate under the general business corporation act of the particular state. About half of the states, however, have adopted a general nonprofit corporation act.[34] The majority of these states enacted the Model Nonprofit Corporation Act with minor variations.[35]

The distinction between a profit and nonprofit corporation is that a profit corporation is organized to earn profit and pays income to shareholders who are entitled to dividends and to a share in the assets of the corporation. A nonprofit corporation is organized primarily to render a service and does not distribute its income to the members, directors, trustees, or officers. This distinction, however, is not always clear.[36] Status as nonprofit does not preclude a corporation from paying salaries or wages to the corporate members, trustees, or officers who are employees of the corporation. The nonprofit corporation uses its profits and reinvests its income for institutional purposes. Since the nonprofit corporation does not have shareholders as such, its owners are referred to as members.

Since the corporation is a legal entity separate and distinct from those who create it or are employed by it, the corporation can sue or be sued as an entity and can hold property in its corporate name.[37] The major advantage of corporate status is the limited liability of the shareholders, owners, or members of the corporation for the actions of the corporation; i.e., they are not held personally liable for the contracts or torts of the corporation.

The articles of incorporation define the corporation's basic structure. Generally, they specify such things as how the board is elected, the number of board members, who votes and how, the frequency, time and place of meetings, manner of distribution of dividends, and other basics of the operation of the corporation. A copy of the articles of incorporation is filed with the state along with the application for corporate status.[38] They may be amended by at least a majority of the members or shareholders of the corporation.

Corporations have express and implied powers. Express powers are granted by statutes, articles of incorporation and bylaws. Implied powers are those which are reasonably necessary or convenient to carrying out the express powers.[39]

If the corporation performs an act outside its powers, it is said to perform *ultra vires*. For example, a gift made by a nonprofit corporation to another institution for a purpose not included in its own charter would be an *ultra vires* gift. *Ultra vires* acts of the board are voidable, that is, challengeable. If unchallenged, or otherwise ratified by the shareholders or members, there are no personal consequences to the board members. Challenged *ultra vires* acts may, however, lead to personal liability of board members. No personal liability arises from good faith mistakes in judgment.[40]

Illegal actions of the governing board are void, i.e., they cannot bind the corporation or the institution. For example, employment by a hospital of an unlicensed professional person is an absolutely void act. An employment contract signed subsequent to this illegal hiring cannot bind the corporation.[41]

§ 7.42 Bylaws

A hospital, public or private, may have two sets of bylaws. The first set is adopted by the governing board and includes such things as the role and purpose of the hospital; the specifics of the governing board itself, i.e., members, elections, officers, maximum service, duties, frequency of meetings, quorum requirements; and the relationships between the governing board and chief executive officer and between the governing board and medical staff.

A second set of bylaws may be developed and adopted by the medical staff. The governing board has approval and adoption power over these bylaws. Because they in effect become part of the corporate bylaws, they are binding on the corporation. It should be noted that the Joint Commission on the Accreditation of Hospitals requires the development and adoption of both sets of bylaws.[42] (See § 7.71, Joint Commission on the Accreditation of Hospitals.)

The medical staff bylaws establish a framework for the operation of the medical staff and its accountability to the governing board,[43] and reflect the current staff practices of the hospital. The bylaws include the qualifications and procedures for appointment and reappointment to the medical staff, various procedures for delineation of privileges, credentials review, organizational structure in departments, frequency and attendance at meetings, and mechanisms for effective communication with the governing board regarding quality of care, continuing education requirements, and ethical pledges.[44]

The medical staff also adopts, subject to governing board approval, rules and regulations specifically related to the role of the medical staff in the care of inpatient, outpatient, emergency, and home care patients. These regulations may be specific to a department or generalized to the whole medical staff.

From the standpoint of hospital liability, the bylaws are significant in that they constitute evidence, for jury consideration, of the standard of care the hospital requires of the medical staff and employees. They reveal what the hospital knew or should have known regarding the practice of its staff and employees.[45] The presence of bylaws with clearly defined and well-monitored procedures is therefore critical to a hospital's avoidance of liability. (See § 7.51, Governing Board.)

CASE ILLUSTRATION

The patient, an 80-year-old woman, was admitted to the hospital's "special care unit" after suffering a heart attack. Nine days later, she was transferred out of that unit to a double room in a regular patient ward. Her bed there had two pairs of side rails, one pair for the upper half of the bed and the other pair for the lower half. The night she was transferred, a hospital nurse gave the patient 15 milligrams of flurazepam hydrochloride (Dalmane). At midnight, the patient awoke and wanted to go to the bathroom. She was confused and thought she was at home. The upper side rails of her bed were raised but the lower side rails were down. Without calling for help, the patient got out of bed and headed for the hallway. In the hall she fell and sustained a fracture of her right hip. The hip could not be operated on as soon as it should have because of the patient's poor general condition. (The patient's physicians suspected that she might have suffered a second heart attack.) Because of the delay, the hip never healed properly and the patient was never able to walk again unaided or without pain.

    The manufacturer of Dalmane provides certain warnings with the drug, one of which states: "Dizziness, drowsiness, lightheadedness, staggering, atoxia, and falling have occurred, particularly in elderly or debilitated persons." The hospital had a regulation which read, "Bedside Rails. With confused or disoriented patients, beds should be in low position at all times with side rails up, except when nursing care is being given. If patient objects to the side rails being raised, a note to that effect should be included in the nursing notes or the doctor may indicate on the order sheet that he does not want the side rails raised."

The patient sued the hospital and submitted the hospital regulations as evidence of negligence on the part of the hospital. The hospital argued that expert testimony was required to show that it had acted improperly. The court imposed liability on the hospital holding that "the hospital regulation is, in a sense, an expert opinion concerning the necessity for raising bed rails in the circumstances to which the regulation applies." (*Polonsky v. Union Hospital*, 1981)[46]

§ 7.50 ORGANIZATION AND ADMINISTRATION

The organization and administration of the hospital define the relationships between various parties, e.g., the relationship between the governing body and the medical staff. A clear understanding of the respective functions of various organizational bodies facilitates horizontal and vertical communications among various personnel and contributes to the efficient functioning of the hospital generally.

§ 7.51 Governing Board

The governing board is the major decision-making body of the hospital. In the case of a private hospital, the governing board is the board of directors. In the case of a public hospital, the governing board is the board of trustees. Election or appointment to the governing board is conducted according to requirements of the articles of incorporation and/or state statute.

Most state incorporation statutes regulate the duties and responsibilities of hospital governing boards and their members quite specifically.[47] Generally the governing board develops policy and articulates plans for short- and long-term institution goals and ultimately controls the performance of both the lay and professional staff of the hospital.[48]

The following JCAH (see § 7.71, Joint Commission on the Accreditation of Hospitals) principle and standards reflect the requirements imposed by most state laws on hospital governing boards:

Principle
There shall be an organized governing body, or designated persons so functioning, that has overall responsibility for the conduct of the hospital in a manner consonant with the hospital's objective of making available high-quality patient care.

Standard I: There shall be full disclosure of hospital ownership and control.

Standard II: The governing body shall adopt bylaws in accordance with legal requirements and its responsibility to the community.

Standard III: Governing body members shall be selected, unless otherwise provided by law, in accordance with the hospital's bylaws and, if applicable, articles of incorporation or charter.

Standard IV: The governing body shall provide for the selection of its officers, adopt a schedule of meetings, and define attendance requirements and the method of documenting governing body proceedings.

Standard V: The governing body shall provide mechanisms for fulfilling the functions necessary to the discharge of its responsibilities.

Standard VI: The governing body shall provide for institutional planning to meet the health needs of the community.

Standard VII: The governing body shall appoint a chief executive officer whose qualifications, responsibilities, authority, and accountability shall be defined in writing.

Standard VIII: The medical staff bylaws, rules and regulations shall be subject to governing body approval. This approval shall not be unreasonably withheld.

Standard IX: The governing body shall hold the medical staff responsible for making recommendations concerning initial medical staff appointments, reappointments, termination of appointments, the delineation of clinical privileges, and the curtailment of clinical privileges.

Standard X: The governing body shall require that the medical staff establish mechanisms designed to assure the achievement and maintenance of high standards of medical practice and patient care.[49]

The governing board may appoint an executive committee which is responsible for the day-to-day operation of the hospital between board meetings. A number of standing committees which advise and make recommendations to the board may also be appointed.

The authority of hospital governing boards is either express or implied. Express authority is granted by the articles of incorporation which delineate the purpose of the hospital and the powers which the corporation through the governing board is authorized to use to fulfill that purpose. Other powers are impliedly authorized for the execution of any and all acts which the corporation and board have expressly been granted the power to perform.[50]

Ultimate responsibility for the quality of patient care in the hospital rests with the governing board.[51] Part of this responsibility involves the appointment and retention of medical staff and the delineation of privileges for individual physicians. Although the medical staff may advise regarding these matters, the board cannot delegate its responsibility.[52] Failure to exercise reasonable care in meeting this responsibility may result in liability of the hospital.[53]

The governing board members are also fiduciaries to the hospital corporation and the shareholders or members. A fiduciary relationship involves both formal and informal relations where a person or institution is placed in a position of trust or confidence by another. This position entails two extra duties—loyalty and responsibility. Loyalty implies that the interest of the institution must be placed above self-interest. Board members are therefore precluded from such acts as making secret profits, taking bribes, or competing with the hospital. Responsibility requires the exercise of reasonable care, skill, and diligence in every activity of the board. Reasonable care is that which an ordinary, prudent trustee would exercise under similar circumstances.[54]

Breach of fiduciary duties may lead to the individual liability of board members for their own torts or wrongs, even though carried out in the name of the corporation.

§ 7.52 Hospital Administrator

The hospital administrator is the chief executive officer of the hospital. The governing board appoints this person and confers authority on him or her consistent with its goals and objectives. The law does not articulate specific qualifications for the hospital administrator, although the JCAH requires the administrator to be qualified by education and expertise appropriate to the fulfillment of his or her responsibility.[55]

Basically, the hospital administrator is responsible for planning, developing and maintaining programs that implement the policies and achieve the goals of the governing board. Specifically, the hospital administrator organizes the administrative functions, establishes accountability, facilitates effective communication between medical staff and departments, organizes the hospital's internal structure, manages the hospital finances and provides for the appropriate use of the physical resources of the hospital.[56]

The relationship between the administrator and the medical staff is not always smooth and cooperative. Antagonism stems from the seemingly different focus of the two groups. Although both groups are ultimately striving for the common goal of quality patient care, the administrator is required to comply with various government and other regulations. These regulations impose cost-containment measures, "red tape" and accountability controls which serve to consume valuable physician time and restrict unlimited freedom and spending by the medical staff.[57] The conflicts that result must be resolved if the hospital administrator is to remain effective in the operation of the hospital.

§ 7.53 Medical and Other Staff

The precise legal nature of the medical staff has been questioned in some states. The New Jersey Superior Court has held it to be an unincorporated association and therefore capable of being sued as an entity for failing to curtail privileges of an incompetent staff member.[58] The more legally traditional and most often followed view is that the medical staff is not a legal entity, but rather, a component of the hospital corporation which is ultimately responsible to the governing board.[59]

Selection of the medical staff is an element of the fiduciary responsibility of the board. Hospitals may be liable for patient injury resulting from the failure to monitor adequately the qualifications and performance of the medical staff.[60] (See § 7.51, Governing Board.)

Functions and duties of the medical staff are specified in its bylaws. (See § 7.42, Bylaws.) The medical staff may be organized into categories such as active medical staff, associate medical staff, courtesy medical staff, consulting medical staff, and honorary staff. These categories and the various responsibilities and privileges associated with them should also be specified in the medical staff bylaws.[61]

Generally, medical staffs contain staff officers who are members of the active staff, as well as an executive committee which performs the day-to-day functions of the medical staff and serves as a liaison between the medical staff and the hospital administrator.[62]

Large hospitals may provide for the departmentalization of their medical staff. Departments are specified by the bylaws, as is the method for appointing department heads.[63]

The nursing staff is organized into a nursing department and directed by a nurse administrator.[64] Unlike the members of the medical staff, the nursing staff members are hospital employees. This is a primary source of hospital liability, i.e., both the nurse and the hospital are generally held responsible for the negligence of the nurse.[65] The nursing department should devise written standards which delineate the authority, accountability and communication lines between administrative, medical staff and nursing.[66] These written standards, along with appropriate governmental regulations, define the standard of care to which a nurse in a particular hospital will be held.

Concern over the scope of practice of nurses has stimulated changes in nurse licensing legislation. The effect of those changes has been to recognize a broader range of activity for professional nurses within the law and to eliminate the artificial definition and unnecessary restriction of nursing practice.[67]

§ 7.60 SERVICES AND PROCEDURES

Requirements of the Joint Commission on the Accreditation of Hospitals specify that a hospital provide at least the following services: dietetic services, emergency services, medical record services, nuclear medicine services, pathology and medical laboratory services, pharmaceutical services, radiology services, re-

§ 7.62   *Emergencies*   207

habilitation programs and services, respiratory care services, social work services and special care services.[68] Each of these services must be organized, directed and integrated with other related services and departments of the hospital. Most services should be the subject of written policies and procedures concerning the scope and conduct of the service.[69]

§ 7.61 Admissions

The governing board establishes admission policies. Beyond the general non-emergency situation, admission to the hospital is handled on a case-by-case basis. Hospitals generally utilize admission forms containing such things as: responsibility for payment, consent for routine medical procedures and diagnostic tests, information regarding the safekeeping of valuables and consent to the release of information to legitimate third parties such as insurers and governmental agencies.[70]

§ 7.62 Emergencies

Governmental hospitals have no right to refuse admission, while private hospitals have no duty to admit patients. These rules do not apply in the emergency admission situation. Some states require certain hospitals to provide emergency care. These hospitals must provide at least a specified amount of physician coverage, as well as adequate facilities for emergency care. Harm to a patient stemming from failure to provide adequate emergency facilities could result in liability of the hospital.[71] These statutes imply that a hospital which holds itself out as treating emergencies has a duty to treat (or refer if unable to treat) emergency cases.[72]

The JCAH requires that any ill or injured individual who comes to the hospital for emergency medical evaluation or initial treatment must be properly assessed by qualified individuals and that appropriate services must be rendered within the defined capability of the hospital. If appropriate services are outside the capability of the hospital, the ill or injured person must be referred to an appropriate facility.[73] (See § 7.71, Joint Commission on the Accreditation of Hospitals.) The degree of evaluation and treatment given to any patient in the emergency care area is the responsibility of a physician.[74] A hospital must have written policies and procedures regarding emergency patient care relating to such things as:

   a. Provision of care to an unemancipated minor not accompanied by parent or guardian, or to an unaccompanied unconscious patient
   b. Transfer and discharge of patient
   c. The emergency medical record, including consent for treatment
   d. Specification of the scope of treatment allowed, including the general and

specific procedures that may not be performed by medical staff members in the emergency department service, and the use of anesthesia

e. Who, other than physicians, may perform special procedures, under what circumstances, and under what degree of supervision
f. The use of standing orders
g. Circumstances that require the patient to return to the emergency department for treatment
h. Handling of alleged or suspected rape and child abuse victims
i. Management of pediatric emergencies
j. Initial management of patients with acute problems such as burns, hand injuries, head injuries, fractures, poisoning, gunshot and stab wounds[75]

When a hospital exerts control over an emergency patient, i.e., begins to render aid, it is generally under a duty to use reasonable care under all circumstances.[76]

In determining the hospital's liability for an emergency patient, older cases distinguished between whether or not an admission had been made. If the emergency treatment did not constitute an admission, recovery for legal liability was denied, since the defendant, a private hospital, owed no duty to accept any patient.[77]

Many states currently follow the rule stated by the Delaware Supreme Court: liability of the hospital may be predicated on the refusal of service to a patient in the case of an "unmistakable emergency."[78] Since courts will often view the extent of the emergency with the benefit of hindsight, the hospital is obligated to screen each emergency patient to determine whether the patient's condition, if left untreated, presents a serious threat to his life, health, or well-being.[79]

A hospital is not required to admit a patient when it is not adequately equipped to provide necessary continuing treatment. The hospital in this case has a positive duty to transfer or refer the patient to a facility where appropriate care can be rendered.[80] Transfers motivated in whole or part by a patient's race, creed, or ability to pay pose the threat of liability for the hospital.[81]

The emergency admission situation is distinguishable from the in-hospital emergency situation. In Michigan, for example, physicians, nurses, or other hospital personnel* who respond in good faith to life-threatening emergencies within the hospital, where their actual duties as defined by hospital rules do not require a response, are exempted by state statute from civil liability. This is not true if their act or omission in the face of the in-hospital emergency amounts to gross

---

*The statute applies to a physician, dentist, podiatrist, intern resident, registered nurse, licensed practical nurse, registered physical therapist, clinical laboratory technologist, inhalation therapist, certified registered nurse-anesthetist, x-ray technician or paramedical person.

negligence or willful and wanton misconduct.[82] The hospital itself may be held liable for ordinary negligence in the treatment of a patient by employees where a hospital-patient relationship exists at the time of the negligent act. A Michigan hospital may not derive immunity from the immunity afforded its employees.[83]

WARNING: *This immunity from liability does not apply to a physician in cases where a physician-patient relationship existed between the patient and the physician prior to the advent of the emergency.*[84]

§ 7.63 Discharge

Discharge from a hospital is also determined generally by hospital policy and on a case-by-case basis by the treating physician. Two major problems may arise concerning patient discharge: first, the restraint of patients who wish to leave, and second, the release of patients who may endanger themselves or third parties upon leaving.[85] In the first case, the refusal to discharge a patient who insists on leaving but who needs further care constitutes the tort of false imprisonment and subjects the hospital or the physician or both to liability.[86] In this situation the hospital should require the patient (or guardian) to sign a form acknowledging that he or she is acting against the advice of the physician or hospital and releasing them from liability for resulting harm.[87] If the patient refuses to sign, he or she may not be forced to do so, nor may release be withheld pending signature. The form should be filled out and witnessed by hospital personnel with the notation "Signature Refused."[88] It should be noted that the detention of a patient for inability to pay a bill also constitutes false imprisonment.[89]

Second, the hospital or the physician or both may be liable for damages resulting from the improper discharge of a patient. This situation usually involves mental patients or patients with contagious diseases. In either case, the hospital is justified in using as much restraint as reasonably necessary.[90] Hospitals have also been held liable in cases in which they have known of the escape of a dangerous patient but have failed to warn foreseeable victims.[91] In such cases the protective physician-patient privilege ends where the public peril begins.[92]

§ 7.64 Utilization Review Committee

A hospital may be required to maintain a utilization review committee which monitors the appropriateness of the continued hospitalization of individual patients. If this committee recommends against continued hospitalization and the patient is not discharged, most third-party payers (insurers) will not assume responsibility for the remaining costs.[93] Obviously, this is of critical importance to the patient, the physician, and the hospital. (See § 7.74, Professional Standards Review Organization.)

§ 7.65 *Abortion and Sterilization*

Once a state has undertaken to provide general short-term hospital care it may not constitutionally prohibit certain medically indistinguishable surgical procedures that impinge on fundamental rights. A public hospital therefore may not refuse to perform a lawful abortion or sterilization.[94]

Since private hospitals are not constrained by the requirements of the Fourteenth Amendment Due Process and Equal Protection clauses, they may refuse to perform abortions or sterilizations regardless of whether or not they receive federal funds.[95]

Some states have enacted "conscience clauses" which allow an institution, physician or other health practitioner to refuse to perform or participate in the performance of an abortion. For example, Michigan provides:

> A hospital, clinic, institution, teaching institution, or other health facility is not required to admit a patient for the purpose of performing an abortion. A hospital, clinic, institution, teaching institution, or other health facility or a physician, member, or associate of the staff, or other person connected therewith, may refuse to perform, participate in, or allow to be performed on its premises an abortion. The refusal shall be with immunity from any civil or criminal liability or penalty.
>
> A physician, or other individual who is a member of or associated with a hospital, clinic, institution, teaching institution, or other health facility, or a nurse, medical student, student nurse, or other employee of a hospital, clinic, institution, teaching institution, or other health facility in which an abortion is performed, who states an objection to abortion on professional, ethical, moral, or religious grounds, is not required to participate in the medical procedures which will result in abortion. The refusal by the individual to participate does not create a liability for damages on account of the refusal or for any disciplinary or discriminatory action by the patient, hospital, clinic, institution, teaching institution, or other health facility against the individual.
>
> 1. A physician who informs a patient that he or she refuses to give advice concerning, or participate in, an abortion is not liable to the hospital, clinic, institution, teaching institution, health facility or patient for the refusal.
> 2. A civil action for negligence or malpractice or a disciplinary or discriminatory action may not be maintained against a person refusing to give advice as to, or participating in, an abortion based on the refusal.
>
> A hospital, clinic, institution, teaching institution, or other health facility which refuses to allow abortions to be performed on its premises shall not deny staff privileges or employment to an individual for the sole reason that the individual previously participated in, or expressed a willingness to participate in, a termination of pregnancy. A hospital, clinic, institution, teaching institution, or other health facility shall not discriminate against its staff members or other employees for the sole reason that the staff members or employees have participated in, or have

expressed a willingness to participate in, a termination of pregnancy.[96]

The Georgia version of the Michigan "conscience clause" was specifically approved by the United States Supreme Court.[97] States' courts have also approved their conscience statutes as a means of supporting the First Amendment right to practice one's religion.

CASE ILLUSTRATION

A certified nurse-anesthetist was asked to assist in a dilatation and curettage accompanied by an abortion procedure. Her observation of the dissection and the part-by-part removal of the fetus caused her to be horrified and upset. She informed the hospital administration the day before her scheduled participation in another tubal ligation that she would not participate. The nurse-anesthetist was fired and, upon request, given a written statement of the reason for her discharge as "untimely refusal to perform customary and needed services," which the hospital claimed placed it in a position with few viable alternatives. The nurse-anesthetist sued the hospital. The court concluded that the nurse-anesthetist's rights under the conscience statute were not outweighed by her employer's necessity, especially since the procedure was elective and there was no showing that the hospital was unduly prejudiced, or that the patient was in danger. The court further held that the nurse-anethestist was not required to specify her reasons for non-participation in the procedure. (*Swanson v. St. John's Lutheran Hospital*, 1979)[98]

A physician who refuses to perform an abortion or sterilization based on moral or religious grounds is required under the general law of malpractice to refer the patient to another competent practitioner to perform the procedures where they are medically indicated.[99]

§ 7.70 REGULATION OF THE HOSPITAL

Hospitals are regulated externally in a number of ways. Generally, noncompliance with requirements of state and federal programs will involve a penalty for the hospital in terms of finances, availability of or eligibility for various funds, or some sanction against the hospital's license. Voluntary compliance with the requirements of the JCAH, however, could provide financial incentives, while no penalties are given for noncompliance.

§ 7.71 Joint Commission on the Accreditation of Hospitals

The standards adopted by the Joint Commission on the Accreditation of Hospitals (JCAH) apply to the quality of services provided by hospitals. They are optimal, yet achievable, and form the basis of the voluntarism movement across the United States.[100] The standards provide incentives for adoption through advantages to compliance rather than through penalties for noncompliance.[101] Perhaps the strongest incentive is that compliance with JCAH standards constitutes automatic compliance with Medicare conditions of participation. These JCAH standards also foster compliance because they are admissible for jury consideration as evidence in determining the standard of care to which a hospital should be held.[102]

To participate in the accreditation process a hospital must request and complete an Application for Survey.[103] The hospital is notified of the survey approximately four weeks in advance.[104] The extent of the hospital's compliance will be assessed through at least one of the following means:

1. Statements from authorized and responsible hospital personnel
2. Certification or other documentation of compliance provided by the hospital
3. Answers to questions concerning the implementation of a standard, or examples of its implementation, that will enable a judgment of compliance to be made
4. On-site observations by Hospital Accreditation Program surveyors[105]

The JCAH will also provide an opportunity during the on-site survey for the presentation of information about the hospital by hospital personnel and staff and public representatives and consumers.[106]

Since the JCAH standards are optimal achievable standards, 100 percent compliance is not necessary and a hospital that substantially complies will be accredited.[107]

The development of JCAH standards is an ongoing process. Technological innovations, advancements in knowledge, changes in governmental regulations or consumer demand for accountability may prompt a revision, or development of new standards.[108] Input for each standard is solicited from specialty organizations and experts in the appropriate area. Feedback is also obtained from concerned governmental agencies, individual health care practitioners and health care groups.[109]

JCAH accreditation is attractive to many hospitals because it offers benefits in the private and public sectors. Some private insurance companies require accreditation for reimbursement. Even if not required, accreditation generally smooths the path for private insurance reimbursement.[110] The federal government gives accredited hospitals "deemed status," that is, automatic eligibility for

§ 7.73   *Certificate of Need*   213

Medicare/Medicaid reimbursements.[111] Accreditation is also one of the criteria for funding decisions, as well as rate setting for hospital liability insurance premiums. Some graduate education or medical specialty programs require JCAH accreditation, and an accredited hospital may have an advantage in recruiting its professional staff.[112]

JCAH interacts with the federal government in several ways. The government validates the survey findings, even though the government generally uses less stringent standards. Since 1976, PSRO and JCAH have formed a joint task force to avoid duplication of efforts and eliminate potential conflicts in review activities.[113] (See § 5.30, Professional Standards Review Organizations.) JCAH and PSRO are not automatic equivalents, however, and JCAH maintains strict confidentiality of its survey results.[114] It is not part of the federal or state government and as yet has no contract of funding from the government.

§ 7.72 Licensure

The passage of the federal Hill-Burton Act of 1946 led most states to adopt a hospital licensing statute, since state licensure was a prerequisite to obtaining federal construction funds and to participating in federal and state Medicare–Medicaid programs. Most standards set forth in these licensing statutes pertain to the adequacy of the construction and design of the hospital physical plant rather than to the quality of care delivered.[115] Some states, however, do cover all aspects of the hospital, including physical plant, services, procedures, administration and medical staff.[116] Some regulations, for example, those which relate to patient's rights, may be worded as recommendations rather than requirements, which makes enforcement difficult.[117] In addition to general licensure requirements, some states impose specific regulations on anesthesiology services within hospitals. (See § 7.80, Anesthesiology Services.)

§ 7.73 Certificate of Need

By 1973, about half of the states had passed certificate of need legislation. Generally, this legislation requires that a facility obtain some certification that there is a public need for a change or expansion in its services prior to beginning such a change.[118] As part of the 1972 amendments to the Social Security Act, Section 1122 provided for a review of the capital expenditures of institutions participating in the Medicare reimbursement program. The National Health Planning and Resource Development Act established a system and scheme for national and local health planning. Part of this scheme includes responsibility and criteria for the administration of the certificate of need program.[119] Basically, the certificate of need program attempts to contain health care costs by restricting the capital expenditures of health facilities in the areas of building, expansion and acquisition of significant equipment. The underlying assumption is that unnecessary facilities or services increase inappropriate utilization and overhead, ultimately increasing the cost of health care.

§ 7.74 Professional Standards Review Organization

One type of indirect regulation of hospital use is carried out by the Professional Standards Review Organization (PSRO). This network of local organizations was established by an amendment to the Social Security Act for the purpose of determining whether hospital care and services are medically necessary and provided according to professional standards.[120] The PSRO reviews provider and practitioner profiles to determine if the services provided are necessary, appropriate and of sufficient quality to be eligible for payment under the Medicare and Medicaid programs. (See § 5.30, Professional Standards Review Organizations.)

§ 7.80 ANESTHESIOLOGY SERVICES

In addition to the general licensure and accreditation requirements mentioned above, hospitals may be required to comply with specific regulations related to a particular service or procedure. The JCAH requires that anesthesia care be available when the hospital provides surgical or obstetrical services.[121] Some states have promulgated specific rules related to anesthesia service as part of their facilities' licensure requirements.

§ 7.81 JCAH Standards

The JCAH standards (see § 7.71, Joint Commission on the Accreditation of Hospitals) serve as guidelines to hospitals for the purpose of ensuring a minimum availability of quality anesthesia services, but they do not prescribe any specific suggestions on matters about which reasonable deference to the professional judgment of the anesthetist has been traditionally recognized. On these matters, the administering anesthetist is held to the more elastic standards of care imposed by the "state of the art."

The standards of the JCAH regarding anesthesia services are set forth in its accreditation manual for hospitals with surgical or obstetrical facilities, and are separated into four categories. These standards are usually modified each year and the most current standards should be consulted.

Standard I requires that anesthesia services be organized, directed and integrated with other related services or departments of the hospital. Interpretation of Standard I requires that anesthesia services be directed by a physician who is a member of the hospital's medical staff, preferably a specialist in anesthesiology, with the following responsibilities:

§ 7.81   JCAH Standards   215

1. Recommending privileges for any individuals with primary anesthesia responsibility
2. Monitoring the quality of anesthesia care provided anywhere in the hospital
3. Recommending the type and amount of equipment necessary, and ensuring through annual review that enough equipment is available for administering anesthesia and related resuscitative efforts
4. Developing regulations concerning anesthetic safety
5. Assuring evaluation of the quality and appropriateness of anesthesia care rendered by the hospital
6. Establishing a program of continuing education for individuals with anesthesia privileges, including in-service training
7. Participating in the development of policies relating to the functioning of anesthetists and administration of anesthesia in the hospital, and participating in the hospital's cardiopulmonary resuscitation program. The director should also provide consultation in the management of acute and chronic respiratory insufficiency and other diagnosis and therapeutic measures when pertinent.[122]

The quality and appropriateness of anesthesia services provided should be reviewed at least quarterly, using pre-established criteria. The review should be performed within the overall hospital quality assurance program. A record of the evaluation as well as resultant action and follow-up should be maintained.[123]

Standard II requires that staffing for the delivery of anesthesia care be related to the scope and complexity of services offered. Anesthesia care must be provided by anesthesiologists, other qualified physician or dentist anesthetists, qualified nurse-anesthetists, or supervised trainees in an approved educational program. Except for emergency situations, the administration of anesthesia should be limited to areas where it can be given safely and in compliance with the policies and procedures of the departments involved. The competence of anesthesia personnel should not vary among procedures, whether elective or emergency.[124]

Physician anesthetists must be able to perform all of the independent services usually required in the practice of anesthesiology, including the ability to:

1. Perform accepted procedures commonly used to render the patient insensitive to pain during pain-producing clinical maneuvers and to relieve pain-associated medical syndromes
2. Support life functions during the administration of anesthesia, including induction and intubation
3. Provide appropriate preanesthesia and postanesthesia patient management
4. Provide consultation relating to such patient care as respiratory therapy, emergency cardiopulmonary resuscitation, and special problems in pain relief[125]

The JCAH has also established standards governing anesthesia services provided by dentists and nurse-anesthetists in hospitals. The nurse- (or dentist) anesthetist must be able to provide general anesthesia under the overall direction of the director of anesthesia services, or his or her designee, or under the overall direction of the surgeon or obstetrician responsible for the patient's care. The qualified nurse- or dentist anesthetist should have the competence to:

1. Induce anesthesia
2. Maintain anesthesia at the required levels
3. Support life functions during the administration of anesthesia, including induction and intubation
4. Recognize and take appropriate corrective action (including requesting consultation) for abnormal patient responses to anesthesia or to any adjunctive medication or other form of therapy
5. Provide professional observation and resuscitative care until the patient has regained control of his vital functions

The responsibilities of nurse- or dentist anesthetists and the corresponding attending physician must be defined in a policy statement, job description, or other appropriate document. The services that they may provide and the level of supervision required must also be described. When the operating anesthesia team consists entirely of nonphysicians, a physician must be immediately available in case of emergency.[126]

Standard III requires that precautions be taken to assure the safe administration of anesthetic agents. Written regulations for the control of electrical and anesthetic explosion hazards should be reviewed annually to assure compatibility with current practice of other services and should include at a minimum such requirements as:

1. Anesthetic apparatus must be inspected and tested by the anesthetist before use.
2. Only nonflammable agents are to be used during or prior to an operation employing an open spark.
3. Flammable anesthetic agents shall be employed only in areas in which a conductive pathway can be maintained between the patient and the floor.
4. Fabrics permissible for use as outer garments or blankets in anesthetizing areas shall be specified in writing.
5. With specified exceptions, all electrical equipment in the anesthetizing areas shall be on an audiovisual line isolation monitor.
6. The condition of all operating room electrical equipment shall be inspected regularly and a written record maintained.
7. Anesthesia personnel shall familiarize themselves with the rate, volume, and mechanism of an exchange within the surgical and obstetrical suites, as well as with humidity control.[127]

§ 7.90   *Medical Staff Privileges*   217

Written policies relating to the delivery of anesthesia care are required by Standard IV. These policies should be approved by the medical staff, reviewed annually, enforced, and provide for at least the following:

1. The preanesthesia evaluation of the patient by a physician with appropriate documentation in the patient's record. The record should at least refer to the use of general, spinal, or other regional anesthesia.
2. The review of the patient's condition immediately prior to the induction of anesthesia, including a review of the medical record.
3. The patient's safety during the anesthetic period including: condition of equipment, cleanliness of reusable anesthesia equipment, pin-index safety system on each anesthetic gas machine, anesthetist's attendance of the patient as long as required relative to anesthesia status.
4. A mechanism for the release of patient from postanesthesia care.
5. The recording of all pertinent events taking place during induction of, maintenance of, and emergence from anesthesia.
6. The recording of postanesthetic visits, including at least one note describing the presence or absence of anesthesia-related complications.
7. Written guidelines developed by an anesthesiologist defining the role of anesthesia services and of all postanesthesia care areas in the hospital's infection control program.[128]

§ 7.82 *State Regulation*

In addition to the JCAH standards and general state hospital licensing requirements, some states specify additional requirements regarding the use of anesthesia in hospitals. These requirements are generally included within the hospital licensing regulations. They may be quite detailed as in the case of California (see Appendix B) or quite general as are those of Massachusetts (see Appendix C). Other states' regulations are essentially a consolidated version of the JCAH Standards (see Appendix E).

§ 7.90 MEDICAL STAFF PRIVILEGES

Given the realities of contemporary American medical practice, affiliation with a hospital is absolutely indispensable to surgeons and other specialists. A physician or surgeon who is denied access to hospital facilities is for all practical purposes effectively denied the opportunity to practice his or her profession fully. Because of the adverse professional and financial effects of not being appointed to or being removed from the hospital staff, many physicians who have been so denied have gone to court to obtain or continue their staff appointment(s). As noted earlier, it is the governing board of the hospital which is ultimately responsible for the quality of patient care and therefore controls admission to, or discharge from, the medical staff. This conflict between the responsibility of the hospital and the needs of the physician has spawned considerable litigation in the area of medical staff privileges.

§ 7.91 Substantive Due Process

The U.S. Constitution provides that a state may not deprive any person of life, liberty, or property without due process of law, or deny to any person the equal protection of its laws.[129] These clauses, referred to as the Due Process and Equal Protection clauses, seemingly apply only to governmental entities or to entities which have such close connections to the government as to be considered its agents. The significance of the clauses from the standpoint of a hospital medical staff is that they impose certain constraints on state hospitals in denying, reducing, or revoking staff privileges. Some state courts have begun to impose similar constraints on private hospitals based on public policy and common law considerations.[130] In addition, the Joint Commission on the Accreditation of Hospitals[131] and Conditions of Participation for Hospitals[132] require that physicians be afforded substantive due process and equal protection.

Substantive due process requires that hospital privileges be determined on reasonable, nonarbitrary and non-capricious standards. This has been interpreted to mean that the standards for determining privileges must be related to such things as the clinical standards of patient care, the objectives and purposes of the institution or the professional, ethical behavior of the physician, and objective application.[133] Hospitals may not restrict privileges based on vague and arbitrary standards such as "the best interests of the patient and hospital."[134]

Various requirements of admission to the medical staff have been tested in court. Briefly, the following requirements of admission to the hospital medical staff have been upheld:

1. References documenting training, experience and current clinical competence, so long as they are not required from current active medical staff members[135]

2. Reasonable geographic limitations regarding the proximity of the hospital to the physician's office, although these limitations cannot require that the office be in the same county as the hospital[136]

3. Documented clinical competence[137]

4. Mandatory medical malpractice insurance[138]

§ 7.91　　　　　　　　　Substantive Due Process

5. Mandatory specialty board certification[139]
6. Documented ability to work with others[140]

In addition, hospitals may restrict or delineate privileges if the restriction can be professionally justified.[141] For example, a Michigan appeals court has allowed a hospital to suspend privileges based on the physician's personal behavior, i.e., rudeness and unacceptable language directed at patients, staff and visitors.[142]

In most states public hospitals may deny privileges to licensed osteopathic physicians and to members of other schools of healing arts if their regulations so permit.[143] Some states, however, have adopted specific legislation which prohibits discrimination between doctors of allopathic and osteopathic medicine.[144] Where licensing statutes or other legislation equate physicians of allopathic and osteopathic medicine, osteopathic physicians must be afforded equal substantive rights and opportunities based on their individual training and qualifications.[145]

Specialty Staff Privileges: Courts have upheld the requirement of an American Medical Association approved residency in a specialty as a prerequisite to admission to the medical staff in that specialty.[146] The JCAH standards specify that delineation of clinical privileges should be based on the staff member's credentials. While one method of delineating clinical privileges is through specialty board certification or current eligibility as defined by the appropriate board, privilege delineation should be reasonably comprehensive and not identified simply as a specialty designation, such as "family practice privileges" or "obstetrics and gynecology privileges."[147]

Physician specialists have been excluded from a medical staff on the grounds that the current staff coverage in that specialty is adequate or that additional coverage would needlessly increase the amount of surgery performed.[148] In these cases, the hospital must be able to support its decision with substantial, credible evidence and may not base such exclusions on fostering the well-being of its present staff members.[149]

A blanket moratorium on new medical staff appointments (except for limited subspecialties or where an applicant had no hospital affiliation), adopted to curb excessive utilization rates, was held by a New Jersey court to be an abuse of the governing board's discretion following a five-year experience demonstrating the ineffectiveness of the moratorium. The court held that the effect of the moratorium was to enhance the economic interests of the current medical staff at the expense of practitioners whose patients would be excluded.[150]

Additionally, courts have upheld closed departments or services which restrict from practice in that specialty or service all physicians except those who have an exclusive contract with the hospital for the rendition of that service.[151] In exclusive contract arrangements, the hospital contracts with one or more physician(s) to provide specialized professional service, closing that service to all other physicians regardless of their qualifications and competence. The hospital must be able to show valid reasons for its decision to enter into an exclusive contract.[152] (See § 7.100, Exclusive Contracts.)

§ 7.92 Procedural Due Process

In addition to the reasonableness requirements of due process, certain procedural safeguards are imposed on hospitals in granting, reducing or revoking staff privileges. Though procedures may vary slightly between initial appointments to the staff and renewals or other actions against the privileges of current staff members, procedural due process generally means that the physician must be granted fundamental fair play given the particular circumstances.[153] At least one state court has specified minimal due process requirements as follows:

1. Written notice of the charges against the physician (or reasons for denial of initial appointment)
2. Opportunity for a hearing
3. A relatively impartial, duly authorized body to conduct the hearing
4. Opportunity to produce positive evidence and witnesses, and to refute adverse evidence and testimony
5. Findings based on substantial factual evidence
6. Written notice of the decisions with reasons for it
7. Opportunity to appeal[154]

The JCAH standards require the medical staff to adopt bylaws which include the establishment of fair hearing and appellate review mechanisms in connection with medical staff recommendations for denial of initial appointments and reappointments, curtailment, suspension, or revocation of staff privileges. These mechanisms should specify the period of time for requesting a hearing, the right to introduce witnesses or evidence, the role of legal counsel, and fixed periods of time for completing action, including final action by the governing board.[155]

Some hospitals may grant protections to staff physicians in their bylaws, such as recognizing the physician's right to be represented by counsel.[156] Although hospitals may summarily suspend a physician's privileges in order to protect the patient, they must provide the physician with an opportunity for hearing within a reasonable time after suspension.[157] Whether public or private, a hospital must follow the procedural due process requirements specified in its own bylaws.[158]

§ 7.100 EXCLUSIVE CONTRACTS

Hospital contracts for the exclusive services of a single or group of specialists have been repeatedly challenged by physicians seeking hospital privileges in the specialty covered by the contract.[159] The courts will look to the hospital's rationale for the exclusive contract in deciding physicians' suits based on civil rights or antitrust claims. The hospital's reasons for the contract must be related to legitimate hospital concerns.

CASE ILLUSTRATION

A public hospital, dissatisfied with the anesthesiology services provided to it, had for some time attempted unsuccessfully to assure "on call" services of anesthesiologists and nurse-anesthetists. As a result, surgery was sometimes performed without an anesthesiologist in attendance. The Joint Commission on Accreditation of Hospitals had indicated a number of deficiencies in the hospital's anesthesiology services in its annual review. The hospital finally contracted with a professional corporation of three anesthesiologists and a number of nurse-anesthetists, to provide 24 hours per day, 7 days per week services. A physician's application to use the house facilities to practice his specialty, anesthesiology, was subsequently denied because of the existence of the exclusive contract. The physician sued the hospital and the court dismissed the physician's suit, which had charged violations of the Sherman Antitrust Act, federal civil rights statutes, and the U.S. Constitution.

The court's specific conclusions of law contained the following listing of legal arguments in general support of a hospital's right to enter into an exclusive contract:

1. A physician has no federal constitutional right to staff privileges at a public hospital merely because of his or her license to practice medicine.

2. A hospital has the right to treat physicians of the same calling differently, provided there is a rational basis for the different treatment.

3. A contract between a hospital and some of its staff members to operate a certain specialized facility to the exclusion of other equally qualified physicians is not necessarily unreasonable or arbitrary, depending on the ends to be met thereby.

4. The hospital administered the plaintiff's application with fairness

and denied it, based on a rationale compatible with the hospital's responsibility.
5. The exclusive contract was justified in view of the ends to be accomplished by the hospital and contractors in providing proper care to surgical patients.
6. None of the plaintiff's rights under the Fourteenth Amendment to the U.S. Constitution or the Civil Rights Act (42 U.S.C. § 1983) were abridged as a result of the existence of the exclusive contract. (*Capili v. Shott*, 1980)[160]

The above listing is an example of the types and extent of consideration given an exclusive contract which is challenged in a court action. Other courts have rejected a physician's argument that denial of hospital privileges due to the existence of an exclusive contract entitles the physician to a hearing.[161]

Generally, courts will uphold the hospital's discretion to adopt a reasonable administrative policy. For example, where a hospital faced with conflicting views chooses to operate a particular hospital unit on a "closed-staff" basis, the court has stated that where the rule-making or policy-making decision was arrived at in substantively rational and fair proceedings, the court would not substitute its judgment for that of the governing board, even if it did disagree with the decision.[162]

NOTES

1. E. Hayt, L. Hayt & A. Groeschel, Law of Hospital, Physician and Patient 83 (1972).
2. *Id.* at 84.
3. A. Donabedian, Aspects of Medical Care Administration 241 (1973).
4. D. Warren, Problems in Hospital Law 303 (1978); A. Southwick, The Law of Hospital and Health Care Administration 79 (1978).
5. Hill v. Ohio County, 468 S.W.2d 306 (Ky. 1971), *cert. denied*, 404 U.S. 1041 (1972).
6. A. Southwick, *supra* note 4, 162-63.
7. Memorial Hosp. v. Maricopa County, 415 U.S. 250 (1974).
8. Mich. Comp. Laws Ann. § 333.20152 (1980).
9. *See, e.g.*, Okla. Stat. Ann. tit. 68, § 2405(j) (West 1966 & 1980 Supp.); A. Southwick, *supra* note 4, at 431.
10. D. Warren, *supra* note 4, at 86.
11. A. Southwick, *supra* note 4, at 431.
12. Joint Commission on Accreditation of Hospitals, Accreditation Manual for Hospitals 93 (1981) [hereinafter cited as JCAH].
13. Southwick, *Due Process Part I: The Physician's Right to Due Process and Equal Protection*, 7 Hosp. Med. Staff 30, 31 (May, 1978).
14. Parker v. City of Highland Park, 404 Mich. 183, 273 N.W.2d 413 (1978); Mich. Comp. Laws Ann. § 691.1407 (Supp. 1980-81).
15. D. Louisell & H. Williams, Medical Malpractice 528-40.7 (1980).

Notes: Chapter VII

16. *See, e.g.*, Calomeris v. D.C., 125 F. Supp. 266 (D. D.C. 1954); Strickland v. Bradford County Hosp. Corp., 196 So.2d 765 (Fla. App. 1967).
17. *See, e.g.*, McMahon v. Baroness Erlanger Hosp., 306 S.W. 2d 41 (Tenn. App. 1951); Mo. Ann. Stat. § 71.185 (Vernon Supp. 1981); Collins v. Memorial Hosp., 521 P.2d 1330 (Wyo. 1974); Vt. Stat. Ann. tit. 29, §§ 1401 *et seq*.
18. *See, e.g.*, Tuengel v. Sitka, 118 F. Supp. 399 (D.C. Alaska 1954); Stone v. Ariz. Highway Comm'n, 93 Ariz. 384, 381 P.2d 107 (1963); Parker v. City of Highland Park, *supra* note 14; Becker v. City of New York, 2 N.Y.2d 226, 140 N.E.2d 262 (1957); Conn. Gen. Stat. Ann. § 7-465 (West Supp. 1981).
19. *See* D. Louisell, *supra* note 15, at 528-40.7.
20. E. Hayt, L. Hayt & A. Groeschel, *supra* note 1, at 91, 93, 95.
21. *Id*.
22. D. Warren, *supra* note 4, at 303.
23. *Id*.
24. *Id*. at 53.
25. *See, e.g.*, Waters v. St. Francis Hosp., 618 F.2d 1106, 1107 (5th Cir. 1980); Hodge v. Paoli Memorial Hospital, 576 F.2d 563, 564 (3d Cir. 1978); Barret v. United Hosps., 376 F. Supp. 791 (S.D. N.Y. 1974), *aff'd mem.*, 506 F.2d 1395 (2d Cir. 1974).
26. Sams v. Ohio Valley Gen. Hosp. Ass'n, 413 F.2d 826 (4th Cir. 1969); Simkins v. Moses H. Cone Memorial Hosp., 323 F.2d 959 (4th Cir. 1963), *cert. denied*, 376 U.S. 938 (1964).
27. Southwick, *supra* note 13, at 31.
28. 42 C.F.R. §§ 405.1021 *et seq*. (1979).
29. JCAH, *supra* note 12, at 94-5.
30. Morton v. Savannah Hosp., 148 Ga. 438, 96 S.E. 887 (1918); Jones v. Baylor Hosp., 284 S.W.2d 929 (Tex. Civ. App. 1955); Norfolk Protestant Hosp. v. Plunkett, 162 Va. 151, 173 S.E. 363 (1934).
31. Sisters of the Sorrowful Mother v. Zeidler, 183 Okla. 454, 82 P.2d 996 (1938); Villarreal v. Santa Rosa Medical Center, 443 S.W.2d 622 (Tex. Civ. App. 1969); Sessions v. Thomas P. Dee Memorial Hosp., 94 Utah 460, 78 P.2d 645 (1938).
32. O'Connor v. Boulder Colorado Sanitarium Ass'n, 105 Colo. 259, 96 P.2d 835 (1939).
33. Tucker v. Mobile Infirmary Ass'n, 191 Ala. 572, 68 So. 4 (1915); Tuengel v. Sitka, *supra* note 18; Ray v. Tucson Medical Center, 72 Ariz. 22, 230 P.2d 220 (1951); Malloy v. Fong, 37 Cal.2d 356, 232 P.2d 241 (1951); Heimbuch v. President & Directors of Georgetown College, 251 F. Supp. 614 (D. D.C. 1966); Wilson v. Lee Memorial Hosp., 65 So.2d 40 (1964); Bill v. Presbytery of Boise, 91 Idaho 60, 297 P.2d 1041 (1956); Darling v. Charleston Community Memorial Hosp., 33 Ill. 2d 326, 211 N.E.2d 253 (1965), *cert. denied*, 383 U.S. 946 (1966); Harris v. Young Women's Christian Ass'n, 237 N.E.2d 242 (1968); Haynes v. Presbyterian Hosp., 241 Iowa 1269, 45 N.W.2d 151 (1950); Noel v. Menninger Foundation, 175 Kan. 751, 267 P.2d 934 (1954); Jackson v. Doe, 296 So.2d 323 (1974); Colby v. Carney Hosp., 254 N.E.2d 407 (1969); Parker v. Port Huron Hosp., 361 Mich. 1, 105 N.W.2d 1 (1960); Mulliner v. Evangelischer Diakonneissenverein of Minn. Dist. of German Evangelical Synod of North America, 144 Minn. 392, 175 N.W. 699 (1920); Miss. Baptist Hosp. v. Holme's, 214 Miss. 906, 55 So.2d 142 (1951); Abernathy v. Sisters of St. Mary's, 446 S.W.2d 599 (1969); Howard v. Sisters of Charity of Leavenworth, 193 F. Supp. 191 (D. Mont. 1961); Myers v. Drozda, 180 Neb. 183, 141 N.W.2d 852 (1966); Welch v. Frizbee Memorial Hosp., 90 N.H. 337, 9 A.2d 761 (1939); Collopy v. Newark Eye and Ear Infirmary, 27 N.J. 29, 141 A.2d 276 (1958); Bing v. Thunig, 2 N.Y.2d 656, 143 N.E.2d 3 (1957); Rickbeil v. Grafton-Deaconess Hosp., 74 N.D. 525, 23 N.W.2d 247 (1964); Avellone v. St. John's Hosp., 165 Ohio St. 467, 135

Notes: Chapter VII

N.E.2d 410 (1956); Hungerford v. Portland Sanitarium & Benev. Ass'n, 235 Or. 412, 384 P.2d 1009 (1963); Flagiello v. Pa. Hosp., 417 Pa. 486, 208 A.2d 193 (1965); Foster v. Roman Catholic Diocese of Vt., 116 Vt. 124, 70 A.2d 230 (1950); Friend v. Cove Methodist Church, Inc., 65 Wash. 2d 174, 396 P.2d 546 (1964); Atkins v. St. Francis Hosp., 143 S.E.2d 154 (1965); Kojis v. Doctors Hosp., 12 Wis. 2d 367, 107 N.W.2d 131, *modified*, 12 Wis. 2d 367, 107 N.W.2d 292 (1961); Lutheran Hosps. v. Homes Society v. Yepsen, 469 P.2d 409 (Wyo. 1970).

34. A. Southwick, *supra* note 4, at 32.
35. *Id.* at 37.
36. R. Anthony & R. Huzlinger, Management Control in Nonprofit Organizations 2-36 (1975).
37. A. Southwick, *supra* note 4, at 33.
38. *Id.* at 32.
39. *Id.*
40. *Id.* at 35.
41. Manuel Tovar v. Paxton Community Memorial Hosp., 29 Ill. App. 3d 218, 330 N.E.2d 247 (1975).
42. JCAH, *supra* note 12, at 51, 103.
43. *Id.* at 103.
44. *Id.* at 103-4.
45. Darling v. Charleston Community Memorial Hosp., *supra* note 33.
46. Polonsky v. Union Hosp., 418 N.E.2d 620, 622 (Mass App. Ct. 1981).
47. D. Warren, *supra* note 4, at 27.
48. A. Southwick, *supra* note 4, at 40.
49. JCAH, *supra* note 12, at 51-6.
50. D. Warren, *supra* note 4, at 28.
51. JCAH, *supra* note 12, at 151.
52. Shields, *Guidelines for Reviewing Applications for Privileges*, 9 Hosp. Med. Staff 11 (Sept., 1980).
53. *See, e.g.*, Purcell v. Zimbliman, 18 Ariz. App. 75, 500 P.2d 335 (1972); Joiner v. Mitchell County Hosp. Auth., 125 Ga. App. 1, 2, 186 S.E.2d 307, 308 (1971), *aff'd*, 229 Ga. 140, 189 S.E.2d 412 (1972); Corleto v. Shore Memorial Hosp., 138 N.J. Super. 302, 309, 250 A.2d 534, 537 (1975).
54. A. Southwick, *supra* note 4, at 51.
55. JCAH, *supra* note 12, at 79.
56. *Id.* at 81-82.
57. Blanton, *Physician's Role in Hospital Continues to Grow*, 9 Hosp. Med. Staff 13, 14 (April, 1980).
58. Corleto v. Shore Memorial Hosp., *supra* note 53.
59. Horty & Mulholland, *The Legal Status of the Hospital Medical Staff*, 1979 Specialty Law Dig.: Health Care 19 (April, 1979).
60. D. Warren, *supra* note 4, at 47.
61. JCAH, *supra* note 12, at 99.
62. *Id.* at 101.
63. *Id.* at 102.
64. *Id.* at 115.
65. D. Warren, *supra* note 4, at 71.
66. JCAH, *supra* note 12, at 116.
67. D. Warren, *supra* note 4, at 79.
68. JCAH, *supra* note 12, at xviii.

69. *Id.* at 9, 28, 126, 142, 157, 174, 179, 184.
70. A. Southwick, *supra* note 4, at 164-66.
71. D. Warren, *supra* note 4, at 91.
72. A. Southwick, *supra* note 4, at 186; *see, e.g.*, Mich. Comp. Laws Ann. § 691.1502 (Supp. 1980-81).
73. JCAH, *supra* note 12, at 23.
74. *Id.* at 26.
75. *Id.* at 29-30.
76. *See, e.g.*, Thomas v. Corso, 265 Md. 84, 288 A.2d 379 (1972); Barcia v. Soc'y of N.Y. Hosp., 241 N.Y.S.2d 373, 39 Misc. 2d 526 (Sup. Ct. 1963).
77. Kucera, *Narrow Definition of 'Emergency' Can Spell 'Litigation,'* 7 Hosp. Med. Staff 21, 23 (Sept., 1978).
78. Wilmington Gen. Hosp. v. Manlove, 54 Del. 15, 174 A.2d 135 (Sup. Ct. 1961).
79. Kucera, *supra* note 77, at 25; *see* Powers, *Hospital Emergency Service and the Open Door*, 66 Mich. L. Rev. 1455 (1968).
80. *See, e.g.*, Carrasco v. Bankoff, 220 Cal. App. 2d 230, 33 Cal. Rptr. 673 (1963).
81. Kucera, *supra* note 77, at 26.
82. Mich. Comp. Laws Ann. § 691.1502 (Supp. 1980-81).
83. Hamburger v. Henry Ford Hosp., 91 Mich. App. 580, 284 N.W.2d 155 (1979).
84. Mich. Comp. Laws Ann. § 691.1502 (Supp. 1980-81).
85. D. Warren, *supra* note 4, at 93.
86. A. Southwick, *supra* note 4, at 179.
87. D. Warren, *supra* note 4, at 95.
88. American Medical Association (AMA), Office of the General Counsel, Medicolegal Forms with Legal Analysis 6 (1973).
89. D. Warren, *supra* note 4, at 93.
90. *Id.* at 95.
91. Tarasoff v. Regents of the Univ. of California, 118 Cal. Rptr. 129, 529 P.2d 553 (Cal. 1974); Rum River Lumber Co. v. Minnesota, 282 N.W.2d 882 (Minn. 1979); Comiskey v. State of N.Y., 71 A.D.2d 699, 418 N.Y.S.2d 233 (1979).
92. *Id.*
93. A. Southwick, *supra* note 4, at 181.
94. Hathaway v. Worcester City Hosp., 475 F.2d 701 (1st Cir. 1973); Doe v. Bridgeton Hosp. Ass'n, Inc., 168 N.J. Super. 593, 403 A.2d 965 (App. Div. 1979).
95. Doe v. Bellin Memorial Hosp., 479 F.2d 756 (5th Cir. 1973).
96. Mich. Comp. Laws Ann. §§ 333.20181-.20184 (1980).
97. Doe v. Bolton, 410 U.S. 179 (1973).
98. Swanson v. St. John's Hosp., 597 P.2d 702 (Mont. 1979).
99. A. Southwick, *supra* note 4, at 270.
100. JCAH, *supra* note 12, at xi.
101. *Id.* at x.
102. A. Southwick, *supra* note 4, at 370, 412.
103. JCAH, *supra* note 12, at xix.
104. *Id.*
105. *Id.* at xvii.
106. *Id.* at xx.
107. *Id.* at xxi.
108. *Id.* at xi.
109. *Id.*
110. Interview with Jan Shulman, Public Relations Dep't, JCAH (Feb. 13, 1980).

111. JCAH, *supra* note 12, at x.
112. Shulman, *supra* note 110.
113. *Id.*
114. JCAH, *supra* note 12, at xxiii.
115. Worthington & Silver, *Regulation of Quality of Care in Hospitals: The Need for Change*, 35 Law & Contemp. Prob. 305, 309 (1970).
116. *See, e.g.*, Mich. Comp. Laws Ann. §§ 333.21501 *et seq.* (1980).
117. G. Annas, The Rights of Hospital Patients 22 (1975).
118. Havighurst, *Regulation of Health Facilities and Services by Certificate of Need*, 59 Va. L. Rev. 1143, 1144 (1973).
119. *See* D. Warren, *supra* note 4, at 263-76.
120. *Id.* at 67.
121. JCAH, *supra* note 12, at 5.
122. *Id.* at 5-6.
123. *Id.* at 6.
124. *Id.*
125. *Id.* at 6-7.
126. *Id.* at 7.
127. *Id.* at 7-8.
128. *Id.* at 9-10.
129. U.S. Const. XIV.
130. Southwick, *supra* note 13.
131. JCAH, *supra* note 12, at 104.
132. 42 C.F.R. §§ 1021 *et seq.* (1979).
133. Southwick, *supra* note 13, at 32; Gouda v. Detroit-Macomb Hospital Ass'n, 52 Mich. App. 516, 217 N.W.2d 905 (1974).
134. *See, e.g.*, Milford v. People's Community Hosp. Ass'n, 380 Mich. 49, 155 N.W.2d 835 (1968).
135. Southwick, *supra* note 13, at 32-33.
136. *Id.* at 33.
137. *Id.*
138. *See, e.g.*, Renforth v. Fayette Memorial Hosp., 267 Ind. 326, 383 N.E.2d 368 (1978); Holmes v. Hoemako Hosp., 117 Ariz. 403, 573 P.2d 477 (1978).
139. *See, e.g.*, Berman v. Florida Medical Center, Inc., 600 F.2d 466 (5th Cir. 1979).
140. *See, e.g.*, Huffaker & Bailey, 540 P.2d 1398 (Or. 1975).
141. Southwick, *supra* note 13, at 33.
142. Anderson v. Caro Community Hosp., 10 Mich. App. 348, 159 N.W.2d 347 (1968); Sosa v. Bd. of Managers of Val Verde Hosp., 437 F.2d 173 (5th Cir. 1971).
143. Hayman v. City of Galveston, 273 U.S. 414 (1927).
144. *See, e.g.*, Mich. Comp. Laws Ann. § 333.20152(1)(b) (1980).
145. *See, e.g.*, Stribling v. Jolley, 241 Mo. App. 1123, 253 S.W.2d 519 (1952).
146. JCAH, *supra* note 12, at 95.
147. Berman v. Florida Medical Center, Inc., *supra* note 139.
148. *See, e.g.*, Guerrero v. Burlington County Memorial Hosp., 70 N.J. 344, 360 A.2d 334 (1976); Davis v. Morristown Memorial Hosp., 106 N.J. Super. 33, 254 A.2d 125 (1969).
149. Southwick, *The Physician's Right to Due Process in Public and Private Hospitals: Is there a Difference?*, 9 Medicolegal News 4, 6 (Feb., 1981).
150. Walsky v. Pascack Valley Hosp., 145 N.J. Super. 393, 367 A.2d 1204 (1976).
151. Dattilo v. Tucson Gen. Hosp., 23 Ariz. App. 396, 533 P.2d 700 (1975) (nuclear medicine); Blank v. Palo Alto-Stanford Hosp. Center, 234 Cal. App. 2d 377, 44 Cal.

Rptr. 572 (1965) (diagnostic radiology); Lewin v. St. Joseph Hosp., 82 Cal. App. 3d 368, 146 Cal. Rptr. 892 (1978) (renal hemodialysis); Rush v. City of St. Petersburg, 205 So.2d 11 (Fla. App. 1968) (pathology); Adler v. Montegiore Hosp., 254 Pa. 60, 311 A.2d 634 (1973) (cardiac catheterization).
152. Southwick, *supra* note 149, at 6.
153. Southwick, *Due Process Part 2: The Elusive Concept of Procedural Due Process*, 7 Hosp. Med. Staff 19, 20 (June, 1978).
154. Silver v. Castle Memorial Hosp., 53 Hawaii 475 (1972).
155. JCAH, *supra* note 12, at 104.
156. *See, e.g.*, Bylaws of the Medical Staff of the University of Michigan, § ix-4 (Jan., 1979).
157. Southwick, *supra* note 153, at 24.
158. Margolin v. Morton F. Plant Hosp. Ass'n, 348 So.2d 57 (Fla. App. 1977).
159. Hyde v. Jefferson Parish Hosp. Dist., 513 F. Supp. 532 (E.D. La. 1981); Capili v. Shott, 620 F.2d 438 (4th Cir. 1980).
160. *Id.*
161. Centeno v. Roseville Community Hosp., 167 Cal. Rptr. 183 (Cal. App. 1979).
162. Lewin v. St. Joseph Hosp. of Orange, 82 Cal. App. 3d 368, 146 Cal. Rptr. 892 (1978).

Part III
Anesthetic Practices

Introduction

Part III of *Anesthesiology and the Law* is unique in today's medical-legal literature. Each drug, device and treatment regimen for which anesthesiologists have been found liable for malpractice is identified and discussed.

As discussed in Part I, the patient-plaintiff must prove that the defendant anesthesiologist deviated from the accepted anesthesia *standard of care* before malpractice can be found. (See § 1.32, Standard of Care.) Because standards of care are so elusive and because most physicians do not know what standard of care applies until they are accused of breaching it, Part III attempts to present a variety of standards from a variety of sources. For this reason this book in general, and Part III in particular, may be useful as a risk management tool.

The sources of anesthesia standards of care used in this text include, (1) the published guidelines of the American Society of Anesthesiologists, (2) interpretations and customary practice, as written by the medical authors, and (3) appellate court reports of trial-jury decisions which found that a particular anesthesia standard of care applied after hearing expert testimony based on a specific set of facts.

These anesthesia standards of care are not offered to direct anesthesia care. Rather, they are offered to help practicing anesthesiologists avoid known medical-legal pitfalls and to stimulate a standard of care debate. It is the authors' view that an open discussion of standards of care will promote quality care by keeping physicians up to date and at the same time provide protection against the penalties of ignorance. Because standards of care are constantly evolving in response to technological advances and increases in knowledge such discussion is essential.

This Part, because it presents standards of care, will be controversial. The controversy will come from those who believe that standards of care are antithetical to the art of practicing medicine. It will also come from those who may propose a different standard for a given drug, device or treatment regimen. Comments from the latter are welcomed by the authors and may be reflected in subsequent editions of this text. Those who believe that standards of care are antithetical to the art of practicing medicine, however, should be prepared for the intrusion of reality.

Chapter VIII

Preoperative Anesthetic Care

§ 8.10 PREANESTHESIA VISIT AND EVALUATION

Liability may be imposed on the anesthesiologist in connection with the preanesthesia visit for: (1) failing to properly examine the patient or otherwise ascertain that a certain anesthetic is contraindicated based on the patient's condition; (2) failing to properly act in administering anesthesia according to a finding of a contraindication based on the patient's condition; or (3) failing to obtain the informed consent of the patient for anesthesia at the appropriate time during the visit.

Basic Standard of Care: With respect to all anesthesia, whether it be general, regional, or local, certain fundamental considerations have been identified by the American Society of Anesthesiology (ASA).[1] The following is a list of these considerations.

Prior to the induction of anesthesia, it is advisable that:

1. A medical evaluation be made and recorded by a licensed physician.
2. The individual responsible for the anesthesia be thoroughly familiar with the medical and surgical problems involved.
3. Pertinent consultations be requested and obtained.
4. Provisions for continuity of care be considered and established.
5. The physician responsible for the anesthesia decisions required during anesthesia management be already identified to the patient and to any technician who may assist in such care and management, and his availability for supervision and direction be established if he is not administering the anesthesia personally.

Certain other guidelines also developed by the ASA that specifically address the preoperative anesthetic evaluation[2] are provided below:

Preanesthetic evaluation and preparation by a responsible physician means that he or she should:
1. Review the chart
2. Interview the patient to
   a. Discuss medical, anesthetic and drug history
   b. Perform any examinations that would provide information that might assist in a decision regarding risk and management
3. Order necessary tests and medications essential to conduct anesthesia
4. Obtain consultation as believed necessary
5. Record impressions on the patient's chart or on anesthesia record

Interpretation and Customary Practice: The preanesthetic visit has been a traditional part of the anesthetic management of patients since the emergence of anesthesiology as a specialty, although the role and the purpose of the preanesthetic visit has changed since its inception. In earlier days, the operation itself was the crucial part of the overall management of surgical patients and the primary role of the anesthesiologist in the preanesthetic visit was to determine whether in fact the patient could survive the surgery. There were relatively few alternatives available in determining preoperative management, and postoperative management was relatively straightforward in those patients whose constitutions were strong enough to survive the stress of surgery. With the evolution of modern surgical and anesthetic practices, the situation has changed. Today, the final outcome for the patient depends to a much greater extent on the preoperative preparation of the patient and the postoperative management of the patient. Consequently, the preanesthetic visit has not only retained its traditional place in anesthetic practice but has also grown in importance, and it now encompasses many purposes other than merely determining whether or not a patient is likely to survive the operation.

The first purpose of the preoperative visit is to allow the anesthesiologist to obtain enough pertinent data on which to base decisions regarding the overall anesthetic management of the individual patient. Considerations for the anesthetic management of an individual patient would include a determination of the requirement for preoperative sedation, the choice of anesthetic agent and technique, and the need for particular monitoring requirements. (See § 9.20, Records, and Table 9.1.)

Several sources are available to assist in forming a decision. Clearly, the admitting history and physical examination, current laboratory studies and pertinent diagnostic studies available on the patient's current chart should be reviewed. The old chart should also be reviewed with particular attention to previous anesthetic records, recovery room notes and anesthesiology follow-up notes regarding any problems which may have arisen in previous anesthetic administration. Often, a review of nursing notes will indicate whether a seemingly stoic patient may in fact be much more anxious than he is willing to admit to his physician and may require higher doses of preoperative sedatives. By reviewing the available data prior to going to the bedside, the anesthesiologist already has a good idea of the overall condition and mental status of the patient and can tailor his interview and physical examination to the needs of the individual patient. While it is probably not necessary to duplicate a complete history and physical examination, it must be realized that determining a rational plan for the preoperative, intraoperative and postoperative management of a patient encompasses many variables.

General considerations include age, weight loss, obesity, deformities, laboratory studies, and blood volume.[3] Simple bedside tests of pulmonary and cardiac function are helpful in identifying patient risk.[4] Cases have been brought alleging that the physician was negligent in administering a particular anesthetic in the face of a claimed contraindication in the patient's history. A 1978 Louisiana case alleged negligence on the part of the physician for his failure to perceive from the patient's medical history that a problem could occur because of known prior reaction of the patient to sulfa drugs. An inadequate assessment of the patient's history may indeed result in liability; however, in this particular case no liability was found because the patient failed to support his allegation with the requisite expert testimony.[5] (See § 1.32, Standard of Care.)

A second purpose of the preoperative evaluation is the determination of surgical requirements. It is important, for example, to know in what position the patient will be placed during surgery; and if more than one position is suitable, it may be necessary to contact the surgeon to determine the surgeon's individual preference. Certain types of surgery may require specialized techniques for airway management, such as nasal tubes or double lumen endotracheal tubes. Neuromuscular blocking agents may be indicated or contraindicated depending on individual surgical requirements. Surgical considerations may also indicate the desirability for special techniques such as hypotensive anesthesia. Finally, in some types of surgical procedures, such as the Harrington-rod procedure, it may be desirable to employ a wake-up technique intraoperatively. In any case, if there is any doubt about the specialized requirements for an individual surgical procedure, the surgeon should be contacted preoperatively so that arrangements can be made in advance to accommodate any special needs.

Yet another purpose of the preoperative visit is to have the opportunity to obtain support or consultation from other services and to coordinate the overall management of the patient. For example, if a patient is found to have a bifascicular heart block, it may be desirable to contact cardiology ahead of time to insure the availability of someone skilled in the insertion of temporary pacemakers. If a patient is likely to require intensive care unit monitoring in the immediate postoperative period, it may be well to coordinate activities with an individual unit. For those patients in renal failure, the intraoperative management of fluid balance may depend heavily on dialysis support in the postoperative period. Obviously, there is a great variability from hospital to hospital and in the degree to which other medical specialists or specialized facilities are available, and it is difficult to make general rules. Nonetheless, it is much more desirable to arrange for the availability of specialized supporting services ahead of time when possible, rather than attempt such arrangements while dealing with an emergent situation.

Perhaps the most important part of the preoperative visit for the patient, and the area closest to the interface of law and medicine, is patient education and the explanation of events and procedures which are planned. This more than anything else helps to allay the patient's anxiety and to establish a favorable physician-patient relationship. The anxiolytic effect of good patient preparation and formation of a favorable doctor-patient relationship is well known among anesthesiologists, and it has become an axiom of anesthesia practice that "an informed patient is a tranquil patient."

Having reviewed the records, performed the history and physical examination, and considered the requirements for surgery, the anesthesiologist should have a good idea about which options are open for the anesthetic management of the individual patient. The expectations of the patient should be determined, and, whenever possible, the wishes of the patient should be given precedence. For example, it may be wiser to administer a general anesthetic than it is to try and talk a patient into having a spinal, assuming of course there are not contraindications to general anesthesia. On the other hand, when a regional anesthetic technique is clearly indicated, a patient explanation of why this technique is more desirable than a general anesthetic will often serve to allay the patient's anxieties and will elicit the patient's cooperation with the planned regional anesthetic.

Some explanation of the risks of the proposed anesthetic technique is mandatory to obtain informed consent from the patient. (See § 1.33, Consent and Informed Consent.) There is, however, considerable disagreement among anesthesiologists regarding which individual risks of a procedure should be mentioned and in what detail. Complications that occur rarely do not need to be discussed in great detail, but if there is reason to suspect that a complication will occur with a patient, the patient should be informed of this risk. The disclosure of risks required will vary with the knowledge of the individual as well as the effect the disclosure may have upon him, and what is reasonable disclosure will depend upon the facts and circumstances of each case. In another Louisiana case, decided in 1966, the attorney for the patient argued that the failure to allay a patient's fear and anxiety prior to an operation constituted negligence. However, this argument failed. The court recognized that it is impossible to identify a standard of care that delineates a procedure which can be followed to calm a patient, even though it is recognized that fear of the effect of an anesthetic or of undergoing an operation is medically undesirable. Furthermore, in this case since no relationship could be shown between the patient's fear and anxiety and the ultimate injury the patient suffered, the court would not impose liability.[6]

Certainly, where the proposed surgery is elective, the anesthesiologist should consider providing as much information as possible to the patient. In a 1975 Vermont case, a patient undergoing surgery to reduce the size of her breasts was not informed of the risks associated with halothane, which was used as the anesthetic. After surgery, the patient suffered from hepatitis. The court noted that where surgery is elective, as in this case, the right of informed choice is of relatively more significance. Failure to furnish such information is negligence and will result in the imposition of liability for harm resulting from the undisclosed risk.[7]

All pertinent variables in the preoperative visit should be included in the preoperative note. (See also § 9.20, Records.) This note, along with the date and hour of the visit, should be recorded in the progress note section of the patient's chart. Although the contents of the note may vary, guidelines have been established by the American Society of Anesthesiologists House of Delegates:[8]

Basic Standard of Care—Preoperative Note

1. System review
2. Review of objective data (lab, EKG, x-ray, etc.)
3. History of
   a. previous anesthetics
   b. family history regarding anesthesia
   c. allergies
   d. medications
   e. last fluid or food intake
4. Determination of physical status. (The documentation of the pre-operative evaluation should be consistent with the physical status designation.)
5. Plan of anesthesia for the proposed operation

Should questions regarding anesthetic management arise later, a clear, concise preoperative note which shows the reasoning behind the choice of a particular agent or technique can be invaluable. Furthermore, any decisions made regarding the choice of an anesthetic should be carefully and painstakingly implemented. Where the choice is proper from a medical standpoint, unless it is actually acted upon, the physician, from a legal standpoint, has breached his duty to the patient.

CASE ILLUSTRATION

The patient entered the hospital for a cholecystectomy. The operating surgeon visited the patient on the day prior to surgery and advised her that she would be given a general anesthesia. He further told her that tests taken at the hospital showed her physical condition as generally normal, but because her history included an episode of hepatitis suffered during childhood, there were "anesthetics that we probably would not be using." The surgery was performed under Penthrane (methoxyflurane) subsequent to which the patient developed a liver dysfunction which resulted in her death twelve days later. The patient's husband sued the operating surgeon, the assisting surgeon, the nurse-anesthetist, and the hospital. At trial, the operating surgeon testified that he decided to avoid using halogenated anesthetics, specifically Penthrane, and he informed the nurse-anesthetist of this decision. The nurse-anesthetist testified that although she was obligated to follow a physician's direct orders relating to an anesthetic agent, the decision not to use Penthrane had *not* been communicated to her. The appellate court held that the physician must communicate his decision to those administering medical treatment and will be held liable for failing to do so. Because of the conflicting testimony with regard to the communication and other procedural errors, the court ordered that the case be retried in light of this holding. (*Carlsen v. Javurek*, 1975)[9]

One method of circumventing this problem of communication is the inclusion of a preoperative assessment section on the anesthetic record to be used during surgery. This is especially important when the anesthesiologist performing the preoperative assessment will not be providing the direct care to the patient. Nevertheless, the court decision cited above makes it incumbent upon the evaluating physician to communicate any special considerations or decisions to the person providing the direct anesthetic care. Whether or not a notation on the anesthetic record will satisfy the requirement for "communication" is uncertain. Thus, although the requirement to communicate such decisions is clear, the method of communication is not.

§ 8.20 PREOPERATIVE MEDICATIONS

While anesthesia malpractice cases rarely revolve solely around preoperative medications, these medications may indicate a pattern of inappropriate administration of drugs or an undesirable interaction with other agents, which causes the patient to suffer an injury such as respiratory depression and cardiac arrest.

Although many good reasons for medicating patients preoperatively exist, some medications are occasionally contraindicated. These decisions most often will depend upon the experience, training, and preferences of the individual anesthesiologist.

Some beneficial effects from preoperative medication include sedation, anxiolytic effect, an amnesia effect, an antisialagogue action, blockade of adverse sympathetic and vagal reflexes, a decrease in anesthetic requirements, and an antistress action.

The anesthesiologist should decide if any of the patient's long-term medications should be continued or discontinued prior to surgery. A general principle is that medical disorders should be brought under control prior to anesthesia and that each organ system be maintained in optimal condition. Most medications for the control of a medical condition should be continued as usual to the time of surgery. For example, patients on chronic antihypertensive medication require their usual morning doses of antihypertensive drugs. Some plan should also be devised and agreed upon for the insulin-dependent diabetic about to undergo major surgery.

Preanesthetic orders must be legible. Doses must be carefully written. A scribbled order or a carelessly placed decimal point can lead to errors and overdoses.

The use of preoperative sedatives is not totally benign. There is always a risk of respiratory depression or obtundation leading to obstruction of the airway, or hypotension. If the medications given are long-acting, their effects may persist not only throughout the surgical period, but may also influence mental status or respiration well into the recovery phase.

Regardless of the particular agents employed, it must be remembered that the time interval between the giving of the preoperative medications and the patient's arrival in the operating room is a relatively unsupervised period in most hospitals and is the period least under the control of the anesthesiologist. If there is doubt about administering preoperative sedatives or narcotics, prudent practice would require the availability in the operating room of a rapidly acting sedative or narcotic in order to sedate the patient on arrival. If the anesthesiologist adopts this approach, it should be explained to the patient so that the patient will not be unduly alarmed at the prospect of arriving in the operating room relatively awake.

In the usual case, prior to the administration of general anesthesia, most conscious patients will be given preoperative medication. Several agents (usually three) are given:

1. A sedative for mental relaxation and for the control of acute apprehension (situational anxiety) or a major or minor tranquilizer for the control of chronic anxiety (trait anxiety).

2. A narcotic to produce some decrease in metabolic rate; to provide a generalized central nervous system decrease in alertness; to decrease anesthetic requirements (decreased MAC); to provide antistress action (block hypothalamus); and to provide an analgesic effect for the pain attendant to preliminary preparations in the administration of anesthesia (venipuncture and/or arterial puncture). Lastly,

§ 8.20 *Preoperative Medications* 239

preanesthetic narcotics contribute to a smooth and minimally painful recovery time.

3. An anticholinergic agent (to decrease adverse cardiovascular vagal reflexes, to decrease to G.I. tone and secretions, to reduce bronchial and salivary secretions and to generally reduce the risk of aspiration).[10]

The purposes of the above combinations of medications are manifold. The agents individually or in combination, may produce an attitude of acquiescence, euphoria, reduction in apprehension, decrease in metabolic rate and oxygen demand, anti-emetic effect, decrease in the overall need for high concentrations of anesthetics, and finally decrease in stress reactions through the autonomic nervous system and a minimization of the release of catecholamines and depletion of cortical steroids.[11]

The most frequent argument for premedication is that it makes the operating room experience more pleasant for the patient and makes the anesthesiologist's job technically a bit easier.[12]

Several significant drug interactions can occur with these medications. Phenothiazines (the major tranquilizers) may potentiate the effects of barbiturates, narcotics and possibly some general anesthetic agents.[13] Failure to reduce the dosages of these agents accordingly may result in undesirable side effects and potential legal liability.

While the use of preoperative medications rarely results in legal liability or litigation, mishaps can occur. If the medication is administered negligently and the patient suffers an injury, the physician may be held liable.

CASE ILLUSTRATION

The physician inadvertently injected Sparine into the patient's artery. The drug company insert warned about the dangers of arterial injection. The patient lost part of the left thumb and left index finger as well as suffering a decrease in the use of his left hand and arm. The patient sued the physician. At trial, the physician argued in his defense that the drug could be properly injected into the vein and still leak into the artery and that a physician could inject into the artery even while exercising the best precautions and the best medical practice. The court rejected these arguments, finding that the physician had failed to follow the generally accepted standards for preventing an inadvertent arterial injection. After inserting the needle, the physician-defendant failed to make adequate observations to determine whether the needle had accidentally introduced into an artery. The court held in favor of the patient. (*Schrib v. Seidenberg*, 1969)[14]

Some preoperative medications may indirectly contribute to cardio-respiratory complications. Many of these agents are sedatives and central nervous system (CNS) depressants which may contribute to respiratory depression, a problem more likely to occur when the patient has also been given barbiturates or muscle relaxants. If a patient did suffer a cardiac arrest, the patient's attorney may suggest that the preoperative medications in combination with other drugs contributed to respiratory depression and hypoxia, leading to the patient's cardiac arrest. Such cases may not be identified specifically as complications of preoperative medications. Direct proof of the role of preoperative medications in contributing to the injury will rarely be possible, but the patient's attorney may suggest an inference that they were involved. Errors in dosage and inappropriately high dosages may be presented as evidence of a general pattern of negligence.[15] Patients have generally been unsuccessful in such cases.

NOTES

1. American Society of Anesthesiologists [hereinafter cited as ASA], *Fundamental Considerations for All Anesthesia*, in American Society of Anesthesiologists Directory of Members III, 426 (46th ed. 1981).
2. ASA, *Guidelines for Patient Care in Anesthesiology*, in American Society of Anesthesiologists Directory of Members IV A 1 (a), 427 (46th ed. 1981).
3. V. Collins, Principles of Anesthesiology 176-78 (2d ed. 1976).
4. *Id.* at 178-80.
5. Brown v. Allen Sanitarium, 364, So.2d 661 (La. App. 1978).
6. Prack v. United States Fidelity & Sur. Co., 187 So.2d 170 (La. App. 1966).
7. Small v. Gifford Memorial Hosp., 133 Vt. 552, 349 A.2d 703 (1975).
8. ASA, *Suggestions for a Record of Anesthesia Care to Facilitate Medical Audit*, in American Society of Anesthesiologists Directory of Members 431 (46th ed. 1981).
9. Carlsen v. Javurek, 526 F.2d 202 (8th Cir. 1975).
10. Lasagna, *Drug Therapy: Hypnotic Drugs*, 287 New England J. Med. 1182 (1972).
11. V. Collins, *supra* note 3, at 214.
12. Ominsky, *Premedication in the Anxious Patient*, in ASA Annual Refresher Course Lectures 228 (1980).
13. V. Collins, *supra* note 3, at 204.
14. Schrib v. Seidenberg, 80 N.M. 573, 458 P.2d 825 (1969).
15. Chapman v. Argonaut-Southwest Ins. Co., 290 So.2d 779 (La. App. 1974).

Chapter IX

Monitoring and Records

§ 9.10 MONITORING

> *Liability may be imposed on the anesthesiologist where the patient suffers an injury due to the failure of the anesthesiologist to properly and adequately monitor the patient's vital signs or the anesthesiologist's failure to utilize physical signs in addition to those supplied by monitoring equipment in the event that such equipment malfunctions or provides inaccurate information.*

Monitoring a patient in the operating room is a basic function of the anesthesiologist. The law recognizes this function as an essential aspect of the anesthesiologist's legal duty and more than one court has held that the standard of care applicable to anesthesiologists includes constant monitoring of the patient's vital signs by the anesthesiologist or a qualified nurse-anesthetist.[1]

The problem of monitoring a patient in the operating room must be approached on several levels of complexity. On the simplest level, the anesthesiologist must have some method of determining the depth of anesthesia and the overall physiological status of the patient. The depth of anesthesia may be determined by clinical signs, pharmacologic analysis, and/or electroencephalography. Overall physiological status must include evaluation of pulse (cardiac performance), blood pressure (circulatory status), and respiration (spontaneous or assisted ventilation and oxygenation). The situation becomes considerably more complex, however, when one considers the diversity of anesthetic techniques available and the fact that the physiological status of any individual patient depends on pre-existing disease as well as on the particular type of surgery to be performed. Monitoring that may be appropriate for a healthy patient undergoing an elective dilatation and curettage might be grossly inappropriate or inadequate for a patient with multiple medical problems who is undergoing coronary artery bypass.

Since some monitoring techniques are invasive, there may be added risks associated with their use. The question must then include some analysis of possible benefit versus potential risk. When invasive monitoring is planned, it is probably prudent to inform the patient during the preoperative visit of potential risks from these monitoring techniques and to make some mention in the chart that these risks were explained. Equipment used in anesthesia may require careful attention. In a New York case decided in 1973 the use of hypothermia was required for a particular surgical procedure. The anesthesiologist used an Aquamatic K-Thermia machine and blanket for this purpose. The blanket lowered the patient's temperature appropriately but apparently failed to raise her body temperature at the proper time. The patient suffered frostbite; her feet, thighs and buttocks became necrotic, necessitating the excision of parts of her legs and buttocks and amputation of her feet. In this case, the patient's injury was caused by defective equipment and the manufacturer of the equipment was held liable along with the anesthesiologist and other hospital personnel. (See § 2.50, Products Liability.) However, the injury suffered was also attributed to the anesthesiologist's failure to monitor and supervise the patient properly: the records indicated that the patient's body temperature had failed to rise when expected and no responsive action had been taken by the anesthesiologist.[2] Perhaps the lesson of this case is that even though the anesthesiologist must often rely on mechanical equipment to accomplish the monitoring function, the duty owed to the patient is not met by mere reliance alone. Monitoring involves going beyond the signals and feedback such equipment provides. The anesthesiologist may often find it necessary to rely on his or her own medical expertise and familiarity with the physical signs and symptoms which the human body may provide. In the New York case, the fact that the patient's skin was mottled and discolored at her extremities was apparently noted in the record but not investigated further.

While it may be difficult to establish an upper limit to the scope of monitoring, there are certain minimum functions which should be monitored regardless of the individual patient or the type of surgery. These include the patient's circulation and ventilation and the adequacy of such functions during the course of surgery.

The assessment of the adequacy of circulation usually entails many more observations by the anesthesiologist than are actually recorded. What is most frequently recorded is a measure of blood pressure and heart rate. In addition to recording a blood pressure and heart rate, however, most anesthesiologists will make a continuous assessment of many other parameters, including the character and quality of the pulse, quality of heart sounds auscultated through either a precordial or esophageal stethoscope, capillary refill times, bleeding in the surgical field, and skin temperature. This aspect of monitoring is so intrinsic to the duty owed to a patient that in a 1976 Pennsylvania case the failure of the nurse-anesthetist to monitor her patient's heartbeat was stipulated by the parties to constitute negligence.[3] In addition to recording the heart rate, most anesthesiologists also continuously observe the regularity of the heartbeat and the quality of heart sounds through the stethoscope and make an assessment of the overall rhythm of the heart. A 1980 Texas decision upheld a judgment against an anesthesiologist who had failed to keep his finger on the patient's carotid artery during surgery. According to the expert testimony offered, if he had so placed his finger,

§ 9.10 *Monitoring* 243

the cardiac arrest the patient suffered would have been diagnosed the second it occurred and corrective measures could have been taken to renew the cardiac function, perhaps preventing the brain damage and death ultimately suffered by the patient.[4] Since electrocardiographic monitors are widely available, an electrocardiographic diagnosis of the rhythm of the heart is often included in the running record. Since 1970, operating room electrocardiography has become routine for all patients.

Similarly, in assessing the adequacy of ventilation, many more clinical parameters are usually monitored than are recorded. For example, many anesthesiologists will monitor several different parameters of lung inflation such as quality of breath sounds and symmetry and bidirectionality of chest wall movement. If the patient is being ventilated by hand, the "feel of the bag" is a vital and continuous monitor of the adequacy of ventilation.

Adequacy of oxygenation can also be determined by several clinical methods. Skin color and the color of arterial bleeding in the surgical field may be used to assess adequate oxygenation. If blood or skin color take on a darkish cast, hypoxia is indicated. To record all of these observations on a continuing basis would be time consuming and laborious and would divert the attention of the anesthesiologist from his patient. However, the recording of observations at least every five minutes does maintain the attention of the anesthesiologist, provide a graphic view of the physiologic trends, and verify the monitoring care. If a problem based on these clinical observations is suspected during anesthesia and surgery, it should be noted on the record, and the steps taken to confirm or deny the presence of the problem should be documented.

CASE ILLUSTRATION

The patient underwent surgery on his left eye to correct a muscle disorder which allowed his eye to wander and turn out. During surgery, the patient was oxygenated by means of a tube connected to his nose. At one point the patient's head moved slightly after which the anesthesiologist instructed the surgeon to proceed. After the surgery, the anesthesiologist told the operating room technician that something had happened to the patient but that he did not know what it had been. The patient awoke from surgery paralyzed on his right side and suffered a spastic right-sided paralysis of 50 percent in the right shoulder, a loss of fine finger movement in his right hand, an inability to heel gait on the right side, a right circumductive walk and numbness. The patient sued the anesthesiologist for negligence in failing to watch and record the patient's breathing during the administration of anesthesia or in allowing a respiratory depression to occur. At trial, expert testimony was proffered that the patient's injuries were due to hypoxia occurring during surgery. The anesthesiologist's failure to chart the patient's respiration during surgery was apparent in the medical record and the expert stated that this suggested that the anesthesiologist may have been casual in his observation of the breathing. The expert further stated that had the anesthesiologist placed his hand on the patient's chest to monitor respiration, the parties would not be in court. Because the medical record did not contain a charting of the patient's respiration, the anesthesiologist introduced evidence of his customary practice and method of monitoring patient respiration generally. The trial court jury exonerated the anesthesiologist from liability but the patient appealed. The Court of Appeals granted a new trial[*] to the patient, rejecting the evidence of the anesthesiologist's customary practice with regard to monitoring in light of the availability of the preferred eyewitness testimony of the surgeon and assisting personnel and the evidence presented by the medical record. *(Vuletich v. Bolgla,* 1980)[5]

This case decision fails to resolve the issue of liability. Presumably the new trial will accomplish that. However, the decision does emphasize the necessity for proper record keeping (see § 9.20, Records) in conjunction with the monitoring of respiration and the type of injuries that may result and may generate lawsuits if monitoring is inadequate. As other cases involving monitoring indicate, the anesthesiologist should evaluate respiration by keeping a hand on the patient's chest or watching the movement of draping or tubing in addition to reading the electrocardiogram and other monitoring apparatus.

Monitoring techniques used intraoperatively may also be of use postoperatively. This is especially important when there is a question of neuromuscular blockade. Because the anesthesiologist is an expert in the use of neuromuscular blocking agents, he or she should be familiar with the use of blockade monitoring devices and the patterns of patient response under varying conditions of depolarizing and nondepolarizing blocks. This type of monitoring could provide invaluable diagnostic information in the recovery room and into the post-operative period. (See § 10.50, Muscle Relaxants.)

In summary, monitoring the patient under anesthesia is a very complex subject. In determining what is appropriate, one must consider the pre-existing condition of the patient, the medical problems of the patient, the type of surgery being performed, the anesthetic technique being utilized, and the potential risks of the monitoring itself.

---

[*] This case was settled before the new trial.

§ 9.20 RECORDS

Where the medical record is admissible in evidence, inadequate or erroneous records may lead to liability if the inadequacy or the error relates to the cause of the patient's injury or the adequacy of the physician's care.

Basic Standard of Care: With respect to the patient's record, the American Society of Anesthesiologists (ASA) makes the following recommendations to facilitate the medical audit of anesthesia for peer review purposes:[6]

The patient's record should contain the following information:

1. Evidence of preanesthetic evaluation and physical status determination by a physician
2. The patient's anesthesia record should include
   a. The dosage of all drugs and agents employed
   b. The type and amount of all fluids administered, including blood and blood products
   c. Evidence of monitoring of the patient
   d. Description of technique or techniques employed
   e. Status of patient at conclusion of surgery
3. Evidence of postanesthesia surveillance
4. Evidence of postanesthetic evaluation by a physician

Interpretation and Customary Practice: Records should reflect the three phases of anesthesia management: preanesthesia, anesthesia and postanesthesia. ASA standards governing the preanesthetic record are provided elsewhere. (See § 8.10, Preanesthesia Visit and Evaluation.) Additionally, the Joint Commission on the Accreditation of Hospitals has promulgated the following standards governing the preanesthesia record to be kept with respect to hospital anesthesia services.[7]

> The preanesthesia evaluation of the patient by a physician [includes] appropriate *documentation in the patient's medical record* of pertinent information relative to the choice of anesthesia and the surgical or obstetrical procedure anticipated. Except in extreme emergency cases, this evaluation should be *recorded prior to the patient's transfer to the anesthesia* and operating area and before preoperative medication has been administered. While the choice of a specific anesthetic agent or technique may be left up to the individual administering the anesthesia, *the preanesthesia medical record entry* should at least refer to the use of a general, spinal, or other regional anesthesia. When other than anesthesia personnel are involved, reference in the medical record to the use of spinal, regional, topical, or local anesthesia should be made by the responsible physician (e.g., surgeon, obstetrician) or dentist when

administered within the limits of his privileges. The preanesthesia record entry should include the patient's previous drug history, other anesthetic experiences, and any potential anesthetic problems.

The preanesthetic note reflects the overall evaluation of the patient and should be written in the "Progress Section" of the hospital's record, usually the day before the operation. It should also be on the checklist of the anesthesia record before the operation commences.

This note should include important statistical data (see Table 9.1; § 8.10, Records). For example, if omitted, the patient's height and weight may cause problems if complications occur because of the relevance of these parameters vis-à-vis the site of injection of a spinal anesthetic, position of the patient, and dosage of the anesthetic agent.

One preoperative notation that is too often overlooked, or not considered sufficiently, is the classification of each patient, first for physical condition and fitness, and second, for the overall anesthetic surgical risk. Classification of physical status was originally devised in 1941 by Dr. Meyer Saklad[8] and was later officially adopted by the American Society of Anesthesiologists. In 1963, this classification of physical status was amended and the present divisions have been approved by the American Society of Anesthesiologists (see Table 9.2).

TABLE 9.1   Preanesthetic Note Form

ANESTHESIA NOTE:

DATE: (Hour)
HABITUS: WGT.(kg)   TEETH
HABITS:
DRUG THERAPY:
OPERATIONS:
ANESTHESIA HISTORY:
ALLERGIES:
C.N.S.:
C.V. SYSTEM: P.R.   B.P.
RESP. SYSTEM: R.R.   MECHANICS   BREATH HOLDING
HEPATO-RENAL:
OTHER SYSTEM REVIEW:
LABORATORY
REMARKS:
CONCLUSIONS:
  1. PHYSICAL STATUS:
  2. ANESTHESIA CHOICE:
  3. OPERATING RISK: EXCELLENT: GOOD: FAIR: POOR:

TABLE 9.2 Division of Physical Status, ASA Saklad Committee, 1941; ASA House of Delegates, 1963

GRADE 1: (PS 1)	A normal healthy patient No disease other than surgical pathology No systemic disturbance
GRADE 2: (PS 2)	A patient with mild systemic disease A general medical disease

GRADE 3:
(PS 3)
	A patient with moderate systemic disturbance:
	    due to medical disease
	    due to surgical disease
	Some limitation of activity
	Not incapacitating.

GRADE 4: (PS 4)	A patient with a severe systemic disturbance A constant threat to life Incapacitating disease
GRADE 5: (PS 5)	Moribund Not expected to survive 24 hours, with or without surgery.
EMERGENCY:	Precede PS grade with "E".

Source: American Society of Anesthesiologists, *New Classification of Physical Status,* 24 Anesthesiology III (1963).

The classification of the patient's physical status may be distinguished from an evaluation of the total operative risk involved. The physical status simply refers to the medical disorders existing in a given patient and the overall performance and function of the organ systems. It is concerned with the medical "state" of the patient and whether or not there are graded systemic disturbances. It reveals the presence or absence of disease, disease severity, and, to some extent, the reserve in function of the affected systems to withstand stress.

On the other hand, the estimation of operative risk involves other variables. These enter into the final determination of risk and include such factors as the type of surgery, the choice of anesthesia, and the operating room conditions. The personnel involved become important factors in determining the chance or risk that a patient accepts and undergoes for a given surgical procedure. It is, of course, recognized that morbidity and mortality rates correlate quite well with the grade of physical status of patients. The higher the grade of physical status, namely, Physical Status III and Physical Status IV, the higher the incidence of probable complications and the mortality rate.

Physical Status gradations also apply to emergency situations. A problem often encountered in this regard is a failure to designate the patient as Class E or lE, or to designate in some way that an emergency procedure is being performed from the point of view of anesthesia. If the operation is an emergency procedure, the patient should be classified as such by the anesthesia staff. To the lawyer reviewing the medical record, whether or not the case has been classified as an emergency anesthetic case can have significance regarding claims of informed consent to the particular anesthetic technique (see § 1.33, Consent and Informed Consent), the anesthesiologist's choice of anesthetic technique and agents (rapid sequence versus slower induction), and the availability of time for the administration of preoperative fluids and/or blood.[9]

Preoperative medications must also be charted accurately. (See also § 8.20, Preoperative Medications.) Dosage, time and route of administration, and effects should be included. The lawyer viewing the chart will look carefully at the dosage and route of administration of the pre-medications because he or she will know, through consultation with experts, the onset, peak time, and duration of these medications. An evaluation will be made as to what effects, if any, the pre-medications were having when the untoward incident occurred during the operation, and whether the effects of the pre-medications were unfavorably interacting with, or potentiated by, the intraoperative agents. The attorney will know this information about pre-medication was needed in order to make sound medical judgments about the dosage and time of administration of intraoperative agents.

Records are kept during anesthesia:

1. To facilitate the care of the patient:
    a. by insuring frequent attention to patient's condition;
    b. by providing information regarding the patient's general condition;
    c. by establishing the sequence of events leading to reactions or complications
2. To provide material for teaching, for study, and for statistical information
3. To establish a medical-legal record[10]

According to suggestions approved in 1977 by the ASA House of Delegates[11] the intraoperative record of anesthesia care should include the following to facilitate a medical audit:

1. The dosage of all drugs and agents employed
2. The type and amount of all fluids administered, including blood and blood products
3. Evidence of monitoring of the patient
4. Description of technique or techniques employed
5. Status of patient at conclusion of surgery

The anesthesia record must represent the actual progress and course of the anesthetic management. To this end, most anesthesiologists currently employ some form of graphic presentation of the parameters monitored and the pertinent events. Usually time is recorded on the horizontal axis in five minute blocks and information such as blood pressure, heart rate, and temperature is recorded on the

§ 9.20 Records 249

vertical axis. Additional space is usually provided for written notes which can be referenced to the time axis. Those parameters which are monitored should be documented on the record. (See § 9.10, Monitoring.) Furthermore, those parameters should be documented on the record as they occur.

A particular problem in documentation occurs when an emergency situation arises, such as cardiac arrest. (See § 12.70, Cardiac Arrest.) During such times, the anesthesiologist is often too busy attending to the patient to record events, drugs, and vital signs as they are occurring. It is probably prudent to instruct whatever operating room personnel are available and not immediately involved in the situation to start and maintain a continuous running record of all observations, vital signs, drugs administered, and other pertinent data. From these accurate and detailed notes, the anesthetic record can be filled out after the resolution of the crisis. If there is disagreement regarding the order of events or the patient's condition, such disagreement should be noted. If additions or changes are made or the record is otherwise completed in other than a routine manner, a plausible explanation for the anomalous nature of the record should be included. In the absence of such, a court may construe such an event to the disadvantage of the anesthesiologist.

CASE ILLUSTRATION

The patient underwent surgery for a gallbladder condition. Towards the completion of the two-and-one-half-hour operation, the anesthesiologist advised the surgeon that he did not feel a pulse. Emergency procedures were undertaken whereby the anesthesiologist administered pure oxygen and drugs to stimulate the heart and restore normal blood pressure. The surgeon massaged the heart internally through the diaphragm and another physician massaged the heart externally. The patient's heart responded almost immediately and quickly resumed a normal beat. It was estimated that the time lapse that occurred before resumption of normal heart beating was somewhere between one-and-a-half and five minutes. As a result of deprivation of oxygen to the brain, the patient suffered permanent brain damage leaving her partially blind, spastic and unable to care for herself.

Ten months after surgery the anesthesiologist was notified that the patient's lawyer wished to examine the hospital records of the operation. The anesthesiologist went to the hospital record room, obtained the records and began making additions to the chart he kept during the operation, until advised by a record room clerk that this was improper. The patient sued the anesthesiologist and the trial court entered judgment for the anesthesiologist. This was affirmed by the Court of Appeals. The patient appealed to the state Supreme Court. At the original trial, the anesthesiologist had testified that during the course of the operation he had checked the blood pressure at least every five minutes and the pulse at least every two minutes and at the same time had kept one hand on the bag to assist in breathing. He had testified further that as a part of his regular duties he kept a chart checking blood pressure and pulse as taken and there had been no signs that the patient was experiencing any difficulty until he failed to detect a pulse. The anesthesiologist asserted that he constantly monitored the anesthetic agents, that they were normal, and that the cardiac arrest was sudden and "just happened." An expert witness had testified that "instant cardiac arrest" is so rare as to be unreportable; he stated that signs of impending cardiac arrest are revealed by the dropping blood pressure and pulse and that these signs should be apparent to the anesthesiologist who would record them. The expert opined that the chart kept by the anesthesiologist was "too regular to be believable in that up to the point of the cardiac arrest it showed no change in blood pressure" and by the very nature of the procedures followed there would be changes. The trial court had ruled that the alterations to the medical record were immaterial to a determination of the cause and subsequent treatment of the cardiac arrest and refused to allow the patient's attorney to question the expert on the matter. The state Supreme Court held that in light of the expert testimony, the anesthesiologist's alterations *were* material to a determination of the actual cause of the cardiac arrest. Since the patient was entitled to have the jury consider the issue and attach whatever weight was appropriate to it, the Supreme Court ordered a new trial. (*Seaton v. Rosenberg*, 1978)[12]

The accuracy of the anesthetic record should never be in question. If an error is made in charting the vital signs, or in making a notation, it should be corrected immediately, usually with a single line drawn through the statement or by a simple initialed notation that an error was made. In 1966 an Alaska court[13] held that it is incumbent upon the physician to describe accurately and fully in the report of the operation everything of consequence which was done and which the physician's trained eye observed during the operation. To have maximum probative force in the event of a lawsuit, the report should be dictated immediately after the operation. If these requirements have been met, the report is more likely to refresh the physician's recollection and supply sufficient facts to permit expert witnesses to testify on the question of negligence. (See § 4.41, Expert Testimony.) The physician is the only person who can prepare a full and accurate report of what was observed and done during the operation. Furthermore, the Alaska court held that the physician is obligated to the patient to prepare such a report as part of the responsibility owed to the patient.[14]

Besides being accurate, the record should also be complete in that all pertinent facts must be recorded. What is pertinent may differ with the individual

§ 9.20 Records

anesthetic technique used. For example, if a regional technique is used, such as a spinal or epidural, then it is important to document which interspace was entered, whether or not the lumbar puncture was successful, how many attempts were made, what level of anesthesia was obtained, whether paresthesias occurred and whether there was a clear return of cerebrospinal fluid if lumbar puncture was done. (See § 11.10, Spinal Anesthesia.) The exact amount of the drug injected and the vehicle in which the drug was injected, as well as total volume, may all be pertinent facts. If complications occur, a note at the side of the graphic chart should include all of the observations which were monitored, especially if such observations were not continuously noted on the graphic chart. For example, many anesthesiologists continually look at the color of the blood in the surgical field, note the color of the skin and the quality of breath sounds and the appearance of the S-T segments and T waves of the electrocardiogram, but may not record all of this information continuously on the graphic chart. If a problem is encountered, these observations might be critical to the assessment of the problem or to the eventual outcome. They should, therefore, be noted somewhere on the anesthetic record. In addition, it is useful to note such things as any changes in anesthetic technique, anesthetic agents, or surgical events, since such information may be very important on later review.

Another routine but extremely important matter that should be accurately noted is the position of the patient during the operation, as well as any changes therein. If, for example, some circulatory difficulties are encountered during the operation, it may be significant for the anesthesia chart to reflect the position of the patient in order to understand and explain the causes thereof. If respiratory difficulties have been encountered, the evaluation of the case may, for example, be significantly affected by the knowledge that at the time of the untoward event the patient was in the extremely problematic prone-jackknife position.[15] (See § 12.50, Faulty Patient Positioning.)

Finally, a record of postanesthesia status and progress must be maintained. JCAH Standards respecting the postanesthetic record[16] are as follows:

> The recording of postanesthetic visits, including at least one note describing the presence or absence of anesthesia-related complications. A note made in the surgical or obstetrical suite, or in the postanesthesia care unit (or nursing floor anesthesia recovery phase when there is no such unit), does not ordinarily constitute a visit. While the number of visits will be determined by the status of the patient in relation to the procedure performed and anesthesia administered, a visit should be made early in the postoperative period and once after complete recovery from anesthesia. Complete recovery is determined by the clinical judgment of the anesthetist or the discharging surgeon/obstetrician. Each postanesthesia note shall specify the date and time. It is recommended that a postanesthesia medical record entry be made by a physician. However, all anesthesia personnel are encouraged to make pertinent postanesthesia entries in the medical record of patients to whom they have admin-

istered anesthesia. When the postanesthetic visit and record entry by anesthesia personnel is not feasible because of early patient release from the hospital, the physician or dentist who discharges the patient from the hospital should be responsible for meeting the requirement.

As in other phases of anesthesia, pertinent variables of the patient's postanesthetic condition should be recorded. The fact that information is omitted from the patient's record will not serve to prevent the patient from proving in court that care was inadequate. Rather, a material omission from the patient's chart may serve to prove just the opposite, that if a record of monitoring in the recovery room is not kept, it was not done. Thus incomplete records will often affect a court's consideration of whether the anesthesiologist's conduct adhered to professional standards.[17]

CASE ILLUSTRATION

The patient underwent surgery to correct an obstruction in the tear sac on the right side of his eye. According to the hospital chart nothing unusual occurred during either the operation or the period of recovery. When released from the hospital, however, the patient experienced spatial disorientation, a reduction in his field of vision and a loss of memory. Several different neurologists examined the patient and determined that he had suffered permanent brain damage. The patient brought suit alleging that he was administered massive overdoses of narcotics by the nurse-anesthetist; that at the conclusion of the surgery inadequate amounts of reversal drugs were administered; that, as a result, unnoticed by recovery room personnel, his respiration was substantially depressed and in turn the amount of oxygen supplied to his brain was reduced, causing diffuse bilateral brain damage. The patient introduced expert testimony supporting these allegations. The patient's expert witnesses also testified that the failure to chart respiration on the recovery room sheet after such a massive dose of narcotics is not good medical practice; that it is "easy to just look at a patient, see them breathe, and . . . go about your business"; that a gradual decrease in the rate and volume of respiration might not be noticed without both observing and charting that information. The patient's recovery room record disclosed that his pulse and blood pressure had been recorded at 15-minute intervals. It was also noted on the chart that the patient was "doing well" and that there were "no apparent complications." The rate and depth of his breathing was not charted despite the fact that the chart provided a place for the charting of respirations. The defendants argued that the fact that the chart was devoid of a record of respiration did not offer evidence that respiration was not monitored. They pointed to hospital policy which was to count and observe respirations of patients in the recovery room without charting them unless something unusual occurred. The court concluded that a blank respiratory chart constituted sufficient evidence for the jury to believe that the recovery room personnel had failed to monitor the patient's respiration properly, and upheld a decision in favor of the patient. (*Wagner v. Kaiser Foundation Hospitals*, 1979)[18]

It has been stated that claims of medical malpractice can be won or lost on the basis of inaccurate or inadequate charts.[19] An important point is the fact that the jury may favor what has been documented at the time of the incident, as opposed to other types of evidence. One commentator has stated:

> A jury of laypersons will believe a black and white copy of a record over a person's memory for several reasons. First, they may feel that someone testifying as to events which occurred several years ago may not fully remember them. Second, the jury may believe that a record made when the event occurred might be more accurate than someone's recollection of the past. Therefore, it is clear that the medical record plays an extremely important role before and during a trial.[20]

The importance that the medical record may play in providing evidence of negligence, i.e., medical malpractice, cannot be overemphasized. The medical record itself may become the most important piece of evidence introduced at the trial.

NOTES

1. McAdams v. Holden, 349 So.2d 900 (La. App. 1977); Thomas v. Seaside Memorial Hosp., 80 Cal. App. 2d 841, 183 P.2d 288 (1947); Willinger v. Mercy Catholic Medical Center, 241 Pa. Super. Ct. 456, 362 A.2d 280 (1976).
2. Fogal v. Genesee Hosp., 41 A.D.2d 468, 344 N.Y.S.2d 552 (1973).
3. Willinger v. Mercy Catholic Medical Center, *supra* note 1.
4. Garza v. Berlanga, 598 S.W.2d 377 (Tex. Civ. App. 1980).
5. Vuletich v. Bolgla, 85 Ill. App. 3d 810, 407 N.E.2d 566 (1980).
6. ASA, *Guidelines for Peer Review in Anesthesiology,* in American Society of Anesthesiologists Directory of Members IA, 429 (46th ed. 1981).
7. Joint Commission on Accreditation of Hospitals, *Anesthesia Services Standard IV,* in Accreditation Manual for Hospitals 9 (1981) [hereinafter cited as JCAH].
8. Saklad, *Grading of Patients for Surgical Procedures*, 2 Anesthesiology 281 (1941).
9. Gore, *As a Lawyer Views Your Chart*, 44 Am. A. Nurse Anesthetists 48 (Feb. 1979).
10. V. Collins, *Principles of Anesthesiology* 31 (2d ed. 1978).
11. ASA, *Suggestions for a Record of Anesthesia Care to Facilitate Medical Audit*, in American Society of Anesthesiologists Directory of Members 431 (46th ed. 1981).
12. Seaton v. Rosenberg, 573 S.W.2d 333 (Ky. 1978).
13. Patrick v. Sedwick, 391 P.2d 453 (Alaska 1966).
14. *Id.*
15. Gore, *supra* note 9.

16. JCAH, *supra* note 7, at 10.
17. Herbert v. Travelers Indem. Co., 239 So.2d 367 (La. App. 1970).
18. Wagner v. Kaiser Foundation Hosp., 285 Or. 81, 589 P.2d 1106 (1979).
19. Yoder, *Legal Aspects of Anesthesia Charting,* Am. A. Nurse Anesthetists 48 (Feb. 1979).
20. *Id.*

§ 10.10   *Principles of General Anesthesia*   257

Stage II: cepted. Depression of the cortex ranges from slight to moderate.

Stage II: The degree of anesthesia may be referred to as "hypersensitivity" and is characterized by a loss of consciousness with uninhibited reaction. Stimulation of any kind during this stage could elicit an injurious response. Thus, the prophylactic use of restraints is routine. There is a slight depression of the subcortex which predominantly controls function.

Stage III: (This stage is subdivided into three planes.)

Plane I. Referred to as "Light Surgical," this plane is characterized by a range of responses from hypoactivity to response to painful stimulus. There is moderate depression of the subcortex. The eyes may oscillate during this plane and often become eccentrically fixed. In all planes, gross ocular movement is minimal or absent during halothane anesthesia. The tendency for rate and depth of respiration to increase in response to skin incision diminishes. Often, increased cutaneous blood flow and onset of peripheral venous dilation signal entry into this plane.

Plane II. Referred to as "Moderate Surgical," this plane is characterized by a loss of somatic response to pain. This plane lasts from the time the eyes cease to move and become fixed concentrically (except with cyclopropane) to the beginning of a decrease in intercostal muscle activity. The conjunctiva lose luster and respiratory response to skin incision disappears. Predominant control of functions is by the midbrain.

Plane III. Referred to as "Deep Surgical," this plane is characterized by a loss of visceral response to pain. Also, intercostal activity decreases until intercostal paralysis is reached in lower plane III. In mid-to-lower plane III, pupils cease to react to light. There is a moderate depression of the midbrain at this plane.

Stage IV: The degree of anesthesia may be referred to as "Impending Failure" and is characterized by a fall in pulse pressure and a cessation of respiration. At this stage there is a moderate depression of the pons.

Once the patient is unconscious (Stage II), the patient should then be carried rapidly to a state of surgical anesthesia (Stage III), when blockage of all special senses and most of the somatic cutaneous senses occurs. Hearing is the last of the special senses to be obtunded. Simultaneously, there is progressive blunting of visceral sensation, which then permits exploration of thoracic and abdominal cavities.

Insufficient recognition of the various stages of anesthesia could precipitate certain problems. With balanced anesthetic techniques, a patient may be unconscious and paralyzed, but not adequately anesthetized. As a result, the patient may retain an awareness of procedures and events in the operating room. Some patients have had sufficient recall of such events to cause psychiatric disturbances or even psychoneurotic episodes. The recorded incidence of such a reaction ranges between one and ten percent.[4]

§ 10.20 AIRWAYS AND VENTILATION

A general anesthetic state can be achieved and maintained as long as adequate ventilation occurs through an unobstructed airway in the presence of adequate cardiovascular function.

The anesthesiologist should have a knowledge of respiratory physiology and possess skill in performing both manual and mechanical ventilation. Although there are special and occasionally unique ventilatory techniques (Liverpool technique, diffusion oxygenation, etc.) employed in anesthetic practice, adequate ventilation is usually considered to include:

1. Provision of sufficient oxygen to meet the metabolic needs of the body
2. Removal of carbon dioxide
3. Preservation of acid-base balance

There are many factors which must be considered in determining which ventilatory pattern will be adequate for any given patient and surgical procedure, and this may change during the course of anesthetic management. The anesthesiologist must have sufficient knowledge of respiratory pathophysiology to determine ventilatory parameters such as tidal volume, respiratory rate, inspiratory/expiratory ratios, and ventilatory pressures which are appropriate for the needs of the patient. He or she must have the skill necessary to perform adequate manual ventilation and the ability to adjust mechanical ventilators to achieve the desired ventilatory parameters.

§ 10.21 *Airway Management without Intubation*

Three inhalation techniques are recognized.[5]

    1. *Spontaneous respiration under a mask with a clear airway provided by*

§ *10.22*   *Airway Management with Intubation*   259

proper positioning of the head. This is simple, but not always easily accomplished. It is not the best method for use in long procedures, anatomical distortions of the face or neck, when deep anesthesia is needed, when relaxants are used, or when assisted or controlled respiration is needed.

2. *Spontaneous respiration under a mask with a clear airway provided by a pharyngeal airway device.* This device may be associated with technical difficulties of oral or nasal type. The purpose is to retain the tongue forward of the pharynx (oral route) or by-pass the tongue (nasal route). In either procedure injury may occur if the device is improperly or forcefully used. Insertion through the mouth may be accompanied by the lips being pushed inward and over the teeth; the lips may be cut by the teeth. Unless carefully inserted, teeth may be injured and loose ones dislodged. Insertion of the oropharyngeal airway upside-down (other than in the small curvature of the tongue) may result in laceration of the hard or soft palate. Too large a device may push the epiglottis against the glottis or larynx and merely block the passageway.

Insertion of a nasopharyngeal airway requires both proper selection of type and route of insertion. First, the anesthetist should know which nasal passage is unobstructed. Second, the bevel of these airways should face the nasal septum medially. A bevel facing lateral may injure the turbinates and/or cause hemorrhage. (These conditions also apply to nasotracheal intubation.)

3. *The third technique of airway management is that of the endotracheal tube.*

§ *10.22 Airway Management with Endotracheal Intubation*

Endotracheal intubation results in legal liability most often for improper insertion into the esophagus rather than the trachea and for failing to respond properly to the emergency which results. Where injury to vocal cords occurs from intubation, the law generally does not hold the anesthesiologist liable unless his subsequent treatment of the injury is inadequate.

Interpretation and Customary Practice: Preservation and protection of the airway is of paramount importance in anesthesia. To this end, endotracheal intubation is frequently employed. Anesthesiologists are considered the hospital experts on endotracheal intubation and airway management. Consequently, the anesthesiologist may be called upon as a consultant to perform intubation outside as well as inside the operating room as part of the overall anesthetic management plan.

Although simple in concept, the actual practice of endotracheal intubation is relatively complex. For example, the choice of tube is based on clinical indications. First, the route of intubation must be considered. Three routes are common: oral, nasal, or transtracheal. In anesthesia practice, the first two are usual. Standards for oral and nasal tubes have been established.[6] The tube may be a relatively simple single lumen tube or a complex double lumen tube designed for endobronchial intubation or preservation of the airway when pulmonary surgery or a pneumonectomy is considered. These tubes may be rubber or plastic; they may be cuffed or uncuffed; and they may have either high pressure or low pressure balloon cuffs. There are other types of tubes available to be used in patients with tracheostomies. Depending on the individual application, any one or a number of these particular types of tubes may be employed.

In an uncomplicated situation, an endotracheal tube is employed to establish and preserve an airway and to help prevent the aspiration of secretions. Since the trachea is not a rigid structure, it is possible to aspirate secretions around the cuff of an endotracheal tube; however, it is generally assumed that the cuff does help prevent or decrease the severity of aspiration. The balloon cuff can be inflated once the tube has been inserted past the vocal cords. This expansion of the diameter of the portion of the tube distal to the vocal cords wedges the tube against the walls of the trachea. The cuff aids in a leak-proof exchange of gases and minimizes the chance of dislodgement of the tube or aspiration of foreign material into the tracheobronchial tree.[7] A cuff should be inflated properly. An over-inflated cuff will injure the mucosa, inhibit ciliary action, and increase the incidence of pulmonary complications. The amount of air that is injected into the cuff should be just sufficient to prevent air leaks.

Vomiting is always a threat in patients undergoing anesthesia or an operation,[8] particularly if there is stimulation of the pharynx and elicitation of the gag reflex. The risk increases in emergency operations where the patient may have eaten shortly before the operation, but vomiting can occur in any patient. If the patient should vomit, the cuff should minimize the risk of aspiration of foreign material into the lungs that can interfere with the exchange of gases and cause damage to the lungs.[9] A cuff may also prevent aspiration of broken teeth.

Endotracheal tubes may be inserted either orally or nasally, depending on the surgical indications or individual circumstances. Intubation can be performed either with or without the aid of direct laryngoscopy. The patient may be fully awake or induced for anesthesia. No matter what type of tube is employed or how it is inserted, the proper position of the tube below the vocal cords and above the carina must be checked and determined to be correct.

There are several methods of ascertaining the appropriate position of an endotracheal tube. If laryngoscopy is employed, the anesthesiologist will usually see the tube pass between the vocal cords. Observation of the chest during ventilation will show the movement of the chest wall which will be bi-directed and symmetrical. Auscultation of the chest reveals breath sounds which will be heard approximately equally when listening to both the right and left lung fields. Furthermore, with the appropriate positioning of an endotracheal tube, there will be an absence of air in the stomach. Having ascertained that the tube is in fact in the correct position in the trachea, the tube should be secured. This is most often accomplished by taping to the maxillary face. Having ascertained that the tube is in the correct position and securely taped, some method must be employed for monitoring the position of the endotracheal tube so that if it becomes dislodged it will be immediately apparent. In addition, all connections external to the patient must be secured. An inadvertent disconnection of the patient from the ventilatory support can be fatal.

Several methods are available for monitoring adequacy of ventilation through an endotracheal tube. The continuous auscultation of breath sounds by a precordial or esophageal stethoscope is perhaps the most simple. Observations of the peak inspiratory pressure of the ventilator are also useful, as are the commercially available pressure- and time-sensitive alarms. Capnographs are becoming popular, as are percutaneous oxygen monitors.

Regardless of which methods of intubation or monitoring are employed, the adequacy of ventilation must be assured and the individual methods of determining this should be documented on the chart or the anesthetic record. Where inadequate ventilation has been shown to be the most likely cause of a patient's injury, a court will probably impose liability on the anesthesiologist. Insertion of the tube into the esophagus rather than the trachea is one manifestation of inadequate ventilation which may cause serious injury and thus lead to a lawsuit.

CASE ILLUSTRATION

A first-year anesthesiology resident and a student nurse-anesthetist inserted an endotracheal tube into an 18-year-old patient prior to a cesarean section. Fifty percent cyclopropane/oxygen was administered for two minutes, followed by ethylene and oxygen. About nine to ten minutes after the endotracheal tube had been inserted, the assistant obstetrician noted dark blood and informed the anesthesiology resident. No decrease in blood pressure, EKG or pulse changes, or difficulty in ventilation had been noted prior to that time. After switching the patient to 100 percent oxygen, the resident and nurse-anesthetist checked chest expansion and breath sounds which were all normal. They checked the placement of the endotracheal tube between the vocal cords with a laryngoscope, then suctioned the endotracheal tube. Cyanosis persisted, the uterus became flaccid, and the patient's pulse rate dropped rapidly. About eight or nine minutes later (roughly 18 minutes after insertion of the endotracheal tube), the anesthesiology resident noted that the bag was becoming "a little hard" to squeeze and removed the endotracheal tube. When attempts to reinsert the tube failed, he inserted a plastic airway and administered oxygen by mask. Cardiac arrest occurred about this time, but arterial blood became brighter. Heart action was restored, and the endotracheal tube was reinserted. Within a few minutes, the patient's blood became bright red and arterial blood gases showed an increase in oxygen concentration and a decrease in carbon dioxide over previous blood gas values. A large amount of gas was noticed in the bowels. The patient died eight days later. The patient's widower and child brought suit.

At trial, an expert for the defendants formed the opinion that an amniotic fluid embolism was more likely the cause of the injury than faulty intubation; the former could produce vasospasm through release of serotonin. Refuting the diagnosis of vasospasm were the absence of any EKG, blood pressure, or pulse changes. Bronchospasm was also unlikely because the difficulties in ventilation, according to the testimony of the anesthesiology resident, were noted long after cyanosis developed. Another expert for the defense believed that the cause of cyanosis and cardiac arrest could be amniotic fluid embolism, but the absence of tachycardia and massive bleeding made this diagnosis unlikely.

An expert called by the plaintiff testified that it was easy to misinterpret the rising of the stomach against the ribs as chest expansion. He doubted that a pulmonary embolus that could cause extensive arterial oxygen desaturation could return to normal within 20 minutes; furthermore, no residual lung problems were found during the patient's postoperative course in the hospital. Another expert testified for the plaintiff that pulmonary vasospasms, amniotic fluid embolism, air embolism, and thromboembolism were unlikely.

The court discounted the testimony of the resident and nurse-anesthetist, concluding that "no other diagnosis comes near fitting the pattern of events, and the diagnosis of improper intubation virtually fits the pattern exactly." The upper court affirmed a judgment against the hospital and held the resident-anesthesiologist and the student nurse-anesthetist individually liable. *(Aubert v. Charity Hospital of Louisiana, 1978)*[10]

When cyanosis and cardiac arrest do occur during an operation, a patient-plaintiff is likely to recover in court if he or she can present strong evidence pointing to the likelihood that the endotracheal tube was not in the trachea and that the physician's conduct subsequent to the discovery of this fact constituted a substandard response to an emergency situation.

§ 10.22   *Airway Management with Intubation*   263

CASE ILLUSTRATION

A plastic surgeon, anesthesiologist, a university medical center, and four of the defendants were sued after a patient became cyanotic and developed cardiac arrest, resulting in brain damage. The operation was for an "obstructed gland." The patient had received a muscle relaxant prior to endotracheal intubation. Three unsuccessful attempts to intubate were made, and the staff anesthesiologist left the tube in after the fourth attempt, approximately 20 minutes after induction had begun. About five minutes later, the plastic surgeon became concerned about the patient's condition and expressed his concern to the anesthesiologist. Cyanosis was then noticed. The chief of the anesthesiology department was nearby and was notified of the problem. His examination for breath sounds did not satisfy him; he found that the patient's blood pressure was dropping and her pulse was inadequate; and he noted that the anesthetic bag was resistant to squeezing. He was able to inflate the bag by pushing on the patient's stomach. However, he and the other physician who were present did nothing more until approximately five minutes later, when the patient had a cardiac arrest. At this point, the chief of anesthesiology removed the endotracheal tube, and when the surgeon began external cardiac massage, the patient's skin color and heartbeat returned to normal.

An expert testifying for the patient formed the opinion that the endotracheal tube had either been placed in the esophagus or else was "kinked." It was held that the chief of anesthesiology was individually liable for failing to make an immediate determination of whether the patient's airway was obstructed and for failing to remove the endotracheal tube within 15 seconds of his arrival. The chief of anesthesiology was also held vicariously liable for the negligence of the staff anesthesiologist, as was the surgeon. *(Schneider v. Albert Einstein Medical Center,* 1978)[11]

When surgery involves the head or neck area, the endotracheal tube and its immediate connections often must be covered in preparation for surgery. This factor, plus the fact that the anesthesiologist is often physically distanced from the patient, either at the patient's side or at the foot of the bed or table, makes the tubing difficult to monitor and observe. Consequently, it is necessary to use long breathing circuits such as a non-rebreathing circuit (Jackson-Rees, Mapleson-D, Bains) to assure ventilation. Problems with disconnection of the endotracheal tube from the breathing circuit employed are probably the most common cause of preventable anesthesia mishaps. As the number of connections which must be made and the distance of the anesthesiologist from the patient's airway is increased, the likelihood of inadvertent disconnection increases. This can have devastating consequences for the patient.

CASE ILLUSTRATION

The patient was undergoing surgery for a cataract in his left eye. The tubing connecting the patient's tube to the anesthetic machine was taped to the patient's chest and then covered with drapes for surgery. A nurse had difficulty adjusting the height of an instrument tray and the tray slipped, striking the patient's chest and drapings. The tubing connection was not examined when this happened. Anesthesia became inadequate, and the patient coughed, leading to the expulsive loss of his left eye. At this point, the anesthesiologist discovered that the connection between the tubes had become dislodged. The patient brought suit against the surgeon, the anesthesiologist and the hospital. At trial, the anesthesiologist testified that the disconnection of the tubing resulted in inadequate anesthetic depth which probably caused the patient to cough. However, there was no evidence of the cause of disconnection other than the possibilities that the instrument tray had touched the tubing, the tubing had been improperly connected, or that it was displaced during taping or draping.

The defendants testified that a cough could occur in the absence of negligence. They testified that it was possible for a patient to rise from an appropriate deep level of unconsciousness despite the exercise of due care. Testimony in this case, however, established that a disconnection had caused the loss of the patient's eye.

After the jury found only the anesthesiologist liable, the plaintiffs and the anesthesiologist appealed. The appellate court reversed and ordered a new trial* on the issue of liability of the hospital, the surgeon, and the anesthesiologist. *(Kitto v. Gilbert*, 1977)[12]

This case illustrates several important points. The inadvertent disconnection of the breathing circuit from the patient was not immediately discovered. It is fortunate for this patient that he was breathing spontaneously at the time, but nonetheless the irritation from the endotracheal tube and the light level of anesthesia caused the patient to cough with the resultant loss of his left eye. This points out

---

* A new trial was held and the jury found the anesthesiologist liable. The other defendants were found not liable.

the medical necessity of maintaining patients undergoing open eye surgery at a level of anesthesia deep enough to prevent the cough reflex. This should not be misconstrued, however, to mean that patients undergoing open eye surgery should be paralyzed to prevent coughing. It simply means that the level of anesthesia must be kept deep as long as the eye is open and irritation to the airway is present. Clearly, in cases such as this where long circuits and multiple connections are employed, the anesthesiologist must be especially alert to the problem and take extra care to assure that connections are tight and that disconnections will not occur. It is probably even more important to monitor respirations rigorously under circumstances such as this, since disconnections can occur even with adequate precautions.

Irritation from the endotracheal tube can lead to sore throats, laryngitis, and even to trauma to the vocal cords or laryngeal structures. The mere stimulation of the trachea can cause hypertension and tachycardia, which may be a considerable problem in patients with coronary artery disease. It is unlikely, however, that trauma from the presence of an endotracheal tube will cause significant problems during the short duration of intubation required for most surgical procedures.

There are also risks inherent in positioning and placing the endotracheal tube. If laryngoscopy is employed, there is a risk of chipped or damaged teeth from the laryngoscope. Laryngoscopy is also known to stimulate sympathetic reflexes and cause hypertension and tachycardia. In a patient with poor dentition or missing or absent teeth, the risk of dental damage should be explained to the patient beforehand. If nasal intubation is anticipated, there may well be problems with trauma to the nasal pharyngeal structures and epistaxis which should also be explained to the patient. Generally, reported case decisions recognize that damage to teeth may occur in the absence of negligence, and the anesthesiologist generally will escape liability for such an injury.

CASE ILLUSTRATION

A patient was hospitalized for an exploratory lumbar laminectomy. Before the operation a nurse gave him an injection and instructed him to tell the doctors in the operating room that he had three capped teeth.

When informed he was to receive spinal anesthesia, the patient insisted on being put to sleep. The anesthesiologist was unsuccessful in convincing him of the advantages of the spinal anesthesia and agreed to give him general anesthesia.

The patient later said that just before he went to sleep he told the anesthesiologist to watch his teeth because they had caps on them. When he awoke in the recovery room, he was given a jar containing pieces of tooth and informed by a hospital attendant that one of his teeth had been broken by accident. In fact two of his teeth were damaged, the upper left and right front incisors.

The patient brought suit. At the trial, the anesthesiologist testified that he had examined the patient's chart before the operation but had found no information about his capped teeth. He said he looked casually at the patient's front teeth but saw nothing to warrant a more detailed examination.

The damage occurred when the operation was over and the patient suddenly bit down hard on the plastic airway in his mouth, breaking one tooth into pieces and cracking another. The anesthesiologist testified that the first thing a patient would do on waking is to clamp down with his muscles. The patient had bitten the airway before anyone could stop him. The anesthesiologist testified that it was standard practice to leave the airway in a patient's mouth until he was awake, in order to keep his tongue away from the air passage. There is no way to anticipate when a patient will react and bite down on the airway; such a reaction can occur regardless of precautions.

Evidence of the standard of care offered by several experts indicated that there was no method that could have been used to safeguard the teeth. The court held in favor of the anesthesiologist. (*Hughes v. Hastings,* 1971)[13]

Where endotracheal intubation results in inflammation of the vocal cords and trachea, the physician is less likely to be held liable, because damage to the vocal cords can occur in the absence of negligence and may not be preventable.

CASE ILLUSTRATION

The patient sustained injury to her vocal cords after a hysterectomy. She was left with a weak and raspy voice after the operation, and the left vocal cord was thin and atrophic; it did not meet the other vocal cord in the midline on phonation. (The cords had been noted to be normal prior to intubation.) The patient sued the anesthesiologist and the surgeon who was a general practitioner and who performed the general surgery. At trial the general practitioner's motion for directed verdict was granted after the plaintiff's opening statement; there was a verdict for the anesthesiologist and a motion for new trial was denied. Experts for both sides agreed that this was a unique injury which few had seen before. One expert for the plaintiff testified that the few cases of vocal cord damage from intubation that he had seen had been bilateral, not unilateral, and that the unilateral nature of this injury suggested that it was not the result of negligence; another expert for the plaintiff thought the unilateral nature of the injury was insignificant.

A metal stylet had been used, but the defendant anesthesiologist denied that it had protruded beyond the tube during insertion. Expert witnesses for the plaintiff testified that improper intubation could injure the vocal cords and that the plaintiff's injury could have been caused by the introduction of the tube, but they also acknowledged that the injury might not have resulted from faulty intubation. In affirming the verdict for the anesthesiologist, the upper court held that plaintiff's evidence was insufficient to permit a determination of negligence, even if viewed in the best light possible. The plaintiff's expert had only established that the cause of the injury was uncertain. (*Rauschelbach v. Benincasa,* 1963)[14]

Plaintiffs generally have difficulty recovering for injuries to the vocal cords after intubation. Direct proof of negligence is difficult or impossible to produce, and it is difficult to draw inferences of negligence because injury to the vocal cords can occur in the absence of negligence.

CASE ILLUSTRATION

The patient sued her anesthesiologist alleging that he had inserted tubes that were too large for her and had used excessive force during intubation, causing her injury. She had developed two granulomas and an anterior adhesion or web that required surgical removal. The patient was left with a hoarse, raspy voice.

The anesthesiologist had at first inserted a number eight tube before trying a number seven, number six, and finally inserting a number five tube. There was no evidence as to which tube had caused the patient's injury; there was testimony for the defense that the smallest tube could have caused the damage. Experts called by the defendant testified that it was a preferred custom in the profession to insert larger tubes first, because they offered less resistance to the flow of air. Due to the absence of direct evidence of negligence, the court found the anesthesiologist not liable. *(Bell v. Umstattd,* 1966)[15]

Although a physician is unlikely to be held liable for the mere occurrence of vocal cord injury after intubation, he or she may expose himself or herself to liability by negligent acts or omissions in treatment of such an injury postoperatively.[16]

The cervical spine, in close proximity to the oropharynx, can be damaged during endotracheal intubation. In a victim with evidence of multiple trauma or head injuries, care must be taken to preserve the integrity of the cervical spine. If the patient is breathing adequately, there is usually time to obtain cross table spine x-rays to rule out fracture dislocations of the spine. This may not be possible, however, if ventilatory function is impaired. Under these circumstances the head should be immobilized in extension by an assistant and blind nasal intubation should be attempted unless there is evidence of facial fractures or cerebrospinal fluid rhinorhea. Tracheostomy under local anesthesia should be considered whenever there is doubt regarding the stability of the cervical spine.

§ 10.30 VOLATILE ANESTHETIC AGENTS

Volatile anesthetic agents commonly in use today include halothane, penthrane, enflurane and isoflurane. Of these, enflurane and isoflurane have not appeared in legal case reports of injuries arising out of the use of such anesthetic agents; however, the same principles that apply to the use of halothane and penthrane apply to these agents as well.

§ 10.31 Halothane

Liability may be imposed on an anesthesiologist when the patient suffers liver damage from the use of halothane and the anesthesiologist fails to adequately predetermine from the patient's history that the use of the anesthetic is contraindicated. Where the injury resulting from halothane is related to its arrhythmogenic effects liability will not be imposed unless it is conclusively proved that the injury is the result of faulty initial administration or subsequent treatment of the resulting complication.

Precautions Regarding the Use of Halothane: A number of recent studies[17] have identified factors which increase the risk of injury associated with halothane. These studies recommend that the anesthesiologist, considering halothane as an anesthetic, should:

1. Avoid multiple patient exposures to halothane
2. Allow an interval of at least three months between exposures
3. Not administer halothane if the patient has suffered a bout of hepatocellular jaundice, especially following a previous operation
4. Not administer halothane to patients with liver disease
5. Avoid the use of halothane if any four of the following factors exist:[18]
    a. Age over 40 years
    b. Long operation
    f. Allergy
    g. Drug dependency

§ 10.31   Halothane

- c. Surgery of biliary system
- d. Females
- e. Obesity
- h. Occupational exposure
- i. Sepsis

Interpretation and Customary Practices: Halothane is a potent anesthetic agent that may be used alone or in combination with other anesthetics. Halothane is a clear, colorless, volatile liquid which remains relatively stable at room temperature and is approximately 12 percent metabolized in the liver with urinary excretion of metabolic products.

The dose of halothane administered is measured as a percentage of vapor concentration in a carrier gas. The carrier gas may be either oxygen or a mixture of nitrous oxide and oxygen. Since halothane is supplied as a liquid and dispensed as a gas, it must be vaporized by some method in order to be administered. Although the physical chemical properties of halothane allow for open drop vaporization, most commonly one of several commercially available vaporizers is used. Although guidelines exist for the approximate vapor concentrations required for induction and maintenance of anesthesia, the actual dose required depends on the individual patient, the presence of preanesthetic medication, and the use of other anesthetic agents.

Halothane has several advantages as an anesthetic agent. Since it is neither unpleasant to breathe nor irritating to the airway, it may be used as an induction agent for general anesthesia. This is a particularly useful approach in pediatric anesthesia where it is often difficult to start intravenous lines without traumatizing the child. It is also a useful approach where there may be problems in establishing an airway when spontaneous ventilation is still allowed. Halothane acts as a respiratory depressant but also has a good bronchodilating effect and does not stimultate bronchial secretions. The bronchodilatory effect is of clinical significance and makes halothane a useful agent in patients with chronic obstructive pulmonary disease or asthma.

Halothane, however, does have some adverse effects. It is a somewhat arrhythmogenic agent, the incidence of arrhythmias being approximately 15 percent in patients with spontaneous ventilation. The incidence of arrhythmias can be reduced by as much as tenfold by controlling ventilation.[19] Nodal rhythms, premature ventricular contractions, and occasionally bigeminal rhythms are very common under halothane anesthesia. Halothane also sensitizes the myocardium to the effects of catecholamines; in surgery, where it is anticipated that local anesthesia with epinephrine will be used, the use of some agent other than halothane is advisable unless there is a clear and overriding indication for its use. Halothane also acts as a myocardial depressant and can lead to hypotension.

In 1963, a syndrome of halothane hepatitis was found to occur after the administration of halothane for general anesthesia.[20] However, considerable controversy surrounds the significance of this syndrome. Clearly, many events occur during a major surgical procedure which may pose a threat to hepatic physiology. The administration of blood products which may be contaminated by the presence of non-A, non-B hepatitis, surgical manipulation of the liver, hypoxia, decreased hepatic blood flow, and pre-existing but subclinical hepatic injury may all be factors contributing to halothane hepatitis syndrome.

In the first several years following the introduction of halothane into the United States in 1958, the anesthetic appeared to compile an admirable record of safety. There soon appeared, however, isolated reports of massive hepatic necrosis following halothane anesthesia. In response, the Committee on Anesthesia of the National Academy of Sciences-National Research Council (NAS-NRC) in December 1961, appointed a study group to report periodically on all clinical aspects of halothane anesthesia, including the possibility of the anesthetic's association with fatal postoperative hepatic necrosis. Although a subcommittee of the study group found no firm evidence to either establish or refute a causal relationship between halothane and postoperative hepatic damage, the issue again came to the fore in May 1963, when the manufacturer issued a drug warning recommending that halothane not be administered to "patients with known liver or biliary tract disease." The warning was issued on the basis of 12 new cases of fatal hepatic necrosis that followed the use of halothane in surgical procedures. That same month the NAS-NCR Subcommittee on the National Halothane Study was appointed, and in June, with funds provided by the National Institute of General Medical Sciences, the National Halothane Study was initiated. This was a retrospective study of over 850,000 anesthetics administered between 1958 and 1962, in 34 institutions.[21]

The National Halothane Study showed that there is about one case of fatal massive hepatic necrosis in approximately 10,000 people who receive general anesthesia. In the large majority (73 of 82 cases) the necrosis could be attributed to shock, overwhelming infection sepsis, congestive heart failure, or pre-existing liver disease. The remaining nine of the 82 cases had no known cause and it is possible that some of these were due to halothane.

In addition to the National Halothane Study, other approaches have been taken to study the problem, but there is currently no definitive answer to this complex question. A recent study has summarized the available data and suggested that:

1. Repeated halothane administrations to individual patients are not hepatotoxic per se.

2. It is possible halothane has a hepatotoxic effect in patients undergoing radium therapy in the pelvis.

3. The true halothane challenges essentially prove the existence of halothane hepatitis.

4. There are no clinical or pathological features which distinguish halothane from viral hepatitis.
5. Health care professionals who work around anesthetic gases have a higher "prevalence" of liver disease.
6. Halothane should be avoided if a patient has developed unexplained hepatitis subsequent to the administration of halothane.[22]

The exact mechanism by which halothane causes liver damage has not been uncovered. It is generally believed to be the result of an immunological reaction such as that seen in the auto-immune diseases. It may be that halothane changes the proteins on the surface of liver cells such that they are recognized as foreign matter by the body's lymphocytes and are therefore attacked by the body's white blood cells. The immunologic theory is consistent with the observation that the more severe liver damages from halothane occur in patients who have received halothane previously, especially within only weeks or months. Other mechanisms are also possible, however, and the following conclusion has been offered:

> All organohalothane compounds used for anesthesia probably possess a capacity for a certain degree of hepatic damage. This hepatic damage is based upon biotransformation to reactive intermediates which adversely effect hepatic cellular function. At least three mechanisms are known by which this can occur: Lipoperoxidation, depletion of antioxidants such as glutathione, and covalent bonding. Hepatotoxicity from any halogenated anesthetic is a multifactorial event. Among the variables having roles are extent of biotransformation, type of biotransformation, genetic metabolic pathways and environmental drug pathways due to induction.[23]

Since other techniques are available which can be used in most circumstances, it may be prudent to avoid the use of halothane in patients with hepatocellular disease, a strong history of alcohol abuse, radium therapy in the pelvis, any history of jaundice or prior administration of halothane to the patient within a three-month period of time.

As a direct consequence of the pharmacology and toxicology of halothane, two general areas emerge where the potential for litigation is greatest. The first area is related to the hepatocellular toxicity of halothane, and the second is related to the arrhythmogenic effects of halothane. Where injury occurs as the result of halothane toxicity and the physician fails to adequately assess the patient's history or condition to assess the risk of such a result, he may be held liable.

CASE ILLUSTRATION

A 50-year-old woman was initially administered halothane for an exploratory laparotomy for what was presumed to be a perforated ulcer. The defendant-surgeon biopsied the cells lining an ulcer in the stomach that appeared abnormal to him. The frozen section interpretation of these cells was that they were benign. However, subsequent studies of parafin sections of the biopsy were interpreted first as "atypical" and later as "cancer." A gastrectomy for carcinoma of the stomach was scheduled for three weeks after the first operation. Laboratory tests performed at an unspecified date revealed an elevated alkaline phosphatase and SGOT value that was "off the chart." More specific tests were never done. The anesthesiologist presumed that these were signs that the cancer spread to the liver and decided to use halothane as the anesthetic for the gastrectomy, since the patient told him she had been happy with the anesthetic used during the laparotomy. He interviewed the patient but did not discuss the test results with her, nor did he disclose any risks associated with halothane. The surgeon noted the abnormal liver function tests and attributed them to metastasis or to a postoperative peritonitis and decided to operate without further tests. The resident assisting him did not recall looking at the results; the patient had mentioned to the resident that her urine was "dark as beer." Jaundice developed three days after the operation. The patient was transferred to a large medical center and died three months later after having received a liver transplant for severe hepatitis. The patient's widower sued all medical personnel, the hospital and the manufacturer of the Halothane. An impression in the hospital record made by a consultant who visited the patient after the second operation described the patient's condition as "halothane hepatitis." This was excluded at trial as the inadmissible hearsay opinion of a non-testifying expert because evidence at the trial showed the existence of a controversy as to whether halothane could cause or intensify hepatitis. Although the appellate court affirmed the jury's verdict finding the anesthesiologist not negligent in his treatment of the patient, the court ordered the case retried on the issue of whether informed consent was adequately obtained.* (*Cornfeldt v. Tongen*, 1977)[24]

Several medical facts are of interest in this case. First, the patient was admitted to the hospital with a perforated ulcer. Although not discussed in the case decision, considerable bleeding may have occurred, requiring several transfusions. The chance of transfusion hepatitis would tend to increase directly with the number of units transfused. It can only be assumed that SGOT levels were either not obtained or were normal prior to this first surgery. The assumption by the

---

* The defendant anesthesiologist was voluntarily released by the plaintiff at the time of retrial; however, the jury returned a verdict against the surgeon for $146,000.

anesthesiologist that the elevated SGOT and alkaline phosphatase levels were signs that cancer had spread to the liver may well have been presumptuous. It is not clear when the hepatic damage actually started in this case, but it seems likely that it occurred some time in the immediate postoperative period. Thus, the use of halothane for the second operation for gastrectomy was probably ill-advised unless there were overriding considerations. In this case, if such considerations existed, they should have been documented on the chart. The development of jaundice three days after the second surgery could indicate an exacerbation of pre-existing hepatic disease, since there was clear evidence of hepatocellular dysfunction prior to the operation.

Because an accurate history is essential to determining whether halothane may be used safely, the anesthesiologist contemplating its use must be certain to rule out any contraindications in a given patient.

CASE ILLUSTRATION

The patient died approximately one month after surgery during which halothane was used as the anesthetic. The patient had a past history of jaundice after surgery. The patient's widower sued the surgeon and anesthesiologist, alleging that they had either failed to take an adequate history, or else had failed to heed the warning from the history. There was questionable evidence whether the surgeon knew of the previous history of hepatitis. "Yellow jaundice, five years ago" was written below the doctor's signature on the patient's record. The surgeon admitted having written this after the operation and after having discovered the patient's liver difficulties. The court of appeals held that in light of expert testimony regarding the taking of a patient's history, the defendants could be found to be negligent in failing to determine the patient's prior history of jaundice. The case was ordered retried. *(Moore v. Francisco*, 1978)[25]

In addition to the medical history taken by the surgeon, the anesthesiologist or nurse-anesthetist who is contemplating the use of halothane should question the patient regarding the history of such things as jaundice or hepatitis prior to the administration of this drug. The negligence of one physician does not excuse the negligence of another.

Litigation may also occur because of the arrhythmogenic properties of halothane. Patients have generally been unsuccessful in such litigation if they are unable to show specific acts of negligence on the part of the physician in administering or choosing the halothane or in responding to the resulting cardiac arrest.

CASE ILLUSTRATION

The patient was receiving halothane with nitrous oxide and oxygen in preparation for surgery to repair a diaphragmatic hernia. Approximately 13 minutes after the administration of anesthesia was begun and before surgery was initiated, the nurse-anesthetist discovered that the patient was cyanotic and that a cardiac arrest had occurred. Two physicians attempted resuscitation, but their attempts failed and the patient was pronounced dead. The patient's widower sued the nurse-anesthetist and the physicians, alleging the improper mixture of halothane with oxygen and nitrous oxide, the improper use of the anesthesia machine, and the improper monitoring of the patient during anesthesia. A medical expert testified that the patient's cardiac arrest was caused by either an overdose of halothane or a lack of proper oxygenation. The nurse-anesthetist should have set the machine so that it would have administered the gas mixture at a flow rate of at least four liters per minute; instead the proof showed that the flow rate was only two liters per minute. This difference would have resulted in an increased delivery of halothane to the patient. The expert also testified that it was necessary to adjust for temperature changes in order to prevent significant changes in the amount of halothane delivered to the patient. Furthermore, the expert stated that blood pressure readings should have been taken at two-minute intervals rather than at the four-minute intervals recorded in the record. However, additional expert testimony postulated that the cardiac arrest could have been caused by an air embolism or other causes. It was argued that cardiac arrest is an often unavoidable risk of surgery. The jury refused to find the defendants liable and their verdict was upheld on appeal. *(Webb v. Jorns, 1975)*[26]

This case is of some medical interest for several reasons. The decision does not reveal whether this patient had pre-existing cardiac disease, a history of arrhythmias, a history of hypertension, or was taking other interfering medications in the preoperative period. The expert witness testimony that the patient's cardiac arrest was caused by either an overdose of halothane or a lack of proper oxygenation seems somewhat simplistic, considering the complex pharmacology of halothane. It seems equally likely that the patient's cardiac arrest was caused by the presence of high circulating catecholamines from too light rather than too deep a depth of anesthesia. This case also highlights problems that may arise with vaporizers. With older vaporizers, a gas flow of four liters per minute or greater was advisable. The newer vaporizers may deliver appropriate concentrations of halothane and other volatile gas anesthetics at lower gas flows. From the facts of this case, specifically the gas flow requirement and the adjustment for temperature changes, it seems likely that halothane was being administered by a copper kettle type vaporizer rather than the newer halothane specific vaporizers. There is, nonetheless, a clear implication that the anesthesiologist is responsible for assuring that vaporizers and other anesthesiology equipment function in a correct fashion and that the appropriate dose of a volatile gas anesthetic is delivered. (See § 2.50, Products Liability.)

§ 10.32 Penthrane

Liability involving the use of Penthrane will be imposed where the anesthesiologist administers the anesthetic without properly determining whether or not it is contraindicated or where such a determination is made, it is ignored, penthrane is administered, and the patient suffers an injury.

Penthrane is a halogenated anesthetic which is now used infrequently. When used as an anesthetic, it is generally administered in combination with nitrous oxide and a neuromuscular blocking agent, since high concentrations can produce cardiovascular depression and if administered for long periods are likely to cause adverse renal effects. High output renal failure is dose related and is thought to be caused by an effect of the inorganic fluoride ion produced by metabolism of the drug; this interferes with the sodium transport necessary for concentrating urine and may also render the appropriate renal tubules unresponsive to antidiuretic hormone. Its use should be avoided with other drugs with possible nephrotoxic effects, such as gentamycin or the tetracyclines.[27] Penthrane is also known to cause liver damage and is therefore probably contraindicated in patients who have developed jaundice and unexplained fever after a previous administration of penthrane or halothane.[28]

The reported lawsuits involving the administration of penthrane serve to emphasize the importance of taking an adequate patient history and determining the proper anesthetic to be used based on that history. The medical literature is definite in its assessment that penthrane is contraindicated in patients with prior kidney or renal problems. Where such a patient is anesthetized with penthrane and suffers an injury, liability will, in all likelihood, be imposed on the anesthesiologist.

CASE ILLUSTRATION

The patient entered the hospital for an elective cholecystectomy. The admitting hospital history disclosed, among other things, that the patient had suffered from hepatitis during her childhood some 16 years prior to admission. The operating surgeon visited the patient, decided on a general anesthetic, but made a medical decision not to use penthrane. Nevertheless, the nurse-anesthetist administered penthrane. Subsequent to surgery, the patient developed a liver dysfunction which resulted in her death ten days later. The patient's widower sued the drug manufacturer, the attending physician (who had also assisted in the surgery), the operating surgeon, the nurse-anesthetist, and the hospital as the nurse's employer. At the trial, the operating surgeon testified that he relayed the decision not to use penthrane to the nurse-anesthetist. The nurse-anesthetist denied that this message had been communicated to her. The trial court's verdict in favor of the drug company was upheld on appeal because the expert witnesses had testified that the package insert gave a proper and adequate warning. The attending physician was not held liable because he had not exercised any control over the operating surgeon. The appellate court ordered the case retried with regard to the liability of the hospital, the surgeon and the nurse-anesthetist, stating that the facts indicated negligence on the part of the surgeon for failing to properly communicate his medical decision to the nurse-anesthetist and negligence on the part of the nurse-anesthetist for failing to follow the surgeon's orders properly. (*Carlsen v. Javurek*, 1975)[29]

§ 10.40 INTRAVENOUS ANESTHETIC AGENTS

Legal liability has generally not been imposed on anesthesiologists for complications resulting from extravascular injections of the anesthetic agent unless the anesthesiologist fails to properly treat the complication, to the patient's detriment.

Drugs included under the general heading of intravenous anesthesia can be divided into three classes of drugs. The first class would include barbiturates; the second class, narcotics; and the third class, neuroleptic agents. The use of barbiturates for intravenous anesthesia generally refers to the use of the ultra short-acting barbiturates such as induction agents. Using short-acting barbiturates to induce anesthesia offers certain advantages. These agents do not irritate the patient's airway and they help move the patient rapidly through stage two, the hypersensitivity stage of anesthesia. (See § 10.10, Principles of General Anesthesia.)

Most legal cases referring to the use of ultra short-acting barbiturates involve extravascular injections. Care must be taken to assure the adequacy and potency of intravenous lines. These drugs are extremely irritating and can lead to a marked phlebitis. In the event that these drugs are administered inadvertently into an artery, the vasospasm that develops can lead to loss of the distal extremity. In the event of an extravascular injection it is important to recognize this complication immediately and to take appropriate steps. Depending upon the particular anatomy of an individual patient, it may not be readily apparent that an IV line has infiltrated.

The barbiturate type drugs are also cardiodepressive agents. In fact, in certain patients, cardiovascular collapse can occur after the injection of small amounts of barbiturates. In patients with compromised cardiovascular function, the dose of barbiturates must be drastically reduced if they are used at all. In such cases alternate induction techniques, such as ketamine or narcotics in low doses, should be used. In addition, there are other well-known contraindications to the use of barbiturates, such as porphyria and adrenal hypofunction, where the usual doses must be reduced. Respiratory arrest can occur from the respiratory depressant action of these drugs, and attention must be directed to assuring an airway when these drugs are used.

Cases where the patient suffered injury from the use of ultra short-acting barbiturates have generally been resolved in favor of the physician. Often this resolution is the result of legal rather than medical considerations, such as a failure of the patient-plaintiff to produce expert testimony.

CASE ILLUSTRATION

The patient complained to the nurse-anesthetist of pain after the injection of sodium pentothal. The nurse-anesthetist noted swelling near the injection site; she then injected the anesthetic into the other arm. The patient had no further complaints while in the hospital, nor were any abnormalities noted then. However, the anesthetic administered initially had apparently entered a muscle, producing some scarring. The patient brought suit. An expert for the defendant testified that the needles could penetrate the muscle even if properly inserted with care and skill. For instance, movement by the patient or accidental jarring of the operating table could make the needle penetrate through the wall of the vein into the muscle. The patient failed to produce any contrary expert testimony that the anesthetist's conduct failed to meet the standard of care; therefore, the court held for the anesthetist. *(Gore v. U.S., 1964)*[30]

In a 1966 Minnesota case sodium pentothal extravasated into surrounding tissues prior to gynecologic surgery. The anesthesiologist noted the delayed onset of the anesthesia and looked for but saw no indications of infiltration of the anesthetic. The patient, who also happened to be an employee of the surgeon, commented on the fact that she was not going to sleep. The anesthesiologist then noted that the anesthetic had infiltrated; he inserted the needle in the arm proximally, and anesthesia followed. During the operation, the anesthesiologist injected Alidase into the area of infiltration to decrease the possibility of damage.* He acknowledged that infiltration had occurred in the medical record ("possible 8-10 cc."). It was held that the question of whether the anesthesiologist had had warning that the anesthetic was infiltrating tissues of the patient's hand was a scientific fact beyond the common knowledge of laymen, and the proof of warning by expert testimony was necessary before an inference of negligence could be drawn.[31] The difficulty in obtaining expert testimony in these cases is probably attributable to the fact that most anesthesiologists recognize that such an injury can occur in the absence of negligent conduct.

The legal outcome is not the same, however, where the anesthesiologist fails to respond properly to the mishap, or his or her conduct tends to exacerbate the problem.

CASE ILLUSTRATION

The anesthesiologist ordered a resident to administer sodium pentothal to the patient. The resident attempted intravenous injection in the left antecubital fossa; the patient cried out in pain, jerked his arm, and the needle came out. The resident called the anesthesiologist, who examined the patient, noted that the patient's hand had blanched, noted the patient's low pulse and attempted, unsuccessfully, to arouse the patient. The anesthesiologist decided to proceed and administered cyclopropane, ether and oxygen and took the patient to the operating room. The surgeon was not informed of the incident until two hours after the injection, at which time, measures were attempted to reverse the effects in the arm. However, the patient's left arm had to be amputated three days later. The patient brought suit. At trial, the anesthesiologist testified that one measure to correct an injection outside a vein was to inject procaine without removing the needle. He also mentioned the use of stellate ganglion block or brachial plexus block to counteract the vasospasm. However, none of these measures were instituted. In light of this fact the court held the anesthesiologist liable for the patient's injury. (*Rockwell v. Stone*, 1961)[32]

The medical facts in this case indicate that this injection was not only outside the vein, but intra-arterial. This situation is more serious than simple extravasation into tissue (as evidenced by the eventual amputation) and requires immediate action. Obviously, the best approach is to assure that injection into an artery does

---

* This treatment is not the treatment of choice and should not be construed as the standard of care.

§ 10.40   *Intravenous Anesthetic Agents*   279

not occur. Unless the patient is in shock, hypoxic, or both, the return of bright red pulsatile blood should immediately indicate that the needle is positioned in an artery.

In a similar case the anesthesiologist was held liable for conduct amounting to abandonment (see § 1.31, Physician-Patient Relationship) after the patient reacted adversely to sodium pentothal.

CASE ILLUSTRATION

The patient suffered a laryngospasm following injection of sodium pentothal and ultimately sustained severe brain damage. The laryngospasm was unresponsive to injections of "relaxing drugs" and manual attempts at ventilation. There was a question of whether intubation as a remedial measure was timely; intubation occurred as late as 50 minutes after the laryngospasm developed. At trial, the plaintiff alleged that the defendant-anesthesiologist had been absent from the operating room while the patient was experiencing laryngospasm for much of the 50-minute delay. The defendant and the anesthesiologist who replaced him testified that one of them was with the patient at all times. However, hospital records that indicated the replacing physician had been present elsewhere at a delivery throughout the emergency were admitted in spite of the contradictory testimony. This record was allowed to support the inference that the replacing physician had not been with the patient during the emergency and therefore that the defendant-anesthesiologist had abandoned his patient. The court held that once abandonment had been proven, the defendant could not argue that his best efforts might not have prevented the patient's brain damage. (*Ascher v. Guttierrez*, 1976)[33]

Laryngospasm can develop in the absence of negligence. Usually it is associated with stimulation of the airway in stage II anesthesia and is generally responsive to positive pressure ventilation. In this case, it may have been a manifestation of an allergic reaction to sodium pentothal. Clearly, the airway must be secured immediately when laryngospasm occurs, and if the spasm cannot be broken with positive pressure ventilation, a rapidly acting muscle relaxant can be used to paralyze the cords and allow the passage of an endotracheal tube if adequate ventilation cannot be obtained with mask and bag.

The second class of intravenous anesthetics includes the narcotics. Potential problems arising from the use of narcotics are centered around the respiratory depressant effect of these drugs. Narcotics are used not only for premedication but also as part of the balanced anesthetic technique using nitrous oxide, narcotics and muscle relaxers. Clearly, under these circumstances, adequate ventilation must be assured. The respiratory depressant activity of narcotic agonists may outlast the analgesic properties of these drugs. Potential problems exist well into the recovery room period. In the case of the longer acting narcotic agonists such as morphine, reversal by a shorter acting agent such as naloxone may lead to respiratory depression some time after the patient has been admitted to the recovery room. The requirements for a postoperative analgesia must be balanced against the respiratory depressant effect of these drugs.

There are several narcotic agonists commonly used in anesthetic practice, as well as newer agents currently undergoing clinical trials. Although it was thought by many physicians that narcotics, as a group of drugs, differed among themselves only in duration of action, it has become apparent that other pharmacologic properties vary from agonist to agonist within the group.[34] Under most circumstances, if modest doses are used, it is unlikely that these differential pharmacological actions will pose a significant problem. If large doses are administered, as is the custom for patients undergoing coronary artery surgery, these differential effects may influence the anesthesiologist's choice of agent depending on the hemodynamic effects desired. A pharmacologic property that differs among the various agonists is the ability to release histamine. Thus, one would probably choose to avoid morphine in a patient with carcinoid syndrome or histamine-sensitive asthma. It is of considerable interest that the newer narcotic agonists also have partial antagonist properties and less respiratory depressant properties (or at least a plateau in the respiratory depression-dose curve). Both nalbuphine and butorphanol have been used as part of a balanced anesthetic technique, and evaluations of these narcotics are continuing.

It is likely that the anesthesiologist will continue to be plagued by the problem of respiratory depression following the use of narcotics, a problem often manifested in the recovery room after the anesthesiologist has left. The reason for this is that during the period of emergence from anesthesia, the patient receives a great deal of stimulation; the patient is extubated, transferred to a litter, transported, and subject to initial attention in the recovery room, etc. Stimulation acts as an antagonist to the depressant effects of narcotics, and consequently a patient may have adequate spontaneous respirations and be reactive during this period, only to become more obtunded when the stimulation ceases. While there is a definite need to provide sedation and analgesia in the postoperative period, care must be taken to assure that this is accomplished without endangering the ventilation of the patient.

The third class of intravenous drugs used in anesthesia are the neuroleptic agents such as diazepam, droperidol or ketamine. Droperidol is most frequently used in combination with fentanyl in a product called Innovar. Innovar is useful for calming an anxious patient on arrival in the operating room and is also useful for the induction of anesthesia. Diazepam is very commonly used as a preanesthetic medication and also as part of balanced techniques, and there are numerous other

§ 10.40　　　　　*Intravenous Anesthetic Agents*　　　　　281

drugs used for their anxiolytic, amnestic, or analgesia-potentiating properties. Many of these drugs belong to the general class of major and minor tranquilizers, and commonly are benzodiazepine, phenothiazine, or butyrophenone derivatives. The use of these agents is largely dependent on the individual preferences and experiences of the physicians who use them, but several principles should be borne in mind when these drugs are used:

1. These drugs may have effects other than those which are intended. An example of this principle is the alpha-adrenergic blocking properties of some of the phenothiazines and butyrophenones. The anesthesiologist who uses these drugs should be familiar with the pharmacology of the agents which he routinely uses and should therefore be aware when the use of a particular drug is contraindicated.

2. The duration of action of these drugs may be quite different. *For example,* lorazepam has a longer duration of action than diazepam, and droperidol may have prolonged effects. Thus, the potential exists for continued pharmacological effects which outlast the immediate perioperative period of intensive monitoring.

3. Interactions with other drugs can occur. In fact, one of the reasons these drugs are used is to potentiate the analgesic effects of narcotic agonists. When a patient is taking several other drugs the potential for drug interaction must be borne in mind.

4. The doses used may vary among patients. The overall status of the patient, nutritionally and physiologically, is a major determinant of the dose which can be considered appropriate. This is a particular problem in the pediatric population and in wasted, cachexic adults.

5. Behavioral effects may be unanticipated. These drugs are generally depressants, but the potential for disinhibition also exists. The occasional elderly patient who becomes very euphoric or agitated after receiving a "sedative" demonstrates the potential for this to occur.[35]

There is enough difference of opinion among practicing anesthesiologists, and the principles referred to above are of sufficient complexity, that expert witness testimony would probably be necessary to establish whether or not the standard of care has been breached in a given fact situation. (See § 1.32, Standard of Care.)

Ketamine differs significantly from other intravenous anesthetic agents. Ketamine produces a state of profound analgesia, preservation of pharyngeal and laryngeal reflexes, increased muscle tone, circulatory stimulation, and elevated intracranial pressure.[36] This agent is most commonly used as an induction agent in the pediatric population, in adults with hypovolemia or compromised cardiovascular function, and as a general anesthetic where repeated use is likely, e.g., for dressing changes in burn patients. The use of this drug in adults is limited because of the delirium and hallucinations seen on emergency and postoperatively,[37] although the incidence of unpleasant emergence phenomena can be reduced with appropriate premedication. Contraindications to the use of Ketamine include:

1. Hypertension
2. Cerebrovascular disease
3. Psychiatric disease-psychosis
4. Increased intracranial pressure
5. Increasing age

Thus, the unique pharmacological properties of this drug may be used advantageously in selected patients, but the incidence of unpleasant side effects is sufficiently high that it is not routinely used. Liability would most likely be imposed for the inappropriate choice of this anesthetic technique if prolonged psychiatric disturbance occurred.

§ 10.50 MUSCLE RELAXANTS

Anesthesiologists are most frequently subject to legal liability in the administration of muscle relaxants (1) for failing to adequately monitor and control the secondary effects of the relaxant on the patient, or (2) where the relaxant is used in combination with other drugs and the drugs prevent the resumption of spontaneous respiration.

Muscle relaxants are frequently administered to patients in combination with other anesthetic agents during general anesthesia, especially in intra-abdominal surgery. Analysis of the many anesthetic agents and techniques available reveals several inadequacies which may be overcome by relaxants. While relaxants are adjuncts to good anesthesia, they are not considered to be a substitute for good anesthesia, nor are they anesthetics. Unless the general anesthetic agent produces muscle relaxation on its own (such as ether), the administration of a muscle relaxant in combination may be indicated. The primary anesthetic indications are:

1. To produce relaxation
2. To reduce the amount of inhalation agent required for a given procedure
3. To facilitate intubation
4. To overcome laryngospasm[38]

The use of the term relaxant is somewhat euphemistic when applied to this class of drugs. These drugs are, in fact, pharmacological blockers of the neuromuscular junction with the potential for causing complete total motor paralysis.

Under the general heading of neuromuscular blocking agents, there are two categories of drugs. The first category is the depolarizing type of muscle blockers, and the second category is the non-depolarizing type of neuromuscular blockers. The prototype depolarizing neuromuscular blocking agent is succinylcholine. Succinylcholine is pharmacologically similar to the neurotransmitter acetylcholine and acts at the neuromuscular junction to cause a persistent depolarization of the motor end plate. Fasciculations are initially present and full paralysis follows the initial fasciculations. Succinylcholine is readily metabolized in the body by pseudocholinesterase.

Since the termination of action of this drug depends on hydrolysis by plasma cholinesterase and since the levels of pseudocholinesterase and the activity of pseudocholinesterase are genetically determined, there is a subsegment of the population which has a markedly decreased pseudocholinesterase activity. Patients may be either heterozygous or homozygous for the deficiency of pseudocholinesterase. Half of the enzyme in heterozygous patients will have normal activity, and while these patients will show a prolonged duration of activity following the administration of succinylcholine, this will often go unnoticed since the duration of their operation will still be longer than the duration of the action of the drug. The rate of hydrolysis in homozygous patients is slow enough to require assisted or controlled ventilation for several hours after the administration of succinylcholine in doses routinely used for normal patients. Laboratory tests are available to determine the activity of pseudocholinesterase, but these tests are not routinely ordered for preoperative screening because of the relatively low incidence of significant problems arising from the enzyme deficiency and the relatively high cost of the tests. Nonetheless, if a patient has prolonged neuromuscular blockade following the administration of this drug, the patient and also family members should be tested to determine the potential for problems in subsequent surgeries. In a normal patient with a full level and activity of pseudocholinesterase, the duration of action of succinylcholine is usually about six to ten minutes.

The most frequent use for succinylcholine is to facilitate endotracheal intubation. When used to facilitate intubation, succinylcholine is typically given after the induction of anesthesia, or if rapid sequence induction is employed because of a full stomach, it may be given simultaneously with a short-acting barbiturate to induce anesthesia. With paralysis of the muscles of mastication and the vocal cords, laryngoscopy and endotracheal intubation is much easier, resulting in less trauma to the teeth and laryngealpharyngeal structures.

In addition to its use to facilitate intubation, succinylcholine can also be used as a continuous drip infusion where muscle relaxation is required for relatively short surgical procedures. The advantage of employing this method over using non-depolarizing muscle relaxers is that succinylcholine has a shorter duration of action and is readily hydrolyzed to plasma pseudocholinesterase in most patients.

Yet another use for succinylcholine is in the emergency situation where a laryngospasm cannot be broken by positive pressure ventilation and muscle paralysis is required to allow for assisted ventilation. Rapid onset of action, short duration of action and good absorption from either intravenous or intramuscular injection are clearly of benefit under these circumstances.

If repeated doses of succinylcholine are employed or if a continuous drip infusion is given, an unusual type of persistent neuromuscular blockade called dual block can occur. Dual block has several of the characteristics of a non-depolarizing neuromuscular blockade, and the exact mechanisms underlying this phenomenon are poorly understood.

There are other problems with succinylcholine as well. In patients with burns or massive tissue destruction, the release of potassium which occurs after the administration of succinylcholine may lead to cardiac arrest. In cases of open eye injuries, fasciculation of the extra-ocular muscles may lead to extrusion of the vitreous and loss of the eye.

Postoperative muscle pain is also related to succinylcholine administration. Originally thought to be due to fasciculations, this pain may occur with or without the presence of fasciculations. The practice of giving small doses of non-depolarizing neuromuscular blockers such as curare seems to be beneficial in decreasing the incidence of postoperative muscle pain, even though the prevention of fasciculation is unrelated to the pain. Where the presence of fasciculation is used to indicate the onset of neuromuscular blockage, such as in rapid sequence inductions, the use of non-depolarizing drugs may be omitted. Pre-curarization is usually not employed in pediatric anesthesia, and a minority of anesthesiologists question its utility in adults. Thus although the technique is widely used, it should not be construed as a breach of the standard of care not to routinely use defasciculating doses of non-depolarizing drugs unless indicated for other reasons, e.g., open eye injuries.

Bradycardia and arrhythmias may occur after the administration of succinylcholine and may well be related to a partial degradation of succinylcholine to succinylmonocholine. There has also been an unconfirmed report that oxytocins may alter the type of block produced by succinylcholine. Offsetting this consideration is the fact that succinylcholine does not cross the uteroplacental barrier and is therefore of considerable use in obstetric anesthesia. There are many drugs which may interact with cholinesterase or at the neuromuscular junction to prolong the duration of the action of succinylcholine.[39] Some of these drugs are:

1. Neostigmine
2. Pyridostigmine
3. Echothiophate
4. Insecticides
5. Alkylating agents
6. Hexafluorenium
7. Procaine

8. Trimethaphan
9. Phenelzine
10. Chlorpromazine
11. Certain antibiotics

The second class of neuromuscular blocking drugs is the non-depolarizing neuromuscular blockers. D-tubocurarine is the prototype drug in this class of drugs. These drugs combine with the motor end plate and prevent acetylcholine from reacting with the end plate receptors. This is a competitive inhibition of the neuromuscular junction. Drugs in this class also will exhibit other nicotinic blocking effects, for example, at autonomic ganglia, and the relative importance of these other effects depends on the individual agents.[40] Histamine release may also occur when these agents are administered. Thus, while the action at the neuromuscular junction is the same for every drug in this classification, individual drugs may differ in the incidence and significance of other direct and indirect effects and there may be differences in onset and duration of action. All of these drugs are relatively long-acting compared to the duration of action of succinylcholine. Although it is possible to use pancuronium to facilitate intubation in rapid sequence inductions where succinylcholine is contraindicated, the major use for these drugs is to provide muscle relaxation during surgery. This may be of particular importance in abdominal surgery in allowing adequate exposure for the surgical procedures contemplated. Since the mechanism of action of these drugs is a competitive antagonism of the effects of acetylcholine at the nicotinic cholinoceptive motor end plate, it is possible to antagonize the motor paralysis caused by these drugs with the use of cholinesterase inhibitors such as neostigmine. Since acetylcholine is the neurotransmitter of the parasympathetic nervous system as well as the neurotransmitter at the neuromuscular junction, there are complex interactions which can occur with the use of these types of drugs. The potential for drug interactions is enhanced because these agents are protein bound and because they also have complex presynaptic actions to decrease the amount of acetylcholine released. These interactions have been recently reviewed.[41] Interacting drugs include:

1. Various ions
2. General anesthetics
3. Local anesthetics
4. Antiarrhythmics
5. Barbiturates
6. Narcotics
7. Tranquilizers

8. Antibiotics
9. Diuretics
10. Steroids

Litigation involving the use of neuromuscular junction blocking drugs most commonly centers around respiratory paralysis. Once a muscle relaxant has been administered in doses effective to cause relaxation of abdominal or other muscles, the diaphragm will also be relaxed and paralyzed, thereby rendering spontaneous respiration impossible. Consequently, with the use of these drugs, the anesthesiologist must guarantee adequate ventilation of the patient. In reported cases of injury to a patient who has been administered a relaxant, the cause has often been linked to inadequate control and monitoring of respiration.

CASE ILLUSTRATION

The patient suffered a shoulder injury in a football game. His injury was initially diagnosed as "a possible dislocation to the left shoulder." X-rays revealed a shoulder separation and surgery was prescribed. The nurse-anesthetist administered sodium pentothal intravenously without waiting the recommended 60 seconds for observation of the patient's reaction to a small dose of the drug. She then gave the larger dose immediately because the patient was apprehensive. The general anesthetic gases were then administered, along with succinylcholine. About half an hour after this it was noticed that the patient was not breathing. The surgeon left the operating room about five minutes later when the patient's breathing was being assisted. About five minutes after that, the nurse-anesthetist ordered a Bennett respirator and began to hyperventilate the patient with excessive oxygen so that he could have a "three-minute supply" of oxygen for his trip from the operating room to the recovery room. The patient was extubated and taken 50-75 feet in less than one minute to the recovery room. Upon arrival to the recovery room, no pulse could be detected. The patient died about an hour later. The patient's widow sued the hospital, the nurse-anesthetist, and the surgeon. The recovery room nurse testified at trial that a patient should not be removed from the operating room if he is not breathing spontaneously. The patient's face was covered during the operation. Because the patient was black, it would have been difficult to detect cyanosis from outward coloration. One expert testified that it was acceptable to leave a patient without assisting respiration for one minute, but that one never transports patients who are not breathing without assisting ventilation. The physician who diagnosed the patient's shoulder separation testified that it was not standard medical practice to leave a patient who is not breathing without resuscitative equipment accompanying him, and that a patient should not be moved unless he is breathing spontaneously. The court found the hospital, the surgeon, and the nurse-anesthetist liable for failing to supervise the administration of anesthesia properly and for failure to remain in the operating room until the patient was breathing without assistance. (*Foster v. Englewood Hospital Association*, 1974)[42]

Patients who seek medical attention for injuries which require urgent surgery should be assumed to have full stomachs. The risk of aspiration of gastric contents exists in such patients, and this case probably represents a rapid sequence induction with endotracheal intubation, although it is not stated as such, to minimize the risk of aspiration. It is noted that succinylcholine was given. Apparently the plan was then to allow the patient to be spontaneously ventilated. It can only be assumed that the patient resumed spontaneous ventilation in the appropriate period of time after the initial dose of succinylcholine. The facts in this case support the following overall implication: if any type of neuromuscular blocking agent is given, respiration must be guaranteed and ventilatory support must not be discontinued until it is ascertained that the patient is breathing spontaneously and has adequate ventilation.

Injuries have occurred as a result of the administration of drugs to reverse the action of the neuromuscular blocking of the relaxant agent. In a case stemming from such a situation, the court concluded that there was a vast difference of opinion among recognized experts concerning the use of such agents (in this case, tensilon following succinylcholine), and such a practice by an anesthesiologist in and of itself does not violate the standard of care.

CASE ILLUSTRATION

A three-year-old girl was undergoing dental restoration of massive tooth decay. The surgery was extensive and a general anesthesia was required. Preoperative medication consisted of meperidine, 25 mg., hydroxyzine, 12-1/2 mg., and 1/25 grain of atropine. The child was taken to surgery and anesthetized through a face mask with a mixture of halothane and oxygen. She was injected intravenously with 1-1/2 cc. of succinylcholine to aid in nasal intubation. She was then placed on assisted respiration which continued for an undetermined period, following which she resumed spontaneous breathing. The assisted respiration was then discontinued. About 50 minutes later, a decrease in spontaneous breathing was noted and the anesthesiologist assisted respiration by bag breathing. Eighty minutes later (more than two hours after succinylcholine had been given and 25 minutes after the operation was completed) the anesthesiologist gave 1/4 cc. edrophonium intravenously to help restore spontaneous breathing. The patient's heart rate dropped after this and breathing improved. After the patient was observed breathing normally for about 15-20 minutes, she was taken from the operating room to the recovery room.

Absence of spontaneous respiration was noted just before the patient arrived at the recovery room and there were immediate efforts to resuscitate the child; however, she died shortly thereafter. An autopsy revealed that the patient had adrenal insufficiency with adrenals about 1/5 of the normal size that had therefore hypofunctioned. The pathologist later explained the abnormally small glands were incapable of producing sufficient adrenal fluids to sustain life under surgical stress. The child's parents brought suit. One expert for the child's parents, testified that the preoperative dose of hydroxyzine was twice as much as necessary in light of its potentiation by and of narcotics. He testified that administration of succinylcholine had been unnecessary, and that administration of edrophonium after succinylcholine was a "gross error." A second expert testified that succinylcholine and edrophonium should never be given together, and agreed that this was "gross error." He did acknowledge that there was a wide divergence of opinion in the medical community about this subject. Edrophonium has a normal duration of action of around ten minutes, and changes in the heart rate can be used to monitor its effects and duration. The defendant-anesthesiologist testified that he customarily gave succinylcholine for intubation. The defendant's expert testified that succinylcholine was widely used to aid intubation and that edrophonium was properly used in certain types of muscular blockade. The court found that in light of the conflicting expert testimony as to the propriety of the use of edrophonium with succinylcholine, neither the giving of edrophonium, the amount given, nor removal of the patient from the operating room constituted medical malpractice. *(Chapman v. Argonaut-Southwest Insurance Co., 1974)*[43]

This case is of interest for several reasons. First, the preoperative sedation with meperidine, hydroxyzine, and atropine does seem to be excessive for a three-year-old child; however, if these doses were, in fact, appropriate on a milligram per kilogram basis, then the weight of this child would have had to have been excessive for a normal three-year-old, implying that the child was either obese or, considering the diagnosis of Addison's disease, edematous. In either case, the risk of anesthesia is greater, and some mention of the patient's condition should have been made in the preoperative note. It would certainly be unusual for a patient with adrenal glands this atrophic to appear perfectly normal. In view of the events of this case and the eventual diagnosis by the pathologist, the dose of preanesthetic medication was certainly excessive, no matter what the weight of the patient, and the most important question seems to be whether or not there were sufficient clinical signs to suggest the diagnosis of Addison's disease prior to the administration of anesthesia. The mask induction with halothane and oxygen is not particularly unusual in the pediatric patient population. Nor is it particularly unusual to use succinylcholine in cases of nasal intubations where it may be necessary to use forceps and direct laryngoscopy to position the endotracheal tube properly.

The patient was appropriately assisted with her respirations and did in fact resume spontaneous respirations. A decrease in spontaneous breathing 50 minutes later is somewhat confusing. Ordinarily one would assume that the resumption of spontaneous respiration indicated that the effects of succinylcholine had entirely worn off, inasmuch as a termination of effect of succinylcholine is by enzymatic hydrolysis. There is a possibility in situations like this that some other neuromuscular blocking agent such as curare may have been inadvertently and mistakenly given. The antagonism of the neuromuscular blockade and decreased respiration associated with edrophonium indicates that the neuromuscular blockade was of the competitive or non-depolarizing type. This would be unusual for succinylcholine unless the presence of dual block had been established. Clearly, the depression of respiration caused by narcotics is not antagonized by the use of edrophonium. In addition, the presence of adequate spontaneous respiration after induction would indicate that the depressed respirations were not due to preoperative medication. The exception to this would be if these drugs were given orally and for some reason the absorption from the gut was delayed. In this case, the delayed absorption could have occurred somewhat later on into the case, and respiratory depression could have occurred. Thus, unless unusual circumstances were in operation, the generous preoperative sedation probably was not a real factor in causing the respiratory depression later on.

Those authorities who do advocate the use of a trial of edrophonium in reversing the dual block caused by succinylcholine usually point out that a longer-acting cholinesterase inhibitor should be used if edrophonium is initially effective. Other than failing to follow with a longer-acting agent, the use of edrophonium under these circumstances should be considered unusual perhaps, and perhaps a low yield procedure, but not improper. Under situations as unusual as those occurring in this case, probably the most prudent course would have been to leave the patient intubated and support ventilation mechanically.

The fact that this child was an undiagnosed Addisonian further complicates the medical picture. This is clearly a unique case, but its principles apply to the more usual circumstance where patients are given non-depolarizing neuromuscular blocking agents to facilitate surgery, and difficulty arises in reversing the effects of these drugs with cholinesterase inhibitors. There may be residual paralysis of the neuromuscular junction causing inadequate spontaneous respirations. It would seem that the medical lesson to be learned from these legal resolutions is that wherever there is doubt about the adequacy of a patient's spontaneous ventilation, steps should be taken to assist the patient mechanically until no doubt exists that the patient can handle his or her own airway and have adequate ventilation unsupported.

NOTES

1. ASA, *Guidelines for Anesthesia Care*, in American Society of Anesthesiologists Directory of Members A.1.b, 427 (46th ed. 1981).
2. Joint Commission on the Accreditation of Hospitals, Anesthesia Services Standard IV, in Accreditation Manual for Hospitals 9-10 (1981).
3. Etsten & Himwich, *Stages and Signs of Pentothal Anesthesia: Physiologic Basis*, 7 Anesthesiology 536 (1946).
4. Blacher, *On Awakening Paralyzed During Surgery: A Syndrome of Traumatic Neurosis*, 234 J.A.M.A. 67 (1975); Mainzer, *Awareness Muscle Relaxants and Balanced Anesthesia*, 6 Can. Anesthesiology Soc. J. 386 (1979); Van Valen, *Baroreceptor Activation Reduces Reactivity to Noxious Stimulation: Implications for Hypertension*, 205 Sci. 1299 (1979).
5. V. Collins, *Principles of Anesthesiology*, 277-310 (2d ed. 1976).
6. American National Standards Institute, *Specifications for Anesthesia Equipment Endotracheal Tubes* (1960).
7. V. Collins, *supra* note 5, at 342.
8. *Id.* at 1598.
9. *Id.* at 1606.
10. Aubert v. Charity Hosp., 363 So.2d 1223 (La. App. 1978).
11. Schneider v. Albert Einstein Medical Center, 257 Pa. Super. Ct. 348, 390 A.2d 1271 (1978).
12. Kitto v. Gilbert, 39 Colo. App. 374, 570 P.2d 544 (1977).
13. Hughes v. Hasting, 225 Tenn. 386, 469 S.W.2d 378 (1971).
14. Rauschelbach v. Benincasa, 372 S.W.2d 120 (Mo. 1963).
15. Bell v. Umstattd, 401 S.W.2d 306 (Tex. Civ. App. 1966).
16. *See, e.g.*, Walstad v. University of Minn. Hosp., 442 F.2d 634 8th Cir. 1971).
17. Carney & Van Dyke, *Halothane Hepatitis-A Critical Review*, 51 Anesthesia & Analgesia 135 (1972); Bunker, *Summary of National Halothane Study: Possible Association Between Halothane Anesthesia and Postoperative Hepatic Necrosis* 197 J.A.M.A. 126 (1966); Klatskin & Kimberg, *Recurrent Hepatitis Attributable to Halothane Sensitization in an Anesthetist* 280 New England J. Med. 515 (1969); Vergani, Mieli-Vergani, Alberti, Neuberger, Eddleston, Davis & Williams, *Antibodies to the Surface of Halothane-Altered Rabbit Hepatocytes in Patients with Severe Halothane-Associated Hepatitis*, 303 New England J. Med. 66 (1980).
18. Carney & Van Dyke, *supra* note 17.
19. Bird, Hayward, Howells & Jones, *Cardiac Arrythmias During Thyroid Surgery*, 24 Anesthesia 180 (1969).
20. Bunker & Blumenfield, *Liver Necrosis after Halothane Anesthesia*, 268 New England J. Med. 531 (1963); Lindenbaum & Leifer, *Hepatic Necrosis Associated with Halothane Anesthesia*, 268 New England J. Med. 525 (1963).
21. Subcommittee on the National Halothane Study of the Committee on Anesthesia, National Academy of Sciences— National Research Council, *Summary of the National Halothane Study*, 197 J.A.M.A. 775-88 (1966).
22. Dykes, *Anesthesia and Hepatic Toxicity: The Clinical Problem*, in ASA Annual Refresher Course Lectures 106A (1979).

Notes: Chapter X

23. Brown, *Anesthetic Hepatic Toxicity: A Scientific Problem?*, in ASA Annual Refresher Course Lectures 106B (1979).
24. Cornfeldt v. Tongen, 262 N.W.2d 684 (Minn. 1977).
25. Moore v. Francisco, 583 P.2d 391 (Kan. App. 1978).
26. Webb v. Jorns, 530 S.W.2d 847 (Tex. Civ. App. 1975).
27. Department of Drugs, American Medical Association, *AMA Drug Evaluations* 294-95 (3d ed. 1977).
28. Klein & Jeffries, *Hepatoxicity after Methoxyflurane Administration*, 197 J.A.M.A. 1037-39 (1966).
29. Carlsen v. Javurek, 526 F.2d 202 (8th Cir. 1975).
30. Gore v. United States, 229 F. Supp. 547 (E.D. Mich. 1964).
31. Miller v. Raaen, 273 Minn. 109, 139 N.W.2d 877 (1966).
32. Rockwell v. Stone, 173 A.2d 48, 404 Pa. 561 (1961).
33. Ascher v. Guttierrez, 533 F.2d 1235 (D.C. Cir. 1976).
34. Hug, *What is the Role of Narcotic Analgesics in Anesthesia?*, in ASA Annual Refresher Course Lectures 138 (1980).
35. *See* Stanley, *Pharmacology of Intravenous Non-Narcotic Anesthetics (Excluding Ketamine)*, in ASA Annual Refresher Course Lectures 235 (1980).
36. R. Dripps, J. Eckenhoff & L. Vandam, Introduction to Anesthesia 187-89 (1977).
37. Way, *Ketamine: What is Fact or Fantasy?*, in ASA Annual Refresher Course Lectures 236 (1980).
38. V. Collins, *Principles of Anesthesiology* 532 (2d ed. 1976).
39. Standaert, *Interactions Among Neuromuscular Blocking Agents and Other Drugs*, in 6 ASA Annual Refresher Course Lectures ch. 9 (1978).
40. Savarese, *Cardiovascular and Autonomic Effects of Neuromuscular Blockers*, in ASA Refresher Course Lectures 124 (1979).
41. Standaert, *supra* note 39.
42. Foster v. Englewood Hosp. Ass'n, 19 Ill. App. 3d 1055, 313 N.E.2d 183 (1974).
43. Chapman v. Argonaut-Southwest Ins. Co., 290 So.2d 779 (La.App. 1974).

Chapter XI
Regional Anesthesia

§ 11.10 SPINAL ANESTHESIA

Liability for injury from spinal anesthesia will be imposed on the anesthesiologist (1) where paresthesia or pain upon insertion of the needle is not properly dealt with by reinsertion and other necessary steps (paresthesia properly dealt with will not, in and of itself, result in liability); (2) where paralysis occurs and the evidence does not sufficiently disprove that it has resulted from a negligently caused spinal cord lesion; and (3) where the use of spinal anesthesia is inappropriate or inadequately achieved with regard to the particular surgical procedure intended; (4) where any of a variety of infections ensue from improper aseptic technique or spinal anesthesia is performed in the presence of bacteremia (superficial abcesses or epidural infection and meningitis are recognized complications).

The following is a compilation from various authorities[1] of recommendations for safe spinal technique:

1. Scrub hands according to aseptic surgical technique.
2. Use sterile gloves.
3. Avoid contaminating blocking solutions with solutions used to prepare the skin.
4. Use aseptic technique when opening tray.
5. Cleanse the skin prior to needle puncture.
6. Touch only sterile articles once gloved.
7. Use introducer prior to insertion of spinal needle.
8. Avoid repeated traumatic punctures.
9. Avoid performing a spinal or epidural puncture if patient's bleeding time is increased.
10. Avoid spinal or epidural blocks in patients with a bacteremia.

11. Never insert a needle through an infected area.
12. Use approved local anesthetic agents in standard concentrations.

Interpretation and Customary Practice: The brain and spinal cord are enclosed in and protected by three thin membranes. The inner two layers enclose the subarachnoid space, which contains a watery substance, the cerebrospinal fluid (CSF). Spinal anesthesia is achieved by inserting a needle into the subarachnoid space and injecting an anesthetic solution. The anesthetic acts on the nerve roots as they pass from the spinal cord through the subarachnoid space.[2]

The spinal cord in most adults extends to the first or second lumbar vertebra (L-1 or L-2); rarely it will extend as low as the mid-portion of the third lumbar vertebra (L-3).[3] Inferior to the termination of the spinal cord, the nerve roots fan out into the cauda equina (horse's tail). Injection of the spinal anesthetic is usually made in the L-3–L-4 or L-4–L-5 interspace to avoid the risk of injection of anesthetic into the spinal cord.

The effect of the anesthetic on nerve fibers increases as the size and degree of myelination of the fibers decrease. Fibers which carry pain sensations are among the smallest, and are therefore more susceptible to the effects of the anesthetic. Sympathetic nerve fibers, which are even smaller, are affected at a spinal cord level higher than the level of anesthesia. If sympathetic nerve fibers are paralyzed in the high thoracic area, sympathetic control of the cardiovascular system is lost, increasing the risk of hypotension.[4] The anesthetic can diffuse as high as the neck and head, possibly paralyzing the phrenic nerves and even the cranial nerves. In an early Oregon case, one expert witness stated that the standard of care (see § 1.32, Standard of Care) with regard to a spinal is to place a pillow under the patient's head when administering the anesthetic in order to elevate the head to guard against this danger.[5]

Spinal anesthesia yields excellent operative conditions for operations involving the lower abdomen, the pelvic region or the lower extremities.[6] In fact, spinal anesthesia is the preferred type of anesthetic for certain urological procedures, such as the transurethral resection of the prostate. Where complications from drug interactions pose a threat, e.g., in patients taking multiple medications or in the pregnant patient at term where consideration must be given to the effects on the fetus, spinal anesthesia is clearly preferable over general anesthesia. Spinal anesthesia may also be indicated in cases where there is a full stomach or the potential for difficulty in airway management exists; however, a high spinal or a drug reaction necessitating urgent airway management may still create problems. Although there is an absence of scientific proof in medical literature, most anesthesiologists feel that patients with significant pulmonary disease fare better under spinal anesthesia than under general anesthesia. When used correctly, this technique affords good operative conditions with a minimum potential for adverse drug interactions and is usually well tolerated by patients affording good postoperative pain relief and relatively few long-term sequelae.

The administration of a spinal anesthetic is a relatively simple procedure involving performance of lumbar puncture in the usual fashion, followed by the injection of a local anesthetic drug into the subarachnoid space. The level of anesthesia attained and the physiological consequences of that level will depend on:

1. The amount of drug and the type of drug injected
2. The volume of solution which is injected
3. The anatomic site of injection
4. The rate of injection
5. The specific gravity and density of the solution employed[7]

The position of the patient may also be used to influence the distribution of the anesthetic in the subarachnoid space. Because of the overlap in the sympathetic nervous system it is generally necessary to have anesthesia at least two dermatomes higher than the major innervation of the area in which the surgery is performed. Occasionally, even in the best of hands, a high spinal will occur, necessitating sedation of the patient and control of the airway. As higher and higher thoracic segments are involved, the resultant vasodilatation and hypotension become more pronounced and declines in blood pressure will be more prominent. Blood pressure can usually be controlled easily with the administration of fluids and, if necessary, the use of vasoconstricting drugs such as ephedrine.

Most contraindications to the use of spinal anesthesia are relative rather than absolute and depend upon varying factors. The performance of the lumbar puncture itself is one such factor. Any condition in which a lumbar puncture is contraindicated, as where increased intracranial pressure is present or infection in the area through which lumbar puncture must be performed is present, also contraindicates the use of spinal anesthesia. Systemic infections may also be considered a relative contraindication to spinal anesthesia. Other factors are related to the administration of the local anesthetic itself, such as spinal cord and peripheral nerve disease, particularly if the disease is characterized by exacerbations and remissions as in multiple sclerosis. Exacerbation of the underlying disease may accompany the use of local anesthetics in the subarachnoid space. Congenital anomalies of the spine or abnormal spinal anatomy may make the spread and distribution of anesthetics patchy or unreliable. Still other contraindications relate to the circulatory effects of sympathetic nerve paralysis. Hypovolemia, shock, or hypotension may all be worsened by the vasodilatation accompanying spinal anesthesia. Patients with aortic stenosis may not tolerate the loss of filling pressure. Although most of these problems may be overcome with the liberal use of intravenous fluids, caution should be exercised under these circumstances.

Psychological factors should also be considered since patient cooperation is necessary for the administration of spinal anesthesia. An uncooperative or unwilling patient or a mentally retarded patient is probably not a suitable candidate for a spinal anesthetic. The anesthesiologist can anticipate most of the complications of spinal anesthesia from knowledge of the technique itself and familiarity with the circulatory and reflex effects that accompany it.

Headaches following the lumbar puncture depend upon the amount of cerebrospinal fluid lost during and following the procedure. The degree of loss of cerebrospinal fluid is related to several other factors, including the sex and age of the patient. Post-spinal headaches are generally more frequent in females, particularly in the gravid female who is undergoing a delivery. There are rapid changes in fluids during delivery and there may be an accompanying dehydration. Further loss of cerebrospinal fluid may occur under the stress of delivery. In general, older patients suffer the lowest incidence of spinal headaches.

The incidence of spinal headaches is also related to the size of the needle used to perform the lumbar puncture and the number of punctures that are required. The larger the needle used, the larger the hole made in the dura will be, which relates directly to the amount of loss of cerebrospinal fluid. The relationship of the bevel of the needle to the longitudal fibers of the dura mater is also important. If the dural fibers are spread apart by the needle rather than lacerated by the needle, less cerebrospinal fluid will be lost. If multiple lumbar punctures are necessary for the induction of satisfactory spinal anesthesia, spinal headaches are more likely. A variety of methods have been employed to treat post-spinal headaches, particularly in the situation of the inadvertent dural puncture by the large needles used for epidural anesthesia.

There seems to be a general public awareness of the possibility of neurological complications following spinal anesthesia. The lay press has devoted a great deal of attention to this problem, and many patients are reluctant to undergo spinal anesthesia because of the fear of paralysis. The incidence of neurological sequelae following spinal anesthesia is actually quite low, however, and there is considerable evidence that there is less morbidity and mortality with spinal anesthesia than with general anesthesia. In fact, many of the minor problems associated with spinal anesthesia also accompany the use of general anesthesia, e.g., backaches in the postoperative period related to the positioning on the table, the incidence of hypotension, and the risk of increasing intraluminal pressures with obstructive ileus. Nonetheless, a low incidence of neurological complications following spinal anesthesia remains. The cause of this damage is often an idiosyncratic reaction of the patient to the local anesthetic used or direct neurotoxic effect of the anesthetic drugs. If the wrong solution is injected intravenously or if the improper concentration or dose of drug is used, then the risk of neurological damage is enhanced. Improper techniques of injection may also result in neural damage.

Although paresthesia is not uncommon and should not be misconstrued to represent negligent technique, care should be taken to deal with the problem adequately when it arises. Although the occurrence of paresthesia has not been held to constitute negligence in any reported case, it is often seen as a precursor to more serious injury.[8]

CASE ILLUSTRATION

The patient entered the hospital for a hysterectomy and, on the evening prior to the operation, she was visited by the anesthesiologist. The two agreed to a spinal anesthesia.

The patient was drowsy from preoperative medication when she arrived at the operating room and was first placed on the operating table in a sitting position with her legs straight out, then held in a position which required her to lean over keeping her head very low. When the needle was first inserted at the L-2—L-3 interspace, she felt a pain down her leg; her leg jerked; and she said, "Oh." The anesthesiologist said, "sit still," and soon thereafter the patient felt another pain and remarked to the anesthesiologist that, "something's wrong, my legs aren't going to sleep." The anesthesiologist then said, "Well, maybe we had better remove the needle" and reinserted it at the L-3—L-4 interspace. About two tenths of a cubic centimeter of anesthetic solution was injected through the needle at the place of its initial insertion before the needle was reinserted at the lower interspace.

The patient sustained paralysis on the left side with total anesthesia to pain as well as temperature and a problem with control of bladder and bowels. The patient sued the anesthesiologist and alleged that he was negligent in proceeding with the injection after she experienced pain down her leg rather than removing the needle and repositioning it before injection. She claimed he was also negligent in not heeding the warning of the first pain, but waiting until she cried out a second time before repositioning the needle.

The patient's nerves which were adversely effected were at L-5, L-4, S-1, and S-2. An expert testified that there was no possible way to "injure four nerves on one side without an injection into the substance of the conus." Other evidence was introduced that 1.8 percent of the population, or one in every 55 persons, has a low-lying conus medullaris which extends down to the L-2—L-3 interspace. The court noted that the evidence presented established a possibility of nerve damage from a spinal injection; however, expert testimony offered at trial supported a finding that the anesthesiologist was not negligent.* (*Funke v. Fieldman*, 1973)[9]

---

*The court also stated that the anesthesiologist in this case could be held liable for failure to obtain the patient's informed consent based on certain facts not discussed above and ordered a new trial. For a

Where adequate care is not taken to deal with paresthesia, the courts have held the anesthesiologist liable.

CASE ILLUSTRATION

The patient entered the hospital for a hemorrhoidectomy. In preparation for surgery, the anesthesiologist injected a local anesthetic, then located the interspace between the third and fourth lumbar vertebrae by feeling and inserted the spinal needle at that level. When the needle punctured the dura and entered the spinal canal, the patient gave out a cry of intense pain and complained that his left leg felt like it had been subjected to a severe electrical shock. Rather than pull back on the needle for subsequent reinsertion, the anesthesiologist gave the patient an injection of nembutal intravenously, made an attempt to attain a free flow of cerebrospinal fluid to determine whether the needle was properly positioned, and proceeded to administer Pontocaine as the anesthesia.

The patient regained consciousness soon after returning to his room after the operation and immediately complained of intense pain. There was no complaint regarding the hemorrhoidectomy which was successful. The patient suffered lesions of the L-5 and S-1 nerve roots, and possibly two others.

The patient brought suit. In addition to other relevant testimony, six medical experts offered the following diagnoses of the patient's condition:

1. A neuritis of the fifth lumbar and first sacral roots as a result of a chemical injection into a root
2. A traumatic neuropathy, meaning an injury to the left fifth lumbar and first sacral nerve root secondary to a spinal anesthetic
3. A mild mechanical injury to the first sacral nerve on the left side causing abnormal function and sensations termed paresthesia
4. Radiculitis, meaning nerve root inflammation; or causalgia, meaning injury to a peripheral nerve; or arachnoiditis, meaning inflammation of the arachnoid. (Causalgia was ruled out by the performance of a sympathetic nerve block.)
5. Radiculitis involving S-1 and L-5 regions on the left without clinical motor involvement
6. Nerve pressure syndrome or nerve root syndrome in the left extremity; a denervation causing a muscular abnormality

---

Continued
discussion of the informed consent issues presented by this case, see § 1.33, Consent and Informed Consent.

The court evaluated the expert testimony as follows:

> The expert medical testimony clearly preponderates in support of the conclusion that there was a causal relation between the administration of the spinal anesthetic and the residual symptoms. It is agreed by all of them that it is not unusual that a nerve root might be struck by the spinal needle and that when this occurs the patient will give an outcry or otherwise evidence severe pain as though subjected to an electric shock. When this occurs the physician should pull back on the needle which will relieve the pain, and then reposition the needle. It is a cardinal rule that the patient must be free from pain, thus indicating that the needle is not pressing against the nerve root, before proceeding with the injection of the anesthetizing solution. They all agree that the injection is never knowingly made into a nerve root.

The court further observed that although the anesthesiologist testified that he had observed all proper procedures (such as obtaining a free flow of CSF after insertion of the needle), the evidence did not support a conclusion that he had not determined the patient was not in pain when the injection was made, as it was his professional duty to do. Rather, the fact that Nembutal was injected, which rendered the patient unconscious immediately, was construed as proof that the anesthesiologist had made a negligent assumption that the cause of pain had been relieved. The court ultimately held that a permanent injury did result and that the anesthesiologist's conduct did not follow prescribed procedures; he was thus held liable for the patient's injury. (*Herbert v. Travelers Indemnity Co.*, 1970)[10]

The presence of a paresthesia indicates a proximity of the needle to a nerve root, and several steps can be taken to minimize the potential risk to the patient under these circumstances. Repositioning of the needle, four-quadrant rotation of the needle to assure free flow of cerebrospinal fluid, or transfer to another interspace may all minimize the attendant risks. It is important to document on the anesthetic record the occurrence of paresthesias, where the paresthesias are located, and what steps were taken to assure that intermedullary injection of local anesthetic was avoided.

Despite all precautions, adequate preparation of the patient, and appropriate attention to detail in the administration of spinal anesthesia, there is still a low risk of neurological damage. Consequently, it is unwise to tell patients that there is no risk of paralysis following spinal anesthesia. The best that might be said is that the risk is exceedingly low, and that for the individual patient spinal anesthetic might be preferred. However, it is equally unwise to downplay the risk. In one case, an anesthesiologist was held liable for failure to obtain the informed consent to spinal anesthesia of a patient who suffered paralysis in her lower body, after he told her that the only risk of a spinal was a headache.[11]

§ 11.10 Spinal Anesthesia 299

Most of the cases arising from the injuries resulting after spinal anesthesia have involved some degree of paralysis. The key to the anesthesiologist's liability lies within the facts of each case. Generally, where the patient's resulting condition more closely approximates arachnoiditis or some other reaction to the anesthetic used, the anesthesiologist has not been held liable. However, where the patient provides sufficiently persuasive expert testimony that his or her injury is due to a lesion in the spinal cord or some other damage precipitated by needle puncture, the anesthesiologist may be held liable.

CASE ILLUSTRATION

The patient was admitted to the hospital for delivery and her child was born the following morning. She was given a spinal anesthetic, and when the needle was inserted, she felt a shock and sharp pains down both legs to her toes. Hours after delivery she came to feel a heavy sensation in both legs and was unable to use them. The following day she had no control over her legs, lower back, bladder and bowels. The patient brought suit. Based on expert testimony offered at trial, the court concluded that the patient suffered from cauda equina syndrome which, in that patient, under the facts, could have only resulted from either (a) chemical trauma from a contaminant in the anesthetic; or (b) an idiosyncrasy or natural sensitivity to the drug. Other evidence ruled out the first possibility and the court held that because the patient's injuries were caused by her own hypersensitivity to the anesthetic, a factor which could not be predetermined, the anesthesiologist could not be held liable. (*Hall v. United States*, 1955)[12]

The following case differs from the one outlined above in two respects: (1) it is a more recent case (1972 as opposed to 1955); and (2) the medical procedure was a hysterectomy rather than a delivery. Otherwise, these two decisions are difficult to distinguish. From the court's opinion it can be inferred that the court was impressed with expert testimony by the anesthesiologist's expert to the effect that arachnoiditis is a slow process which results from the build-up of scar tissue around nerve roots and does not manifest itself abruptly.

CASE ILLUSTRATION

The patient entered the hospital for a hysterectomy and agreed, after discussion with her anesthesiologist, to undergo spinal anesthesia in lieu of a general anesthetic. When she was brought into the operating room, she was instructed to lie on her left side, after which she was placed in a "boiled shrimp position" with her spinal column forming a convex curve. The anesthesiologist inserted a 20 gauge needle into her back at which point the patient experienced pain. The anesthesiologist withdrew the needle, which he later insisted at trial was initially inserted in the L_2–L_3 interspace, and reinserted it at the L_3–L_4 interspace. The anesthetic was administered and the operation performed. The patient experienced initial pain and eventual paralysis in her left leg. The patient brought suit. At trial, expert testimony offered by the patient attributed this to a lesion of the lower end of her spinal cord as a result of the needle puncture made to administer anesthesia. The anesthesiologist offered expert testimony that such an injury could result from arachnoiditis, a condition over which the anesthesiologist had no control. Another expert, also testifying for the anesthesiologist, stated that he felt that the patient's condition was arachnoiditis but that he could not determine how, when or why the condition developed. He characterized the condition as a gradual process resulting from scar tissue accumulation around nerve roots. He agreed that the condition could not have pre-existed the operation and that the spinal injection could have precipitated it. The finding of the trial court that a negligent puncture by the anesthesiologist caused the patient's injury was upheld on appeal. *(Buras v. Aetna Casualty and Surety Company,* 1972)[13]

Finally, liability will be imposed on the anesthesiologist where spinal anesthesia is inadequate or incomplete for the operation performed on the patient.

CASE ILLUSTRATION

The patient had a severe trimalleolar fracture of the right ankle; general anesthesia was not administered because the patient had eaten before she injured her ankle. The anesthesiologist presumed the operation would take about two hours; he later testified that had the surgeon informed him that the operation might take longer, he could have added epinephrine to the anesthetic to prolong its duration of action. After about two hours, when it became apparent that the effects of the anesthetic were wearing off, the surgeon decided to halt the operation before be had completed reduction of the third fracture. He did not communicate the need to prolong the anesthesia to the anesthesiologist or ask him whether it was possible to prolong anesthesia. The patient suffered from osteoarthritis in the ankle joint and brought suit to recover for this injury. According to expert testimony, the osteoarthritis might have resulted from the fracture anyway, but the chance of its development was increased by the failure to complete the reduction.

The anesthesiologist was held liable for choosing spinal anesthesia

§ 11.20 *Epidural and Caudal Anesthesia* 301

under the circumstances, although merely using spinal, rather than general, anesthesia was not negligent by itself. The surgeon was held liable for failing to advise the anesthesiologist of the need for an anesthetic of longer duration and for deciding to terminate the operation without communicating with the anesthesiologist about the possibility of prolonged anesthesia. *(Clark v. Gibbons,* 1967)[14]

In summary, spinal anesthesia offers several advantages over general anesthesia in certain patients. The overall incidence of morbidity and mortality is less with spinal than with general anesthetic and there are relatively few contraindications for the use of spinal anesthesia. Nonetheless, misconceptions still exist about the overall safety of spinal anesthetics and the potential for litigation remains high. Several steps may be employed by the anesthesiologist to minimize the chance of litigation. Procedures as well as the advantages and disadvantages of any alternative type of anesthesia should be explained in full to the patient in the preoperative period. Diagrams may be used to explain spinal anesthesia; these diagrams should be preserved in the chart or on the back of the anesthetic record as part of the permanent medical record. It should be explained that although the risk of permanent nerve damage from a spinal anesthetic is exceedingly low, it can occur. The site of injection and details of administration of the anesthetic should be recorded on the anesthetic record as well as the level of anesthesia obtained. If paresthesias are elicited, subsequent developments should be dealt with properly and recorded accurately and completely. Following these steps can greatly minimize the potential for litigation in cases involving a spinal anesthetic.

§ 11.20 EPIDURAL (AND CAUDAL) ANESTHESIA

Legal liability will be imposed on the anesthesiologist where due care is not exercised in the administration of the anesthesia or where the anesthesiologist fails to disclose the risks of epidural or caudal anesthesia or otherwise misrepresents the patient's prognosis. However, liability will not be imposed soley for a bad result where the anesthesiologist can show that injury occurred due to some cause other than his or her own negligence.

Epidural anesthesia is accomplished by blocking spinal nerves in the epidural space as they emerge from the dura and pass into the intervertebral foramina. Anesthetic solution is deposited outside the dura rather than in the subarachnoid space, as with spinal or subdural anesthesia. The result is a segmental block chiefly of spinal sensory and sympathetic nerve fibers. A partial block of motor fibers may also be produced.[15]

Medical commentators[16] have offered the following recommendations for safe epidural or caudal technique:

1. Scrub hands according to aseptic surgical technique.
2. Use sterile gloves.
3. Avoid contaminating blocking solutions with solutions used to prepare the skin.
4. Use aseptic technique when opening tray.
5. Cleanse the skin prior to needle puncture.
6. Touch only sterile articles once gloved.
7. Avoid repeated traumatic punctures.
8. Do not do an epidural puncture if patient's bleeding time is increased.
9. Avoid epidural blocks in patients with bacteremia.
10. Never insert a needle through an infected area.
11. Use approved local anesthetic agents in standard concentrations.

Interpretation and Customary Practice: The use of epidural anesthesia is becoming more and more popular, particularly in obstetrical anesthesia. Although epidural anesthesia is more difficult technically than spinal anesthesia, a longer duration of action can be obtained and the area of anesthesia can be better controlled and defined. By avoiding lumbar puncture, headaches, meningitis and arachnoiditis are minimized.

Certain risks and contraindications are associated with epidural anesthesia. Blockade of the thoracolumbar sympathetic outflow tracts and laceration of epidural venus plexus may result. Relative contraindications to the use of epidural anesthesia include shock or hypovolemia, and the presence of infection or inflammation in the area in which the epidural will be administered. Patients with coagulation defects are not suitable candidates for epidural anesthesia. A previous laminectomy may obliterate the epidural space and make accurate localization of the needle impossible. Situations in which lumbar puncture is contraindicated, such as an increase in intracranial pressure, probably also contraindicate the use of epidural anesthesia, since inadvertent dural puncture can occur. Because large doses of local anesthetic solutions are employed for epidural anesthesia, an unrecognized inadvertent dural puncture can lead to the total spinal and all its inherent complications.

In general, the risk of neurological sequelae following epidural anesthesia is less than that for spinal anesthesia. Nonetheless, direct trauma from the needle or catheter or reactions to local anesthetics (especially 2-chloroprocaine) may result in prolonged paralysis.[17] The same considerations as discussed previously for spinal anesthesia apply to epidural anesthesia.

§ 11.20   *Epidural and Caudal Anesthesia*   303

A 1967 Washington decision involving epidural anesthesia demonstrates that a physician may expose himself to legal liability if he or she fails to reveal the severity of the patient's prognosis to the patient when the prognosis is known to the physician.

CASE ILLUSTRATION

The patient was paralyzed in both legs after receiving epidural anesthesia prior to an appendectomy. The surgeon was aware of the permanent nature of the patient's paralysis but failed to discuss the results and implications of the neurologic findings and the EMG. The patient, believing his disability would not exceed one year, initiated settlement talks with the hospital's insurance agents and suggested one year's wages as an amount of settlement in exchange for signing a release. The surgeon was held liable for breaching his duty to inform the patient of his prognosis, when such failure to inform led the patient to act to his detriment. *(Lockett v. Goodill,* 1967)[18]

This case suggests that the physician's duty to inform the patient extends beyond the treatment period. The issue the court dealt with involved the physician's breach of the fiduciary duty owed the patient rather than the breach of the duty of skill and care. Although the initial injury may have been caused by the latter, liability in this case was imposed because of the former. (See § 1.31, Physician-Patient Relationship.) Another case, involving the administration of epidural anesthesia to facilitate obstetrical procedures considers both of these duties.

CASE ILLUSTRATION

One day after the patient entered the hospital for the delivery of her child, labor was induced, her contractions subsequently became regular and she went into "good" labor. Her obstetrician requested an epidural or caudal anesthetic and the anesthesiologist was called by the nurse on duty in the labor room to administer it. When the anesthesiologist entered the labor room, he identified himself and told the patient he had been notified that she desired an epidural. He said something to the effect that "I understand you're ready for an anesthetic" or "would you like to have one now." The patient responded affirmatively and he described the procedure to her. She would be put on her side, a local would be injected in her back, then a needle would be inserted, the anesthetic would be injected, and she should expect to become numb from the waist down. He also told her that with any kind of anesthetic there was some risk involved, but that the risk of serious complication was one in a thousand. He asked if she had any questions and she did not. The patient was in much discomfort at that time and was anxious to receive an anesthetic. The anesthesiologist determined that the patient understood the nature of his questions and there was no impairment of her ability to consent to the anesthetic.

Shortly after the anesthesia was administered the patient started to show signs of difficulty in breathing and her blood pressure dropped. The patient became cyanotic and went into cardiac arrest which lasted for less than a minute. In response to the drop in blood pressure, the anesthesiologist administered the drug Ephedrine through an intravenous device set up and placed in the operating room prior to the administration of the anesthetic. To assist the patient in breathing he first used an oxygen mask and then an ambu-bag until the patient was able to resume breathing on her own. The fetus was born subsequently without further complications.

The patient sued the anesthesiologist alleging that he negligently failed to obtain her informed consent to the epidural anesthesia and, in conjunction with the hospital's negligent failure to have necessary emergency equipment on hand, negligently failed to adequately deal with the emergency.

With respect to the consent issue, the court noted that consent to medical treatment may be oral or written. Under the facts, the patient's consent was adequate to protect the anesthesiologist from liability. The patient claimed she had no memory of the exchange between herself and the anesthesiologist regarding consent. The court noted that the patient had not presented any evidence that she had suffered any brain damage or that the anesthesiologist's treatment caused an impairment of memory. Without an explanation as to why the patient could not remember the consent conversation, the allegation could not overcome the strength of hospital records and testimony that it had taken place. Consequently, the court held for the anesthesiologist on the consent issue.

With respect to negligence, the court was persuaded by expert testimony offered on behalf of the anesthesiologist which concluded that the actions of the anesthesiologist and the hospital were in full accord with proper procedures for treatment of such emergencies. The patient failed to offer any testimony to refute this analysis. The court held in favor of the anesthesiologist and the hospital on all issues. (*Patterson v. Van Wiel*, 1977)[19]

Caudal anesthesia is a type of epidural anesthesia of the lumbar and sacral nerves which is accomplished by placing the anesthetic agent in the epidural space via the caudal canal.[20] Like saddle block, this type of anesthesia is most often used in obstetrics.

Complications that may arise from caudal anesthesia include systemic reactions to the local anesthetic and, in obstetrics, high levels of anesthesia with arterial hypotension and interference with the forces of labor. Infection has also been noted as a serious delayed complication.[21]

When complications result, the courts do recognize that the physician does not warrant that his treatment of the patient will be successful. Where a bad result occurs and the physician can show that it did not occur due to any negligence on his part but due to some recognized risk, liability will not be imposed.

CASE ILLUSTRATION

Caudal anesthesia was administered to the patient to prepare him for hemorrhoidectomy. Xylocaine, the anesthetic agent used, was taken from a tray holding a container of uncolored alcohol. The anesthesiologist had to combine two different containers of xylocaine before he injected the anesthetic. After the operation, the patient was paralyzed from the waist down and brought suit to recover for his injury. The patient alleged that the anesthesiologist had been negligent in injecting alcohol into the epidural space and in keeping uncolored alcohol on the same tray with the uncolored, and therefore indistinguishable, xylocaine. Consequently, the patient suggested that the anesthesiologist had accidentally added the alcohol to the xylocaine in the mixing process.

The defendant anesthesiologist and the nurse who had observed him testified that the defendant had not injected alcohol. The anesthesiologist's defense was that the paralysis was the result of thrombosis, and that it was customary in that community to have uncolored alcohol and xylocaine on the same tray. The upper court did not disturb the jury's verdict that the defendant had not injected the patient with alcohol. Consequently, the physician was found not liable. (*Oberlin v. Friedman*, 1965)[22]

§ 11.30 REGIONAL NERVE BLOCKS

Injury resulting from regional nerve block anesthesia is usually of such a minor nature that patients are unsuccessful under legal theories of negligence, informed consent and res ipsa loquitur. However, lawsuit may possibly be avoided completely by obtaining a fully documented informed consent after disclosing all possible risks to the patient.

For certain procedures, it is possible to avoid the greater risks of general anesthesia by anesthetizing only a region of the body. This is achieved by injecting the anesthetic around that portion of the nervous system which carries pain impulses from the operative site. The patient remains conscious and the risks of general anesthesia, including cardiovascular and pulmonary complications, are decreased.

Various authorities[23] prescribe the following recommendations for safe regional and local (infiltration) anesthesia technique:

1. Scrub hands according to aseptic surgical technique.
2. Use sterile gloves.
3. Avoid contaminating blocking solutions with solutions used to prepare the skin.
4. Use aseptic technique when opening tray.
5. Cleanse the skin prior to needle puncture.
6. Touch only sterile articles once gloved.
7. Avoid repeated traumatic punctures.
8. Never insert a needle through an infected area.
9. Use approved local anesthetic agents in standard concentrations.

Interpretation and Customary Practice: Regional nerve blocks are becoming more and more important to the practicing anesthesiologist, not only for patients at high risk from general anesthetics, but also in the treatment and diagnosis of chronic pain syndromes. Although there are a great many types of regional nerve blocks, the general principle is the same for each specific nerve considered: a quantity of local anesthetic solution is injected into the fascial plane through which the affected nerve runs.

Among the more commonly used types of nerve blocks is the brachial plexus block, an extremely useful technique for surgery involving the upper extremity. There are several approaches to the brachial plexus and the incidence of specific complications depends on the type of approach used as well as the skill of the anesthesiologist. Among the complications of brachial plexus block are pneumothorax, injection into a major vessel, or injection of a nerve trunk.[24]

Patients have generally been unsuccessful in suits brought to recover for injuries resulting from regional nerve block anesthetics. The following case illustration is an example of the axillary approach to brachial plexus block. Using this approach, the correct position of the needle can be identified by one of two techniques: either purposeful puncture of the axillary artery or by the elicitation of paresthesias. In the following case, it would appear that paresthesias were elicited, and damage to the axillary nerve occurred either from intramedullary or perineural injection of local anesthetic.

§ 11.30   Regional Nerve Blocks   307

CASE ILLUSTRATION

The patient entered the hospital to have a tumor removed from his right hand. The anesthesiologist administered a brachial block anesthetic by a hypodermic injection into the brachial plexus area of the patient's right shoulder. The patient felt two sharp pains when the anesthetic was administered and then lost consciousness. After the operation the patient's shoulder was numb; and after the numbness wore off, he had a severe pain in his shoulder that lasted six weeks. The patient brought suit, and at the time of trial, three years after the operation, he had not regained the full use of his arm. He had suffered a partial loss of the axillary nerve supply to the deltoid muscle. The patient was never advised of possible complications inherent in the administration of the anesthetic, nor were possible alternatives ever discussed with him. The patient sued the anesthesiologist on two theories, lack of informed consent (see § 1.33, Consent and Informed Consent) and res ipsa loquitur (see § 1.52, Res Ipsa Loquitur).

The court held, with respect to informed consent, that the evidence established that injuries such as those the patient suffered occurred so infrequently that they could not be considered a material risk. Thus, under the informed consent rule adhered to by the court, there could be no liability for failure to disclose an immaterial risk. With regard to res ipsa loquitur, evidence was submitted that the injury could have been caused at multiple points during the operative procedure, and the patient failed to establish the likelihood that his injury was not caused by such things as anatomic variation, pre-existing disease or positioning of the arm. The court held the anesthesiologist not liable. *(Martin v. Stratton,* 1973)[25]

While the result in this case was favorable to the anesthesiologist, there is no guarantee the result may not be otherwise in future cases with similar facts. Although the opinion does not so state, the court may have been influenced by the relatively minor nature of the injury sustained. The possibility that such an injury can occur is ever present in this anesthetic technique, and a patient's consent, obtained after all risks have been disclosed, should be sought on a routine basis.

In another case involving another type of injury resulting from a brachial plexus block, the informed consent theory again failed to impose liability.

CASE ILLUSTRATION

The patient's right hand was severely lacerated by the fan of his car. His physician advised an operation. Brachial block anesthesia was administered by inserting the needle at the base of the neck, near the collarbone, and injecting into the brachial complex of nerves, during which the needle used punctured the patient's right lung, causing a partial deflation or pneumothorax. At the trial, the patient alleged that the anesthesiologist had been negligent in administering the brachial block and had done so without the patient's informed consent. Because the expert testimony offered at trial failed to prove the anesthesiologist administered the brachial block negligently in any regard, the court held that the anesthesiologist had not been negligent. As to the informed consent issue, the court referred to evidence admitted at the trial that the chance of a pneumothorax resulting from such a procedure is about one percent and implied that the anesthesiologist need not inform of so small a risk. Additionally, the court stated that the medical testimony established that a pneumothorax is not, when properly treated, a serious injury or one that results in any damage to the affected lung. The court held for the anesthesiologist. *(Napier v. Northrum,* 1978)[26]

§ 11.40 INFILTRATION (LOCAL) ANESTHESIA

Liability for injury resulting from local anesthesia will most likely be imposed where local anesthesia is administered to a hypertensive patient without first determining that the patient is hypertensive or without monitoring the patient's blood pressure in conjunction with anesthetic administration. Where injury results from an allergic reaction, liability will not be imposed.

The term local anesthesia refers to either topical or infiltrative anesthesia or surgical field block. Although local anesthetics are employed by anesthesiologists for regional nerve blocks or conduction anesthesia, the use of local anesthetics for field block is usually done by the surgeon. In fact, unless anesthesiology standby is requested by the surgeon, the presence of an anesthesiologist is not usually considered necessary for the performance of local anesthesia in this context.

Epinephrine is often included in the local anesthetic solution because its vasoconstricting action limits absorption and thereby prolongs the duration of action of the local anesthetic. The vasoconstrictor activity of epinephrine also limits its own absorption into the circulation.[27] Advantage can be taken of this property to minimize blood loss in the surgical field. This is of particular importance in highly vascular areas such as the face and for plastic surgery procedures.

Several complications may arise from the use of local anesthetics with or without epinephrine. Allergic reactions to local anesthetics may occur, but are exceedingly rare. More commonly, the reactions experienced stem from systemic absorption of the local anesthetics and are predictable from the pharmacology of these agents. Inadvertent intravascular injection can lead to the rapid development of toxic reactions from the local anesthetic, or the epinephrine.[28]

CASE ILLUSTRATION

A dentist administered a local anesthetic containing epinephrine to a patient with a history of high blood pressure; the dentist had not obtained this history before administering the anesthetic. The patient died of a stroke (probably an intracerebral hemorrhage) and her widower brought suit.

The dentist had made no record in the chart regarding the patient's medical history, and he could not recall specifically asking the patient about her past medical history. He testified that he usually asked patients about their "general health," and he "guessed" that he had asked this patient about her general health and that since there was no notation on the chart, she probably had not said anything about high blood pressure. He testified that if he had known of this history, he would have contacted her physician; he also testified that he was not aware that xylocaine with epinephrine was contraindicated in hypertensive patients. However, a brochure, prepared by the drug manufacturer which accompanies each container of xylocaine, stated that xylocaine without epinephrine is adequate in those cases where vasopresser drugs are contraindicated.

The court stated that although the information contained in the drug manufacturer's brochure could not be used to set the standard of care for the dentist, the court recognized that it could be used as evidence that the dentist was, or should have been, warned of the possibility of a stroke in hypertensive patients who receive epinephrine.

The court ordered the case retried, stating that the plaintiff had presented facts adequate to support a cause of action for negligence based on the dentist's failure to determine the patient's medical history. *(Sanzari v. Rosenfeld, 1961)*[29]

Inquiring into the patient's past medical history alone may not be sufficient. In the following case it was established that the physician also has a duty to measure the patient's blood pressure prior to administration of epinephrine, even if the patient has no history of diagnosed hypertension.

CASE ILLUSTRATION

The patient came to an oral surgeon with an impacted wisdom tooth; he had had severe headaches for several days prior to the operation as well as on the day of the operation. There was no indication of a history of hypertension in the written medical questionnaire filled out by the patient, and the patient told the dentist that he was in good health. (The patient's age is not mentioned in the opinion.) The oral surgeon did not measure the patient's blood pressure prior to injecting xylocaine with epinephrine. After the operation, the patient had fever and chills and was disoriented and unresponsive; he was vomiting as he was helped into his car by his wife and the oral surgeon. A subarachnoid hemorrhage was diagnosed the following day. The patient sued, alleging that the oral surgeon had been negligent in failing to measure his patient's blood pressure, failing to disclose the risk of local anesthesia with a vasoconstrictor, failing to observe and treat the patient properly after surgery, and discharging a patient who was getting worse, not better.

A physician testifying as an expert for the patient believed that he probably had hypertension at the time of the operation; the patient's attending physician testified that he could not be sure about the cause of the subarachnoid hemorrhage but could only speculate about whether it was caused by hypertension. An oral surgeon called by the patient testified that the preanesthetic history was not adequate because the dentist had failed to determine whether the patient had hypertension. The court noted that the oral surgeon's history would pick up only patients with previously diagnosed high blood pressure or cardiovascular disease who were under a doctor's care. The court also said that a physician has a duty to disclose the risk of the proposed procedure, alternative procedures and their risks, and the risk of no treatment to the patient, so that the patient can choose his therapy. (The opinion also does not mention what the patient's blood pressure was in the hospital after the stroke.) *(LeBeuf v. Atkins, 1979)*[30]

These cases suggest that a health care professional, who fails to discover hypertension on history or physical exam, will be liable if the patient develops a stroke or other complication of epinephrine with a local anesthetic.

The first case creates the impression that a standard of care has been established that contraindicates the use of local anesthetics with epinephrine in hypertensive patients. However, there are many patients who are hypertensive who could benefit medically from infiltration of local anesthetics with epinephrine. In the second case, there was no history of hypertension. The patients in both cases suffered neurological sequelae from cerebrovascular disease. Thus, a history of hypertension or the lack thereof may be of no consequence because patients who are healthy and without hypertension can develop significant hypertension following intravascular injection of epinephrine. Thus, the logical assumption to be made from these cases is that if this technique is employed, it should be done with great

§ 11.40 *Infiltration Anesthesia* 311

care to avoid intravascular injection and blood pressure should be monitored before and after injection.

In the usual anesthetic practice, the use of local anesthetics with epinephrine may also be a potential problem under general anesthesia. If volatile gas anesthetics are being used, such as halothane, the sensitization of the myocardium to the effects of circulating catecholamines may be significant enough that the choice of epinephrine should be carefully weighed prior to the administration. In the absence of an intravascular injection, however, the absorption of epinephrine and local anesthetics is sufficiently slow so that this will usually not be a major problem.

Physicians are less likely to be liable for allergic reactions to local anesthetics, since these reactions are generally more difficult to detect and, thus, less preventable.

CASE ILLUSTRATION

Prior to a cystoscopy for evaluation of hematuria, an anesthetist (a paramedic) administered pyribenzamine, an antihistamine which is sometimes used as a local anesthetic. After injection of 1-1/2 cc., the patient developed sharp pain and then blanching of the skin near the urethral meatus. The anesthetist ceased the injection and the procedure was cancelled by the urologist. The patient brought suit and the court ultimately held in favor of the defendants because the defendants had no control over the condition and allergic reaction of the patient. The injury was not the type that ordinarily occurs only with negligence. Common experience suggests no strong inherent probability of negligence in this fact situation. *(Mogenson v. Hicks,* 1961)[31]

NOTES

1. Adriani, Labat's Regional Anesthesia 332-34 (1967); D. Moore, Complications of Regional Anesthesia 208 (1955)
2. V. Collins, Principles of Anesthesiology 637 (2d ed. 1976).
3. *Id.*
4. *Id.* at 664-65, 670, 683-84.
5. Mayor v. Dowsett, 400 P.2d 234 (Or. 1965).
6. V. Collins, *supra* note 2, at 657.
7. *Id.* at 648.
8. *See, e.g.,* Ayers v. Parry, 192 F.2d 181 (3d Cir. 1951), *cert. denied,* 343 U.S. 980 (1952); Buras v. Aetna Cas. & Sur. Co., 263 So.2d 375 (La. App. 1972).
9. Funke v. Fieldman, 212 Kan. 524, 512 P.2d 539 (1978).
10. Herbert v. Travelers Indem. Co., 239 So.2d 367 (La. App. 1970).
11. Funke v. Fieldman, *supra* note 9.
12. Hall v. United States, 136 F. Supp. 187 (W.D. La. 1955).

13. Buras v. Aetna Cas. & Sur. Co., *supra* note 8.
14. Clark v. Gibbons, 66 Cal. 2d 399, 426 P.2d 525, 58 Cal. Rptr. 125 (1967).
15. V. Collins, *supra* note 2, at 698.
16. J. Adriani, *supra* note 1, at 332-34; D. Moore, *supra* note 1, at 208.
17. V. Collins, *supra* note 2, at 711-12.
18. Lockett v. Goodill, 71 Wash. 2d 654, 430 P.2d 589 (1967).
19. Patterson v. Van Wiel, 91 N.M. 100, 570 P.2d 931 (1977).
20. V. Collins, *supra* note 2, at 699.
21. R. Dripps, J. Eckenhoff & L. Vandam, Introduction to Anesthesia 286 (5th ed. 1977).
22. Oberlin v. Freidman, 5 Ohio St. 2d 1, 213 N.E.2d 168 (1965).
23. J. Adriani, *supra* note 1, at 332-34; D. Moore, *supra* note 1, at 208.
24. Bridenbaugh, *Complications of Regional Anesthesia,* in ASA Annual Refresher Course Lectures 222 (1980); V. Collins, *supra* note 2, at 959-61.
25. Martin v. Stratton, 515 P.2d 1366 (Okla. 1973).
26. Napier v. Northrum, 264 Ark. 406, 572 S.W.2d 153 (1978).
27. V. Collins, *supra* note 2, at 888-90.
28. *Id.* at 637.
29. Sanzari v. Rosenfeld, 34 N.J. 128, 167 A.2d 625 (1961).
30. LeBeuf v. Atkins, 22 Wash. App. 877, 594 P.2d 923 (1979), *rev'd on other grounds,* 93 Wash. 2d 34, 604 P.2d 1287 (1980).
31. Mogenson v. Hicks, 253 Iowa 139, 110 N.W.2d 563 (1961).

Chapter XII

Anesthesia Mishaps

§ 12.10 HUMAN ERROR AND PREVENTABILITY

Despite the fact that the risk associated with anesthesia is considered to be low, injuries do result. It is clear that injuries are not the result of intentional misconduct; most are attributable to human error. Because such error is denominated "human," it is thought to be preventable. This perspective is inherent in the law and perhaps, more than any other factor, accounts for the resentment many physicians feel when faced with a malpractice lawsuit. Physicians may conclude that the law does not allow them to be an imperfect human, an impossible expectation to fulfill. Actually, the law is concerned primarily with compensating the injured rather than pointing the finger of blame. In order to provide compensation, it is unavoidable that the party most clearly responsible, despite that party's intent, be identified.

With respect to anesthesia mishaps, a superficial assessment leads to the conclusion that their root cause is lack of vigilance. Vigilance has been found to decrease with time and with the level of mental or physical energy required.[1] This general conclusion may be further explicated by a review of recent studies conducted to explore the etiology of anesthesia mishaps. Preventable human error is a surprisingly common factor in anesthesia-related injuries. A recent study based on interviews with a large number of practitioners concluded that 82 percent of anesthesia mishaps involve human error; the remainder is attributable to mechanical failure. Most of the mishaps reported were "near misses" with either no effect or only transient effect on the patient. Only 17 percent produced more than a transient effect; 3.6 percent contributed to mortality.[2] The following specific factors have been associated with preventable anesthesia mishaps:[3]

1. Inadequate total experience
2. Inadequate familiarity with equipment/device
3. Poor communication with team, lab, etc.
4. Haste
5. Inattention/carelessness

6. Fatigue
7. Excessive dependency on other personnel
8. Failure to perform a proper checkout/history
9. Supervisor not present enough
10. Visual field restricted
11. Inadequate familiarity with surgical procedure
12. Teaching activity underway
13. Inadequate familiarity with anesthetic techniques
14. "First time" incident

Haste and fatigue are two common factors well known to any physician. The frequency of replacement of the anesthesiologist is a factor with a variable effect. On the one hand, inadequate replacement can contribute to fatigue. On the other hand, replacements made too frequently can lead to a lack of continuity of care and can create problems when the anesthesiologist is less familiar with the patient. Generally, replacement anesthetists are more likely to discover a problem or its source than to cause a problem.[4]

Similar problems may arise in the context of procedures done under local anesthesia where general or regional anesthesia is made available on a standby basis. Problems can arise when the anesthesiologist's involvement commences in the middle of the operation after problems have already developed, or they may arise from a preanesthetic evaluation that is inadequate or not done at all.

Inexperience in the use of equipment can first become apparent at the precise moment when it is imperative that the equipment be used correctly. Even experienced practitioners may have problems in the operation of EKG monitors and oscilloscopes. Taking the time needed to understand the operation of complex equipment better may prevent future mishaps.

The most frequently occurring mishaps fall into three general categories: airway or oxygenation problems, drug-related problems, and fluid management problems.[5]

Airway or oxygenation-related problems

1. Breathing circuit disconnection
2. Wrong gas flow setting
3. Gas supply problem
4. Laryngoscope malfunction
5. Breathing circuit misconnection
6. Tracheal airway device position change
7. Ventilator malfunction

8. Premature extubation

Drug-related problems

1. Incorrect drug dose
2. Syringe swap
3. Other (e.g. vial) drug swap

Fluid management-related problems

1. Intravenous line disconnection
2. Hypovolemia

Interference with the breathing circuit connection or with gas flow or supply is a recurring problem and one that is frequently the result of human error. Most breathing circuit disconnections involve the endotracheal tube; contributing factors include visual restriction, fatigue, distraction, and lack of familiarity with the equipment. The site of most breathing circuit disconnections has been found to be the endotracheal tube connection to an elbow or Y-piece.[6] Intubation of the esophagus rather than the trachea is another airway management problem that has resulted in suit.[7] (See § 10.22, Airway Management with Endotracheal Intubation.)

The belief that induction and emergence are the most dangerous periods of anesthesia for the patient may be a trap for the unwary. Sixty percent of anesthesia-related incidents occur during the procedure, as opposed to 27 percent during the induction phase and 13 percent at the end or after the procedure while the patient is still in the operating room.[8]

With respect to drug-related anesthesia injuries, syringe swaps are common examples of human error. One syringe may be inadvertently exchanged for another, sometimes resulting in the administration of the wrong drug. Muscle relaxants and their antagonists have been found to be involved in syringe swaps 65 percent of the time.[9]

Experienced anesthesiologists will recognize that some of these frequently occurring mishaps can occur even when appropriate steps are taken to minimize their occurrence and that appropriate monitoring and vigilance are needed to detect their occurrence. Implementing the following steps may avoid these mishaps:[10]

1. Know the equipment.
2. Eradicate equipment and procedural design pitfalls.
3. Select appropriate vigilance aids.
4. Organize the workspace.
5. Check out the equipment.
6. Maintain the equipment. (Preventive maintenance and repair should be performed only by qualified technicians.)

7. Recognize and neutralize the precursors and catalysts of errors. (This refers to the prior 14 item list of factors associated with preventable anesthesia mishaps.)

Cognizance of the possibility of human error requires that preventive measures be taken to assure that mishaps will be minimized. While it may be impossible to eliminate all errors and equipment failure, reasonable actions taken to eliminate the more frequently occurring incidents should prove fruitful.

§ 12.20 ELECTRICAL, GAS, AND FIRE HAZARDS

The Joint Commission on the Accreditation of Hospitals has devised the following standards identifying precautions to be taken to ensure the safe administration of anesthetic agents:[11]

> Anesthetic apparatus must be inspected and tested by the anesthetist before use. If a leak or any other defect is observed, the equipment must not be used until the fault is repaired.
>
> Only nonflammable agents shall be used for anesthesia, or for the preoperative preparation of the surgical field, when electrical equipment employing an open spark is to be used during an operation, for example, cautery or coagulation equipment.
>
> Flammable anesthetic agents shall be employed only in areas in which a conductive pathway can be maintained between the patient and a conductive floor.
>
> Each anesthetizing location shall be identified by a prominently posted permanent sign denoting whether the anesthetizing location is designed for flammable or nonflammable anesthetic agents.
>
> Rooms in which a flammable agent is employed for anesthesia or preparation of the surgical field shall be identified by appropriate signs while the anesthetic agent is in use.
>
> The administration of a flammable anesthetic to a patient being moved from one area to another shall be prohibited.
>
> All personnel shall wear conductive footwear, where required, which should be tested for conductivity before entering the area.
>
> All equipment in the surgical suite shall be fitted with grounding devices, where required, to maintain a constant conductive pathway to the floor.
>
> Fabrics permissible for use as outer garments or blankets in anesthetizing areas shall be specified.
>
> With the exceptions of certain radiologic equipment and fixed lighting more than five feet above the floor, all electrical equipment in anesthetizing areas shall be on an audiovisual line isolation monitor. When this device indicates a hazard, the administration of flammable anesthetic agents should be discontinued as soon as possible; the use of any electrical gear should be avoided, particularly the last electrical item

put into use as well as any item not required for patient monitoring or support; and the hospital engineer or maintenance chief shall be notified immediately. Following completion of the procedure, the operating room from which the signal emanated should not be used until the defect is remedied. All personnel who work in such areas shall be familiar with the procedures to be followed.

The condition of all operating room electrical equipment shall be inspected regularly, preferably on a monthly basis, and a written record of the results and any required corrective action shall be maintained.

The results of any required monthly conductivity testing shall be made known to personnel who work primarily in these areas.

Anesthesia personnel shall familiarize themselves with the rate, volume, and mechanism of air exchange within the surgical and obstetrical suites, as well as with humidity control.

§ 12.21 Ether

Legal liability for injury resulting from ether has usually arisen out of the occurrence of an occasional explosion or fire, accounting in part for the general decrease in use of this anesthetic. More compelling in its loss of popularity among practitioners is the pungent odor and high incidence of nausea and vomiting.

Ether was one of the first anesthetics used, initially administered by Dr. Crawford Long in Georgia in 1842 and then by Dr. William T.G. Morton, a dentist turned medical student in 1846. It was Morton's public demonstration at Massachusetts General Hospital which resulted in worldwide acceptance of ether specifically and of anesthesia generally for surgery.[12]

As a general anesthetic, ether has many advantages. It is a totipotent agent, easy to administer, and effective in low concentrations with minimal toxicity. It provides excellent muscle relaxation, eliminating the need for a muscle relaxant. It does not sensitize the myocardium to the catecholamines, nor does it depress the cardiovascular system. Ether may even protect against cardiac arrhythmias.[13] Unlike several other widely used general anesthetics, it is nontoxic to the liver and kidneys.[14] The major disadvantages of ether are slow induction, irritation of the respiratory mucosa causing unpleasant induction for the patient, and flammability.[15]

The use of ether has decreased greatly with the development of nonflammable halogenated anesthetics. However, a discussion of ether is worthwhile because it will still be used occasionally in some areas of the country. If a halogenated anesthetic is contraindicated in a given patient, ether may be administered. A discussion of ether will also remind health care professionals of the need for precautions in the operating room whenever explosive or flammable chemicals are used in the presence of electrocauterizing surgical instruments. (Static electricity is always possible with inadequate grounding of equipment or personnel in the operating room.)

Cases involving explosions in the operating room are rare. When ether was commonly used, the overall incidence with explosive agents was estimated to be about one in 200,000. For ether, it was set at one in 58,000.[16] In the last 10 years, no explosions have been reported either in the major journals or by anecdotal stories. However, when a fire or explosion does occur and the injured patient brings a lawsuit, both the surgeon and the anesthesiologist are likely to be held liable for negligence. It should also be noted that laser surgery of the oxygen-rich airway has resulted in fire damage, and special precautions, e.g., metal endotracheal tubes, may be necessary for this type of surgery.

CASE ILLUSTRATION

The patient, a nine-year-old boy, was having trouble with his breathing although he had previously had his tonsils removed. The physician recommended an operation to remove an obstruction in the nasal passage. The patient was admitted to the hospital for this purpose. The machine from which the anesthetic was administered by the nurse-anesthetist had a large gauge on the front of it which indicated by color the anesthetic being used and showed at the moment the physician began the operation that the nurse-anesthetist was using ether. However, the surgeon had not been informed that ether was to be used; nor did he notice the color of the dial or inquire regarding the nurse-anesthetist's choice of anesthetic. The physician proceeded and an explosion occurred when the physician applied an electrical cauterizing instrument to the patient's throat, causing the boy's lungs to be so severely burned that he died a few hours after the explosion. The jury found the nurse-anesthetist to be negligent in failing to communicate the potentially hazardous choice of ether anesthesia to the physician. The court of appeals held the surgeon vicariously liable (see § 2.30, Vicarious Liability) for the nurse-anesthetist's negligence. *(McKinney v. Tromly,* 1964)[17]

The paucity of recent cases involving ether reflects either the relative safety of this general anesthetic agent or the fact that its use has been supplanted by halogenated hydrocarbons that are noncombustible.

§ *12.22 Burns*

An anesthesiologist is most likely to be subject to legal liability in connection with burns suffered by the patient where (1) burns are caused by faulty electrocautery or thermal equipment, or (2) properly maintained equipment is improperly used.

§ 12.22 Burns 319

The patient's insensitivity to pain and extremes of temperature while under anesthesia make it particulary important to avoid burns during the operation.

High frequency current from an electrocautery apparatus is a common cause of burns. The active electrode of the cautery cuts or cauterizes with intense heat because all current flows through a small area. When this current leaves the body through the large ground plate, the current density is small and significant heating is not produced. If, however, the ground wire is broken or disconnected and the current exits through an ECG electrode, via a conductive face mask, or by contact with the metal table, a burn may result. Large ECG electrodes provide a greater surface area and burns are less likely to result when currents accidentally pass through them.[18]

Chemical burns resulting from the use of direct current have also occurred. If a few volts are applied to a saline solution, electrolysis occurs with sodium hydroxide formed at the positive pole and chlorine at the anode; the hydroxide then formed is caustic. Flammable chemicals (e.g., alcohol compounds) have ignited and caused burns when applied to the operative area prior to the use of electrocautery.

Optical lasers constitute another potential source of burns. The energy of a laser beam can obviously cause deep burns and ignite a rubber endotracheal tube, which must be protected by a reflecting metal tape or foil covering.[19]

Electrode equipment must not only be well-designed but properly maintained. Maintenance is ordinarily beyond the ability of the physicians and should be delegated to an expert. Certain deficiencies, however, should be obvious even to the unsophisticated. Equipment with frayed or broken cords, plugs that do not seat firmly in outlets, and damaged instruments should not be used but set aside for repair. If the operator of an instrument receives a shock, use of the instrument for a patient should be avoided.[20]

As noted, burns caused by faulty equipment are a common source of liability. The anesthesiologists who use the equipment, however, may avoid liability if they neither supplied the equipment nor held the responsibility for its proper maintenance.

CASE ILLUSTRATION

The two-year-old patient entered the hospital for surgery to correct a congenital defect in the blood vessels of the heart. During the operation the anesthesiologist used an Aquamatic K-Thermia Machine to control the patient's temperature. The machine was owned by the hospital and kept on the premises for use in the anesthesiology department and on other occasions when physicians in charge of patients ordered its use. The anesthesiologist observed the functioning of the machine for ten minutes at the outset of the operation and then set the machine on automatic control. The machine was turned off one and one-half hours into the operation when it was damaged by an observing physician who tripped over one of its cords. While it was on, however, the machine had malfunctioned. At the conclusion of the operation it was discovered that the patient's right side, hip, and chest, which had been resting on the thermal mattress attached to the machine, had been severely burned.

The patient's parents brought suit. At trial, the hospital's efforts to shift responsibility for the defects in the machine to the anesthesiologist were unsuccessful. The court noted that there was no evidence to indicate that the defects were obvious, or that the anesthesiologist was an electronics expert capable of detecting electronic malfunctions in the machine. The evidence also established that the accidental damage to the machine during the course of the operation was not the source of the patient's injury. The court refused to admit into evidence the internal hospital regulations assigning responsibility for proper maintenance of the machine because the regulations were contradictory. One rule placed the burden of maintenance upon the hospital, while another placed it upon the chief of the anesthesiology department. The court then directed a verdict against the hospital, holding that the evidence presented conclusively established its liability. The appeals court affirmed, stating that the patient "had the right to rely upon the hospital to furnish a properly functioning device to aid the operative procedures." *(Weeks v. Latter-Day Saints Hospital,* 1969)[21]

Of course, even though not responsible for its maintenance, the anesthesiologist who uses an obviously defective piece of equipment may well be found negligent.

Most operations, if properly conducted, are unlikely to result in burns. Some courts have therefore held that the presence of burns creates an inference that the operation was performed negligently. This inference may enable the patient to recover damages even if the patient cannot prove a specific act of negligence, and even if the physician-defendant suggests possible non-negligent causes of the burns. An anesthesiologist also faces liability for the negligence of his assistants, and the fact that his assistants at a particular operation were employed by the hospital and not by the anesthesiologist himself may be held irrelevant. (See § 2.30, Vicarious Liability.)

CASE ILLUSTRATION

The patient underwent an operation to correct a vascular circulatory problem. After the anesthesiologist administered an anesthetic, the physician removed an atherosclerotic obstruction of the aorta, both common iliac

§ 12.22 *Burns* 321

arteries, and the right femoral arteries. As part of an electrocautery procedure used in the operation, a flat metal electrode was placed directly beneath the patient's buttocks. The buttocks were separated from the plate with K-Y Jelly. While the patient was in the recovery room it was discovered that he had suffered second to third degree burns on both buttocks. After the patient died from unrelated causes, his wife brought suit against the hospital, the physician, and the anesthesiologist, alleging that the patient's burns had been caused by negligence. A jury verdict for the plaintiff was affirmed, the court holding that since the proper performance of vascular surgery is extremely unlikely to result in burns on the buttocks, the existence of the burns created an inference that the operation had been conducted negligently. Possible non-negligent causes of the injury suggested by the defendants (pressure necrosis or a chemical reaction between the prepping solution and the cautery plate) were held insufficient to rule out the possibility of negligence. The anesthesiologist's argument that, since he did not employ them, he was not responsible for the negligence of any hospital employees who assisted him in his duties was also rejected. Instead, said the court, if the anesthesiologist "charged with the patient's care so neglected him as to allow the injury to occur, he would be liable for the negligence of those who became his temporary assistants while performing the duty owed by him to (the patient), regardless of whether he paid or employed them." *(Wiles v. Myerly,* 1973)[22]

The physician may be held liable for the negligence of his assistants even if they disregard express instructions. In a New York case decided in 1956, an anesthetist applied an alcoholic antiseptic (tincture of Zephiran) to a portion of a patient's back prior to spinal anesthesia. The same solution was then applied to the operative area. The hospital's nurses had been instructed to inspect the sheets beneath the patient and to remove any that had been stained with the solution; however, they made no inspection. When the surgeon applied electrocautery, gaseous vapor from the solution ignited, burning the patient. The surgeon was held liable.[23]

The equipment used at an operation, whether supplied by the physician or the hospital, need not be of the latest design so long as it is reasonably suited for the use to which it is put. However, regardless of the technological sophistication of the equipment, it must be used properly or liability may result. Misuse of even the simplest piece of equipment creates a potential for liability.

CASE ILLUSTRATION

A seven-day-old baby underwent an emergency operation to correct intestinal blockage. He was kept warm during the operation by being placed atop an inverted flash pan which, in turn, covered a hot water bottle. Although the surgery corrected the intestinal blockage, the baby suffered a third degree burn over most of the surface area of his buttocks. The baby's parents brought suit against the hospital, the anesthetist, and the operating physician, contending that the placement of excessively hot water in the hot water bottle caused the burn. The trial court directed a verdict in favor of all three defendants. The appeals court affirmed the verdict for the hospital, holding that even if, as plaintiff asserted, the operation would have been safer had the hospital provided a K-thermal blanket in place of the hot water bottle, that fact alone did not establish negligence. The hospital, said the court, "is not required to furnish the latest or best appliances, or to incorporate in existing equipment the latest inventions or improvements even though such devices may make the equipment safer to use. . . . At most, the hospital is required to furnish equipment which is reasonably suited for the purposes for which it is intended." The verdict for the physician was also affirmed, the court holding that in the absence of some conduct or situation which should reasonably warn him of the presence of negligence, the physician is entitled to rely on the expertise of the anesthetist. The verdict for the anesthetist, however, was reversed, and a new trial was ordered on the issue of her liability. Since a jury could reasonably infer a duty on the part of the anesthetist to see that the bottle is filled with water of the proper temperature, said the court, it was an error to take the question of her liability away from the jury. *(Starnes v. Charlotte-Mecklenburg Hospital Authority,* 1976)[24]

§ 12.30 IMPROPER MANAGEMENT OF FLUID AND ELECTROLYTE IMBALANCES

Liability for improper management of body fluids will be imposed on the anesthesiologist where anesthesia is given despite the presence of a fluid imbalance which contraindicates anesthesia or where injury results from a failure to maintain proper fluid levels.

Proper management of fluid and electrolyte levels in the surgical patient about to undergo general anesthesia requires consideration of factors not usually present in non-surgical cases. Although a patient may be well compensated on the ward, cardiovascular depression and alteration of peripheral vascular tone and autonomic nervous system mechanisms may lead to impaired cardiovascular function with the induction of general anesthesia. In addition, the surgical procedure may lead to shifts in blood and fluid balance. To the extent that these changes can be anticipated, it is important to correct deficits and improve cardiovascular reserve when possible.

§ 12.30 *Fluid and Electrolyte Management* 323

Fluid and electrolyte therapy involve control of vascular volume, electrolyte concentrations, metabolic and energy requirement considerations, and the maintenance of appropriate red cell volume. Maintenance fluid requirements will vary from patient to patient, but the average healthy patient may require from two to three liters of fluid per day to account for both sensible and insensible water losses. Sensible losses are those losses which can be measured, such as loss in the urine or in the feces. If bowel surgery is planned, bowel preparation may involve considerable fluid loss through the fecal route. Insensible losses include losses which are not easily measured, such as losses from respiration and losses through the skin. Rapid respiratory rates and the breathing of dry air may increase loss through the lungs; fever or burns may markedly increase loss through skin. Thus, the preoperative evaluation must include some estimate of hidden volume deficits.

If patients have received no food or drink by mouth (NPO) from midnight until the time of operation, fluid losses have continued without replacement. Even under the best of circumstances at the time of the induction of anesthesia, patients may be a liter or more behind in fluids. Depending on the patient's status, preinduction volume loading may be desirable. For example, it may be important to prepare very ill patients with impaired cardiovascular function for general anesthesia by giving intravenous fluids preoperatively. Intraoperative maintenance of vascular volume will depend on surgical considerations as well. For certain types of surgical procedures, it may be necessary to keep the patient in a relatively dehydrated state. For example, this may be necessary in the patient undergoing a craniotomy, where vascular volume is kept to a minimum to decrease the risk of cerebral edema. Renal failure or cardiac failure may also necessitate managing patients at a relatively low intra-vascular volume. For most types of surgery, however, fluid loss will be in excess of maintenance requirements. It is then the goal of the anesthesiologist to maintain fluid administration at a level appropriate to assure cardiovascular stability.

Consideration must also be given to the composition of body fluids. Electrolyte concentration should be kept close to normal levels. Metabolic decompensation may ensue at the extremes of levels of sodium, potassium or bicarbonate. Other ions such as calcium or magnesium may also become important considerations. The serum sodium levels and vascular volume are interrelated. A low serum sodium in the presence of hypovolemia has different implications than hyponatremic normovolemia, or hyponatremic hypervolemia.[25]

Because of the problem of cardiac arrhythmias, serum potassium levels are also very important. This factor is well recognized among anesthesiologists and under most circumstances elective surgery will not be performed in patients with serum potassiums of less than 3.2 mEg/liter.

Bicarbonate levels are of extreme importance for maintenance of normal acid-base equilibrium. This may be very important in a patient with a metabolic acidosis or in a patient receiving large amounts of blood products. Although specific electrolyte considerations will vary greatly from patient to patient, depending upon the surgical procedure being performed, the anesthesiologist has a duty to:

1. Give advice on preoperative correction of electrolyte imbalances
2. Diagnose and treat electrolyte imbalances intraoperatively
3. Provide appropriate therapy to ensure electrolyte balance into the postoperative period

Providing glucose for cellular metabolism is another consideration in fluid and electrolyte therapy. Although a liter of five percent dextrose intravenous solution contains 50 grams of glucose, this amount is inadequate to provide daily caloric requirements. Nevertheless provision of glucose may prevent some breakdown of protein, depletion of glycogen stores, and excessive mobilization of fatty acids leading to ketoacidosis. If glucose administration is excessive, serum glucose levels may exceed the renal threshold for clearance of glucose, and glucosuria will result. The resultant osmotic diuresis may make urine output inaccurate as a measure of monitoring volume status. Obviously the diabetic patient has requirements quite different from that of normal patients. The anesthesiologist may advise appropriate preoperative insulin therapy as well as monitoring glucose levels intraoperatively to prevent hypoglycemia or extremes of hyperglycemia.

The other component of vascular volume of major importance is the red cell mass. Red cell mass is measured as the hematocrit. Most anesthesiologists would consider a hematocrit of 30 to be the minimum acceptable level for undertaking elective surgery. This level is not absolute, however, and consideration must be given to the patient's overall condition and existence of other disease processes. For example, if a patient is in renal failure, hematocrits in the 20s may be acceptable for elective surgery. The decision to administer an intraoperative transfusion will be based on the preoperative hematocrit, current blood loss, and probability of continued blood loss. Additional consideration should be given to the patient's overall condition and ability to manufacture red cells in the postoperative period. Volume loss alone is not an indication for blood transfusion, since volume loss can be managed effectively by the administration of crystalloid solutions. When it does become necessary to provide additional red cell mass, either whole blood or packed cells are available. In patients with impaired ability to handle potassium loads, washed packed cells may be considered. The advantage of using packed cells is that the other components of whole blood are available for component therapy and the usefulness of each individual unit of blood is increased. The advantage of using whole blood is that colloid in the form of protein is also administered and colloid oncotic pressure is maintained. Expansion of the interstitial space will occur if noncolloid solutions are used to maintain vascular volume. This is usually of no consequence, however, and most anesthesiologists will transfuse at least the first one or two units of red cells as packed red blood cells. As requirements for blood transfusion increase, other problems occur. Hyperkalemia resulting from cell lysis may occur, particularly with older units of blood, and the acid-base balance may be disturbed because of the anticoagulant solutions employed in blood banking. Because citrate lowers ionized calcium levels, hypocalcemia may become a significant problem with massive blood transfusions. Obviously the risk of a transfusion reaction or transference of hepatitis increases directly with the number of units of blood transfused. (See § 12.40, Blood Transfusions.) Thus the duty of the anesthesiologist is to assess the degree of blood loss intraoperatively in terms of the patient's preoperative hematocrit and overall condition and to determine the need for the transfusion of blood. The serum hematocrit should be maintained at a level sufficient to provide adequate oxygen carrying capacity, giving due consideration to the problems inherent in transfusion therapy.

There are a few cases in which patients have brought actions against anesthesiologists for failure to diagnose or treat fluid or electrolyte derangements properly. Evidence that a patient was suffering from acidosis prior to the administration of anesthesia has resulted in liability for the anesthesiologist.

CASE ILLUSTRATION

The 15-year-old diabetic female came to her physician with a history of diarrhea for one day and abdominal pain. On examination she had right lower quadrant tenderness without rebound; she was dehydrated and lethargic. Laboratory tests indicated that her urine was positive for glucose and ketones; her hemoglobin and hematocrit were elevated, as was her white blood count. Her internist diagnosed diabetic ketoacidosis and a possible appendicitis and admitted her to the hospital. The patient was nauseated. While in the hospital her hematocrit and white blood count dropped (she was receiving intravenous fluids). Her pH and potassium levels were also below normal. The patient was noted to be less dehydrated and less lethargic. A progress note by the internist stated that appendicitis was "less likely." The patient was given 30 mgs of Talwin for severe headache, but had severe abdominal pain a little bit more than two hours later. At that time, the decision to operate was made. Prior to the operation the patient was given 40 milliequivalents of potassium chloride to bring her into metabolic balance. The anesthesiologist suggested spinal anesthesia, but the surgeon and the anesthesiologist made a joint decision to use general anesthesia because they were reluctant to have a patient of that age conscious during surgery. Before the operation, the patient was given atropine and sodium pentothal. Inhalation anesthesia with cycloproprane and oxygen was used. The patient was also given succinylcholine. The dosage of succinylcholine was titrated; the total dosage administered was not recorded and could not be recalled by the anesthesiologist.

The surgeons were working in a bloodless field. After about 20 minutes, the anesthesiologist noted and announced that blood pressure was falling, and then that there was no pulse or blood pressure obtainable. External cardiac massage was begun immediately and the patient was resuscitated in 70 seconds. During the resuscitation, the anesthesiologist inserted an endotracheal tube; only an oropharyngeal airway had been used earlier. The operation was completed. Pathological examination of the appendix showed it to be normal. Postoperatively, the patient was given dilantin for prevention of convulsions and digitalis for tachycardia. Her internist began treatment with decadron one day later, when her level of consciousness failed to improve. The patient survived but was left with hypoxic brain damage.

The patient brought suit. At trial several experts testified that a patient in metabolic acidosis is both a surgical and an anesthetic risk. The anesthesiologist testified that the previous physical status of the patient, the fact that she had been in a state of ketoacidosis, contributed to the weakening of her heart, and the sudden change in condition had caused the cardiac arrest. A directed verdict was granted for the hospital; the jury returned a verdict against the surgeon, the anesthesiologist, and the internist. *(Burrows v. Widder,* 1977)[26]

The maintenance of proper fluid levels, which is the anesthesiologist's responsibility, also encompasses the responsibility for dealing with blood loss. In cases where the anesthesiologist fails to meet this responsibility, liability will be imposed.

CASE ILLUSTRATION

The female patient died as a result of shock caused by internal bleeding following delivery of a normal baby by cesarean section performed in the hospital. The patient's widower brought suit. At the trial there was expert testimony that the amount of blood which had been given the patient by transfusion as a replacement was inadequate; otherwise the patient's condition would have stabilized and she would not have reached the point of irreversible shock. An expert also testified that the responsibility for dealing with the shock rested on the anesthetist and that it was his duty to replace the blood lost through bleeding. The court held that under the facts the anesthetist was negligent. *(James v. Holder,* 1970)[27]

§ 12.40 BLOOD TRANSFUSIONS

Liability may be imposed on the anesthesiologist for injury resulting from blood transfusions where the blood transfused is incompatible with the patient's blood type; where hepatitis is the injury suffered, liability will probably not be imposed since the courts recognize the difficulty in ascertaining the presence of blood-borne hepatitis.

Administration of blood transfusions during operations is an area of potential legal liability for anesthesiologists.

A physician may be sued for failing to replace fluid losses or blood losses adequately or for giving unnecessary transfusions. There is also a potential for legal liability if the patient's consent to transfusion has not been obtained. Most of these cases involve Jehovah's Witnesses.

Lawsuits involving blood transfusions, however, will arise either from administrations of incompatible blood or for hepatitis occurring after a blood transfusion. As might be expected, patient-plaintiffs are generally more successful in recovering for damages from incompatible transfusions than for post-transfusion hepatitis. Usually hospitals or blood banks are the only parties held liable, but it is common for the surgeon and even the anesthesiologist to be named as defendants.

Despite the trend towards strict liability in tort law, courts in most jurisdictions are still applying a negligence standard in imposing liability for hepatitis acquired from a blood transfusion. (See § 2.50, Products Liability.) For this reason, blood transfusion is termed a "medical service" (which requires the plaintiff to prove negligence to recover), not a "sale of a product" (to which strict liability would apply). Thus, a patient's chances of recovery are much greater if he or she can prove that the hospital or blood bank used paid donors or failed to meet the standard of customary practice of screening donors and units of blood for any transmissible disease.

Courts have struggled with the problem of blood-borne hepatitis, just as the medical profession has. Often liability will turn on whether a court considers a blood transfusion "unreasonably dangerous."[28] Other courts have proposed less abstract tests, such as weighing the means of avoiding the risk and extent of risk against the utility of the product.[29]

In a 1970 decision, the Supreme Court of Illinois applied strict liability to blood transfusions.[30] This decision understandably alarmed many physicians and other health professionals. In response to this decision and what was perceived as a threat of application of strict liability to blood transfusions, Illinois and other states have passed statutes which specifically define blood transfusions as a service, not the sale of a product, and proscribe the application of strict liability to the administration of blood transfusions.[31]

The discovery of the Australia antigen and further sophisticated serologic tests allowing for identification of individuals who have had hepatitis in the past has led to the hope that ultimately the risk of hepatitis from blood transfusions can be eliminated entirely. However, the recent discovery that most cases of post-transfusion hepatitis are non-A, non-B hepatitis has reminded physicians that, at least for now, it is not possible to detect all asymptomatic carriers of hepatitis in the donor population.

Administration of incompatible transfusions, on the other hand, is an area in which anesthesiologists, as well as other health professionals, can actually reduce both medical risk to patients and legal risk to themselves. Realistically, the anesthesiologist can do little to reduce the chance of hepatitis after a transfusion, other than by avoiding unnecessary transfusions, although the transfusion decision is often made jointly with the surgeon. Incompatible transfusions, on the other hand, are the result of clerical error by at least one person between the time the patient's blood is drawn for typing and cross-matching and the time the transfusion has begun.

CASE ILLUSTRATION

During the course of the patient's surgery, the anesthetist told the surgeon that he had the patient's blood ready and asked, "Shall I give it?" The surgeon said yes. The circulating nurse had come into the operating room with a bottle of blood on which there was a slip inscribed with the name of the patient, type of blood and the name of the patient's physician. The slip showed that the blood was for another patient, previously operated on, not by the surgeon. However, the circulating nurse and anesthetist had also been present at that operation. The surgeon knew that he had not ordered the blood and later stated that it had occurred to him "to inquire as to how that blood got to the operating room," but he did not do so. The patient died as the result of the transfusion of incompatible blood.

The patient's widower sued the surgeon, the anesthetist and the hospital. At trial, the anesthetist testified that it was his duty to check the blood to be transfused with a chart he kept showing the patient's blood type. He failed to perform that duty. The court held that the concurrent active negligence of the three defendants caused the patient's death. *(Weiss v. Rubin,* 1961)[32]

§ 12.50 FAULTY PATIENT POSITIONING

An anesthesiologist is most likely to be subject to legal liability in connection with the positioning of the patient where (1) the patient suffers an injury, the cause of which cannot be accounted for except as arising out of faulty positioning or (2) injury results from the failure to exercise due care in moving the patient.

A patient is susceptible to injury under general anesthesia, because the patient has been paralyzed and rendered unconscious. The anesthesiologist must pay particular attention to the positioning of the patient's body to avoid injury. All postures to some degree affect circulation and respiration, influence various reflexes, and place stress on anatomical structures. It is the obligation of the anesthesiologist to protect the anesthetized patient against the adverse effects of positioning. Extremes of position are to be avoided: patients should be moved slowly and gently; all personnel must realize that the patient under general anesthesia is subject to profound changes in physiology and thus lacks the ability to compensate for changes in posture.[33] Also, the fact that the patient does not complain of pain or pressure does not mean that he or she is not susceptible to injury from pressure or incorrect positioning.

The following test is recommended as a guide to proper positioning: (1) estimate whether or not a particular position can be tolerated in the conscious state; (2) note if the position is comfortable, and whether it will continue to be so; and (3) determine if the musculoskeletal mechanics will permit the position without injury.[34]

Generally, positions which require extreme variations from normal anatomical positions, such as the jackknife and knee-chest positions, should be avoided. For example, the prone jackknife position presents problems, both because of its deviation from normal posture and because, in the event that emergency resuscitation becomes necessary, it often requires repositioning, a process that often wastes precious time. In two recent lawsuits, anesthesiologists paid hefty settlements out of court to compensate patients for injuries incurred during operations in which the jackknife position was used.[35]

The types of complication due to positioning in the operating room may be categorized as physiological reactions, and anatomical effects. Physiological reactions may occur in either the respiratory or circulatory system, both of which systems may be influenced by either mechanical-gravitational factors or by reflex factors. Anatomical effects will principally concern injuries to the patient's nerves, and may involve cervical or brachial plexus palsy.[36] Nerves are especially vulnerable to errors of positioning,[37] usually in one of three situations: (1) the nerve may be pressed between a hard metal or wood table or stirrup and underlying bone, especially if there is little protective subcutaneous tissue; (2) hard objects may be placed on or against the patient's body—this includes the undesirable practice by operating room personnel of leaning on an unconscious patient's body; (3) injury may result from traction on nerve plexuses, especially those leading to an upper extremity which is extended and externally rotated, such as an arm bound to an arm board.

At all times due care must be exercised in moving the patient. A sufficient number of persons should assist in the transfer of the patient to and from the operating table to ensure that a fall does not occur. Transfers should not be unduly abrupt, since excess haste and force may result in injury.[38] Many injuries are the result of simple carelessness. In at least one reported case, an unconscious and unstrapped patient fell off the operating table simply because no one was looking.[39] Because accidents of this kind are easily prevented, failure to exercise due care in moving the patient may well result in a finding of liability. Once a patient is taken from the operating room, liability may also arise if injury results from incorrect positioning during the postoperative period.

Injuries resulting from improper positioning during anesthesia give rise to lawsuits involving unique problems of proof. Such an injury usually occurs to an unconscious patient, and its cause is often unrelated to a strictly medical treatment procedure, as in the case referred to above where the patient's injury was due to an unattended fall from the operating table. The more common injuries sustained as a result of faulty positioning are paralysis or other nerve damage in the neck, shoulder or arm.[40] These cases are particularly appropriate for the application of the doctrine of res ipsa loquitur. (See § 1.52, Res Ipsa Loquitur.) In order to apply the doctrine, the patient-plaintiff must prove the following:

1. The event or injury is of a kind which ordinarily does not occur in the absence of someone's negligence.
2. The injury was caused by an agency or instrumentality within the exclusive control of the defendant.
3. The injury was not due to any voluntary action or contribution on the part of the plaintiff.
4. The evidence for the explanation of the events causing the harm is more accessible to the defendant than to the plaintiff.[41]

The applicability of res ipsa loquitur to cases arising out of positioning injuries is supported by an early opinion that first extended the doctrine to multiple defendants. This decision, illustrated below, is still recognized in most jurisdictions as authoritative with respect to multiple liability under res ipsa loquitur.

CASE ILLUSTRATION

Prior to an appendectomy, the anesthetist placed the patient on the operating table. An anesthetic was then administered, but before losing consciousness, the patient felt two hard sharp objects at the top of his shoulders, about an inch below his neck. When the patient regained consciousness following the operation he felt a sharp pain about half way between the neck and the point of the right shoulder. After the patient was released from the hospital, his condition grew worse. He was unable to rotate or lift his arm, and he developed paralysis and atrophy of the muscles around the shoulder. The patient sued the surgeon, the anesthesiologist, the nurses in the operating room, and the physician who owned the hospital. At trial, the patient was unable to identify the member of the operating team or the instrumentality that had injured him, and judgment was entered for the defendants. Upon appeal, the judgment was reversed, the court holding that the facts of the case created such a strong inference of negligence that the patient did not need to prove a specific act of negligence. Instead, res ipsa loquitur was held to be applicable, and the court stated, "where a plaintiff receives unusual injuries while unconscious and in the course of medical treatment, all those defendants who had any control over his body or the instrumentalities which might have caused the injuries may properly be called upon to meet the inference of negligence by giving an explanation of their conduct." Upon retrial, judgment was entered for the patient. The defendants' testimony that they had not seen an accident which could have caused the injury was held to be insufficient to overcome the inference of negligence. *(Ybarra v. Spangard,* 1949)[42]

More recently decided cases dealing with injuries arising out of faulty positioning have held res ipsa loquitur inapplicable, generally because the cause of the injury has been ascertainable. Where the injury may be shown to be due to some factor other than the physician's negligence, liability will not be imposed.

CASE ILLUSTRATION

The patient was admitted to the hospital for a hysterectomy and the repair of a ventral hernia. Surgery was performed and the patient's recovery progressed well for about a week until bleeding was discovered at the lower incision following a coughing spell. The patient complained of pain in the pelvic region; following an examination, the physician discovered an infection that required drainage. A second operation was performed to drain the abscess. The operation was successful, but immediately upon regaining consciousness the patient began to experience pain in her cervical spine area that radiated into her shoulder and arms. The patient sued the physician, the anesthesiologist present at the second operation, and the hospital. At trial, the patient attributed her neck injury to hyperextension during surgery. It was revealed, however, that six years prior to the surgery, the patient had undergone a laminectomy to remove a ruptured disk between L-5 and S-1 on the left side, which had been caused by disk degeneration. Additionally, the neurosurgeon who later operated on the patient's injured neck confirmed a diagnosis of herniation of disk material between C-5 and C-6 vertebrae. The neurosurgeon testified that the patient was undergoing "advanced degenerative changes when the foramina became narrowed" and that coughing, sneezing, or merely awakening in the morning could cause the patient's disk herniation. Additionally, the anesthesiologist testified that he had not hyperextended the patient's neck for the purpose of administering anesthesia in the second operation performed to drain the abscess. The court concluded that ample evidence had been submitted to support a finding that the patient's injuries were not due to the hyperextension of her neck, but could have been due to entirely natural acts such as coughing, sneezing, or rolling over in sleep. Because the evidence did not prove that a negligent act of the defendants was a more likely cause of the patient's injury than any other possible cause, res ipsa loquitur was held inapplicable and the court exonerated the defendants from liability. *(Faris v. Doctors Hospital, Inc.,* 1972)[43]

Other reported cases involving neck injury resulting from allegedly faulty positioning have received similar resolutions by the courts. In a Florida case involving an injury to the eleventh cranial nerve sustained during open-heart surgery, the court declined to impose liability based on res ipsa loquitur. In that case, expert testimony had been presented that such an injury had:

> . . . never been seen nor even been recorded in medical literature. Further, the expert medical testimony was to the effect that an injury to the eleventh cranial nerve can occur in an "infinitesimal" number of ways including degenerative diseases, inflammation of the nerve, pressure from neoplasms, tumors, emboli, enlarged masses of boils or lymph nodes.[44]

A similar result was reached in a Louisiana case involving a hysterectomy patient who sustained a loss of feeling and mobility in her left arm that she attributed to faulty positioning. This patient's history, however, indicated a long-standing cardiovascular problem involving a significant blockage of the arteries supplying the left arm and the left side of her brain. This had been discovered when the patient underwent a transfemoral aortic angiogram. Because direct evidence of the cause of the injury existed, the court declined to impose liability based on res ipsa loquitur.[45]

Physicians have also escaped liability for malpositioning injuries to patients in cases where the patient has failed to show that the physician-defendants had control over the instrumentality causing the injury. Such results have been due to the failure of the patient's attorney to include all the appropriate parties as defendants in the patient's claim. These cases should be distinguished from the early *Ybarra* decision which imposed liability on multiple defendants under the doctrine of res ipsa loquitur. The *Ybarra* court concluded that any or all of the defendants might have been responsible for the injury; the more recent decisions

§ 12.50　　　　　　　　Faulty Patient Positioning　　　　　　　　333

involve a determination that a party who is most likely responsible has not been made a defendant to the lawsuit.

CASE ILLUSTRATION

The patient underwent surgery at the hospital to correct gynecological and suspected abdominal problems. Three surgical procedures were conducted: a dilatation and curettage performed by the patient's physician; a laparoscopy, performed by a second physician who was assisted by the patient's physician; and a laparotomy performed by the patient's physician. Prior to surgery, the patient was given a general anesthetic by the nurse-anesthetist. An intravenous apparatus was set to run into the patient's left arm, and her arm was extended on an arm board out from the side of the operating table to facilitate this process. During the D. & C., the patient was placed in a modified dorsal lithotomy, or supine, position in which she lay on her back in a flat position with her feet in stirrups. To facilitate the laparoscopy, the patient was placed in the Trendelenberg position, whereby her abdomen and legs were raised and her head and shoulders lowered. The Trendelenberg position was retained for the laparotomy, but the degree of slant was increased. Upon awakening in the recovery room, the patient experienced severe pain in her neck, left shoulder and left arm. This pain was diagnosed as resulting from suprascapular nerve palsy allegedly caused by the malpositioning of the patient. The patient sued the physician who performed the D. & C. and the laparotomy, the nurse-anesthetist, and the hospital, but failed to sue the physician who performed the laparoscopy. The court refused to impose liability on the named defendants based on res ipsa loquitur. The court recognized that the operating surgeon during the laparoscopy was responsible for the patient's positioning at that time, according to his own testimony. Thus the injury may have occurred during the laparoscopy and the unnamed surgeon's negligence could have been the cause. (*Jones v. Harrisburg Polyclinic Hospital,* 1980)[46]

This case illustrates a general reluctance on the part of the courts to impose liability in malpractice cases based on res ipsa loquitur. Another court may have recognized the independent duty of the nurse-anesthetist rather than the operating surgeon to exercise care with respect to patient positioning.[47] Based on the evidence it has before it, each court individually determines who has that responsibility. Furthermore, the decision reached does not necessarily indicate that physicians as a general rule will escape liability for malpositioning injuries.

Although other recent cases have declined to impose liability based on res ipsa loquitur where a presumably responsible party was not included as a defendant,[48] the courts acknowledge that the doctrine itself may still be applicable in a faulty positioning case.[49] Therefore, the anesthesiologist is well advised to exercise due care in protecting the anesthetized patient from injury associated with positioning. Such care should also be exercised when the patient is moved during or after the operation.[50]

A problem arises for the anesthesiologist confronted with a patient who may face great risk from being placed in a position requested and favored by the surgeon performing the procedure, but which is not required by other surgeons for the same procedure. An example would be the knee-chest position (versus the prone position) for laminectomy. If the surgeon insists that the knee-chest position is required despite advice to the contrary, the anesthesiologist might gain some medicolegal protection if the additional risks are clearly outlined in the preoperative note or if the additional risks from positioning are discussed with the patient as part of the informed consent discussion. (See § 1.33, Consent and Informed Consent.) Such preventive measures could conceivably shift responsibility to the surgeon, although no cases addressing this issue have been decided.

As is indicated by the available cases, responsibility for positioning injuries generally rests on the anesthesiologist. Therefore, if the surgeon is steadfast in his or her insistence in the use of a contraindicated position, in the absence of hospital policy or other guidelines resolving such dispute, the anesthesiologist's best recourse is to decline to take the case.

§ 12.60 MALIGNANT HYPERTHERMIA

Legal liability resulting from the onset of malignant hyperthermia will probably not be imposed due to the unpredictability of a predisposition to the disease. However, if the anesthesiologist should have reason to know of a predisposition through, for example, family screening or if the anesthesiologist is negligent in his or her treatment of the disease when it occurs, liability may be imposed.

Malignant hyperthermia (M.H.), also called malignant hyperpyrexia, is a rare disease which can confront any anesthesiologist. It is a clinical syndrome characterized by a rapid rise in temperature during anesthesia, most commonly occurring in young adults.[51] Although detection is difficult, its high mortality rate makes detection during the preanesthetic examination or during the intraoperative period crucial.

Thorough preanesthesia evaluation may be helpful in preventing malignant hyperthermia. Inquiries should be made about personal or family history of pyrexia or difficulty during anesthesia in relatives. When such a history is noted succinylcholine and halogenated agents should probably be avoided.[52]

Creatine phosphophinase (CPK), aldolase, and serum phrophosphate (P-P) levels should be evaluated to identify carriers. CPK is nonspecific but may be elevated in 30 percent of asymptomatic malignant hyperthermia carriers (relatives).[53]

A semi-open or semi-closed high flow system provides an additional avenue of heat loss for patients determined to be at risk. Acceptable agents include: intravenous neuroleptanesthesia, thiopental, ketamine and althesin. Nitrous oxide is also a safe inhalation agent. Regional anesthesia also serves to avoid the hazards of disruptive biological oxidation.[54]

Intraoperative detection of malignant hyperthermia and prompt, appropriate treatment are part of the anesthesiologist's duty. The syndrome develops with tachycardia, hypertension, tachypnea, cyanosis, sweating and muscle rigidity, and possibly cardiac arrhythmias. Dark blood is another symptom to be noticed by the surgeon. A rapid rise in temperature is the most dramatic characteristic; a rise of 1°F every 15 minutes, reaching levels of 105° to 112°F may be seen.[55]

The presence of malignant hyperthermia syndrome constitutes a life-threatening emergency. Treatment of the syndrome must therefore take precedence over other procedures. The specific treatment is dantrolene, 1 mg/kg as the initial dose.

Other treatments include:

1. Discontinuance of anesthesia and termination of the operation
2. Hyperventilation of the lungs with 100 percent oxygen
3. Correction of associated severe lactic acidosis by means of bicarbonate injection
4. Cooling of the body by any available means (surface cooling, intravenous infusion of iced saline, gastric and rectal lavage, irrigation of body cavities, extracorporeal cooling)
5. Treatment of hyperkalemia by administration of dextrose and insulin
6. Aggressive hydration
7. Treatment for tachycardia (do not move patient)
8. Administration of intravenous procaine to stabilize cell membranes and calcium storage vesicles
9. Administration of magnesium to protect against oxidative uncoupling
10. Use of alpha-blocking agents[56]

Few cases involving malignant hyperthermia have been reported in the courts. Consequently, the lack of legal precedent makes it difficult to define what duties an anesthesiologist must meet to avoid liability. However, some estimates about the appropriate standard of care can be made from the medical literature.

The unpredictability of malignant hyperthermia syndrome may spare the anesthesiologist from liability for resulting injuries. This result has been seen in other cases where the patient has an unforeseeable adverse reaction to a drug. (See § 10.31, Halothane.) As in those cases, if the anesthesiologist knew or should have known of a predisposition towards malignant hyperthermia or if the anesthesiologist fails to diagnose or treat the disease properly, liability may be imposed. To date, because the onset of the disease in unpredictable, it has only been treated as a defense in legal decisions.

CASE ILLUSTRATION

An eleven-year-old boy fractured his wrist and jaw in a sledding accident. During an operation to reduce the jaw fracture, the patient had a cardiac arrest and died. The patient's family sued, alleging negligence on the part of the general surgeon who examined the boy initially in failing to discover the rib fracture, and negligence on the part of the anesthesiologist for failing to examine the patient. The plaintiff alleged that the undiagnosed rib fracture led to a tension pneumothorax, causing anoxia, cardiac arrest, and death. The initial autopsy report described the rib fracture and essentially agreed with the plaintiff's theory of causation. Shortly before the beginning of the trial, however, an addendum to the autopsy report was made, stating that the rib fracture was probably caused by resuscitative efforts. The addendum stated that presence of a rectal temperature of 107.8 degrees "strongly suggests" that the boy's death was due to malignant hyperthermia, and not a tension pneumothorax.

On appeal, the plaintiffs sought to overturn the judgment in favor of the anesthesiologist on the grounds that the addendum should not have been admitted into evidence. Although the court held it was error to allow the addendum into evidence, the error was harmless. The court noted that the anesthesiologist's defense to the lawsuit was predicated on establishing that the patient had died from malignant hyperthermia, which the medical profession has no known method of predicting. Because other admissible medical testimony had been offered to this effect, the court upheld the decision in favor of the anesthesiologist. *(Vogan v. Byers, 1971)*[57]

§ 12.70 CARDIAC ARREST

The physician may incur liability for failure to initiate CPR when the patient is his or her responsibility or when he or she has failed to perform in a manner judged to be the most likely to succeed, i.e., according to established standards.

Cardiac arrest can occur under general anesthesia, under spinal anesthesia, or even under regional nerve blocks. It is not always readily apparent what the mechanism of the arrest is, and the courts have recognized that cardiac arrest can occur even in the absence of negligence.[58] Among the non-negligent causes of cardiac arrest are such things as thromboembolic disease and intrinsic heart disease. Nonetheless, if negligence on the part of the anesthesiologist has contributed to cardiac arrest, the anesthesiologist may be held liable for that negligence.

Perhaps the current state of what is known about the cause of cardiac arrest is expressed by Harold Engel, M.D., J.D., in a letter to the editor of *Anesthesiology* in January of 1980:

> For the last ten years I have devoted full time to defending medical malpractice suits both as a trial attorney and as a consultant performing medical-legal reviews of files. Scores of these cases have involved anesthesiologists and instances of cardiac arrest resulting in brain damage and death. In only a handful has it been possible to determine the etiologic factor. Almost invariably, in spite of autopsies, record reviews and personal interviews, the cause remains undiscovered. Obtaining second opinions from other anesthesiologists has not given any substantial help.
>
> Early in this work I came to the same conclusions as Dr. Hamilton. These unexplained arrests and deaths must be due to negligence on the part of anesthesiologists. In all probability there was an overdose, hypoxia, hypoventilation, or some combination of these errors. Or, the records and the deposition testimony were inaccurate, altered, or perjured. But as time has passed and I have become exposed to more cases, I have begun to change my thinking towards these views expressed by Dr. Keats. I have simply seen too many instances of cardiac arrest occurring during anesthesia administered by individuals whom I know personally do not lie and who keep accurate records. Repeatedly, I am confronted by instances where everything has been done properly, where there has been careful ongoing monitoring, where the dosages are minimal and the oxygenation more than adequate, and the ventilation satisfactory, only to have a sudden, unexpected cardiac arrest. It seems to happen too frequently to be explained by error by the anesthesiologists. More and more I am led to believe that we do not know enough about drug action and interaction or about the physiology of the neurologic and cardiovascular system to rule out unknown factors to put the blame upon anesthesiologists unless there is clear evidence that he [sic] was at fault.[59]

While it is true that cardiac arrest can occur in the absence of negligence, it is equally true that negligence can precipitate cardiac arrest on the operating table. Where anesthesia may be contraindicated due to the patient's condition and the anesthesiologist proceeds despite this fact, he or she will be held liable. This factor in conjunction with a failure to treat the arrest when it occurs constitutes negligence.[60]

CASE ILLUSTRATION

A six-year-old boy was admitted to the hospital for a second operation to correct an inner deviation of his eye. Before the operation the patient was febrile and had symptoms of an upper respiratory infection. The patient was apprehensive, uncooperative, and agitated the night before and on the day of the operation; his response to sedating preoperative medication was called "unsatisfactory" in the records. The patient's temperature was recorded as slightly below normal prior to the operation, but there was evidence of an erasure in the record under this recorded temperature; this erasure was unexplained. During administration of anesthesia, the patient suffered first a respiratory arrest and then a cardiac arrest. When immediate resuscitative efforts were unsuccessful, the anesthesiologist asked the ophthalmologist to perform open cardiac massage. The ophthalmologist stated that he did not feel competent to do this operation and rushed out of the operating room to find someone to perform a thoracotomy. He found a surgeon (who had never performed a thoracotomy) who opened the patient's chest and began cardiac massage within a few minutes. The patient nevertheless suffered brain damage resulting in spastic quadriplegia.

The patient's family brought suit. It was generally agreed that the cardiac arrest was caused by vagal stimulation; the cause of the vagal stimulation was unknown and became a major issue in the case. The failure of the ophthalmologist and the anesthesiologist to cancel the operation in the face of an elevated temperature and a possible infection (that might have made vagal stimulation and cardiac arrest more likely) was criticized by expert witnesses. Based on expert testimony that fever is usually an indication of infection that might stimulate the vagal nerve, and that apprehension causes adrenalin to be pumped into the circulatory system further stimulating the vagal nerve, the court held that the anesthesiologist and the ophthalmologist negligently failed to postpone the operation. The ophthalmologist was further held to have a duty, as does any surgeon, to be able to perform appropriate resuscitative measures such as a thoracotomy, since cardiac arrest is a rare but foreseeable event during any operation involving general anesthesia. *(Quintal v. Laurel Grove Hospital,* 1964)[61]

Because cardiac arrest is often an admittedly unexplainable occurrence, res ipsa loquitur is sometimes a central consideration in anesthesia-related cardiac arrest lawsuits. (See § 1.52, Res Ipsa Loquitur.) Where specific acts by the anesthesiologist suggest that probable negligence can be proved by the patient, the doctrine will be involved.

CASE ILLUSTRATION

The patient suffered cardiac arrest while a surgeon was closing the abdomen

§ 12.70   Cardiac Arrest   339

after completion of a laparotomy for a ruptured appendix. The patient brought suit alleging that the defendant had been negligent in failing to bag-breathe the patient and in failing to monitor and record the pulse rate at any time during the operation.

The defendant was a general practitioner without formal training in anesthesiology who administered anesthesia one to three times a week. He first saw the patient in the operating room. Among the medications he administered to the patient were demerol 75 mg., sodium pentothal, and 7 cc. tubocurare. The defendant did not assist the patient's ventilation by bag-breathing until he noticed that the bag had ceased expanding and contracting spontaneously near the end of the operation. He then noticed that he could not obtain a blood pressure or pulse and announced this to the surgeon. At this time he began bag-breathing the patient with 100 percent oxygen. The patient sustained severe brain damage as a result of the cardiac arrest. The patient alleged that the anesthesiologist's failure to bag-breathe was a specific act of negligence which failed to meet the standard of care as represented by the patient's expert witness. Expert testimony that failure to bag-breathe was not a violation of the medical standard was offered by a witness for the general practitioner. Similar conflicting expert testimony was offered on many of the issues in the case. The appellate court reversed the holding of the trial court in favor of the anesthesiologist and held that the rarity of the occurrence of the accident did not in itself bring res ipsa loquitur into operation, but that the doctrine applies when other elements exist which, when combined, give the plaintiff the right to use res ipsa loquitur. Here there was expert testimony from which reasonable persons could infer that negligence was the probable cause of the injury as well as specific negligent acts or omissions. The court ordered the case retried. *(Edelman v. Zeigler,* 1965)[62]

Courts have recognized that the fact that a particular injury suffered by a patient as the result of an operation is something that rarely occurs, such as a cardiac arrest, does not in itself prove that the injury was probably caused by the negligence of those in charge of the operation.[63] Consequently, where no specific act suggesting negligence by the anesthesiologist is proved, res ipsa loquitur will not be applied. Where the injury is the result of an undetermined cause and the patient is not entitled to res ipsa loquitur, the anesthesiologist will not be held liable.

CASE ILLUSTRATION

The patient suffered a cardiac arrest after completion of closed reduction of an ankle fracture under general anesthesia. This occurred after the cast had been applied, the x-rays taken and read, and the anesthesia turned off. External cardiac massage was begun four to five seconds after the absence of blood pressure was noted. The patient died three days after the operation.

The patient's family brought suit and introduced only the medical record and the testimony of the autopsy surgeon. Neither the nurse-anesthetist, the surgeon, nor his assistant were called as witnesses or named as defendants. The autopsy surgeon stated that the patient had an infarction of the left internal capsule, but could not be certain whether this was the cause or a result of the cardiac arrest. He listed other possible causes of a cardiac arrest, including emboli (air, fat, or thrombus from the fracture site), drugs, an allergic reaction, intrinsic heart disease, or a cerebrovascular accident. There was no evidence that the nurse-anesthetist had failed to monitor the patient. The court stated that no evidence had been presented that the cardiac arrest was a result of anything the anesthetist did or failed to do and therefore that he had not been negligent. *(Crawford v. County of Sacramento,* 1966)[64]

Where the patient fails to communicate a condition to the physician which may contraindicate a particular anesthetic technique or which may require additional treatment to safeguard against the risk of cardiac arrest during surgery, the physician may escape liability.[65] The courts will interpret the patient's failure to give a comprehensive history to constitute negligence on the part of the patient. Such negligence contributes to the patient's own injury; the physician will not be held responsible for the patient's contributory negligence. (See § 3.20, Contributory Negligence.)

The legal doctrine of informed consent (see § 1.33, Consent and Informed Consent) is also frequently seen in litigation involving anesthesia-related cardiac arrest. Where the anesthesiologist fails to warn the patient that cardiac arrest is a risk of administration of anesthesia and such an injury ensues, the anesthesiologist may be held liable.

CASE ILLUSTRATION

A 23-year-old patient suffered a cardiac arrest and died after extraction of 23 teeth by a dentist. The anesthesia was administered and monitored by the oral surgeon and two assistants who lacked any anesthesia, surgical or dental training. One assistant noticed that the patient "looked dark" during the recovery phase after surgery. The oral surgeon then noticed cyanosis, fixed and dilated pupils, and cardiopulmonary arrest. Resuscitation was begun and the patient seemed to respond after five minutes; however, she suffered a second cardiopulmonary arrest while being placed in an ambulance for

§ 12.70   Cardiac Arrest   341

transportation to a hospital. She was in a coma for three days before expiring. Her widower brought suit and a verdict for the oral surgeon was ultimately reversed on the issue of informed consent. The oral surgeon had asked the patient if she wanted a local anesthetic, but did not compare the relative risks of local and general anesthesia. *(Sauro v. Shea,* 1978)[66]

Other courts have failed to find lack of informed consent even when the patient was not warned of the risk of cardiac arrest in cases where there is no evidence that it is customary to inform the patient of such a risk.[67]

In most cases involving cardiac arrest, if the factors already discussed are not present, the anesthesiologist will not be subjected to liability. Courts have characterized the cardiac arrest as "rare, . . . unexpected, indeed an unforeseeable development."[68] In fact, one court adopted the view that a cardiac arrest constituted an emergency situation that required the anesthesiologist's conduct to meet a modified standard of care.

CASE ILLUSTRATION

A child sustained severe brain damage when a cardiac arrest occurred during a tonsillectomy and the family brought suit. The jury was allowed to determine whether a cardiac arrest was in fact an "emergency." Although due care must be used in an emergency, in judging the defendant's conduct the jury was properly allowed to consider that less time is available for thought and contemplation about alternatives than in a nonemergency situation. *(Linhares v. Hall,* 1970)[69]

Often, patients who bring lawsuits to recover from injuries suffered from cardiac arrest allege that the anesthesiologist was negligent in failing to monitor the patient properly.

CASE ILLUSTRATION

A five-year-old patient suffered a cardiac arrest in an operation to correct a kidney disorder and his family brought suit. At the trial, the anesthesiologist testified that he left the operating room for about five minutes to answer a telephone call. While he was gone, he was relieved by a nurse-anesthetist. The patient suffered a severe neurological deficit as a result of the cardiac arrest. The patient maintained that this injury was due to the anesthesiologist's failure to monitor. The court found no evidence that the patient was ever left unattended or that his vital signs were not constantly monitored. It was held that the standard of care applicable to anesthesiologists included a constant monitoring of the patient's vital signs by the anesthesiologist or qualified nurse-anesthetist and that the defendant anesthesiologist had met this standard. *(McAdams v. Holden,* 1977)[70]

Cardiac arrest can occur during spinal anesthesia as well as general anesthesia. It may be as difficult to determine the exact cause in these cases as it is in general anesthesia cases. Excessive sedation leading to hypoventilation, high spinal anesthesia, altered sympathetic or vagal responses, or hypotension may contribute. (See § 11.10, Spinal Anesthesia.) In a 1966 California case,[71] the patient suffered cardiac arrest immediately after delivery of a child. It was held that the physician need not prove the exact cause of the cardiac arrest; it was sufficient to prove that the accident could not have occurred from want of care, but was due to some unpreventable (though unknown) cause. The anesthesiologist was held not liable.

§ 12.80 POSTOPERATIVE ANESTHETIC CARE

An anesthesiologist is most likely to be subject to legal liability in connection with postoperative care where he or she has (1) failed to monitor a patient's recovery from general anesthesia adequately, or (2) has used an inappropriate drug or procedure during the postoperative period.

Basic Standard of Care: With respect to postanesthesia care, the American Society of Anesthesiologists (ASA) has provided the following basic guidelines.[72] Under these guidelines, postanesthesia care means:

1. Availability of adequate nursing personnel and pertinent equipment necessary for safe postanesthesia care
2. Awareness by responsible physicians of competence level of personnel who carry out postanesthetic care
3. Informing personnel caring for patient in immediate postanesthetic period of any specific problems presented by each patient
4. That the individual responsible for administering anesthesia remains with patients as long as his presence appears necessary
5. That a physician participates in establishing policies for the discharge of patients from any postanesthetic care facility
6. At least one visit with appropriate notation on patient's chart during early postanesthetic period where feasible

7. Management of related anesthesia complications

The ASA has also provided the following suggestions[73] for preparing a postoperative care record* to facilitate a medical audit:

1. Evaluation of the status of the patient on admission and discharge from the postoperative recovery suite
2. A record of vital signs
3. A record of IV fluids administered, including blood and blood products
4. Record of all drugs employed
5. Record of unusual events or postoperative complications, including management thereof
6. The anesthesiologist shall determine and document when the period of postoperative surveillance has terminated.

Interpretation and Customary Practice: Numerous problems may arise following the completion of an operation. Even the transfer of the patient to the recovery room presents the potential for mishap. Poorly attended patients have fallen to the floor and been injured. Abrupt transfers have resulted in muscle and ligament strains, brachial plexus injury, or dangerous degrees of hypotension. An adequate number of individuals should assist in the transfer to avoid incidents of this kind. Once the patient is moved, the sides of the litter or bed should be elevated, a restraining strap put in place, and the patient constantly attended.[74]

The anesthesiologist should be prepared to respond to at least four categories of postanesthetic problems: respiratory, cardiovascular, and metabolic complications, and postoperative pain and delirium.[75]

Respiratory Problems. Airway obstruction, laryngospasm, accumulation of secretions, and inadequate gas exchange may be present. Perhaps the most common postoperative respiratory problem is residual neuromuscular block. Hypoventilation with resultant hypoxemia and hypercarbia is a threat. Hyperventilation too, is commonly observed after anesthesia. Because secretions accumulate and atelectasis may develop, hypoventilation should be searched for and treated promptly. Other problems which may arise include pneumothorax, aspiration of vomitus, and inadequate ventilation or respiratory obstruction caused by excessively tight surgical dressings.[76]

Cardiovascular Problems. While the anesthesiologist is disconnecting the apparatus from the anesthesia machine, turning off the gas supply and preparing to move the patient from the room, blood pressure or pulse may not be observed for a time, even if monitoring devices are in place. Thus, hypotension could reach

---

*For Joint Commission on Accreditation of Hospitals requirements with respect to the postanesthetic record, see § 7.81, JCAH Standards.

serious proportions before being recognized. In other patients hypertension may be present. The anesthesiologist should also keep in mind the possibilities of hypoxia, cardiac arrhythmias, and unreplaced blood loss.[77]

Metabolic Problems. Most patients returning from air-conditioned operating rooms are hypothermic, particularly following prolonged procedures and extensive dissection. A hypothermic patient is intensely vasoconstricted, which results in impaired peripheral perfusion, metabolic acidosis, and, frequently, hypertension. Postanesthetic shivering is commonly experienced upon emergence from general anesthesia. The reduction of body temperature that causes shivering may be minimized by maintaining room temperature at 21°C or higher. Hyperkalemia may be observed in connection with chronic renal disease or abnormal administration of potassium.[78]

Pain and Delirium. The incidence and severity of postoperative pain are so variable that the approach to each patient must be individualized. The very young, the emotionally stable, and the elderly tend to show lesser responses to pain. Excitement following emergence from general anesthesia is displayed particularly by the younger patient who, without analgesia, may be difficult to control.[79] Agitation may also be experienced by patients who have psychomotor disturbances, who are fearful of the findings of the operation, or who cannot tolerate pain.[80]

One of the more common sources of liability in this area is a failure to monitor a patient's recovery from general anesthesia adequately. However, proof that the patient suffered an injury during the postoperative period does not by itself prove negligence on the part of the anesthesiologist. The anesthesiologist cannot be liable, for example, for an *unavoidable* injury occurring during the course of an operation. This is true even if the patient's injury is significantly aggravated during the postoperative period by the negligence of hospital employees not under the direction of the anesthesiologist.

CASE ILLUSTRATION

The five-year-old patient was admitted to the hospital for a tonsillectomy and myringotomy. During the operation absence of pulse and cardiac arrest were noted. The patient's heartbeat was restored within two and one-half minutes. The patient was transferred to the recovery room, where hypothermia was applied. From there, at the direction of a member of the anesthesiological firm, the patient was moved to the hospital's intensive care unit. The unit had no monitor or defibrillator, and the use of a defective telethermometer resulted in the maintenance of the patient's body temperature at a temperature higher than that prescribed. Although the nurse on duty in the unit noted the continuing rise in the patient's temperature, she took no action in response. No neurological response charts were kept. Three hours after being transferred to the unit, the patient suffered the first of three grand mal seizures. Permanent brain damage and cortical blindness were the ultimate result.

The patient's parents brought suit. In holding that the anesthesiologists who participated in the operation and in the patient's recovery room care had not been negligent, the court noted that there was no evidence to indicate that the cardiac arrest suffered during the operation was the result of negligence. In contrast, said the court, the defective equipment in the intensive care unit and the nurses' failure to exercise ordinary care clearly established negligence on the part of the hospital. (It should be noted, however, that the anesthesiological firm which was sued in this case, wishing to avoid jury trial, paid a settlement of $175,000 to the patient's father prior to trial.) Despite the later specific findings of "no negligence," established legal doctrines precluded recovery of this money from either the father or the hospital. *(Rose v. Hakim,* 1974)[81]

When circumstances so demand, it does not constitute negligence to depart from customary postoperative procedures. Thus, a hospital is not necessarily negligent if it fails to provide a patient with the facilities of a recovery room, nor is an anesthesiologist necessarily negligent for unsuccessful postoperative care so long as the care provided conforms to the standard of care.

CASE ILLUSTRATION

Following the completion of an emergency operation to relieve intestinal blockage, the patient was returned to her own hospital room, rather than to the recovery room, because the latter had closed for the evening. The patient's room was provided with the customary equipment, and a special registered nurse had been employed to care for the patient during the postoperative period. After accompanying the patient to her room, the anesthesiologist reintubated her, attached the Levin's tube to a suction pump, affixed an oxygen nasal catheter and then, satisfied as to the condition of the patient, left to administer an anesthetic at another emergency operation. Shortly thereafter, the patient suffered a cardiac arrest, and the anesthesiologist, who was requested to bring an oxygen pressure machine from the operating room and to use it upon the patient, was delayed for several minutes by his duties at the second operation. Although the patient's heartbeat was restored by a thoracotomy and internal cardiac massage, she never regained consciousness, and died ten months later.

The patient's widower brought suit. In upholding a jury verdict rendered for the physician-defendant and the hospital, the court stated that the hospital's failure to take the patient to the recovery room did not constitute negligence. The court noted that hospitals in the area customarily closed their recovery rooms late in the day. The court also found a lack of causal connection between the hospital's actions and the patient's injuries, noting that while the machine needed to help the patient was not available in her room, it would not have been available in the recovery room either. And the anesthesiologist was not negligent in scheduling the second operation, said the court, because at the time he did so there was no reason to suspect that the patient would need his continued attention. *(Prack v. United States Fidelity and Guaranty Co.,* 1966)[82]

In the absence of extenuating circumstances, however, a hospital which fails to provide skilled medical personnel during the postoperative period may find itself liable for malpractice. Similarly, a physician entrusted with the general postoperative care of a patient should not unnecessarily leave the hospital or otherwise fail to attend the patient if he or she wishes to avoid liability.

CASE ILLUSTRATION

The patient was admitted to the hospital with a fractured jaw suffered in an automobile accident. The fracture was reduced by a dentist after a nurse-anesthetist administered a general anesthetic. Although made responsible by a hospital rule for the patient's general medical care, the admitting physician left the hospital shortly before the operation began in order to take his afternoon off. No physician attended at the operation, and there were no other physicians present in the hospital. After being moved to the recovery room, the patient suffered convulsive seizures which resulted in brain damage. The patient was not examined by a physician until one and one-half hours after the convulsions began, and he did not regain consciousness for one month.

The patient brought suit to recover for disabling brain damage. Expert testimony at trial indicated that the patient's brain damage was due to cerebral anoxia or hypoxia, which in turn was caused by inadequate ventilation of the patient during the anesthesia or postoperative period. In overturning a judgment rendered for the hospital, dentist, and physician, the court held that the hospital was negligent as a matter of law in permitting the operation to take place without an attending physician. The court also concluded that the facts of the case would support a finding that the physician and dentist had been negligent, and a new trial* was ordered. *(Pederson v. Dumouchel,* 1967)[83]

---

* This case was settled before the new trial.

§ 12.80   Postoperative Anesthetic Care   347

The degree of care owed to a patient during the postoperative period depends upon the patient's condition. Failure to exercise a degree of care consistent with the patient's known needs and self-care capabilities may result in a finding of negligence.

CASE ILLUSTRATION

An eight-month-old baby was placed under general anesthesia for the surgical removal of a hemangioma from the child's shoulder. Following successful completion of the operation the baby, still sleeping, was returned to her crib in a room with five other children. No one else was present in the room except for a nurse's aide, who was engaged in removing soiled clothes and bedding. When the baby's mother returned to the room one-half hour later, she found her child's body to be very white and her fingernails blue. A graduate nurse and two or three physicians were summoned, but all attempts at resuscitation failed; the child was dead.

The child's parents brought suit. At trial, a surgeon testified that the cause of death was atelectasis. He also testified that it is the usual custom in hospitals to watch a child coming out of anesthesia until consciousness has returned, and that such observation may reveal the onset of an atelectasis. In holding that a suit brought by the baby's parents could proceed, the court stated: "It is clear that a reasonably careful management of (the hospital) would have had a proficient nurse at the bedside of the baby during the time it was under the effect of the anesthetic and that reasonable care and diligence was not exercised when the only person in the room was an unskilled nurse's aide who was not watching over the baby but was changing the clothing and the bedding of other children." The court also stated that because of the baby's age and complete inability to care for itself the hospital owed a higher degree of care to her than it would have owed to an adult. *(Thomas v. Seaside Memorial Hospital of Long Beach, 1947)*[84]

NOTES

1. Cooper, *Avoiding Preventable Mishaps,* in ASA Annual Refresher Course Lectures 201 (1980).
2. Cooper *et al., Preventable Anesthesia Mishaps: A Study of Human Factors,* 49 Anesthesiology 399-406 (1978).
3. Cooper, *supra* note 1.
4. Cooper, Long, Newbower & Philip, *Multi-Hospital Study of Preventable Anesthesia Mishaps,* 51 Anesthesiology 5348 (Sept, 1979).
5. Cooper, *supra* note 1.
6. Cooper, *et al., supra* note 4.
7. *See, e.g.,* Aubert v. Charity Hosp., 363 So.2d 1223 (La. App. 1978); Schneider v. Albert Einstein Medical Center, 257 Pa. Supr. Ct. 348, 390 A.2d 1271 (1978).

Notes: Chapter XII

8. Cooper, *supra* note 1.
9. *Id.*
10. *Id.*
11. Joint Commission on Accreditation of Hospitals, Anesthesia Services Standard IV, in Accreditation Manual for Hospitals 7-9 (1981).
12. V. Collins, Principles of Anesthesiology, at 7 (2d ed. 1976).
13. Dobkin, Harland & Fedoruk, *Comparison of the Cardiovascular and Respiratory Effects of Halothane and the Halothane-Diethyl Ether Azeotrope in Dogs,* 21 Anesthesiology 13 (1960).
14. V. Collins, *supra* note 12, at 1441-44.
15. *Id.* at 806.
16. V. Collins, *supra* note 12, at 806; Jacoby, *Electrical Safety and the "Safe" Power Center,* 13 Anesthesiology 19 (1971); Horton, *Present Status of the Problems of Preventing Anesthetic Explosions,* 2 Anesthesiology 121 (1941).
17. McKinney v. Tromly, 386 S.W.2d 564 (Tex. 1964).
18. R. Dripps, J. Eckenhoff & L. Vandam, *Introduction to Anesthesia,* at 437-38 (5th ed. 1977).
19. *Id.* at 438.
20. *Id.*
21. Weeks v. Latter-Day Saints Hosp., 418 F.2d 1035 (10th Cir. 1969).
22. Wiles v. Myerly, 210 N.W.2d 619 (Iowa 1973).
23. Bing v. Thunig, 1 A.D.2d 887, 149 N.Y.S.2d 358 (1956).
24. Starnes v. Charlotte-Mecklenburg Hosp. Auth., 28 N.C. App. 418, 221 S.E.2d 733 (1976).
25. Wong, *Electrolyte Disturbance and Anesthetic Considerations,* in ASA Annual Refresher Course Lectures 187-98 (1978).
26. Burrows v. Widder, 52 Ill. App. 3d 1017, 368 N.E.2d 443 (1977).
27. James v. Holder, 34 A.D.2d 632, 309 N.Y.S.2d 385 (1970).
28. Brody v. Overlook Hosp., 127 N.J. Super. 331, 317 A.2d 392 (1974); *aff'd per curiam,* 66 N.J. 448, 332 A.2d 596 (1975).
29. Jackson v. Muhlenberg Hosp., 96 N.J. Super 314, 232 A.2d 879 (1967).
30. Cunningham v. MacNeal Memorial Hosp., 47 Ill. 2d 443, 266 N.E.2d 897 (1970).
31. Ill. Rev. Stat. ch. 91, § 181-83 (1977); N.Y. Pub. Health Laws § 420.4 (McKinney 1971 & Supp. 1980–81); Idaho Code § 39-3702 (1977).
32. Weiss v. Rubin, 9 N.Y.2d 230, 173 N.E.2d 791, 231 N.Y.S. 2d 65 (1961).
33. V. Collins, *supra* note 12 at 164.
34. V. Collins, *supra* note 12, at 157.
35. Legal Perspectives on Anesthesia, Feb./Mar. 1981, at 1, col. 3.
36. V. Collins, *supra* note 12 at 164-65.
37. *See, e.g.,* Guzman v. Faraldo, 373 So.2d 66 (Fla. App. 1979).
38. R. Dripps, J. Eckenhoff & L. Vandam, *Introduction to Anesthesia,* 460 (5th ed. 1977).
39. Beadles v. Matayka, 135 Cal. 366, 311 P.2d 711 (1957).
40. *See, e.g.,* Guzman v. Faraldo, *supra* note 37; Spannaus v. Otolaryngology Clinic, 308 Minn. 334, 242 N.W.2d 597 (1976); Jones v. Harrisburg Polyclinic Hosp., 487 Pa. 506, 410 A.2d 303 (1980).
41. Hass v. United States, 492 F. Supp. 755 (D. Mass. 1980); Kitto v. Gilbert, 39 Colo. App. 374, 570 P.2d 544 (1977); Warrick v. Giron, 290 N.W.2d 166 (Minn. 1980); Spannaus v. Otolaryngology Clinic, *supra* note 40.
42. Ybarra v. Spangard, 25 Cal. 2d 486, 154 P.2d 687 (1944); *op. remand,* 93 Cal. App. 2d 43, 298 P.2d 445 (1949).
43. Faris v. Doctors Hosp., Inc., 18 Ariz. App. 264, 501 P.2d 440 (1972).

Notes: Chapter XII

44. Guzman v. Faraldo, *supra* note 37.
45. Bertrand v. Aetna Cas. & Sur. Co., 306 So.2d 343 (La. App. 1975).
46. Jones v. Harrisburg Polyclinic Hosp., *supra* note 40.
47. Miller v. Hardy, 564 S.W.2d 102 (Tex. Civ. App. 1978).
48. *See, e.g.*, Spannaus v. Otolaryngology Clinic, *supra* note 40.
49. Miller v. Hardy, *supra* note 47.
50. *Id.*
51. Editorial, *Malignant Hyperpyrexia During General Anesthesia*, 13 Can. Anesthesiology Soc. J. 415 (1966).
52. V. Collins, *supra* note 12, at 1256.
53. Solomons & Myers, *Hyperthermia of Osteogenesis Imperfecta and its Relation to Malignant Hyperthermia*, in Int'l Symp. on Malignant Hyperthermia ch. 26 (1973); Isaacs & Barlow, *Identification of Asymptomatic Carriers of Malignant Hyperthemia*, 42 Brit. J. Anesthesiology 1077 (1970).
54. V. Collins, *supra* note 12.
55. *Id.* at 1252-53; R. Dripps, J. Eckenhoff & L. Vandam, *supra* note 38, at 429.
56. V. Collins, *supra* note 12, at 1256-57; R. Dripps, J. Eckenhoff & L. Vandam, *supra* note 38, at 429.
57. Vogan v. Byers, 447 F.2d 543 (3d Cir. 1971).
58. Rose v. Hakim, 335 F. Supp. 1221 (D.D.C. 1971), *op. on remand*, 345 F. Supp. 1300 (D.D.C. 1972), *aff'd in part, remanded in part*, 501 F.2d 806 (D.C. Cir. 1974); McAdams v. Holden, 349 So.2d 900 (La. App. 1977).
59. Engel, Anesthesiology (Jan. 1980).
60. Dalen, Howe, Membrino & McIntyre, *CPR Training for Physicians*, 303 New England J. Med. 455 (1980).
61. Quintal v. Laurel Grove Hosp., 62 Cal. 2d 154, 397 P.2d 151, 41 Cal. Rptr 577 (1964).
62. Edelman v. Ziegler, 233 Cal. App. 2d 871, 44 Cal. Rptr. 114 (1965).
63. Silverson v. Weber, 57 Cal. 2d 834, 372 P.2d 97, 22 Cal. Rptr. 337 (1962).
64. Crawford v. County of Sacramento, 239 Cal. App. 2d 791, 49 Cal. Rptr. 115 (1966).
65. Mackey v. Greenview Hosp., Inc., 587 S.W.2d 249 (Ky. App. 1979).
66. Sauro v. Shea, 257 Pa. Super. Ct. 87, 390 A.2d 259 (1978).
67. Dunlap v. Marine, 242 Cal. App. 2d 162, 51 Cal. Rptr. 158 (1966).
68. Prack v. United States Fidelity & Guar. Co., 187 So.2d 170 (La. App. 1966).
69. Linhares v. Hall, 357 Mass. 209, 257 N.E.2d 429 (1970).
70. McAdams v. Holden, *supra* note 58.
71. Dunlap v. Marine, *supra* note 67.
72. ASA, *Basic Guidelines for Anesthesia Care*, in American Society of Anesthesiologists Directory of Members IV A1.C at 427 (46th ed. 1981).
73. ASA, *Suggestions for a Record of Anesthesia Care to Facilitate Medical Audit*, in American Society of Anesthesiologists Directory of Members 431 (46th ed. 1981).
74. R. Dripps, J. Eckenhoff & L. Vandam, *supra* note 38 at 460.
75. Cullen & Cullen, *Postanesthetic Complications*, 55 Surg. Clin. North Amer. 987 (Aug., 1975).
76. R. Dripps, J. Eckenhoff & L. Vandam, *supra* note 38, at 461-62.
77. *Id.* at 461.
78. Cullen & Cullen, *supra* note 75, at 994-95.
79. *Id.* at 995-96.
80. R. Dripps, J. Eckenhoff & L. Vandam, *supra* note 38, at 463.
81. Rose v. Hakim, 335 F. Supp. 1221 (D.D.C. 1971), *op. on remand*, 345 F. Supp. 1300 (D.D.C. 1972).
82. Prack v. United States Fidelity & Guar. Co., 187 So.2d 170 (La. App. 1966).

83. Pederson v. Dumochel, 72 Wash. 2d 73, 431 P.2d 973 (1967).
84. Thomas v. Seaside Memorial Hosp. of Long Beach, 80 Cal. App. 2d 841, 183 P.2d 288 (1947).

Appendix A

Controlled Substances Schedule

The following controlled substances are included in Schedule 1:

(a) Any of the following opiates:
Acetylmethadol
Allylprodine
Alpha-acetylmethadol
Alphameprodine
Alphamethadol
Benzethidine
Betacetylmethadol
Betameprodine
Betamethadol
Betaprodine
Clonitazene
Dextromoramide
Diethylthiambutene
Difenoxin
Diampromide
Dimenoxadol
Dimepheptanol
Dimethylthiambutene
Dioxaphetyl Butyrate
Dipipanone
Ethylmethylthiambutene
Etonitazene
Etoxeridine
Furethidine
Hydroxypethidine
Ketobemidone
Levomoramide
Levophenacylmorphan
Morpheridine
Noracymethadol
Norlevorphanol
Normethadone
Norpipanone
Phenadoxone
Phenampromide
Phenomorphan
Phenoperidine
Piritramide
Proheptazine
Properidine
Propiram
Ecemoramide
Trimeperidine

(b) Any of the following opium derivatives:
Acetorphine
Acetyldihydrocodeine
Benzylmorphine
Codeine Methylvromide
Codeine-N-Oxide
Cyprenorphine
Desomorphine
Methyldesorphine
Methyldihydromorphine
Morphine Methylbromide
Morphine Methylsulfonate
Morphine-N-Oxide
Myrophine
Nicocodeine

Appendix A

Dihydromorphine
Drotebanol
Etorphine
Heroin
Hydromorphinol

Nicomorphine
Normorphine
Pholcodine
Thebacon

(c) Any material compound, mixture, or preparation which contains any quantity of the following hallucinogenic substances, their salts, isomers, and salts of isomers, unless specifically excepted, when the existence of these salts, isomers, and salts of isomers is possible within the specific chemical designation:

3,4-methylenedioxy amphetamine
   5-methoxy-3,4-methylenedioxy
   amphetamine
3,4,5,-trimethoxy amphetamine
   Bufotenine
   Some trade and other names:
   3-(B-dimethylaminoethyl)-5 hydrozyindole
   3-(2-dimethylaminoethyl)-5 indolol
   N,N-dimethylserotonin; 5-hydroxy-N-dimethyltryptamine
   Mappine
2,5-Dimethoxyamphetamine
   Some trade or other names:
   2,5-dimethoxy-a-methylphenethylamine; 2,5-DMA
4-Bromo-2,5-Dimethoxyamphetamine
   Some trade or other names:
   4-bromo-2,5 dimethoxy-a-methylphenethylamine;4-bromo
   2,5-DMA
Diethyltryptamine
   Some trade and other names:
   N,N-Diethyltryptamine; DET
Dimethyltryptamine
   Some trade or other names:
   DMT
4-methyl-2,5-dimethoxyzmphetamine
   Some trade or other names:
   4-methyl-2,5-kimethoxy-a-methyl-phenethylamine
   DOM,STP
4-methoxyamphetamine
   Some trade or other names:
   4-methoxy-a-methylphenethylamine; paramethoxy amphetamine;
   PMA
Ibogaine
   Some trade and other names:
   7-Ethyl-6,6a,7,8,9,10,11,12,13
   Octahydro-2-methoxy-6,9-methano-5H-pyrido

(s,2:1,2 azepino 4,5-b) indole
  Tabernanthe iboga
Lysergic acid diethylamide
Marijuana
Mecloqualone
Mescaline
Peyote
N-ethyl-3, piperidyl benzilate
N-methyl-3 Piperidyl benzilate
Psilocybin
Psilocyn
Triophene analog of Phencyclidine
  Some trade or other names:
  1-(1-(2-thienyl cyclohexyl) piperidine)
  2-thienyl analog of phencyclidine; TPCP

(d) Synthetic equivalents of the substances contained in the plant, or in the resinous extractives of cannabis and synthetic substances, derivatives, and their isomers with similar chemical structure or pharmacological activity:

  (i) ^{1}cis or trans tetrahydrocannabinol, and their optical isomers.
  (ii) ^{6}cis or trans tetrahydrocannabinol, and their optical isomers.
  (iii) ^{3,4}cis or trans tetrahydrocannabinol, and their optical isomers.

(e) Compounds of structures of substances referred to above, regardless of numerical designation of atomic positions, are included.

The following controlled substances are included in Schedule 2:

(a) Opium and opiate, and any salt, compound, derivative, or preparation of opium or opiate excluding naloxone and its salts, and excluding naltrexone and its salts, but including the following:

Raw opium	Etorphine hydrochloride
Opium extracts	Hydrocodone
Opium fluid-extracts	Hydromorphone
Powdered opium	Metopon
Granulated opium	Morphine
Tincture of opium	Oxycodone
Codeine	Oxymorphone
Ethylmorphine	Thebaine

(b) Substances which are chemically equivalent to or identical with substances referred to in 1, except that these substances do not include the isoquinoline alkaloids of opium.

(c) Opium poppy, poppy straw, and concentrate of poppy straw, accrued extract of poppy straw in either liquid, solid or powder form, which contains the phenanthrine alkaloids of the opium poppy.

(d) Cocoa leaves and its derivatives. The substances include cocaine, its salts, isomers, and salts of isomers.

(e) Any of the following opiates:
Alphaprodine   Fentanyl
Anileridine   Isomethadone
Bezitramide   Levomethorphan
Dihydrocodeine   Levorphanol
Diphenoxylate   Metazocine

                      Methadone
Methadone-Intermediate, 4-cyano-1 diamethylamino-4
4-diphenyl butane
Moramide-Intermediate, 2-methyl-3-morpholino-1,
1-diphenylpropane-carboxylic acid

                      Pethidine
Pethidine-Intermediate-A, 4-cyano-1-methyl-4-phenylpiperidine
Pethidine-Intermediate-B, ethyl-4-phenylpiperidine-4–carboxylate
Pethidine-Intermediate-C, 1-methyl-4-phenylpiperidine-4-carboxylic acid
Phenasocine   Racemethorphan
Piminodine   Rademorphan

(f) Unless listed in another schedule, any material, compound, mixture or preparation which contains any quantity of the following substances having potential for abuse associated with a stimulant effect on the nervous system:

    (i) amphetamines

    (ii) any substance which contains any quantity of methaphetamine

    (iii) Phenmetrazine

    (iv) Methylphenidate

(g) Any quantity of the following substances having a potential for abuse associated with a depressant effect on the central nervous system: methaqualone, emobarbital, pentobarbital, or secobarbital.

The following controlled substances are included in Schedule 3:

(a) Unless listed in another schedule, any material, compound, mixture or preparation, which contains any quantity of the following substances having a potential for abuse associated with a stimulant effect on the central nervous system is included in Schedule 3:
Benzphetamine   Mediatric tabs

Clorphentermine
Clotermine
Edrisal tabs
Genegesic caps
Hovizyme tabs
Mazindol
Mediatric liquid
Phendimetrazine
Special formula 711 tabs
Thora Dex No. 1 tab
Thora Dex No. 2 tab

(b) Also, any material with any quantity of the following substances having a potential for abuse associated with a depressant effect on the central nervous system:

Chlorhexadol
Glutethimide
Lysergic acid
Lysergic acid amide
Methyprylon
Phencyclidine
Sulfondiethylmethane
Sulfonethylmethane
Sulfonmethane

(c) Nalorphine

(d) Substances containing any quantity of a derivative of barbituric acid.

The following substances are included in Schedule 4:

(a) materials which contain any quantity of the following substances having potential for abuse associated with a depressant effect on the central nervous system:

Barbital
Chloral Betaine
Chloral Hydrate
Dextropropoxyphene
Diazepam
Ethchlorvynol
Ethinamate
Flurazepam
Lorazepam
Mebutamate
Meprobamate
Chlordiazepoxide
Clonazepam
Clorazepate
Methohexital
Methylphenorbarbital
Oxazepam
Paraldehyde
Petrichloral
Phenobarbital
Prazepam

(b) Fenfluramine and its derivatives

(c) Materials containing any quantity of the following substances having a potential for abuse associated with a stimulant effect on the central nervous system: diethylpropion, phentermine, pemoline.

The following substances are included in Schedule 5:

Amodrine
Bronkaid
Tedral anti-H
Tedral one-half strength

Bronkolixir
Bronkotabs
Beckman buffer B-1
Beckman buffer B-2
Primatene
Tedral

Tedral pediatric suspension
Tedral suppositories double strength
Tedral suppositories regular strength
Verequad tablet
Verequad suspension

Appendix B

California Anesthesia Service Regulations

70223. Surgical Service General Requirements.

    (d)   Prior to commencing surgery the person responsible for administering anesthesia, or the surgeon if a general anesthetic is not to be administered, shall verify the patient's identity, the site and side of the body to be operated on, and ascertain that a record of the following appears in the patient's medical record:

    (f)   A register of operations shall be maintained including the following information for each surgical procedure performed:
        (1)   Name, age, sex and hospital admitting number of the patient.
        (2)   Date and time of the operation and the operating room number.
        (3)   Preoperative and postoperative diagnosis.
        (4)   Name of surgeon, assistants, anesthetists and scrub and circulating assistant.
        (5)   Surgical procedure performed and anesthetic agent used.
        (6)   Complications, if any, during the operation.

70227. Surgical Service Equipment and Supplies.

    (a)   There shall be adequate and appropriate equipment and supplies maintained related to the nature of the needs and the services offered, including at least the following monitoring equipment and supplies:
        (1)   Cardiac monitor, with a pulse rate meter, for each patient receiving a general anesthetic.
        (2)   D.C. defibrillator.
        (3)   Electrocardiographic machine.
        (4)   Oxygen and respiratory rate alarms.
        (5)   Appropriate supplies and drugs for emergency use.

Source: California, Title 22, Health Facilities and Referral Agencies, Register 78, No. 30-7-29-78.

70231. Anesthesia Service Definition.

Anesthesia service means the provision of anesthesia of the type and in the manner required by the patient's condition with appropriate staff, space, equipment and supplies. A postanesthesia recovery unit is a specific area in a hospital, staffed and equipped to provide specialized care and supervision of patients during the immediate postanesthesia period.

70233. Anesthesia Service General Requirements.

(a) Written policies and procedures shall be developed and maintained by the person responsible for the service in consultation with other appropriate health professionals and administration. Policies shall be approved by the governing body. Procedures shall be approved by the administration and medical staff where such is appropriate. The policies and procedures shall include provision for at least:
  (1) Preanesthesia evaluation of the patient by a physician, with appropriate documentation of pertinent information relative to the choice of anesthesia and the surgical or obstetrical procedure anticipated.
  (2) Review of the patient's condition immediately prior to induction of anesthesia.
  (3) Safety of the patient during the anesthetic period.
  (4) Recording of all events taking place during the induction of, maintenance of and emergence from anesthesia, including the amount and duration of all anesthetic agents, other drugs, intravenous fluids and blood or blood fractions.
  (5) Recording of postanesthetic visits that include at least one note describing the presence or absence of complications related to anesthesia.

(b) The responsibility and the accountability of the anesthesia service to the medical staff and administration shall be defined.

(c) Rules for the safe use of nonflammable and flammable anesthetic agents which conform with the rules of the State Fire Marshal and Section 70849 shall be adopted.

(d) Periodically, an appropriate committee of the medical staff shall evaluate the service provided and make appropriate recommendations to the executive committee of the medical staff and administration.

(e) The requirements in this section do not apply to special hospitals unless the special hospital provides this service.

70235. Anesthesia Service Staff.

Appendix B 359

(a) A physician shall have overall responsibility for the anesthesia service. His responsibility shall include at least the:
  (1) Availability of equipment, drugs and parenteral fluids necessary for administering anesthesia and for related resuscitative efforts.
  (2) Development of regulations concerning anesthetic safety.
  (3) Operation of the postanesthesia service.

(b) Anesthesia care shall be provided by physicians or dentists with anesthesia privileges, nurse anesthetists, or appropriately supervised trainees in an approved educational program.

(c) Anesthesia staff shall be available or on call at all times.

(d) A registered nurse with training and experience in postanesthesia nursing care shall be responsible for the nursing care and nursing management in the postanesthesia recovery unit.

(e) There shall be sufficient licensed nurses assigned to meet the needs of the patients.

(f) Nurses assistants, where provided, shall not be assigned patient care duties unless under the direct supervision of a licensed nurse.

70237. Anesthesia Service Equipment and Supplies.

(a) There shall be adequate and appropriate equipment for the delivery of anesthesia and postanesthesia recovery care.
  (1) The anesthetist shall check the readiness, availability, and cleanliness of all equipment used prior to the administration of the anesthetic agents.
  (2) At least the following equipment shall be provided in the postanesthesia recovery room:
    (A) Cardiac monitor, with pulse rate meter, in the ratio of 1 monitor for each two (2) patients.
    (B) D.C. defibrillator.
    (C) Mechanical positive pressure breathing apparatus.
    (D) Stripchart electrocardiographic recorder.
    (E) Sphygmomanometer.
    (F) Crash cart, or equivalent, with appropriate supplies and drugs for emergency use.

70239. Anesthesia Service Space.

(a) Postanesthesia recovery unit shall maintain the following spaces as required in Section T 17-314, Title 24, California Administrative Code:
  (1) Floor area of at least 7.5 square meters (80 square feet) per bed exclusive

of the spaces listed below in (2) through (6).
- (2) Space for a nurses' control desk, charting space, locked medicine cabinet, refrigerator and handwashing lavatory not requiring direct contact of the hands for operation.
- (3) A utility space including a rim-flush clinic sink and countertop work space at least one meter (3 feet) long. Clean and dirty areas shall be separated.
- (4) Storage space for clean linen.
- (5) Storage space for soiled linen.
- (6) Storage space for supplies and equipment.
- (7) Air Conditioning.

(b) The postanesthesia recovery unit is classified as an electrically sensitive area and shall meet grounding requirements in Section 70853.

(c) Beds in the postanesthesia recovery unit shall not be included in the licensed bed capacity of the hospital.

70749. Patient Health Record Content.

(a) Each inpatient medical record shall consist of at least the following items:
- (11) Anesthesia record including preoperative diagnosis, if anesthesia has been administered.

Appendix C

Massachusetts Anesthesia Service Requirements

130.510: Anesthesia Facilities

(A) All equipment for the administration of anesthesia shall be readily available, kept clean, maintained in good repair and comply with the National Fire Protection Association Codes.
(B) There shall be provided a suction apparatus and resuscitation apparatus and equipment for the administration of oxygen.

130.511 Anesthesia Procedures

(A) In hospitals not providing an organized anesthesia service, all anesthetics shall be given under the supervision of a competent staff physician.
(B) No general or intrathecal anesthesia shall, for any reason, surgical or otherwise, be administered, except in extreme emergencies, until the patient has had a preliminary physical examination and necessary laboratory procedures.
(C) After the administration of a general or intrathecal anesthetic, the patient shall be under the constant observation of a competent individual specifically assigned to that duty until the patient has regained consciousness or until the effects of the anesthesia have disappeared.

Source: Massachusetts 105 CMR § 130.510 and .511 (1/1/78)

Appendix D

Illinois Anesthesia Services Regulations

(11-1)	ANESTHESIA SERVICE
(11-1.1)	The Anesthesia Service shall be organized under written policies and procedures regarding staff privileges, the administration of anesthetics, and the maintenance of strict safety controls. In hospitals where there is no organized Anesthesia Service, the Surgery Service shall assume the responsibility for establishing general policies and supervising the administration of anesthetics. The Anesthesia Service is responsible for all anesthetics administered in the hospital.
(11–1.2)	The anesthesia service shall be under the direction of a physician who has had specialized preparation and/or experience in the area or who has completed a residency in anesthesiology. An anesthesiologist, Board certified or Board eligible is recommended.
(11–1.3)	A physician or registered professional nurse shall supervise the work of all nonmedical personnel working in the anesthesia service.
(11–1.4)	Responsibility for regular inspection, maintenance, and repair of anesthesia equipment and supplies shall be established.
(11-1.5)	The anesthesia service, hospital administration, and medical staff shall collaborate to establish policies, procedures, rules and regulations for the control, storage, and safe use of combustible anesthetics; oxygen and other medicinal gases; types of anesthesia to be administered and procedures for each; personnel permitted to administer anesthesia; infection control and safety regulations to be followed.
(11-1.6)	The hospital shall recognize the dangers of accidental ignition of anesthetic gases to patients and others and shall make provisions to minimize this hazard in accordance with National Fire Protection Association standards.
(11-1.7)	Appropriate measures shall be taken to acquaint all personnel with the rules and regulations established and to assure enforcement.
(11-1.8)	Anesthetic agents and medicinal gases shall be administered only on the order of a member of the medical staff and shall be administered only by

---

Source: Illinois Administrative Case, Hospitals, Part II, Anesthesia Services §§ 11.1 et seq. effective 12/29/80.

Appendix D

persons qualified in the management of such materials. Refer: (11-1.5)

Comment: It should be noted that State law requires that persons who administer medication must hold a license or certification permitting them to administer medication, such license or certification issued by the Illinois Department of Registration and Education. See Illinois Attorney General Opinion No. S-1033.

(11-1.9) The use and storage of anesthetic gases shall be in accordance with the current edition of the National Fire Protection Bulletin 56A, Inhalation Anesthetic-1973, and 56F Non-Flammable Medical Gases-1973. Areas for cleaning, testing, and storing anesthesia equipment shall be provided.

(11-1.10) An anesthetic record on special forms shall be made a part of the patient's chart. Drugs used, vital signs and other relevant information shall be recorded at regular intervals during anesthesia.

(a) There shall be a history, and physical examination by a physician within 48 hours prior to the surgery with findings recorded in the patient's record.

(b) Except in emergency, no anesthetic shall be administered until the patient has had a history and physical examination by a physician, and a record made of the findings.

(11-1.11) Patients under or recovering from anesthesia and those who have received sedatives or analgesic shall remain under continuous, direct nursing supervision until vital signs have become stabilized. Any nurse performing this duty shall have been instructed in the management of postanesthetic patients, shall have no other clinical duties during the time she is supervising such patients, and shall have immediate recourse to the attending surgeon or anesthesiologist, or qualified substitute, present in the hospital.

(11-1.12) Postanesthetic follow-up visits shall be made within 24 hours after the operation, by the anesthesiologist, nurse-anesthetist or responsible physician who shall note and record any postoperative abnormalities or complications from anesthesia.

Appendix E

Joint Commission on the Accreditation of Hospitals Anesthesia Services (1981)

PRINCIPLE

Anesthesia care shall be available when the hospital provides surgical or obstetrical services.

Standard I
Anesthesia services shall be organized, directed, and integrated with other related services or departments of the hospital.

Interpretation: Anesthesia services shall be directed by a physician member of the medical staff. Whenever possible, the director of anesthesia services shall be a physician specializing in anesthesiology. The director shall have overall administrative responsibility for anesthesia services. The director's responsibilities shall include, but not necessarily be limited to, the following:

- Recommending privileges for all individuals with primary anesthesia responsibility. Clinical privileges shall be processed through established medical staff channels.
- Monitoring the quality of anesthesia care rendered by anesthetists anywhere in the hospital, including surgical, obstetrical, emergency, ambulatory care, psychiatric, and special procedure areas.
- Recommending to the administration and medical staff the type and amount of equipment necessary for administering anesthesia and for related resuscitative efforts, assuring through at least annual review that such equipment is available.
- Developing regulations for anesthetic safety.
- Assuring evaluation of the quality and appropriateness of anesthesia care rendered throughout the hospital.
- Establishing a program of continuing education for all individuals having anesthesia privileges. The program shall include in-service training and be based in part on the results of the evaluation of anesthesia care. The extent of the program shall be related to the scope and complexity of anesthesia services provided.

- Participating in the development of policies relating to the functioning of anesthetists and the administration of anesthesia in various departments or services of the hospital, and participating in the hospital's cardiopulmonary resuscitation program. When pertinent, the director should provide consultation in the management of problems of acute and chronic respiratory insufficiency as well as in a variety of other diagnostic and therapeutic measures related to patient care.

Representatives of the anesthesia department/service should participate as instructors in the hospital's program of continuing education. The extent of their participation should be related to the scope and complexity of anesthesia services, and may include provision of programs involving cardiopulmonary resuscitation and respiratory therapy, as well as the use of related equipment.

The quality and appropriateness of the anesthesia services provided shall be reviewed and evaluated at least quarterly, and shall involve the use of preestablished criteria. The review and evaluation should cover the scope of anesthesia services provided and should not be limited to morbidity and mortality review. The review and evaluation should be performed within the overall hospital quality assurance program. The director of anesthesia services shall assure that the work performed in the hospital by all categories of personnel administering anesthesia is included in the review and evaluation. Depending on the size of the hospital, such personnel shall include anesthesiologists; other qualified physician, dentist, and nurse anesthetists; individuals in an approved anesthesia training program; and those physician, nurse, or dentist anesthetists who are not employed by the hospital but who are associated with or employed by a surgeon or group of surgeons. A record shall be maintained of the findings of the anesthesia care evaluation as well as all resultant action and follow-up. Refer also to the Quality Assurance section of this *Manual*.

Standard II
Staffing for the delivery of anesthesia care shall be related to the scope and complexity of services offered.

Interpretation: Anesthesia care shall be provided by anesthesiologists, other qualified physician or dentist anesthetists, qualified nurse anesthetists, or supervised trainees in an approved educational program. A qualified anesthetist shall be available to provide anesthesia care for patients whenever and wherever it is required in the hospital. Except for specific emergency situations, the administration of anesthesia shall be limited to areas where it can be given safely, in accordance with the policies and procedures of the anesthesia, surgical, obstetrical, emergency, ambulatory care, and other concerned departments or services. The same competence of anesthesia personnel shall be available for all procedures requiring anesthesia services, whether elective or emergency.

Physician anesthetists must be able to perform all of the independent services usually required in the practice of anesthesiology, including the ability to:

- perform accepted procedures commonly used to render the patient insensible to pain during the performance of surgical, obstetrical, and other pain-producing clinical maneuvers, and to relieve pain-associated medical syndromes;

- support life functions during the administration of anesthesia, including induction and intubation procedures;
- provide appropriate preanesthesia and postanesthesia management of the patient; and
- provide consultation relating to various other forms of patient care, such as respiratory therapy, emergency cardiopulmonary resuscitation, and special problems in pain relief.

Qualified nurse or dentist anesthetists must be able to provide general anesthesia. Their performance shall be under the overall direction of the director of anesthesia services or his qualified anesthetist designee when a full-time anesthesiologist heads the department/service; otherwise, their performance shall be under the overall direction of the surgeon or obstetrician responsible for the patient's care. When the physician primarily responsible for a patient's care is other than a surgical specialist or obstetrician, the approval of the director of anesthesia services shall be obtained before any elective general anesthesia is administered to the patient. Qualified nurse or dentist anesthetists shall have the competence necessary to:

- induce anesthesia;
- maintain anesthesia at the required levels;
- support life functions during the administration of anesthesia, including induction and intubation procedures;
- recognize and take appropriate corrective action (including the requesting of consultation when necessary) for abnormal patient responses to anesthesia or to any adjunctive medication or other form of therapy; and
- provide professional observation and resuscitative care (including the requesting of consultation when necessary) until the patient has regained control of his vital functions.

The responsibilities of nurse or dentist anesthetists and the corresponding responsibilities of the attending physician must be defined in a policy statement, job description, or other appropriate document. The services that may be provided by nurse or dentist anesthetists and the level of supervision they require must also be defined in a policy statement, job description, or other appropriate document. When the operating/anesthesia team consists entirely of nonphysicians (for example, dentist with nurse anesthetist, dentist with dentist anesthetist, podiatrist with dentist or nurse anesthetist), a physician must be immediately available in case of an emergency, such as cardiac standstill or cardiac arrhythmia.

Standard III
Precautions shall be taken to assure the safe administration of anesthetic agents.

Interpretation: Controls shall be established to minimize electrical hazards in all anesthetizing areas, as well as hazards of fire and explosion in areas in which flammable anesthetic agents are used. Anesthetic safety regulations should be developed by, or under the supervision of, the director of anesthesia services and in conjunction with the hospital safety committee. Such regulations shall be approved by appropriate representatives of the

Appendix E

medical staff and administration, reviewed annually to assure compatibility with current practice, and enforced. Refer to the Emergency Services, Functional Safety and Sanitation, Hospital-Sponsored Ambulatory Care Services, Infection Control, and Special Care Units sections of this *Manual* for other standards related to anesthesia services.

Written regulations for the control of electrical and anesthetic explosion hazards shall include, but should not necessarily be limited to, the following requirements.

- Anesthetic apparatus must be inspected and tested by the anesthetist before use. If a leak or any other defect is observed, the equipment must not be used until the fault is repaired.
- When electrical equipment employing an open spark (for example, cautery or coagulation equipment) is to be used during an operation, only nonflammable agents shall be used for anesthesia or for the preoperative preparation of the surgical field.
- Flammable anesthetic agents shall be employed only in areas in which a conductive pathway can be maintained between the patient and a conductive floor.
- Each anesthetizing location shall be identified by a prominently posted permanent sign that clearly states whether the anesthetizing location is designed for flammable or nonflammable anesthetic agents.
- Rooms in which a flammable agent is employed for anesthesia or preparation of the surgical field shall be identified by appropriate signs while the anesthetic agent is in use.
- The administration of a flammable anesthetic to a patient being moved from one area to another shall be prohibited.
- When required, all personnel shall wear conductive footwear, which should be tested for conductivity before entering the area.
- When required, all equipment in the surgical suite shall be fitted with grounding devices to maintain a constant conductive pathway to the floor.
- Fabrics permissible for use as outer garments or blankets in anesthetizing areas shall be specified in writing.
- With the exception of certain radiologic equipment and fixed lighting more than five feet above the floor, all electrical equipment in anesthetizing areas shall be on an audiovisual line isolation monitor. When this device indicates a hazard, the administration of flammable anesthetic agents should be discontinued as soon as possible; the use of any electrical gear should be avoided, particularly the last electrical item put into use as well as any item not required for patient monitoring or support; and the hospital engineer or maintenance chief shall be notified immediately. Following completion of the procedure, the operating room from which the signal emanated should not be used until the defect is remedied. All personnel who work in such areas shall be familiar with the procedures to be followed.
- The condition of all operating room electrical equipment shall be inspected regularly, preferably on a monthly basis, and a written record of the results and any required corrective action shall be maintained.

- The results of any required monthly conductivity testing shall be made known to personnel who work primarily in these areas.
- Anesthesia personnel shall familiarize themselves with the rate, volume, and mechanism of air exchange within the surgical and obstetrical suites, as well as with humidity control.

Standard IV
There shall be written policies relating to the delivery of anesthesia care.

Interpretation: Because individuals with varying backgrounds may administer anesthetic agents, the medical staff must approve policies relative to anesthesia procedures, including the delineation of preanesthesia and postanesthesia responsibilities. Written policies of the anesthesia services shall be approved by the medical staff, reviewed annually, and enforced. These policies shall provide for at least the following:

- The preanesthesia evaluation of the patient by a physician, with appropriate documentation in the patient's medical record of pertinent information relative to the choice of anesthesia and the surgical or obstetrical procedure anticipated. Except in extreme emergency cases, this evaluation should be recorded prior to the patient's transfer to the operating area and before preoperative medication has been administered. While the choice of a specific anesthetic agent or technique may be left up to the individual administering the anesthesia, the preanesthesia medical record entry should at least refer to the use of general, spinal, or other regional anesthesia. When other than anesthesia personnel are involved, reference in the medical record to the use of spinal, regional, topical, or local anesthesia should be made by the responsible physician (for example, the surgeon or obstetrician) or dentist when administered within the limits of his privileges. The preanesthesia record entry should include the patient's previous drug history, other anesthetic experiences, and any potential anesthetic problems.
- The review of the patient's condition immediately prior to induction of anesthesia. This should include a review of the medical record with regard to completeness, pertinent laboratory data, and time of administration and dosage of preanesthesia medication, together with an appraisal of any changes in the patient's condition as compared with that noted on previous visits.
- The safety of the patient during the anesthetic period. The policies shall include at least the following requirements.
  - Prior to administering anesthesia, the anesthetist shall check the readiness, availability, cleanliness, sterility when required, and working condition of all equipment used in the administration of anesthetic agents.
  - Laryngoscopes, airways, breathing bags, masks, endotracheal tubes, and all reusable anesthesia equipment in direct contact with the patient shall be cleaned after each use.
  - Each anesthetic gas machine shall have a pin-index safety system. It is recommended that each machine also be provided with a gas-scavenging system and an

oxygen pressure interlock system. A system that functions as well as, or more effectively than, an interlock system shall be considered acceptable.

- Following the procedures for which anesthesia was administered, the anesthetist or his qualified designee(s) shall remain with the patient as long as required by the patient's condition relative to his anesthesia status, and until responsibility for proper patient care has been assumed by other qualified individuals. Personnel responsible for postanesthetic care should be advised of specific problems presented by the patient's condition. The same degree of care should be provided when there is no postanesthesia care unit and the patient is returned to the nursing floor to recover.

- A mechanism for the release of patients from any postanesthesia care unit. The basis for the decision to discharge a patient from any postanesthesia care unit shall be made only by a physician and not by nursing service personnel. However, the actual release of a postanesthetic patient by a physician and documentation thereof does not necessarily require the presence or signature of a specific physician at the time of release. When discharge criteria are used, they shall be comprehensive, approved by the medical staff in order to assure the same standard of care for all patients, and rigidly enforced. When the responsible physician has not issued a written order or authenticated a verbal release, the name of the physician responsible for the patient's release shall be recorded in the medical record.

- The recording of all pertinent events taking place during the induction of, maintenance of, and emergence from anesthesia, including the dosage and duration of all anesthetic agents, other drugs, intravenous fluids, and blood or blood components.

- The recording of postanesthetic visits, including at least one note describing the presence or absence of anesthesia-related complications. A note made in the surgical or obstetrical suite, or in the postanesthesia care unit (or nursing floor anesthesia recovery phase when there is no such unit), does not ordinarily constitute a visit. While the number of visits will be determined by the status of the patient in relation to the procedure performed and anesthesia administered, a visit should be made early in the postoperative period, and once after complete recovery from anesthesia. Complete recovery is determined by the clinical judgment of the anesthetist or the discharging surgeon/obstetrician. Each postanesthesia note shall specify the date and time. It is recommended that a postanesthesia medical record entry be made by a physician. However, all anesthesia personnel are encouraged to make pertinent postanesthesia entries in the medical records of patients to whom they have administered anesthesia. When the postanesthetic visit and record entry by anesthesia personnel is not feasible because of early patient release from the hospital, the physician or dentist who discharges the patient from the hospital should be responsible for meeting the requirement.

- Written guidelines defining the role of anesthesia services and of all postanesthesia care areas in the hospital's infection control program.

Written guidelines for the safe use of all general anesthetic agents used in the hospital shall be developed by an anesthesiologist. Such guidelines shall apply to all personnel, both physician and nonphysician, who administer anesthesia. In the absence of a staff anesthesiologist, a practicing consultant anesthesiologist should provide the specific guidelines based on an on-site assessment of the personnel, equipment, and overall anesthesia environment.

Appendix F

Sample Release from Liability

TO MY PATIENTS

We have always tried to give you the very best medical care of which we are capable. We will continue to do the same. However, with all medical treatment, there is the possibility of permanent disability . . . to you or even death. We have no insurance. If you wish to receive injections or treatment under these circumstances, we will be willing to administer them. The above, if accepted, is an assumed risk and is therefore not a matter for litigation. If you don't understand this, consult your attorney before coming in.

DOCTOR-PATIENT CONTRACT

I understand that in seeking medical treatment from either_____M.D. or Associates, who will hereinafter be referred to as "the Doctor", whether speaking of one or more of them, I am not required to use him as my doctor for myself or my family as there are many other doctors in_____, Michigan, as well qualified who practice medicine in the specialty of obstetrics and gynecology and that he is willing to refer me to them. As an example he has advised me that two of such doctors are Dr._____and Dr._____ I understand that if I waive any liability for his care of me or my family, I will help the Doctor keep down the expenses of his practice of medicine due to savings in avoiding malpractice insurance and malpractice lawsuits, the expenses of which would otherwise be passed on to me and his other patients in higher fees. I enter into this contract freely and voluntarily and I understand I am waiving my right to bring a claim against the Doctor for any negligent act or omission he may commit in his treatment of me or for any breach of the contractual obligation to me to render to me that standard of medical care which is rendered in this or similar communities. I understand that this contract applies to all of his medical care to me.

I specifically release the Doctor from any liability to me and I hereby release; discharge and acquit the Doctor from any and all claims for loss, damage or injury of any nature whatsoever to my person, my family, or estate resulting in any way from or in any fashion arising from, connected with or resulting from the Doctor's medical treatment of me or my family whether caused by malpractice or negligent acts of the doctor, his agents, or employees or servants or otherwise. This contract is clearly intended to protect the doctor against his own negligence and I so understand it.

Further, I specifically release the Doctor from any liability to me and my family which I may claim resulting from a lack of consent or lack of informed consent on my part to the particular treatment he or his agents or employees may render to me or my family, including any effects of that treatment which the Doctor may or may not have discussed with me.

I voluntarily enter into this contract in order to induce the Doctor to render to me medical care at his most reasonable cost.
In witness whereof, I have signed this Contract this____day of_____, 1976.

Witnesses:

_____   _____
                                                          (Patient)
_____

Appendix G

Sample Complaint

State of Michigan
in the Circuit Court for the County of Wayne

JAMES SMITH, Personal
Representative of the Estate of
CLIFFORD SMITH, Deceased,
          Plaintiff,

-vs-   No. 80   NM

MEMORIAL HOSPITAL,
WILLIAM DAVIS, M.D. and
GERALD BROWN, M.D., Jointly
and Severally,
          Defendants.

COMPLAINT AND DEMAND FOR JURY TRIAL

NOW COMES the above named plaintiff by and through his attorneys, Jones and Jones, P.C., and complains against the defendants and for his cause of action states as follows:

1. That plaintiff, JAMES SMITH, is the duly appointed personal representative of the estate of Clifford Smith, Deceased, and brings this lawsuit in that capacity.

2. That the defendant, MEMORIAL HOSPITAL, is doing business and is situated in the City of Detroit, County of Wayne, State of Michigan.

3. That the defendant, WILLIAM DAVIS, M.D., is a duly licensed physician doing business in the City of Detroit, County of Wayne, State of Michigan.

4. That on or about July 24, 1978, the deceased, CLIFFORD SMITH, presented himself for treatment at the emergency room of Memorial Hospital, Detroit, Michigan.

5. That on or about July 24, 1978, Memorial Hospital referred CLIFFORD SMITH to defendant, WILLIAM DAVIS, M.D., for an office visit.

6. That on or about July 24, 1978, the deceased, CLIFFORD SMITH, was seen by defendant, WILLIAM DAVIS, M.D., in his office, at which time defendant, WILLIAM

DAVIS, M.D., recommended an emergency I & D of the peritonsillar abscess and an emergency tonsillectomy.

7. That at the time of the office visit with Dr. Davis, on or about July 24, 1978, the defendant, WILLIAM DAVIS, M.D., noted that Mr. Smith had a chronic right ear drainage for approximately 20 years, a history of chronic shortness of breath, hypertension and flank pain for two years.

8. That on or about July 24, 1978, the deceased, CLIFFORD SMITH, was admitted to Memorial Hospital, Detroit, Michigan.

9. That on or about July 24, 1978, the deceased, CLIFFORD SMITH, was 46 years of age.

10. That on or about July 24, 1978, the defendants provided surgical and medical care to CLIFFORD SMITH and he died on that date while a patient at the defendant's hospital.

11. That the medical, surgical and hospital care provided CLIFFORD SMITH, the deceased, deviated from the accepted standards of care and was the proximate cause of his death.

DEFENDANTS AND CAUSES OF ACTION

12. That plaintiff hereby incorporates by reference each and every allegation contained in paragraphs 1 through 11 of his Complaint as though the same were set forth herein word for word and paragraph by paragraph.

13. That defendant, MEMORIAL HOSPITAL, is liable to the plaintiff for the following reasons on the following cause of action:

A. Negligence:
1. That the defendant hospital, through its agents, servants and employees, had a duty to properly monitor CLIFFORD SMITH.
2. That the defendant hospital had a duty to conduct a preoperative anesthesia evaluation.
3. That the defendant hospital had a duty to provide adequate ventilation to CLIFFORD SMITH.
4. That the defendant hospital had a duty to treat the tachycardia of CLIFFORD SMITH.
5. That the defendant hospital had a duty to conduct intraoperative determinations of electrolytes and blood gases.
6. That the defendant hospital had a duty to provide adequate oxygenation.
7. That the defendant hospital had a duty to prevent aspiration.
8. That the defendant hospital had a duty to use proper drugs.
9. That the defendant hospital had a duty to properly place the endotracheal tube.
10. That the defendant hospital had a duty to make sure its hospital was staffed by reasonably competent and skillful physicians and nurses.
11. That the defendant hospital is liable for the wrongful acts of its employees.
12. That the defendant hospital and its employees were negligent in failing to do (1 through 10) all of the above.

Appendix G 375

14. That defendant, WILLIAM DAVIS, M.D., is liable to the plaintiff for the following reasons on the following cause of action.

   A. Negligence:
   1. That a reasonable and prudent physician would take an adequate medical history.
   2. That a reasonable and prudent physician would make an adequate preoperative assessment of a patient's status and suitability for surgery.
   3. That a reasonable and prudent physician would properly medicate his patient.
   4. That a reasonable and prudent physician would properly assess the impact of a patient's obesity (e.g. is this patient a poor risk for general anesthesia?).
   5. That a reasonable and prudent physician would choose a proper anesthetic.
   6. That a reasonable and prudent physician would order proper tests prior to, during and following the course of surgery.
   7. That a reasonable and prudent physician would not perform a contraindicated tonsillectomy.
   8. That a reasonable and prudent physician would timely treat a tachycardia.
   9. That a reasonable and prudent physician would not abandon a patient following a cardiac arrest.
   10. That defendant, WILLIAM DAVIS, M.D., was negligent in failing to do all of the above.

15. That defendant, GERALD BROWN, M.D., is liable to the plaintiff for the following reasons on the following cause of action.

   A. Negligence:
   1. That a reasonable and prudent physician would provide timely treatment to a patient in extremis.
   2. That a reasonable and prudent physician would properly medicate and oxygenate a patient.
   3. That a reasonable and prudent physician would adequately ventilate a patient.
   4. That a reasonable and prudent physician would conduct proper tests.
   5. That a reasonable and prudent physician would make a timely replacement of an endotracheal tube.
   6. That a reasonable and prudent physician would not lift an obese patient having a difficult time breathing through an obstructed endotracheal tube.
   7. That a reasonable and prudent physician would properly place an endotracheal tube.
   8. That defendant, GERALD BROWN, M.D., is negligent in failing to do all of the above.

16. That as a direct and proximate result of the defendants' negligence, plaintiff, JAMES SMITH, personal representative of the estate of CLIFFORD SMITH, deceased, claims damages under the wrongful death act of Michigan for all damages allowable under said act.

17. That the plaintiff reserves the right to add additional claims of negligence against the defendants as well as additional claims for damages as they are discovered during the course of pretrial discovery.

18. That the amount in controversy exceeds TEN THOUSAND ($10,000.00) DOLLARS.

WHEREFORE, the plaintiff prays for a judgment in his favor and against the defendants in whatever amount he is found to be entitled together with interests, costs and attorney fees so wrongfully incurred.

JONES AND JONES, P.C.

Dated: July 15, 1980

By: David Jones
Jones and Jones, P.C.

DEMAND FOR JURY TRIAL

NOW COMES the above named plaintiff by and through his attorneys, Jones and Jones, P.C., and hereby demands a trial by jury of the within cause.

JONES AND JONES, P.C.

Dated: July 15, 1980

By: David Jones
Jones and Jones, P.C.

Appendix H

Sample Answer

State of Michigan
in The Circuit Court for the County of Wayne

JAMES SMITH, Personal
Representative of the Estate
of CLIFFORD SMITH, Deceased,
                Plaintiff,
-vs.-   No. 80   NM
MEMORIAL HOSPITAL
WILLIAM DAVIS, M.D. and
GERALD BROWN, M.D., Jointly
and Severally,
                Defendants.

ANSWER TO COMPLAINT
AND DEMAND FOR JURY TRIAL

NOW COMES WILLIAM DAVIS, M.D., by his attorneys, Blount and Swiss, who in answer to Plaintiff's Complaint says that:

    1. Neither admits nor denies.
    2. Admits.
    3. Admits.
    4. Neither admits nor denies.
    5. Neither admits nor denies.
    6. Admits.
    7. Admits, excepting on information he denies noting a history of chronic shortness of breath, hypertension and flank pain for two years.
    8. Admits.
    9. Admits.
    10. Admits.
    11. Denies insofar as Paragraph 11 applies to him.
    12. Realleges and repleads his answers to Paragraph 1 through 12 above.

13. Inasmuch as Paragraph 13 applies to another defendant he neither admits nor denies the same excepting he denies at any time committing any negligence himself.

14. Denies any negligence on his part as alleged in Paragraph 14 and in support of his denial says that he at all times cared for his patient in a careful and prudent manner and in full accord with a good standard of medical practice.

15. Denies and in support of his denial states upon information that Gerald Brown treated the deceased patient at all times in a careful and prudent manner and in full compliance with the standard of good medical practice at the time.

16. Lacks information sufficient from which to form a belief and therefore leaves Plaintiff to his proofs excepting that he denies any negligence on his part and excepting that he further denies that any damages or conditions or problems that came by the Plaintiff are causally related to anything he did or anything he omitted to do.

17. He does not plead thereto since no answer is required.

18. Lacks information sufficient from which to form a belief as to the matter as set forth in Paragraph 18 and therefore leaves Plaintiff to his proofs.

WHEREFORE this Defendant prays that Plaintiff's Complaint be dismissed with whole prejudice to all relief requested of this Defendant together with costs.

Blount and Swiss

DATED: August 28, 1980

By_____
JOHN SWISS

AFFIRMATIVE DEFENSES TO PLAINTIFF

PLEASE TAKE NOTICE Defendant, WILLIAM DAVIS, M.D., says by way of affirmative defenses that:

1. Plaintiff's claims may be barred by the applicable statute of limitations, wherefore, this Defendant reserves the right to move for accelerated judgment on completion of discovery or at the pre-trial conference, which ever comes last.

2. He reserves the right to assert and plead affirmative defenses on completion of discovery.

BLOUNT AND SWISS

DATED: August 28, 1980

BY_____
JOHN SWISS

Appendix H

DEMAND FOR JURY

NOW COMES, Defendant, WILLIAM DAVIS, M.D., by his attorneys, and hereby makes a demand for trial by jury of the within cause.

BLOUNT AND SWISS

DATED: August 28, 1980

BY_____
JOHN SWISS

Glossary

ADMISSIBLE. Any evidence which may be properly received and considered in a legal proceeding.

ADMISSION (against interest). A statement made by one person to another in conflict with the interests of the person making the statement.

AFFIDAVIT. A written account of a declaration made under oath.

AGENCY. Any relation in which one person acts for or represents another by the latter's authority. *See* Respondeat superior.

ALLOPATHY. A system of therapeutics in which diseases are treated by producing a condition incompatible or antagonistic to the condition to be cured or alleviated. Licensed practitioners of this system generally hold M.D. degrees. *Compare with* Osteopathy.

ANSWER. A defendant's written response to a complaint against him or her.

APPEAL. A petition to a higher court to review and correct or reverse an alleged error committed by a lower court.

APPELLANT. A party who appeals a case or issue from a lower court to a higher court.

APPELLATE COURT. A court to which a party may submit a petition to review the decision of a lower court, usually a trial court. Appellate courts include a court at an intermediate appellate level and a supreme court, the court of last resort in the legal system.

APPELLEE. A party against whom a case or issue is appealed from a lower to a higher court.

ARBITRATION. An alternative to a formal court hearing; the investigation and determination of a dispute between contending parties is made by one or more persons chosen by the parties and called arbitrators or referees.

BATTERY. The unauthorized and offensive touching of a person by another.

BLUE CROSS PLAN. An independently operated, nonprofit plan organized for the prepayment of hospital care.

BLUE SHIELD PLAN. An independently operated, nonprofit plan organized for the prepayment of physicians' services.

BURDEN OF PROOF. The duty or responsibility at trial to present sufficient evidence to establish the truth of a position or set of facts asserted by a party to be true.

CASE. A general term for an action, cause, suit, or controversy.

CASE LAW. Legal principles derived from judicial decisions. Case law differs from statutory law which is derived from laws written and adopted by legislatures. Case

Glossary

law is sometimes referred to as "common law." *See* Common law.

CAUSE OF ACTION. A claim or occurrence which gives rise to litigation.

CAVEAT EMPTOR. Literally translated, this phrase means, "Let the buyer beware." This maxim summarizes the rule that a consumer must examine, judge or test a potential purchase for himself or herself and take the risk that the quality of the item purchased is acceptable.

CERTIORARI *or* CERT (petition). A request made to an appellate (higher) court asking it to command a lower court to certify and send its records of a case to the higher court for purposes of appellate review.

CHALLENGE FOR CAUSE. A legal right allowing each party to challenge the selection of a juror because of juror bias.

CIRCUMSTANTIAL EVIDENCE. Any evidence of an indirect nature. *Compare with* Direct evidence.

CIVIL LIABILITY. Being amenable to a suit or action brought by an individual to enforce a private right. *Compare with* Criminal liability.

COMMON LAW. Unwritten law grounded in custom, natural justice, and reason, sanctioned by usage and adopted in judicial decisions. *See* Case law.

COMPARATIVE NEGLIGENCE. A legal doctrine which allows the jury to compare the negligence of the alleged wrongdoer with the negligence of the plaintiff. For example, if the plaintiff is found to have contributed 20 percent to his or her injury, the jury's award to the plaintiff will be reduced by 20 percent. *Compare with* Contributory negligence.

COMPLAINT. The first or initiatory pleading on the part of the plaintiff in a civil action.

CONFIDENTIAL COMMUNICATION. A statement made in confidence to a lawyer, physician, or clergyman with the implicit understanding that it shall remain a secret. Case law and/or statutes in most states recognize privileged or confidential communications.

CONSPIRACY. A combination of two or more persons formed for the purpose of committing, by their joint efforts, some unlawful act or for the purpose of using unlawful means for the commission of an act lawful in itself.

CONSTRUCTIVE NOTICE. Notice to a person not having received actual notice imputed by the occurrence of events that would give notice to a reasonable and prudent person observing those events.

CONTEMPT (of court). A willful disregard or disobedience of the court's orders, as well as conduct tending to bring the authority of the court and the administration of the law into disrepute. The court may issue money or penal penalties to those found to be in contempt.

CONTRACT. An agreement between two or more parties, upon sufficient consideration, to do or not to do a certain thing which is enforceable by law.

CONTRIBUTION. The sharing of a loss or payment by one or more parties having a common interest of liability. Apart from statute, the general rule is that there can be no contribution between tort-feasors, it being against public policy to adjust equities between wrongdoers or to allow a person to base an action on his or her own wrongdoing.

CONTRIBUTORY NEGLIGENCE. Negligence on the part of the plaintiff which results in injury to his or her person or property and precludes the plaintiff from making a recovery against the alleged wrongdoer. *Compare with* Comparative negligence.

CONVERSION. A wrongful exercise of dominion over the personal property of another. Civil stealing.

COUNTERCLAIM. A cause of action existing in favor of the defendant against the plaintiff.

COURT. An organ of the judicial branch of government whose function is the application of laws to controversies brought before it and the public administration of justice.

CRIMINAL LIABILITY. Being amenable to prosecution for wrongs against a public right or interest. *Compare with* Civil liability.

CUSTOM. A usage or practice of the people, which, by common adoption and acquiescence, and by long and unvarying habit, has become compulsory and has acquired the force of a law.

DECREE. A declaration of the court announcing the legal consequences of the facts found.

DEFAMATION. A communication to a third party which tends to diminish the esteem, respect, goodwill, or confidence in which a party is held, or which excites adverse, derogatory, or unpleasant feelings or opinions against the party. *See* Libel, Slander.

DEFAULT JUDGMENT. A judgment entered after the defendant has failed to appear when properly served with a summons and complaint; also, same result but for a variety of additional reasons usually found in the court rules of the various states.

DEFENDANT. The party against whom relief or recovery is sought in a legal action or suit.

DEFENSIVE MEDICINE. The alteration of patterns of medical diagnosis to include more diagnostic tests and procedures than would normally be required for adequate diagnosis of a given condition; the practice of defensive medicine has arisen primarily in response to increased malpractice suits, allowing physicians to document fully the reasons for making a given diagnosis and prescribing a given treatment in the event a lawsuit should arise from the patient encounter.

DEMONSTRATIVE EVIDENCE. A type of evidence which consists of things—e.g., weapons, photographs, wearing apparel—as distinguished from the assertion of a witness.

DEPOSITION. Sometimes used as synonymous with oath, but the term is specifically applicable to the testimony of witnesses taken in writing and under oath before some officer in answer to oral and written questions.

DIRECT EVIDENCE. Proof of facts by witnesses who saw acts done or heard words spoken. *Compare with* Circumstantial evidence.

Glossary

DIRECTED VERDICT. When there is no substantial evidence which would support a judgment for the one party, the court may, on motion of the other party, direct the jury to bring in a verdict for that other party. *Compare with* Verdict.

DISSENTING OPINION. A minority opinion in the decision of a case.

DUE CARE. The degree of care which would be exercised by the ordinary careful person in the same circumstances.

DUE PROCESS. A provision of the Fourteenth Amendment to the United States Constitution which provides that no one may be deprived of life, liberty, or property without "due process"—e.g., a notice of a hearing, a hearing, and an opportunity to confront witnesses. Due process concepts also appear in the American common law.

DUTY OF CARE. Every person owes a duty to conduct himself or herself as the average, reasonable person would conduct himself or herself in the same or similar circumstances. A professional's duty is to conduct himself or herself as a reasonable professional.

EMANCIPATED MINOR. One who is freed from the custody, control, and service of the parent prior to attaining the age of majority.

EMERGENCY PATIENTS. Acutely ill or injured patients requiring immediate care in a special treatment complex that may include an operating room, x-ray facility, and other services.

ENTRY OF JUDGMENT ON VERDICT. A procedural rule applied where a jury returns a verdict following its deliberations and a trial judge enters an order of judgment certifying the jury's findings.

ESTOPPEL. A state of affairs which arises when a person's own acts preclude him or her from stating anything to the contrary.

ETHICS. A moral-philosophic inquiry into the duties a member of a profession owes to the public, to colleagues, and to his or her patients or clients.

EVIDENCE. Proof presented at trial through witnesses, records, documents, concrete objects, etc., for the purpose of proving or defending an issue or case.

EXECUTOR (of estate). A person designated in a will to administer an estate.

EXEMPLARY DAMAGES. Damages awarded because of the malicious, fraudulent or wanton character of the acts committed by the wrongdoer.

EXPERT OPINION. The testimony of an expert stating his or her opinion on a question of science, skill, or trade.

EXPRESS CONTRACT. An agreement between parties stated in distinct and explicit language either orally or in writing.

FELONY. A crime considered graver than those designated misdemeanors and that may result in a sentence of death or imprisonment in a penitentiary. *Compare with* Misdemeanor.

FIDUCIARY. One holding a position of trust or confidence with respect to the money or property of another.

FRAUD. A general term embracing all the multifarious means which can be devised by human ingenuity and resorted to by one individual to gain an advantage over another by false suggestions or by suppression of the truth.

GARNISHMENT. A court-ordered process by which the plaintiff makes claim to property of the defendant in the hands of a third person for money owed by the third person to the defendant.

GOODWILL. The advantage a business has from its establishment or from the patronage of its customers, over and above the mere value of its property and capital.

GOVERNMENTAL IMMUNITY. An ancient common law doctrine that a government is protected from suit by private persons unless it waives that immunity. The federal government and a number of states have waived the immunity by statute or court decisions.

GROSS NEGLIGENCE. The intentional failure to perform a manifest duty in reckless disregard of consequences to the life or property of another. *See* Negligence.

GUARDIAN AD LITEM. A person appointed by the court to look after the interests of a minor or incompetent in litigation.

HEARSAY EVIDENCE. What the witness says he or she heard another person say, and although generally inadmissible as evidence, there are exceptions to the rule.

HYPOTHETICAL QUESTION. A combination of assumed or proved facts and circumstances, presented as a question upon which the opinion of an expert is asked, to provide evidence in a trial.

IMPEACHMENT. The process of calling in question the veracity of a witness by showing through evidence or process that the witness is unworthy of belief.

INCOMPETENT. The legal status of one who is considered to be unable or unfit to manage his or her own affairs by reason of insanity, imbecility, or feeble-mindedness.

INDICTMENT. A formal accusation based on legal testimony of a direct and positive character, and the concurring judgment of at least 12 of the grand jurors that upon the evidence presented to them the defendant is guilty of a crime.

INFORMED CONSENT. The duty of a physician to disclose to a patient the risks involved in a proposed course of treatment or surgery as well as the optional or alternative courses of treatment available to the patient.

INJUNCTION. An order issued by a court requiring a person to whom it is directed to do or refrain from doing a particular act.

INSTRUCTION (by the court). The rules or principles of law applicable to the entire case or to some phase of it, which the jury is bound to accept and apply.

INTERROGATORIES. A series of written questions drawn up by one party asking an adversary for answers that may be used as evidence in a judicial proceeding.

JUDGMENT. The final word in a judicial controversy entered upon the record and binding on the parties unless overturned or modified by appeal. *Compare with* Verdict.

JUDGMENT BY DEFAULT. A judgment rendered against a party because of that party's failure to plead or defend his or her case or issue.

Glossary 385

JUDGMENT NOTWITHSTANDING THE VERDICT (N.O.V.). A court reversal of a jury decision on its own motion or on the motion of the aggrieved party.

JUDICIAL NOTICE. Court recognition of facts so well-known that the production of evidence would be unnecessary.

JURISDICTION. The authority provided by law to courts that allows them to hear and decide cases.

LIABILITY (in tort). The legal responsibility a wrongdoer assumes for doing a civil or private wrong that causes an injury.

LIBEL. Written or printed accusations against the character of a person which adversely affect that person's reputation. *Compare with* Slander.

LIMITED LIABILITY. Owners or shareholders of a corporation are not held personally liable for the obligations of the corporation, except to the extent of their interest in the property of the corporation.

MALPRACTICE (medical). Any deviation from the accepted medical standard of care, due a given patient, which causes an injury.

MANDAMUS, WRIT OF. A command directing an inferior court, officer, corporation or person to perform a particular duty.

MANSLAUGHTER. The unlawful killing of a human being without malice or intent.

MATERIAL (evidence). Evidence relevant to the matters in dispute or which has a legitimate and effective influence or bearing on the decision of the case.

MINOR. A person under the age of legal competency, which is currently 18 years of age for most purposes.

MISDEMEANOR. A crime that may result in short-term imprisonment and/or a fine. *Compare with* Felony.

MOTION. An application made to the court to obtain a rule or order directing some act to be done in favor of the applicant.

NEGLIGENCE. The intentional or unintentional violation of a duty owed to another. *See* Gross negligence.

OSTEOPATHY. A system of therapy based on the theory that the body provides its own disease remedies when it is in a normal structural relationship and has favorable environmental conditions and adequate nutrition. It emphasizes the importance of normal body mechanics and manipulative methods of detecting and correcting faulty structure. Licensed practitioners of this system generally hold D.O. degrees. *Compare with* Allopathy.

PERJURY. The willful giving, under oath, of false testimony material to the issue in a judicial proceeding.

PLAINTIFF. A person who brings a legal action; the party who complains or sues in a personal action.

POLICE POWER. The power vested in the states and legislatures to make laws for the health, safety and welfare of the people.

PRECEDENT. A principle of law stated in a case decision that serves as authority for subsequent decision-making cases involving similar questions of fact or law. *Compare with* Stare decisis.

PREPONDERANCE OF EVIDENCE. The greater weight of evidence or evidence which is more credible or convincing to the mind; that which best accords with probability and reason.

PRIMA FACIE CASE. A case established by sufficient evidence which can be overthrown only by rebutting evidence offered by the other side.

PRIVILEGED COMMUNICATION. Communication between parties to a confidential relation such that the recipient cannot be legally compelled to disclose it as a witness nor may it be voluntarily disclosed without the permission of the person making the disclosure. Privileged communications include communications between attorney and client, husband and wife, physician and patient, etc.

PROFESSIONAL CORPORATION. An organization established as a corporation pursuant to state law, composed of professionals offering professional services.

PROXIMATE CAUSE. An act or omission which, in a natural sequence, unbroken by any intervening cause, produces an injury, and without which the injury would not have occurred.

REGULATIONS. Rules promulgated by administrative agencies based on authority conferred in statutory enactments which have the force of law.

RELEASE. A written contract by which some claim or interest is surrendered to another person, often in exchange for consideration, e.g., money.

RELEVANT (evidence). Evidence that bears directly on the issue or fact in question and proves or has a tendency to prove the proposition alleged.

RES IPSA LOQUITUR (literally, e.g. "the matter speaks for itself"). An evidentiary presumption that a defendant is negligent because the instrumentality causing the plaintiff's injury was in the defendant's exclusive control and the injury was one that does not ordinarily happen in the absence of negligence.

RESPONDEAT SUPERIOR. The legal principle that an employer is vicariously liable for civil wrongs committed by employees within the course and scope of their employment; this is true whether or not the employer has the actual ability to control the employee's conduct.

SLANDER. Oral accusations against the character of a person which adversely affect that person's reputation. *Compare with* Libel.

SOCIAL SECURITY ACT. A federal act originally enacted in 1935; includes authority for Medicaid and Medicare programs, social services programs, and financial assistance to the aged, blind, disabled and families in need of such assistance; see Titles IV-A, V, VI, XI, XVI, XVIII, XIX, XX of the Social Security Administration.

STARE DECISIS. The principle that the law by which we are governed should be fixed, definite, and known, and that when the law is declared by a court of jurisdiction competent to construe it, such declaration in the absence of palpable mistake or error is itself evidence of the law until changed by competent authority. *Compare with* Precedent.

STATUTE. A law enacted by a legislature.

STATUTE OF LIMITATIONS. Legislative statutes and court decisions which define the period of time during which an action must be brought. The failure to bring an action within this period may bar the action.

STIPULATION. Any agreement made by the attorneys engaged on opposite sides of a case regarding any matter related to the case, proceedings or trial.

STRICT LIABILITY. Liability imposed where certain types of accidents happen, irrespective of whether anyone was at fault. The policy of the law in these cases is that the injured party must be given redress, even though there is nothing legally or morally wrong in what the defendant did.

SUBPOENA. A writ or order directed to a person requiring that person's attendance at a particular time and place to testify. It may also require that the person bring to court any books, documents, or other things under his or her control, in which case it is known as a *subpoena duces tecum*.

SUBSTITUTED JUDGMENT RULE. A rule which authorizes the court to sit in the place of an incompetent to make a decision for the incompetent, such as a decision regarding the incompetent's donation of an organ, as the court believes the incompetent would if able to do so. *See* Incompetent.

SUMMARY JUDGMENT. A procedural rule which allows an attorney to make a motion for a judgment in a case on the pleadings without the necessity of going to trial. If a court issues an order of this type, it is in essence saying that the case has no merit, regardless of what the pleadings say and should not proceed any further on the trial court level.

SUMMONS. A writ directed to the sheriff or other proper officer requiring him or her to notify the person named that an action has been commenced against him or her in the court and that he or she is required to appear on a day named and answer the complaint.

TESTIMONY. The words heard from a witness under oath in court.

TOLL THE STATUTE. To stop the running of the statute of limitations.

TORT. A private or civil wrong or injury for which one sues for money damages.

TORTFEASOR. One who commits or is guilty of a tort. To be "joint tortfeasors," the parties must either act together in committing the wrong or their acts, if independent of each other, must unite in causing a single injury.

ULTRA VIRES. This phrase is used to refer to acts committed which are not within the power of the person or organization committing them. Literally translated, it means "beyond the power" and is used most commonly in reference to unauthorized acts of corporations.

VERDICT. The definitive answer given by the jury to the court concerning the matters of fact presented to the jury for their deliberation and determination. *Compare with* Judgment.

VICARIOUS LIABILITY. Civil liability to one for the tortious acts of others.

WAIVER. The voluntary relinquishing of a known right.

WILLFUL AND WANTON MISCONDUCT. The failure to exercise ordinary care to prevent injury to a person who is known to be within the range of one's dangerous act.

WRONGFUL DEATH (statutes). Statutory provisions which override the common law rule that the death of a human being may not be complained of as an injury in a civil action. The provisions allow beneficiaries to sue for their loss.

Selected Bibliography

Abouleish, Ezzat. *Pain Control in Obstetrics*. Philadelphia: J.B. Lippincott, 1977.
Adriani, John. *Labat's Regional Anesthesia: Technology and Clinical Applications*. Philadelphia: W.B. Saunders, 1967.
Albright, George A. *Anesthesia in Obstetrics: Maternal, Fetal, and Neonatal Aspects*. Menlo Park, CA: Addison-Wesley, 1978.
Aldrete, J. Antonio. *International Symposium on Malignant Hyperthermia* (Denver, CO, 1977). New York: Grune and Stratton, 1978.
Alling, Charles C. *Facial Pain*. 2d ed. Philadelphia: Lea and Febiger, 1977.
Bastron, R. Dennis and Deutsch, Stanley. *Anesthesia & the Kidney*. New York: Grune and Stratton, 1976.
Bennett, Edward John. *Fluids for Anesthesia and Surgery in the Newborn and the Infant*. Springfield, IL: Thomas, 1975.
Branthwaite, Margaret Annie. *Anesthesia for Cardiac Surgery and Allied Procedures*. Oxford: Blackwell Scientific Publications, 1977.
Burton, George G. *Respiratory Care: A Guide to Clinical Practice*. Philadelphia: J.B. Lippincott, 1977.
Cohen, Ellis N. *Metabolism of Volatile Anesthetics: Implications for Toxicity*. Reading, MA: Addison-Wesley, 1977.
Collins, Vincent J. *Principles of Anesthesiology*. 2d ed. Philadelphia: Lea and Febiger, 1976.
Covino, Benjamin G. *Local Anesthetics: Mechanisms of Action and Clinical Use*. New York: Grune and Stratton, 1976.
DeJong, Rudolph H. *Local Anesthetics*. 2d ed. Springfield, IL: Thomas, 1977.
Dorsch, Jerry A. *Understanding Anesthesia Equipment: Construction, Care, and Complications*. Baltimore: Williams & Wilkins, 1975.
Dripps, Robert Dunning. *Introduction to Anesthesia: The Principles of Safe Practice*. 2d ed. Philadelphia: W.B. Saunders, 1961.
Eger, Edmond I., II. *Anesthesia Uptake and Distribution*. Baltimore: Williams & Wilkins, 1974.
Ellis, Harold and McHarty, Margaret. *Anatomy for Anesthetists*. 2d ed. Oxford: Blackwell Scientific Publications, 1969.
Feldman, Stanley A. *Tracheostomy & Artificial Ventilation in the Treatment of Respiratory Failure*. 3d ed. London: E. Arnold, 1977.
Ganong, William Francis. *The Nervous System*. Los Altos, CA: Lange Medical Publications, 1977.
Gifford, R.W. and Manger, W.M. *Pheochromacytoma*. New York: Springer-Verlag, 1977.
Goldberger, Emanuel. *Treatment of Cardiac Emergencies*. Saint Louis: C.V. Mosby, 1974.
Goudsouzian, Nishan G. and Karamamian, Agop. *Physiology for Anesthesia*. New York: Appleton-Century-Crofts, 1977.

Gray, Thomas Cecil and Nunn, J.F. *General Anesthesia.* 3d ed. New York: Butterworths, 1971.

Heironimus, Terring W. *Mechanical Artificial Ventilation: A Manual for Students and Practitioners.* 3d ed. Springfield, IL: Thomas, 1977.

Hedley-Whyte, John et al. *Applied Physiology Respiratory Care.* 1st ed. Boston: Little, Brown, 1976.

Henschel, Ernest O. *Malignant Hyperthermia: Current Concepts.* New York: Appleton-Century-Crofts, 1977.

Jacox, Ada K. *Pain: A Source Book for Nurses and Other Health Professionals.* 1st ed. Boston: Little, Brown, 1977.

Katz, Arnold M. *Physiology of the Heart.* New York: Raven Press, 1977.

Katz, Arnold M. *Anesthesia and Uncommon Diseases: Pathophipiologic and Clinical Correlations.* Philadelphia: Saunders, 1973.

Lipton, Sampson. *Persistent Pain: Modern Methods of Treatment.* London: Academic Press, 1977.

Little, Robert C. *Physiology of the Heart and Circulation.* Chicago: Year Book Medical Publishers, 1977.

MacDonnell, Kenneth F. and Segal, Maurice C. *Current Respiratory Care.* Boston: Little, Brown, 1977.

Moir, Donald D. *Obstetric Anesthesia and Analgesia.* New York: Macmillan, 1976.

Moore, Daniel C. *Complications of Regional Anesthesia.* Springfield, IL: Thomas, 1955.

Nunn, John Francis. *Applied Respiratory Physiology.* 2d ed. Boston: Butterworths, 1977.

Redding, Joseph Stafford. *Life Support: The Essentials: An Introduction to Sound Principles of Intensive Care in Cardiorespiratory Crisis.* Philadelphia: J.B. Lippincott, 1977.

Safer, P. and Elam, J.O. eds. *Advances in Cardiopulmonary Resuscitation.* New York: Springer-Verlag, 1977.

Scheinberg, Peritz, ed. *Modern Practical Neurology: An Introduction to Diagnosis and Management of Common Neurological Disorders.* New York: Raven Press, 1977.

Schroeder, John S. and Daily, Elaine K. *Technology in Bedside Hemodynamic Monitoring.* St. Louis: C.V. Mosby, 1976.

Schneider, Sol M. and Moya, Frank, eds. *Anesthesia, Mother and Newborn.* Baltimore: Williams & Wilkins, 1973.

Siegel, John H. *Aged and High Risk Surgical Patient: Medical, Surgical and Anesthesia Management.* New York: Grune and Stratton, 1976.

Snow, John C. *Manual of Anesthesia.* 1st ed. Boston: Little, Brown, 1977.

Vickers, Michael Douglas. *Medicine for Anesthetists.* Oxford: Blackwell Scientific Publications, 1977.

Wallace, John. *Blood Transfusion for Clinicians.* New York: Churchill Livingstone, 1977.

West, John Bernard. *Pulmonary Pathophysiology: The Essentials.* Baltimore: Williams & Wilkins, 1977.

West, John Bernard. *Ventilation of Blood Flow and Gas Exchange.* 3d ed. Oxford: Blackwell Scientific Publications, 1977.

Wood-Smith, Francis Geoffrey, et al. *Drugs in Anaesthesia Practice.* 3d ed. New York: Appleton-Century-Crofts, 1968.

Wylie, William Derek. *Practice of Anaesthesia.* 3d ed. London: Lloyd-Luke, 1972.

Wylie, William Derek. *Practice of Anaesthesia.* 4th ed. Philadelphia: W.B. Saunders, 1978.

Index

Abandonment, 11, 12
Abortion, 210–11
Abuse of Process, 134
Agency. *See* Vicarious Liability
Airway Management: with endotracheal intubation, 259–68; without endotracheal intubation, 258–59
Alabama Law, 143
Alaska Law, 166
Alexander's Jury Instructions on Medical Issues, 14
Allopathy, 18
American Association of Medical Colleges, 147
American Association of Nurse-Anesthetists: guidelines for practice, 186–88, 190, 193; standards of practice, 183–86
American Association of Professional Standards Review Organizations. *See* Professional Standards Review Organizations
American Board of Anesthesiology, 177, 181; Residency Review Committee, 177–79
American Board of Medical Specialties, 176
American Medical Association (AMA), 9, 162, 176, 219; Council on Medical Education, 177
American Osteopathic Association, 181, 182; Committee on Postdoctoral Training, 181
American Society of Anesthesiologists, 188, 191; abortions, 210–11; anesthesiology services, 214–17. *See also* Joint Commission on Accreditation of Hospitals; classification of physical status, 246–47; postoperative care record keeping, 343, preanesthesia care record keeping, 245; record keeping, 245–53. *See also* Records; responsibilities of anesthesiologists, 189; standards for anesthesia care, 255; standards for postanesthesia care, 342–43; standards for preanesthesia care, 232–33; state regulation, 217
American Society of Anesthesiologists House of Delegates, 236; Guidelines for Preoperative Notes, 236; intraoperative monitoring, 241; intraoperative record keeping of anesthesia care, 248
Anesthesia: history of, 192; risks, 5; stages of, 256–58. *See* specific headings
Anesthesia Mishaps and Hazards, 313–22
Anesthesiologists: liability of, 71–73
Answer: sample, 377. *See also* Pleadings
Arbitration, 6
Ascher v. Gutierrez, 11–12, 279
Assault and Battery, 19–21
Assumption of Risk, 105–6
Aubert v. Charity Hospital of Louisiana, 47, 261–62

Baird v. Sickler, 76
Baker v. St. Agnes Hospital, 92
Barbiturates. *See* Intravenous Anesthesia
Battery. *See* Assault and Battery
Beauvais v. Notre Dame Hospital, 26
Bell v. Umstattd, 267
Bertrand v. Aetna Casualty and Surety Company, 32
Blood Transfusions, 327–28
Board of Medical Examiners, 143
Board of Pharmacy, 165
Borrowed Servant Doctrine, 67, 69–70
Breach of Duty. *See* Duty
Brown v. Allen Sanitarium, 29, 234
Bull v. McCuskey, 134
Buras v. Aetna Casualty & Surety Co., 13, 300
Burden of Proof. *See* Evidence
Bureau of Narcotics and Dangerous Drugs, 163
Burns, 35, 318–22
Burrows v. Widder, 325–26
Byrne v. Boadle, 34

California Anesthesia Service Regulations, 357
California Law, 79, 81, 119, 143, 145–48, 157, 191–92, 217

Canterbury v. Spence, 25
Capili v. Shott, 221–22
Captain of the Ship. *See* Vicarious Liability
Cardiac Arrest, 4, 5, 8, 40, 336–42
Carlsen v. Javurek, 16, 236–37, 276
Caudal Anesthesia. *See* Epidural Anesthesia
Causation, 7, 30. *See also* Res Ipsa Loquitur; cause in fact, 32; proof of, 31–32; proximate cause, 32–34; substantial factor formula, 31
Central Nervous System: depressants, 240
Certificate of Clinical Competence. *See* Specialty Certification (Anesthesiology)
Certificate of Need Program, 199, 213–14
Certification. *See* Specialty Certification (Anesthesiology)
Certification Standard, 142
Certified Registered Nurse-Anesthetists, 12, 183
Chalmers-Francis v. Nelson, 192
Chapman v. Argonaut-Southwest Insurance Company, 15, 287–88
Charitable Immunity. *See* Defenses
Circumstantial Evidence. *See* Res Ispa Loquitur
Clark v. Gibbons, 301
Collateral Estoppel, 112–15. *See also* Defenses
Colorado Law, 48, 143, 166, 189
Common Knowledge: scope of, 39
Comparative Negligence, 103–4. *See also* Defenses
Competing Professions: regulation of, 191–94
Complaint: sample, 373. *See also* Pleadings
Computerized Axial Tomography, 88. *See also* Products Liability
Confidentiality, 3, 133. *See also* Privileged Information
Connecticut Law, 14, 81, 144
Conscience Clause, 210–11. *See also* Abortion
Consent, 5–6; assault and battery, 19–21; cardiac arrest, 340; emergency admission, 20–21; exclusions and exceptions from duty to disclose, 24–27; informed consent, 22–27, 105, 235; minor or incompetent, 25; preanesthetic explanation of risks, 235; standard preprinted forms, 5
Consortium: loss of, 48
Conspiracy of Silence, 14, 35
Constitution, United States, 149, 198, 218; due process, 149–50, 198–99, 216, 218–20; equal protection, 199, 216, 218; privacy, 82
Contempt, 122

Continuing Medical Education, 148–49. *See also* Licensure
Continuous Treatment Doctrine, statute of limitations, 110
Continuum of Education in Anesthesiology, 178
Contracts: damages, 63; exclusive contracts, 221–22; express agreements, 9; hospital services, 221–22; implied, 62; legal theory, 3, 4, 61–65; limitations period, 63, 106–9; products liability, 84; release from liability, 9, 114–15
Contributory Negligence, 43–44, 100–103. *See also* Defenses
Controlled Substances. *See* Drugs
Cornfeldt v. Tongen, 271–72
Corporations, 200–201
Council on Medical Education of the American Medical Association, 177
Countersuits, 134–35
Court-Appointed Experts. *See* Expert Witnesses
Courtroom Procedure, 126
Crawford v. County of Sacramento, 339–40
Cross-Examination, 126; use of textbooks, 131

Damages, 6, 7, 44–51, 63, 135; alteration of damage award, 51; apportionment, 51; categories, 45; mitigation, 51; punitive damages, 12, 45, 49–50; purpose of, 45, 118; special damages, 45, 48–49
Deep Pocket Recovery, 65–66
Defamation, 81–82, 134
Defective Medical Devices. *See* Products Liability
Defenses: assumption of risk, 105–6; comparative negligence, 103–4; contributory negligence, 100–103; immunity, 198, 200; release from liability agreements, 114–15; res judicata and collateral estoppel, 112–14; statute of limitations, 106–12
Defensive Medicine, 6
Delaware Law, 208
Department of Justice, 163
Deposition. *See* Discovery
Direct Examination, 126
Discharge. *See* Hospital
Disciplinary Proceedings, 143, 149–57; ex parte actions, 151–52; grounds, 152–56; hearing, 150–51; incompetence, 153; judicial review, 151; notice, 149–50; procedural aspects, 149

Disclosure. *See* Consent
Discovery, 106, 120-24; depositions, 120-22; interrogatories, 122
District of Columbia Law, 166
Documents: production of, 123; work product exception, 123
Drugs: defective, 3, 87, 91-94; Federal Controlled Substances Act, 163-67; license to dispense or prescribe controlled substances, 165; manufacturer recommendations and warnings, 16, 92-94; Uniform Controlled Substances Act, 164-67
Due Process. *See* Constitution, United States
Durenberger, David, 157
Duty, 7-30. *See also* Negligence; breach, 27-30; consent and informed consent, 19-27; disclosure of risks, 22-27. *See also* Negligence; physician-patient relationship, 9-12; standard of care, 13-19

Edelman v. Ziegler, 338-39
Education. *See* Licensure
Educational Council for Foreign Medical Graduates, 146
Emergency, 8, 10, 197, 199, 207-9. *See also* Consent; good samaritan legislation, 10-11
Endotracheal Intubation. *See* Intubation
Engel, Harold, 337
Epidural Anesthesia, 301-4
Equipment. *See* Products Liability
Equipment-Related Injuries, 88
Ether, Hazards in Administration, 317-18
Ethicon, Inc. v. Parten, 86
Ethics. *See* Principles of Medical Ethics
Evidence, 6, 15, 18, 27, 37, 64, 124-34; adverse witnesses, 131-32; burden of proof, 31-32, 36; circumstantial, 35; court-appointed experts, 129; disciplinary hearings, 150; discovery, 120-24; expert testimony, 124-29. *See also,* Expert Testimony; federal rules, 121-30; hearsay, 134; hypothetical question and opinion testimony, 129-30; medical records, 133-34; physician-patient privilege, 132-33; preponderance of, 7; textbooks, 130-31
Exclusive Hospital Contracts. *See* Contracts
Expert Testimony, 14-17, 29, 124-25, 129-31; cross-examination, 126-27; direct examination, 126; exceptions, 15-16; hypothetical questions, 129-130; textbooks, 130-131
Expert Witnesses, 125-30; court appointment, 129; cross-examination, 127; defendant as, 131-32; deposition of, 121-22; direct examination, 126; fees, 125; guidelines for trial preparation, 127-29; interrogation of, 126; nurse-anesthetists as, 15; opinion testimony, 129-30; pharmacologists as, 15; preparation for trial, 125; qualifications, 125
External Equipment. *See* Products Liability

False Imprisonment, 209
Faris v. Doctor's Hospital, 40, 331-32
Federal Controlled Substances Act. *See* Drugs
Fiduciary Relationship, 132
Florida Law, 143, 146-48
Fluid and Electrolyte Levels: management, 322-26
Food and Drug Administration, Regulation of Drug Manufacturers, 91
Foreign Medical Graduates, 146-47
Foreign Object Rule, 111. *See* Statute of Limitations
Foreign Trained Physicians, 146
Foster v. Englewood Hospital Association, 68, 286-87
Fourteenth Amendment, Due Process Clause. *See* Constitution, United States
Funke v. Fieldman, 22, 296

Garcia v. Tarrio, 73
General Damages. *See* Damages
Gentry v. Department of Professional and Occupational Regulation, 154
Georgia Law, 217
Good Samaritan Legislation. *See* Emergency
Gore v. U.S., 277
Governmental Immunity. *See* Defenses
Gravis v. Physicians and Surgeons Hospital of Alice, 20-21

Haas v. United States, 38
Hall v. United States, 299
Halothane, 17, 92, 268-75; halothane hepatitis, 269-70, 272; medical history of patient, 273; postoperative hepatic necrosis, 270. *See also* National Halothane Study

394   Index

Health and Human Services, Department of, 158–59, 161
Hearsay. *See* Evidence
Hepatitis. *See* Blood Transfusions
Herbert v. Travelers Indemnity Co., 297–98
Hill-Burton Program, 197, 199, 213
Hirsch, Harold, 5
History of Development of Anesthesia in the United States, 192–94
Hospitals: abortion and sterilization, 210–11; administration, 203–6; admissions, 197, 199, 207–8; anesthesiology services, 214–17; bylaws, 201–3; Certificate of Need Program, 199, 213–14; contracts, 221–22; corporations, 200–201; discharge, 209; governing board, 201, 203–5; Hill-Burton program, 197, 199, 213; JCAH. *See* Joint Commission on the Accreditation of Hospitals; liability, 35, 66, 72, 74, 76–79; licensing of, 197, 213–14, 217; medical records, 80–81; medical staff, 201–2, 205–6; organization, 203–6; origin and development, 196–97; PSRO. *See* Professional Standards Review Organization; private hospitals, 199–200; privileges, 217–20; public hospitals, 197–99; regulation, 142, 196–223; services generally, 206–11; staff privileges, 197, 199, 217–20; types, 197–200; Utilization Review Committee, 160, 209
Hughes v. Hastings, 265–66
Hunter v. Robison, 33–34
Hutton v. Davis, 115
Hypothetical Question. *See* Evidence

Illinois Anesthesia Services Regulations, 362
Illinois Law, 81, 143, 148, 150, 191
Immoral Conduct, 154
Immunity. *See* Defenses
Implied Contracts. *See* Contracts
Infiltration Anesthesia, 308–11
Informed Consent, 105, 235. *See also* Consent
Inhalation Techniques, 258–59
Interrogatories, 122. *See also* Discovery
Intervening Cause. *See* Causation
Intravenous Anesthesia, 276–82; barbiturates, 276–79; narcotics, 279–80; neuroleptic agents, 279–82
Intubation, 11–12; cardiac arrest and cyanosis, 262–63; cervical spine damage, 267–68; damage to vocal cords, 266–67; endotracheal, 259; laryngoscopy, 265; methods of intubation, 260; monitoring, 260–61; open eye surgery, 264–65; surgery of head and neck area, 263–64
Invasion of Privacy. *See* Constitution, United States

James v. Holder, 326
Joint Commission on the Accreditation of Hospitals (JACH): anesthesia care, 255–56; anesthesia services, 364; emergencies, 207–9; hospital administrator, 205; hospital bylaws, 201–2; hospital governing boards, 203–4; hospital operations, 200; hospital regulation, 212–13; medical and other staff, 205–6; postanesthesia record keeping, 251–52; preanesthesia record keeping, 245–46; precautions in administering anesthetic agents, 316–17; regulation of nurse-anesthetists, 189; services, 206; specialty staff privileges, 219
Joint Enterprise, 79–80. *See also* Vicarious Liability
Jones v. Harrisburg Polyclinic Hospital, 333
Jury, 38–39

Kansas Board of Healing Arts v. Seasholtz, 153
Kentucky Law, 191
Ketamine, 281–82. *See also* Intravenous Anesthesia
Kincl v. Hycel, 91
Kitto v. Gilbert, 264

LeBeuf v. Atkins, 309–10
Levett v. Etkind, 105
Licensure, 141–57, 165, 176; continuing medical education, 6, 14, 148–49; disciplinary proceedings, 143, 149–57; dispensation or prescription of controlled substances, 165; educational requirements, 144; foreign training, 146–47; hospitals, 213; personal qualifications, 145–46
Limitation of Actions. *See* Statute of Limitations
Linhares v. Hall, 341
Local Anesthesia. *See* Infiltration Anesthesia
Lockett v. Goodill, 303
Long, Crawford, 317

Index

Louisiana Law, 50, 81, 190

McAdams v. Holden, 341–42
McFadden v. Turner, 67
Mackey v. Greenview Hospital, 102
McKinney v. Tromly, 318
Maine Law, 166
Malignant Hyperthermia, 334–36; detection and treatment, 335–36
Malpractice: defenses, 100–115; definition, 3; insurance, 4; malpractice crisis, 4, 6, 134; Professional Standards Review Organizations (PSRO) immunity, 162; statistics, 4, 5
Martin v. Stratton, 307
Marvulli v. Elshire, 72
Maryland Law, 143, 146
Massachusetts Anesthesia Services Requirements, 361
Massachusetts Guidelines for Nurse-Anesthetists, 191
Massachusetts Law, 81, 143, 190, 217
Maternal and Child Health Program, 157
May v. Brown, 78
Mediation, 6
Medicaid, 157, 161, 213
Medical Devices. *See* Products Liability
Medical Examiners, Board of, 144–45, 147
Medical Records. *See* Records
Medical Societies, 144
Medicare, 157, 161, 197, 200, 213
Medvecz v. Choi, 50
Merritt v. Deaconess Hospital, 40
Michigan Conscience Clause, 210
Michigan Law, 4, 18, 63, 133, 143, 146, 148, 152, 154–57, 190, 198, 208–9, 216–17, 219
Michigan, University of: anesthesiology program, 178–79
Minnesota Law, 16, 104
Mississippi Law, 81
Model Nonprofit Corporation Act, 200
Mogenson v. Hicks, 311
Monitoring patient, 241–44; defective equipment, 242. *See also* Products Liability; intraoperatively, 241–44; postoperatively, 244; record keeping, 244. *See also* Records
Montezuma, 196
Moore v. Francisco, 273
Morton, William, 192, 317

Napier v. Northrum, 307–8
National Association of Insurance Commissioners, 4
National Board of Medical Examiners. *See* Medical Examiners, Board of
National Halothane Study, 92, 270
National Health Planning and Resource Development Act, 213
National Professional Standards Review Council, 161–62
Negligence: breach of duty, 27–30; causes of in anesthesia mishaps, 5; causation, 30–44; comparative negligence, 103–4; contributory negligence, 43, 100–103; damages, 44–51; duty, 7–27; elements of, 6–7; emergencies, 10; legal theory, 3, 27, 32, 63; products liability, 82–85. *See also* Products Liability
Nelson, Dagmar, 192
Neuroleptic Agents. *See* Intravenous Anesthesia
Neuromuscular Blocking Agents, 282; depolarizing blockers, 282–85; nondepolarizing blockers, 285
Nevada Law, 134
New Hampshire Law, 166
New Jersey Law, 81, 143, 205–6, 219
New York Law, 143, 166
Nonprofit Hospitals. *See* Hospitals
Nurse-Anesthetists: certification, 183; Council on Nurse Anesthesia Practice, 187–88; expert witnesses, 15; guidelines, 186–87; JCAH regulations, 189, 216; liability, 69, 73–77; regulation, 182–94; standards of practice, 183–86; state regulation, 189–91

Oberlin v. Friedman, 305
Ohio Law, 148
Opinion Testimony. *See* Expert Witnesses
Osteopathy, 18, 19, 143, 145, 181–82
Outrageous Conduct, 49

Patient Positioning, 328–34
Patterson v. Van Wiel, 303–4
Pederson v. Dumouchel, 346
Pennsylvania Law, 51, 70, 143, 190
Penthrane, 16, 275–76
Pharmacologists, 15
Physical Examination, 123
Physical Status: classifications, 246–47
Physician-Patient Privilege, 132–33

Physician-Patient Relationship, 5, 9–12; abandonment, 11, 12; consent, 19; creation, 9
Pleadings, 118; patient's complaint, 119; physician's answer, 119; sample answer, 377; sample complaint, 373
Polonsky v. Union Hospital, 202–3
Police Power, 141–43
Postgraduate Programs in Anesthesiology, 177
Postoperative Anesthesia Care, 11, 12, 342; cardiovascular problems, 343; hospital liability, 345–46; interpretation and customary practice, 343; metabolic problems, 344; pain and delirium, 344; postanesthesia records, 251–52; respiratory problems, 343; standards, 342–43
Prack v. United States Fidelity and Guaranty Co., 345–46
Preanesthesia Visit and Evaluation, 232–37
Preanesthetic Care, 11
Preoperative Medications, 237–40
Principles of Medical Ethics, 9
Privacy, 82
Private Hospitals. *See* Hospitals
Privileged Information, 121, 132, 133
Privileges. *See* Hospital
Products Liability, 82–94; blood transfusions, 327; burden of proof, 85; contract theory, 83; defective devices, 87–91; defective drugs, 87, 91–94; defective monitoring equipment, 242; disclaimers, 84; manufacturer instructions and warnings, 85; negligence theory, 82–85; procedural defenses, 106–14; strict liability theory, 84; warranty theory, 84
Professional Standards Review Organizations (PSRO), 141, 142, 157–63, 214; immunity, 162, 163; peer review, 159, 160; quality review, 160, 161; utilization review, 160, 209–11
Proximate Cause. *See* Causation
Public Hospitals. *See* hospitals
Punitive Damages. *See* Damages

Quality Review. *See* Professional Standards Review Organization
Quintal v. Laurel Grove Hospital, 337–38

Rauschelbach v. Benincasa, 266–67
Reasonable Man, 8
Reasonable Prudence, 8

Recertification, 176
Records, 5, 6, 130, 133–34; accuracy, 250–51; emergency care, 248, 249; evidence, 133; intraoperative records, 248; liability, 80–82; ownership, 80; patient monitoring and record keeping, 244; patient requests to be informed, 24, 81; physical status data, 246–47; postanesthesia records, 251–52; preanesthesia notes and records, 236, 245–48. *See also* Hospitals; preoperative medications, 248
Regional Nerve Block Anesthesia, 4, 305–8
Regulations, Governmental, 141–42; California Anesthesia Service Requirements, 357; Illinois Anesthesia Service Requirements, 362; Massachusetts Anesthesia Service Requirements, 361; state regulations, 142–57
Releases, 9, 114–15. *See also* Defenses
Relicensure, 148–49
Res Ipsa Loquitur, 34–44, 83; absence of contributory negligence, 43–44; cardiac arrest, 338–40; causation, 34–44; defendant-controlled instrumentality, 41–43; faulty patient positioning, 330; injury caused by negligence, 37–41
Res Judicata, 112, 113
Respondeat Superior. *See* Vicarious Liability
Risk Management, 4
Risks, Disclosure of, 24
Rockwell v. Stone, 278
Rose v. Hakim, 90, 344–45
Rothman v. Silber, 39, 111

Saklad, Meyer, 246–47
Sanzari v. Rosenfeld, 309
Sauro v. Shea, 340–41
Schneider v. Albert Einstein Medical Center, 263
Schrib v. Seidenberg, 239
Seaton v. Rosenberg, 249–50
Seneris v. Haas, 43
Sesselman v. Muhlenberg Hospital, 76
Small v. Gifford Memorial Hospital, 27
Social Security Act, 157, 213–14
Spannaus v. Otolaryngology Clinic, 43
Special Damages. *See* Damages
Specialty Boards, 176; Certificate of Clinical Competence, 177; clinical material, 180; didactic program, 180-82; faculty, 179, 180; postgraduate programs, 177–79

Index

Specialty Certification (Anesthesiology), 14, 176–82
Spinal Anesthesia, 4, 13, 35, 43, 292; contraindications, 294–95; interpretation and customary practice, 293–301; paresthesia, 295–98; safe spinal techniques, 292–93
Staff Privileges. *See* Hospitals
Standard of Care, 7, 8, 13–19, 27, 141, 231; community standard, 13, 14; emergency situations. *See* Emergency; expert testimony, 14, 15; failure to follow manufacturer recommendations, 16–17; manufacturer's duty, 87; medical textbooks, 17–18; schools of medicine, 18–19; specialty standards, 14, 176
Standards of Practice of American Association of Nurse-Anesthetists, 183–86
Starnes v. Charlotte-Mecklenburg Hospital Authority, 74, 321–22
State Action, 198–99
State Licensure. *See* Licensure
State Regulation of Nurse-Anesthetists, 189–91
Statute of Limitations, 6, 63, 85, 106–12; foreign object rule, 111; "tolling" the statute, 110, 111
Sterilization, 210–11
St. Paul Fire and Marine Insurance Company, 4
Subdural Anesthesia. *See* Spinal Anesthesia
Subpoena, 122
Substitute Physician, 12
Succinylcholine, 283; interacting drugs, 284–85. *See also* Neuromuscular Blocking Agents
Swanson v. St. John's Lutheran Hospital, 211

Teeth, 4, 15
Testimony. *See* Expert Witnesses
Texas Law, 19, 49, 50, 152, 153
Textbooks, 130–31
Therapeutic Privilege, 24–25
Thomas v. Seaside Memorial Hospital of Long Beach, 347

Tomer v. American Home Products, 93
Torsiello v. Whitehall Labs, 94
Tort. *See* Negligence

Uniform Business Records Act, 134
Uniform Controlled Substances Act. *See* Drugs
Unlawful Conduct, 154
Unprofessional Conduct, 152
Utilization Review. *See* Professional Standards Review Organization

Ventilation, 258
Vergott v. Deseret Pharmaceutical Co., Inc., 89
Vermont Law, 166
Vicarious Liability, 61, 65–80; anesthesiologists, 70–73; borrowed servant doctrine, 65, 67–70, 76; captain of the ship, 65, 70, 73; hospitals, 72, 74, 76–79; joint enterprise, 79–80; nurse-anesthetists, 69; respondeat superior, 65, 70
Vogan v. Byers, 336
Volatile Anesthetic Agents, 268. *See also* Halothane; Penthrane
Vuletich v. Bolgla, 243–44

Wagner v. Kaiser Foundation Hospitals, 252–53
Washington Law, 48, 119
Webb v. Jorns, 17, 274
Weeks v. Latter-Day Saints Hospitals, 319–20
Weiss v. Rubin, 328
White, Edward, 5
Widlitz v. Board of Regents, 156
Wiles v. Myerly, 69, 320–21
Wisconsin Law, 18, 81, 143
Withdrawal from Case, 12
Witnesses; adverse, 131-132. *See also* Expert Witnesses
Wright, Charles, 118
Wrongful Death Statutes, 107, 112

Ybarra v. Spangard, 41, 330-31

About the Authors

J. DOUGLAS PETERS, J.D., is a partner in the law firm of Charfoos, Christensen, Gilbert and Archer, P.C., Detroit, Michigan, and an adjunct assistant professor of law and medicine at the University of Toledo College of Law and the Wayne State University School of Medicine. Mr. Peters has also served as Chairperson of the State Bar of Michigan Committee on Medicolegal Problems and is the author of numerous articles on the subject of law and medicine. He is co-author of *The Law of Medical Practice in Michigan* and the *Social Security Disability Claims Manual* and co-editor of *Legal and Ethical Aspects of Treating Critically and Terminally Ill Patients*. Before moving to Michigan, Mr. Peters served as Executive Director of the Fourth Ohio Area Professional Standards Review Council, Toledo, Ohio.

KEITH S. FINEBERG, J.D. is senior attorney at ComLaw, Inc., a computer-assisted legal research service. He is past program director of the Michigan Medical Schools Council of Deans, Medical-Legal Project. Mr. Fineberg has also served as editor at the Lawyers Cooperative Publishing Company, writing legal reference material for attorney use. He has also practiced law as an associate with Sanders, Hester, Holly, Askin and Dye in Georgia and is a member of both the Georgia and Michigan bars. Mr. Fineberg is co-author of *The Law of Medical Practice in Michigan*.

DONALD A. KROLL, M.D., Ph.D, was co-project director and medical director of the Michigan Medical Schools Council of Deans, Medical-Legal Project. He received his M.D. degree from The University of Michigan Medical School, and his doctorate in Pharmacology from The University of Michigan. Dr. Kroll is currently serving as a physician and an assistant professor in the Departments of Anesthesiology and Pharmacology at The University of Michigan Medical School. He is co-author of *The Law of Medical Practice in Michigan*.

VINCENT J. COLLINS, M.D., M.S., is professor of anesthesiology and Coordinator of Education in Anesthesiology at the University of Illinois Medical Center, and professor of anesthesiology at Northwestern University School of Medicine. From 1961 to 1981, he was director of the Department of Anesthesiology at Cook County Hospital, which he helped build to one of the largest training programs in anesthesiology in the country. The author of *Principles and Practices of Anesthesiology*, now in its third edition, Dr. Collins received his M.D. degree from Yale University School of Medicine, and his M.S. degree in Biology and Endocrinology from Brown University.